MAHON, John K. The War of 1812. Florida, 1972. 476p il map bibl 79-137856. 12.50. ISBN 0-8130-0318-0

CHOICE   JUNE '73

History, Geography &

Travel

  North America

In his preface Mahon claims to have placed the military operations of the War of 1812 "precisely within the politics and culture of the time," to have exhausted the sources on every battle, to have analyzed "the important command decisions which went into the grand strategy at the uppermost level, and into tactics at the lowest," to have presented the British side of the war more fully and accurately than any previous account, and to have written a definitive history, "for a while at least." Unfortunately, the body of the work does not bear out these rather extravagant claims. Mahon has done considerable research in original sources and he has made a conscientious attempt to be accurate in presenting the details of battles. But a pedestrian style, failure to grasp larger issues, and a certain naïveté combine to make this expensive volume of limited interest either to the general reader or to the specialist.

650

**NORTHERN
THEATER**

The War of 1812

About the Author

John K. Mahon is Professor of History and Chairman of the Department of History at the University of Florida. He is a past trustee of the American Military Institute and a former civilian military historian in the Office of the Chief of Military History, Department of the Army. He has taught at Colorado State University and the University of California at Los Angeles.

Dr. Mahon's many articles on military history have been published in *Military Affairs*, *North Carolina Historical Review*, *Current History*, *Civil War History*, *Florida Historical Quarterly*, and other scholarly journals. He is the author of *The American Militia: Decade of Decision, 1789–1800*, and the editor of *Reminiscences of the Second Seminole War*, by John Bemrose. He wrote the introduction to the Floridiana Facsimile and Reprint Series edition (1964) of Sprague, *The Origin, Progress, and Conclusion of the Florida War* (1847). He also wrote *History of the Second Seminole War* (1967), which received the Award of Merit from the American Association for State and Local History.

The War of 1812

John K. Mahon

★★

1972

UNIVERSITY OF FLORIDA PRESS

Gainesville

A University of Florida Press Book

MANUFACTURED FOR THE PUBLISHER BY THE
ROSE PRINTING COMPANY, INCORPORATED
TALLAHASSEE, FLORIDA

To Enid and Johnny

Preface

Henry Adams remains one of our finest historians. About ninety years ago he wrote an operational history of the War of 1812 as a part of his great *History of the United States of America during the Administrations of Thomas Jefferson and James Madison.* This incidental account, in spite of occasional errors and known prejudices, is still the best one on that war. I have not improved on Adams' insights and fine writing, but I have used indispensable materials which he did not have, especially British and Canadian documents. Indeed, the present work shows the British side of the war more fully and accurately than any previous one.

I have not dwelt much on the causes of the war, since a few able scholars, working during the last two decades, have made that unnecessary.

Mine is a detailed narrative for several reasons. The past can live for present readers only when it is presented in detail. This fact is particularly true of warfare. There is no use presenting a highly generalized account of a battle, for the generalizations will have no meaning for a reader who does not already intimately know the details of the action. My history is intended to be definitive, for a while at least, which means that it will serve in part as a reference work. Readers who want data on specific participants, places, and things will be able to find many of them here, and there is a comprehensive index to simplify their search. Readers who feel no need for the details can easily skim them.

I am aware of the danger of a historian's getting lost in detail. I am equally aware of the futility of his spinning out theories which will not stand up under analysis of the detailed events upon which they are supposed to rest. I have tried not to do either.

Why bother with military affairs unless they can be related to the rest of society's affairs? This work tries to place the operations of the War of 1812 precisely within the politics and culture of the time.

Every battle account in the work rests upon an analysis of all the data I could find. Each account of a battle is a mosaic, and that is why I cite a block of sources for it instead of giving a separate citation for each detail. I have done my best to analyze the important command decisions which went into the grand strategy at the uppermost level, and into the tactics at the lowest. I have especially done this on the British side of things. The informed scholar is invited to study my account, say, of the Battle of New Orleans, and to compare it with the best he can find elsewhere. Certain controversies persisted after the war, and I have analyzed and presented these. Perhaps the most notorious controversy, though rarely noted in latter-day narratives, was the one between Oliver Hazard Perry and Jesse D. Elliott over what happened during the Battle of Put-in-Bay. It will be found in this work.

I have adopted a short form of citation for the notes and have put them at the back of the book. This will occasion denunciations among some of my associates, but I am not sorry I did it. As presently arranged, the notes will not interrupt the narrative, but they are easily accessible to persons who want to follow my tracks. They need only refer to the note at the back and go on to the bibliography where they will find full information on each work cited. This arrangement results in a healthy division of labor. A scholar can check my sources with less labor than the editors, printers, and I would have expended in leading them in the conventional way.

Scholars can learn from the War of 1812 how a war ought not to be conducted. If that is not sufficient justification for studying it, let me point out that the war is worth studying as a part of each one of us. The American past is an active part of every one of us. Educated persons are those who know what baggage they are carrying from history. My objective here has been to show them accurately one piece of that history, so that some of what we carry from it will be plain to them. One thing we need to know is this: the war was fought when rationalism was giving way to romanticism. The people then saw the glory, not the gore, in warfare. Inasmuch as we see the reverse today, it is vital for us to know that a different mood did once exist.

JOHN K. MAHON

Contents

x   CONTENTS

1814–1815—337

Peace—373

Notes—387

Bibliography—427

Index—451

Illustrations

Prologue

The United States

On 22 June 1807 the English frigate *Leopard* attacked the United States frigate *Chesapeake*, and took from her certain of her sailors who, the *Leopard*'s captain claimed, were British citizens. Not since 1798 had an English warship presumed to halt and board an American ship-of-war. The people of the United States reacted passionately, but President Thomas Jefferson calmed them and kept the peace. Jefferson, however, could not prevent a military augmentation from growing out of the affair. In April 1808 Congress added 8 regiments to the 20 companies of infantry and 20 companies of artillery which had survived the heavy cut in the army made by Jefferson in 1802. This legislation tripled the authorized number of enlisted men (from 3,068 to 9,311), but despite the authorization the total of men actually in the service never rose above 6,500.[1]

Three years passed without further addition to the military establishment; then because of deteriorating relations with England, Secretary of War William Eustis asked in 1811 for 10,000 men to be added to the regular army. Senator William Branch Giles, a Virginia Democrat but violently anti-Madison, proposed 25,000 instead of 10,000. Since neither Giles nor anyone else thought it possible to raise 25,000 men, it has usually been assumed that his purpose was to embarrass the administration. Now began a lively debate in Congress between supporters and detractors of standing forces. Supporters insisted that a regular army of 30,000 could not possibly endanger civil control of the military. Detractors, on the other hand, drew upon history to prove that standing armies had more often than not overthrown free governments.

Some detractors wanted to see the regular army abolished, for then the country would be forced to engage in nothing more than defensive military operations.[2]

Neither geographical origin nor party seemed wholly to govern the way men voted on the choice between regulars and militia. Federalists from Massachusetts and Connecticut favored reliance on militia because of the excellence of their own citizen soldiery, while Federalists from most other states usually spoke in favor of regulars. Elisha Potter, representative from Rhode Island, saw a need for both types; he called the militia the shield of the nation and the regular forces the sword. His metaphor displeased most of the Democrats because they did not want to see the nation brandishing a sword.[3]

In the end all the Federalists in the Senate joined with some Democrats to enact Giles' augmentation. Then Henry Clay of Kentucky and Peter B. Porter of New York pushed the Senate bill through the House, and it became law on 11 January 1812. The result on paper was 10 new regiments of infantry, 2 of artillery, and 1 of light dragoons, but the ranks of these units were never more than half filled. The new law made provision for two major generals and five brigadiers, but not for a general-in-chief to give professional advice to the civilian secretary of war.[4]

Twice in four years, in 1808 and again in 1812, Congress had tripled the size of the regular army on paper. One month after the second tripling it gave the President permission to alert 50,000 volunteers, and appropriated $1 million to support them. If these volunteers were called into federal service, they were to serve for one year. Senator Joseph Anderson of Tennessee, among others, approved them and others like them as being more efficient than newly raised regulars, and as being far safer for a free society to employ. In any case, there had been a rush since 1807 to form volunteer companies. The drawback with this movement was that it endangered what little integrity the standing militia still possessed. In 1807 President Jefferson had called upon the states to alert 100,000 militiamen to be ready to spring to arms, but as late as 1810 several states had not bothered to reply and some never did. Nevertheless, in April 1812 Congress authorized the President to alert another 100,000. These militiamen, if called into federal service, were to serve from three to six months.[5]

By late spring of 1812 the authorized land forces of the United States had been pushed to formidable levels: 35,925 regulars, 50,000 volunteers, and 100,000 militia. War Department appropriations were up from $2,633,000 in 1811 to $11,818,000, but the new large sum was to be raised by a loan rather than by taxation. If the English government was aware of the new figures, it was scarcely worried, for it certainly knew how wide the gap was between authorized and actual numbers.

Next, Congress turned its attention to the organization of the War Department. That department, unlike all others except the navy, contained two separate establishments within it, a civilian and a military. The former consisted only of the secretary of war and eight clerks, but the secretary was theoretically a host of persons himself: quartermaster general, commissioner of pensions, commissioner of public lands, commissary general, master of ordnance, and superintendent of Indian affairs. If war came he could not possibly discharge all these positions, so the President asked for two deputy secretaries. Congress denied his request on the grounds that compliance might lay the entire United States government open to sinecures. As it happened, congressmen were also influenced to vote against the request because of the incumbent secretary, Dr. Eustis.[6]

Dr. William Eustis had first been selected by Jefferson to be secretary of war in 1809, and had been reappointed by Madison. He had been a medical student under Dr. Joseph Warren, and had served as a surgeon's assistant during the Revolutionary War. Afterwards he practiced medicine for a time, then moved into politics as a profession. He was elected as an Antifederalist to the General Court of Massachusetts, and later for two terms to the United States House of Representatives. Being genial and courteous, he made friends easily. He was always a staunch party man, and considered party when making decisions concerning the military posture of the United States. By 1812 he was fifty-nine years old and apparently not capable of distinguishing between important and unimportant duties. William H. Crawford said that he consumed his time "reading ads of petty retailing merchants to find where he [might] purchase 100 shoes or 100 hats." All in all, he had become a liability to the administration. Influential members of the party began to put pressure on the President to remove him, but for various reasons Madison was reluctant to let him go.[7]

The secretary of the navy was Paul Hamilton, a fifty-year-old rice planter and slaveholder from South Carolina. He had been governor of that state from 1804 to 1806. At the start of his term Madison must have chosen him for his political value. He knew little of the sea and the navy. As long as the work load was moderate, Hamilton performed well enough, but French Minister Serurier asserted that he was too drunk by noon each day to be able to work. As the burdens upon the navy department increased, mutterings against the secretary did so too.[8]

On 1 May 1811 British frigate *Guerrière* impressed an American sailor from a United States coasting vessel. Seeking revenge for this and other actions, Captain John Rodgers, commanding the frigate *President*, 44 guns, on 16 May at dusk overhauled and hailed a strange ship-of-war. Although both commanders denied firing the first shot, guns flared in a few minutes. The unidentified vessel escaped in the darkness, but the next morning Rodgers discovered her nearby, badly crippled. Instead of the sought-for *Guerrière* she proved to be the British sloop-of-war *Little Belt*, 18 guns, hardly a match for *President*. She had suffered 9 men killed and 23 wounded, but her captain declined an offer of aid from Rodgers and sailed limping away to Halifax. Even though both governments played down this fight, public sentiment was aroused. Fortunately it was not followed during the next twelve months by any equally inflammatory incident, but tempers remained touchy.[9]

About a year later Secretary Hamilton ordered Rodgers to put to sea to resist impressment and to "inflict merited punishment on foreign insolence." Acting on these orders, Rodgers patrolled near Norfolk with *President*, *Essex*, and *Congress*. When *United States* was ready for sea, he took two of the ships northward to cruise off Sandy Hook, and left the others to guard Chesapeake Bay.[10]

On 21 May Secretary Hamilton asked Rodgers to submit a plan of operations which would enable the "little navy" to annoy England to the utmost. The commodore recommended that a squadron of three frigates and a sloop cruise off the British Isles, where the coasts were relatively unprotected, while lighter vessels harassed the English trade in the West Indies. The frigates were to be kept in constant motion.[11]

At the same time Hamilton called upon Captain Stephen Decatur for a strategy. He got back almost the exact opposite of Rodgers' recommendation. Decatur wanted the frigates to cruise singly and to stay at sea until starved into returning. Under such a system the vessels could remain away from American shores on an average of about six months. Part of the idea was to keep the enemy also distant from the home coasts and to force him to disperse his squadrons.[12]

Almost a century later Admiral Mahan repudiated both these strategies. If Rodgers and Decatur had combined at the start, he said, they could have beaten the British squadron in American waters. To give proper credit, Rodgers soon shifted to a similar analysis. When he learned that the British North American squadron consisted of a 64-gun ship, 7 frigates, 7 sloops, 7 brigs, and 2 or 3 schooners, he too concluded that the entire United States squadron ought to seek out the British ships individually and beat them before they combined or before help came from England.[13]

The point at which American interests conflicted with British was, of course, on the oceans. President Madison considered England as great a threat as Napoleon to freedom in the world because of the apparent English attempt to dominate the sea-lanes by force. In this attempt she seemed determined to treat the United States as if it were still a colony. The President could not forgive the New England Federalists that they seemed willing, for the sake of profits, to sink docilely into colonial status again.[14]

Continuously from late in 1811 through the first half of 1812 British frigates had been blockading New York, seizing vessels bound for France, and impressing American seamen mercilessly. Their pressure induced a debate in Congress on the navy, which produced at least one novel argument. Representative Richard M. Johnson of Kentucky insisted that plunder, piracy, and perpetual war had resulted from the creation of every navy in history. He specified those of Tyre, Sidon, Rhodes, Athens, and Carthage. This line of reasoning was common enough relative to land forces, but it was novel applied to the sea service. We cannot know whether it had any influence or not, except that on 27 January 1812 the House defeated by a vote of 61 to 59 the proposal to build additional frigates.[15]

British Orders in Council and Napoleon's Continental System were designed primarily to affect England's manufacturing and shipping. It was incidental that they cut off an essential part of America's trade with Europe. That trade was running in early 1812 at about three-fifths of its level of five years earlier. A shrinkage of this order was bearable, but impressment was a continuous insult to American sovereignty. If the United States could not protect her own nationals from British press gangs, she could hardly expect to be considered sovereign. On the other side of the proposition, England insisted that her national life depended on impressment. Desertions from her ships were running at an annual rate of 2,500 men per year. To fill the gap, English captains had taken an estimated 6,000 sailors from United States merchant ships. In desperate response to this the United States reimposed in April 1812 a full-scale embargo to run for ninety days. Its primary purpose seems to have been to keep American ships out of the way of the British navy.[16]

The core of the American navy consisted of seven of the best frigates in the world. Three of them, *United States, Constitution,* and *President,* were rated at 44 guns, but actually carried 50 to 54. Of these guns 20 to 22 were carronades, throwing 32- to 42-pound shot, which were mounted on the spar deck. The other 30 were long guns, usually 24-pounders, situated on the main deck. British frigates carried similar guns, except that their long ones were 18- instead of 24-pounders. Ranging from 175 to 155 feet in length and 43 feet at the beam, the 3 American frigates were 20 feet longer than their British counterparts. They carried a large crew of about 400 men, which provided numbers for boarding, for working the guns, and for sustaining a fight when losses were heavy.[17]

Constellation, Congress, and *Chesapeake* were rated at 38 guns, but carried 46. Twenty-eight of these guns were long 18- or 24-pounders on the gun deck, the rest were 32-pound carronades on the spar deck. These 3 frigates were 12 feet shorter than the 44's and 4 feet narrower across the beam, but they still were larger than frigates of other nations of the same rating.

The smallest of the frigates was *Essex,* 140 by 26½ feet. Rated as a 32, she actually mounted 24 32-pound carronades and 2 long 12-pounders on her gun deck, with 16 32's and 4 long 12-pounders on the quarterdeck and forecastle. She had no spar deck. Her crew of 328 was large for her size. Like the other American frigates, she could defeat enemy frigates of the same rating because of her extra size, heavier guns, and enlarged crews. Another advantage the American ships had was 20 inches of planking for armor. If they encountered a ship-of-the-line too big to fight, they had a good chance of outrunning her because of their clean lines and large sail surfaces.

The other 9 United States naval vessels fit for the high seas were brigs, sloops, and corvettes ranging from 104 to 84 feet in length and from 28 guns for *Adams* (a frigate rebuilt as a corvette) to 12 for *Viper.* Nearly all these vessels had been rebuilt as schooners; then between 1806 and 1811 they had been rerigged. As a result they were overcrowded with both men and armament. C. S. Forester call ships of this class eggshells armed with hammers.[18]

The United States had around 200 gunboats in 1812. Some of them had been purchased in the Mediterranean, some built on our western rivers, and some on the east coast, but the last contracts to build any of them had been let in 1810. They varied in length from 47 to 80 feet, but all of them were armed with one heavy gun, fired over the bow. Since this was usually a 24-pounder, it was almost more than the smallest of the gunboats could carry. The small boats had to dismount the gun and store it in the hold to avoid swamping during violent storms.[19]

Carronades could throw heavy shot short distances, long guns could throw light shot long distances. Carronades were also well suited to firing shells, that is, rounds which contained an explosive charge inside them set off by a fuse, but these were not much used. A 32-pound carronade and a long 12-pounder were roughly equivalent in range: 260

yards point blank, and 1,260 yards at 5 degrees elevation. The balls were round, except for certain special varieties, such as bar and chain shot. The latter were used to tear up rigging. When the object was to injure the hull of a ship, solid shot was the charge, and if the object was to eliminate personnel, canister or any sort of scatter-shot was used. Fewer British-made guns burst than American, and British-made shot were also more reliable. On the other hand the English naval historian William James claimed that an improved type of cartridge case gave the Americans an advantage of one gun in every three over their foes. An Englishman, Captain Truscott, invented a sight for naval guns, but although it was tried aboard a few selected ships, it was not put into general use.[20]

In the spring of 1812 there were 4,010 enlisted sailors in the American navy and 1,523 men in the Marine Corps. Nine-tenths of them were Americans, perhaps one-twentieth Englishmen, and the rest of diverse origins. The officer corps numbered 234, with nearly half of them coming from the southern states.* All captains who commanded ships were under forty. No higher rank than captain existed, but the commander of a squadron was given the honorary title of commodore. There was no senior captain or professional head of the navy to advise the secretary and the President. In consequence, the secretary, aided by 20 clerks, 11 of whom were accountants, had to keep up direct communication with no less than 16 commanders of naval yards and separate squadrons, 14 naval agents, the captains of all ships, including gunboats, and any other naval person who chose to write him.[21]

The London *Times* described the United States Navy as a "few fir built frigates with strips of bunting, manned by sons of bitches and outlaws."[22]

In 1812 the population of the United States was estimated at 6,000,000 white people, and 1,700,000 others, mostly Negroes. Even though nine-tenths of this population were farmers, somebody produced or imported enough manufactured goods to carry on a war. Probably about 695,000 men were enrolled in the state militias, which provided an adequate reserve of men of fighting age to draw upon.†

---

* The officers came from the various regions in the following numbers: New England 42, Middle Atlantic 78, District of Columbia 4, South 110.

† The reports of 1811 from the state adjutant generals accounted for 695,000 militiamen. Of these only 13,500 were artillerymen, only 20,000 cavalrymen, the rest infantrymen. The only states with anything like balanced forces were Massachusetts and Connecticut; 20 per cent of all militia cannon belonged to them. They also had an average of 9.1 firearms for every 10 men, while Delaware and Maryland had only 1 firearm for every 10 men. Massachusetts and Connecticut claimed they had the best militia in the world.

Federal indebtedness, the price of independence plus the purchase of Louisiana, stood at $55,963,000 ($7.25 per capita).[23]

Few Americans attempted to estimate the ability of the United States to wage war. None of them doubted that the inherent strength was available, but many, such as John Randolph, questioned the ability of the government to channel that power. Randolph jeered at his own party's jingoism; he said it was supported by insufficient money, arms, and navy, and had only courage enough to pass resolutions. Randolph and other skeptics knew that there was too much factionalism, sectionalism, and individualism at large in the nation. Nevertheless, conviction drove these and others to advocate war or else to oppose it. Some persons were primarily influenced by their economic interests. Different motives impelled others. None knew whether or not the Madison administration could form a team from the welter.[24]

Whatever the diverse factions thought or knew or did, war itself was drawing ever closer in the spring of 1812.

England and Canada

Except for eighteen months in 1801 and 1802 England had been at war since 1793, and before that for almost a century. War had piled up a funded debt of £609,600,000 by 1811 (only £80 million short of the level at the outbreak of World War I). Political economists like Adam Smith felt that so massive a burden would ruin the nation unless corrective action was taken at once. The Bank of England had been given permission to suspend specie payment, which to conservatives seemed a sure route to financial disaster. British taxes in wartime aggregated about $25.00 per person, as compared with $2.00 in America. The laboring class was much closer to pauperism in Britain than in the United States. Also, the common people owned very little land in England, whereas they owned a good deal of it in the United States.[1]

Wheat was priced at $3.50 a bushel and remained so until the fall of 1813. British exports fell off one-third in 1811 after the closing of American ports to English ships in February. The high price of bread and loss of jobs brought substantial portions of the population close to starvation. The Luddites, striking out blindly in their misery, smashed cotton machinery which they thought was taking away their work, and other underprivileged groups rioted and pillaged. The Tory government, unmoved by the problems of the needy, sternly repressed their uprisings. Adding to public uneasiness was the final decline of George III into unrelieved insanity. This made necessary the establishment of the formal regency of the Prince of Wales. A majority of the governing classes did not believe that the Prince Regent had the qualities needed for effective rule, while the common people called him "Prinny," in part derisively. As if this were not enough, Napoleon had succeeded in subduing all of Spain and Portugal except Cadiz and Lisbon, while Sweden had elected one of Napoleon's marshals, Bernadotte, to be king, and had declared war on England. Had an American declaration of war struck the nation so beleagured in 1811, it might have produced immediate concessions.[2]

Fortunately for England, her position in the world improved substantially during the first half of 1812. After the siege of Badajoz in April, Wellington's entire force was free for operations on the Iberian Peninsula, whereas the French there were tied down trying to garrison a vast, turbulent country. Next, Russia and Sweden detached themselves from France and resumed their trade with England, closed four years earlier. Britain was now able to transfer her substantial Baltic squadron into the Atlantic. With these improvements in their international affairs, Englishmen became more resentful than ever of American belligerence. This hostility seemed to them at once cold-blooded patricide and alliance with a despot who threatened the liberty of the entire Western world.[3]

A demented Englishman named John Bellingham murdered Spencer Perceval, the prime minister, on 11 May 1812. The loyal opposition expected to be called upon to form a government, but instead the Prince Regent dipped into Perceval's Tory ministry. Robert Banks Jenkinson, second earl of Liverpool, became prime minister on 8 June at the age of forty-two. He had entered the government in 1793 and had since then held office continuously, except for 1806. Relatively speaking, he was well trained for his task, which, as matters fell out, he labored at for the next decade and a half. During the previous three years he had been secretary of state for war and the colonies (the two secretaryships had been combined in 1801). He had been on excellent terms with George III and was on the same footing with the Prince Regent, which aided him in the operation of the clumsy apparatus of the British government. Clever persons considered him and the associates he asked to govern with him mediocre. That may have been a correct estimate, but at least Liverpool was well balanced and moderate with regard to America. Also, he and his ministers, being all in their forties, had the advantage of youth. Even though Liverpool had always been inclined to respect American neutrality, his administration embodied the national will to defeat Napoleon.[4]

Henry Bathurst, third Earl Bathurst, became secretary of state for war and the colonies in the Liverpool ministry. He had advanced in politics almost stealthily as a protégé of the younger William Pitt. Aged fifty in 1812, never conspicuous before the public, quiet and unobtrusive, but regarded by his peers as efficient, he, as one of His Majesty's principal secretaries of state, occupied a key position. He proved to be the minister most concerned with America. This fact helped America, because Bathurst, like Liverpool, had throughout the years of gathering crisis favored keeping the United States neutral in the Napoleonic conflict, and he had avoided vindictiveness toward America.[5]

In common with most of the British government, the administration of the army was cumbersome and riddled with peculation. Its flaws in organization reflected a government which was weakened by powerful countervailing forces, such as the independent aristocracy, strong commercial interests, the almost holy sanctity of property, and the innumerable civil liberties imbedded in the common law. In theory strategic decisions had to be made by the King in Council, but in practice an informal inner cabinet made them, or often single ministers or other officers who were knowledgeable and willing to accept responsibility. Lord Bathurst was one of these.[6]

The second of George III's sons, Frederick, duke of York and Albany, was intimately connected with army operations, but not with strategy. Always accessible and willing to look into complaints, he did much to keep the unwieldy system running fairly well. Unfortunately, his influence at the time was at a low ebb because of scandals involving his mistress. Without his knowledge, she had sold influence in the army. Even so, Sir John Fortescue, historian of the British army, felt that Frederick could have run the war from his office at the Horse Guards more effectively than it actually was run.[7]

An English colonel rarely actually commanded, but rather owned, a regiment and left its handling to the lieutenant colonel. Commissions from colonel down were often for sale, but they could be acquired in other ways. It was possible to fill vacancies caused by death on a merit basis, and lowly sergeants sometimes earned battlefield commissions. No one could buy a commission as adjutant, quartermaster, or paymaster, nor one in either the Royal Artillery or the Royal Engineers. In those arms officers came from the middle class and were promoted on merit and on seniority.[8]

Henry, Earl Bathurst

At the beginning of 1812 the British regular army totaled about 220,000 men. It was nearly as top-heavy with infantry as the American militia. In addition there were no less than 150,000 militiamen who were deemed well enough organized to be placed on the official roster. But because of England's preoccupation in Europe, not much of this force was available to serve in North America.[9]

Unlike the army, the Royal Navy had a representative in the Ministry. He was the first lord of the Admiralty, the head of a seven-man commission denominated the Lords Commissioners of the Admiralty. He was not subject to control by the other commissioners, except that at least two of them had to sign a directive to make it official. The Lords Commissioners, called for short the Admiralty Board, were responsible for all aspects of the navy, except for strategy. But the first lord sat in the Ministry and in the inner cabinet, and was at least present when strategy was made.[10]

The Navy Board, not to be confused with the Admiralty Board, consisted of specialists who directed the actual operation of the navy. Together with the Victualling and the Sick and Wounded Boards and the Treasury of the Navy, it was nominally under the Lords Commissioners. These units were made up of specialists, and it was hard for amateurs such as the Lords Commissioners actually to direct them. But the Lords, subject to the King in Council, made all appointments in the Royal Navy, and they were able to achieve some surveillance over the boards through the admirals they designated to command fleets.

Robert Saunders Dundas, second Viscount Melville, was appointed first lord of the Admiralty on 25 March 1812 (he remained in the office until 1827). Of greater importance in the conduct of the war with America, although of lesser status, was Secretary of the Admiralty John Wilson Croker. Like his predecessors, of whom Samuel Pepys was the best known, he owed his appointment to this office in 1809 to political favor. He was a literary figure of some reputation and a formidable debater in Parliament. Many of the most important strategic decisions concerning America were published through him to subordinate commanders, and probably a number of them were formulated by him. He was well enough connected and efficient enough to retain the post until 1830.[11]

Of the 650 to 700 vessels in the British navy only 3 ships-of-the-line, 23 frigates, and 53 sloops, brigs, and schooners were in the waters of the New World, and only 25 of these were off North America.[12]

In June 1812 the British minister to the United States, Augustus John Foster, finally realized that the Americans meant to fight. Having theretofore deceived his government as well as himself, he now sought to avoid naval humiliation. He warned Vice Admiral Herbert Sawyer, in command at Halifax, that British captains ought to avoid single-ship engagements with American ships of the same class, for it would be bad policy to lose so much as one ship to the Americans.[13]

Ever since the American Revolution, the United States had loomed as a menace to Canada. In 1811 Canada's population, perhaps 500,000, was about 7 per cent of that of the United States. Sir George Prevost looked over the situation and said, "The Canadas now unequivocally become the object of indemnity to the government of the United States for the commercial restraints and privations it complains of." Almost a century later Sir John Fortescue asserted that there were never enough men to defend the whole of Canada "except against so unmilitary a nation as the Americans." Upper Canada had not more than 77,000 people in it and was especially vulnerable.[14] The only hope there was help from the Indians, and to insure this help early governors of Canada had sought to create an Indian buffer state. Beginning in 1807 Lieutenant General Sir James Craig and Francis Gore, governors of Lower Canada and Upper Canada respectively, had commenced an enlarged program to ally the Indians with Great Britain. Americans feared such an alliance, and charged England with inciting the Indians to aggression.[15] Neither the Americans nor the British realized that warrior strength in the Great Lakes region did not exceed 1,500.

British authorities assumed that as long as Britain controlled the ocean and Quebec remained in her hands, Canada could not be conquered. The St. Lawrence River was the main artery and Quebec the heart of British power in Canada. Quebec, therefore, must have a large enough garrison at all times to fight off assault at least until winter shut down campaigning. An invader could not continue the fight in the winter weather. When navigation opened up once more, succor from the home islands would be waiting to ascend the river and relieve the city. Control of the ocean extended all the way up the arterial St. Lawrence to Montreal, but above Montreal perilous rapids interrupted the continuous flow of sea power. However the realm of sea power began again on the Great Lakes.[16]

Sir James Craig, being recalled, left for England on 19 June 1811. An interregnum of three months followed, ended when Sir George Prevost arrived. His title (when in July 1812 it became official) was Captain General, Governor in Chief, Vice Admiral, Lieutenant General, and Commanding Officer of His Majesty's forces in Upper Canada, Lower Canada, Nova Scotia, New Brunswick, Prince Edward Isle, Cape Breton, Newfoundland, and the Bermudas. No more controversial figure than Prevost appears in this segment of history. He was

Lieutenant General Sir George Prevost

forty-four at the time of his appointment. His father, although Swiss-born, had been a major general in the British army and had secured for the son his initial commission. In the ensuing three decades Prevost rose to be major general in 1798 and lieutenant general ten years later. Most of his service had been in the West Indies, where in 1798 he had become governor of St. Lucia. His success and popularity there brought him the governorship of Nova Scotia and then of Canada. From the start he seems to have had better rapport with the French element in the population than his predecessors, and to have drawn it into a closer allegiance with Great Britain. The consensus is that he was an able peacetime administrator, but that he lacked the dash and daring to be a wartime governor and commander. He fussed too much over petty problems, correctness of uniform and the like. Old army officers looked somewhat askance at him because he was Swiss and because he had never found his way into the central combat arena in the fight against Napoleon, but only served around the fringes.[17]

Sir James Craig had had many bitter fights with the Canadian parliaments, but Prevost enjoyed better relations with them. He held the power to appoint members of the upper chambers for life, establish electoral districts for the houses of commons both of Upper and of Lower Canada, and assign the numbers of representatives to each district. He could also convene, prorogue, and dissolve the parliaments, and refuse his assent to any bills they passed. The governor of Upper Canada had similar power, but subordinate to Prevost's. At the governor's prodding, the Parliament of Lower Canada, in spite of sharp opposition, passed a bill to enlarge the militia and appropriated £60,000 for the purpose.[18]

The British land forces in North America totaled 8,125 early in 1812. Of this number 2,100 were Canadian auxiliaries. One Canadian unit of the regular establishment was the Tenth Royal Veterans Battalion, 473 steady veterans, formed in 1806. Another was the Canadian Fencibles, aggregating 668, organized as light troops in 1808. Next was the regiment of Glengary Light Infantry, with an authorized strength of 600, to be recruited from Scotsmen in Canada. Roughly an additional 1,000 Fencibles were stationed in Newfoundland and Nova Scotia, but they were not readily available for use in the interior. Prevost relayed the need for more troops to Liverpool, who promised that he would do all he could. But he made it clear that most of the available British strength had to be concentrated in Europe.[19]

General Prevost selected Major General Sir Isaac Brock to replace Francis Gore as governor and commander of Upper Canada. Brock was two years younger than his superior. He had been a soldier since boy-

Major General Sir Isaac Brock

hood and had first commanded a regiment when twenty-eight. He had many advantages Prevost had not: extensive combat duty, distinguished service against the French in Europe, ten years in Canada, and a large measure of dash and daring. Because Prevost respected his ability but regarded the dash and daring as impetuosity, he sent only a minimum of forces to Upper Canada. This was his way of preventing Brock from making rash moves. Brock therefore had only about 1,600 regulars at his command. "Most of the people have lost all confidence," he said, "I however speak loud and look big." He had scant confidence in the civilian population, but he was not the kind to lose heart. He knew of course that he had to remain on the strategic defensive.[20]

Governor Brock's experience with the Parliament of Upper Canada, which met at York, was different from Prevost's. He proposed to suspend the privilege of the writ of habeas corpus, but could not persuade the Parliament to agree, probably because the members really did not expect war with the United States. United States influence was rife in Upper Canada; indeed the area was infested by "the most abandoned characters who seek impunity in this province from crimes committed in the states."[21]

Like his predecessors, General Brock understood that Britain needed to have the Indians as allies in order to save Upper Canada. To secure them it would be necessary to capture Detroit and Mackinac from the Americans and to control the other trading posts on the Great Lakes. From these centers British influence could radiate outward along the waterways as far south as New Orleans and as far west at the Great Plains. Control of the head of Lake Erie and access to Lake Huron meant influence with the Indians as far away as the Missouri River. Sanguinary as Brock was, even he admitted that reinforcements would be necessary to secure the redmen as allies.[22]

Generals Brock and Prevost thus conducted themselves as if they must prepare Canada for war. Their judgment was sound, for all the while, in the spring of 1812, war was coming closer.

Tippecanoe

The Indians in America rarely realized the advantages of forming an intertribal confederation to halt the advance of the white men. One Indian leader lived at this time, however, whose vision was wide. Tecumseh was born in 1768 of a Creek mother and a Shawnee father. Through extended contacts with white society as a young man, he had become familiar with Shakespeare and the Bible. He is said to have fallen in love with Rebecca Galloway, who returned his love. She refused to marry him, however, unless he gave up Indian ways, and so the affair ended. As the years went by he grew to hate white men and to seek revenge upon them for his people. Spurning liquor and white society, he gathered about him a group of dedicated warriors and formed a village in western Ohio, within the cession which Anthony Wayne had wrung from the Northwest tribes in 1795. This settlement caused much uneasiness to the white frontier dwellers, and they were relieved when Tecumseh voluntarily moved outside the treaty boundaries in 1807 to a new site near the confluence of the Wabash and the Tippecanoe rivers.[1] They did not know that he did so in order to try to carry into execution his project to unite all the tribes of the Mississippi Valley.

William Henry Harrison, governor of Indiana Territory, concluded on 30 September 1809 a land cession of about 3 million acres with some chiefs who purported to represent the Delaware, Eel River, Kickapoo, and Wea tribes. These chiefs ceded the ground right out from under Tecumseh and his band, but Tecumseh threatened to kill them and refused to abide by the terms of their treaty. Harrison was convinced that the combination being put together by Tecumseh and his brother the Prophet had to be broken up lest all tribes in the region unite, and the governor sought a conference with the Indians. The first meeting took place on 20 August 1810. Tecumseh is supposed to have talked very plainly to the governor. "How can we have confidence in the white people?" romantics quote him as saying. "When Jesus Christ came upon earth, you . . . nailed him to a cross." Although what he said impressed even those listeners who could not understand Shawnee, the conference came close to turning into a donnybrook. Yet Harrison developed a high opinion of his antagonist's talents. He wrote of Tecumseh: "The implicit obedience and respect which [his] followers pay to him is really astonishing and more than any other circumstance bespeaks him one of those uncommon geniuses which spring up occasionally to produce revolutions and overturn the established order of things. If it were not for the vicinity of the United States, he would perhaps be founder of an Empire that would rival in glory that of Mexico and Peru. No difficulties deter him. His activity and industry supply the want of letters. For four years he has been in constant motion. You see him today on the Wabash or on the banks of the Mississippi, and wherever he goes he makes an impression favorable to his purpose."[2]

In July 1811 Tecumseh appeared with 300 warriors at Vincennes, the capital of the territory, though Harrison had asked him to come unarmed. He let it be known that he was traveling south to contact the tribes there. He did not so state it, but everyone present knew that his purpose was to unite all Indians against the United States. He asked that white settlers stay out of the so-called new purchase until his return the following spring, at which time he would go and negotiate directly with the President. He started southward on 5 August with an elite band of 20 to 30 warriors, clad and ornamented alike and trained to conduct impressive ceremonials. Governor Harrison believed that there would be no hostilities until he returned.[3]

Tecumseh and his band drew large crowds. It was necessary for the influential Choctaw Chief Pushmataha to follow him from town to town to undo his influence. An important faction of the Creek Confederation, because Tecumseh had Creek blood and because the faction opposed the civilizing, de-Indianizing program of Benjamin Hawkins, the United States Indian agent, prepared the way for the touring chief. Tuscanea, the oldest son of the head chief of the Creeks, saw to it that 5,000 Creeks came to hear his talks. In the end no alliance resulted from this council, but for a time the outcome was in the balance. One after another, the powerful Choctaw, Chickasaw, Cherokee, and Creek tribes refused the proposed union, mostly because it implied a connection with Great Britain which the leaders reasoned was neither safe nor sound.[4]

In predicting that there would be no violence while Tecumseh was in the South, Harrison either was concealing his own intentions in a Machiavellian way or was underestimating the capabilities of Tecumseh's brother Tenskwatawa. The brother, a medicine man called the "Prophet" by white men, was Tecumseh's junior by seven years. Tenskwatawa had been an idler in his youth, more interested in liquor than in hunting or war. Then after a sudden conversion he became an impassioned advocate of an ascetic life devoted to winning back from the whites the spoils taken from his people. The year 1811 was a good one for him, since it was filled with frightening spectacles of nature which he ascribed to his own supernatural powers. While his brother was gone, the Prophet worked into a frenzy the people at Prophetstown on the Tippecanoe.

Governor Harrison became certain that it was necessary to break up Prophetstown. For western whites the place had become a symbol of British influence. Only Federalists denied the charge that England was inciting the Indians against the United States, but even they had to be aware that Britain's gifts to the natives had at least doubled. In any case, party fervor attached itself to the issue of war or peace with the Indians. Governor Ninian Edwards of Illinois Territory, and later Governor Benjamin Howard of the newly formed Missouri Territory, agreed with Harrison and looked to him for leadership in the conduct of Indian affairs. Harrison promised Secretary Eustis that he would not act without the advice and consent of the two governors.[5] They approved his suggestion in August for a "peaceful" march up the Wabash River to the outer limits of the purchase of 1809. Harrison now informed Secretary Eustis of the projected foray. Upon receipt of the plan Eustis wrote to President Madison, who was in Virginia, saying that he would like directions from him at once on the matter. But in the end he chose not to wait for Madison's order, and sent his own ideas to Harrison, "to be observed or departed from as your judgment shall direct." He favored approaching the Prophet, ordering his band to disperse, and attacking him if he refused to comply. He authorized Harrison to establish a post on the new purchase if it seemed necessary. As the administration believed that the British were not inciting the Indians to war, Eustis added that whatever the general did must not exasperate England.[6]

Harrison did not wait for the approval of Washington, but he did wait for the arrival of the Fourth United States Infantry to start his advance. That regiment marched out of Philadelphia on 3 June 1811 and made its painful way on foot and in keelboats for 1,500 miles to Vincennes, which it reached on 19 September. Even at the end of this grueling march it dazzled Vincennes with its brass buttons and stovepipe hats, the gaudiest costumes that had appeared so far on the frontier. Harrison praised Colonel John Boyd for the appearance and quality of his regiment. But when the general issued the march order six days later, only 350 out of the 533 men of the Fourth were physically able to respond. They moved out with 400 Indiana militia infantry, 84 Indiana mounted rifles, 123 Kentucky dragoons, and 13 spies and guides, a total of 970 men.[7] Their surprise-proof order of march was something Harrison had learned from Anthony Wayne during the Fallen Timbers campaign. A company of riflemen preceded the infantry column by 150 yards. Fifty yards behind the riflemen rode a mounted troop, and another followed 100 yards in the rear of the main column. One hundred yards off to the right and to the left were companies of flankers. The right side of the main column was trained to face right to repel attack from that quarter, and the left side to the left, and if there was an attempt at envelopment, the two ranks would be back to back. The Indiana militia had trouble with these evolutions, but Harrison said the men had the best spirit he had ever seen.[8]

Since the column prepared a strong defensive position each night, it took more than two weeks to cover the sixty-five miles to the high ground where the Wabash River bends and where Terre Haute now stands. The men completed Fort Harrison there on 27 October, and moved forward on the next leg of the march to the mouth of the Vermillion River. There Harrison ordered a blockhouse to be built which was later called Fort Boyd. In all this deliberate advance, including moving supplies by boats on the rivers, there was fearful manual labor for the enlisted men. Harrison pointed out to the secretary of war that citizen soldiers had never before been successfully employed to do so much building and at so low an extra cost as half a gill of whiskey per man. Colonel John Boyd did not see in the citizen soldiers the virtues Harrison discovered, and he harassed them with impetuous punishments. Since Boyd's conduct threatened the cooperation between citizen soldiers and regulars, Harrison stepped in tactfully and restricted Boyd's disciplinary power even within the Fourth Infantry. This preserved the working team, but left Boyd with a grudge.[9]

Harrison had warned the Indians that the distance his expedition advanced depended upon their conduct. Thus, when a supposed Indian stole horses and when on 10 October someone fired shots into his camp, wounding a man, the general considered that the Indians had challenged him to advance. Across the Vermillion River went the column, into territory claimed by the redmen. More long shots dropped harmlessly among the white soldiers. By this time—perhaps before—Harrison had made up his mind not to turn back until Prophetstown was destroyed. His officers urged an attack at the earliest possible moment, but on 6 November a deputation of Indians for the first time requested a parley. They assured Harrison that they had been trying to find him along the Wabash and had failed because he had veered out into the prairie (to avoid, as it happened, certain dangerous defiles). Against the counsel of the officers, he determined to go into bivouac and to talk to the Prophet the next day.[10]

The campsite, picked for the invaders by the Indians, was about two miles west of Prophetstown on an oak-covered knoll which ex-

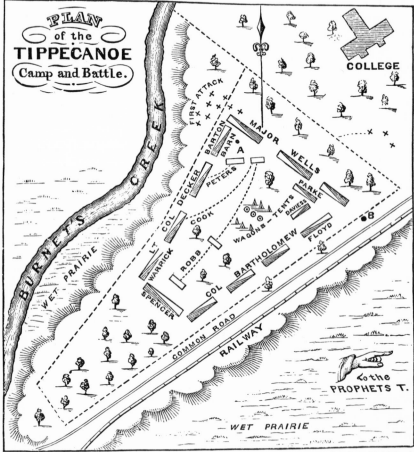

PLAN of the TIPPECANOE Camp and Battle.

COLLEGE

BURNET'S CREEK

FIRST ATTACK

BARTON

BARN
A

MAJOR WELLS

LT. COL. DECKER

PETERS

COOK

PARKE

DAVIESS

WAGONS-TENTS

WARRICK

ROBB

COL

BARTHOLOMEW

FLOYD

SPENCER

B

WET PRAIRIE

COMMON ROAD

RAILWAY

To the PROPHETS T.

WET PRAIRIE

Lossing, Field Book

tended like a small pointed peninsula into a wet prairie. Enemies later accused Harrison of permitting the redmen to place him where he could be secretly surrounded, but in fact there was no more secure situation in the vicinity. Ten acres in extent, it afforded enough room for Harrison's men to move about without interfering with each other. On the east side it was ten feet above the prairie, on the west twenty. Burnet's Creek ran at the foot of the west-side bank. The encampment formed a hollow trapezoid, roughly following the edges of the pointed peninsula. The right flank was about seventy-five yards long, the left twice that. The men lay down to sleep in order of battle, with their guns loaded and bayonets fixed. In case of attack they were to rise, advance a pace or two, and form a single line of battle. Since Indians did not rely on shock action, Harrison saw no need for a depth of more than one line of two ranks. Also, he held most of his mounted men within the trapezoid as a disposable reserve. For lack of axes, no breastworks went up. Harrison reasoned that the Indians had already let slip their best opportunities for surprise, but he still ordered a night watch of 108 men. At first the moon came out, then black clouds blotted out all light, and cold rain fell. The volunteers who lacked blankets were cold and miserable.[11]

There was no problem of keeping warm in Prophetstown. Shabonee, a Potawatomi chief, later testified that two Englishmen were present, urging the Indians to strike. The Prophet forced a captured Negro wagon driver to talk. He said that the whites had no cannon and that Harrison meant to attack after the conference. He was correct on both counts. In any case, 550 to 700 Kickapoos, Wyandots, Potawatamis, Piankeshaws, Shawnees, Mucos, Hurons, Ottawas, Chippewas, and probably some Winnebagos, worked themselves into a frenzy during the night. The Prophet, engaged in incantations and exhortations, convinced the warriors that the enemy gunpowder had already turned to sand and the enemy bullets to soft mud. The result was that the warriors swarmed out into the inky darkness, without waiting for leaders, and surrounded the knoll at about 4:00 A.M.[12]

Stephen Mars, a sentinel at the northwestern angle, heard the stirring, nervously fired a shot or two, and fled for camp. He had alerted his fellows, but he was killed before he could reach safety. The Indians now yelled hideously and opened fire. They worked their way into the northwest angle, where for a time they badly hurt the two companies stationed there, one of regulars and the other of Kentucky volunteers. The first white men to arms were silhouetted against campfires, and many were hit before the fires were put out.

They were under orders to keep their stations until it was light enough to see. Harrison was awake when the shooting began, and he mounted and rode toward the noise. His white horse had broken its tether during the night, and he rode a dark one to the point of attack. This accident saved his life. The Indians were looking for his white horse, and killed the officer who found and rode it. Because of superior discipline, Harrison was sure that his army could hold during the darkness and throw the enemy back in the daylight.[13]

Firing now broke out at the eastern angle, and Major Joseph Daviess, a celebrated Kentucky citizen soldier, moved his part of the reserve there. Eager for glory and convinced of his own military talent, he sent repeated demands to Harrison that he be allowed to attack and dislodge sharpshooters firing from behind logs in his front. After the third demand Harrison told him to use his own judgment. Thereupon, without waiting to form his men, he showed more courage than discretion. Clad in a white coat which made him an easy target, Daviess raced for the pinpoints of gunfire, calling for the men to follow him. After a few steps he was killed, probably by bullets (not aimed at him) fired from his own lines into the darkness.[14]

Firing now became heavy all around the perimeter. The infantry were using cartridges with twelve buckshot in them. As a dull day broke on 7 November, the Indians were concentrated at the two ends of the camp and had good cover among the oaks. Many appeared in the open, though, because they believed in the Prophet, who was continuing his incantations on a high rock some distance to the east. Using a tactic rare for Indians, they rushed forward in groups to fire, and retreated to load while other groups rushed.[15]

When it was light enough, Harrison sent out the mounted men to encircle the foe's flanks. This time-honored tactic worked once more, and the horse soldiers were soon pursuing the Indians across the wet prairie.

Harrison had lost 62 killed and 126 wounded, a casualty rate of 20 to 24 per cent. Indian losses totaled perhaps 200. When word reached Harrison that Tecumseh was close by with many fresh warriors, he ordered his army to dig in. The following day a cautious reconnaissance revealed that Prophetstown had been abandoned. The army marched in and found good new equipment supplied by the British. Having taken what they wanted, they applied the torch to all the rest, including the town.

With many wounded men and the menace of Tecumseh, Harrison feared for his column. He ordered valuable private property, including his own, to be burned in order to free wagons for the wounded. Public property was saved. Now began the retreat to Vincennes, 150 miles of anguish for the wounded men jolting in the wagons. An average of two of them a day died from the punishment.[16]

The Indians, suffering too, came near to killing the Prophet. He saved himself only by claiming that his wife had touched some of his sacred vessels during her menstrual period, and thus had broken the spell. Though they spared his life, the warriors trussed him up and carried him like a captured wolf. Weeks later Tecumseh stood among the ruins of his village in the wan light of a grim winter day and swore, it is said, eternal enmity to the white man. When reunited with the tribe he banished his brother, lest the Prophet do more harm.[17]

News of the so-called Battle of Tippecanoe was soon widespread. Andrew Jackson was much pleased and offered to raise 1,000 men to come to Harrison's aid against "those unrelenting barbarians." "The blood of our murdered countrymen must be revenged," he said, "that banditti ought to be swept from the face of the earth." Like most frontiersmen, he was sure that British agents lay behind it.[18] In general, people interpreted the battle according to their politics. Harrison's political foes, of whom he had many, charged him with shameless aggressiveness and bad leadership. Friends, on the other hand, insisted that he had saved the Northwest from devastation. Friends also emphasized his cold nerve in the battle, but Daviess' followers contended that he had purposely sacrificed their leader. Colonel Boyd of course found fault with the citizen soldiers and with Harrison's use of them. In all cases, the spotlight was upon Harrison. This made it virtually certain that if there was military activity in the West again, Harrison would lead it.[19]

The Battle of Tippecanoe pushed Tecumseh and his followers irrevocably into alliance with England, it convinced British officials in Canada of the need to aid the Indians, and it inflamed western Americans with the idea that they would never be safe and would never be able to expand peaceably as long as a powerful British influence remained among the Indians. For these reasons it has been called the opening battle of the War of 1812.

1812

Reaction to the War

On 1 June 1812 President James Madison sent to Congress a message recommending a declaration of war against Great Britain. Within three days, that is, on 4 June, the House passed a war bill, but the Senate took time to deliberate. Federalist Senator James A. Bayard of Delaware asked that consideration of it be postponed until October. The people were not prepared for the declaration, he said, and did not expect it. Moreover, a few months' delay would enable a great many valuable ships to reach home safely. He was not heeded; on 18 June the Senate passed the House bill. The Senate Committee on Foreign Relations took the opportunity to get in a verbal salvo at the new enemy. "The mad ambition, the lust of power, and commercial avarice of Great Britain, arrogating to herself the complete domination of the ocean, and exercising over it an unbounded and lawless tyranny, have left neutral nations [no alternative] . . . it must be evident to the impartial world that the contest which is now forced upon the United States is a contest for their sovereignty and independence." The same day the President proclaimed a state of war.[1]

The news reached New York on 21 June 1812, Boston the next day, Quebec on 25 June, remote Amherstburg by 28 June, and New Orleans on 10 July.

Now repeal of the nonimportation of English goods was proposed in the House. The argument in favor of repeal was that war costs had to be paid by duties on imports from England, or else there would have to be some internal taxes, which were generally hated.

Although the debate was sharp, in the end nonimportation was continued, but only by the Speaker's breaking the tie vote. Congress made a gesture toward financing the war by issuing $5 million in treasury notes and by doubling existing import duties. Even though this was not enough, the solons turned to regulating the size of the army. They set the number of regiments of regular infantry at 26, and reduced the size of some of them. The surprising result of their action was to raise the total authorized strength no more than 100 men to 35,603, but the actual enrollment in July stood at 6,686 enlisted men. They increased the number of brigadier generals from five to seven. This done, Congress adjourned on 6 July without attempting to meet the need for money.[2]

Major General Henry Dearborn requested militia from Connecticut in June, but he got instead a note from Acting Governor John Cotton Smith. The state council had convened, the governor said, to consider the general's request and had concluded that it was unconstitutional on two grounds: (1) the President had not indicated that there existed any of the three exigencies stipulated in the Constitution—an invasion, an insurrection, or a combination to break the laws—and (2) Connecticut militia could not be placed under the immediate command of federal officers when proper state officers were already designated for them. The secretary of war, entering the dialogue, insisted that an invasion did exist or was imminent. The governor countered that neither a declaration of war nor the nearby cruising of a hostile fleet constituted an invasion or even the threat of one. He would send no troops.[3]

Upon receipt of the declaration of war, Governor Caleb Strong of Massachusetts proclaimed a fast day to mourn fighting "against the nation from which we are descended." Not until 3 July did he issue general orders to the militia. He called upon the citizen soldiers "duly to notice the solemn and interesting crisis [and to] meet the occasion with constancy and firmness." Massachusetts organized and properly reported her share of the 100,000 detachment, but when General Dearborn went to Boston to tend to the defense of the coast, he met inertia and hostility. Governor Strong on 5 August finally put his state's case into writing. His premises and conclusions were much the same as those of Connecticut, but the emphasis was slightly different. Governor, Council, and three justices of the Supreme Court agreed that the call of the President was unconstitutional. The power to determine whether or not there was an invasion rested as much with the governors of the several states as with the President. Acting on this reasoning, the governor surveyed the scene, saw no invasion, and refused to release Massachusetts militia to the United States.[4]

At least one citizen of Massachusetts regarded the war as just and necessary. This was John Adams who, because of the hostile attitude of England, had been expecting war for a quarter of a century.

The reaction of the other New England states varied. Rhode Island provided no militiamen for federal service during 1812, but the state did supply one company of volunteers to guard Newport. The company was accepted into United States service, but with the stipulation that it could not be marched elsewhere without its own consent. New Hampshire sent only 246 militiamen into federal service during 1812. Nevertheless each of these states received 1,000 stands of arms under the act of 1808 for arming the militia. Vermont leaned more toward New York than toward New England. Governor Jonas Galusha of Vermont was an ardent supporter of the administration and saw to it that his state supplied 2,434 militiamen for federal service in 1812.[5]

Public sentiment in Maryland favored the war, at least in Baltimore, but the state found only 318 men for federal service in 1812. There were hard-core Federalists in Maryland who opposed the war at great personal loss. One of them ran a press in Baltimore which poured out denunciations of administrative policy. A mob wrecked his press, but he procured another and continued his output. Light-Horse Harry Lee and some other Revolutionary officers who were Federalists undertook to defend his new office. The mob attacked again and killed a defender or two, but Lee and his supporters were whisked off by the authorities and put into jail for their own protection. The mob broke into the jail, severely beat them, and left them lying helpless all night, exposed to the weather. Although General Lee lived to 1818, he never fully recovered. This episode, the "Baltimore Massacre," caused Federalists in New England to look to their guns, not for protection against England, but for possible use against their political enemies, the friends of the war.[6]

The *Montreal Herald*, commenting on the declaration of war, bitterly announced that the United States sought to crush religion and venerable laws and customs in Canada and to replace them with anarchy. The now-declared foe, if victorious, would be "the most cruel and unrelenting of tyrants."[7]

When Sir George Prevost learned of the American declaration, he suspended the order from the government to ship out the Forty-first, Forty-ninth, and One Hundredth Foot Regiments, drew the elite companies of both regular and militia regiments into a special battalion to protect the areas south of Montreal, and ordered 2,000 militia to be drafted for training. When some of the latter mutinied, he forced them to comply by threatening them with regulars armed with cannon. He moved his headquarters from Quebec to Montreal to be closer to operations, and left in command at Quebec Major General George Glasgow of the Royal Artillery. Glasgow had served twenty-three years in Canada and had never experienced combat. When ordered to proceed to England, he petitioned to remain where he was, in the hope of finally seeing some action.[8]

General Sir Isaac Brock constantly warned of the unreliability of the population of Upper Canada. Many Canadians were primarily concerned, he said, to determine which side would promote their own interests and then to adhere to it. The militia were fairly well trained, but would probably go home at harvest time. He felt it necessary to prorogue the Parliament of Upper Canada and to declare martial law. "My situation is most critical," he wrote, "not from anything the enemy can do, but from the disposition of the people. The population is . . . essentially bad—a full belief possesses them that this province must inevitably succumb." United States citizens, he said, wielded great influence there. Prevost was apparently certain that the same situation prevailed also in the lower province, and he ruled that Americans who refused either to swear an oath to the king or to take up arms must, with a few exceptions, leave Canada. He also cautioned Brock once more against rash actions. Canada lacked the manpower for offensive use, and besides it was important not to drive New England into joint action with the ·warlike sections.[9]

Prevost bore the labor and worry of defense from the moment of his arrival, but he did not actually receive his commission as governor and commander until the middle of July 1812. Even after he had detained three regiments, he still lacked enough regulars and trained militia to defend so long a frontier. There were besides himself only two general officers of the line in all Canada: Brock and Major General Francis DeRottenburg who was commanding at Montreal. He was therefore obliged to use General Glasgow at Quebec, an artillery officer, and Major General Sir Roger Sheaffe, a retired officer living in Canada. In order to finance operations he called the Parliament of Lower Canada into special session on 16 July 1812. It voted to issue £250,000 of "Army Bills," and appropriated £40,000 to pay the interest on them. A similar issue was authorized for Upper Canada. The citizens recognized the army bills for what they were, a sort of printing-press currency, and were mistrustful of them.

It was necessary to gain the aid of Catholic Bishop Joseph-Octave Plessis before the French-Canadians would accept them.[10]

Forty-one days after Congress declared war, the word arrived in London on 29 July. Two days later, 31 July 1812, the Ministry ordered its first countermeasures. It forbade English ships to sail except in convoys and restrained American ships in English ports. The Orders in Council had been repealed on 23 June and the ministers did not intend to take additional measures until they could learn the American reaction. Word of the repeal of the Orders did not reach President Madison until 12 August, that is, fifty days later. Even then he refused to halt hostilities because he did not know how Britain had reacted to the declaration of war. The lack of swift communications hindered these last chances to settle the war peacefully.[11]

The Ministry had assumed until recently that America would not fight under any circumstances. Preoccupied as they were with Napoleon, they therefore took no time to think about a strategy for use against the United States. But they did not lack advice on the matter, much of it unsolicited. They could choose between two diametrically opposite grand strategies. The first was to make a pre-emptive strike against America to cripple her as a dangerous future trade rival. She had neither fleet, nor army, nor money, nor unity against England. But she was rapidly gaining power, and if left unchecked she would in the future involve Britain in a series of ruinous wars. She coupled hatred for Britain with a determination to drive her out of the Western Hemisphere. Finally, no European power would come to the aid of the United States in 1812. Strike, therefore, before she became a rival too big to eliminate! Force her to return Florida and Louisiana to Spain. Free the slaves, set up Negro governments in the South, and split the South off from the North. Return all territory north of the Ohio River to the Indians and help them retain it. Take possession of the shores of the Great Lakes and of the St. Lawrence River. If English troops would not carry out this firm policy, hire Cossacks from Russia. Blockade all American ports and land enough troops on the coasts to harass the enemy relentlessly.[12]

Lieutenant General Sir George Prevost made himself the spokesman of the softer strategy. Some ministers, who were preoccupied with France, sided with him. They traced the animosity of the war party in the United States to insidious French influence. France would welcome a British invasion of the United States, in part because it would afford her a diversion and in part because it would unite the States against England as nothing else could do. Moreover, a harsh strategy might fix the fire-eaters in permanent control. Those fire-eaters would strive primarily not to win a war but to destroy British seaborne commerce. When that was accomplished, France could then move upon America, overcome her, almost without a struggle, and achieve dominance on land and sea.[13]

The Liverpool ministry did not pay much attention to the proposals for a harsh strategy. Only when there were a few resources left over from the struggle against Napoleon did they consider America at all, and then they chose the milder course. Perhaps a mild strategy won favor only because the means for the opposite were not at hand. The only offensive ingredient in it was a limited naval blockade. But even this was based upon the milder mood, which in turn rested upon the desire to exploit the cleavage in the States.

Aside from its naval aspects, British strategy was not generated at the seat of government. After the first few months it originated with officers on duty in America. Generals Prevost and Brock, for example, urged that Britain must dominate the Great Lakes. Otherwise numerous invasion routes into Upper Canada lay invitingly open. Britain needed the lakes to control the Indians too, and needed the Indians to have any chance of coping with the United States. Bathurst ruefully stated that he would have preferred the Indians to be neutral, but that if England did not woo them they would ally themselves with the United States. Accordingly, he did not attempt to cut back the £29,600 paid annually to maintain the Indian service in Canada.[14]

As soon as the British commander at Kingston knew of the state of war, he occupied Carleton Island, which dominated the head of the St. Lawrence, and stationed militia cavalrymen in pairs westward along the northern shore of Lake Ontario to keep open communication with York. Convoys went out from Kingston to protect the indispensable fleets of bateaux which carried supplies through the rapids above Montreal. Soon, however, three American farmers overpowered the four Canadians who constituted the garrison on Carleton Island. This was the United States' first success on the lakes, and the last for some time. Now Prevost replaced the resident commander at Kingston with Colonel Robert Lethbridge, an elderly half-pay officer. Lethbridge led an expedition to shoot up the nearby American naval base at Sackett's Harbor, but accomplished little.[15]

Canada's military strength was placed primarily in the area downriver from Montreal. Here in mid-1812 were stationed 4,744 regular British troops, more than twice as many as in Upper Canada. In spite of the attitude of New England, President Madison had to take this concentration into account. He therefore designated the senior of the two major generals in the American service to command in the North-

Major General Henry Dearborn

east. This senior was Major General Henry Dearborn, who, like Secretary Eustis, had been trained in medicine. The American Revolution had interrupted his brief practice. He had been at Bunker Hill and with Arnold in Canada in 1775, where he was taken prisoner and then exchanged. He had been present when Burgoyne surrendered at Saratoga in 1777 and at Valley Forge during the following grim winter. He had taken part in the battle at Monmouth Court House in the summer of 1778 and had joined General John Sullivan to fight the Indians in 1779. He was also in the Yorktown campaign. After this extended tour, he never returned either to his native New Hampshire or to the practice of medicine. He became instead an influential politician in the Maine District of Massachusetts, and represented Massachusetts in the United States House of Representatives from 1793 into 1797. When Jefferson became President, it was important to him to have New Englanders in his cabinet. He appointed Dearborn secretary of war, and kept him as such during his two terms. After Jefferson left, Dearborn resigned and accepted a lucrative political appointment as customs collector of the Port of Boston. He was still serving in that office when in April 1812, at the age of sixty-one, he received his commission as major general.[16]

Thereafter such strategy as the United States developed was concerted by Dearborn, Secretary Eustis, and the President. The secretary of the navy was not included in the inner policy-making circle. Indeed, he at first proposed that the American navy be laid up during the war, since it was hopelessly outclassed, but he was overruled. The navy instead was to harass British commerce and cooperate with the land forces to protect American coasts. The only place where the United States could possibly take the offensive was in Canada, and the triumvirate decided to invade that province. They proposed to advance three columns: one along the line of Lake Champlain toward Montreal, the middle one 250 miles southwestward along the Niagara River, and the westernmost 200 miles yet farther southwest at the Detroit River. The President and secretary assumed that General Dearborn would give the three columns some sort of coordination, but Dearborn never accepted this responsibility.[17]

The general went off to Boston to try to win New England over to the war, and stayed there too long for the secretary's liking. But Eustis could not bring himself to give Dearborn a peremptory order to get to the northern frontier. "You have a full view of the intentions of the government," he wrote the general, "take your own time. . . ." Meanwhile the President had designated Brigadier General William Hull to command in the Detroit theater, and had promised him that there would be diversions in his favor to the eastward. Eustis informed Dearborn that Hull was expecting help, but could not tell him anything about the specific timing of Hull's campaign.[18]

When the western column had been in motion for some time, Dearborn was still in Boston and wrote plaintively to the secretary, "I begin to feel that I may be censured for not moving." Finally, after much breast-beating, he departed Boston on 22 July and arrived at Greenbush, his campsite close to Albany, on 26 July. Albany was the place for him, since the line of Lake Champlain northward and the line of the Mohawk River westward were both open there, and it was a fine spot from which to coordinate the three columns. What was principally lacking was knowledge in the general's head. He did not then know who was in charge of either the commissary or the ordnance departments in the Northeast, nor did he know the extent of his authority. "Who is to have command of the operations in Upper Canada?" he asked Eustis. "I take it for granted that my command does not extend to that distant quarter." In reply Eustis gave him a specific order: "You will make a diversion in [Hull's] favor at Niagara and at Kingston as soon as practicable." But neither Eustis nor Dearborn seemed to feel any sense of urgency about creating a diversion for General Hull.[19]

From late June onward Secretary Eustis assumed that preparations were under way to advance all three of the projected columns into Canada. Dearborn's reactions and his requisitions for men and materiel, however, changed Eustis' viewpoint. In the end he virtually abdicated his authority to Dearborn, who thus far had shown no tendency to pick up responsibilities. The secretary's words of abdication were these: "How far the plan originally suggested by you for attacking Niagara, Kingston, and Montreal at the same time can be rendered practicable, you can best judge." Vigorous action fell down somewhere between the secretary and the senior major general and was lost.[20]

President Madison himself would have been content with one rapier thrust at Montreal, for it could throttle the St. Lawrence waterway, choke off supplies to the Great Lakes, and virtually reduce Upper Canada without a fight. But such a strategy required the full cooperation of New England, which could not be obtained. In contrast to the surliness of New England was the enthusiasm of the South, especially Kentucky and Tennessee. That enthusiasm must be directed against Canada through the Mississippi Valley and the Great Lakes.[21]

The British at the start intended only to protect their own shipping and to harass America's. Except for the blockade, they left the initiative, even at sea, to the United States. The only offensive the United States could mount was an assault by single ships on British merchantmen and on naval vessels below the rating of ship-of-the-line. For the defense of the coast she had some fortifications and the old Jeffersonian gunboats: 10 of them at Baltimore, 53 at New York (only 28 of which were in commission), 2 at Charlestown, Massachusetts, and 8 at Portland, Maine. The crew of each gunboat was supposed to be 24 men and boys, but at the moment of their heaviest use, Congress reduced it to 8 men. If more were needed they would have to come from local volunteers. The gunboats were to be placed where they could cooperate with such forts as existed.[22]

As soon as notice of war reached Commodore John Rodgers on 21 June, he put to sea at the head of a squadron of five vessels to try to capture the rich West Indies fleet, then sailing for England. Rodgers flew his broad pennant on *President,* which became detached some distance from the other ships. The lookouts in the flagship sighted an unidentified vessel at 4:40 A.M. on 23 June. The stranger made off under full sail and *President* pursued, but not until 11:30 A.M. did either ship show its true colors. The stranger's colors were British, and *President* slowly drew close enough to fire her bow guns. One of them blew up and broke Rodgers' leg. The frigate *Belvidera,* 36 guns, Captain Richard Byron commanding, replied with her stern guns. At the same time Byron ordered excess stores, ship's boats, and fourteen tons of water jettisoned. Thus lightened, *Belvidera* began to pull away, and soon passed over the horizon. Rodgers lost the race in part because in trying to bring his guns to bear he yawed the ship too much.* In any case, he and the squadron were too far northward now to intercept the Indies fleet, so he had to return without making a capture.[23]

For a cruise similar to Rodgers', Secretary Hamilton assigned to Stephen Decatur *United States, Congress,* and *Argus,* but as these ships were part of Rodgers' squadron, Decatur had to wait until they returned to port. Afterwards Rodgers was to range northward from Chesapeake Bay with two frigates and three brigs. He and Decatur were directed to unite if necessary, but each of them was given discretion, and, as was to be expected, Decatur elected to send his ships out to cruise individually.[24]

Hamilton's suggestion that the two squadron leaders might like to unite was the closest thing to an order to organize into a fleet which came out of the Navy Department. The suggestion might better have been issued as an order. C. S. Forester, analyzing the naval scene later, stated that Rodgers could have swept sixty miles of ocean, and

* To yaw is to deviate from a straight course.

that with Decatur's vessels added, he could have fanned out wide enough to have captured the West Indies fleet. Admiral Mahan agreed.[25]

Captain Isaac Hull sailed out of Boston to assist returning merchantmen. Several of his crew, who were deserters from British warships, feared hanging if captured. They, with others, had to stand to their duty when the lookouts sighted sails on the horizon on 17 July 1812, and *Constitution* made for them. Night halted the approach, but when dawn broke, Hull found himself in the midst of seven British ships: *Africa* 64, *Shannon* 38, *Guerrière* 38, *Belvidera* 36, *Aeolus* 32, and two smaller ones. Fortunately for him the closest of them was five miles. They made up the squadron of Captain P. B. V. Broke, which was sailing southward to try to find the West Indies fleet.[26]

Constitution could outsail the fastest of these British ships, but the wind died down, seemingly leaving her at their mercy. Hull put out his boats to tow, and the British did the same. He now took two guns from the main deck and ran them out the cabin windows to shoot astern. His pursuers steadily gained because they could man more boats to tow the leading ships, and by 8:00 A.M. on 18 July four of them were close enough to open fire. Hull now switched to kedging with two anchors.* When the foe made the same shift, Hull began to drain off ten tons of water to raise the ship an inch and thus gain perhaps 100 yards in half a day. At 11:00 P.M. a light breeze sprang up, and Hull ordered the sails to be kept wet to make the most of it. *Constitution* began to slip ahead and to pick up her boats without losing headway. By nightfall on 19 July only three British sail remained visible. When a squall blew up, Hull held full sail to the last moment, then shortened it at just the right second to avoid loss of speed. During 20 July the enemy was finally outdistanced. *Constitution* had been handled with maximum seamanship.[27]

Reluctantly Hull made for Boston to take on water and make repairs. When the story of the race was known, the captain received much honor, but in spite of this he worked his crew twelve hours without relief to get supplies aboard and without orders from anyone, once loaded, sailed again on 2 August. The idea was to clear Boston before being blockaded in once and for all.[28]

Rumors of war reached Captain William Bainbridge in St. Petersburg, Russia. He started at once upon the grueling journey of 1,200 miles by land and 53 days more by ship to reach the United States. The moment he reached Washington he advised the secretary of the

---

* To kedge is to carry anchors forward and then haul the ship up to them by winching the anchor lines on a capstan.

navy that he had traveled far to receive orders for active duty. Hamilton assigned him to command *Constellation*, then at Charlestown, Massachusetts. There the British schooner *Brim* delivered to him two Americans taken from *Chesapeake* five years before. Bainbridge did not show very much respect for this tardy gesture, or much appreciation of the hardships the two prisoners had endured. He said to them, "Your country now offers you an opportunity to revenge your wrongs." Their opportunity was to join his crew.[29]

Captain David Porter, commanding *Essex*, had fabulous success in capturing valuable prizes. He took seven in his first two months, with good profit to himself and to his crews. All the while that he marauded, he himself was sought by Captain James Lucas Yeo of the Royal Navy, commanding *Southampton*. Yeo wanted revenge for the depredations and for the alleged atrocity of having tarred and feathered an English sailor who refused to swear loyalty to the United States. Yeo and Porter never met.[30]

Porter's lookouts sighted sails off the banks of Newfoundland on 13 August 1812. The captain ordered drags put out at the stern, but at the same time he sent men into the tops to unfurl sail to give the impression of trying to escape. The stranger gave chase, as Porter had hoped he would, and soon appeared within pistol shot. At 11:30 A.M. she ran up British colors, and revealed her identity as the brig-of-war *Alert*, 22 guns, half *Essex*' force. Porter swiftly wore his ship out of position to be raked and received the first broadside with minor damage.* Because the British ship was shorter and more maneuverable, Porter drew back to musket-shot distance. He wore to do this and raked *Alert* in the process. She was hurt and tried to escape, but instead she had to surrender almost at once. Superb American gunnery and shiphandling had wrecked her in eight minutes. She was the first British naval vessel to surrender to an American, and her loss occasioned a shock in the Islands. British frigates had habitually defeated French counterparts with heavier armament, and Britons had assumed that the pattern would remain the same.[31]

---

* To wear is to turn around on another tack by turning away from the wind. To rake is to fire along a vessel from bow to stern or vice versa.

William Hull

William Hull, governor of Michigan Territory since 1805, called himself to the attention of the commanders in Washington. In December 1811 he wrote to Secretary Eustis to express approval of the firm line being taken against England. In the letter, too, he ran over his own military qualifications. He had been graduated from Yale at nineteen, then had studied law with Tapping Reeve at Litchfield, Connecticut. Thereafter he had been plunged into extensive military service in the Revolutionary War in which he had well earned a commission as lieutenant colonel in the Massachusetts line. Since that time, as governor of Michigan, he had organized the territorial militia and had commanded it now for seven years. Hull claimed a thorough knowledge of Canada, of the border people, and of the Indians, but an examination of his career as governor indicates that he had remained eastern in orientation and had never in fact understood western ways. Hull was fifty-eight, but he described himself as strong, well, and eager for service.[1]

On some account he was in Washington in the spring of 1812. The President offered him the western command, but he declined it. Jacob Kingsbury accepted the post, but before he could report for duty he developed such a severe case of the gout that he had to resign. When a second offer was made him, Hull accepted it, possibly because this time he was allowed to continue as governor of Michigan Territory.[2]

Two-thirds of his army was to come from Ohio. Secretary Eustis called upon Governor Return Jonathan Meigs of Ohio for 1,200 men, whereupon Meigs asked 300 from each of the four militia divisions in the state. The men assembled at once, but they were without supplies. The governor called upon each family in the state to donate one blanket. The response was generous, but supplies still remained inadequate. Nevertheless, out of the confusion emerged three infantry regiments and one company of dragoons to fill the Ohio quota. The men elected James Findlay, Duncan McArthur, and Lewis Cass to be their regimental commanders, and in the face of the federal requirement that they be lieutenant colonels, Meigs commissioned the three as colonels.[3]

Detroit was a vital center for trade and diplomacy with the Indians, and Secretary Eustis ordered Hull to advance toward it. According to the general's intelligence, there were fewer than 100 regulars there. Except for this estimate, his figures were distorted; he calculated the British regulars west of Montreal to be in the neighborhood of 20,000, whereas in fact there were only 2,257. Hull's first view of a

proper strategy was to concentrate on building ships on the Great
Lakes. Without American control, the foe could overrun all of the
western United States. The man for the naval command was Captain
Charles Stewart, but Stewart declined the honor. With that, Hull gave
up the lake-centered strategy and began to argue that a strong showing at Detroit might bluff the English into letting the western country
go by default. In that case, no fleet would be necessary.[4]

Hull's first task was to cut a road for 200 miles from Urbana in
Ohio to Detroit. Once well settled at Detroit, he was to prevent British thrusts into the United States. He insisted that this defensive action
was impossible unless he was assigned some regulars, and Eustis ordered the Fourth Infantry to join him. The Fourth left Vincennes,
where it had been since Tippecanoe, and got to Urbana on 11 June,
450 strong. When the regiment had been joined to Hull's column, its
commander, Lieutenant Colonel James Miller (who had succeeded
John Boyd), became subordinate to the three Ohio militia colonels,
Findlay, McArthur, and Cass. Since the colonels said they would disband their regiments if their ranks were reduced and since Governor
Meigs sustained them, Miller was obliged to swallow his pride.[5]

General Hull traveled 900 miles from Baltimore to Cincinnati in 16
days. He was weak from cold and fever when he arrived, but he at
once ordered his command to move northward. One Ohio unit demanded pay before marching, but the company was pricked into motion by a company of the Fourth Infantry. The Ohio regiments, taking
turns cutting the road through the wilderness, averaged a remarkable nine and one-half miles a day. Even though Meigs had induced
the Ohio Indians to give the army peaceful passage, Hull adopted a
secure marching order. His two main columns had front, rear, and
flank guards of riflemen and horse troops. The bivouac was always a
defensive square. Finally, he caused five blockhouses to be erected
along his line of communications. Heavy rains fell, supplies came hard,
and the going was generally rough, but Hull stoically concentrated on
surmounting his difficulties rather than complaining of them.[6]

He arrived below the rapids of the Maumee River on 30 June, and
loaded some supplies and his sick on board *Cuyahoga* for easy transport across the head of Lake Erie. Unknown to Hull, his son had also
put aboard the general's official papers. Hull must have known that
the chances of war were greater than peace, but he did not know
that war had already been declared. The British did know, and they
captured *Cuyahoga*. Hull's papers were of great use to them. Not until 1 July did Hull find out about either the declaration of war or the
loss of his ship.[7]

Hull's orders appeared inflexible: to go to Detroit. He would like to have paused to reduce Fort Malden, close by Amherstburg, which otherwise would always threaten his communications. *Queen Charlotte* in the Detroit River was also a threat. Neither the fort nor the war vessel seemed vulnerable at the moment, so he continued northward in spite of them.[8]

Meanwhile the American commander at Detroit had opened a bombardment across the river upon the parties of British workmen who were preparing gun emplacements on their side. Hull reached Detroit on 5 July and halted the cannonade. His orders from Washington were to secure the surrounding countryside and await further directives, but they were quickly modified. In one of the modifications Secretary Eustis told him to take Fort Malden as soon as his force was up to it. Eustis did not bolster the general's morale when he added, "an adequate force cannot be relied on for the Reduction of the enemies [*sic*] posts below you." Hull had all along been led to expect a diversion in his favor to the north and east, but this now seemed to be withdrawn. By 9 July he had become convinced that he lacked the strength to take Malden.

The Canadian commanders across from Detroit judged the American forces to be too strong for them, and they abandoned Sandwich and concentrated upon Amherstburg. Aware of this movement, Hull made bold to cross the river into Canada on 12 July, and he occupied Sandwich without a fight. He issued a proclamation which promised protection to all persons except those found fighting beside the Indians: "Everyone else will be emancipated from Tyranny and oppression and restored to the dignified station of freemen." Forthwith Canadian militiamen deserted to him in such droves that Lieutenant Colonel T. B. St. George, in command at Malden, had only 470 left with him.[9]

Hull's move into Canada had raised for the first time the problem of the use of militia outside the country. About 188 men of the Ohio militia asserted that they could not be required to fight outside the United States, and they refused to cross into Canada. Their captain was at once court-martialed and dismissed, but was immediately re-elected to the command. Neither he nor his men made the crossing.[10]

General Brock at Fort George sent off his most reliable subordinate, Colonel Henry Procter, Forty-first Foot, to assume command at Fort Malden. He could only hope that Procter would not be too late, for if Malden fell, so would the entire peninsula.[11]

A party of 280 Americans, foraging under the command of Lewis Cass, reached the Aux Canards River very close to Malden and captured the lightly guarded bridge over it. Robert Lucas, an Ohio militia general serving as a field officer, claimed that, except for failures of the officers, they could have captured 150 British soldiers and 50 Indians. Cass had exceeded his instructions, but he now sent to Hull for permission to hold the bridge and asked for reinforcements to do it. Hull responded with a small detachment, all he could spare, but left the bridge decision to Cass and his officers. With only Cass and Josiah Snelling dissenting, the bridge was destroyed, though it was the key to any advance upon Fort Malden. There is grave question whether or not it could have been held because *Queen Charlotte* could fire upon it from the river. Nevertheless, this episode convinced the Ohio colonels that their commander was not equal to his task, a viewpoint toward which they had been tending for some time.[12]

While Cass and others looked toward Amherstburg, Hull cast glances apprehensively along the trail behind him. The *Queen Charlotte* on the water and Tecumseh on the land could cut it almost any place. Hull informed Governor Meigs that Ohio must use its militia to keep his lifeline open. Meigs and his people were eager to help, and when supplies were collected and ready to go forward to Detroit, he called for volunteers to provide a military escort. Two hundred men volunteered in one hour and did not sleep until preparations were completed. Women sewed uniforms in a single day, and old men and children put powder, ball, and three buckshot together in each of 2,000 cartridges. Canteens and knapsacks were provided at public expense. Within 24 hours after the call, 195 citizen soldiers, physically soft but enthusiastic, were on their way under the command of Captain Henry Brush.[13]

Tecumseh's band cut the road at the River Raisin. When Brush's column got to the river on 9 August, it had to stop until it was reinforced from Detroit, 33 miles away. Brush's men settled down in tents borrowed from the local militia to await help. Meanwhile, Major Thomas Van Horne, an Ohio brigadier general of militia serving as a field officer, was on his way toward them from Detroit. He had only 150 Ohio riflemen with him and was following the main road because he could not find the little known trail he was supposed to take. At Brownstown, still some 18 miles short of meeting Brush, in spite of warnings, he was engulfed on 4 August in a skillful ambush by a small party under Tecumseh. The citizen soldiers stood bravely at first, but, unable to see the enemy, became progressively demoralized. Squads broke contact and began to straggle back toward Detroit. In small knots they became vulnerable; they lost 17 men killed and many more wounded. All that saved the detachment from annihilation was the courageous behavior of Robert Lucas and some other cool heads, fighting as a rear guard. Toward the end, Lucas came upon a soldier bloody and dazed and closely pursued by the Indians. He gave his horse to the soldier and himself outran the pursuers on foot. Tecumseh captured the mail, and Brock learned more of the American situation than Hull knew. And the supplies on the River Raisin remained out of reach.[14]

Aware that the defeated detachment had been too small and badly led, Hull selected Lieutenant Colonel James Miller to command the second relief column and assigned to him 300 of his own regiment, the Fourth, 200 Ohio volunteer riflemen, 60 Michigan militiamen, and 40 volunteer dragoons from Ohio. This was triple the strength Van Horne had commanded and represented one-third of Hull's disposable force. Colonel Miller directed his officers to kill stragglers and exhorted his men to "Remember Tippecanoe." With these hard words and only two days' rations the second relief expedition took to the trail.[15]

The advance was systematic, very slow, and easily observed by the Indians every moment of the day and night. Miller insisted on hauling two small cannon, and the parts of the column kept in touch by drumtap. The men were regularly drilled in forming line of battle, and they did it handily on 9 August when they encountered about 150 British soldiers under Captain A. C. Muir behind a breastwork at the Indian village of Monguagon, about 14 miles from Detroit. An undetermined number of Indians were in the woods on the flanks. Miller ordered a bayonet charge, which broke through the works on the right and started a British retreat there. At this moment Van Horne, in command on the other flank, sent word that he had to have support. Miller decided to recall the pursuit on the British right and turn the men over to Van Horne. Van Horne's untimely call for help now enabled Muir to retreat about a mile and take up another well-organized position. Once in front of this one, Miller ordered the Ohio dragoons to charge it in the flank, but they never did. The British position remained intact. Miller now bivouacked where he was and sent a request back to Hull for men and rations. Hull forwarded food for one meal only, but could spare no men. During the next two days Miller permitted himself to be immobilized by a very small white force and the fear of an unknown army of Indians. Out of his small detachment Muir had lost 6 killed and 16 wounded, while the Americans had suffered 18 killed and 57 wounded. There had been no change in the position when Miller received Hull's order to return to Detroit, which he carried out with almost no protest.[16]

Fort Malden was enclosed in a palisade of logs 14 feet high, interrupted with some bastions, and armed with 24 cannon. It contained a garrison of less than 300 regulars and some local militia. Hull began to build carriages for his 24-pound cannon and for his mortars, because if these could be used the place would fall with minimum loss. By 7 August two 24-pounders and three howitzers were ready, but they could not be brought into firing position. It had not been foreseen that they were too heavy to pass over the bridges at Turkey Creek and the Aux Canards River. Nor could they be sent by water because of *Queen Charlotte*. Hull told his officers he would lead an assault without the aid of siege cannon if they would guarantee the good conduct of their men. Only the regular, Miller, would do it.[17]

Far to the north beyond the tip of Lake Huron, British Captain Charles Roberts became convinced that he could not hold his station at St. Josephs if the Americans continued to possess Mackinac. Accordingly, he began steadily to petition General Brock for permission to assail the American position. After considerable vacillation Brock agreed, and on 16 July 1812 Roberts sallied forth from St. Josephs with his entire garrison strengthened by 180 Canadians, 300 Indians, and two 6-pounders. He hauled one cannon to a point where it dominated the American fort, and at 10:00 A.M. on 17 July demanded surrender. Lieutenant Porter Hanks, the United States commander at Mackinac, had not heard that a state of war existed. He had 57 effectives and counted the enemy at no less than 900. His officers concurred that there was no choice, and the garrison surrendered before noon. The numbers involved were insignificant, but the position was not. The Indians swayed toward Britain. General Hull learned of the episode on 29 July and began to look for swarms of savages to come upon him from the north. Harrison, watching at Vincennes, predicted that Detroit would fall and that Chicago was in serious danger.[18]

Mackinac and the failure to reach the River Raisin drove out of Hull's mind all hope of advancing upon Fort Malden. At this critical moment, word reached him that General Brock himself was on the way to Amherstburg with an unknown number of reinforcements. Without asking any advice, Hull on 8 August drew his army back to the American side of the Detroit River. Had he followed his better judgment he would have continued his withdrawal clear back to the line of the Maumee River, but Cass told him bluntly that this would produce mutiny among the Ohio troops. Nearly all of Hull's officers, disapproving of the retrogression, became sullen toward their commander. Lewis Cass circulated on 12 August a round robin letter proposing to replace Hull, by force if need be. He asked Colonel Miller to take over; when Miller declined, the intrigue slowed down but did not die.[19]

Hull now ordered Colonels Cass and McArthur to select 400 of the best men from their regiments and force their way through a circuitous route to Brush at the Raisin. The two colonels assumed that Hull knew of their attempts to displace him, and that he was primarily interested in getting them out of camp. They therefore delayed throughout the day. Toward evening on 13 August, however, stimulated by a second peremptory order, they finally began their march. Meanwhile, General Brock had collected 300 men, loaded them in boats, and against adverse winds made his way to Amherstburg. He arrived there about the time Cass and McArthur left the American camp, but his subsequent actions were full of energy, whereas theirs were languid. On 14 August, without harassment from the American side, he laid one 18-pounder, two 13-pounders, and two 5½-inch mortars to bear on Detroit. Although he really did not expect it to work, he now undertook a colossal bluff. On Saturday evening 15 August he sent Hull a demand to surrender and hinted that if it came to a fight, he might not be able to restrain his Indians. Hull, though shaken, refused. The Canadian batteries opened fire upon Detroit.[20]

Hull made no effort to dislodge the hostile cannon; indeed, his primary concern seemed to be that Tecumseh might attack at night. To counter this expected attack, he disposed the Ohio and Michigan militia about the town and concentrated the regulars at the fort or in the shore batteries. The overall effect was to scatter his manpower so that he did not have enough to watch the natural crossing place, Spring Wells, three miles downstream from Detroit. He sent messengers with orders to Cass and McArthur to return at once. The two Ohio colonels had advanced farther than either of the previous relief expeditions, but still without finding Captain Brush. They were returning toward Detroit when Hull's order came to hand. They did not inform him where they were and did not obey the order.*[21]

Where Hull was proving ultracautious, Brock now demonstrated the streak of impetuosity which Prevost had detected in him. He reopened the cannonade at dawn on 16 August, and the shots this time took effect. Next he passed 30 men of the Royal Artillery, 250 of the Forty-first Foot, 50 from the Royal Newfoundland Regiment, 400 Canadian militiamen, and 600 Indians under Tecumseh across the river at Spring Wells. With these went three 6-pounders and two

---

*Quaife ("Hull," pp. 168–82) offers proof that Cass and McArthur had returned within sight of Detroit, then withdrew and camped while the surrender occurred.

3-pounders. He did not expect to capture Detroit, but hoped to lure Hull out to meet him in open battle. Now the Indians informed him that the McArthur-Cass detachment was three miles in his rear. If the garrison sortied, if the outparties in town held their ground, and if Cass and McArthur came up on his rear, he might be trapped. His solution to this precarious situation was to attack the fort. Advancing within one mile of it, he began his desperate preparations.[22]

A detachment of 400 Ohio militiamen, behind a picket work with two 24-pounders and a good stock of grapeshot, commanded Brock's flank as he marched into attack position. Before it could commence to fire, Hull ordered it to withdraw into the fort. The Indians filtered into Detroit with orders to take the town. Just at this moment two companies of Michigan militia defected, leaving a gap in the American perimeter. Still the fort itself, with 40 cannon, was strong. Its three interior acres were badly crowded, it is true, but the spirit of the troops was good, and their expectation was to have to fight. Some observers reported that Hull seemed to be collapsing under the pressure. Tobacco juice dribbled out of the corners of his mouth, and his detractors claimed that he tried to duck incoming artillery rounds. What went on in his mind cannot be known, but in the end, after a talk with Lieutenant Colonel Miller, he sent his son with a flag of truce to surrender. Included in the surrendered troops were not only the garrison, but also the detachments at a distance: Brush's men and those of Cass and McArthur. Cass and others said that the troops deeply resented the surrender.

General Brock listed 2,500 men captured, but this number was at least 500 too high. He said that he had achieved the surrender with 750 white men and around 600 Indians. Actually he probably had twice as many men close by the fort where they counted as Hull had. The Cass-McArthur detachment never entered the battle. The two colonels heard no small-arms fire, assumed the place was already lost, drew back a few miles, and roasted an ox.[23]

Brock proclaimed Michigan henceforth to be part of Britain, and he promised humane treatment to its citizens. He paroled the captured militiamen, but interned the regulars in Canada.[24]

Hardly anyone on either side could believe that the major United States offensive had come to this end. Americans, as is customary, ascribed the debacle to inside treachery. It was alleged that two British officers had secretly seen Hull on 13 August and that he had probably sold out to them. Canadians had expected no such outcome, and they now began to fear the power of the British government and to hesitate to flout it.[25]

When he came once more within the jurisdiction of the United States, Hull was charged with treason, cowardice, neglect of duty, and bad conduct. A court-martial finally heard his case in the early spring of 1814. On 26 March 1814 it cleared him of the charges of treason and cowardice, but it condemned him to be shot for neglect of duty and bad conduct. It did recommend mercy because of his age and his excellent war record, and President Madison remitted the sentence.[26]

Hull spent the rest of his life (he died in 1825) virtually an outcast trying to defend himself. The main arguments he used were these: his line of communications could be cut at any time either by the Indians or by water-borne forces, and no one could have kept it open better than he had; the continuous threats of the three Ohio militia colonels robbed him of essential flexibility; the militia failed him—some would not cross into Canada, some deserted to the enemy at the most critical moment, and nearly all of them were poorly trained and underarmed; he was critically short of supplies; he had been outnumbered two to one. Finally, he had been promised diversions in the East to distract the enemy, but none had been made. On the contrary, General Dearborn had agreed to an armistice at precisely the wrong moment.[27]

The story of that armistice is in order at this point. Augustus John Foster, the British minister to the United States, had gone to Halifax in Nova Scotia when forced to leave Washington. There he received from the government in England both the news that the Orders in Council had been repealed and an order to try to stop hostilities. Foster persuaded Prevost to ask for an armistice while the import of the repeal of the Orders became known to the government and people of the United States. Prevost consequently wrote a letter to Dearborn and sent it on 2 August by his adjutant, Colonel Edward Baynes. Baynes appeared at Dearborn's headquarters on 8 August, and in a few hours Dearborn made up his mind to go along with Prevost. But all he could do was agree that there would be a suspension of hostilities until a final ruling came from President Madison. When Colonel Baynes returned to Canada, he reported to Prevost, on the basis of what he had seen, that the United States was in no position to carry on the war with vigor and could not possibly overrun Canada. Prevost accepted this view and reported it to his government.[28]

Whatever claims Hull later made, it now is clear that General Brock had sent reinforcements to the Detroit area before he knew of the suspension of hostilities. Even then he disapproved of it. Thus, all in all, the cease-fire was not a factor in Hull's surrender. It is possible, of course, that if Dearborn had notified Hull of the suspension by special courier, Hull might have used the knowledge to slow Brock down. As it was, the message took nine days to arrive and fell into Hull's hands at the moment of his surrender.[29]

During the truce Major General Sir Roger Sheaffe made at the Niagara front a special arrangement with Major General Stephen Van Rensselaer that neither of them would send reinforcements west of the Niagara River. General Brock annulled this arrangement. Meanwhile, waiting for word from the President, Dearborn continued his bootless speculations about what he might do next. Nothing firm came from them.[30]

Returning to General Hull's defense of himself, the best scholarly analysis would grant that his line of communications was indefensible, that the militia were an inadequate instrument, that he had been injured by the failure to stage a diversion to the eastward, and that he was outnumbered two to one, as he said. It would not grant that he was critically short of supplies, and would emphasize his own shortcomings. If Hull had struck the foe soon after reaching Detroit on 5 July, he could have taken Fort Malden, but the longer he waited, the less were his chances. If he had shown one-quarter of Brock's daring, the outcome would have been different. Even if he was outnumbered two to one, his chances of a successful defense were good and any fight at all would have forced Brock to scurry back to Canada.[31]

The failure to gain control of Lake Erie was, of course, not charged against Hull, nor was it charged especially against the government. Much later Admiral Mahan said that there would have been no question of Hull's success if as much energy had gone into dominating Erie as was soon to go into the effort to control Lake Ontario.

The news of this fateful surrender reached President Madison while he was on his way home to Virginia. He turned back to the capital and called a meeting of the cabinet. Its decision, which he ratified, was to retake Detroit and to concentrate on building ships on the Great Lakes.[32]

Encouraged by British successes, the Indians in the vicinity of Chicago grew bolder and more bloodthirsty. Captain Nathan Heald, with two other officers, a surgeon, and fifty-four enlisted men of the regular army, made up the garrison of Fort Dearborn at Chicago. Their friendly relationship with the Potawatamis and Winnebagos was not good enough to detach the tribes from their British connection. The Potawatamis grew more hostile, and on 17 April they attacked the houses outside the fort. Cannon firing to warn soldiers who were outside to hurry back scared the warriors away before they could complete their destruction. All the inhabitants of Chicago now moved to the Agency, a short distance from the fort, and threw up an earthwork around it. The Indians hovered in the vicinity for a time, then left. Chicago remained apprehensive but unmolested for the next four months.[33]

On 7 August, Winnemeg, a friendly Potawatami chief, brought a dispatch from General Hull. It told of the loss of Mackinac and ordered Heald, if practicable, to evacuate Fort Dearborn. Knowing the temper of the redmen, Winnemeg counseled against leaving the shelter of the fort. With six months' supplies on hand the garrison could hold out indefinitely. The officers sided with Winnemeg, but a fatal destiny drove Heald. He was determined to carry out the order. After the delay of a critical week, pursuant to Hull's orders and to his own promise to the Indians (for the purpose of good relations), he distributed among the redmen the goods which could not be carried, except for powder and whiskey which he dumped into the river in the night. This waste made the Indians furious. Now Captain William Wells, an adopted son of Little Turtle, arrived from Fort Wayne.* He had great influence with the Potawatamis and hoped to use it to save the garrison.

Since Heald was adamant, abandonment of the fort begin on 15 August while the garrision band played the "Dead March" from *Saul*. Nobody but Heald seems to have expected much safety from the band of 500 Potawatamis who were supposed to act as escort. In the sand hills hard by the fort they slipped off, took cover, and opened fire on the column they were purportedly defending, composed of 54 soldiers, 12 civilian men, 3 or 4 women, and several children. Following the best tradition of Indian fighting, Heald ordered a charge and it broke through the ring. With his party badly reduced, he reached the protection of some oak woods. After a while a parley was arranged and then a surrender. Heedless of whatever they had promised, the Indians killed and scalped the wounded. Americans claimed that the British paid for the scalps. Twelve children, all the civilian males (except a family named Kinzie), Captain Wells, 2 military officers, and 26 enlisted men lost their lives. Certain warriors, who had admired Wells' manliness, chopped off his head, cut out his heart, and ate it raw.

* Little Turtle was a Miami war chief who played a large part in the defeats of General Josiah Harmar in 1790 and of General Arthur St. Clair in 1791. He tried and failed to hold together an Indian force to oppose Anthony Wayne in 1794, and he was one of the signers of the Treaty of Greenville in 1795. By this treaty vast areas of the Ohio country were transferred to the United States.

Following this disaster and the fall of Mackinac, the area of American control shrank back into southern Illinois and Indiana, and to the line of the Maumee River in Ohio.

British Strategy

Even though in June 1812 Napoleon turned away from England and invaded Russia, the British Ministry were too deeply engaged with the army he had left in Spain to give more than passing attention to America. Early in August, perhaps unwittingly, they added a third strategist to the two, Prevost and Brock, already at work in North America. On 3 August Sir John Borlase Warren, Admiral of the White, received orders to assume command of a new North American station consolidated from three previously independent naval commands, Halifax, Jamaica, and the Leeward Islands.*[1]

Warren at fifty-nine was a decade older than most of the British commanders of the Napoleonic era. After graduation from Cambridge he had been first associated with the navy in 1771, and had joined it full time in 1777 when the war in the United States began to turn into a war against France. He received no important commands during the American Revolution, but afterwards he rose steadily to become a flag officer in 1794. He harassed the French coast with vigor and cut up a French fleet which attempted in 1798 to land troops in Ireland. When younger, Warren had been an aggressive officer, but there is some evidence that the edge had worn off him by 1812. John Wilson Croker, or someone else in the London office, seemed to feel that he required more supervision than most of the admirals.[2]

Admiral Warren reached his station at Halifax on 26 September 1812. He found his squadron dispersed, reduced, and disheartened.

* The highest rank in the Royal British Navy at that time was admiral of the fleet. Next came admirals of the red, then admirals of the white, then admirals of the blue. During the seventeenth and eighteenth centuries a fighting fleet was habitually divided into three squadrons. An admiral of the red commanded the front squadron, an admiral of the white the center, and an admiral of the blue the rear. If a fleet admiral was present, he usually took station with the center squadron. Each of the squadrons—red, white, and blue—was itself broken down into three divisions. A vice admiral commanded the van, an admiral the center, and a rear admiral the rear division.

The need for sailors being chronic, he published a proclamation summoning all British seamen in the United States to return to their true allegiance. Not only would they receive full pardon; they also would be privileged to fight for "the Preservation of the Liberties, Independence, Religion, and Laws of all the remaining nations of the world against the Tyranny and Depotism of France." Then on 30 September he sent off a proposal to the United States to suspend hostilities because of the repeal of the Orders in Council. If the United States concurred, he was to halt operations; if not, he was to open negotiations with disaffected parts of the nation, expressly with New England. In about thirty days Secretary of State James Monroe replied that before his country could enter an armistice, Britain must give up impressment. That ended the exchange.[3]

Warren, after enough time to look around, recommended: active operations to be launched against the southern portions of the United States and forbearance toward the Northeast; three war vessels to be built on the Great Lakes during the winter and a naval captain assigned to command on the lakes; Sir George Prevost to be sent 5,000 additional soldiers to retake the Indian territory absorbed by the United States in the 1790s; this Indian territory to be erected into an effective buffer zone; and another 3,000 soldiers and marines to be directed to Halifax. Generals Prevost and Brock had suggested to him the importance of a diversion on the southern coast of the United States to relieve beleaguered Canada. The troops sent to Halifax would be assigned to attack New Orleans. Success there would cut supplies off from Ohio, Kentucky, and Tennessee, the most militant of the states in favor of the war. It would also incline the eastern states toward a separate peace. Once New Orleans was captured, Warren proposed to hold it with a corps of Negro troops and to direct his "flying army and squadron" toward the naval resources and vessels at Charleston, Savannah, Chesapeake Bay, Delaware Bay, and New York City.[4]

By the third week in August the Admiralty had issued 180 licenses to American, Swedish, Portuguese, and Spanish vessels for carrying grain and other provisions to Wellington's army in Spain. Not all of the captains of His Majesty's ships were informed of the government policy, and some of them sent American ships into Halifax as prizes in spite of the licenses. Warren released these and sought to enlarge licensing to include United States ships carrying food to the West Indies.[5]

At this time England was too hard pressed in Europe to divert specie or reinforcements to America. Only one battalion already on the way to Quebec and another to Halifax could be spared from Europe. Some precious specie was shipped to America, but one ship went aground and sank, carrying down $63,000.[6]

General Prevost was especially concerned about the Great Lakes. He cautioned Brock not to stir up opposition around Lake Erie, because there were no reinforcements to send west unless they came straight from England. Brock was even given permission to abandon at his discretion Detroit and all of Michigan Territory. Chronic shortages made the governor peevish, and he blew off steam to Brock. The lack of reinforcements was "strong proof," he said, "of the infatuation of his Majesty's Ministers on the subject of American affairs." Having got this out of his system, he cautioned Brock that the ministers were not eager to inflict a major disgrace upon the United States while they were principally committed in Europe. He must rely on attrition, not offensive victories, to weaken the United States' forces opposing him.[7]

Brock in turn warned his superior that British policy must not become so flabby as to allow the Indians to align themselves with the United States. This would be a disaster for Upper Canada. Control of the Niagara area and an open line of communications to Montreal were essential to sound Indian relations. Prevost replied pessimistically that the government probably would not actively embrace the Indian cause, and Brock must be careful both to make no promises to his red neighbors and to firmly restrain them. Nevertheless Prevost added his own endorsement to Brock's ideas and sent them along to Lord Bathurst.[8]

The latter was grateful to Prevost for the restraint in calling for reinforcements and did his best to divert some units from the Napoleonic campaigns to North America. He sent off 550 dragoons, but only 150 horses for them. He also promised several foot regiments for use in the spring, and Prevost warned Major General J. C. Sherbrooke, commander of the Marine Provinces, not to hold any of them back. The lifeline of Upper Canada depended on them. The governor believed that the United States intended to concentrate its effort in the Detroit region, the remotest and hardest of all for Britain to defend. The strategy was to cut off British intercourse with the Indians. He had, by dint of the rapid switching of scanty forces, foiled that strategy so far.[9]

Problems crowded upon Governor Prevost. By June 1813 his army bills were beginning to depreciate. This made the need for specie all the more acute, but specie could come only from England. Naturally, the cost of labor and of military supplies rose dangerously in Canada.

American privateers captured the mail packets during the spring of 1813, causing Prevost to go for five months without any word from his government. This made him, when he was at his most peevish, complain that he was not receiving adequate direction from the Ministry.[10]

Naval Actions on the Oceans

Captain Isaac Hull sailed aboard *Constitution* for the Gulf of St. Lawrence to intercept the ocean traffic from England to Canada. From 10 to 15 August 1812 he captured three vessels and burned two of them. Cruising south of the grand banks, his lookouts sighted a vessel east by south of them. *Constitution* and the sighted ship bore toward each other and at 4:14 P.M. hoisted national colors. The stranger was the British frigate *Guerrière*, Captain J. R. Dacres commanding. The opposing forces compared thus: American crew 456, British 272; American broadside 684 pounds, British 556.

At extreme long range Dacres fired one broadside, then wore ship and fired the other. He now turned to run before the wind, but not under full sail; he apparently meant to bring on close action. Boarding would be risky for him because his crew was small, but he may not have been aware of the discrepancy. Hull followed on the same course under full sail, and by 6:05 P.M. drew abeam of *Guerrière* at very close range. Up to this moment he had reserved his fire while receiving several hits, but now he ordered the gunners to fire at will with a combined load of solid and grape shot. The first blast knocked *Guerrière*'s mizzenmast overboard and crippled her mainsail. This reduced her headway and enabled Hull to draw ahead, cross her bow, and open a raking fire. Within thirty minutes *Guerrière* was totally dismasted, and her gunports were rolling under water. A council of British officers decided that no course was open but surrender, and Dacres hauled down his colors. When the crew had been removed, Hull ordered his captive burned as a useless wreck.[1]

Even though the vanquished was not equal to the victor, the outcome was not encouraging to Englishmen. *Guerrière* had 30 shot in her hull, *Constitution* had none at all. Thirteen British sailors had

United States Frigate President 44

The facing drawing depicts *President*. The frigate was built in New York and launched 1 April 1800. As was the case with her sister ships *Constitution* 44 and *United States* 44, she frequently carried more than the rated 44 guns. *President* was slightly longer than the other two, but she was considered the fastest ship of her class.

There follows a key to the sails.

Square Sails

1. Foresail (pronounced *for's'le* by seamen).
2. Fore-topsail (*for'tops'le*).
3. Fore-topgallant sail (*for'to'ga'ns'le*).
4. Fore-topgallant royal sail (*for'to'ga'ns'le royal*; usually *for'royal*).
5. Fore-topgallant skysail (*for'to'ga'ns'le skys'le*; usually *for'skys'le*).
6. Mainsail (*mains'le*).
7. Main-topsail (*maintops'le*).
8. Main-topgallant sail (*mainto'ga'ns'le*).
9. Main-topgallant royal sail (*mainto'gallant royal*; usually *main royal*).
10. Main-topgallant skysail (*mainto'gallant skys'le*; usually *main skys'le*).
11. Mizzentopsail (*mizzentops'le*).
12. Mizzentopgallant sail (*mizzen to'ga'ns'le*).
13. Mizzentopgallant royal sail (*mizzento'ga'ns'le royal*; usually *mizzen royal*).
14. Mizzentopgallant skysail (*mizzento'ga'ns'le skys'le*; usually *mizzen skys'le*).

Fore and Aft Sails

15. Jib (*jib*).
16. Fore-topmast staysail (*for'to'm'st stays'le*).
17. Forestaysail (*for'stays'le*).
18. Main-topgallant staysail (*mainto'gallant stays'le*).
19. Main-topgallant royal staysail (*mainto'gallant royal stays'le*; usually *main royal stays'le*).

20. Main-topgallant sky staysail (*mainto'gallant sky stays'le*; usually *mainskystays'le*).
21. Mizzentopgallant staysail (*mizzen to'gallant stays'le*).
22. Mizzentopgallant royal staysail (*mizzen to'gallant royal stays'le*; usually *mizzen royal stays'le*).
23. Driver or spanker (*spanker*).
24. Driver or spanker topsail (*spanker tops'le*).

The sails were made from canvas of varying weights. The heaviest, designated no. 1 canvas, was for the mainsail and foresail, known as the *courses*. The lightest canvas was a no. 8. The higher the sail was set on the mast, the lighter the canvas. The sails were made from long panels of canvas, called *cloths*. The square sails were secured to wooden booms, called *yards*, which were slung from the mast and braced (that is, pivoted about the mast) by blocks and tackles. The square sails were trimmed (that is, hauled in or eased off) by lighter blocks and tackles, known as *sheets*. The fore and aft sails, except the spanker, were secured to stays and trimmed by sheets. The upper portion, or "head," of the spanker was secured to a gaff, and the lower portion was "loose footed" to the spanker boom.

The amount of sail shown in the rendering could be carried only in relatively light air. Certain of the gunports are shown in open position, for ventilation. The boat griped to the stern davits is the captain's gig. Ships of *President*'s class frequently carried quarter boats, here shown griped to quarter davits. The launch, pinnace, and other boats were nested over hatches amidship, as shown. The sail plan in the rendering is from the sail plan indicated for *President* when her lines were "taken off" by the British, as described in Howard I. Chapelle, *The History of the American Sailing Navy* (New York: Bonanza Books, 1949), p. 267. The use of skysails in *President*'s sail plan is unusual for frigates of the 1812 period, which normally did not cross yards higher than the royals.

For complete details as to the sails and rigging of men-o-war, merchantmen, and East Indiamen of the 1812 period, see *The Young Sea Officer's Sheet Anchor*, originally published in London, 1807, and reprinted from the "First Philadelphia Edition from the Second London Edition," by Charles E. Laurait Company, Boston, 1938.

been killed, 7 Americans; 62 British and 7 Americans had been wounded. Clearly the American ship was stronger and better handled. Thereafter the order went out for British frigates to avoid single combat with American frigates, but the English public never heard of it for fear of a violent reaction. Where possible, English vessels were formed into squadrons of two frigates and one sloop each. These squadrons were expected to keep a vigil outside all major United States ports.[2]

Hull entered the port of Boston on 30 August, and once again he met a hero's welcome. One of his sailors who had lost both legs received a pension, and the one who had climbed the rigging to retrieve the flag and nail it to the mast was rewarded with one month's extra pay. Hull's request for a boon comes as a shock to hero worshipers; he desired to be relieved of the command of *Constitution*. He needed to be ashore to provide for his dependents. William Bainbridge cheerfully went to sea in *Constitution*, while Hull moved into his berth as commandant of the Charlestown Naval Yard.[3]

On the last day of August Captain Rodgers brought his ships back to Boston. With the largest squadron that the United States assembled during the war, he had captured only seven insignificant prizes. He claimed, however, that he had obliged the British to concentrate their forces, and had enabled many American merchantmen to get home safely. British agents in Boston must have been efficient, for Admiral Herbert Sawyer at Halifax learned of Rodgers' return as fast as news could travel. His comment was that even so unsuccessful a cruise was possible only because two-thirds of the American crews were Englishmen held by force to uncongenial duty.[4]

The secretary of the navy created on paper three squadrons patterned after the British. Rodgers on *President* commanded one, Decatur on *United States* another, and Bainbridge on *Constitution* a third. For a second frigate the senior captain could choose from *Chesapeake*, *Congress*, and *Essex*, and so on down the line. Finally, each was assigned a brig. For practical purposes these squadrons never got off paper, and the American warships continued to operate singly.[5]

On 18 October, Captain Jacob Jones of the United States ship-sloop *Wasp* found the English brig *Frolic* repairing damage done the day before by a gale. When *Frolic* was not impaired in speed or armament, she had 1 more gun than *Wasp*, 14 more pounds in her broadside, and 135 to 110 men. At 11:32 A.M. the two brigs were running parallel in heavy seas about sixty yards apart. British gunners, firing as fast as they could, shot as the vessel rolled upward and in twenty minutes brought down *Wasp*'s main topmast and badly damaged most of her rigging. In contrast, the American gunners, firing on the downroll, severely hulled *Frolic* and almost wiped out her crew. Bit by bit *Wasp* pulled ahead, cut across *Frolic*'s bow, and raked her deck. When on the close turn the English brig's bowsprit jabbed between masts across the American deck and tangled in the rigging, Jones started across a boarding party. Not 20 men of the opposing crew were able to stand up and fight it off. *Frolic* was captured. British losses were four times those of the Americans. The humiliation of this surrender was not much eased when His Majesty's ship-of-the-line *Poictiers* captured the crippled *Wasp* the next day.[6]

More severe humiliation lay in store for the British. *United States* was sailing south of the Azores, close-hauled into a southerly wind, when about daybreak on 15 October her lookouts sighted a sail to the windward. Decatur made out that the stranger was the British frigate *Macedonian*, Captain John S. Carden commanding. The two ships compared thus: *United States* crew 478, armament 56 guns (the long guns were 24-pounders), broadside 200 pounds the heavier; *Macedonian* crew 300, guns 49 (the long guns were 18-pounders). The power ratio between them was 3 to 1 in favor of *United States*.

Captain Carden was approaching before the wind and could have overcome the American advantage in long guns by closing fast and crossing in front of his antagonist. Fearful of losing the weather gauge, however, he hauled into the wind to slow his approach.* Decatur now fired his long guns, but the shot fell short. Carden resumed his advance, but this time only part of his guns could bear, while the well-served American guns beat shot into his hull and rigging. Decatur maneuvered to avoid close quarters, thereby losing the advantage of the musketry of his numerous crew but gaining the use of his superior long guns. For two hours his gunners fired twice as fast as their foes were; they dismasted *Macedonian* and pierced her hull 100 times. The casualties were 36 British and 6 Americans killed, 68 British and 6 Americans wounded. The damage was on the order of 9 to 1; nonetheless, after she had struck her colors, *Macedonian* was carried as a prize into New York, the first captured British war vessel ever to make an American port. She was appraised at $200,000, and that amount was paid over to Decatur's agent for distribution to his crew. The navy took the ship for its own use. Captain Jacob Jones had been captured along with *Wasp*, but he was

---

* You have the weather gauge when you are windward of your foe. You can make a direct approach to him, but he cannot do the same to you. He is leeward of you.

soon exchanged. The navy put him in charge of getting *Macedonian* back into shape.[7]

Before year's end the tiny United States Navy achieved another brilliant single-ship victory. About thirty miles off the coast of Brazil, *Constitution*'s watch sighted sails on her land and windward side. Bainbridge made for the vessel until he identified her as a British frigate, then wore and headed southeast in order to draw her away from the coast. She turned out to be the frigate *Java*, Captain Henry Lambert commanding. She had 49 guns to *Constitution*'s 54 and fired a broadside about 80 pounds lighter. Her crew was the smaller by 50 men. Whether Lambert knew the relative strengths or not, he gained fast with the advantage of the windward position. For such a moment as this Captain Bainbridge had hurried home from Russia, and he at 2:00 P.M. fired one gun across *Java*'s bow from half a mile to force her to show her colors. *Java* replied with a crippling broadside. Lambert now sought to use his speed advantage to get across *Constitution*'s bows and to rake, but under the cover of heavy black smoke Bainbridge thwarted him. Jockeying for position occupied the next hour and a half. *Java* managed to keep the weather gauge, but *Constitution* avoided the fatal crossing of her T.*

All this while, gunfire at pistol-shot distance took a heavy toll, particularly of the English crew. Musketry from the American tops heightened the carnage. Superior marksmanship bit by bit began to win an advantage. When some of *Java*'s headsails were shot away, she commenced to handle awkwardly and finally fell into an unfavorable position. American gunners poured in a murderous raking broadside across her stern. At this Captain Lambert ordered his ship to close for boarding, but the raking fire cut down his boarders as fast as they gathered. Sometime between three-ten and three-thirty an American maintopman mortally wounded Lambert. The command passed to Lieutenant Henry Chads, who soon was badly wounded. The two ships became fouled, and American fire carried off every British mast. Still *Java* did not surrender. *Constitution* disengaged and lay for a short time out of range, making repairs, then moved toward the raking position. Now *Java* was dead in the water and could do nothing but surrender. It was none too soon: 48 of her crew were dead, 102 wounded, against 12 Americans killed and 22 wounded. This battle of two and a quarter hours had been more fiercely con-

---

* When a warship crossed the T, it brought its broadside to bear on either the bow or stern of another ship. In this position it could rake the entire length of the enemy's deck, but the enemy could train almost none of its guns on the attacker.

tested than any other during all the War of 1812. The British, both
crew and vessel, had done their best, but the Americans had out-
fought them, from the leeward position at that, and had outshot them.
Java was too badly damaged to be brought into port and was destroyed at sea.[8]

The human and medical side of this engagement, and of naval
battles in general, is seen in the fate of Captain Henry Lambert. The
fatal musket ball entered his chest and chipped off bone splinters
which lacerated his lungs. Where the surgeon could reach the
splinters, he probed them out with his fingers. The first night Lambert ate a morsel and talked rationally, but he was in great pain all
along the spine. The following day he was weaker, but was revived
a little by an enema and a saline injection. The surgeons drew off
eight ounces of his blood and six more the next day. He received
opium and an enema each night. On the sixth day he became irrational
and then died. The surgeon traced the bullet and found that it had
lodged in his spine.*

The American single-ship victories of 1812 at once humiliated
Britain and lifted the United States in the estimation of other
rulers. European governments had for many decades been resigned to
British domination of the seas, but the American exploits gave them a
new outlook. Otherwise the single-ship victories had scant effect upon
the outcome of the war. But there were some 600 United States
privateers prowling the oceans, and these were a real makeweight
in the final outcome. In four months they captured 219 vessels
carrying 574 guns and 3,108 men.[9]

Reacting to the threat, the Admiralty increased the ships-of-the-
line in American waters from 3 to 7, frigates from 24 to 34, sloops-
of-war from 35 to 40, and retained 2 troopships, 14 brigs, and some
smaller vessels. British vessels-of-war in American waters rose from
83 to 98. It was a significant rise compared to American resources,
but it still left the Admiralty in other theaters 113 ships-of-the-line,
111 frigates, and about 350 ships of various other types.[10]

---

* "Medical Report," *Naval Chronicle* 29:416–17. According to today's standards, military hygiene and medicine were then in a primitive state. American
medical officers insisted that the safest way to serve meat was to cook it in soup
because in that form it was least likely to cause diseases of the bowels. Medical
opinion on "ardent spirits" was divided. A minority held that liquor ought to
be eliminated from the daily ration, but the majority insisted that it had medic-
inal value. Surgeons bled patients for almost every ailment, used mercury to
combat venereal diseases, recognized that psychic trauma could produce physical
disabilities, and found that mental patients when fed well and kept warm could
often regain their faculties.

William Henry Harrison

While Hull's campaign was in progress, Kentucky was abustle. In July 1812 the War Department requested that 1,500 Kentucky militiamen be sent at once under Brigadier General James Winchester, U.S.A., to aid the Detroit army. Kentucky raised the 1,500 with ease and added 500 men. Rather than dampen their zeal, Secretary Eustis accepted the entire enrollment. Governor Isaac Shelby reviewed the men, Henry Clay harangued them, and the United States gave them two months' pay in advance. There was a good deal of bickering over details, but it was supply which delayed the march. Just before the column was ready to leave in late August, the news of Hull's surrender arrived. Governor Shelby reacted by calling the rest of the Kentucky quota of 5,500 into active service.[1]

Supply for citizen soldiers became impossible. Men took the field promptly, but lacked essential equipment. Subordinate officers of the Ohio militia wrote directly to the War Department to beg for supplies. Eustis, borne down by detail work, bypassed the chain of command and corresponded with them directly. He even gave them directions about the movement of troops to be executed before they informed their Ohio superiors. No one in Ohio got very much out of sorts about this because every commander was absorbed in trying to find enough provisions to keep his men in service. Due to sickness, essential blockhouses were ungarrisoned. Short-term soldiers, seeing the privations which existed in camp, refused to enlist for longer tours.[2]

The only surge of patriotic stirring in Indiana Territory seemed to be in William Henry Harrison who had been governor of the territory since its inception in January 1801. Harrison had been an officer in the United States Army from 1791 to 1798 and had gained valuable experience as aide to General Anthony Wayne. He had had at least the sanction of the secretary of war to command the Tippecanoe operation, but the reaction to that event had been so violent that he had resigned his military command on 20 December 1811. Less than a month later he made his first overture to obtain a commission in the regular service, and he continued to press for one whenever he had a chance. In July he enlisted the help of Charles Scott, then governor of Kentucky, for Scott knew how enthusiastically the citizen soldiers of Kentucky would serve under Harrison. Next Harrison wrote directly to the secretary of war. Ever so delicately he suggested that he did not seek to avoid any responsibility the government might want to lay upon him.[3]

Eustis heeded Scott and Harrison, and perhaps others, and on 22 August 1812 he mailed Harrison a commission as brigadier general in the United States Army. The new general's orders were to cooperate with Hull—Hull's surrender on 16 August was not yet known in the capital—and above all to protect the frontiers of Indiana and Illinois territories in conjunction with the other territorial governors.[4]

William Henry Harrison was forty-one years old when he received his commission as brigadier. His father Benjamin had been one of Virginia's signers of the Declaration of Independence. His wife was the daughter of Judge John Cleves Symmes of the federal court. These were solid connections, but not wealthy ones. Harrison had been secretary in the government of the Northwest Territory before he received the governorship of Indiana Territory. He favored allowing slavery in the territories and permitted ownership of slaves while he was governor, but not legal sales. There was of course opposition. "Between the difficulties of introducing Negroes and expelling Indians," Henry Adams said, Harrison "found that his popularity had been lessened if not lost." Adams suggested that the governor's reawakened interest in military command might have resulted from the desire to get back some popularity.[5]

When the administration learned of the disaster at Detroit, it picked Brigadier General James Winchester to succeed Hull as commander of the western army. Winchester had been brought up in Virginia and had served well as a captain in the Virginia line during the Revolutionary War. Afterwards he migrated to Tennessee where he made a reputation as an Indian fighter. But he never attained the charisma for westerners which Harrison had. Kentucky, after all, had made Harrison—even though he was not a resident—a brevet major general of her militia.

Harrison now transferred his duties as governor to his deputy, John Gibson, and devoted his full time to military matters. He and Winchester began a subtle and gentlemanly duel for the western command. The place of decision was Washington. There Secretary Monroe advised the President, at home in Virginia, that there were many complaints about the selection of Winchester. The secretary hinted rather broadly that to avoid a stalemate and to placate the westerners he would himself be willing to assume the western command. Madison inclined toward this solution at first, but changed his mind because of Harrison's supporters. Richard M. Johnson wrote, ". . . no event is now so important to the cause as giving Governor Harrison com-

Major General William Henry Harrison

mand of the forces from Kentucky . . . he has the confidence of
the forces without a parallel in our History except in the case of General Washington in the revolution." Under pressure from Johnson
and others the President rescinded the directive to Winchester on
13 September and gave Harrison the command, with orders to retake
Detroit when the force of 10,000 allotted to him was gathered, and
to penetrate as far into Canada as possible.[6]

Of course it was some time before the order from Washington
reached the western theater. Thus, when Harrison and Winchester
both appeared at Fort Wayne in mid-September, Harrison argued
that his brevet major general's commission gave him precedence,*
while Winchester stated that he had government orders to take command. On 18 September Harrison appeared to yield gracefully to his
rival, but three days later he wrote Eustis that the move "which would
name me from the chief to the second in command [as a final arrangement, would be] an event which has perhaps never before occurred in
any army." Madison had already made his decision, and it reached
Fort Wayne on 24 September. Winchester accepted his displacement
genially enough and agreed to serve thereafter as general in command
of the left wing of the western army under Harrison.[7]

Kentucky made an additional bid to be arbiter of the war in the
West. Governor Shelby proposed that the President appoint a Board
of War of "respectable characters" living in the West to direct operations, naturally under the distant supervision of the secretary in
Washington. Had such a board been in existence, he said, it might
have prevented Hull's disaster. Moreover, George Washington himself had created a similar body in Kentucky in 1791. Distant as the
western theater was, President Madison still could not agree to this
delegation of the war power.[8]

Secretary Eustis called upon Pennsylvania and Virginia to supply
part of the 10,000 men allotted to Harrison. Pennsylvania's quota was
2,000, added to another draft upon her for men to serve on the New
York front, which taxed her inefficient militia system beyond its capacity. Officers and men were to elect a brigadier general at the rendezvous in Pittsburgh. Supply was pretty much in confusion, and no
one knew who would feed the men as they made their way to Pittsburgh. They would have to start and find out.[9]

Michigan Territory had fallen back under British domination. The
task of organizing government there belonged to Colonel Henry Proc-

---

* A brevet commission was mainly a way of rewarding an officer for accomplishment by naming him to an honorary higher rank. Ordinarily he received neither the command authority nor the pay of the higher rank.

ter. He wisely sought, as far as possible, to keep American laws in force and American officials in office. He designated Judge A. B. Woodward territorial secretary. Woodward accepted the office after some soul-searching, he said, in order to protect American citizens. In all ways Procter and the British authorities displayed moderation.[10]

None of this was known in London. Not until late in September did word of Brock's triumph at Detroit get there. "This news is a great relief to me," Liverpool wrote to Wellington. "After the strong representations which I had received of the inadequacy of the force in those American settlements, I know not how I should have withstood the attack against me for having sent reinforcements to Spain instead of sending them for the defense of British possessions."[11]

It was Tecumseh, not the English commanders, who now took and kept the offensive. He peppered the western frontier with destructive raids. At Pigeon Roost in Indiana on 3 September a small party wiped out about 20 white people and burned down their houses. A large band of fierce Winnebagos attacked Fort Madison near St. Louis for three days, but could not capture it. The heaviest blow was directed at Fort Harrison, fifty miles up the Wabash River from Vincennes. Here Captain Zachary Taylor commanded a garrison of 50 men, 38 of whom were ill when the attack came. Two of his men were killed outside the fort on 3 September. Thereafter pressure on the garrison was steady, night and day, and at midnight 4 September the attackers set the lower blockhouse on fire. Whiskey stored there went up in an awesome blaze. Taylor, with unexpected immodesty, took credit for preventing a panic. "Most of the men immediately gave themselves up for lost, and I had the greatest difficulty in getting my orders executed—from the raging of the fire—the yelling and howling of several hundred Indians—and cries of nine women and children . . . and the despondency of many of the men . . . and indeed there were not more than ten or fifteen men able to do a great deal . . . and to add to our other misfortunes, two of our stoutest men . . . jumped the picket and left us. But my presence of mind did not for a moment forsake me." First it was necessary to prevent the fire from spreading into the barracks. This was done, but the blockhouse was entirely consumed, leaving a gap of twenty feet in the curtain of the fort. Taylor put up a breastwork there, under fire, and successfully defended it. The Indians, unable to get into the fort, killed all the cattle in the vicinity but left the corn standing. Finally, on 16 September a column of 1,200 men under Colonel William Russell reached Fort Harrison and relieved it after thirteen days of sporadic siege. Zachary Taylor received a majority for his stout conduct.[12]

While Fort Harrison was under siege, Tecumseh himself began to invest Fort Wayne. It guarded one of the Indian factories (that is, trading posts) run by the United States and was a key to the lake country. The garrison consisted of only 70 men with 4 small cannon, commanded by Captain James Rhea. On the night of 6 September Tecumseh hurled 600 warriors against this tiny force, but was repulsed. The next day he set up logs (quaker guns) which were supposed to convince the garrison that British artillery had arrived. But this ruse, rare enough for Indians, failed.[13]

Reinforcements were on the way for both sides. Colonel Procter dispatched about 600 English troops under the command of Major A. C. Muir. Their objective was not only to help capture Fort Wayne, but also to prevent massacre of the garrison by the Indians. Harrison himself arrived with 2,000 men on 12 September, ahead of Muir. When General Winchester got there, Harrison directed him to fan his force out from Wayne to lay waste the Indian villages, but Winchester sent a strong detachment down the Maumee River on 22 September to find and engage Muir's column. Muir knew that the force in front of him was twice his size. Therefore, when small parties of Indians began to peel off and disappear, he gave the order to retreat. Governor Prevost was not aware that Muir's advance was in part to prevent a massacre and disapproved of it as a violation of the indispensable defensive strategy.[14]

The American policy was now to punish the ringleaders of the attack upon Fort Wayne. A detachment of 350 men obliterated a town of Ottawas on the Auglaize River. A second struck the Potawatamis at Elkhart. A third hit the Miami towns at the forks of the Wabash River. All three destroyed their targets during the third week in September.[15]

By far the most ambitious attempt against the Indians was conducted by Kentucky volunteers under Brigadier General Samuel Hopkins. Hopkins issued ten days' rations to about 2,000 mounted Kentucky riflemen at Fort Harrison, then headed out across the prairie toward the Kickapoo and Peoria towns along the Illinois River, a hundred miles away. He covered thirty miles a day, but at the end of five days his guides admitted they did not know where they were. Now the redmen lit a prairie fire to engulf the invaders, and the riflemen showed signs of panic. Even though the fire was stopped by a backfire, morale was gone and provisions were running low. In spite of Hopkins, his horde turned back toward Fort Harrison, and he trailed along behind them.[16]

Early in 1812 seven companies of mounted United States Rangers had been constituted to help the territories defend themselves. Two were to be raised in Ohio, the rest in Kentucky and in the Indiana and Illinois territories. In February 1813 ten more companies were authorized: four to be recruited in Indiana, three in Illinois, and three in Missouri. Since there was considerable patronage in raising and officering these companies, they were a boon to the areas assigned to recruit them. Even so, the last ten companies were never fully manned.[17]

It was expected that the territorial governors would build block-houses at key points and use the Rangers to scour between them across the important lines of access leading from the Great Lakes into the Mississippi Valley. When large numbers were needed, the Rangers could alert the local militias. In practice, the companies operated separately, and Colonel William Russell, who had theoretical command over all of them, was skeptical of their ability to protect 500 miles of wilderness. On one rare occasion, Russell drew six companies together and traversed Indiana Territory diagonally from the northeast for a distance of 500 miles.

In spite of the Rangers, the Indians gained control of the land as far as the Illinois River. Governor Ninian Edwards of Illinois Territory personally supervised the defense of the territory. With difficulty he arranged for a garrison to hold Fort Edwards at the mouth of the Des Moines River. When he failed to make contact with Hopkins' expedition, he gathered together 360 men, mostly United States Rangers and a detachment of Illinois riflemen, and with them he destroyed the Indian town at the head of Lake Peoria. He was proud of this march and was nettled when credit for it fell mostly to Colonel Russell. The Territorial legislature assured the President that the credit belonged to Edwards and used the opportunity to ask for added help against "inhuman and ferocious enemies." It suggested extermination.[18]

Edwards' goal was to build a line of forts, and by mid-March 1813 he had brought seventeen of them nearly to completion. One stood on each of the Rock, Wisconsin, and Illinois rivers to interdict the canoe routes from Lake Michigan. His plan was to keep armed boats at the mouths of these rivers too.

General Hopkins, meanwhile, brooded over his previous failure and made plans to try again. He assembled three regiments of militia infantry from Kentucky, Zachary Taylor's company of regulars, a company of Rangers, and some scouts, for a total of 1,200 men, and led them out of Fort Harrison on 11 November 1812. This time he destroyed the forty huts of Prophetstown without a fight and wiped out a Kickapoo village of 160 huts. His men cut down all the growing corn they came upon. Detachments now split off for pursuit. One fell into an ambush and lost eighteen men. The rest returned intact, and Hopkins was proud to lead them back through the snow to Fort Harrison, confident that he had permanently crippled the Indians in that quarter.[19]

All the while General Harrison gave his own attention to mounting a campaign against the British. His left column, commanded by Winchester, was to move from old Fort Defiance down the Maumee River to the rapids, where the others would rendezvous with it. This column was to build a new fort near Defiance and call it Fort Winchester. One of the Kentucky regiments was directed to build a road along the Auglaize River from St. Marys (sometimes called Girty's Town) to Fort Winchester. He formed his center column at Urbana, 1,200 Ohio citizen soldiers under Brigadier General Edward Tupper, to protect Hull's Road, the supply line. The right column, volunteers from Pennsylvania and Virginia, was to assemble at Upper Sandusky.[20]

When all columns had taken their assigned positions by the third week in October, Harrison said, "I know of no arrangement which would be better calculated to protect the frontiers and support each other than that which the several Corps of the Army at present form." Deputy Quartermaster William Morrison did not agree, but communicated his reservations to persons other than Harrison. Each column, he said, had a staff as large as the combined army would have needed, and this and other unnecessary frills pushed the cost of maintaining the three columns through the winter up to $1 million, according to his estimate. He wrote directly to Henry Clay, and it was obvious that he wanted to be sure that his exertions to do the extra work imposed by Harrison's system were not overlooked. He found fault too with the people around Harrison's depots. Mostly Dutchmen and Yankees, they intended to profit as much as they could from the military needs of the nation.[21]

Harrison's orders were to retake Detroit when he could. In late September he decided that it was first necessary to clear the Indians away from the essential routes. He believed, as Hull had, that he must neutralize Malden before advancing farther northward. During the fall he vacillated between a winter campaign and a delay until the next proper campaigning season, but by December he had come to a firm conclusion that nothing but an overwhelming political need would justify the enormous costs of a winter operation. It would be far better to spend the money to gain dominance on Lake Erie, for if that was achieved, Detroit and the other enemy posts in the west would automatically fall. Late in December the secretary of war, then James Monroe, ratified Harrison's decision and left the timing of the attempt upon Detroit altogether up to him.[22]

Harrison remembered that Wayne's legion had nearly starved in the same area in the 1790s. He therefore insisted that there be a million rations within reach of his columns before he started toward Canada. The government agreed, but the contractors blundered. One supplier, who stood to make $100,000 from his contracts with the army, was willing, Harrison said, to see the men starve before he would lose $5.00 of his profit. In the end, he failed to lay down the rations according to contract. Harrison discarded him in favor of John H. Piatt, who had provisioned Hull's army.[23]

Horses strained through the mud and were given only grass for feed. Soon they broke down. In mid-October the general bought 100 wagons and converted to oxen. Oxen could forage in the woods and keep alive where horses could not. The next problem was to find ox-drivers; they were both scarce and high priced. In addition, since wagons could not go along the last stage of the trail, pack horses would have to take up the loads. These too were in short supply. Moreover, from 2,000 to 3,000 of them would be loaded with nothing but forage. One pack horse carrying a normal burden of three bushels for sixty miles would eat up eight-ninths of its own load. And since forage cost a dollar a bushel, the outlay was nearly, but not quite, prohibitive.

William Henry Harrison never forgot that politics and military activities were inexorably intertwined in a people as political as the Americans. When he appointed a deputy inspector general for Kentucky volunteers, he not only stressed the candidate's ability to do the job, but he also took pains to add that he was "a warm advocate for the present administration, the brother-in-law of Mr. H. Clay, and mainly connected with Governor Scott." He knew the value of having good friends in Washington and counted Senator Thomas Worthington of Ohio as one of them. Worthington reassured him when he was required to resign as governor of Indiana Territory in order to accept a commission as brigadier general that this was standard practice. Worthington further assured him that his friends were watching for the opportunity to make him a major general, but could not force the issue.[24]

The Army of the Northwest was not in condition late in 1812 to advance as a whole, but its parts were in motion. Harrison sent General Winchester toward the rapids of the Maumee River to cut down Indian corn. Winchester crossed the river and advanced to within a few miles of the rapids, but at that point typhus broke out in his

army and brought him to a halt. Perhaps the most significant consequence of his reconnaissance was the death of Logan, a loyal
Shawnee chief, who was shot while scouting for him.[25]

Winchester next issued an order to General Edward Tupper, commander of the center column, to pursue and punish some prowling
Indians. Tupper never denied that Winchester could give him orders,
but instead of moving gave a detailed itemization of the difficulties
which prevented his moving. When Winchester learned that the
marauding party of Indians was only forty strong, he removed
Tupper and designated Lieutenant Colonel Allen to take command.
The Ohio troops, however, refused to march under anyone but
Tupper. It turned out, in fact, that no more than 200 of them would
follow even Tupper, and he marched them to Urbana and discharged
them. When all the backing and filling to carry out Harrison's order
about the Indian corn at the rapids was completed, General Winchester preferred charges against Tupper for insubordination. Tupper
was never punished for this conduct, and he had the consolation at
least of having got closer to the rapids than Winchester did.[26]

The Delaware and Miami Indians who lived in villages along the
Mississinewa River in Indiana were in a position to intercept the
quantities of supplies General Harrison was trying to lay down at
the rapids of the Maumee River. Therefore he designated Lieutenant
Colonel John B. Campbell, Nineteenth Infantry, to command 600
men to neutralize them. Campbell received Colonel James Simrall's
regiment of Kentucky dragoons, a squadron of the Second United
States Dragoons, one company of the Nineteenth Infantry, the Pittsburgh Blues, and Alexander's Pennsylvania Riflemen. These units
came together at Dayton and marched to Fort Greenville, which was
to be their point of departure into the dreary, bitter, cold wilderness.[27]

Each man carried twelve days' rations for himself and a bushel of
corn for the horses. This freed some pack horses, and the foot troops
were put up on them. Every man had a short rifle. Thus accoutered
for rapid movement, Campbell's column started out on 14 December
in severe cold. It covered forty of the eighty miles in two days, and
during the third day drove day and night in order to cover the
last forty miles. At the end of this exhausting march, without rest, it
charged silently in ten files at the gallop into a principal Indian village.
In spite of the speed and silence, most of the redmen had already
escaped, but 8 were killed and 42 taken prisoner. Campbell ordered
all the Indian cattle shot and three towns burned down, then returned
to the first village and camped in it. There was a gap in the perimeter
of his defensive square, and before dawn on 18 December 1812 the

Indians attacked and forced their way into it. Only after an hour of heavy fighting were they repulsed. Besides the wounded, 40 men were crippled by the cold, and 303 others so badly frostbitten as to be virtually invalids. In addition, 10 men had been killed, 48 wounded, and 107 horses had perished. Campbell at once ordered withdrawal to Fort Greenville. Seventeen men were transported on litters, but the severe frostbite cases had to walk or be left behind. Fortunately snow made sledding possible, and cold bridged the rivers with ice, while at night the moon made it nearly as light as day.

According to customary European practices, the Mississinewa march had occurred after the end of the campaign season. It demonstrated the difficulties of winter campaigning in the wilderness. It also showed the capacity of men, including citizen soldiers, when well led, to endure extreme hardship. General Harrison chose to refer to it as a great success, but knew that it did not eliminate the threat of the Delawares and Miamis upon his flank.

Meanwhile, the three columns of Harrison's army were trying to get into position. The Ohio troops reached the edge of Black Swamp and came to a halt. There was nothing for them to do but settle down in the mud and wait. Inaction was certain to bring out their worst qualities, and it was aggravated by a lack of food, clothes, and medicine. After three months in camp some of the Ohio troops still had not received one cent of pay. The generals and other officers were not well enough trained in camp sanitation to prevent the spread of disease. Camps and hospitals soon stank fearfully. Many soldiers who had turned out in summer clothes suffered the winter chill in rags. A British officer said, "They had the air of men to whom cleanliness was a virtue unknown . . . their clothes . . . had undergone every change of season and were arrived at the last stage of repair."[28]

In Winchester's camp, where no flour had been issued for a week, the men lived on stringy beef and hickory roots. They threatened to leave unless conditions improved. By Christmastime 100 Kentuckians had died. Numbers of men were discharged at the end of their short terms, and just as many deserted to accompany them home. Even severe punishments, such as riding the wooden horse, did not stop the deserters.*[29]

To hold this army of citizen soldiers together at all, camped in the mud without enough tents, clothes, medical supplies, and food,

* To ride the wooden horse was to be forcibly lifted astride a two-by-four or other narrow timber which was then manipulated up and down and sideways. Aside from the anguish, such punishment could injure the testicles and the tailbone.

required a particular sort of genius. Harrison had it. Clad in common hunting garb, he rode over his sprawling theater, talking with the citizen soldiers. He ruled by harangue. Some listeners said that his addresses inspired everyone to try to be a hero. With his superb voice he persuaded men over to his side "as a father would his children." One night in the heavy rain it was necessary to stop in a thick woods without fire or camp equipment. Like the others, Harrison wrapped himself in his cloak and sat on his saddle, leaning against a beech tree. He urged his officers to sing to forget the cold and wet, and himself joined in. During the fall he had to return to Chillicothe to expedite supplies and while there received an invitation to a grand dinner. He declined it on the grounds that he had no right to eat in luxury as long as his army was cold and hungry. Showmanship, demagoguery, sincerity—no one will ever know which, or what mixture, of these it was, but the men loved him for it. He understood the ways in which a successful leader of citizen soldiers had to behave.[30]

Since the general could not be everywhere, other officers who lacked his particular gifts were obliged to try as best they could to hold the army together. Some of them did really remarkable things. Leadership of the militia literally meant going first into hardship and danger. It also meant the application of a great deal of simple but often overlooked psychology. Sometimes the officers lied about supplies being on the way and so kept up hope. Sometimes even the generals got down in the mud and labored alongside the privates.[31]

All the while, the main effort was to supply the northwest army and to accumulate the required million rations and other stores. In this prodigious task the militiaman was the main burden-bearer. He guarded supply trains, and he often had to put his shoulder to the foundered wagons. He slept in mud, marched hip deep in it, and usually ate it in his food. What Harrison saw as a grand movement to provide future bases for his army, the citizen soldier saw as mere wallowing in the mud. When freezing weather came, he gained some relief, but then he often had to pull sleds because the horses and oxen had fallen exhausted in their harness.

The Niagara Theater

No governor was more loyal to the national administration than Daniel D. Tompkins of New York, none more plagued by dissensions within his state. Tompkins was himself an unswerving Democrat, but the Federalists dominated a unique New York bureau called the Council of Appointments. This council selected Federalists to be generals, but Tompkins left most of them unemployed and created good Democrats to be generals by brevet and actually to handle the active commands. His reason was that, like many Democrats, he truly believed most Federalists to be British at heart. "Our Republicans," he said, "will illy brook it that the command of an army in a contest with Great Britain should be entrusted to such men."[1]

Tompkins' problems relative to the parts of New York which were closest to Canada were not unlike those in New England. Every congressman from a district which bordered on the St. Lawrence River had voted against the war. In addition there were tensions between citizen soldiers and regulars. Accordingly, the governor requested Secretary Eustis either to appoint a general officer from the United States Army to command in western New York, or to allow him to designate a militia general. Eustis on 3 July gave him permission to install a major general of New York militia, but with the understanding that a regular might supersede him at any time.[2]

To gain support for the war effort, and perhaps for political reasons, Tompkins maneuvered an influential Federalist, Major General Stephen Van Rensselaer, into accepting the western command. When Van Rensselaer had a chance to inspect his resources, he may have regretted accepting the post. He found less than a thousand men along the Niagara River, many of them shoeless, ill equipped, and badly in arrears in pay. There was not enough artillery nor enough artillerists. Tents, camp equipment, and medicine were very scarce. The citizen soldiers seemed to him insubordinate, undisciplined, and unreliable.[3]

General Dearborn, who had always disclaimed responsibility for the Niagara area, nevertheless felt some sensitivity about the diversion in favor of General Hull which had never taken place there. He argued that he had acted as fast as he could, and that his armistice had not hurt Hull. On the other side General Prevost saw the truce as wholly in the British favor. It gave him a chance to "augment [his] resources against invasion, whilst the Enemy, distracted by Party broils and intrigues, are obliged to remain supine. . . ." President

Madison took the same view as Prevost and sharply ordered Dearborn to cancel the cease-fire. The very day that Dearborn received Madison's directive, 26 August 1812, he notified Prevost that in four days the truce would end.[4]

The British commanders expected an American offensive on the Niagara front. General Brock worried less about his opponents there than about the restrictions placed upon him. If he were unleashed, he confided privately, he could clear the Americans away from the Niagara River with such poor forces as he already had. But if obliged to remain on the defensive, he would need strong reinforcements when the assault against him finally came.[5]

General Dearborn hurried toward Niagara the Fifth and Thirteenth United States Infantry Regiments and a brigade of recruits under Brigadier General Alexander Smyth, erstwhile inspector general. Smyth reached Buffalo on 29 September 1812 and reported his arrival to Van Rensselaer in writing. This was highly irregular, and he did it because he apparently could not bring himself to appear in person as a subordinate to a major general of militia. Van Rensselaer understood perfectly well what was going on, but did not choose to make an issue of it. To make up for his own professional deficiencies he relied heavily on his kinsman, Colonel Solomon Van Rensselaer, who had held a commission in the regular army from 1792 to 1800 and had been severely wounded serving with Wayne at Fallen Timbers. After Solomon had resigned from the army he had been adjutant general for New York State.[6]

By the second week in October there were about 6,300 American and 2,200 British troops near the Niagara River, one-half militia on each side. Not being sure where the inevitable attack might be made, the British commanders had to disperse their inferior numbers widely, for the American army was strung out along the entire river. The American commanders, unaware of their three-to-one advantage, estimated the enemy strength as high as 8,500.[7]

Major General Van Rensselaer's militiamen told him he must either march them into action or let them go home. Secretary Eustis too wanted action. The New York Democrats would accuse the general of treason if he remained inactive. Van Rensselaer therefore planned a two-pronged attack, one wing to go by water to the rear of Fort George to storm it, the other wing to cross the river at Lewiston and assail Queenston and the heights behind it. The British feared such a plan, but General Smyth unwittingly frustrated it. He did not approve of an attack below the falls and so successfully avoided subordinating himself to Van Rensselaer that he and his troops were finally left out of the plans. This meant that there would be no assault on Fort George and that 25 per cent of the American troops close by would not take part in the planned attack.[8]

Only 600 men were designated to make the attempt against Queenston. While they were assembling on 10 October, Lieutenant Colonel John Chrystie arrived near Fort Niagara with 350 recruits for the Thirteenth Infantry. When he learned of the invasion, he hastened to offer his detachment for it, but was turned down for lack of boats. Only thirteen rowboats had been assembled, and put under the direction of one Lieutenant Sims. The troops waited in a severe storm on the morning of 11 October to put out in Sims' flotilla, but in vain. Sims himself pushed off in a boat with the oars for all the boats, drifted downstream, landed, and disappeared. There seems to be no way of knowing whether his conduct was cowardly, treasonable, or something else. Van Rensselaer was disposed to give up the undertaking, but his officers demanded another attempt.[9]

The second try was scheduled for the night of 12–13 October. Now came the customary scramble for command between regular and citizen officers. Major General Van Rensselaer insisted that his relative have charge. Chrystie was welcome to bring his detachment, but had to agree that he would not interfere with Solomon's authority. By the time all this was settled, Chrystie complained that it was almost too late for him to bring his men up. He brought them, however, at night from Fort Niagara to deceive General Brock, who was expecting the main attack out of that fort. Late in the afternoon of 12 October, Lieutenant Colonel Winfield Scott arrived near Fort Schlosser with the Second Artillery. He, too, pleaded to join the invasion, and was allowed to do so but only in a volunteer capacity. He was ordered to post his cannon so as to shoot at the heights across the river.[10]

Under cover of intense darkness, with noise blotted out by the roaring of the falls, 4,000 American troops assembled across from Queenston. The river before them was about 200 yards wide, and the current four miles an hour. The bank where they were to land was steep, and the heights behind it towered 345 feet above the river level. As before, only thirteen boats were on hand, each of which, it was planned, would have to make seven separate crossings.

The first increment of regulars stepped in the boats, Colonel Van Rensselaer with them. Lieutenant Colonel Chrystie, too, entered one of the first boats, which got lost in the darkness with two others and was swept far downstream. Ten boats carrying 300 men made the crossing in the first quarter of an hour. It took the waiting British

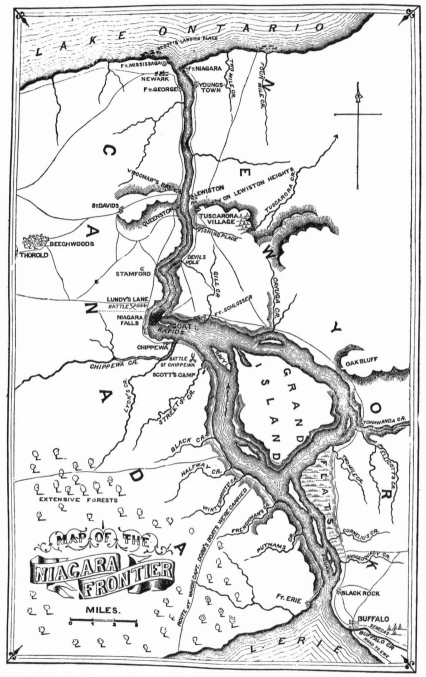

MAP OF THE
NIAGARA
FRONTIER

MILES.

some time to locate them, but then they opened fire effectively, threw the beachhead into disorder, and severely wounded Colonel Van Rensselaer. When the British began to fire, Scott's cannon across the river were aimed and fired at their muzzle flashes. They forced English parties to climb to the top of Queenston Heights. After them went a body of United States regulars led by Captain John E. Wool. Aged twenty-three, Wool had been commissioned from civil life only seven months before and had never up to that moment been under fire. Once on the flats in the vicinity of Queenston, he halted his men and sent down a messenger to ask Van Rensselaer for orders. Van Rensselaer ordered him to storm the heights north of the town, but as he formed to do so, another directive arrived rescinding the first. Meanwhile, strengthened by local reinforcements, the British attacked. Wool beat them off, but the fire from the heights became so galling that he was obliged to return to the river bank, and there under the shelter of the bluffs hang onto the beachhead.[11]

Northward at Fort George, General Brock heard the firing and rode at full gallop toward it. He arrived at the British battery near the top of the heights just as daylight came. Wool too at first light had once more begun to climb toward the top by a little-used, unguarded path. He arrived in Brock's rear and opened fire. Brock and the artillerists had just time to spike the guns and make their escape on foot. At the base of the hill he sent an order to Sheaffe to come on with reinforcements, and then turned to organizing about 100 men for another thrust up the hill. Up they went, but were repulsed. Once more Brock organized about 300 stragglers and led them for another try. Being six feet four inches tall and in a general's uniform, he was an almost certain target, and he dropped at once, fatally shot in the chest. This was a fearful loss to the British cause, and his regiment, the Forty-ninth Foot, charged recklessly against superior numbers to gain revenge. They had pushed the Americans perilously close to the cliff when their commander, Lieutenant Colonel John Macdonnell was killed. By 7:00 A.M. on 13 October 1812 their attack had melted away.[12]

Captain Wool's detachment of 240 men now held the heights. Wool retained command, though he had been shot through both thighs. His time was limited, however, for numbers of higher ranking officers were crossing over, among them Major General Van Rensselaer, Brigadier General William Wadsworth of the New York militia, and Lieutenant Colonel Winfield Scott, Second United States Artillery. Van Rensselaer ordered earthworks to be dug, then he recrossed to the United States to bring over the balance of his force. Before he left, however, Scott pleaded with him for the command and received it after Brigadier General Wadsworth had waived his militia rank. Without additional reinforcements, Scott at 10:00 A.M. commanded 350 regulars and 250 volunteers.[13]

Americans had now held the heights for about five hours. There was a lull until early afternoon, when between one and two a large body of Indians attacked. They were repulsed by three o'clock, and at that time Lieutenant Colonel Chrystie made his first appearance on the battlefield.

Americans, high on the hill, could see Sheaffe's red column, 800 strong, approaching from Fort George. They were not much concerned because they expected larger reinforcements to reach them soon. They had no way of knowing that the generals and colonels had been riding among the citizen soldiers on the American side, exhorting them in vain to line up and prepare to cross. Few militiamen were willing to do it. Many perhaps would have crossed if they had been given enough advance notice to replenish their supply of ammunition. As it was, they chose to stand on their known right not to serve except voluntarily in a foreign country. They reminded their officers that any attempt at retaliation would be remembered at the forthcoming elections. But even those who were willing to cross could not get over. British cannon firing from Queenston and from Vrooman's Point so successfully interdicted the crossing place that civilian boatmen refused to risk the trip.[14]

Major General Sir Roger Sheaffe, who was approaching with reinforcements for the British, had been born in Boston. He had been a loyalist during the Revolutionary War and had risen in the king's service. He was living in Canada on half pay when the second war broke out, and because of the grave shortage of experienced general officers he at once re-entered the service. Sheaffe now made a wide detour in order to stay out of artillery range and to pick up a small detachment marching from Chippewa. He attacked with the bayonet about 4:00 P.M. and drove the exhausted Americans down to the very edge of the river. Winfield Scott, after consultation with his officers, displayed signs of capitulation, but the Indians would not heed them. Finally, Scott at great peril to his life reached Sheaffe and got the battle halted.

Sheaffe had fought the action well, but followed it up badly. He could easily have captured Fort Niagara, but instead agreed to a truce. He was, nevertheless, astonished at the number of American prisoners rounded up on the Canadian side. There were 958 of them, far more volunteers than the American commanders believed to have crossed the river. He paroled the militiamen and sent the regulars to Canada as prisoners of war.[15]

Thus ended the second United States invasion of Canada. It was not a disaster of the same order as Hull's, but it cost 90 Americans killed and 100 wounded, besides all the prisoners, at a price of only 14 British killed, 84 wounded, and 15 missing. The highest price to England, though, had been the death of General Brock. On the other hand, the American officers, such as Wool and Scott, had shown fitness which would rapidly boost them up the promotion ladder.

One lesson from the Queenston campaign was that militiamen could not be counted on for offensive warfare on foreign soil. Another was that invasion just to be invading might well produce disaster. Even if the United States had held Queenston Heights, it would have had little more than a precarious foothold on Canadian soil, with no plan to go farther in any direction. This tiny campaign stood in sharp contrast with the collapse of Napoleon's invasion of Russia, which was going on at the same time.[16]

The Queenston failure brought recriminations and a change of command. General Smyth charged that Van Rensselaer had purposely kept him and his recruits out of the action. Van Rensselaer countered that Smyth had simply refused to cooperate. He also asked to be relieved. On 16 October 1812 the Niagara command was transferred to Smyth, who accepted with bombast. The choice, he said, was most "gratifying as it has exhibited the imbecility of the relentless malice of my foes." He considered himself bound by the armistice Van Rensselaer had made with Sheaffe, which gave him a month to get organized. He needed this time, since even his regulars were green recruits. The Fourteenth United States Infantry was considered by the inspector general as mere militia, or "if possible even worse." In a fight, he said, they would harm more friends than enemies. One of Smyth's colonels advised him against forming a mixed brigade of volunteers and regulars because the volunteers were so undisciplined that they would infect the regulars. Smyth himself had little confidence in militiamen. After Queenston he said, "they have disgraced the nation."[17]

General Dearborn increasingly involved himself in the Niagara theater. He established an express route over which messages could pass in forty-two hours between his headquarters near Albany and Niagara. By this channel he urged Smyth not to try to cross the Niagara River with less than 3,000 men and to be sure to have enough boats. There was apparently no need to caution Smyth on this count. He had already made up his mind to ask for 400 boats (contrasted with Van Rensselaer's 13), plus 20 or 30 scows to carry artillery and a total of 8,000 men. Dearborn wanted an early attack because he believed the British force was no more than 1,400 men, but Smyth could not oblige. Measles and dysentery played havoc with his troops, and since their pay was fearfully in arrears they were close to mutiny. Finally, he would not move until the arrival of 2,000 men from Pennsylvania.[18]

When the War Department had called on Pennsylvania in early September for these men, Pennsylvania's clumsy militia system had at once gone into operation. Brigade inspectors were made responsible for getting the detachments from their brigades to Pittsburgh, where the adjutant general was to command until officers for the detachment were elected. The men elected Adamson Tannehill, a peacetime major general, to be brigadier general in command.[19]

Smyth on 10 November published a florid proclamation. The nation, he confided to the soldiers, had been unfortunate in its field commanders; one had shamefully surrendered an army, and the other had sacrificed another army "by a precipitate attempt to pass it over at the strongest point of the enemy's lines. . . . The commanders were popular men destitute alike of the theory and practice of war." He was in the second case talking about Van Rensselaer and his officers, and apparently did not realize that this might be resented by the New Yorkers on whom he had to rely. Those who followed him, he continued, would "plant the American standard in Canada . . . they will conquer or they will die. . . . Has the race degenerated? Must I turn from you to ask the Six Nations to support the government. . . . Shame where is thy blush. . . . The present is the hour of renown. Have you not a wish for fame. . . . Yes!"[20]

Persons who may have been inspired by this exhortation left no record, but some who were offended replied in print. "You, General, who are taking the place of . . . mercenaries, cannot appeal to us. The renown you seek is not our renown. It is the renown of Europe, not of America." President Madison himself took a rather dim view of Smyth's proclamation. Secretary Eustis asked Smyth if General Dearborn had agreed to planting the standard in Canada. If he had not, Smyth must call a council of officers and be guided by their judgment before he undertook another invasion.[21]

As soon as the armistice was ended, General Sheaffe ordered a bombardment of Fort Niagara from Fort George. He hoped to distract the American commanders from the southern end of the Niagara River, where he believed lay the greatest danger to his country. The cannonade he had ordered evoked a reply, and an artillery duel went on through 21 November. When it was over, half a dozen men were dead, a few wounded, and some property damaged, but no important objectives had been achieved.[22]

Late in November Tannehill's brigade straggled in from Pennsylvania. Smyth asked Tannehill if his men would be willing to cross into Canada, and received the reply that they would do so if part of an adequate force. This convinced the general that he could rely on at least 3,000 men, Dearborn's minimum, and that with them he would invade, without regard to those who "prefer staying . . . and guarding the constitution . . . to crossing into Canada . . . in triumph."[23]

Under cover of darkness on 27 November 1812 Lieutenant Colonel Charles Boerstler led 200 men of the Fourteenth Infantry across the river to destroy a bridge over which reinforcements would have to pass to get to Queenston. At the same time Captain William King with 130 soldiers of the Fifteenth Infantry and 70 sailors went over to try to destroy the batteries across from Black Rock. General Smyth had so often proclaimed his intentions, that the British were ready for him above the falls, and both advanced parties came under heavy fire. King's men, nevertheless, overran some batteries and spiked the guns, but became separated in the darkness. They could find no boats to return in, and in the end had to surrender. Boerstler's detachment could not destroy its target because of the approach of a superior British force. Indeed, it escaped encirclement only because Boerstler in a series of loud orders to fictitious field grade officers convinced his opponents that his force was greater than theirs. Thus, when his men charged with bayonets, they opened up an escape route to the bank of the river. Most of them returned to the American side, but a few were left on the other shore with no boats. In these sharp encounters the British had lost 15 to 17 killed, 47 to 57 wounded, and 32 to 56 missing.[24]

All the while, the main invading force was standing by on the American shore, cold and wet, waiting for the order to follow the advance parties across. The order never came, and late in the day they returned to camp in a mutinous mood. They did not understand why they had waited poised all day, and Smyth never told them that he could not assemble his minimum of 3,000 men. It turned out, for example, that only 413 of the 1,500 men of the Pennsylvania Brigade would consent to cross into Canada.[25]

Smyth's officers now contended that the next attempt ought to be made at some other point on the river, but Smyth held to the same site across from Queenston. He issued an order for the invasion to take place on 1 December, and with it one of his inimitable proclamations: "Neither rain, snow, or frost will prevent the embarkation. While em-

"Those Are Regulars, by God!"

The facing drawing depicts a brigade of infantry led by Winfield Scott (on horseback) at the Battle of Chippewa, 5 July 1814. The brigade had been drilled by Scott during the previous winter into a professional unit. At Chippewa the precise maneuvering of Scott's brigade as it crossed a bridge under fire and deployed into line of battle brought from Major General Phineas Riall, the British commander, the exclamation "Those are regulars, by God!"

In the War of 1812 the heart of a battle was a line of infantry formed like this one. The fire of the enemy's artillery and the exertions of his cavalry were chiefly directed against the line. When these efforts, or the action of the enemy infantry, or a combination of the three broke the cohesion of the line, the battle was usually decided. In an ideal situation the line was formed on an open plain just outside the effective range of the enemy's artillery. The enemy would also be formed in a line of battle with its supporting units. Thus, the opposing lines were in most cases within 500 yards of each other. Cannon fire was very destructive to an advancing line, but it was not really effective in support of such a line.

The American line was two ranks deep, with a prescribed distance of 32 inches between the ranks. Within a rank, the men worked elbow to elbow. The objective of such a formation was to preserve the line's cohesion while it moved precisely in any direction. If a line could be handled skillfully enough to strike its opponent in the flank, it could enfilade the opposing line and swiftly bring the action to a victorious finish. The commanding officer sometimes rode his horse ahead of the line, as Scott is doing here. The company officers, depicted here in dark jackets, marched in the line to give orders and to keep the line dressed and intact. Subalterns marched with drawn swords behind the line to cut down any soldier who deserted his place.

As long as the colors were aloft, the unit was known to be in action. The men, if scattered, were expected to rally on the colors.

They could be seen above and through the black-powder smoke of the battle. So could the uniforms, which were gaudy and glittering, partly for that reason. The uniforms were also expected to awe the foe, who waited while the line advanced upon him slowly, inexorably, and by beat of drum.

The effective range of the muskets shown in this picture was between 50 and 100 yards. When an advancing line came within musket shot, it halted and fired volleys by orders from the officers. The effect sought was not an aimed fire from one soldier to another who was seen in the sights of the shooter's gun, but rather a sheet of lead. Behind that sheet the attackers would go in on the double to break the enemy line by means of the bayonet.

barking the music will play martial airs. Yankee Doodle will be the signal to get underway. . . . Hearts of War! Tomorrow will be memorable in the annals of the United States." Reality did not measure up to his proclamation. Only 865 regulars, 506 twelve-month volunteers, and about 100 militiamen were on hand to embark on 1 December. This was far below the minimum 3,000. Councils and recriminations followed, but in the end the men were ordered out of the boats and the campaign declared over.

After two false starts, the Pennsylvania brigade, which had arrived late and had been of little use, decided to go home. When the men made the decision, General Tannehill said, "With volunteers this is a crime which the english [*sic*] language cannot give a name equal to the Offense." In spite of him 1,150 officers and men went home; only 300 stayed. Smyth ordered the remainder made into a battalion on 9 December, then a week later discharged it.[26]

Smyth's reputation as a general, justly or unjustly, was destroyed. The volunteers threatened him, so he camped among the regulars. Brigadier General Peter B. Porter of the New York militia made no attempt to conceal his scorn, and on 12 December he provoked Smyth into a duel. Each fired and missed. Next Smyth asked permission to return to Virginia on leave, and the President willingly granted it. A mob in Buffalo hooted at him as he started home, and a militiaman got off a shot in his direction. He traveled the rest of the way to Virginia on back roads. In the ensuing months he was dropped from the army rolls. He blamed his fall upon the militia. "The affair at Queenston," he said, "is a caution against relying on crowds who if they are disappointed . . . break their muskets; or if they are without rations for a day desert." The enemy took comfort from Smyth's campaign. "My apprehensions for the safety of the province," said Prevost, "are considerably diminished; such an enemy cannot be considered as formidable."[27]

Thus ended the campaigning season on the Niagara front in 1812.

Throughout the Niagara campaign the commanders on both sides were trying to approximate their battles to the European practice of the time. The heart of a battle was the line of infantry. It was this line which had to be broken if victory was to be won; therefore, the heavy fire of the artillery and the maneuvers of the cavalry were for the most part directed against it. When it was possible, the battle line of infantry was formed on an open plain, just outside the effective artillery range of the enemy. This meant that the two opposing lines took their positions within 500 yards of each other. Cannon which fired solid shot could, it is true, span three times that distance, but they were not especially accurate. At about 300 yards the charge for cannon became grapeshot, which scattered and thus had a multiple effect; then at 200 yards or less the charge became canister, which scattered even more but had a short range. In 1784 Lieutenant Henry Shrapnel of the British army had invented a variation of close-range scatter shot which came to bear his name. His variation was a hollow shell filled with small metal balls and carrying an explosive charge set off by a fuse. This type of shot received limited use in the War of 1812.

The effective range of the infantryman's musket was not over 100 yards, and this range dictated the battle formations. Infantry organization was founded on the need to form the line, control it in battle, renew it when it was decimated, and maneuver it so as to place the enemy at a disadvantage. Battle formations were thus lines of men two ranks deep, with the men virtually elbow to elbow. They were maneuvered much as men are today in the close-order drill used for training and for display. In other words, the close-order drill formations of the twentieth century were the battle formations of the time of the War of 1812. Battles were won by infantry lines which held their cohesion in battle and in cooperation with cavalry and artillery destroyed the cohesion of their foes.

The Great Lakes and the St. Lawrence River

Both belligerents knew that the Great Lakes were a critical theater, but neither of them had an impressive naval strength there. The British commanders were officers of the Provincial Marine, which was primarily a transport service and was administered not by the Royal Navy but by the quartermaster department. These officers were senior indeed, the one on the upper lakes being eighty-five years old, while the Ontario commander was seventy-five. General Brock tried to get the former replaced, but it was the junior on Ontario who resigned first. Prevost at once sent off to England an appeal for a vigorous replacement.[1]

On the United States side, the Navy Department in June designated Captain Isaac Chauncey to repair to the lakes and take command.

Chauncey was forty and had been serving as a ship captain since the age of eighteen. He had been an officer in the United States Navy since 1799 and had served in the pseudo-war with France and in the Tripolitan War. For leadership qualities and for coolness in the face of danger, he had been promoted to captain in April 1806. At the time of his appointment to the lake command he was commandant of the New York Navy Yard and in a good position to forward supplies and men to the Great Lakes. During the three weeks following his notification—which for some reason was delayed until 3 September—he caused gun carriages and ammunition to be manufactured at forced paces, established a courier system which could complete the round trip from New York to Sackett's Harbor in six days, started forward 140 ship's carpenters and 700 seamen and marines from New York, and ordered shipped more than 100 guns and many tons of ammunition.[2]

Sackett's Harbor was the only really good harbor on the American side of the lake, and it had been made the United States Navy base on Lake Ontario. It did not lie on any of the lines of internal communication with the rest of the United States, and it had to be maintained by coasting vessels from Oswego, forty miles southward. From Oswego the line of communications ran along the Oswego and Oneida rivers, Lake Oneida, the Mohawk River, and thence down the Hudson River to New York City. Kingston, only thirty-six miles away across the mouth of the St. Lawrence, was the British counterpart. It had the advantage of being better connected with the interior than Sackett's, but it was vulnerable and its harbor was likely to freeze solid in the winter. General Prevost considered York a better base and sought to move the operation there, but he never brought it off.[3]

Before Chauncey's regime, the United States had only one war vessel on Lake Ontario, and it was of course based on Sackett's Harbor. This was *Oneida*, which from April through July brought in two prizes.* Her depredations and the strategic importance of Sackett's made the elderly British commander, Lieutenant Hugh Earle, determined to plan an attack. He sent word ahead that if resisted he would burn Sackett's; then on 29 July 1812 he sallied from Kingston with what seemed an overwhelming force: *Royal George* 24 guns, *Prince Regent* 16, *Earl of Moira* 22, *Simcoe* 8, and *Seneca* 8. Lieutenant Melancthon Woolsey of the United States Navy was not overawed and made preparations to resist. He brought ashore at Sackett's one entire broadside from *Oneida* and dug it in with his cannon. When the

* *Oneida* had been launched in 1809 at a cost of $20,505.00 and 110 gallons of liquor. She was 85'6" × 22'6" and carried 1 long 32-pound carronade in the bow and 18 long 24-pounders on her broadsides.

British flotilla arrived, this artillery punished it so severely that Earle had to withdraw.[4]

The duel between Woolsey and Earle was not over. Earle sent two of his heaviest ships down the St. Lawrence to Ogdensburg to destroy six American schooners moored there. Woolsey had available a vessel just recently acquired and fitted out with guns. This was *Julia*, a schooner which carried one 32-pound carronade and two 6-pounders. He sent her in pursuit, and she overtook the two Britishers before they reached Ogdensburg. The rival ships shot at each other for three hours on 31 July. Since *Julia* inflicted more punishment than she received, in spite of her very inferior armament, the British ships withdrew on the following day and unslung their guns to be mounted in shore batteries at Brockville. *Julia* and the six schooners she had protected were shut in the river until the armistice in September enabled them to reach the lake.[5]

Bearing the honorary rank of commodore, Isaac Chauncey left New York City on 26 September, and the Canadian newspapers noticed his departure. Governor Tompkins soon joined him, and the two struggled along over nearly impassable roads. On account of the road conditions, Chauncey ordered the supplies to be diverted to Oswego. He arrived at Sackett's Harbor on 2 October and at once accelerated matters there. He hurried Lieutenant Woolsey off to Oswego to supervise the gathering of supplies and to buy some schooners. In no time the lieutenant acquired eight schooners, which with *Julia* (purchased earlier by him) cost a total of $39,500, plus $6,000 to carpenters to fit them for naval service. After his purchases the United States naval squadron on Lake Ontario consisted of ten vessels which could carry 56 to 63 guns and 600 men. The British ships there carried 88 guns.*[6]

Captain Chauncey behaved at his boldest during the late fall of 1812. With his flagship *Oneida* and one other he hovered off Kingston to intercept British vessels. At dawn on a November day he discovered *Royal George* and two schooners anchored five miles away. This was too big a force for him, and he sailed south hoping but scarcely ex-

---

* The American ships: *Oneida*, 18 long 24-pounders, 1 32-pound carronade; *Julia*, 1 32-pound carronade, 2 6-pounders; *Conquest* (purchased as *Genessee Packet*), 2 32-pound carronades, 4 6-pounders; *Governor Tompkins* (purchased as *Charles and Anne*), 1 32-pound carronade, 4 6-pounders; *Hamilton* (purchased as *Diana*), 1 32-pound carronade; *Fair American*, 1 32-pounder, 4 6-pounders; *Ontario*, 1 32-pounder, 4 6-pounders; *Pert* (purchased as *Collector*), 2 24-pound carronades; *Growler* (purchased as *Experiment*), 8 small guns; *Scourge* (purchased as *Lord Nelson*), 6 6-pounders. The British ships: *Royal George*, 22 32-pound carronades, 2 long 9-pounders; *Earl of Moira*, 18 9-pounders, 4 6-pounders; *Prince Regent*, 16 9-pounders; *Gloucester*, 10 guns; *Seneca*, 8 guns; *Simcoe*, 8 guns.

pecting to escape attack. Although the British lookouts could hardly have failed to sight him, they made no move. Such conduct convinced him that his antagonists were not eager to fight, and he kept his eyes open for opportunities. When word reached him that the three principal British warships had gone westward to reinforce Fort George, he gathered a large detachment and lay in wait off Kingston for their return. Although outgunned and outnumbered he relied on the dispersion of his guns among several vessels and on their longer range to win. In fact, it would have been 40 American versus 56 British guns, but the two flotillas did not meet.[7]

On 8 November the Americans sighted *Royal George* alone and chased her into Kingston. They followed her in at 3:00 P.M. the next day, and *Conquest, Julia, Pert,* and *Growler* opened on her with their guns, while *Oneida* held her fire for forty minutes. They forced *Royal George* to cut her cables and tie up to the wharf, where ground troops could assist her. Chauncey ordered his gunners to direct their fire so as not to destroy Kingston. Whether he was being chivalrous or canny, to avoid later retaliation upon Sackett's Harbor, is not known. The wind continued to blow inshore, and as dusk fell Chauncey began to beat out into the lake. He anchored outside the harbor and prepared to renew the attack the next day on what he believed was a badly crippled ship. But in the morning the onshore wind was unmanageable, and he beat back toward Sackett's. *Royal George,* in fact, had only suffered injuries to her rigging and the loss of one man killed and eight wounded. American casualties totaled one killed and three wounded. Four more were wounded when a cannon burst on *Pert.* The sailing master was wounded by this explosion and in the heavy weather was washed overboard and drowned.[8]

This episode was the only instance during the war when the American navy entered the harbor at Kingston. Chauncey might have run the risks of the weather if he had had a truer evaluation of the defending force. Whereas he believed there were 108 cannon, there were in fact only 52; whereas he thought there were 2,000 defenders, in fact there were only 700. Whatever the force, the penetration of the harbor demonstrated that the United States had control of Lake Ontario. American vessels captured four merchant ships and by adapting them for naval auxiliary use further upset the balance of power, until ice closed down operations.

The Ontario navies were active to the last moment. Four American schooners patrolled constantly off Kingston, while the rest of the flotilla lay in Sackett's Harbor as a ready reserve. Chauncey dashed out with some of the reserve to try to cut off *Earl of Moira,* but he lost track of her in a severe snowstorm. Meanwhile, weather permitting, he enjoyed the ability to carry supplies and men at will anywhere on the lake. His superiority went up significantly when on 26 November a new corvette was launched at Sackett's; she had been converted from standing timber to a ship in 45 days. Named *Madison*, she had a length of 112 feet and a beam of 32½ feet; she carried twenty-four 32-pounder carronades. She was one-third larger than the ocean-going, victory-winning sloops-of-war *Wasp* and *Hornet*.[9]

Madison was launched only to be laid up for the winter. During the first week in December, Chauncey winterized all his ships and himself hastened to Buffalo to lay plans for a fleet on Lake Erie during the coming season. His main concern was that the British might try to cross the lake on the ice during his absence and assail Sackett's Harbor. Well he might be concerned, for that was exactly the plan of Deputy Quartermaster Andrew Grey of the British service. In addition to his quartermaster duties Grey was responsible for the Provincial Marine. This service was declining and in his opinion would be totally unable to repel the Americans when the next campaigning season came around. There was no solution he thought but to destroy Sackett's Harbor during the winter. General Prevost, however, vetoed his attack.[10]

On the other hand, Prevost ordered a substantial naval building program for the winter. Three ships were to be constructed, one each at Kingston, Amherstsburg, and York, to carry a total of sixty-six 32-pound carronades. Prevost was as aware as anyone of the difficulties of winter shipbuilding at these remote places, where both labor and materials, except for standing timber, were scarce. Accordingly, he sought to hire 100 shipwrights in Quebec. In writing of the building race upon the Great Lakes, he was cheerful to his subordinates but gloomy toward his superiors in England. His theme was that the navy must take control on the lakes. Conscientious though the deputy quartermaster was, he was not qualified to supervise the building of ships. Without naval control and navy officers and men, England had no future on the Great Lakes.[11]

There were five English warships on Lake Erie and one on Lake Huron in the fall of 1812: *Queen Charlotte*, twenty 32-pounders, *Hunter*, ten 12-pounders, *Prevost*, fourteen 9-pounders, *Nancy*, eight 6-pounders, *Caledonia*, eight 6-pounders, and *Detroit*, fourteen guns (captured in August as *Adams*). Against these the United States had nothing except hopes. The first erosion of British superiority occurred on 9 October. Lieutenant Jesse D. Elliott, the American commander on Lake Erie, embarked at 1:00 A.M. with 100 men in two boats from Buffalo, and began to row silently across the Niagara toward Fort Erie. Undetected, his party boarded *Caledonia* and *Detroit* at 3:00 A.M., overpowered their crews, and cut their cables. When the captures were secured, the captors fired a signal volley, whereupon the American shore was illuminated. Now British shore artillery began to fire and forced the beaching of *Detroit* on the Canadian side. There was nothing to do but destroy her; *Caledonia* was saved to become the nucleus of the American flotilla on Lake Erie. Elliott had two 20-gun brigs and three gunboats under construction at Black Rock. Work on them was irregular because the building places were within range of the British artillery. General Brock longed to lead an infantry detachment to destroy the skeleton vessels, but he was restrained by Prevost's orders not to invade the United States.[12]

During the winter Captain Chauncey made a visit of inspection to the eastern end of Lake Erie. What he saw convinced him that Black Rock could not serve as the base for the squadron to be built upon Erie. He ordered a shift to Presque Isle, which was virtually in the wilderness. But it could be supplied from Philadelphia by way of Pittsburgh, which would take some of the strain off New York. Elliott was to finish the five vessels begun at Black Rock, but in the end he would have to shift them to the new base. In order to do so, it would be necessary to neutralize the British strong points along the Canadian bank of the Niagara River.[13]

Unaware of the American preparations, Governor Prevost did not worry about the British position on Lake Erie. As 1812 came to an end, he saw no threat to British dominance and consequently ordered the building of only one schooner of twelve guns.[14]

Upstream from Montreal the St. Lawrence River, Canada's lifeline, consisted of numerous and dangerous rapids. Cargoes could be carried through them only in bateaux manned by experts. On 16 September an American gunboat opened fire on a brigade of bateaux above the rapids near Prescott, and it was supported on shore by units of citizen soldiers. The entire precious brigade might have been captured save for one voyageur who escaped and spread the alarm. Canadian militia assembled, and they and the bateaumen beat off the American attempt.[15]

The last westward point for staging British river convoys in the Thousand Islands was at Gananoque. Captain Benjamin Forsyth with a company of the United States Rifle Regiment and 30 militiamen attacked that place at dawn on 21 September. He killed 10 men, wounded some, took 4 prisoners, and burned the installation. In retaliation, Colonel Robert Lethbridge, British commander at Prescott,

Major General Jacob Brown

prepared to attack Ogdensburg, the main American station for harassing river traffic. On the morning of 4 October he directed a heavy cannonade across the river and under its cover launched 25 bateaux and 2 gunboats to carry 750 men, mixed regulars and militia, to the American shore. Fire from Ogdensburg forced them back in midstream, with 3 killed and 4 wounded. Governor Prevost censured the expedition as a violation of his injunction against offensive action, relieved Lethbridge, and reassigned him to a minor position in Montreal. For some reason Lethbridge was promoted on 4 June 1813 to be major general.

Jacob Brown, brigadier general of New York militia, had arranged the withering fire which drove Lethbridge back. Brown had been born in 1775 in Bucks County, Pennsylvania, of a line of Quakers who had come over with William Penn. At eighteen he had to fend for himself, by teaching school for a while and then by surveying. As a result of his surveying he acquired in 1799 several thousand acres of wild land on Lake Ontario. On it he established Brownstown. His first military experience came in 1809 when he became colonel of a militia regiment. Brown had a feeling for the problems of citizen soldiers, understood their limitations, and showed great power to lead them.[16]

His home was close to Sackett's Harbor, but he had been transferred to Ogdensburg to harass river traffic. Unable at his new post to raise a regiment, he drew together 600 volunteers from among friends and supplied them by buying provisions without any authority but his own. He hastened to inform Governor Tompkins of their hardships. With bounty pay, clothing, three months' extra pay, and 160 acres promised, the regulars were well cared for, whereas the militiaman in federal service had nothing but $6.66 a month. Brown casually added that he had drawn a draft upon the governor for $5,000 to equip his unit. His Quaker background eliminated in him deference to rank, and he often talked to Tompkins like a Dutch uncle.

Whatever the scope of General Dearborn's command, he could not divert his attention very far from the region south of Montreal. Plattsburg on Lake Champlain was the key to that country. Dearborn was instrumental in shifting Brigadier General Joseph Bloomfield, commandant at New York City, to the command of the Champlain area. Bloomfield had been governor of New Jersey for twelve years prior to the war, and was a staunch Democrat. In addition, Dearborn sought to build up a force of 5,000 regulars. His informants told him that 2,000 British soldiers had traveled to Upper Canada during July and August, and he inferred that no more than 1,600 of them and around 3,000 Canadian militia remained near Montreal.[17]

Secretary Eustis directed the deputy quartermaster to purchase six vessels on Lake Champlain. Then on 28 September the secretary of the navy selected Lieutenant Thomas Macdonough to take command of them and two gunboats. Both military secretaries stressed the need for interservice cooperation on Lake Champlain. Secretary Eustis recommended the naval appointee, "whose name as well as I can remember is McDonough," to General Dearborn. In years to come few would forget Macdonough's name. Dearborn, as one might expect, now asked for clarification of the chain of command in the Champlain theater.[18]

Skirmishes were frequent along the border south of Montreal. Major Guildford D. Young of the New York militia led a detachment on 22 October to capture a small British force at St. Regis on the St. Lawrence. Some of the captives were bateaumen who were nearly impossible to replace. Almost exactly one month later, on 23 November, a British party of 20 regulars and 70 militiamen retaliated by raiding the United States fort at French Mills on the Salmon River. They captured 44 men, 4 boats, and 57 stands of arms.[19]

In spite of these skirmishes General Dearborn saw the time drawing near for a thrust toward Montreal. If major British reinforcements did not arrive, a winter campaign was in order, for when the ice formed in the river the commanders in Montreal would have to make the best of what little force they had. Therefore Dearborn himself went to Plattsburg. He found there not the 5,000 men he had been building toward, but 2,500 regulars, with 2,500 New York and Vermont militiamen promised. This force could not attack Montreal, but could enter Canada and cut communication on the river. He recommended such a movement to Bloomfield, and a council of officers concurred. Bloomfield fell ill and stayed so, and by mid-November Dearborn decided to act without him. He advanced his force northward and put it into bivouac about a mile and a half short of the boundary line, near Champlain.[20]

In front of the advancing Americans were 3,000 British, half regulars, half militia, who had felled trees across the roads and set up other obstructions. On 19 November Dearborn found that two-thirds of his militia would not cross into Canada. His regulars were much reduced by illness, and Macdonough had not yet arrived to help on the lake. A council of eight officers agreed with him that it was sensible to withdraw toward Plattsburg and go into winter quarters. It has been hinted that Dearborn never intended with his abortive advance to do more than keep up appearances.[21]

One of Dearborn's officers was not content to march to the border, sniff the wind, and march back. Colonel Zebulon M. Pike asked permission to advance into Canada. As soon as permission was granted, he took 600 regulars across the line at dawn on 19 November. About 400 New York militiamen, who were willing to cross, advanced by another path. Pike's regulars concentrated around a blockhouse at La Cole Mill, only to find that its defenders had fled. They were in the act of occupying it when the American militia column marched up. The dawn light was dim, the blockhouse was known to be Canadian, and the citizen soldiers opened fire. Then the two American columns battled each other for a while, at a cost of 50 casualties, until the error was discovered. This left no fight in the invaders, and no course but to return to Plattsburg and to winter quarters.[22]

Even General Dearborn must have sensed the comic-opera nature of the year's end in his theater. With Smyth's report before him as his men settled into winter quarters, he subtly shifted the responsibility away from himself. His march to the border, he claimed, had been successful as a diversion in favor of operations at Niagara and Lake Ontario. But to provide double coverage he said, "It would appear that something like fatality has pervaded our military operations through the course of this campaign." He added that he would be happy to be relieved if the government found anyone whose talents and popularity would impress it more than his.[23]

The Nations at War

Although not on a pay-as-you-go basis, Canada was forthrightly meeting its share of the cost of war. Governor Prevost was proud of the way his army bills had performed. His government had issued £150,-000 of them, but only the smallest fraction had been presented for redemption. Most of the cost of the war was piled on top of the already heavy burden of the British taxpayers. The English public debt stood at £626 million and was steadily rising. Gone were the profits from £12 million of trade per year with the United States. Bad weather during the growing season had forced the price of food up, while the income of many families had dropped or disappeared due to widespread unemployment. Laborers without work broke up machinery in factories and rioted because they were hungry. *Niles' Register*, militantly pro-war and anti-British, reported to American readers that "a fearful crisis is approaching in England. . . . Though every ramification of the government is corrupt, and the putridity is daily increased, we had rather that the pruning knife than the axe should be laid to the political tree. We sincerely wish that England may remain on the map of the world, a great and mighty nation." Niles built his prediction of doom partly on evidence generated in England by members of the opposition party campaigning for election. He quoted Sir Francis Burdett that the stamina of the British nation was sapped by a ruinous public debt, inland fortresses denominated barracks, an army of spies and informers, a phantom for a king, a degraded aristocracy, an oppressed people, irresponsible ministers, and an intimidated press. Underlying all these evils was the corruption of the House of Commons. If all sinecures held by its members and their retainers were terminated there would be 50 shillings available for each of 71,224 poor families.[1]

Not many British citizens shared Niles' sense of impending doom or cared especially what Americans thought. They analyzed America as having "an aspiring, grasping commercial character" and a military capability, if the campaigns of 1812 were a measure of it, "almost beneath contempt." Many Canadians were quite sure that there was no chance for the war to become any more popular in the United States, or for the dissident geographical sections to be reconciled. On the other hand they believed that the United States could not possibly sustain the military effort beyond one year.[2]

Governor Prevost considered the arming of the Canadian "peasantry," for which he himself was primarily responsible, as a great step forward, because it had drawn the French population closer to Britain. Despite this, reinforcements from the home islands were needed without delay, not in the peripheral areas such as Prince Edward Island, New Brunswick, and Bermuda, as in the past, but in the interior of Canada. Bathurst replied that during the winter the Thirteenth and Ninetieth Foot Regiments and the second battalion of the Forty-first Foot would cross to Canada. Also, 200 sailors would be sent for use on the Great Lakes.[3]

Prevost warned the ministry not to count on an early peace. George Beckwith, governor of Barbados, apprised them of the failure of the navy in his area. He commanded 15,000 troops at 18 stations, scattered from Cayenne to Puerto Rico, but the navy was not equal to the task of keeping open communications among them. The waters were infested with United States privateers which could outsail His Majesty's frigates. The Lords Commissioners of the Admiralty sharply denied his charges.[4]

Viewed from almost any angle the British military establishment appeared impressive. The navy listed 740 vessels in commission, 290 of them frigates or larger, and 267 vessels being built or repaired. It gazetted 64 admirals, 69 vice admirals, 68 rear admirals, 802 post captains, 602 commanders, 3,268 lieutenants, 629 masters, and 140,000 seamen and marines. The British army showed 62,018 men at home, and 167,131 abroad, which was 11,000 more than at the start of 1812. In addition there were no less than 150,000 militiamen and other sorts of citizen soldiers who were considered efficient enough to be listed in strength reports. Monies appropriated for military purposes totaled £20,500,000, a sum substantially in excess of the total income of the United States government.[5]

During 1812 the presidential election dominated politics in the United States. A coalition of Democrats put forward DeWitt Clinton, who had strong Federalist support, to try to defeat Madison. Meanwhile in early elections Federalists gained power in Massachusetts, picked up congressional seats in New Jersey, and won control of both houses of the New York state legislature. Seeking to gratify Federalist New England, Madison backed a bill to increase the navy. Also, his supporters persuaded John Adams, who was slipping away from the Federalists anyway, to head the ticket of Madison electors in Massachusetts. In addition, he retained Dr. Eustis as secretary of war partly because he was from Massachusetts, though doing so cost him some Democratic support. In a bid to gain Federalist support south of the Mason-Dixon Line, he appointed an influential South Carolina Federalist, Thomas Pinckney, to command in the South with the rank of major general. Finally, he did not try to cut off the grain trade with Spain, partly because Pennsylvania, one of the principal gainers from that traffic, had 25 electoral votes.[6]

Some northerners considered that slave power would elect Madison again. Madison's sure states contained 980,000 slaves who, at the ratio of 45,000 of them for each elector, generated 21 electoral votes. War barely seemed to touch the priceless slave labor supply in the South. On the other hand Congress was considering a bill to allow boys of eighteen to enlist without parental consent. Josiah Quincy complained that such an act would deprive northern farmers of their only sure source of labor. In spite of Quincy the bill passed the House, but it failed in the Senate. While this went on, the seemingly ineluctable trend toward the re-election of Madison goaded Federalist Benjamin Stoddert, the first secretary of the navy, into making a radical statement: "If Virginia should persist in fastening upon the middle and eastern states the obnoxious and fatal administration of Mr. Madison, we may bid adieu to the Union, and prepare for the horrors of intestine commotion."[7]

The electoral college cast its votes on 3 December: 128 for Madison, 89 for Clinton; 131 for Elbridge Gerry for vice president, and 86 for Charles J. Ingersoll. The results were not known publicly until late December. Then it was seen that Madison had carried every state south and west of the Delaware River, and lost every one north of it except Vermont.[8]

As soon as President Madison was assured of re-election, he undertook overdue alterations in his cabinet. Early in December he finally got rid of Dr. Eustis and installed James Monroe in his place as acting secretary of war. Madison had needed Monroe's popularity, especially in the West, to help him win the election. Monroe in turn needed the President's support to insure his succession to the presidency. But when Madison offered him the war position as a permanent appointment, he turned it down on the grounds that he could not stand up under the burden of two secretaryships, war and state.[9]

While acting as secretary of war, Monroe spun off with characteristic diligence a broad theory for the use of manpower. He wanted to divide the east coast into six military districts and place a small cadre of regulars in each of them. If the occasion arose, the main defensive force, the citizen soldiery, could form around these cadres. He urged that the laws be changed to permit the President to select the colonels of volunteer regiments. The colonels would in turn pick their subordinates, and the officers would go forth together to recruit the regiments. By awarding a bounty of $40.00 to each volunteer and a bonus of $5.00 per recruit to each recruiting officer, it would be possible to secure as many volunteers as were needed. The administration should then use them for one decisive offensive which would end the war. The country could not bear the cost of a long war.[10]

Setting aside Monroe's scheme, the lame duck session of the Twelfth Congress at year's end debated the raising of regulars. Congressman Timothy Pitkin of Connecticut, who felt a large measure of the traditional fear of a standing army, argued that to vote more regulars was to give to a president, who already had excessive power, immense additional patronage. Certain of his colleagues from the Northeast saw an enlarged standing army as destructive of an important check written into the Constitution. One of the functions of the militia was to hold off the regular forces if the central government became too strong and arbitrary and sent its army against a state or states, but if the standing army grew too large, the militia would not be able to repel it. Josiah Quincy of Massachusetts opposed the increase on other grounds: the regulars were for the invasion of Canada and he was against invasion. Harmanus Bleeker of New York opposed the enlargement, but took pleasure in pointing out that the militarists could not achieve the army they sought regardless of what Congress did. There was no source for the manpower of armies except the idle, dissolute, and disorderly elements of society, but in the United States there were not enough of these to fill up an army of 50,000. For some reason Representative Benjamin Tallmadge of Connecticut was at the opposite pole from his associate Pitkin. To his way of thinking, military skills required a lifetime to learn, therefore regular forces were essential. Following the same line of reasoning, he opposed Monroe's scheme for a single smashing blow to be delivered by one-year volunteers.[11]

In spite of Tallmadge and others, Congress adopted Monroe's recommendation that the President with the consent of the Senate appoint the officers of the one-year volunteer units. This act made these volunteer units identical in organization with those of the Federalist era of the 1790s, an organization which at that time had been considered unconstitutional by Jefferson and other Jeffersonian Republicans. It did not, however, disturb the Democratic war party of 1812 to be inconsistent with the Jeffersonian past of the party.[12]

Staggering as the year 1812 had been to the United States, it did not kill the aggressive spirit of some congressmen. Speaking just after the New Year, Matthew Clay of Virginia (not an expansionist of the stripe of Henry Clay) said: "We have the Canadas as much under our command as [England] has the ocean; and the way to conquer [her] on the ocean is to drive her from the land. . . . Her fleets cannot then rendezvous at Halifax as now, and having no place to resort in the North cannot invest our coast as they have lately done. It is as easy to conquer them on land, as their whole Navy could conquer ours on the ocean. As to coping with them at sea, we cannot do it. . . . I would meet them and hurt them, however, where we can. We must take the continent from them. . . . God has given us the power and the means and we are to blame if we do not use them. If we get the continent, she must allow us the freedom of the seas."[13]

Three days later Josiah Quincy of Massachusetts undertook to lay bare the real instincts underlying this utterance. When the United States had gone to war, he said, some skeptics had looked upon it as a joke, for the country had had no men and scant resources ready for use. They had discovered, however, that the invasion of Canada was just another mode of carrying on an election. Such political use of war was immoral, and the "satraps" who had instigated it would parcel out the conquered land into feudal demesnes for themselves. At the top of the hierarchy of satraps were two Virginians and one foreigner (Madison, Monroe, and Gallatin). The only comfort Quincy could find in the situation was his own clear conscience. "If by the machinations of wicked, ambitious men [my] children should become slaves, and be yolked with a negro to the carriage of some southern despot, they should at least have the consolation to say, 'Our father was guiltless.'" Brought to his feet by a bill to classify the militia, Benjamin Tallmadge of Connecticut underlined the sectional animosity revealed by Quincy. Militias, he said, were state armies. Their classification would destroy the effective northern militia systems. Indeed, classification was a project of the southern states, which states never bothered to keep their citizen soldiery well organized and begrudged any other state an efficient militia.[14]

In response to trying conditions, the several states made adjustments in their militia systems. In general they enlarged the power of the governors to acquire military equipment, and altered unsatisfactory details relative to the raising of detachments. Most of them, too, raised the wages of their citizen soldiers to a minimum of $10.00 per month. Pay for regulars went up in December 1812 to $8.00 a month. In all states volunteer units were regulated by individual legislative enactments, but New Hampshire now passed an act which laid down general rules by means of which her volunteers might organize and choose their officers. Pennsylvania attempted to mitigate the humiliation of the behavior of Tannehill's brigade by providing a bounty of $10.00 for men who would agree to serve thirty days in Canada. North Carolina had no special manpower problem at this point in time, but found it expedient to deny free Negroes the right to enroll in the militia.[15]

Some 50,000 militia, drafted or volunteer, were formally received into federal service during 1812,* and an unknown number were called out by the states and urged upon the government but not formally accepted. At one extreme were Rhode Island, Connecticut, and Delaware, which did not supply a man, and at the other were

---

* Militia furnished in 1812 by the states and territories: New Hampshire 246; Massachusetts 208; Rhode Island none; Connecticut none; Vermont 2,434; New York 14,866; New Jersey 808; Delaware none; Pennsylvania 4,494; Maryland 318; District of Columbia none; Virginia 901; North Carolina 595; South Carolina 1,046; Georgia 378; Kentucky 7,805; Tennessee 510; Ohio 10,135; Louisiana 550; Indiana Territory 1,694; Mississippi Territory 651; Illinois Territory 963; Missouri Territory 44; Michigan Territory 555—*Sen. Doc. 100*, 16 Cong., 2 sess. Upton, *Military Policy*, gives 19,036 in the regular army in Feb. 1813.

New York and Ohio, which provided 14,866 and 10,135 respectively, or more than 60 per cent of the whole number. There cannot have been many one-year volunteers, and of the 36,700 regular soldiers authorized, only half that number were actually in service. Nothing but a national draft could have filled the authorized vacancies, if indeed that would have produced men instead of riots. Conscription at the state level was legal, but at this stage was very little used.

After Monroe had declined appointment as permanent secretary of war, President Madison offered the post to General Dearborn, who also turned it down. Now Madison leaned toward Daniel D. Tompkins, the energetic governor of New York. If the War Department was not inducement enough, Gallatin, who valued Tompkins' capabilities, offered to take war and vacate the treasury for Tompkins. But in the end Tompkins dared not leave New York, lest Federalists gain control there. The War Department therefore was given to another New Yorker, John Armstrong. He was a longtime Democrat, erstwhile Revolutionary officer, erstwhile United States senator, and erstwhile minister to France. He was also a Clintonian who liked to pit the northern and southern wings of the Democratic Party against each other. For many Democrats he had a faint odor of treason due to his authorship of the notorious Newburgh Addresses at the close of the Revolutionary War. Gallatin was reluctant to serve with Armstrong, but Madison called in the influence of his wife upon Mrs. Gallatin to keep him in the cabinet for a few months.[16]

The principal hater of Armstrong in the administration was James Monroe. He was convinced that Armstrong from the start intended to try to be both secretary of war and commander of the field armies. As such he would menace civilian control over the military. Monroe insisted that Armstrong lacked the brains for the job, besides being indolent and insubordinate. He would ruin both the administration and the party. William Jones sized him up as cunning, vain, caustic, and pretentious about military knowledge which he did not possess. In fine, Jones concluded, he was "without one useful quality either social, civil or military."[17]

In spite of these harsh opinions, when John Armstrong took over the duties on 5 February 1813, affairs in the War Department began to move faster. His impact was felt first among the general officers. Most of those who had been called to high command during 1812 had proved themselves unequal to their tasks. Even if the tasks were too big for mortal men, William Hull, Henry Dearborn, and Alexander Smyth cannot be rated very high. Neither can those civilian officials who picked them, that is, James Madison, James Monroe, and

Secretary of War John Armstrong

William Eustis. With Armstrong's advice, Madison appointed four major generals: James Wilkinson, Wade Hampton, William Henry Harrison, and Morgan Lewis. If these four were not dazzling as generals, they were all at least well connected. Wilkinson had been associated with Armstrong during the Revolution. Lewis had been a friend of the President for many years, and in addition was related to Armstrong through marriage with the powerful Livingston family of New York. Harrison enjoyed a national reputation, with special popularity in the West. Hampton had great power in South Carolina. By chance, Wilkinson and Hampton were bitter enemies. Harrison was only forty years old, but the other three averaged fifty-seven. All were confirmed on 2 March 1813. Monroe sadly watched these commissions go, for he had craved one, but since there was no rank of lieutenant general and since his enemy John Armstrong would be making assignments, he let the President know that he did not want to be considered.[18]

Ten days later Madison made recess appointments of seven brigadier generals: Zebulon Pike, George Izard, Lewis Cass, Duncan McArthur, William Winder, Benjamin Howard, and Thomas Parker. Pike and Izard were professionals with fine training. Cass and McArthur had extended experience, some notoriety with William Hull, and political strength in Ohio. William Winder was the nephew of the governor of Maryland, while Ben Howard was himself governor of Upper Louisiana Territory and then of Missouri Territory. Parker, an older man, had revolutionary experience and was a colonel in the regular service. This batch of brigadiers was younger and a good deal more promising than the new major generals.[19]

On 19 March 1813 the nation was redivided into nine military districts, with a general officer assigned to command each one.[20]

A full year before his appointment to be secretary, Armstrong had communicated his ideas on strategy to Dr. Eustis. Since it was still peacetime, he had advised the doctor to take advantage of the low prices then prevailing to accumulate supplies, stressed the need to gain military intelligence, designated the Great Lakes as the focal point for American strategy, and insisted that the United States must gain control of them. During his tenure as secretary of war, the Great Lakes held a good share of his attention.[21]

In January 1813 Madison relieved his administration of Paul Hamilton, his tippling secretary of the navy. Into the cabinet to replace him came William Jones, a Democrat from Pennsylvania, who was fifty-three years old. Before the American Revolution, Jones had served on merchant ships but had fought with the ground forces at

Trenton and Princeton. After that he found his way back aboard ship as a lieutenant on the United States frigate *Constellation*. Under Thomas Truxtun he had been promoted to first lieutenant for gallant conduct. After the Revolution he had commanded in the merchant marine for three years, and then had returned to land pursuits at Philadelphia. Jefferson had asked him to become secretary of the navy in 1801, but instead Jones had served in Congress until 1803.[22]

When William Jones finally arrived to be head of the Navy Department in February 1813, he took the helm firmly. To begin with, he fired Charles W. Goldborough who had been chief clerk since 1807 and was to continue so, except for the Jones interval, until 1843. Jones' knowledge of ships and sea lanes was extensive. He did not defer even to the most seasoned captains, but told them where they should take position most effectively to harass British shipping and to stay there until forced to come home, when they must approach the coastal waters with caution. The secretary told Captain J. D. Dent at Charleston that his costs were too high and his use of schooners was not efficient. Before making decisions in the future, he said, "You are within six days by mail, and can consult with me." He answered special requests from the naval commander at New York by saying, "The force allotted to you must be with reference to the relative force employed at other places, and to the general naval wants and resources, of which you will permit this department to be the exclusive judge." He criticized Oliver Hazard Perry for paying $4,000 for lead to be used as ballast on the Great Lakes, when stones would have done as well and been much cheaper. He had enough technical knowledge to speak of a defective barge in such terms as these: "the resistance of the water on the lee bow pressing her to windward, having so little hold of the water abaft, to resist her flying to; but this cannot be remedied without a leeboard on her quarter, or adding a skag to her keel abaft which would greatly injure her other qualities." President Madison said that he was "the fittest minister who had ever been charged with the Navy Department. With a strong mind, well stored with requisite knowledge, he possessed great energy of character and indefatigable application to business." It is ironic that the President relied on Jones to administer the navy, and for a time to be acting secretary of the treasury, but not to take part in such sporadic strategic planning as was done.[23]

The editors of the London *Times* watched these substitutions with characteristic sourness. Sorry as their own Ministry had sometimes seemed to them to be, they felt it to be brilliant when compared with Madison's. They interpreted the President's changes of personnel as

Secretary of the Navy William Jones

the sacrifice of scapegoats. He could, they said, cover up his own errors by charging all his failures to Dr. Eustis and Paul Hamilton. Eustis, in the same manner, had victimized William Hull. The individual bravery and skill of Commodore Decatur, the editors continued, "had been laid hold of," by the President, "to strengthen his own political influence."[24]

1813

Riverine Warfare and Blockade

Not until seven months after the United States' declaration of war did the British government make a formal statement about this unwelcome development. Finally, on 9 January 1813 it set forth its reasons for war with the Americans. It denied any intention of conquest and vowed that it fought only because the United States had sided with France to destroy British commerce. In the struggle for survival, which it insisted the French had begun, it had to enforce the right of search of neutral ships and the removal of English sailors. The Prince Regent denied that his country had incited the Indians against the Americans.[1]

As the year 1813 began, prospects seemed at least not unfavorable to the Ministry to divert some military resources to America. Napoleon's army was retreating out of Russia in a shattered condition at the same time that word came from Canada that the United States could not possibly sustain the war effort much longer. The London *Times* thought the moment right to censure the Ministry for failing to mount a strong offensive against the United States.[2]

The Lords Commissioners of the Admiralty added significantly to Admiral Warren's duties when in November 1812 they directed him to supply escort vessels for convoys of merchant ships and to establish a blockade to cover Chesapeake and Delaware bays. Six weeks later they informed him that they intended to build up his squadron to 30 frigates and 50 sloops-of-war, but that in return they expected from him positive results against the tiny American navy. Croker reproved him in his usual didactic style for asserting that his squadron was too small, and told him that he ought to know better than to expect to equal the number of privateers carrying the American flag. The Lords Commissioners believed that his figures on American privateers were unrealistic, and that if he would take pains to convoy all merchantmen and properly conduct the blockade, few privateers would be able even to put to sea.[3]

Late in March, Earl Bathurst directed the Admiralty to extend the blockade (heretofore confined to Chesapeake Bay) to include New York, Charleston, Port Royal, Savannah, and the mouth of the Mississippi River. These were points which they thought could be blockaded the year around, but in addition Admiral Warren had the power to impose a de facto blockade anywhere else he desired. Some volunteer advisers urged one for the entire coast, but the admiral found it difficult enough to keep watch over the stipulated areas. He did not formally proclaim the extension until 16 November, eight months after the directive originated in London. At that time he announced blockade over the ports stipulated by the Lords Commissioners. Exercising his discretion, he also covered Long Island Sound and all ports, creeks, bays, harbors, and rivers of the seacoast of New York, New Jersey, Pennsylvania, Delaware, Maryland, Virginia, North Carolina, South Carolina, and Georgia. Meanwhile on 30 April 1813, taking advantage of fog and foul weather, *President* and *Congress* eluded *Shannon*, *Tenedos*, *Nymph*, and *Curlew* and reached the open sea. The Lords Commissioners of course censured Warren for this, and the Earl of Darnley was alerted by the incident to propose in the House of Lords a full-scale inquiry into naval failures. His motion was beaten in May, 125 to 59.[4]

Word reached the Admiralty in the spring that the Americans intended to destroy the Greenland fisheries. In response British warships virtually crisscrossed the northern sea lanes. Farther south the object of their restless cruising was to intercept *President* and *Congress* and to keep the other American frigates sealed in where they were: *Constellation* at Norfolk, *Adams* at Alexandria, *United States* and *Macedonian* at New London, *Constitution* and *Chesapeake* at Boston. *Essex* was out of reach in the Pacific. All British frigates were under orders not to engage the American frigates alone.[5]

Off New London, *Ramillies* captured the sloop *Eagle* which was trying to reach the sea with a load of flour. Captain Hardy of *Ramillies* now sent a gang of workmen aboard to transfer the flour, but the cargo blew up, killing ten. Local merchants had filled *Eagle* with explosives and had set a device to explode when the cargo was moved. These merchants, the British papers said, were "now held in detestation by every friend of humanity." The papers also denounced Robert Fulton's submarine and its use to attempt to fasten a torpedo* to the bottom of *Ramillies*. Thereafter, Captain Hardy caused the ship's bottom to be swept every two hours with a cable, and he warned Americans that if they continued to violate the rules of civilized warfare, he would burn their coastal towns. Even Admiral Cockburn, whom Americans soon came to think of as an unfeeling brute, called Fulton's torpedoes "infernal" machines, while Admiral Warren added "cowardly" to the vocabulary of denunciation.[6]

On 31 October 1812 Admiral Sir George Cockburn had received orders to wind up his command on the Spanish coast and to report to Warren at Bermuda. He had been thoroughly conditioned from the age of ten to the harsh life of the sea. Upon reporting to Warren, he was given command of the Chesapeake operation, which had assigned to it four ships, six frigates, and several small boats. His orders to his subordinates were to be prepared to chase at a moment's notice, and his officers and men understood that failure to obey orders could bring disgrace and professional ruin to an officer, or as many as 350 lashes to an enlisted sailor. Cockburn was known to be a working and a combat officer. His face was browned by the sun, and his gold-laced cap was rusty with wearing. One midshipman marked him as "an officer who never spared himself either day or night, but shared the same toil, danger and privation of the foremost man under his command." The American image of him was in contrast that of a brutal, rapacious marauder. "To Admirals Warren and Cockburn," proposed a toastmaster in Annapolis, "may the eternal vengeance of Heaven hurl them to some station that will terminate their inhuman butcheries and savage cruelties—they disgrace human nature."[7]

On 8 February 1813 nine boats put out from *Belvidera* and *Statira* to confront a strange schooner coming down Chesapeake Bay. It turned about and tried to flee, but they overtook it. Under heavy fire the English boats advanced and the crews boarded the schooner. The defenders put up a game fight on deck too, but in the end they had to surrender when 19 of the crew of 28 men were killed or wounded. At a cost of 13 men the British thus took the privateer schooner *Lottery*, six 12-pounders, their first prize captured in Chesapeake Bay. Six days later the blockaders captured *Cora*, 8 guns and 40 men, said to be the fastest schooner out of Baltimore.[8]

Due to the arrival of the blockading fleet, Captain Charles Gordon, the American naval commander at Baltimore, asked permission to take

---

* The torpedo of that time was not self-propelled. It could be attached to the hull of a ship, but when free-floating, it moved only with the water's motion.

several privateers into service to cruise between Annapolis and the Potomac River. The secretary promptly authorized him to borrow schooners from private citizens, with the stipulations that the captains would be appointed sailing masters in the United States Navy and that the crews would receive navy pay and rations and the right to share in prize money. Gordon now experienced difficulty in obtaining crews because Maryland was paying a $16.00 bounty per recruit. Nevertheless, by the third week in May he had four small schooners and one gunboat, with 51 guns, incorporated as a Baltimore flotilla.[9]

There was no American unity of command in Chesapeake Bay. The governors of Maryland, Virginia, and Delaware were implicated, but no one except the secretary of the navy could coordinate them. Governor Levin Winder said that his state of Maryland, in spite of calls upon the militia, was virtually defenseless. To try to correct this, he appointed Samuel Smith to take command of the defenses of Baltimore. Smith had powerful local influence and along with it great energy and determination. He and his brother Robert Smith had fallen out with the Jeffersonians during Madison's first term, but now Samuel opened up communications with Secretary Armstrong and slashed determinedly away at tangles of red tape. Convinced that the British intended to attack Baltimore, he called for militia help from Pennsylvania and Virginia and begged the federals to make effective delegation of authority to persons in the vicinity. When Colonel Decius Wadsworth inspected the Baltimore defenses late in April 1813, he found them stronger than those of any other American seaport. Fortunately, heavy ships could not get in close enough to destroy Fort McHenry with their guns. Soon thereafter the British came to the head of the bay and took some soundings. They too decided that Baltimore was too strong for present attack.[10]

As Admirals Cockburn and Warren saw it, the fingers of Chesapeake and Delaware bays laid open three states to naval attack. Therefore one month after his arrival Cockburn detached Captain George Burnett with three ships to enter the York, Rappahannock, and Potomac rivers and destroy United States shipping there. On 1 April five boats under the command of Lieutenant James Polkinghorne were rowed all night up the Rappahannock in pursuit of four American schooners. The captain of the schooner *Arab* ran his ship aground and escaped, but the British captured *Dolphin*, *Racer*, and *Lynx* intact with 31 guns and 219 men. *Arab* was refloated, and all four vessels were put to use in the British squadron. Carrying American colors, they infiltrated a flotilla of American vessels and captured them at a cost of 2 men killed and 11 wounded.[11]

Rear Admiral Sir George Cockburn

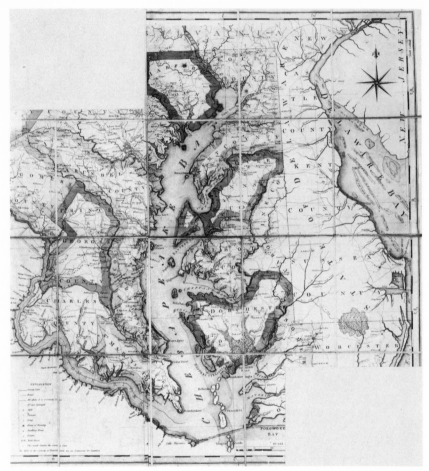

Chesapeake Bay

Admiral Cockburn organized another detachment of four vessels under Captain John P. Beresford to enforce the blockade of Delaware Bay and River. Once in position, Beresford demanded provisions from the town of Lewes at the mouth of the bay. He offered hard money and Philadelphia prices for goods delivered, but let it be known that he would take what he needed if necessary. Governor Joseph Haslet of Delaware sent word to the mayor of Lewes to resist, and appealed to the War Department for cannon. The mayor is said to have told Beresford, "We solemnly refuse to commit legal or moral treason at your command. Do your worst!" Beresford replied with a cannonade on 6 April in which his ships fired 1,000 rounds or so in 22 hours. His bombardment did not cost one life and no more than $2,000 worth of damage because the range was so great. The townsmen returned the fire with an 18-pounder and some smaller pieces, sometimes returning the same rounds fired at them. The DuPont works close by supplied them with all the powder they needed. Seeing no advantage in a land attack, Beresford drew off his squadron.[12]

The town of Wilmington, 50 miles from Lewes, begged the navy for a gunboat. On condition that the citizens would man and operate it, Secretary Jones loaned them one from the naval stores at Philadelphia. At the same time he assigned a lieutenant to command one cutter, one schooner, and three gunboats to protect the Potomac River. If the enemy entered the river with superior force, he ordered the lieutenant to take refuge under the guns of Fort Warburton, and try to repel him.[13]

In the middle of March, Admiral Warren himself took charge of the harassing operations in Chesapeake Bay. He approached within 25 miles of Washington, but decided that he fell 2,500 men short of having enough to attack the capital. Lacking such a force, he moved northward toward the head of the bay and directed Cockburn to penetrate the rivers there in order to intercept the trade between Philadelphia and Baltimore. Cockburn did this so efficiently that the Americans charged him with loving to loot and to burn. He was aided by numbers of Negro slaves who came seeking liberty and brought with them an intimate knowledge of the terrain. With them as guides he moved secretly in the night; for example, he sent a detachment up the Elk River on 28 April, which after a sharp fight burned Frenchtown and the five vessels at its docks.[14]

Cockburn announced that resisters would be destroyed, but that citizens and communities who submitted peacefully would be spared. For several days the citizens of Havre de Grace, near the mouth of the Susquehanna River, had stood guard around the clock. All night on 1 May, having special warning, they stood to their posts without sleep. When Cockburn learned of this through the Negroes, he delayed his approach and made sure that the defenders knew it. The watchers at Havre de Grace gratefully went to bed. Now Cockburn, guided by Negroes at night, approached through shallow water with 150 marines and 5 artillerymen, and at dawn on 3 May he surprised the town. There was however a brief battle. When the other citizen soldiers had fled, John O'Neill tried to serve his cannon all alone. He was injured, captured, and threatened with hanging, but in the end he went free. Later, Admiral Warren said that he would surely have hanged him had he known O'Neill was an Irishman. Cockburn now burned 40 of the 60 houses of Havre de Grace, and his men looted the town. After this episode *Niles' Register* began to refer to Cockburn's detachments as "water Winnebagoes," after the most ruthless of the northern tribes. The only person to be killed at Havre de Grace was struck by a Congreve rocket. He had the distinction of being the sole fatality inflicted by that weapon during the war. This rocket had been developed as early as 1805 by Sir William Congreve, English ordnance expert. It was supposed to fill the gap between the musket and the 12-pound field gun, but although it terrified soldiers with its screaming, it was too inaccurate to have significant effect. An American, William Clark, claimed that he had invented it and offered to reveal his secret to the secretary of war for $4,000. His offer was turned down.[15]

At Havre de Grace, Cockburn was astride the main highway between Philadelphia and Baltimore. He stayed there for some hours, but hugged his water base. His men rowed far up the Susquehanna, burning boats. At Principio, where there was one of the principal cannon foundries in the United States, Cockburn destroyed 68 cannon. He then drew back from the head of the bay and passed eastward toward the Delaware, using the Sassafras River. The admiral now sent two Americans ahead to warn Georgetown that resistance would bring destruction. Defiantly the local militia confronted him with a column of about 400 men, which he easily brushed aside; true to his threat, he burned the town. Next he crossed the river to the north bank, and looted and burned Fredericktown, Maryland. The village close by offered no resistance, and was not molested.

At the end of twelve days Cockburn rejoined Admiral Warren. His skillful harassment, using the rivers as avenues, had fearfully shaken the morale of the tidewater area. Cockburn had earned a niche in history, however unpopular he might be with Americans, as the first practitioner in North America of riverine warfare on an organized scale.

Early in the spring of 1813 the English Ministry issued orders to set in motion the long-promised diversion on the American coast. Too distant and too preoccupied with Napoleon to direct the operation, it assigned 2,300 troops to Admiral Warren, 50 of them marines with special training in the operation of Congreve rockets, and left it up to him to select the point of attack. Earl Bathurst himself prepared the instructions for Colonel Sir John Beckwith, who was placed in command of the land forces. He ordered Beckwith to use his army as directed by Warren, except that once ashore Beckwith, not Warren, was to command. Beckwith must remember that his mission was purely one of harassment, must avoid general action, and must strike without attempting permanent occupation of any place. He might exact money from individuals but not from governments, and he could accept runaway Negroes as free persons but was under no circumstances to encourage slave insurrection.[16]

The Chesapeake squadron re-entered Lynnhaven Bay on 12 May. American scouts counted 15 warships. Admiral Warren left it there on 17 May to go to Bermuda to pick up Beckwith's army, but Beckwith did not arrive until 3 June. Meanwhile Warren proudly wrote to Governor Prevost that his Chesapeake squadron had greatly inconvenienced the enemy at a loss of only 20 men.[17]

While Warren was in Bermuda, Cockburn continued the daily business of blockade and harassment. So many Negroes joined him that they became a nuisance. Under the orders from the government he could not remand any Negro against his will to slavery. He was supposed either to enlist them in the British military service or to ship them out as colonists to British possessions. The directive did not stipulate what British areas would cheerfully receive Negro colonists. The only concession the admiral made was to permit American owners to come aboard to try to persuade their ex-slaves to return.[18]

On 12 June 1813 crewmen of *Narcissus*, 32 guns, boarded the United States revenue schooner *Surveyor*, 6 guns and 25 men. The defending crew fought so bravely that when their captain tendered his sword in surrender, the British commander returned it. The British loss was 4 killed, 5 to 7 wounded; American, 5 wounded. A few days later 15 boats were launched from *Constellation* to attack *Junon, Barossa*, and one razee, becalmed in Hampton Roads about three miles away from the other blockading ships.* At dawn on 20 June the boats opened a sharp fire and seemed for a time about to overpower *Barossa*, but the wind shifted and took away their advantage. This attack probably

---

* A razee is a ship whose upper deck has been cut away; she is thus reduced to a lower rating.

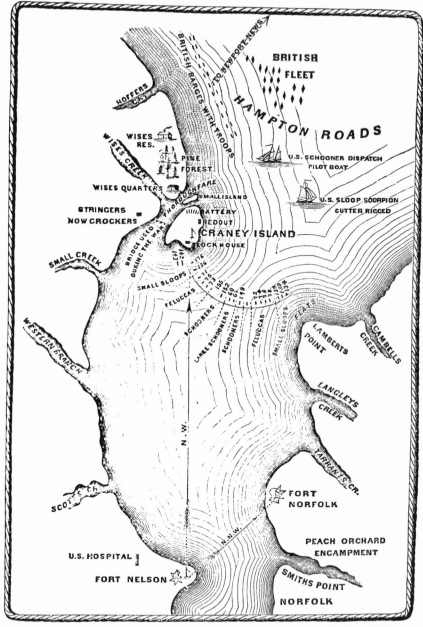

Battle of Craney Island

convinced the British commanders that they must try to capture Norfolk, the center of American maritime resistance in the Chesapeake area. Meanwhile, the British blockaders had difficulty provisioning themselves. When refused a herd of cattle at the market price, the captain of the brig *Atlanta* sent ashore a party of 10 marines to retaliate. Under gunfire from 50 "armed peasants" the retaliators set fire to two mills and then reboarded.[19]

By mid-June Admiral Warren was back in Chesapeake Bay with Colonel Sir John Beckwith's reinforcement. He now had, counting sailors, approximately 5,000 men. *Niles' Register* quoted Cockburn as saying, "We will storm Ft. Nelson and be in Norfolk to supper. There you will find two banks . . . and for your exertions and bravery you will have three days' plunder and the free use of a number of fine women." James Scott, a lieutenant with Cockburn, indignantly denied that the admiral said any such thing, but the Americans wanted to believe it and they did.[20]

Norfolk had been trying to prepare herself in the same unilateral way as had the other parts of Chesapeake Bay. Brigadier General Robert B. Taylor of the Virginia militia directed the land defense. He had about 275 regulars and presumably 2,000 citizen soldiers in the vicinity, but he did not consider more than 100 of the latter available on quick call. Governor James Barbour of Virginia by dint of uncommon effort alerted many more militiamen, but they remained scattered and were never under effective central command. Commanders on both sides recognized that Craney Island was the strategic key to Norfolk. General Taylor erected a battery there, one 18-pounder, two 24-pounders, and four 6-pounders, facing the strait which separated the island from the mainland. He placed another battery at Lamberts Point which sat on the mainland southeast of Craney Island and commanded the throat of the bay into Norfolk. The artillerists prepared a furnace for hot shot and kept a fire in it around the clock. *Constellation*, Captain Charles Stewart, was penned in at Norfolk, and her guns were available for the final defense. Even though there were four hulks sunk in the harbor, it was still possible to bombard Norfolk from the water.[21]

Brigadier General Taylor arranged his forces on the supposition that the British would not attack Norfolk without first capturing Craney Island. His men on the island struck their tents and repitched them in different places to give the impression of a large force. But on the evening of 21 June 1813 they actually totaled only 737. It would be difficult for these men to leave the island if the foe arranged his forces properly. Now Admiral Warren, to gain control of the channel and to get at *Constellation*, ordered an attack. His ships-of-the-line could not get close enough to bombard Craney Island, and he projected two landing parties, one to strike straight for the island and one to capture the mainland across the strait from Craney.[22]

Admiral Cockburn had submitted a plan for the reduction of the island, but Warren did not adopt it. He turned the command over to Colonel Beckwith, whereupon Cockburn characteristically asked to command the boats to be used from ship to shore. At 9:00 A.M. on 21 June 2,500 men landed on the mainland and worked their way opposite the island under cover of brush and trees. Taylor's island battery hit them there so hard that they had to take refuge in the woods. At the same time 50 barges carrying 1,500 men started from the fleet toward the island. The gunners at the island battery could bring them into their field of fire too, and they waited until the range was just right. When they opened fire, it was with devastating effect. They hit and sank three or four of the lead boats and filled the water with men swimming for their lives. Englishmen claimed that the Americans fired at the swimmers. Be that as it may, some Americans ran into the shallows to capture prisoners. The loss was so heavy that Admiral Warren signaled a recall.

Commodore John Cassin, commandant of the local naval yard, reported that the gunners of *Constellation*, handling their shore battery with the accuracy of riflemen, had saved Norfolk. Soldiers, however, gave the principal credit to the land artillerymen. Someone, it is certain, saved Norfolk. Warren had issued orders to Cockburn to use eight ships and take the American vessels in port at Norfolk, but after the rebuff at Craney Island the order was rescinded. Americans estimated the British losses at 200, but accurate figures are not available.

Foiled at Craney Island, the invaders passed northward across Hampton Roads to attack the small town of Hampton, Virginia. As before, they moved at night and attacked at daylight on 25 June. The 450 Americans could not hold out long against Beckwith's 2,000, but the British lost 5 killed, 33 wounded, and 10 missing, against American casualties of 30, one-third of whom, reported as missing, had simply retreated to their own homes. Nothing about the skirmish made it notable except its aftermath. The Chasseurs Britannique (French prisoners enlisted in British service) looted and raped in European style. The American report said, "The sex hitherto guarded by the soldier's honor escaped not the rude assault of superior force." For their excesses, the Chasseurs were withdrawn from combat and sent off to Halifax late in June, but Americans as usual blamed Admiral Cockburn for their behavior.[23]

Minor harassment continued on the shores of the two great bays. Early in July, British detachments battled the crews of the United States gunboats *Asp* and *Scorpion* in the Yeocomico River. *Asp* was damaged by fire, but was saved and returned to American service. Next, Admiral Cockburn sailed southward to examine Okracoke Inlet off the coast of North Carolina. Moving at night as usual, he landed on Okracoke Island on 11 July, and captured the small town of Portsmouth. Finding the vicinity without major ports, he returned to Chesapeake Bay. He reported no resistance, hence no retaliation, but Americans charged his force with looting. The slaves in the Carolina region, it was said, were ready to respond to the coming of a liberator, but only a modest number made their way to Cockburn.*[24]

Now the British flotilla moved up Chesapeake Bay once more. Washington, Annapolis, and Baltimore were frantic. Washingtonians expected an attack on their navy yard and on the cannon foundry north of Georgetown. On 14 July the ships reached the mouth of the Potomac, where 5 vessels and 600 troops were detached to push upstream as far as possible. Thirty miles were the maximum; the frigates could not sail beyond Cedar Point, and Warren called the detachment back. Considering the penetration as far as Alexandria in 1814, one assumes that the will to overcome obstacles was less strong in 1813 than in 1814, probably thanks to Admiral Warren.[25]

After Washington was deemed inaccessible, the flotilla again moved northward. Admiral Cockburn took Kent Island as a place to load water and provisions and to get some rest. There he threatened both Annapolis and Baltimore. Therefore, the secretary of the navy ordered Captain Charles Morris to leave the frigate *Adams* and take his crew to Annapolis. *Adams*, bottled up by the blockade, was anchored in a strong position near Washington with a cluster of gunboats about her.[26]

Admiral Warren became convinced that 11,000 persons were on hand to defend Baltimore and 5,000 at Annapolis. His conviction deflected him from the cities toward the Eastern Shore. At St. Michaels and at Queenstown, his men met a rough reception. These rebuffs, the strength around the cities, the high rate of desertion, and above all the arrival of the fever caused him to bring the Chesapeake campaign to a close for the season. He took part of his command to Halifax to recover in the cool weather, and reported his own arrival there on 18 September 1813.[27]

From Halifax, Admiral Warren set out to convince others that his

---

* Lossing, *Field Book*, pp. 689–90, claimed that Cockburn sold the Negroes in the West Indies, but his information was in error.

Chesapeake campaign had been a success. He assured Prevost that it had prevented 25,000 men from marching against Canada, had weakened the United States, and had taken away around 600 Negro slaves who had come to him for liberation. Most of these, unwilling to enlist, had been shipped to Bermuda. Their care fell upon Commodore Andrew Evans who complained that they were riotous and little disposed to earn their keep.[28]

Of course the blockade had to be maintained, season in and season out; when Warren sailed off to Halifax, Cockburn took command. His resources in ships were as follows: six major men-of-war with suitable support vessels for Chesapeake Bay; one 38-gun, one 36, and one 18 for Delaware Bay and River; two small vessels to hover off the North Carolina inlets; one warship to cruise near Charleston; and two 18-gun vessels for Savannah. To the northward of Cockburn's blockading command were two 74's, one 60, one 36, and two small ships for keeping the United States frigates sealed in their harbors.[29]

The blockade was in fact the dominant item in the naval conflict during 1813. By the end of the year American trade, except that part which continued with British collusion, was practically extinguished. There were no exports save from Georgia and New England. Even the coasting trade was interdicted, and most of it was driven ashore. The use of wagon trains multiplied many times, and so did shipping costs. Naturally, prices rose. Sugar sold for $9.00 per hundred pounds at New Orleans, but for $40.00 in New York. Coffee rose during the last six months from 17 to 38 cents a pound. Moreover, the blockade either sealed in or sealed out the vessels of the United States Navy. *President* was bottled up at Bristol; *Enterprise* and *Rattlesnake*, operating from Portsmouth, New Hampshire, could get to sea for short runs only; *John Adams* was confined in New York harbor, *Constellation* in Norfolk, and so on.[30]

Naval Actions on the Oceans

On 24 February 1813 the English brig *Peacock* was cruising off the northern coast of South America. Around 3:30 P.M. she sighted a strange ship lying off the mouth of the Demerara River. As *Peacock* approached her, the stranger moved. Although displaying British colors, the latter actually was the United States sloop-of-war *Hornet*. *Peacock* was then on the weather quarter of *Hornet*.* About 5:10 Captain James Lawrence of the American sloop, satisfied that he could gain the weather gauge, hoisted true colors and tacked.† The two vessels now bore down on each other on opposite courses. At 5:25, half a pistol shot apart, they exchanged broadsides. The American shot killed Captain William Peake of *Peacock*. Then Lieutenant F. W. Wright, Peake's successor, wore his ship, apparently in an attempt to flee. Lawrence bore up, then wore, and thus placed *Hornet* in a raking position on *Peacock*'s starboard quarter. From this position the American gunners poured in so accurate a fire that within half an hour *Peacock* had six feet of water in her hold. Wright struck his colors. Lawrence sent a relief party to his aid, but *Peacock* sank so fast that 3 of the Americans and 13 of her own crew went down with her. The casualties were 17 Englishmen killed or drowned and 33 wounded, compared with the 3 Americans who had drowned aboard *Peacock*.[1]

The victory over *Peacock* brought Captain Lawrence the responsibility of a frigate. He took command of *Chesapeake* on 18 May at Boston, but he was not able to assemble an experienced crew until late in the month. He was under orders to put to sea "as soon as the weather and force and position of the enemy admit." The position of two of His Majesty's frigates was menacing in the extreme. *Tenedos* 38 and *Shannon* 38 were prowling at the mouth of the harbor itself, waiting for combat with either *Chesapeake* or *Constitution*. The latter was undergoing repairs at Boston.[2]

The commander of *Shannon* was Sir Philip Bowes Vere Broke. He had trained his crew to a rare level of skill, was sick of blockade duty, and was spoiling for a fight. He sent *Tenedos* to cruise elsewhere, hoping that the chance of a ship-for-ship battle might bring out *Chesapeake*. Rather than deplete his skilled crew by scattering them in

---

* To be on the weather quarter is to be on the windward side at a 45-degree angle abaft (to the rear of) the beam, the center line across the width of the ship.

† To tack is to change course by bringing the bow through the wind. It is also a way to sail obliquely into the wind.

prizes, he had burned 25 captures and in doing so had suffered a great loss of loot. Finally, too impatient to wait any longer, he sent in a challenge to Lawrence and promised his ship unaided against *Chesapeake*. It was a fair match: *Chesapeake* threw a broadside of 542 pounds and carried a crew of 379; *Shannon* had a broadside of 550 pounds and 330 men. Lawrence did not need the challenge and never received it, for he was already on his way to the mouth of the harbor. It was 1 June 1813, summery and beautiful, when his lookouts sighted the sails of the foe. He gave the order to prepare to engage.

After running parallel, the two ships began to draw together. As *Chesapeake* was to the windward, Lawrence had the opportunity to cut across *Shannon's* stern and rake. Broke ordered his men to lie down for shelter, but the raking never came. Through chivalry or bad judgment Lawrence had lost his chance. About 5:50 P.M. he ran in for a close-range duel at a half-pistol-shot distance. Broke's expert gun-crews were able to fire into the open American gunports. Three broadsides decimated *Chesapeake's* crew and seriously wounded Lawrence. The command now passed to Lieutenant George Budd who also was soon knocked down. Up to this point neither ship was badly damaged, but now *Chesapeake's* foresail was hit, causing the ship to swing into the wind and present her stern to the mercy of the foe. A murderous raking fire swept her deck and mowed down more of the crew. Now the stern gear on the larboard quarter* tangled with the forerigging of *Shannon*. As soon as the two ships were locked together, Captain Broke himself led a boarding party into a lusty hand-to-hand fight in which he was wounded twice. At the same time Midshipman Smith climbed from *Shannon's* foretops into *Chesapeake's* and drove her topmen down onto the decks. All the American officers were wounded except Acting Lieutenant William Cox who had carried Captain Lawrence below. Cox took no part in the battle on deck. *Chesapeake* was rendered powerless and unable to continue her fight fifteen minutes after the first gun blasts. The loss was 70 Americans and 24 British killed, 100 Americans and 59 British wounded.

News of *Shannon's* victory greatly heartened Englishmen. *Chesapeake* became the first American frigate to be captured by a British ship during the war. Moreover, this battle put an end to the unbroken sequence of American triumphs and seemed to reconfirm Britain's supremacy at sea. English gunnery too was vindicated, for *Shannon's* men had made twice as many hits as the Americans.

Captain Lawrence died of his wounds, but he bequeathed a slogan to the United States Navy with his dying words: "Don't give up the

---

* Abaft the beam on the left side of the ship.

ship." There was need for a scapegoat, and Budd filed charges against Lieutenant William Cox. Budd insisted that Cox should have taken charge of the fighting on deck instead of hauling the dying captain below. Some persons claimed that Lawrence ordered him to do it, but the facts cannot now be known for sure. Cox was tried, found guilty on two counts, and sentenced to be dishonorably discharged from the navy. This verdict stood for more than 130 years, indeed until modified in 1952 by a joint resolution of Congress which exonerated Cox and made him a third lieutenant to rank from 1874, the year he died.[3]

Fierce actions between small ships were taking place up and down the eastern coastline and in the deep waters offshore. They provided opportunities for courage and self-sacrifice and for greed and brutality. Typical of the best privateers was *General Armstrong*, commanded by Captain Guy R. Champlin. Wounded during an action, Champlin was carried below and laid directly over the powder magazine. He sent word to the deck that if there was any move to give up the ship he would fire into the powder and blow the ship and crew beyond the reach of captors. On 29 April boarders from *Orpheus* captured the American letter of marque *Wampoc*. About a month later, a British vessel of 5 guns and 50 men fought off an American schooner of twice its force, but lost 30 per cent of its crew killed and wounded.[4]

The British tender *Eagle* was active in the area of Sandy Hook, forcibly gathering supplies. Certain local American seafarers assembled 40 well-armed men, secreted them below deck on a fishing smack, and put out from shore on 5 July 1813. *Eagle* drew alongside, and seeing only three men, confiscated the load of livestock on board for British use. Someone on the American deck yelled "Lawrence," whereupon the 40 musketeers rushed into the open and commenced a destructive fire. In a few minutes the British crew was swept from the deck, and the ship surrendered. The use of ruse was reversed when the brig *Borer* passed over the shoals between Martha's Vineyard and the mainland, displaying a Swedish flag. The pilot supposed that he was guiding a neutral ship into the main stream of intercoastal traffic, but once safely over the shoals *Borer* began to play havoc with the merchant shipping. She captured no less than five ships and destroyed many more.[5]

On 5 August the privateer schooners *Decatur* and *Dominica* fought a very bloody battle. Although British *Dominica* had more guns, she passed the chance to make the most of them. In the end she had to surrender, but not until 13 men had been killed and 47 wounded, which amounted to a 68 per cent loss for her crew of 88. The Americans lost 20 per cent of a crew of 103.[6]

Late in July when the brig *Martin* ran aground in Delaware Bay, ten American gunboats took position a mile and three-quarters away and opened fire. Since the British frigate *Junon* drew too much water to enter the action, her captain sent some of his long guns to help in the defense. *Martin* returned the American fire, but the captain knew that he would have to attack or suffer the loss of his ship. He therefore dispatched a boat detachment to assail one of the gunboats which had drifted apart from the others. The American lieutenant, seeing his isolation, kept firing his 32-pound carronade, and at the same time attempted to return to the squadron by the use of sweeps. When the British boats overtook him, he anchored to try to beat off the boarders, but outnumbered 7 to 1, he had to surrender. With this setback the Americans called off the attack, and *Martin* was able to release herself from the sandbank.[7]

The United States brig *Argus* chose the English Channel itself and the coasts of Devon and Cornwall during the summer of 1813 to disrupt British commerce. The lookouts on the English brig *Pelican*, Captain John F. Maples, caught sight of her in the late afternoon on 13 August, off the coast of Ireland. Captain W. H. Allen of *Argus* made no attempt to escape; indeed, when dawn came on 14 August and the foe was still in view, he shortened sail to let him approach. At 6:00 A.M. he wore in order to run parallel with *Pelican*, and when he came within grapeshot distance, he fired his larboard broadside. His crew shot badly and received much more than they gave. Within four minutes, Captain Allen lost a leg, and Lieutenant W. H. Watson assumed command. Crucial gear was blown away with every enemy salvo. At 6:15 Watson was wounded, and Allen, suffering severely and doomed to die of his wound, took over again. Now Captain Maples edged off to try to attain a raking position under the stern, but *Argus* forestalled this by backing the main-topsail, and for some minutes herself held a perfect raking angle across the bow. The favorable moment was for some reason lost. Many of *Argus'* sails became useless and the ship grew unmanageable. This enabled *Pelican* to reach her stern and rake effectively. By 7:00 A.M. *Argus* was forced to strike her colors.[8]

Theodore Roosevelt asserted that this was the least creditable of all American single-ship battles. The British broadside advantage was somewhere between 35 and 70 pounds, not enough to have assured such a clean-cut victory if the American ship had been handled well. Coming soon after *Shannon's* triumph, *Pelican's* exploit smartly raised English morale.

Early the following month the tables were turned again. The English brig *Boxer* convoyed a neutral Swedish ship to Kennebec with

English woolens on board for American merchants. Upon separating from the merchant ship, *Boxer* fired a few rounds, which drew the American brig *Enterprise* toward her. On 5 September the two brigs-of-war came within view of each other. *Enterprise*, as the British saw it, tried to run away, but *Boxer* overtook her at 2:40 P.M. Close-in action began at 3:35 and raged for an hour and ten minutes. English Captain Samuel Blyth and American Captain William Burrows were both mortally wounded in the first exchange. At the end of an hour *Boxer* was so badly wrecked that her acting commander surrendered without suffering boarding.[9]

Commenting on this encounter, William James pointed out that the American carronades were superior. They were heavier, thus steadier; were longer in the tube, thus longer in range; and were heavier in the breech, and so heated less. Grudgingly he also admitted that American gunners were usually better trained. He noted too that *Enterprise*, though about the same length, was in most ways a much bigger ship than *Boxer*. She was much heavier, her mainmast was 15 inches greater in diameter, and she had in all ways greater sailing power. Finally, her crew was 102 men to *Boxer*'s 66.

Except for the privateers, the balance of the story of the war at sea in 1813 can be briefly told. In recognition of the fact that Admiral Warren's duties had been much enlarged, the Admiralty sent Rear Admiral Edward Griffith to Halifax to take over the construction and repair of ships. Nature compounded Griffith's task when on 12 November a hurricane of unprecedented violence clutched Halifax for an hour and a half. It drove more than 50 ships ashore and damaged most of those which rode it out afloat.[10]

Admiral Warren took advantage of Griffith's arrival to go south for the winter. He assigned 16 vessels to Griffith to keep the American navy bottled up in New England ports, and on 3 December he sailed off to Bermuda where on 18 December he raised his broad pennant. From that vantage point he expressed concern to the Lords Commissioners over the rate at which the Americans were building ships.[11]

One 74-gun ship was under construction at Portsmouth, New Hampshire, under the supervision of Isaac Hull, and another at Charlestown, Massachusetts, under Commodore Bainbridge. Ten other vessels were also being built along the Atlantic coast, while elsewhere there were still more. The ships America was building ranged from barges 45 feet long to the massive *New Orleans*, 212 feet long, being built on Lake Ontario. On Lake Champlain there was a brig 110 feet long on the ways and some small galleys. At the same time an effort was made to improve the sailing qualities of the rebuilt frigate *Adams*

and to put old reliable *Constitution* in shape. But when Bainbridge
sought to heave the latter out for coppering, he found that the only
suitable drydock in Boston was privately owned and that the owners
would not make it available to him for a United States naval vessel.[12]

Cannon foundries were nearly all located south of the Mason-Dixon
Line. If their products were needed at distant places, there was little
likelihood of supplying them because of the problems of transportation. The blockade interdicted coastal shipping, and naval guns were
too heavy to travel over the roadways. In consequence it was often
necessary to arm vessels by taking guns from some local fort or from
an old ship close by.[13]

The principal gun foundry for iron cannon used by the army was at
Georgetown, close to Washington, but it did not directly supply guns
to the navy. Naval guns came from the Dorsey Works in Baltimore
and the Foxall Foundry in Washington. A number of the guns tested
at the Dorsey plant in 1813 blew up, but Secretary Jones did not lose
faith in their product. The only crisis at Foxall was a shortage of coal,
and this was overcome by lending some of it from the Washington
Navy Yard.

The River Raisin

During the fall of 1812 and into the winter of 1812–13 William
Henry Harrison was accumulating provisions for 10,000 men for one
year along a concave base from the St. Marys River on the left to the
Sandusky on the right. His impression from Dr. Eustis was that he
could spend whatever was needed to carry this out.[1]

A winter campaign depended on ice thick enough to be used to cross
the river to strike at Malden. One of Harrison's senior subordinates,
Richard M. Johnson of Kentucky, wanted to attack the Indian villages, but Harrison overruled him because the Indians were not there.
The men were hunting and the women were gathering maple sap and
rendering it into sugar. As the winter slipped away with no campaign,
Harrison waxed more and more emphatic concerning the need to control the Great Lakes. Only by this means, he said, could the United
States break British control over the western Indians. The costs of a

winter campaign would easily pay for the creation of a fleet on Lake Erie, a fleet which would have twice the effect of a land action.

President Madison found time to write a directive to General Harrison, through James Monroe. Madison agreed that if the army advanced at all during the winter it must be upon the ice. He also agreed that control of Lake Erie was essential, and he expected the commanders to gain it in the spring. Meanwhile, he ordered Harrison to move only if success was assured, for the nation could not bear another major failure.[2]

Harrison, without intending to do so, disobeyed the President's directive. In keeping with the master plan, he ordered Brigadier General James Winchester, who commanded the left wing of his army, to march from St. Marys (often shown on maps as Girty's Town) to the concentration point at the rapids of the Maumee. Winchester started his advance on 29 and 30 December 1812 with about 1,300 men. In the meantime, Harrison had heard that Tecumseh was on the upper waters of the Wabash, and, fearful that the chief might move east and cut Winchester's line of communications, he sent a note recommending, but not ordering, that the march be abandoned. Winchester chose to continue it. When his horses broke down, weak from lack of grain and insufficiently nourished on the frozen grass, the men were obliged to drag the sleds. Reduced to less than half rations, they often had to eat bitter roots, but they reached the rapids on 10 January 1813. Anxious appeals came to them there from the inhabitants of Frenchtown to protect them from British-Indian marauders. Frenchtown lay on the River Raisin, 40 miles ahead. Winchester convened a council of officers, and it strongly urged the general to heed the cries for help. Since the troops were close to mutiny, Winchester agreed in order to keep them employed. (Later Harrison asserted that he was virtually coerced into the advance.) On 17 January, Winchester started Colonel Will Lewis forward with 550 men, and shortly afterwards, Colonel John Allen with 110 more. These troops reached the river and began to form line at 3:00 P.M., 18 January. The French inhabitants watching the formation cried "Kentuck, by God" and scurried for cover. The line swept across the river on the slick ice under heavy fire from about 200 Canadian militiamen and 400 Indians. When darkness ended the ensuing fight, the Americans held the village at a price of 13 killed and 54 wounded. They now camped on the north bank of the Raisin in the midst of the village of 33 families, and since they were cold and hungry they settled in to gorge themselves on cider and tasty foods. On 20 January, Winchester, his staff, and 300 more men arrived, raising the American force at the Raisin to about 800 Kentucky militiamen and

175 other soldiers. Most of the American army lay behind an eight-
foot puncheon fence which protected the village on the north and
west, but the regulars were on the right, unprotected. Winchester
himself, possibly to get away from his disaffected men, withdrew to a
house on the south side of the river, a quarter of a mile at least from
the general bivouac.[3]

The same day that Winchester reached Frenchtown, Harrison
reached the rapids of the Maumee. Convinced that the position at the
Raisin must be maintained, he ordered reinforcements and worried lest
the British strike too soon. His worry was justified, for Colonel Henry
Procter, the British commander at Malden, was at that very moment
eying the vulnerable American salient. Without delay he assembled a
force of around 500 white men and 600 Indians with six 3-pound cannon, and crossed the river on the ice from Malden. General Winchester heard of his approach several times on 21 January, but he did not
credit the reports. He also did not check the guard around the American camp, for he assumed that this task would have been routinely
taken care of. There were too few pickets when the British attacked
at dawn on 22 January and achieved complete surprise. Had they
worked silently with bayonets, they might have annihilated the Americans, but the uproar they created with musketry and cannon gave
brief warning. The unprotected American right wing crumpled back
nearly to the river, and the Indians got upon its flank. In contrast, the
units behind the puncheon fence kept their positions and maintained a
very hot fire.[4]

The battle was fully joined before Winchester could arrive from his
withdrawn headquarters. He tried several times with Colonels Lewis
and Allen to rally the troops to make a new stand, but they were
pushed farther and farther southward. Winchester himself was soon
captured by the Wyandot chief, Roundhead. He was then forced to
witness some atrocities committed by the Indians, and he was thus persuaded to write an order directing the 400 men behind the fence to
surrender. Major George Madison was the Kentucky officer in command of them; he would not comply with the order until Procter himself had guaranteed that he would protect the prisoners from his Indians. But Procter, fearing a reinforcement from Harrison, almost at
once returned to Malden and left a very thin detachment to guard the
wounded prisoners at Frenchtown. When an American officer inquired
if there ought not to be more medical aid left for the wounded men,
he was told that "The Indians are excellent doctors."

The redmen later swarmed into Frenchtown, looted it, and then,
heated by liquor, massacred 33 of the prisoners. British officers, includ-

ing Procter, deplored this, but Procter's hasty withdrawal had brought it about.[5]

In spite of the advantage of surprise, Procter had lost 24 killed and 158 wounded from a total force of about 540. Although he was later censured for these heavy casualties, he was at the time promoted to the local rank of brigadier. Indian losses are not known, but the American cost was also high: 300 killed, 27 wounded, and the entire army, except for a handful of men, taken prisoner. This terrible price, like Hull's surrender, fell heaviest on Kentucky. "What shall I say or how begin," wrote a participant to his brother, "My God, my God, hast thou forsaken us?" The horror produced an American battle cry, "Remember the Raisin," and the foe who heard it could not expect mercy.[6]

Still ignorant of the disaster, Harrison ordered an Ohio battalion and a cannon forward, and the next day himself led 600 men toward the Raisin. On the way he received word of the defeat and, on the advice of a council of officers, turned back. Had he continued the march, he almost certainly would have recaptured Frenchtown and possibly forestalled the massacre, but of course he could not know this.[7]

Leaving behind many valuable stores, he now hastily abandoned the line of the Maumee and withdrew behind the Portage River. Once there, he tried hard to prove to himself and to others that he was not responsible for Winchester's debacle. He admitted, however, that he had not categorically ordered Winchester back from his exposed position, but made it clear that on the other hand Winchester had gone forward contrary to his recommendation.

In response to the continuous threat of an American winter campaign, Governor Prevost ordered a detachment of Royal Artillery and part of the 104th Foot Regiment to march overland from New Brunswick to Quebec. Six companies, 550 men on snowshoes, with a toboggan for each two men to haul supplies, made the march of 350 miles in the dead of winter in 24 days. This was some kind of record, accomplished without the loss of a single man. The column reached Quebec on 15 March 1813 and set out for Kingston six weeks later. This leg of the expedition was more costly; 19 men died of overexertion and exposure before this 350 miles was accomplished. Later, the rest of the 104th Foot arrived in Canada and passed by water to the upper country. Meanwhile, throughout the winter, Prevost, in fear of unseasonal attack, kept 5,000 militiamen enrolled.[8]

Fifteen days of warm weather in February ruined the ice and the chance for an American winter campaign. As the time of the volunteers ran out, General Harrison's army shrank from 6,300 to 2,000.

He sought to recruit it back to 3,300 to man the posts on the Auglaise and St. Marys rivers and the new stronghold he was having built at the rapids of the Maumee. During February, Captain Eleazer D. Wood, one of the first graduates of the United States Military Academy, supervised construction of the new fort. He divided the work so as to create constructive competition among the units. "In the use of axe, Mattock, and spade," he said, "consists the chief military knowledge of our army." Under his capable direction the labor of the soldiers produced a very sturdy outpost, which was named Fort Meigs.[9]

The Kentucky and Ohio troops went home in mid-February. Their departure left a garrison of less than 500 Virginia and Pennsylvania militiamen to hold a fort designed for 2,000 defenders. General Harrison vested the command in Brigadier General Joel B. Leftwich of the Virginia militia, and himself went to his family in Cincinnati. Captain Wood ardently admired Harrison, but described Leftwich as an "old phlegmatic Dutchman, who was not even fit for a packhorse master." Wood worried about the chance of attack, for in addition to being very shorthanded, the defense was jeopardized by Leftwich's permitting the men to burn the picketing for warmth.[10]

In time additional troops entered the fort, until there were three types: 6-month militia, 12-month volunteers, and some newly recruited regulars. All were so green that they had to be punished for relieving themselves wherever they felt like it, for careless shooting, and for depredations upon civilians. Also, the sentinels fell asleep at their posts. Adding to the problems was the presence of some women. One married woman, living in a different tent from her husband, was drummed out of camp.[11]

Because of the River Raisin disaster, the new secretary of war, John Armstrong, had lost confidence in Harrison. Although he said nothing to the general, his every order indicated mistrust. In March he told Harrison that his campaign must be considered at an end until the navy gained control of Lake Erie. Harrison might demonstrate against Malden, but he was to do little more in the way of offensive action. Boats were to be prepared to transport the troops to Canada when Lake Erie was cleared. Armstrong designated Cleveland as the place to build them. Next, he ordered Harrison to dispose of his heavy train of draft horses and oxen, and forbade him to draw upon the department in excess of $20,000 per month.[12]

Harrison, for his part, found much to complain about in the conduct of his superiors. On 19 March they created the Eighth Military District, composed of Indiana, Missouri, Michigan, and Illinois territories, and the states of Kentucky and Ohio. They gave him the command, deprived him of it in less than a month, soon restored him to it, but delayed promoting him to major general. As a result his commission was junior to certain generals under his command, who did not bother to channel their projects through him. All of this brought him to say the following, either with remarkable ingenuousness or with false humility: "Candor obliges me to say that there are in the Western states many persons better calculated for the command than I am, and that if I have manifested either neglect or incapacity, a fair opportunity for another selection is offered by the tender of my commission as brigadier. . . . In this event I should retire from the Regular service. But so deeply impressed on my mind are the injuries which our country has received, from the nation with which we are at war, and so ardent is my desire to participate in the honor of retrieving . . . the disgrace we have sustained, that I am determined to continue to serve if I can get a regiment or even a company of volunteers to follow me."[13]

In March Harrison received from the secretary word that the United States would no longer pay for militia service unless it had been requested by a general officer in the United States service. Nor would it accept militia units with their full complement of officers, because they were too often topheavy and completely at variance with federal tables of organization. Armstrong told Harrison that he must maintain his position with seven regiments of regulars, which it was hoped would soon be fully recruited. Harrison took exception to these restrictions. Without the use of some militia he could not, he insisted, protect the millions of dollars worth of stores he had deposited. Moreover, recruiting for the regular units did not promise to produce results. The quality of the citizen soldiers was far higher than that of such regular recruits as were coming in; indeed, he claimed the irregulars who had fought at the Raisin were "superior to any militia that took the field in modern times." Kentucky could produce citizen soldiers without equals if the troops were allowed to travel on horseback. Finally, Harrison insisted that his supply depots made waste motion unnecessary and rendered it possible to call out the militia only when actually to be used. They could be employed when their enthusiasm was at its highest and be back home in two months. He was not far from the truth.[14]

His passionate argument, however, did not move Armstrong. During the first week in April the secretary positively ordered him to leave militia out of offensive operations. Congress had augmented the regular army to 52 regiments purposely to provide an alternative to the militia. Harrison's 7 assigned regiments totaled 7,000 men, and they must do. Only if recruiting failed in patriotic Kentucky and Tennessee would recourse to the militia be allowed. Finally, he directed the general to send in regular reports, a duty in which he accused him of having been badly remiss.[15]

The secretary sought to use such irregular units as were still in service as recruiting preserves for the regular army. Citizen officers were notified that they could receive personally a $4.00 bounty for every man they secured for a five-year hitch or for the duration. Early in the year Congress had extinguished twelve-month volunteers and replaced them with one-year regulars, but Armstrong sought long enlistments and did not emphasize this alternative. He also played down the fact that the President was empowered to raise 20 regiments of the new short-term regulars at the same pay as five-year men, but without a land bounty.[16]

The area Harrison's army was guarding was organized into four territories, containing 65,000 Americans. Indiana Territory had 24,500 inhabitants, Missouri Territory 20,000, and Michigan and Illinois territories the remaining 20,000. In these areas no one could for a moment forget the Indians. If they were British-dominated, the redmen were as serious a threat on the frontier as British ships were on the Atlantic coast. By holding Michilimackinac and Detroit, England could retain control over them. General Prevost appointed Robert Dickson to be Indian agent because of the great influence he had with them. Dickson, confident of his own power, said that he could assemble 1,000 warriors on short notice from the Sioux, Winnebago, Fox, Chippewa, and Ottawa tribes.[17]

Southward, in the United States, Benjamin Howard, governor of Missouri Territory, was thought to have influence with the Indians. Perhaps on that account, he was given for a time command of the Eighth Military District. This meant that the governors of the territories in that district were subordinate to him. The arrangement did not suit Ninian Edwards of Illinois Territory, who temporarily divested himself of all military responsibility and went off to southern Kentucky to visit his family. In his absence, Howard, who held a commission as brigadier general, organized a force of 1,300 men to go to Peoria and build a fort. Two columns, acting separately, followed the Mississippi River by land, while 200 regulars ascended the Illinois River in armed boats. These units, after some minor engagements, reached Peoria and occupied it without a major battle. All hands were now turned to building a fort before winter set in. By mid-October it was completed and designated Fort Clark. It constituted a strong bastion against Indian incursions, and symbolized the deterioration of British power at the extreme end of the English supply line.[18]

Lake Champlain

General Prevost did not feel that Admiral Warren's diversion in the Chesapeake area had done very much to relieve American pressure upon Canada. He therefore found it necessary to mount a diversion himself. It was directed against the United States on Lake Champlain, a natural spot because of the disaffection of the New England states. Lake Champlain was a dart aimed at the jugular vein of Canada, but because of the mood of New England it remained in 1813 a peripheral rather than a major theater of the war.[1]

A few miles from the point where the Richelieu River runs out of Lake Champlain there is a tiny island in the river called Isle aux Noix. Under the direction of General Francis DeRottenburg, commanding at Montreal, it had been made into the southern bastion of the defenses of Montreal. The two principal vessels of the United States Navy on Lake Champlain approached the island on 3 June 1813. They sailed heedlessly into narrow waters where they could not maneuver, whereupon Major George Taylor, commanding on the island, sent three gunboats to oppose them and a swarm of rowboats to carry men to the shores from which they could rake the vessels. Literally trapped in the narrows, the sloops *Eagle* and *Growler* withstood heavy fire for three and one-half hours, then surrendered. Between them they carried twelve 18-pounders and ten 6-pounders, and a crew of 50 men each. Their capture cost 1 American killed, 3 wounded, and 3 British wounded. It shifted the naval balance on the lake, for both ships were purchased from their captors (1 share for each private, up to 100 shares for the commander) and taken into the British lake service as *Chub* and *Finch*.[2]

The immediate problem was to provide crews for them. This could be done only by persuading some salt-water commanders, temporarily at Quebec or Montreal, to bring their crews for a short tour of duty on the lake. Captain Thomas Everard, whose ship *Wasp* was at Quebec for two weeks, agreed to take 80 of his men to Lake Champlain and serve there for a fortnight, but no more. On the way he encountered Captain Daniel Pring, whom Admiral Warren had sent to command on the Great Lakes, but who was displaced instead to Lake Champlain. Major General Richard Stovin, already on duty at Chambly, took command of the land forces.[3]

On the American side Secretary Jones ordered an investigation into the loss of the two sloops. He instructed Lieutenant Thomas Macdonough to regain the ascendancy on Lake Champlain. Jones qualified Macdonough's authority only by ordering him to cooperate with the newly appointed army commander in the area, Major General Wade Hampton. Hampton reached Burlington, Vermont, on 3 July. He was so overwhelmed by the problems he found there that he did not report to the secretary of war for ten days. When he did report, he described such chaos as in his opinion had probably never existed before. All his troops were recruits, and to handle them he had only one experienced staff member, Colonel James Bankhead, who was prostrated by rheumatism. Hampton and Secretary Armstrong both wrote for aid to Governor Tompkins of New York, and both received Tompkins' usual swift cooperation. Armstrong believed that Hampton, with the aid of the New York militia, could advance against Montreal, but Hampton himself did not consider his band capable of advancing anywhere.[4]

To carry out General Prevost's diversion, Captains Everard and Pring loaded 950 men aboard 5 vessels and 47 bateaux at Isle aux Noix on 29 July 1813. They landed at Plattsburg on 30 July, where they were joined by 935 Canadian militiamen. Colonel John Murray, commanding the landing force, now led his column toward the town. Major General Benjamin Mooers of the New York militia was frantically trying to assemble some citizen soldiers to oppose them, but when Murray's advance came in sight, he had gathered only 300 men and one 6-pound cannon. Murray with five times this number walked into Plattsburg virtually unopposed, where he energetically began to destroy public property. Blockhouses, barracks, and military storehouses went up in flames. So did the public property at the villages of Champlain and Swanton. Murray's orders were to respect private property, but Americans claimed they were disobeyed. By 3 August, Plattsburg was reduced and the invaders gone. Mooers dismissed his meager force, and directed militiamen straggling belatedly toward Plattsburg to turn around and go home.[5]

Meanwhile Captain Everard cruised at will around the lake. Three American sloops were being built in the harbor at Burlington, but he could not touch them due to the protection of the formidable fort high on the bluffs. Neither did Everard elect to land a force to attack Burlington, for he knew that Hampton had around 4,000 men in the vicinity. After capturing some commercial vessels, he returned to pick up the landing party at Plattsburg and then recrossed into Canada. Governor Prevost claimed for this diversion substantial help in saving the Great Lakes for Britain.[6]

Lake Ontario

Even though Secretary Armstrong finally vetoed a winter campaign conducted by General Harrison, he did not want total inactivity during the winter. At one of the first cabinet meetings which he attended, he proposed some sort of sweep from Prescott clear to Niagara. But apparently this project did not find favor with the President and cabinet, for two days after proposing it Armstrong gave orders to General Dearborn to gather 4,000 troops at Sackett's Harbor on the east end of Lake Ontario and 3,000 at Buffalo on the west end. The objectives which he established for these were first, Kingston, second, York, and third, the British forts on the west bank of the Niagara River. He told Dearborn to launch an offensive as soon as Lake Ontario opened for navigation. Later in February it apparently occurred to him that there might be no need to wait for the ice to melt. A force under Colonel Zebulon Montgomery Pike could move across country from Lake Champlain, cross the St. Lawrence on the ice, and attack Kingston. Kingston would be weak because the British troops were scattered widely in defense of the western posts.*[1]

It was apparently because of Commodore Isaac Chauncey that Armstrong gave Kingston the highest priority. Yet by the end of February Chauncey had concluded that the place was too strong to attack. The initiative on the lakes thus fell to General Prevost. He adjourned the parliament of Lower Canada in order to go in person to Upper Canada. En route he took pains to give the impression of having with him a very large army, and he convinced at least one person. General Dearborn hurried with uncommon speed to Sackett's Harbor, where he expected an attack from Kingston. The British had 3,000 to 4,000 men at Kingston, but Dearborn read them as twice that many. By mid-March, however, he had lost his fear of an attack upon Sackett's from Kingston. Yet he and Chauncey agreed that Kingston was too strong for them to attack. They would continue to appear to menace the British base, in order to prevent Prevost from reinforcing Upper Canada.[2]

They made a decision more important than this one. They would attack York instead of Kingston. Once navigation was open, according to their plan, 1,500 picked men could swoop down upon York and take it. This would give the United States control of Lake Ontario, and would open the way to the capture of Fort George. When the

* The reader is referred to the map on p. 78.

latter was in American hands, the United States vessels lying useless at Black Rock could be taken into Lake Erie to obtain superiority there. That would open the way for the conquest of the entire western country. Chauncey requested brevet rank for these operations so that he could not be outranked by land officers with whom he would have to cooperate.[3]

Secretary Armstrong permitted the general and the commodore to shift from his number one strategic objective to number two because it seemed to be "necessary or at least proper." But he became afraid that Dearborn might weaken the York thrust in order to defend Sackett's, and warned him against half measures: "How then would it read that we had lost our object on the Niagara while we had another brig at Sackett's Harbor doing nothing?" As he saw it, the United States was in the same sort of doldrums it had been in during the Revolution just before Trenton and Princeton, and there was need for a morale boost of the Trenton-Princeton sort.[4]

He accepted Dearborn's estimates of 6,000 to 8,000 English troops at Kingston, but his interpretation of them was different from anyone else's. He surmised that the enemy might intend to abandon Kingston, and was concentrated there only preparatory to withdrawing to Montreal. If so, Montreal, always a primary strategic objective, now became a more feasible one. The line of attack against it could be down the St. Lawrence from Sackett's Harbor instead of down the Richelieu River through hostile New England.[5]

While Secretary Armstrong formulated strategy for the Great Lakes region and the military commanders maneuvered him into modifying it radically, the Ministry in England was taking action to strengthen its position on the Great Lakes. The Prince Regent directed that the Royal Navy assume control of the naval establishment, whereupon the Lords Commissioners selected Sir James Lucas Yeo to take command, with the rank of post captain and the local rank of commodore. They assigned 3 commanders, 8 lieutenants, 10 midshipmen, and 400 sailors to accompany him from England. His first duty was to defend Canada, and in discharging it he was to cooperate cordially with General Prevost. The army system would supply him as it had done the Provincial Marine establishment which he was replacing. Finally, he must expect only enough trained personnel to form cadres for his crews, and must be alert lest insinuating United States agents seduce them away.[6]

Yeo sailed for Quebec under these instructions in late March 1813. His command line was fuzzy. He appeared to be responsible directly to the Admiralty, but he seemed also to be a part of Admiral Warren's command and was subject to General Prevost's requisitions.

Captain Sir James Lucas Yeo

He had been in the naval service twenty out of his thirty-one years. In the wars against France and Napoleon he had seen enough action to become a captain in 1807. Two years later he had successfully besieged Cayenne in French Guiana, and had been knighted for it in 1810. His vessel *Southampton* took the American *Vixen* prize in 1812; then on the passage to Jamaica both ships struck a reef on 27 November 1812 and sank, with no loss of life. A court of inquiry absolved him of blame. Since that time he had cruised up and down the American coast seeking combat with the American frigates.[7]

On 4 February 1813 a British detachment from Prescott crossed the St. Lawrence River on the ice and took a few prisoners in Ogdensburg. Two days later, Benjamin Forsyth, major in the United States Rifle Regiment, left Ogdensburg at 10:00 P.M. at the head of about 200 regulars and volunteers; he marched to Morristown, twelve miles up the river, crossed over at 1:00 A.M., and took Elizabethtown by surprise. He freed the American prisoners from the Elizabethtown jail, and took 52 British prisoners at a cost of one man wounded on each side and a 28-mile march in the bitter cold. His performance convinced the British commanders that Ogdensburg had to be neutralized.[8]

Prevost's orders to remain on the defensive stood in the way of retaliation. When Sir George himself appeared in Prescott during the evening of 21 February, Lieutenant Colonel George Macdonnell strongly represented to him the danger from Ogdensburg. He gave permission to make a "conditional" attack. As soon as Prevost was off to the westward, escorted by all the local cavalry, Macdonnell put his 600 men, half militia and half regulars, in motion across the ice, dragging three cannon. Destructive musket fire hit them from the windows in the town, which they answered with their cannon. Soon the defenders fled, and Macdonnell captured 60 prisoners, 16 cannon, 800 muskets, 400 rifles, 2 tons of ammunition, and 1,500 barrels of pork. His men also burned two American schooners. They had killed and wounded 26 persons at a cost to themselves of 7 killed and 63 wounded. Macdonnell claimed he could have captured every American if he had had the cavalry which had gone away with Prevost. Americans complained that there was much looting of private property.[9]

Major Forsyth withdrew nine miles to the eastward and asked for reinforcements of 300 men. With them he said he could recapture Ogdensburg and take Prescott as well, but as they never came he marched on to Sackett's Harbor.

When General Prevost read Macdonnell's report he had misgivings about his conditional approval of such a successful expedition. He therefore altered the report from "I availed myself of the conditional permission I received . . ." to read, "In consequence of the commands of His Excellency to retaliate. . . ." This made him appear better in England, and Macdonnell, even if he knew of it, did not dare to complain.[10]

When General Dearborn heard of the Ogdensburg affair, he lamented Chauncey's absence in New York, because, he said, he and Chauncey might together have taken the opportunity to attack Kingston. As usual Brigadier General Jacob Brown's response was more forthright. He heard of the battle while it was in progress and raced toward it from Sackett's Harbor, but arrived too late. He made an inspection of Ogdensburg and advised against re-establishing a garrison there. The town remained without one for the balance of the war.[11]

As spring approached, the American commanders began to prepare to carry out their inversion of Secretary Armstrong's strategy. Their objective, the village of York, contained only 625 people, but it was the capital of Upper Canada and an important center for shipping. The British commander there was Sir Roger Sheaffe. He expected an attack but was able to do little to prepare for it. As the plans to attack York progressed, Secretary Armstrong made no strong objection to the inversion of his strategy; indeed, he said no more than to point out that Kingston was still the primary objective and that Dearborn must keep Prevost's forces divided by continuously threatening several points.[12]

Meanwhile, the United States quartermaster was trying to assemble a fleet of troop transports for use on Lake Ontario. By April Fools' Day he had gathered 48 at Sackett's Harbor and 85 at Oswego. Since some of them were converted salt boats capable of carrying 100 men, the total boat capacity came to 10,000 men. But in naval power the balance was shifting in favor of England. On 20 April *Wolfe* and 2 gunboats were launched at Kingston, raising the British force on Ontario to 6 vessels, carrying 96 guns. The United States had 3 ships and 14 schooners, with 111 guns, but the broadside weight of these was no more than the British.[13]

At Sackett's Harbor, about 150 miles from York, 1,700 American troops began to board 14 vessels on 22 April 1813. Only half of them could enjoy shelter at a time. Hardly had the flotilla got under way on 24 April when a violent storm drove it back to port. Chauncey tried again on 25 April. General Dearborn was aboard, but had vested the command of the troops in Brigadier General Pike (promoted in March 1813). At thirty-four, Pike was a soldier in the finest romantic tradition. "If success attends my steps," he wrote his father, "honor and glory await my name—if defeat, still shall it be said we died like brave men; and conferred honor, even in death on the American Name. Should I be the happy mortal destined to turn the scale of war—will you not rejoice, O my father . . . but if we are destined to fall, may my fall be like Wolfe's—to sleep in the arms of victory." Leaving little to chance, Pike trained his men meticulously. He advised them that the people of Canada were innocent and that he would punish looting with death. On the other hand, captured public stores would be handled as spoils of war, with all ranks sharing in the proceeds.[14]

The American flotilla reached the waters before York on 26–27 April, but a heavy east wind forced it to anchor about three miles west of the town. There Pike began his debarkation about 8:00 A.M. on 27 April. Forsyth's riflemen, who went first, encountered heavy fire on the beach, mostly from Indians, a scattering of Grenadiers from the Eighth Foot Regiment, and some Newfoundlanders. General Sheaffe had perhaps 800 men in the area, but they were dispersed because he did not know where the foe might land. Once Forsyth's riflemen were ashore, they opened up a smart fire to cover the landing of the Sixth, Fifteenth, Sixteenth, and Twenty-first Infantry Regiments. Pike himself formed them all into a line to charge up the low bank and into the woods. By 10:00 A.M. the American debarkation was completed, the beachhead established, and the flotilla had moved eastward to bombard Fort York and the western battery.[15]

The fighting rolled slowly eastward toward the town. Seeing that the attackers had difficulty moving their cannon, General Sheaffe beat at their flanks with two light pieces of his own. But about eleven o'clock the Americans emerged into the open and came under the fire of the western battery. It halted them. Pike deemed it necessary to storm this battery, and was arranging to do it when the battery blew itself up. Someone had carelessly ignited an open powder magazine. The English survivers scrambled to reach Fort York. Bugles called the formations for the Americans, and with muskets unloaded they advanced to "Yankee Doodle" played by fifes and drums. The general intended to rely on cold steel, not only bayonets but also some pikes, in the use of which he had trained his regulars. The bugles and fifes, heard above the din, seemed to demoralize the British Indians and they slipped away. Meanwhile the American ships at a range of 600 yards rained grapeshot upon the artillery positions and upon Fort York. Fire from the fort dwindled to nothing because General Sheaffe was already withdrawing his regular units and commencing a retreat to Kingston. A few militiamen were left in the fort, but neither they nor those outside knew that the regulars were leaving the field.

As there was an obvious lull in the battle, General Pike halted his

line and sat down on a stump to interrogate a few prisoners. A little
before noon the main British powder magazine at the water's edge
blew up with the force of a volcano. A few British militiamen were
injured, but the American toll was heavy. General Pike was crushed
by a huge stone and died soon afterwards. Under the direction of Colonel Cromwell Pearce, the Americans entered the town of York. By
4:00 P.M. the casualties stood at 52 Americans killed, 180 wounded,
62 British killed, 34 wounded, and 50 missing. Local citizens saw the
need for a formal surrender and began to hunt an American with
whom they could negotiate.

As long as Pike lived, it was meant to be his show, but upon his
death General Dearborn came ashore. By this time discipline was largely
gone in the American force. Forsyth's riflemen were systematically
plundering, but they did not generally bother houses in which the
residents had remained. Bishop John Strachan sought out Dearborn
and accused him of refusing to talk surrender terms so that his men
could plunder. Dearborn replied that neither he nor anyone else could
stop the plundering, as his men were infuriated by word that a scalp
had been found hanging in the Government House.[16] At any rate,
some depredation continued throughout 28 and 29 April, and on the
latter date the Government House itself burned down. Dearborn denied that he or any of his officers had ordered this arson, but it is
likely that American soldiers had started the fire without official orders.

Surrender terms, finally negotiated, were very humane toward the
Canadian militia. On the other hand, they stipulated that all government property be turned over to the Americans. This provision, however, had already been blunted because the warship on the building
stocks had been burned, and many supplies had been carried away or
destroyed. Public money of £2,144, or $8,600, was surrendered, but
Strachan claimed that this did not stop the looting.

Adverse winds kept the United States forces at York until 8 May
1813. Thus the chance to surprise Fort George was lost. Later analysts
have argued that Dearborn ought never to have pulled his whole force
out of York, where a limited detachment could interdict both land
and water routes to Lower Canada and to Lake Erie. As it was, the
American attack had hurt the British establishment on Lake Erie, for
it had destroyed 20 guns and other stores destined for the embryo
Erie fleet.[17]

Probably General Dearborn should have pursued Sheaffe on his long
march to Kingston. Chagrined at the outcome, especially since his own
strategy had been set aside, Secretary Armstrong implied in his annual

report that Dearborn had disobeyed orders in attacking York. Nor did he alter the report even when the general protested. General Sheaffe fared worse than Dearborn. It was charged that he should have concentrated his men behind the unfinished blockhouse, and from there he should have attacked the beachhead with all his might. Instead he had wasted his troops in piecemeal thrusts. In the end, Sheaffe, in bad health, was sent back to Montreal. There Prevost wrote him, "You will not, I hope, again disappoint my expectations as regards yourself." But Sheaffe apparently did not measure up, and in August he was recalled.[18]

Prevost complained to the government that since Brock's death the generals, except for Major General Francis DeRottenburg, had not supported him well. He may not have known it, but the practice was to keep the most promising generals for use against Napoleon and send the leavings to America. The better to use DeRottenburg, Prevost installed him as military commander and lieutenant governor of Upper Canada. DeRottenburg, aged sixty-four, was apt to be phlegmatic, but sometimes he initiated bursts of feverish activity. He did not formally relieve Sheaffe at Kingston until 29 June 1813.[19]

Prevost placed Henry Procter in command of what he called his right wing. He put the center, operating around the head of Lake Ontario, under the direction of John Vincent, with the temporary rank of brigadier. He himself directed from Quebec the left division, which extended from Kingston eastward. If he was absent, Major General George Glasgow took over. In case of combined operations the senior officer in either service would be what we would now call the unified commander. But army forces were always to be under the immediate orders of army officers, the same for the navy, and enlisted men were in all cases to be commanded by officers from their own service.

In due time word came from Lord Bathurst that the Ministry did not hold General Prevost responsible for the loss of York.

General Dearborn and Commodore Chauncey sent an advanced party from York to the Niagara area, where they selected a campsite at the mouth of Four Mile Creek, four miles east of Fort Niagara. On 8 May the troops disembarked there, and Chauncey sailed for Sackett's Harbor to gather supplies and reinforcements. Sickness had taken such toll at Sackett's that only 1,000 men were fit for duty. Chauncey waited at Sackett's for Winfield Scott to arrive with 700 men. On 16 May he sent all but two of his vessels, with 1,100 men on board, back to the Niagara camp. Another ship left Sackett's Harbor on 19 May carrying Brigadier General John Chandler and his staff, and on 22 May Chauncey himself in his flagship *Madison* commenced the return with 350 replacements. On 25 May both he and Oliver Hazard Perry reached the Niagara camp. Perry had heard word of the impending attack at Presque Isle, and had at once started eastward in an open boat. A day and a night in the boat brought him to Buffalo. He reached Fort Schlosser by water, but from there he started out walking. A sailor found him a horse, and without a saddle, with a rope for a bridle, he rode into the camp.[20]

On 24 May some 70 American cannon began the bombardment of Newark, near Fort George. The defenders could answer with only 20 pieces. Brigadier General John Vincent, commander of Fort George, had a garrison of 1,900 men, most of them unreliable militia. Lieutenant Colonels John Harvey and Christopher Myers patrolled the extended British lines all night and slept in the daytime. On 27 May at 4:00 A.M. the Americans boarded their ships and moved westward to a landing place from which they could approach the fort by land and also assail the unfortified side of the detached batteries. In spite of a high wind, the debarkation proceeded in good order because Perry was in charge of it. As the boats came in, the ship's guns gave them protective fire at a range of 300 yards. Grape and canister more than once drove back counterattacking detachments. Too ill to go ashore, General Dearborn watched through a glass from the deck of *Madison*. Major General Morgan Lewis was nominally tactical commander, but in fact the fight was directed by Colonel Winfield Scott and Major Benjamin Forsyth.

These two young officers landed with the advance troops at 9:00 A.M. Under the efficient protection of navy guns, three brigades came ashore, but in an hour the wind was blowing on shore so hard that Chauncey ordered the vessels to proceed farther offshore. Now seeing that he was hopelessly overpowered, General Vincent gave orders to abandon the fort and spike the guns. All detachments were to move southward and meet somewhere on the road to Queenston, or on the road which ran west from Queenston to St. Davids and the head of the lake. By noon Fort George, the several batteries, and Newark were in American hands. General Lewis now came ashore and entered the fort. At the time Scott was in hot pursuit of the enemy, but Lewis, ignorant of the situation, sent out an order recalling him. Scott kept going, but upon receiving a second peremptory order, could only give up the chase and let the enemy escape. Vincent, thus relieved, gathered his 1,500 to 1,600 survivors at Beaver Dam about 18 miles from Fort George. His losses had been heavy: about 50 killed, and 500 wounded, taken prisoner, or missing. Such losses were unjustified, since no significant military objective had been gained by them, yet it cannot be denied that Vincent had drawn off his survivors in good style and had reunited them where they were a threat to the American flank. The American cost had been 40 killed, 100 wounded.

Lieutenant Colonel Cecil Bisshop was in command of the British garrison at Fort Erie, across from Buffalo. What had begun there as a Saint Patrick's Day frolic firing cannon had ended up causing one British death and seven wounded men, with a few United States casualties. When Bisshop learned that Fort George was being evacuated, he blew up the magazine at Erie and started by the back roads to join Vincent. The next day an American detachment crossed from Black Rock and took possession of the remains of the fort. Thus, on 28 May it appeared that the United States forces had driven the British out of the valley of the Niagara and westward to the head of Lake Ontario.[21]

The Americans now controlled Lake Ontario, and General Prevost let it be known that the Ministry had not done enough to help him save this strategic body of water. Still, British power was not extinct. Captain Robert H. Barclay had seven war vessels and six gunboats at Kingston. On 5 May Sir James Lucas Yeo reached Prevost's headquarters and continued on to Kingston, accompanied by the governor. He arrived and took the command from Barclay on 16 May. He was not impressed by what he found and reported that the ships Barclay had concentrated were in a weak condition. Of course he asked for added supplies and reinforcements to support an accelerated building program. He organized a convoy of nine gunboats on the river to guard his St. Lawrence supply line, and directed that no supplies were to leave Prescott to go upriver except under its protection. The crews for the gunboats were drawn principally from the Royal Newfoundland Regiment. A privately owned steamboat carried supplies from Quebec to Montreal.[22]

General Prevost was at Kingston when he learned of the movement toward Fort George. He and Yeo decided that they had been presented with a chance to strike at Sackett's Harbor. To this end they loaded 1,200 men aboard 6 war vessels and 40 bateaux, and sailed from Kingston during the evening of 27 May 1813. An American scout vessel carried the news to Sackett's. The populace looked to Brigadier General Jacob Brown to save them, but he was reluctant to assume the command because Colonel Electus Backus, a seasoned regular, was present. Backus himself waived the command, whereupon Brown took over. He found only 400 regulars and 250 volunteers on hand, but he fired prearranged signal guns to summon the militia. Many more volunteers poured in, but some were unarmed and all were untrained. Unabashed, Brown organized them into units, and planned to use them to fire a few rounds on the beach, after which they could retreat behind the regulars to form a reserve line.[23]

By noon on 28 May the British flotilla was in sight, but for some reason it turned around and started back to Kingston. After another vacillation, Prevost turned it about a second time, and by evening it was once again off Sackett's Harbor. At 1:00 A.M. on the dark, rainy morning of 29 May the British troops began to climb into the boats for the trip to the shore. There were delays, and in the end the approach to the beach was made in broad daylight. The landing was on Horse Island. Formation took shape quickly, and the column waded across the narrows to the mainland under fire but supported by their own ships' shelling the woods.

General Brown had assembled about 500 citizen soldiers behind the gravel heap which constituted the shoreline. They were supposed to fire a volley or two, but when the British troops came out of the shallows and deployed into line, displaying the bayonet, the advanced line broke, after sporadic firing, and retreated toward the village through the woods and stumps. General Brown ran among them, exhorting all and even striking a few men, but to no avail. The attackers meanwhile advanced in good order along the shoreline toward Sackett's. They were stubbornly opposed all the way by a body of regulars and a few militiamen commanded by Colonel Backus. Relentlessly, however, they pushed the Americans back toward the log barracks between them and the town. The day seemed lost to most Americans, but not to General Brown. When he found a few knots of citizen soldiers who had fled from the shoreline but had not left the field, he tried to rebuild his defense upon them. Dragoons galloped out on all the roads, announcing victory. This reversed the flow of stragglers, and soon Brown had several hundred men formed into some semblance of a military formation south of Sackett's. He started them through the woods toward the right flank of the foe.

The battle around the town, which had now gone on for about an hour and a half, hung in the issue. Smoke billowed up from the depot in the American rear. If British troops had landed there the American situation was desperate. Brown sent runners to find out, and learned from them that the depot and *General Pike*, a war vessel on the building stocks, had been ignited by Lieutenant Chauncey Wolcott of the United States Navy, who had received word that the day was lost. The result was a property loss of half a million dollars, but not an envelopment by the enemy.

General Prevost watched the action through a glass from a tall stump. He saw the column which Brown had put in motion and judged it a

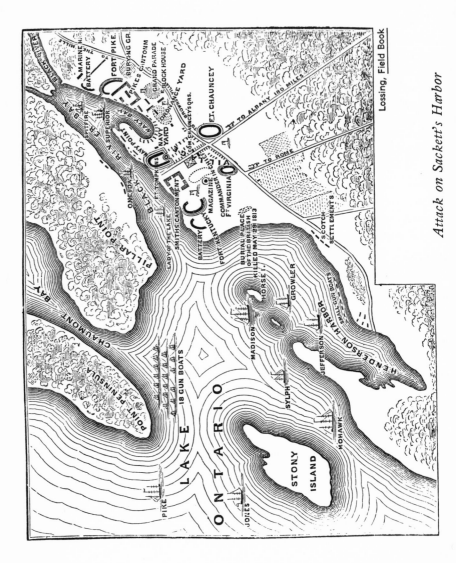

Lossing, Field Book

Attack on Sackett's Harbor

serious threat. He concluded that the day was too far advanced to win a decisive victory, and that he would not be able to hold his ground overnight. To the dismay of his officers, he ordered withdrawal to the boats and a return to the ships. Many Britishers felt that they were on the verge of victory when this order stopped them. General Brown, on the other hand, asserted that if Prevost had not withdrawn, he would have lost his army, an opinion with which Sir John Fortescue concurred more than a century later. The British loss was around 260 men killed and wounded, the American loss about 160 men.

All the while the Niagara campaign had been proceeding. Having through ignorance of the situation halted Winfield Scott's effective pursuit on 27 May, General Lewis too late ordered its renewal the next day. Lewis himself got as far as Queenston in the pursuit and there "succumbed to comfortable quarters." He was not the man for swift action. Peter B. Porter said, "His own baggage moves in two stately wagons . . . carrying the various furniture of a Secretary of State's office, a lady's dressing room, an alderman's dining room, and the contents of a grocer's shop." Nothing came of the pursuit.

General Dearborn's plan was to send troops by water to the head of the lake and cut the retreating British off in that way, but on 30 May Commodore Chauncey refused to participate. He insisted that he must return to Sackett's Harbor because he had just received word of the attack there. He took 2,000 troops with him and sailed out of the Niagara campaign once and for all. As a result, the British reached the head of Lake Ontario on 31 May without much trouble. General Vincent had there 1,763 men, but almost no supplies for them.[24]

Not until 1 June did Morgan Lewis begin an advance upon Vincent. He sent forward two columns under a pair of political generals, William Winder and John Chandler. On 4 June these two established a bivouac of 1,300 behind Stoney Creek, 7 miles from the British force. They had 1,300 more men 3 miles distant, guarding boats on the lake. Those at Stoney Creek lay down on their arms and slept in combat formation.

On the British side, Lieutenant Colonel John Harvey convinced Vincent that the American position was vulnerable to a night attack. Accordingly, with 700 regulars, accompanied by General Vincent, Harvey started from the British camp at midnight under heavy clouds. He had learned the American countersign. He attacked at 3:00 A.M. on 5 June and his men, using the countersign to get close, bayonetted the sentries. Nothing but their sleeping in combat formation saved the Americans from a rout. They were driven out of their camp and up to the top of an escarpment from which they could look down on the

British camp. Aiming by the fires burning in the camp, they opened a destructive fire with small arms and cannon. In time the British captured the American cannon. But at the end of an hour, Harvey was convinced that his force was too badly scattered and cut up to do more, and he gave the order to withdraw.

In the confusion and darkness, both General Chandler and General Winder had wandered into British units and had been made prisoners. This fact became known in the American camp, and the command fell to Colonel James Burn of the Second Light Dragoons. Burn convened a council of officers which decided to draw back to Forty Mile Creek. At this point General Dearborn ordered an advance. His order was foiled by the arrival of Yeo on 7 June from the far end of the lake with reinforcements. Chauncey had gone in the other direction, so Yeo dominated the western end of the lake. He slipped a schooner into Forty Mile Creek and opened a bombardment upon the newly opened American camp. On 10 June a raiding party assailed the American camp, captured 80 prisoners, and destroyed valuable supplies. Even before this Morgan Lewis had been under orders to break camp and return to Fort George, but now the retreat was made in such haste that large piles of stores were abandoned.[25]

Harvey's night fight came to be called the Battle of Stoney Creek. It was plainly a fiasco for the Americans, and in spite of Dearborn's excuses, Secretary Armstrong bluntly expressed the government's surprise that the British army had been allowed to escape after being forced out of Fort George and into the open.[26]

Armstrong ordered Dearborn to concentrate his force, and Dearborn decided to abandon all installations on the Canadian side of the Niagara River except Fort George. The American detachment at Fort Erie set fire to that place and evacuated it on 9 June. Its short occupation had achieved one important thing. As long as Black Rock was under British guns at Fort Erie, the American ships there could not depart, but when Erie was held by the United States the five American ships could sail to Presque Isle and become part of the American flotilla on Lake Erie. Lieutenant Colonel Charles G. Boerstler, American commander at Black Rock, had again and again requested permission to assail British Fort Erie, but had to his indignation been denied it. Now the American evacuation of the fort did not ease his humiliation.[27]

British Brigadier John Vincent had disappeared during the night fight at Stoney Creek. Thrown from his horse, he had got lost in the darkness and had had to hike in the woods and then gradually pick his way westward until, exhausted, he found the British lines on 6 June. He arrived in time to write a report of the Battle of Stoney Creek which muted Lieutenant Colonel Harvey's role as the real commander. Harvey, suspecting this, also wrote a report, addressed to Prevost's adjutant general, in which he took credit for originating the idea of the attack and for carrying it out. By ignoring channels he was assured that his account of the action would reach the commander in chief. Apparently he was not much afraid that Vincent would be able to retaliate against him.[28]

Stoney Creek had resulted in British losses of 23 killed, 136 wounded, and 55 missing, or one-third of the force engaged, but it had succeeded in cooping the Americans up in Fort George. Since they could be supplied only by the lake, there was good hunting for Yeo's squadron, which captured as many as 15 supply boats at a time. Prevost directed Vincent to remain inactive for awhile, and gave Yeo freedom to prey upon American communications. Besides being penned up, the Americans too had heavy losses: 17 killed, 38 wounded, and 99 missing.[29]

For a few days both sides relied on parties of mounted men who knew the country to scour roads and trails and to skirmish. Some of the American bushwhackers were Canadian defectors. Two of these, Joseph Willcock and a man named Chapin, were especially hateful to their erstwhile countrymen. The two were put in charge of the interrogation of prisoners, which they performed very roughly. Of course Canadian partisans retaliated, and did so much damage that General Dearborn directed Lieutenant Colonel Boerstler to take a detachment and attack their point of rendezvous, the headquarters of Lieutenant James Fitzgibbon, who had trained a company of rangers for woods fighting.[30]

Boerstler started from Fort George at night on 23 June in order to preserve secrecy, with 570 men, 2 cannon, and 2 four-horse wagons. When his column passed through Queenston, loyal Canadians learned of its destination. Someone had to warn Fitzgibbon. No men were available, so Laura Secord started across country alone on foot. Indians captured her, but she was able to communicate her mission to them, and as they had British sympathies, they conducted her to Fitzgibbon's blockhouse. She had hiked 20 miles in 6 hours of darkness. Her warning was given to a Frenchman, Captain Dominique Ducharme who commanded Indians, and he at once started out to prepare an ambush. At dawn on 24 June, a very hot day, his Indians were arranged in a heavy beech forest westward of St. Davids and Queenston.

Between 8:00 A.M. and 9:00 A.M. the point of the American column, already suffering from the heat, entered the cool of the beechwoods. When the entire column was strung out upon the narrow path, where brush and trees gave scant opportunity for maneuver, Ducharme's

Indians fired. Their first volley knocked down all 20 men of the point and threw the whole column into confusion. Boerstler at the start showed considerable tactical skill. He restored order, worked his men into a single rank, and sent them on a bayonet charge into the woods on each side of the path, while his cannon sprayed the brush with grapeshot and canister. After a while, feeling hemmed in by the woods, he fought his way into the open and to the top of a hill, where for a couple of hours, perfectly exposed, he continued the fight. The force opposing him enlarged until there were about 80 British regulars in it, around 200 militiamen, and 500 Indians. Late in the action Lieutenant Fitzgibbon arrived and assumed command. He opened a parley with Boerstler during which he employed all sorts of ruses to impress the Americans with the size and power of his force. At the end of three hours, Lieutenant Colonel Boerstler, wounded and convinced that he could not escape, agreed to surrender. Thus, the British neutralized nearly 600 men and captured 2 cannon and the supply wagons, all at a cost of 15 Indians killed and 25 wounded.

Recognizing the importance of this achievement, Lieutenant Colonel Bisshop reported it to General Vincent as if Bisshop had been in command. He gave scant credit to Lieutenant Fitzgibbon and to Ducharme. Neither of these officers chose to protest this hogging of the credit, or perhaps did not dare. In contrast, Lieutenant Fitzgibbon gave the Indians full credit for the victory and stated that his principal contribution had been to prevent them from abusing the surrendered Americans.

This action became known as the Battle of the Beechwoods or the Battle of Beaver Dam. Two years later a board of inquiry examined into Lieutenant Colonel Boerstler's conduct of it. Of course it exonerated him, but he was still criticized for having led his men into the open and for having remained there too long under heavy fire. Secretary Armstrong blamed General Dearborn for having sent so small a detachment into hostile country and for failing to insist on more careful preparations.

When Commodore Chauncey returned to Sackett's Harbor, he found the base still in the possession of the United States, but now without the supply depot and with *General Pike* a charred hull on the building stocks. He had entered the harbor and felt it necessary to stay there, convinced that he was sealed in by a superior fleet. Even when he could get out, he stayed close by, for he was almost pathologically aware that if his fleet were destroyed, the American cause in the West would be lost. He sent out scouting and raiding vessels sometimes, and they now and then captured a vessel. His main effort was to complete *General Pike*, because she would swing the naval balance to the United States. He also began a very fast schooner to carry three long 32-pounders. Secretary Jones, heeding Chauncey's calls for more strength, ordered Captain William Crane to take the entire crew of *John Adams*, which was blockaded in anyway, and go to Lake Ontario. Knowing that fresh-water service was not popular with the sailors, he assured Crane that it would only be for a short time.[31]

The British squadron roamed Lake Ontario virtually at will. On 19 June 1813 it appeared off Oswego and stood in as if to bombard the town. Oswego was an important way station on the supply route from New York to Sackett's Harbor by the Hudson River, the Mohawk River, Lake Oneida, and the Oswego River. The base was under the able command of naval Lieutenant Melancthon Woolsey. Expecting a visit, Woolsey had worked his people night and day to construct batteries, and this foresight paid off. His cannon drove the invaders away without a landing. The British sailed off westward to continue to support their own army at the head of the lake and to cut down the flow of supplies to the Americans.[32]

Early in July, Prevost reassured Lord Bathurst that what had happened to York would never happen to Kingston. At the same time he told of a plan, concocted by Vincent and Yeo, to surprise Sackett's Harbor. It called for the use of only 1,000 picked men; thus, without surprise it could not succeed. It was rendered useless, then, when two Newfoundlanders deserted and warned the Americans. Though known for his daring, Yeo without hesitation called off the attack and rowed all night to get safely back to Kingston.[33]

The bill of particulars against General Dearborn had been growing longer and longer. During the first week in July 1813 Secretary Armstrong wrote the general that the President wanted him to retire until his health improved. John Boyd, Moses Porter, Winfield Scott, Abraham Eustis, John Wool, and Benjamin Forsyth informed Dearborn that the security of the army required him to remain in command, but they must have done so from policy rather than conviction. Dearborn was offended by the tone of Armstrong's letter, and sent it to the President. As he had suspected, Madison had never seen it, had indeed been too ill during most of the summer to discharge his duties. The President found strength, however, not to overrule the secretary, but to advise Dearborn to retire.[34]

Temporarily Brigadier General John Boyd was installed at Niagara, but he was to obey the orders of both Morgan Lewis at Sackett's Harbor and Wade Hampton at Burlington, Vermont. He was also forbidden any military action which could be avoided.[35]

General Peter B. Porter, New York militia, "with the freedom of a Republican about errors," transmitted to Secretary Armstrong his unsolicited opinion of the officers involved in the command changes. The generals, he said, planned nothing except for their own safety. General Lewis was competent but not aggressive. Boyd was not capable of commanding 4,000 men. Dearborn was better than all the others in the North put together, but even he had nothing. The only way to win in the North, he concluded, was for Wilkinson to take the command or the secretary himself.[36]

In the Niagara valley the British maintained a punishing harassment. On the night of 4 July 1813 a party of 34 Indians and Canadian militia under Lieutenant Colonel Thomas Clark crossed the Niagara from Chippewa and attacked the blockhouse called Fort Schlosser. By surprise, they seized the place and a large quantity of supplies. Had they remained, they could have cut the land route for supplying Fort George from Buffalo, but instead they took the supplies and returned to Canada. Success was attracting more Indians to the British interest. A war party of western redmen ambushed Lieutenant Joseph C. Eldridge, who had gone out from Fort George with 39 men to relieve the guard on 8 July, and killed all but 5 of the men.[37]

When the British had evacuated Fort George late in May, they had buried a large cache of medical stores in the vicinity. Medicines became so scarce that a detachment was sent to dig them up. To do so they had to approach perilously close to the fort. They were discovered and a skirmish resulted, but in the end they carried away the precious drugs.[38]

General DeRottenburg now ordered that a small picked force cross to Black Rock, said to be thinly garrisoned, and destroy the depot there. He gave the assignment to Lieutenant Colonel Cecil Bisshop, who was known for enterprise. Bisshop left Chippewa at 2:00 A.M. on 11 July 1813 at the head of 200 regulars and 40 militiamen. The American pickets abjectly fled without giving warning, and the invaders passed into Black Rock unopposed. They burned the military installations, sent off many useful supplies, and made ready to withdraw. At that moment they were struck by a vigorous counterattack. It was led by Peter B. Porter, who had narrowly escaped capture in the initial surprise, but afterwards with characteristic energy had gathered together some men and launched a concentric attack as the invaders tried to reach their boats. The sharp skirmish at the landing lasted 20 minutes. When it was over, 13 British were dead, about the same number missing, and 27 wounded. One of the wounded was Colonel Bisshop who died five days later, not yet thirty years old.[39]

General DeRottenburg moved his headquarters from the head of the lake to St. Davids, not ten miles from Fort George. Attacks on the American pickets were virtually continuous. The net around Fort George was being drawn tighter.[40]

During the third week in July 1813 the naval balance on Lake Ontario once again changed. The keel of *General Pike* had been laid on 4 April, but the hull had been burned during the Battle of Sackett's Harbor. In spite of the burning and of labor problems, *General Pike* was ready to sail by 20 July. On that day Chauncey put out with 3 warships and 10 schooners to try to find the enemy. The British had 6 war vessels which sailed well as a squadron, but the American schooners could not keep up with the 3 warships. American superiority in long guns was 4 to 1, but in carronades the British excelled 2 to 1. These capabilities, of course, set the tactics both sides tried to use.[41]

The cynosure was now the head of Lake Ontario. Chauncey's squadron reached a position before the British stronghold at Burlington Bay on 29 July 1813. The wind was adverse for a landing, and the British position obviously strong. During the night reinforcements came by forced march from York. When Chauncey learned of this he gave up the idea of an attack and turned to York. His sailors and a small detachment of soldiers landed there on 31 July, virtually unopposed. They destroyed or gave away several hundred barrels of provisions, captured 5 cannon and 11 boats, and burned the barracks and public warehouses. For the second time in three months York was gutted. But in spite of its importance, the victors once again abandoned it.[42]

Next Chauncey crossed the lake and on 6 August 1813 held a conference with General Boyd. Because of the favorable balance of naval power on the lake Boyd had been released from his restrictions. Chauncey agreed to take 1,500 men in his ships to Burlington Bay. Until this should take place, the American squadron anchored off Fort Niagara. During the night of 7 August a violent storm struck the anchorage and overturned two schooners, *Hamilton* and *Scourge*. These carried all but 16 of the crews and 19 irreplaceable guns to the bottom. In the morning the British flotilla appeared, and Chauncey, with some misgivings, went out to meet it. Now began two days of maneuvering to gain the advantage of the wind and favorable range for the guns. Each commander reported to his government that he was trying to bring on an engagement, but his opponent was running away.[43]

On 10 August, Yeo spent the day becalmed off Twelve Mile Creek, until late in the afternoon a smart southwest breeze put him in motion. He was proceeding eastward in line when his lookout sighted the

Americans in two lines. Six small vessels were in the line nearest the British and five larger ones in the other. The British squadron came from the rear with the weather gauge and ran parallel with the Americans. Neither side fired. For unknown reasons, perhaps darkness, Chauncey decided to break off the contact. He ordered his lines to wear, thus turning them away from the foe toward the land. But the two lead schooners, *Julia* and *Growler,* either misread the signal or did not see it. They tacked instead of wearing, which turned them toward the foe. Seeing this, Yeo led his line forward until the two strays were cut off, then turned back to capture them. The American squadron paused for a moment. The gunners were standing to their guns, and although night had fallen, the moon was so bright that they could see the red pennants of the enemy. To their amazement and chagrin the order came to continue toward the shore. They were abandoning the two strays. As surprised as the American crews, the British closed in to capture them.[44]

Chauncey played down the capture in his reports, but Yeo reported it as a disgrace to the United States Navy. Whatever the truth was, within two days the American squadron had been deprived of 4 schooners, 170 men, and 23 guns. Now for a few days the two fleets were nearly equal in both guns and manpower. But on 18 August 1813 the Americans launched the schooner *Sylph,* 16 guns, only 21 days after her keel had been laid. She tilted the balance once more in favor of the United States. The British ran to York harbor, where they were safe, and the Americans to Sackett's Harbor. Chauncey stayed just 12 hours, only long enough to take on provisions, then sailed off in the direction of Niagara.[45]

A skirmish occurred on 11 September amidst the Duck Islands, which might have turned into a decisive action had either commander acted differently. With the wind in his favor, Sir James Yeo ran swiftly toward the Americans in order to exert the superior power of his carronades before the American long guns could cut him up. Then the wind turned about, and he scrambled to escape to Amherst Bay. He had already lost 4 men killed and 7 wounded to the long guns without having been able to place a single telling round. Perhaps he could have successfully continued the battle had he shifted all his own long guns to one side and thus temporarily equaled the foe. Chauncey pursued him but persisted in towing his schooners, and Yeo safely reached his sanctuary.[46]

American ascendancy on Lake Ontario perforce cut down the flow of supplies to British installations farther west. Late in the summer of 1813 it became necessary to reduce provisions supplied to the Indians, and as a result the redmen began to desert the British cause in large numbers. Late summer and early fall were oppressively hot, and lake fever took a heavy toll. Five or six soldiers deserted daily from General DeRottenburg's forces. Commodore Yeo had to win a naval victory or the right and center wings of the British army could waste away. General Prevost grew tired of the endless jockeying for position by the Ontario flotilla and complained both to Yeo and to the government of the "protracted contest." He implied that Yeo could do something decisive if he would. As Prevost saw it, the British army in the Niagara Valley was confining an American force twice its size, but was languishing for lack of naval cooperation. He therefore ordered Yeo and DeRottenburg to concert an attack upon Fort George. He himself appeared in the Niagara theater, and on 24 August 1813 he directed an attack upon the American outposts. He did this, he said, in order to get close enough to the fort to study its defenses. But after incurring some losses, he came to the conclusion which DeRottenburg had already reached, that Fort George was too strong to be assaulted.[47]

On 17 September 1813 Commodore Chauncey conferred at Sackett's Harbor with Secretary Armstrong, who had traveled to that theater. The next day Chauncey once more started for the western end of the lake, but adverse winds delayed his arrival until 24 September. Meanwhile orders had been issued by the army commanders to strip Fort George down to a skeleton force and ship most of the garrison to Sackett's Harbor. This transfer would of course require the assistance of the lake squadron.[48]

On 25 September Commodore Chauncey reported a rumor that Perry had captured the entire enemy flotilla on Lake Erie. The next day he learned that the British Ontario squadron was at York, and on 27 September he sailed in that direction. As usual, *General Pike, Madison,* and *Sylph* each towed a schooner. On 28 September, when his ships were coming in before the wind, the British sailed out of York Bay to meet them. As Chauncey bore down on their center, they tacked in succession. In the cannonade *Wolfe*'s mizzen and main topmasts were carried away. Yeo chose to try to save *Wolfe* by running before the wind for Burlington Bay, with *Royal George* protecting his rear. The Americans pursued with schooners still in tow and were soon outdistanced. At 2:45 P.M. they gave up the chase. Meanwhile, one of *General Pike*'s heavy guns had burst, killing and wounding 22 men and tearing up the deck. Also, the American vessels had suffered a good deal in the riggings. Finally, the wind had risen to gale strength and was blowing straight into the western shore. For these reasons, even though the portion of Burlington Bay where Yeo sought refuge was not defended by shore cannon, Chauncey decided not to follow him in.

After this running fight a firm American superiority was established on Lake Ontario. It helped to make the British cause in the West more precarious. But one factor which eased matters for the British was the American decision to concentrate at Sackett's Harbor. Chauncey's fleet was now called upon to transport 3,000 troops from Fort George to that place. Only 1,800 men were left at Fort George, and the British did not expect much trouble from them.[49]

Elated by his clear supremacy, Chauncey found troop-transport duty very irksome. Therefore, as soon as he saw the transports clear the mouth of the Niagara River, he took away his heavy vessels to hunt the enemy. He sighted the British squadron at 10:00 A.M. on 2 October under full sail for the Niagara, perhaps to attack the transports. He added sail and chased it all that day and the next, always towing his schooners. By the evening of 3 October the British ships had sailed away from him. His problem now was necessarily to protect the transports, and he ran eastward before a smart north-northwest wind. Off the False Duck Islands he found seven enemy sloops and schooners. Casting off his tows at last, he ran down and captured five of them. Two of the captures were *Julia* and *Growler,* which the British had taken from the Americans early in August. The crew of a sixth burned their ship, and only the seventh escaped. This was Chauncey's greatest triumph. Governor Prevost criticized Yeo for this loss, but the commodore offered no explanation.

Throughout the campaign of 1813 Chauncey's most persistent error had been to hold his squadron together for fear the parts might be beaten in detail. In order to keep this sort of integrity his ships had to tow his schooners—which were notoriously bad sailors—most of the time. The schooners were subject to swamping in heavy weather, and being without bulwarks they were especially vulnerable to grapeshot and canister. With these faults they were not worth the loss of speed which their towing entailed. Chauncey might better have unleashed his fast ships to catch and engage the enemy, as he did in the action near the False Ducks. It would then have become his responsibility to whip the slowpokes forward in time to tip the balance of the battle in favor of the United States.[50]

As the year 1813 drew to a close, the naval building race on Lake Ontario approached the grotesque. Britain built the *St. Lawrence,* 120 guns, and launched her in the fall. She was bigger and more powerful than Nelson's flagship at Trafalgar. In response the United States began to build *New Orleans,* 110 guns.[51]

Fort Meigs

During the first four months of 1813 General William Henry Harrison was obliged to conduct his logistics under much heavier restrictions than before. Secretary Armstrong said that the nation had no more than $1,400,000 per month to spend on the war, with only $20,000 of this available to Harrison. He had appointed one deputy quartermaster in Harrison's Eighth Military District, and the general had appointed another. These two competed in Ohio for supplies and naturally boosted prices. There remained the problem of advancing the purchased goods to the depots. When the pack animals broke down, straining through the deep mud, they were almost irreplaceable. Harrison, hard pressed, began to suspect nearly everyone of peculation.[1]

Fort Meigs was a vital key to his line, and Captain Wood kept his men digging in the frozen ground to continue to improve the fort. By spring he had completed a potato-shaped work, 2,500 yards in circumference, containing 9 acres. It was ringed with picket logs 12 feet tall, reinforced with mounded dirt. It contained 8 strong blockhouses and 4 large batteries which could rake all the ditches and scour the surrounding high ground. Unaccountably, the only water supply was rain.[2]

General Harrison had a sort of love affair with the state of Kentucky and carried on by mail a constant dialogue with Governor Isaac Shelby. Expecting an attack upon Meigs during the spring, he called upon Shelby for reinforcements. The governor was fully committed to the war, but he was also determined to protect his state from another River Raisin. He told the administration that to strive for naval dominance on Lake Erie was the best investment of manpower and resources. Once the lake was won, he wanted to employ 10,000 to 15,000 men to invade Canada. For this, Shelby said, Kentucky would turn out en masse. But with the current indications that the government would not utilize a big enough invasion force, he was having trouble raising men. Those already enlisted were substitutes for men drafted to meet local quotas and did not measure up to Kentucky standards.[3]

Early in April, when their six months were completed, all but 250 of the citizen soldiers from Virginia and Pennsylvania, who made up the garrison at Fort Meigs, went home. Those remaining 250 agreed to stay only for another two weeks. Indians, scouting for the British, watched the departure of the Virginia and Pennsylvania detachments and reported it to Tecumseh. He in turn told General Procter that the time had come to strike this key position. He and his people had been promised the land north of the Ohio River and were impatient to occupy it. General Procter agreed with their strategy, but he did not act fast enough to intercept the Virginians and Pennsylvanians on their way home. Deliberately, he put together a column of 450 regulars, 475 militiamen, and around 1,200 Indians. Bad weather and scarce supplies made it impossible for him to embark his army at Amherstburg until 23 April, and it did not sail into the mouth of the Maumee River until 26 April 1813.[4]

When word of this advance reached Harrison at home in Cincinnati, he hastened northward. As he crossed Ohio he called upon Governor Shelby to speed his men forward. If he was violating the secretary's order to limit the use of the militia, no one chose to make an issue of it. With 300 men from scattered posts, he entered Fort Meigs and thereafter anxiously looked southward toward Kentucky.

The British army landed 28 April on the left bank of the river across from the fort and a little north of it. Although short of men, Harrison was never short of words. The next day he published the following general orders: "Can the citizens of a free country . . . think of submitting to an army composed of mercenary soldiers, reluctant Canadians, goaded to the field by the bayonet, and of wretched, naked savages? Can the breast of an American soldier, when he casts his eyes to the opposite shore, the scene of his country's triumphs over the same foe, be influenced by any other feelings than hope of glory? Is not this army composed of the same materials with that which fought and conquered under the immortal Wayne [at the Battle of Fallen Timbers in 1794]? Yes, fellow-citizens, your general sees your countenances beam with the same fire that he witnessed on that glorious occasion. . . . To your posts, then, fellow-citizens, and remember that the eyes of your country are upon you." Either this pronouncement did not reach the British or they were not impressed by it.

On 30 April, Procter completed two batteries with five heavy cannon in them. To counter this, Captain Wood constructed a mound of dirt which ran the entire length of the enclosure. Late in the morning on 1 May 1813, in the rain, the British opened a heavy bombardment. Hundreds of rounds of solid shot struck Wood's mound and bored harmlessly into it. The next day a third battery with three cannon opened fire, and the next day a fourth. Because American ammunition was scarce, Harrison now offered a gill of whiskey for each solid shot recovered. This produced 1,000 rounds fired harmlessly by the enemy and able to be fired back at them. During the night of 2–3 May, British engineers crossed the river and planted some cannon within 250 yards of the rear angles of the fort. In response, Captain Wood threw up another traverse which protected the tent area. When morning came, the fire of the 18–pounders in the fort drove the new battery back into a deep ravine. Otherwise, American cannon were fired sparingly, for even with the shot salvaged from the foe the ammunition was low.

On 4 May a well was completed which freed the garrison from dependence on rainwater. That same day General Proctor sent a demand to surrender, to which Harrison replied, with mock concern for Procter's honor, that the British would gain more glory if they took the fort by fighting. Although Meigs was well prepared to withstand siege, the general was much relieved when two men came in near midnight to announce the approach of 1,200 Kentucky militiamen under the command of Brigadier General Green Clay. Clay left his bivouac a few miles above the fort about dawn on 5 May. A messenger from Harrison presented him with an order to split his army, send the smallest part on toward the fort, and cross the other to the far bank of the river to try to destroy the British batteries. Clay detached 800 men under Colonel William Dudley to attack the batteries. Dudley's detachment stormed the batteries with very slight loss. Then, not bothering to spike the guns, they loped off into the woods in an uncoordinated and unauthorized pursuit. Officers threatened but could not stop their men. As a result, the retreating British rallied and began to defeat one by one the scattered groups of Americans.

Dudley's detachment was wiped out. Eighty of the men were killed, 250 to 300 of them wounded, and the rest made prisoners. The blow, as with past blows, fell altogether upon Kentucky. Dudley had won his objective, and then, because of poor discipline, had lost it and his detachment. "That confidence," Harrison said, "which always attends militia when successful proved their ruin." It would have been possible, he continued, to have spiked the guns without losing one man.

Affairs progressed better on the south bank, where the remaining 400 men were ordered to fight their way into the fort in two detachments. Sorties by 350 men from the fort helped bring both detachments safe inside, but Captain William Sebree's company held its ground against four times its numbers until a sortie could come to the rescue. The cost of this reinforcement on the south bank was 28 killed and 25 wounded. Lockjaw contracted from a scratch by a shell fragment killed one of Harrison's supporters, Major Amos Stoddard, in a few days.

Once reinforcements had made their way into the fort, General

Procter gave up the siege. It had cost him 15 men killed, 47 wounded, and 40 to 45 captured. Moreover, when the Indians saw that the siege was failing, they began to desert him in large numbers. He blamed heavy rains for spoiling his plans. Privately, too, he blamed his immediate superior, General DeRottenburg, because he would not send out to the ultimate tip of the British line the men and supplies needed there. On 1 July, DeRottenburg wrote him an instruction which brought his resentment into the open. If the British lost control of Lake Ontario, which seemed likely, the center division would have to move eastward to Kingston. This would leave the right division, Procter's command, no choice but to retreat westward instead of eastward. Procter's route would have to be Lake Huron to Lake Superior, thence on the Ottawa River, finally back to Montreal. General Procter reacted to this by complaining directly to General Prevost. Such a contingency was never likely to occur, and it was harmful even to plan for it. Prevost agreed and sent a mild reprimand to DeRottenburg.[5]

General Harrison's problems were of a different sort. He had to do something to placate the state of Ohio. Although he had made no call on it, Ohio had nevertheless prepared an army to help repel Procter's advance. Governor Return Jonathan Meigs was himself advancing at the head of 3,000 mounted men when Harrison stopped him. Harrison employed his most gracious phrases. He observed "with warmest gratitude the astonishing exertions" of Ohio men. But there was no longer any use for them in the field. Many of the citizen soldiers had put themselves out considerably to help repel the foe, but were given no chance to do it, whereas General Harrison had called Kentucky specifically to come to his side. Ohioans did not like such discrimination.[6]

The Ohio experience gives good insights into the working of the militia system. Major General John S. Gano found much to complain of in the demands made upon his First Division. The governor kept ordering out so many small detachments, without notifying the division commanders, that it was impossible to know who was or was not on duty. All the while that he strove with his full energy to meet the quotas laid upon his division, he grumbled how "arduous, troublesome, expensive, and strictly unthankful" high-level militia duty was. It was his fate to grapple with the details at home while someone else gathered glory in the field.[7]

Hard duty and grumbling occurred all down the militia hierarchy. One of the Ohio brigadiers was confused because of conflicting proclamations issued in his area by General Harrison and Governor Meigs. When he called for 250 men to appear at a rendezvous, only 40 did so, and one colonel categorically refused to obey his order. Even the privates had their tribulations. "The big folks yesterday talked of leaving me here," one of them wrote, "but I told them before I leave my company I will be lashed to one of the cannons on the slide, but from one dam'd thing and another being out of order and wanting repairs we have not got started as yet."[8]

As the summer wore away with no land action in the West, Tecumseh once again exerted pressure on General Procter to invade Ohio. Although Procter could not employ heavy cannon and could not count on the cooperation of the navy, he decided that he must make another attack on Fort Meigs or lose once and for all the use of his red allies. British reinforcements did not come, but he had close to 5,000 men, half of whom were Indian warriors. The Americans under Major General Green Clay could not match this strength, but they had the advantage of a strong fort.[9]

Clay sent notice of the arrival of the enemy to Harrison at Lower Sandusky, but received no reinforcements. Harrison had none to send, and besides he believed that the fort could withstand the impending assault with the garrison it had. Accordingly, he withdrew to Old Seneca Town, a few miles up the Sandusky River from Fort Stephenson. Here he could move either toward Fort Meigs or Fort Stephenson, but he had to cope with the Black Swamp which lay between them.[10]

The British attack plan was Tecumseh's. On 25 July 1813 the Indians began a noisy sham battle where the road from Lower Sandusky crossed the Maumee River. Tecumseh intended it to appear to be an attack on the column supposed to be coming from Fort Stephenson, and assumed that Clay would have to sally from the fort to save the column. When the troops were outside the fort and in the forest, the Indians could cut them up. Clay withstood heavy pressure to sally forth, and therefore he did not fall into the trap. The besiegers did not feel that they had the strength to storm the fort and began to drift away on 28 July. Clay assured Harrison that he could hold the place against twice the numbers left there, while Harrison, believing the feeble feint at Meigs to be a diversion, watched for a main attack to hit Lower Sandusky or Cleveland. Both were points in the defense perimeter for his depots, and Cleveland was the place where Captain Thomas S. Jesup was collecting boats for later use against Canada.

After reconnaissance, General Harrison concluded that Fort Stephenson was indefensible. On 29 July 1813 he wrote to Major George Croghan, the commander there, "Immediately on receiving this letter, you will abandon Ft. Stephenson, set it on fire, and repair with your command this night to Headquarters. Cross the river and come on the opposite side." Croghan did not reply until the next day. Then he said, "I have just received yours of yesterday, 10 P.M. ordering me to destroy this place and make good my retreat, which was received too late to be carried into execution. We have determined to maintain this place, and by heavens we can." This insubordinate note got through to Harrison the same day it was written and produced an instant reply: "An officer who presumes to aver that he has made his resolution," the general wrote, "and that he will act in direct opposition to the orders of his General, can no longer be entrusted with a separate command." Croghan was to be relieved at once.[11]

But the enemy intervened. General Procter had loaded his command aboard ships after the second failure at Meigs, and with 385 officers and men and an indeterminate number of Indians had sailed eastward against Fort Stephenson. His intelligence reported it to be as vulnerable as Harrison thought it was. The garrison numbered only 160 men, but the fort itself was menacing. Its stockade measured about 100 by 50 yards and was encircled by a ditch 8 feet wide and 8 deep. One 6-pounder, aimed to rake the northern part of the ditch, was masked. There was a bayonet driven horizontally through the tip of each picket log.[12]

General Procter did not want to assault the place, but he felt that he would lose the power to command his forces if he did not. On 2 August he sent an officer to demand surrender, and made his preparations to attack. Lieutenant Edmund Shipp went outside to parley with the bearer of the demand. An Indian tried to tear off the lieutenant's coat. Indignant, Croghan ordered Shipp back inside and opened fire. Unmoved by the bullets, Procter formed his men in a column, 15 ranks deep, and ordered it forward. He did this prematurely because he believed that Harrison had sent forward a relief detachment which might appear and shift the balance. The advance went well until it gained the ditch, where Croghan fired upon it with his concealed cannon. The dense column of men now became a mob, and 150 of its number were maimed or killed. The attack was broken.

Procter made no second attempt, but returned by ship to Amherstburg. He frankly admitted that he had made the assault because the Indians had demanded it, and referred to his heavy losses as "a more than adequate sacrifice to Indian opinion." General Prevost acknowledged his report very bluntly: "I cannot refrain from expressing my regret at your having allowed the clamour of the Indian warriors to induce you to commit a part of your valuable force in an unequal and hopeless conflict."[13]

On the American side, General Harrison found himself in the embarrassing position of relieving an officer who had just won a victory against five times his numbers. Moreover, Croghan added to his embarrassment by explaining his insubordination. By the time he had received Harrison's order, he said, it was more dangerous to carry it out than to stay and fight. His officers had concurred in that. He had then written his reply in strong terms because he had expected that it would fall into enemy hands, and wanted it to impress them. There was little Harrison could do but reinstate the major, who at twenty-one was a national hero.[14]

Lake Erie

Commodore Chauncey was keenly aware of his heavy responsibility on all the Great Lakes, and he popped into Presque Isle on New Year's Day 1813. Daniel Dobbins, in charge there, had already begun four gunboats, which Chauncey saw were too small to cruise on the lakes. He gave orders to add ten feet to two of them, but he could do nothing about the other two.[1]

In temperatures below zero Chauncey now turned eastward, and on 8 January he was at Black Rock on the Niagara River. The vessels being built at Black Rock were for the Erie squadron, but they could not be finished before spring. One disadvantage of the place was that it was within range of British cannon, and the garrison had to haul the unfinished hulks up a small creek where they were safe both from ice and from enemy artillery. The men of the garrison lived in miserable shacks in the woods.[2]

Chauncey issued orders to build a small blockhouse to protect the unfinished ships and to shelter the garrison, then he set out for Sackett's Harbor. Once there, he worked furiously for a time, then whisked off to Albany to consult with General Dearborn and to hurry on supplies. At Albany on 28 February 1813 he met Oliver Hazard Perry for the first time.[3]

Perry had been in command of a detachment of gunboats at Newport, Rhode Island, but he longed to go where there would be some military action. Accordingly, he requested permission to join Chauncey's Great Lakes command. Pleased by the request, although he did not know Perry, Chauncey asked the secretary of the navy to transfer him. In response Secretary Jones on 8 February 1813 ordered Perry to proceed to Sackett's Harbor, with the rank of master commandant, and report there to his new chief.[4]

The naval service ran in Perry's blood. His father, five brothers, and two brothers-in-law were naval officers. At the age of fourteen he himself had signed as midshipman on *General Greene*, commanded by his father. Three years later he had become a lieutenant, and at twenty he was captain of a schooner in the Mediterranean squadron. There was just one blot on his record. The gunboat *Revenge* had struck a reef and sunk in 1811 while under his command. He was acquitted of blame for this loss, but the shadow of bad luck lingered. It may have been the reason why he could not get a much desired salt-water command, and why he turned to Chauncey and the fresh-water navy.[5]

Commodore Chauncey ordered Perry to take command on Lake Erie. Perry, accompanied by 100 men, set out from Newport at once. He reached Sackett's Harbor on 3 March and Presque Isle on 27 March 1813. Presque Isle was no more than a frontier outpost, but it offered a good place to build ships, was healthful, could be fairly easily defended, and had a large harbor. These advantages offset the major disadvantage: there was no more than six feet of water over the bar at the mouth of the harbor. When Perry got there the place was nearly defenseless, and the intense cold had halted all building.

Perry, aged twenty-seven and often ill, now drew upon the deep reservoirs of willpower and energy in his makeup. The first evening he was there, he issued orders to resume shipbuilding in spite of the cold. He was informed that there was in the woods an abundance of oak and chestnut for the hulls and pine for the decks, but that other supplies had to come from Pittsburgh, over the Allegheny River and French Creek. At his urgent request four guns were shipped at once from Pittsburgh. Pennsylvania sent him 500 militiamen to help defend the building site. From the first, Perry drove himself and his associates mercilessly to build a United States squadron which would control Lake Erie. His object seemed unattainable, since the British absolutely dominated the lake when he started.[6]

About one month after Master Commandant Perry came to Presque Isle, English Captain Robert Heriot Barclay arrived at Quebec from England. His orders to enter the lake service went back to February, but bad weather had delayed him. By 9 May he was at Kingston in command of the Ontario Squadron, but in a few days was superseded by Sir James Lucas Yeo. Meanwhile Yeo offered command on Lake

Commodore Oliver H. Perry

Erie to Captain W. H. Mulcaster, and, when Mulcaster declined, gave
it to Barclay. The new appointee had to travel on Dundas Street,
which ran along the north shore of Lake Ontario, because the waterways were controlled by the Americans. By 1 June he was at Long
Point with 3 lieutenants, a surgeon, a purser, a master's mate, and 19
sailors. There he found *Lady Prevost* and *Chippewa*. These carried
him to Amherstburg, the British naval base on Erie, and deposited him
there by 3 June.

His first problem was to try to prevent Oliver Hazard Perry from
consolidating the vessels at Black Rock with those being built at
Presque Isle. Barclay came back to cruise between the two places.
Commodore Chauncey recognized the importance of uniting Perry's
units into a squadron and sent 55 sailors and carpenters to Black Rock,
to the detriment of the Ontario program, to expedite the completion
of the vessels there. General Dearborn contributed 200 soldiers to
serve as guards. During the third week in June the vessels started the
voyage from Black Rock to Presque Isle, and squeezed unperceived in
a fog past Barclay's cruisers. Then with heavy exertions they were
safely maneuvered inside the harbor at Presque Isle on 19 and 20 June
1813. Now Perry's fleet, built and under construction, was united; but
with six feet of water at the harbor's mouth, could it ever get out?[7]

Barclay's timing had been very unfortunate. He had been off Presque
Isle on 16 June, but somewhere else when the Black Rock vessels made
their painful way over the bar three days later. Be that as it may, he
recognized the need to destroy the American installation there. He
asked for 500 soldiers and 1,000 Indians from General Procter's command. But Procter, who also recognized the menace of Perry's operation, said he could not supply them or act himself against Presque Isle
without reinforcements. Above all, he wanted the balance of his own
regiment, the Forty-first Foot. When it did not come, he began to
suspect that persons farther back on the route to England were sacri-
ficing public policy to personal comfort. By 4 July he considered that
the best moment for the liquidation of Presque Isle had passed. He
now complained directly to General Prevost: "If means had been
afforded me, which were no more than what your Excellency has
repeatedly directed should be sent me, I could, in all probability, have
effected the destruction of the enemy's vessels at Presque Isle, and have
secured superiority on this lake." This was a barb at DeRottenburg for
having, as Procter believed, shortstopped men and materiel sent him by
Prevost. In the end, no one in the British command could find the
force to wipe out Perry's operation.[8]

The balance of the Forty-first Foot at last reached Lake Erie on 10

July, and Captain Barclay was so desperate for crew that he commandeered 70 men from it. Strengthened by these makeshift sailors, he left for Presque Isle, but now, since the Black Rock vessels had got into Presque Isle's harbor, he could do no more than try to maintain a blockade. Accordingly, he cruised between Long Point and Presque Isle, awaiting word from Yeo.

On the American side, Commodore Chauncey announced to Perry in mid-July that he intended to force a showdown with Yeo on Ontario, then would come to Lake Erie and join in the conflict there. In the midst of his attempts to meet and defeat his opponent and to man *General Pike*, he dispatched at considerable personal sacrifice 120 men to join Perry. Perry's response was, "The men that came are a motley set, blacks, soldiers, and boys. I cannot think you saw them after they were selected." Chauncey's reply was justifiably sharp: "I regret you are not pleased with them; for, to my knowledge, a part of them are not surpassed by any seaman we have in the fleet; and I have yet to learn that the color of the skin, or the cut and trimmings of the coat, can affect a man's qualifications or usefulness. . . . As you have assured the secretary that you should conceive yourself equal or superior to the enemy, with a force in men so much less than I had deemed necessary, there will be a great deal expected from you by your country. . . ." When this letter was delivered to him by Jesse D. Elliott, Perry replied that he was glad to see "anything in the shape of a man." But the tone of the letter had offended him, and he asked to be relieved. Chauncey now became apologetic, others interceded, and Perry was persuaded to remain at his difficult post.[9]

Captain Barclay's expectations for some reason rose so high in mid-July that he loaded field artillery aboard his ships for an attack on Presque Isle. But when word came from DeRottenburg that there would be no reinforcements, Barclay could do nothing but unload them again. The British completed the 20-gun *Detroit* on 20 July, but they lacked stores, sails, guns, and men for her. Presque Isle remained unassailed.

Master Commandant Perry had within the bar 9 warships: brig *Lawrence* 20 guns, brig *Niagara* 20, brig *Caledonia* 3, schooner *Ariel* 4, schooner *Scorpion* 2 guns and 2 swivels, sloop *Trippe* 1 gun, schooner *Tigress* 1, schooner *Porcupine* 1, and schooner *Ohio* 1. On the last day of July 1813 he observed that the British blockading vessels had disappeared from the mouth of the harbor. Except that he had only 490 men where he needed 740, his squadron was ready, and he now decided to try to get his vessels over the bar.[10]

The wind was blowing from the east, piling the water up on the

Canadian shore, and reducing it to five and one-half feet over the bar. August 1 being a Sunday, the country people of the vicinity turned out to watch the five vessels from Black Rock go over the bar and be posted and anchored so as to fight if the foes should appear. *Lawrence* and *Niagara* had to go over without rigging or guns, so their guns were mounted in shore batteries 500 yards from the channel. The sixth vessel was to defend *Lawrence* while she was unarmed. Camels (sunken watertight boxes attached to the hull and then pumped empty) were used to raise *Lawrence* three feet, and then she had to be dragged a mile across the bar through shoal water. This heavy task took a night and a day. Still no enemy was in view, and on 4 August *Lawrence*, of course minus her armament, was afloat in deep water. Now the camels were applied to *Niagara*, and the long drag commenced, but she stuck. At this moment when *Lawrence* was unarmed and *Niagara* was stuck, Barclay's flotilla once again appeared. No one knows why Barclay had been absent at the critical time. Folklore has it that he sailed off to Dover to attend a dinner. Colonel Cruikshank wrote that "stress of weather and lack of provisions" forced him off his station. Barclay himself never explained, but simply reported that "one morning [he] saw the whole of the enemies [*sic*] force over the bar and in a most formidable state of preparation." Apparently unaware of the danger-ous plight of the ships before him and on the surface of it outnum-bered, he decided to wait until his own force could be increased by *Detroit*, and sailed away. So it happened that by nightfall on 4 August *Lawrence* and *Niagara* were fitted out. This remarkable exploit had cost Oliver Perry three nights without sleep.[11]

Perhaps because he was exhausted he wavered for a few days, but when during the evening of 8 August word reached him of the approach of Master Commandant Jesse D. Elliott with 101 seamen, he decided to wait for them. He would then move westward to find and attack Barclay. Strengthened by Elliott's detachment sent by Chaun-cey, he led the squadron up the lake on 10 August. In conjunction with General Harrison, Perry chose Put-in-Bay on Gibralter Island as his base. During the August days he came and went between this new base and the British anchorage in the mouth of the Detroit River. About 21 August he prepared to strike before *Detroit* was fitted for action, but he became gravely ill and had to delay. Lake fever pros-trated him and as many as 30 men on each of his ships.[12]

With no more than 180 to 200 trained sailors on hand, Barclay had to draw most of his crew from two foot regiments, the Royal New-foundlanders, who had so manfully marched 700 miles in the depths of winter, and the Forty-first. Neither he nor Procter expected much additional help from the eastward, but they continued to petition for it. General Procter believed that General DeRottenburg and Commodore Yeo were knowingly withholding supplies and reinforcements meant for him. Because Yeo kept all the prime sailors, he said, Barclay had to use landsmen for his crews. It did not improve his outlook when DeRottenburg criticized him for allowing the Indians to bully him into the Fort Meigs fiasco.

Barclay and Prevost considered their condition to be desperate. *Detroit* could not join the squadron because of lack of sails, supplies, guns, and men. There were piles of stores at Long Point, but the American squadron prevented their transfer. Meanwhile Procter had to try to feed 14,000 Indians in addition to his own complement. Finally convinced of the gravity of the situation, DeRottenburg ordered a detachment of men to go into the back country, impress all the wagons along Dundas Street, and use them to haul supplies to the Thames River where boats could carry them on to the right wing.

Since no flow of necessities came from DeRottenburg's scheme, Barclay began to feel that he must fight to open up his supply line. But as late as 26 August Procter counseled him not to risk an encounter while he was so shorthanded. General Prevost, however, wrote in a different tone: "The experience obtained from Sir James Yeo's conduct toward a fleet infinitely superior . . . will satisfy Captain Barclay that he has only to dare and the enemy will be discomfited." General DeRottenburg began to talk in the same vein. On 5 September a small reinforcement of 2 lieutenants, a master's mate, and 36 sailors switched Procter over to the Prevost-DeRottenburg point of view. But the reinforcements came from Prevost, not from Yeo. On 14 September the issue had been settled, but Prevost, not knowing this, again urged action: "I cannot hesitate in desiring some bold attempt may be made without delay by Captain Barclay to gain the ascendancy and open an outlet for the supplies now lying at Long Point for the Right Division of the Army."

Captain Barclay himself was a man of established reputation. He had served well in the wars against Napoleon and had lost an arm at Trafalgar. His initial instructions told him to rely on his own judgment, but he could not help being influenced by the representations of army commanders much higher than he in rank. Thus, as soon as he was convinced that no more reinforcements were coming to him, he announced that he would "risk everything to gain so great a point, as that of opening the communication by water." To expedite action he stripped the fort at Amherstburg to arm *Detroit*; the new flagship now carried 21 guns of four different calibers.

Barclay on *Detroit* moved his 6 vessels out onto the lake on 9 September. They were H.M.S. *Detroit* 19 guns and 2 howitzers, H.M.S. *Queen Charlotte* 17 and 1, schooner *Lady Prevost* 13 and 1, brig *Hunter* 10 guns, sloop *Little Belt* 3, and schooner *Chippewa* 1 gun and 2 swivels. Perry had been expecting 7 ships, but *Erie* did not emerge with the rest, nor is it known what became of her. The British squadron had about 440 men aboard, but only 10 men in each ship's crew were trained sailors. The opposing squadron carried 530 persons, and a larger proportion of them were experienced seamen. Moreover, some of the United States personnel were Kentucky marksmen from General Harrison's army, who could deliver an accurate rifle fire from the tops. The 6 British ships threw a broadside of 459 pounds, 195 of them from long guns, whereas the 9 Americans rated 896 pounds total broadside, 288 of which came from long guns. Barclay knew that his squadron was in all respects inferior, but he did not know to what degree.

At a gathering of his officers during the evening of 9 September 1813 Perry expressed his determination to attack the enemy the next day, if need be at anchor, for he did not yet know that Barclay had sailed. He ordered each ship commander to engage at close range a specified enemy ship. He then brought out a blue pennant carrying the motto "Don't Give Up the Ship" in large white letters. This pennant when it was displayed on the flagship *Lawrence* was to be the signal for attack.

At dawn on 10 September lookouts announced the British fleet in view to the northwest. Perry at once began to beat out toward it against the wind, and even though it became clear that he could not secure the weather gauge, he signaled his captains to be prepared to fight either to the windward or to the leeward. Now the wind shifted to the southeast, and he ran down upon the enemy with the wind upon the port beam. At about nine miles from Put-in-Bay and the same distance from the mainland, Barclay hove to and, facing southwest almost stationary, awaited the impact. Perry saw that *Detroit* was second in the British line, and he signaled Elliott on *Niagara* to drop from second to third place in the American. As prearranged, this maneuver would enable *Lawrence* to close with *Detroit* and *Niagara* with *Queen Charlotte*, which was fourth from the British van. *Somers*, *Porcupine*, *Tigress*, and *Trippe* were nearly a mile behind *Lawrence*.

At noon Perry signaled his ships to close in and brought *Lawrence* toward the British line at a 25-degree angle. This approach avoided a raking fire and gave him the opportunity to use his broadside at the earliest possible moment. He knew that he had to close in fast, for *Lawrence* was weak in long guns in comparison with *Detroit* (2 to 18) and strong in carronades (18 to 2). *Ariel* and *Scorpion* kept close to *Lawrence* to give her the benefit of their 5 long guns. For twenty minutes *Lawrence* took much heavier punishment than she could inflict. For two hours from 11:45 *Detroit*, *Queen Charlotte*, and *Hunter* concentrated their bombardment on the American flagship. One by one every officer fell except Perry, and the crew dropped too. Perry got only a light wound. One by one the ship's lines and braces were shot away, and *Lawrence* became increasingly unmanageable. The 4 American vessels in the rear still had not closed in, but they were using their long guns well. *Caledonia*, *Ariel*, and *Scorpion* were heavily engaged. Of the 9 Americans only *Niagara* had not contributed effectively to the battle.

After two hours of fighting, 21 men were dead and 63 wounded aboard *Lawrence*, out of a starting crew of about 100 fit for duty. Perry sent word to the ship's surgeon to return to the deck any man who could pull a line, though it be his last. *Niagara*, which for some reason had not closed with *Queen Charlotte*, now began to move toward the head of the line, but keeping the American vessels between herself and the enemy. Jesse Elliott, or members of his staff, later explained that the ship had not closed as ordered because the wind was too light to bring *Niagara* up after *Queen Charlotte* had darted forward to take *Lawrence* under fire. Elliott claimed that he had had to back sails to keep from colliding with *Caledonia*, and had finally had to order her out of his way. His enemies asserted that he had backed sails to keep from closing. In any case, *Caledonia* now moved forward between the two battle lines much faster than *Niagara*, and centered her fire on *Detroit* and *Queen Charlotte*. These two were already badly damaged. At around 2:00 P.M. *Niagara* came athwart *Lawrence* at a distance of about half a mile, unscarred and fresh and except for long-gun shot carrying a full load of ammunition. Actually, her 2 long guns had throughout been firing with effect at *Queen Charlotte*.

Perry abandoned his riddled flagship and with 4 or 5 sailors entered a rowboat and made for *Niagara*. At first he stood up for morale's sake, but the British gunners began to find the range and the sailors pulled him down. Virtually unhurt, therefore, he boarded *Niagara* and came face to face with Jesse Elliott. Their dialogue is lost in myth and polemics. The Elliott version of it said that Perry blurted out, "The day is lost!" Elliott then reassured him and added, "Take charge of my battery while I bring the boats in close action and the day will yet be ours." He next rowed from schooner to schooner—in much greater danger than Perry had earlier been—and ordered them forward. They obeyed him and their fire won the battle. Elliott returned to *Niagara,* and Perry is supposed to have told him, "I owe all this to your exertions."

Scant credit can be given the Elliott story. It was not in character for Oliver Perry to have behaved as he had up to that moment and then to have blubbered to a subordinate that all was lost. Perry's entire record was one of stubborn determination. Besides, all the other accounts testify that he never lost his composure. Nor is it accurate to credit Elliott with bringing the lagging schooners in line. The fact is, they had all along been a vital force in the battle. They had inflicted much damage with their long guns at a range which kept themselves safe from enemy hits. Morover, they were closing in before Elliott ever reached them.

Elliott did leave *Niagara* and go toward the schooners, and the murderous raking fire of the schooners at the end did tip the balance for the United States. *Lady Prevost* became unmanageable and drifted beyond the head of the line. Perry now cut right through the British position, simultaneously firing *Niagara*'s larboard broadside at *Lady Prevost, Little Belt,* and *Chippewa* and her starboard broadside at *Detroit* and *Queen Charlotte.*

Captain Barclay had witnessed Perry's transfer without realizing what he was seeing. Soon afterwards the Englishman was struck in the thigh and carried below deck. Very shortly his second in command was also hit, and Barclay returned to the deck to resume the direction of the battle. He ordered *Detroit* and *Queen Charlotte* to wear in order to use their starboard broadsides, but the ships were virtually helpless and ran afoul of each other. While they were in that tangle, *Niagara* raked them across the bows while the American schooners raked them across the sterns. Barclay's remaining arm was hit and mangled; Lieutenant George Inglis had to take over. In the British squadron every ship's commander and his deputy had by now been killed or wounded. There was little choice but to strike colors— some four hours after the firing of the first shot.

Soon after Perry left *Lawrence,* the ship had to surrender, but the foe never had time to take possession of her. Certain British officers later accused Perry of surrendering and then continuing to fight, but the Americans denied the accusation. Perry chose to return to the crippled flagship to receive the surrender. The human cost of the victory had been 44 Englishmen and 21 Americans killed, 103 Englishmen and 63 Americans wounded. Perry composed two simple, eloquent victory messages. The one to Secretary Jones, written at

4:00 P.M., said, "It has pleased the Almighty to give to the arms of the United States a signal victory over their enemies on this Lake. The British squadron consisting of two ships, two brigs, one schooner, and a sloop, have this moment surrendered to the force under my command after a sharp conflict." The notice to General Harrison was terse and more powerful: "We have met the enemy and they are ours—two ships, two brigs, one schooner, and a sloop."

Perry's victory swept the British off Lake Erie for the balance of the war. In doing so, it opened the way for General Harrison to advance against the British right division. Every Englishman even remotely connected with it sought to avoid blame for the defeat. Commodore Yeo charged the army commanders with having put undue pressure on Barclay to meet a superior foe. He also observed that if the British officers had not fallen, the result would have beeen different. Barclay himself, when he could write again, revealed bitterness at Yeo for not having sent him more help. General Prevost forgot his own part in the episode and asserted that Barclay had been unwise in sailing out to bring on a showdown. Only Barclay and Procter continued to insist that there had been no alternative to the attack.[13]

Earl Bathurst first learned of the defeat on 4 November 1813 from a United States newspaper. He at once wrote to Prevost asking the governor to explain how the entire fleet could have been made to surrender. He ordered Prevost to bend every effort during the winter to re-establish a British force on Lake Erie in order to keep control of Upper Canada and to maintain contact with the Indians. *Gentleman's Magazine*, published in London, informed its readers, probably through ignorance, that the defeated fleet was not a part of the British navy, but was a local organization.[14]

Five weeeks after the Battle of Lake Erie the massive maneuvers of the Battle of Leipzig began in Europe. When they were concluded on 19 October 1813, the French army had been forced to seek security west of the Rhine. Both battles were decisive, but that was all they had in common. The Battle of Lake Erie involved 15 small ships, 117 guns, and about 970 men, whereas Leipzig involved 2,000 cannon and 500,000 men. Small wonder that the statesmen in England looked east rather than west. If they slighted Lake Erie, they at least started Napoleon on the road to ruin.

About a year after the defeat Captain Barclay was tried for the loss of his squadron, but the navy court honorably acquitted him on the following grounds: (1) The means at his disposal were insufficient and defective; (2) the early fall of most of the seasoned officers hastened the defeat (the case of *Queen Charlotte* illustrated this fact—

during the first half-hour the two senior officers were killed, and within the next few minutes the third was knocked senseless; the command of the ship then passed to an officer of the Provincial Marine who had courage and ability, but lacked the necessary experience); (3) each vessel had no more than 10 experienced sailors aboard; (4) matches were so defective that the gunners had to fire pistols at the touchholes to discharge their guns; and (5) Barclay's leadership was withdrawn because of his wounds and could not be replaced.[15]

Except for the single-ship triumphs, the Battle of Lake Erie was the clearest victory the United States had so far won in the war. There were celebrations across the country. Perry at once became a national hero, and everyone directly involved on the American side profited financially. The commanders, living and dead, received several medals, Congress voted three months' extra pay to the officers involved, and midshipmen and sailing masters each received a sword. In 1814 Congress authorized the purchase of the captured vessels at a price of $250,000 in order to add them to the Erie squadron. From this fund Commodore Chauncey received $12,750, the largest sum awarded to an individual. Next came Perry who got $7,140, but Congress, to bring the commander's up almost to the share Chauncey got, voted him another $5,000. Elliott received $7,140, and the common seamen had $95,625 to divide in equal shares with the landsmen and marines. In all 596 persons shared in the distribution.[16]

Master Commandant Jesse Elliott placed a blot on the otherwise pure image of the Battle of Lake Erie. No one could understand why *Niagara* had not closed as ordered with *Queen Charlotte* and done its share in the early phases of the battle. Perry avoided the matter in his official report, dated 19 September 1813, but he gave Elliott generous credit for bringing up the gunboats at the end and for having "evinced his characteristic bravery and judgment." Elliott, however, soon began to demand testimonials from Perry which went far beyond this restrained sort of credit. There must have been some question about Elliott's share of the prize money, for the correspondence grew acrimonious in 1818, the year the shares were paid. On receiving an offensive communication from Elliott in that year, Perry replied, "you reduce me to the necessity of reminding you of the abject condition in which I had previously found you . . . sick (or pretending to be sick) in bed in consequence of distress of mind." We cannot know the details of the incident to which he here refers. He continued, "The reputation you have lost was tarnished by your own behavior on Lake Erie. Mean and despicable as you have proved yourself to be, I shall never cease to criminate myself . . . for screening you from public contempt." The implication of this last sentence was that he should in his report of the battle have accused Elliott of malingering. When Elliott received this blast, he challenged Perry to a duel, but Perry replied that he was preferring formal charges against Elliott. Only when cleared of these charges would Elliott have a right to "assume the tone of a gentleman." The commodore sent the charges directly to the President. There was never a trial, but Elliott was accorded a court of inquiry and it did not find against him. Perry died in 1819, but Elliott kept on asserting that in reality he had won the victory. He continued to serve the navy honorably and also became a staunch Jacksonian. He always claimed that his "persecution" had been a consequence of his republican principles.[17]

Elliott was not the sort of man who would have hung back from combat out of fear. There is no trace of cowardice in his record. His failing probably was an uncontrollable ambition. When he observed the British force concentrating its fire upon *Lawrence*, he may have concluded that neither the flagship nor the commodore could possible last very long, in spite of anything Elliott could do. The result of this reasoning would have been Elliott's belief that the battle could be won without *Lawrence* and Perry, and won by Elliott if he entered it at just the right moment with the full power of his ship undiminished.

The Northwest

While waiting for naval action to release his army to invade Canada, General Harrison as usual turned to Kentucky for support. He had asked Governor Shelby to send him no less than 400 and no more than 2,000 Kentuckians. "To make this last effort why not come in person," he continued. "I have such confidence in your wisdom that you in fact should be the guiding Head and I the hand . . . Scipio the conqueror of Carthage did not disdain to act as the lieutenant of his younger and less experienced brother Lucius."[1]

Governor Shelby did decide to join the campaign, but not as the guiding head. He was a veteran of the critical Revolutionary battle of King's Mountain and a man of tremendous personal influence, and by taking the field at sixty-three, he inspired the already sanguinary Kentuckians. He caused handbills to be posted all over the state, and sent fast couriers out to the militia officers, even to the remotest areas. "I will lead you to the field of battle," his message went, "and share with you the dangers and honors of the campaign." Since he put no limit on the numbers to be raised, it was virtually an invitation to a *levée en masse*. Each man who brought a group into the field was to have the command of it.[2]

Much correspondence about details passed among Armstrong, Harrison, and Shelby. The governor succeeded in persuading the other two to let the Kentuckians ride to the seat of war, and to accept the whole number of men who turned out. Although this course threatened to put more men at the general's disposal than he could subsist, he approved it. "I am determined," he said, "not to have it believed again, that I am the head of an army, when I have only the amount of a regiment, as was the case lately."[3]

While the Kentuckians rode toward the Great Lakes, General Harrison had to cope again with Ohio. Governor Meigs of Ohio, reacting to the dangers on the lakes, had issued a circular urging the militia of his state to turn out en masse. Around 10,000 citizen soldiers responded and took up the march toward the threatened region. Having called for an army of Kentuckians, Harrison did not need these men, and now he had to tell them so. For use in this ticklish situation he found the honeyed phrases which came very easily to him. "The exertions which you have made," he wrote to Meigs, "and the promptitude with which your orders have been obeyed . . . is truly astonishing and reflects the highest honor on the State." But he did not offer the slightest explanation as to why he had called for Kentuckians when Ohioans were already at hand and were willing. Governor Meigs was obliged to disband the entire mass, whereupon the Ohio militia lost all chance to share in the honor of the conquest of Canada. Ohio citizen soldiers were bitter, and many of them vowed they would not turn out again.[4]

The Kentucky army, with Governor Shelby at its head, reached Lake Erie in the middle of September. It numbered between 3,000 and 3,500 men, formed into 11 regiments, 5 brigades, and 2 divisions. Its organization did not in any way conform to that of the regular army. The Kentucky brigades, not as big as regular regiments, were top-heavy with generals. One general or two at most would have been proper by army standards, but the Kentucky expedition had seven general officers besides its commander in chief. Nevertheless, since the Kentuckians had the will to fight, no one tried to reorganize them.

Harrison could not take a mounted army into Canada, so it was necessary to make provision for the horses on which the Kentuckians had ridden to the margin of Lake Erie. He selected a little peninsula, only a mile and a half wide at the neck, extending into the lake. Next, the army corps were given sectors of the neck to fence off, and in no time they had their mounts confined on a splendid pasture where a minimum number of men could guard them. Because all the Kentuckians wanted to take part in the invasion, the guards finally had to be drafted.[5]

There was one regiment of citizen soldiers from Pennsylvania with Harrison's army. They were not as eager to invade Canada as the men from Kentucky. Unfortunately, they would not agree to be used as horse guards. But when the embarkation commenced on 20 September, only 150 of them were willing to leave the United States. They stood on what they alleged to be their constitutional rights. As a result, the invasion force consisted of 150 Pennsylvanians, 2 brigades of regulars numbering about 2,500, and close to 3,000 Kentucky volunteers. One sow, which had followed the Kentucky troops all the way from home, was the only creature from Kentucky which refused to cross into Canada.[6]

General Procter learned of the destruction of Captain Barclay's squadron two days after it occurred. It made his deteriorating situation all but hopeless. His men had not been paid in several months and had scant hope of a payday in the foreseeable future. The Indians, offended by the reduction in their supplies, were falling away in substantial numbers. Tecumseh still remained close by with 500 warriors, but Procter found it harder to find supplies for them and for the large crowd of their women and children. He drew upon the authority granted him by General Prevost and for the second time declared martial law in his region.[7]

As soon as Secretary Armstrong learned of Perry's victory on Lake Erie, he authorized General Harrison to resume operations. The first step for Americans to invade Canada was to transport the troops from the American shore to the islands in the Detroit River just off Malden. For this and other purposes, Perry put his fleet at General Harrison's disposal, and the movement began on 23 September 1813. Perry reported fine harmony between army and navy. Harrison issued detailed general orders on 27 September, from army headquarters aboard *Ariel*, for the landing on the Canadian mainland. Leaving Brigadier General Duncan McArthur with 700 men to protect Detroit, he began the invasion the very same day. His orders for landing under enemy fire were never tested because the British did not oppose the movement

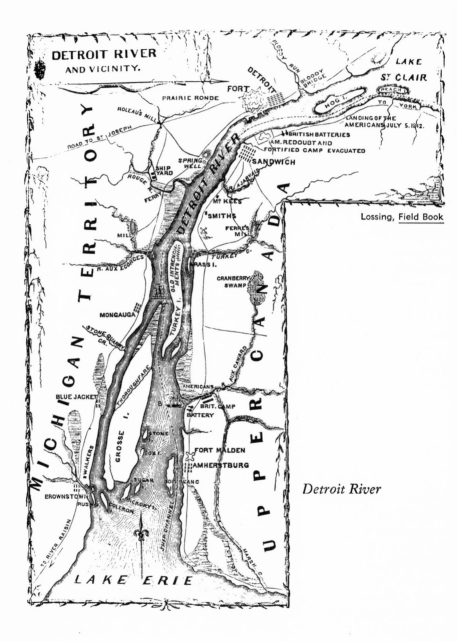

DETROIT RIVER
AND VICINITY.

Detroit River

Lossing, Field Book

from ship to shore. His army occupied Amherstburg without opposition 17 days after the Battle of Lake Erie. At about the same time, General Procter left Sandwich and headed eastward toward the Thames River.[8]

Now a race in slow motion began. Procter's column averaged only nine miles per day, and it took Harrison five days to get from Amherstburg to Sandwich. After that, though, the American pace accelerated. Harrison departed Sandwich on 2 October and the next evening was close behind the retreating column. General Proctor himself left his troops in order to go ahead and meet his family at Moraviantown, and presumably to scout out good places to make a stand. The area through which pursuer and pursued now moved was a virgin forest of walnut trees, some with trunks six feet in diameter. Underbrush could not grow beneath this great stand of timber, nor could the sunlight penetrate there. Procter's men labored through the cathedral-like twilight, overencumbered with baggage. The general did not order them to destroy bridges or fell trees or construct other obstacles. He may have lost interest and may have become interested only in the safety of his own family.[9]

Except at the source, the Thames River was navigable, and both belligerents used it to carry their impedimenta. Perry provided three small gunboats to escort the freight boats, but above Dolson's the stream was too narrow for them and the freighters had to go it alone. On 4 October 1813 the American column reached the third unfordable branch of the Thames. Tecumseh's Indians had removed the bridge, and were waiting on the other side. Harrison brought two 6-pounders to the head of the column, drove the Indians away, and repaired the bridge, all within two hours. He had increasing evidence that the main force of the enemy was close by. Richard M. Johnson's mounted regiment seized a mill and lost two men killed and three wounded. The British now set fire to their own water freighters.

The highly mobile unit in General Harrison's army of invasion was Colonel Richard M. Johnson's regiment of mounted Kentucky riflemen. As far back as the winter of 1812–13 Johnson had asked permission to form this unit, but Harrison had discouraged him. Secretary Armstrong, on the other hand, even though Congress had repealed the volunteer acts in January, had authorized its formation on 26 February 1813. Nominally, the governor of Kentucky had the power to name the officers, but he followed Johnson's suggestions. On the grounds that it was an illegal sort of force, and that the colonel had too much power, a faction in Kentucky had opposed the new regiment. Nevertheless, it had filled up with 1,200 men in a few weeks.

Its members, described as "hardy, keen, daring, and ruthless," wore leather hunting frocks and trousers and bright headkerchiefs. Each was armed with a tomahawk, a scalping knife, and a rifle. They carried the long rifle on horseback with as much ease as other persons might carry a hand gun. Johnson trained them far beyond the level usually attained by citizen soldiers. He prescribed a battle formation and practiced it so often that men and horses fell automatically into their places. He made them charge into lines of infantrymen who actually fired, until they learned to carry a charge straight into the hostile line. Their tactics were unusual in America.[10]

During its first months in service, Johnson's regiment had made a 700-mile circuit through the Indian country south of Lake Michigan. When it came back from this, it was ordered to proceed at once to Kaskaskia. Johnson protested the order on the grounds that men and horses were worn out, and that they wanted to serve with General Harrison. They wished above all to be a part of the force which would defeat the British army in Canada, for Kentucky had suffered cruelly in the war. Nevertheless they started for Kaskaskia, but were recalled after Secretary Armstrong studied the protests from Johnson and Harrison. This regiment alone among Harrison's troops was permitted to ride its horses into Canada.

On the morning of 5 October 1813, it was clear to General Procter that he had to stand and fight. By 6:00 A.M. he had his men awaiting attack in a single line at extended order. His left rested upon the river beside which the road ran to Moraviantown, three and one-half miles eastward. Thence the line stretched about 250 yards northward to a small swamp which divided his front, and from that extended onward another 250 yards to a larger swamp. The Forty-first Foot Regiment (Procter's own), 540 strong, and 290 men of the Royal Newfoundland Regiment held the line to the left of the swamp. Five hundred Indians under Tecumseh manned the balance of it. No fallen timbers or abatis of any kind protected it.[11]

Governor Shelby's infantry manfully kept up with Johnson's regiment because Johnson's men often took them up on the crupper. They did this not only from kindness, but to assure themselves of an infantry screen when the time came. In this manner they arrived before the British position at 8:00 A.M. There were present 140 regulars, 1,000 of Johnson's regiment, and about 2,300 Kentucky volunteers. Master Commandant Perry was with the command party.

As Harrison was arranging his men according to the plan, Colonel Johnson discovered that the British troops south of the swamp were deployed in a single line, with the men standing three feet apart. The situation was made for the kind of charge in which his unit had been trained, and he asked permission to attack at once. Harrison was aware of the capabilities of the mounted riflemen, and also of the unorthodoxy of the proposed charge. Balancing the two against each other, he authorized the movement. Johnson's men at once galloped forward and struck the British formation, which was totally unprepared for what had hit it. In just a few minutes the Kentuckians had ridden through the thin line, dismounted behind it, and opened fire with their rifles upon its rear. Caught between two murderous fires, the British soldiers surrendered. But the Indians, being protected by the swamp, continued to resist. Soon it became known among them that Tecumseh had been killed, and they too quit.

Eleazer Wood, the builder of Fort Meigs, said, "It is really a novel thing that raw militia stuck upon horses, with muskets in their hands instead of sabres, should be able to pierce British lines with such complete effect." He recognized that Johnson's charge was in a class by itself. Cavalry charges are rare enough in American history, but this was not a cavalry charge. Rather, it was the standard movement by mounted infantrymen, to ride to the firing line, then to dismount and continue the battle on foot. What was unique about this charge was the fact that they rode through the enemy formation, and established the firing line behind it. Added to the uniqueness was the fact that they carried long shoulder guns instead of sabers, pistols, or carbines, the standard weapons of Americans who have charged on horseback.

Tecumseh is said to have had premonitions of his death at the Battle of the Thames, and to have awaited it calmly. True to his vision, he here disappeared at the age of forty-four. Years later Colonel Johnson himself claimed to have killed the chief, and whether he did or not, he derived much benefit politically from alleging it. Sometimes it is said that white men mutilated the great chief's body, but the fact is, white men never saw or found it. The Indians steadfastly believed that Tecumseh was invulnerable to white men's weapons, and that he had simply been lifted into the sky. The total of Indian losses is not known, but British figures were 12 killed, 22 wounded, 600 captured. The Americans suffered 7 killed, 22 wounded.

Procter's first report of the battle was so opaque that General DeRottenburg asked for a second, but since it was long delayed, he forwarded the original to Prevost. General orders issued at Montreal on 24 November 1813 treated the battle as a disgrace to British arms. They stated that the retreat was encumbered by private baggage, forbidden by regulations, that official impedimenta were discarded, and that no actions proper to delay a pursuer had been taken.[12]

Procter blamed the troops. Their conduct was not "such as I have on every other occasion witnessed with pride and satisfaction . . . nor did I receive that cordial aid I sought and was entitled to." The men serving the one cannon on the line abandoned it, he said, without firing a shot. In general his orders were not carried out. His supply boats were of the wrong sort, and his ammunition was scarce. The Indians, he claimed, began to desert before the action commenced. Soon after the attack started, he saw that the battle could not be won, and he left the field to avoid capture.[13]

In spite of the criticism of him, Procter remained in the West, trying to hold some sort of British position together. He demanded a court of inquiry, and when none was forthcoming wrote directly to the commander in chief, Frederick Duke of York. This produced a court-martial late in December 1814. The charges against him were: delaying his retreat too long after the naval defeat; attempting to save useless baggage; neglecting proper preparations; failing to choose a suitable place to make a stand; and failing to exercise sufficient command during the battle. The court found him guilty of failing to prepare for his retreat and of making faulty tactical arrangements. It said he had erred both in judgment and in execution, and recommended that he be reprimanded and suspended from duty for six months. In the end his punishment was restricted to a reprimand issued by the Prince Regent on 26 July 1815.[14]

The court did not make anything of the poor morale of the Forty-first Foot Regiment. Procter was on bad terms with his regiment, and its low morale may have been due to his management. In addition, the men were weakened by fever and exhausted by their slow march and heavy baggage. It was not kind, neither was it uncommon, for a general to blame the troops for a failure. This was a safe alibi, for the enlisted men were voiceless.[15]

The Battle of the Thames, like the Battle of Lake Erie which had triggered it, was small but decisive. It destroyed the British army west of the head of Lake Erie and broke the Indian power in the Northwest. It was achieved by a 2 to 1 supremacy over a force which was unpaid, outflanked, far from any support, and very poorly led. Yet for the citizen soldiers of Kentucky it was a great victory. They had gathered 3,500 strong, organized themselves, marched at forced paces, kept fairly decent order in the homeland of a people they hated, and finally, using a tactic peculiarly suited to their talents, had attacked decisively and defeated the enemy—all this in two months. Not the least of the results of the battle was its effect on Kentucky politics. For decades it was worth thousands of votes to have been there. Governors, judges, senators, and representatives, and even one vice president, owed their elections in part to this fight.[16]

Almost as swiftly as they had come, the American troops left Canada. Many of them were angry when they found that instead of being shipped across the head of Lake Erie, they had to march all the way around it; but Harrison, with his usual success, explained to them that the little squadron was needed elsewhere. Governor Shelby invoked the honor of the state to insure good order during the march home, and he secured it. At the peninsula every man caught his own horse and rode it back to Kentucky. On 4 November, two months and four days after the original rendezvous, the troops were discharged in their native state.[17]

The Thames campaign, taken by itself, was almost the perfect use of the citizen soldier. Because supplies were available in depots along the way, there was not the usual delay on their account. Crops and businesses suffered a minimum because the men were not away from home quite three months. Also, the morale of the men was raised by their being allowed to ride, not walk, to the combat zone. Finally, morale was high because the citizen soldiers respected the officers who led them.

Viewed as a part of a planned and coordinated war effort, on the other hand, the Thames campaign was by no means perfect. The administration had hoped to employ an army of 7,000 regulars, but instead fielded one of 2,500 regulars and the balance of citizen soldiers. Moreover, the militia was raised on conditions judged proper, not by any federal official, but by the governor of Kentucky. Lastly, the army was useful for only one campaign; its training, such as it was, could not be utilized to clean the British completely out of Upper Canada.

General Harrison and Master Commandant Perry, who worked well together, now concerted an expedition to reduce Mackinac and St. Josephs on Lake Huron, but the weather turned foul and they decided that they could not carry it to a successful conclusion. The truth is, both of them had lost interest in the western theater.[18]

For reasons not clear, Oliver Perry asked to be relieved of his command on the lakes. Probably he did not feel that he could work effectively any longer with Commodore Chauncey. He and his superior had different codes of conduct. Chauncey made a fortune from percentages of the costs of building vessels under his jurisdiction. The same perfectly legal resource was open to Perry, but he would not take the money on the grounds that it might influence his judgment. When Chauncey learned that Secretary Jones had accepted Perry's resignation, he protested. He held that an officer had no right to complain of his service, and that others would want to leave if Perry was allowed to. Then he revealed how his own feelings were involved. He had not won laurels for himself, he said, but had opened the way for Perry to do so. During his thirteen months of command on the lakes, the American naval force had risen from one vessel to two substantial squadrons. He did not say it, but he implied that the administration must take into account the hard duty which supported victory in battle and too often went unnoticed. His lament did not change the secretary's mind, and on 25 October 1813 Perry turned the command on Erie over to Jesse Elliott and started at once to Rhode Island to become the captain of the first frigate which was available. His progress across the country was a triumphal procession.[19]

General Harrison lingered about Detroit long enough to make some recommendations to the government relative to the Indians. He granted an armistice to all the tribes who asked for it, but he advised the government to show no mercy to the Miamis and Potawatamis. There was constant communication between the Indians around the lakes and those from the far South. He suggested that a firm example in the North of how the British connection brought ruin might deter aggression in the South.[20]

By the end of October 1813 Harrison had traveled to the Niagara end of the Ontario Peninsula. His departure from the Detroit theater shifted the duty of providing garrisons for the numerous forts and blockhouses to the governments of Michigan Territory and the state of Ohio. As late as December 1813, 2,000 of their militiamen were still on duty in them. They were truly forgotten men; many were ill and most of them had drawn no pay for four months. Lack of pay was in part a result of the federal regulation which required state troops to be mustered for pay by an officer of the United States Army. The local commanders resented the implication that there were no honorable men in the state organizations. General John Gano of the Ohio militia expressed his bitterness as a citizen soldier to a friend: "The militia of Ohio have been made pack horses and merely served as convenience for others to receive the honor and glory."[21]

The strategic focus late in 1813 shifted from the western to the eastern end of the Great Lakes. On the British side General Prevost became discouraged and ordered the withdrawal of all his forces to Kingston, but bad weather and the stubbornness of the local commanders prevented this movement. Brigadier General John Vincent, for example, bluntly said that he would cling to the installation at Burlington, at the head of Lake Ontario, until given a peremptory order to get out. If he had to quit the area, he said, it would be necessary to take the Indians with him, as they could not be left to the mercy of the Americans. He succeeded in convincing General Prevost that he should hold Burlington, and, more than that, should prevent the United States from establishing outposts between that place and Fort George. Prevost directed the local commanders to assure the redmen that Great Britain would not abandon them.[22]

When it became known in the Niagara theater in September that all the United States regulars were to be withdrawn for an offensive at the eastern end of Lake Ontario, the ambitious militia officers in the West saw an opportunity for a vigorous offensive of their own. Peter B. Porter and two others petitioned General James Wilkinson (who had become commander in the lake region) to allow them to launch an attack into the Ontario Peninsula. If the United States would finance this expedition, they guaranteed to raise 1,000 volunteers and large numbers of militiamen to clear the British out of the eastern tip of the Peninsula. Wilkinson gave them permission, and they proceeded to assemble their force. Colonel Winfield Scott, a regular, watched them depart Fort George. A determined enemy, he said, would easily annihilate them, for many men had joined only to loot. Whatever the quality of Scott's estimate, which was of course a biased one, the expedition had one brush with the enemy, in which it sustained a few casualties, but otherwise did nothing of note.[23]

George McClure, brigadier general of New York militia, was the United States commander at Fort George. Late in September 1813 he issued a call for volunteers to serve for two months. Men with scruples against serving in Canada need not apply. The response to his call was thin indeed, and some of the volunteers remained at hand only long enough to receive the $2.00 bounty McClure offered, after which they decamped.[24]

Late in October, General Harrison reached the Niagara theater. He at once felt heavy pressure to lead an expedition against the British at the head of the lake. He agreed and set 15 November as the day for launching his campaign. Then he found that he could get naval aid from neither Chauncey nor Elliott. He thereupon refused to proceed with the plan. When on 9 November he was ordered by Secretary Armstrong to go to Sackett's Harbor, the hope of a thrust from Fort George seemed at an end once and for all. Nevertheless McClure begged the general to make an attempt before obeying the order. Harrison was virtually won over once more when on 14 November Commodore Chauncey appeared, bearing orders to take all the regulars on his ships to Sackett's Harbor. He would not wait. Harrison loaded 1,100 soldiers aboard the squadron and on 16 November left the Niagara theater.[25]

Upon his arrival at Sackett's Harbor late in November, General Harrison, although he was not then aware of it, was nearing the end of his military career. Offered no suitable command at Sackett's, he started southward. In Albany he met Secretary Armstrong for the first time. Passing on down the Hudson River, he received scant attention in New York City. Next he traveled to Washington. He found the political mood unfriendly to him there and the President was too ill to receive him. Harrison left on 22 December for Cincinnati.[26]

His pride was continually jolted. Jacob Brown and George Izard were both promoted to major general and given the important commands to the northward, although both of them were junior to Harrison. Secretary Armstrong appeared to be doing everything in his power to force Harrison to resign. He issued orders directly to Harrison's subordinates without bothering even to inform the general. Harrison protested but the practice continued. Finally, in April 1814 the War Department ordered him to render a full accounting of all supplies purchased in his district. It hinted a suspicion that he had profited personally from them. Smarting from the series of indignities, Harrison tendered his resignation on 11 May 1814. Secretary Armstrong accepted it without waiting to consult the President. Almost at once he offered the vacated commission to Andrew Jackson. When President Madison returned to Washington, he learned of this episode for the first time, but chose to let it stand. Harrison's resignation became effective at the end of May, at which date the command of the Eighth Military District passed to Duncan McArthur.[27]

Norfolk County in Upper Canada seemed to attract renegades of various sorts. Some of them sacked the little town of Dover. Certain notorious deserters from the Canadian cause were identified among the looters. Their rendezvous was known, and in November a party of Canadian militia, under Captain John Bostwick, set out to capture them. Bostwick and Lieutenant Jonathan Austin walked boldly into the house where they were gathered, and were set upon. This gave several columns of militiamen a chance to converge upon the house, overpower the occupants, and take 18 prisoners. Four of them, John Dunham, Adam Crysler, Dayton Lindsay, and George Peacock were hanged as traitors on 20 July 1814. The elimination of this band enabled General Vincent to keep his hold at Burlington.[28]

On the American side, General McClure found it increasingly difficult to keep a garrison at Fort George. He even offered illegal bounties to militiamen who would stay on duty, but he could not stem the drain. Secretary Armstrong would neither employ Indians, as McClure requested, nor send any of the regulars from winter quarters near Lake Champlain to strengthen Fort George. Early in November the American militiamen left Fort George when their terms expired. McClure complained that his militiamen had been ruined by neglect on the part of both the state and the nation. Upon discovering that they were to be discharged without pay, they became no better than a mob. Unable to hold the fort with the hundred men remaining, he made plans to evacuate it and burn it down.[29]

But before he did so, his attention was distracted to the village of Newark, which contained about 150 homes. As early as 4 October 1813 Secretary Armstrong had given him permission to destroy the hamlet if this was necessary to the defense of the fort. Now, on 10 December, with a British force approaching Fort George, McClure put the fate of the place to a council of war, and the council voted to destroy it. It was zero weather when the inhabitants were given a few hours' notice to clear out. Then their homes went up in flames. The British detachment quickened its pace and drew so close that McClure dared not take time to destroy the fort. He hurriedly spiked the cannon, threw them into the ditch, and then scrambled across into the United States. Thus the village of Newark was destroyed, but Fort George was left standing.[30]

McClure said he destroyed the town to deny shelter to the British army, but he left tents for 1,500 men pitched close by. Lieutenant General Sir Gordon Drummond, the new British commander, demanded to know from him whether the burning of Newark had been authorized by the United States government. McClure replied that he was accountable only to the American authorities, and would not answer Drummond. He cited as precedents for what he had done the British destruction of Havre de Grace and Frenchtown. Not satisfied by these interchanges, the British commanders prepared to obtain revenge.[31]

On 18 December 1813 about 560 British regulars with scaling ladders and axes landed three miles from Fort Niagara. At ten o'clock that night a detachment of them surprised the men of the advanced American picket in a tavern at Youngstown. They extorted the watchword from them and then stabbed them to death. Next they surprised and dispatched the second picket in the same way. Their Lieutenant Colonel Christopher Hamilton, because he had only one leg, was the only person who rode, and his horse violated the silence by neighing loudly. The American garrison however heard nothing. Indeed, Captain Nathaniel Leonard, the commander there, was asleep with his family in a farmhouse two miles distant. At 1:45 A.M. in the zero weather the attackers listened to the sounds of the gate of the fort being opened, the drawbridge let down, and the guard being changed. A select few of them advanced, gave the password, and then strangled the sentry. The column now charged swiftly over the drawbridge and took the fort with slight resistance. The attackers lost 6 men killed, 5 wounded, the defenders 65 killed, 12 wounded, and 344 captured. Twenty-seven cannon, 3,000 stands of arms, and quantities of blankets, stores, and shoes were also captured. After destroying the houses close by, Colonel John Murray left 500 men to garrison Fort Niagara and crossed with the balance of his command to the British side of the river. At the same time he fired a signal cannon to alert Major General Phineas Riall. Riall then embarked from Queenston and laid Lewistown waste. Resistance was light except for a company of 40 Canadian volunteers, attached to the United States cause, who fought a stubborn rear guard action for two days. Meanwhile the Indians ranged far and wide to plunder and burn. General Drummond in fact deplored the Indian depredations, but the Americans charged him with having incited them. A panic gripped the American countryside.[32]

McClure and other local officers now did their best to encourage the New York militiamen to arise and defend their hearths. He issued a call from Buffalo for the local militia to come out en masse. Most of them, however, were more concerned to take care of their own families, and too short-sighted to see that only cohesive military action could save them. Thus by 21 December only 400 men had answered the call. Plaintively McClure wrote to Governor Tompkins, "Will not the government help soon?"[33]

By this time McClure had lost his authority, and some of the militia officers flatly refused to work with him any longer. Major General Amos Hall of the New York militia superseded him. Hall made his headquarters at Batavia, thirty miles east of Buffalo, where there was a state arsenal. Here he collected men, tried to outfit them, and sent them to Buffalo or Black Rock. But the militia in the Niagara theater had stood so many drafts and had been away from home so much that they would not turn out willingly. Nevertheless, by 27 December there were around 2,000 of them—at least 500 of whom were Canadians, or Americans living in Canada—milling around Buffalo. General Hall went to that place and found confusion rife, arms scarce, and men unattached.[34]

When the British advanced toward Black Rock, Hall sent 4 battalions, loosely thrown together, to oppose them; but after firing a few rounds these battalions melted away. Their defection left the general on the morning of 30 December with only 1,200 men. He paraded them very early and set them to making cartridges as fast as they could. The British force, about 965 regulars and 400 Indians, attacked before noon. Half of Hall's men stood their ground with the "shady coolness of veterans," but the rest broke ranks and ran. They would not rally, although here and there knots of men held together and gave a good account of themselves. Lieutenant John Seely, a carpenter and an artillery officer in the militia, fought his cannon until only 7 men and 1 horse remained, then hitched the horse to the piece and retreated, still pausing from time to time to fire a round. But the American force had lost its cohesion. Hall said, "experience proves that with militia a retreat becomes a flight, and the battle once ended the army is dissipated."[35]

When the British had dispersed the American citizen soldiery, they burned Black Rock and Buffalo and five war vessels that had been part of Perry's fleet. Drummond had ordered Riall to restrain the Indians, but they ran wild. Hall could do nothing but attempt, with 300 men, to cover the flight of civilians. Consternation replaced all order in the militia organization, and the Niagara frontier lay naked before the invader.[36]

The Southeast

Even before the war all observers recognized the great military importance of the Gulf coast and especially of New Orleans. Captain John Shaw, naval commander at New Orleans, felt that his force was not equal to his risks. In the fall of 1812 he purchased *Remittance* and renamed it *Louisiana*, but he implored the secretary of the navy to raise some crews on the Atlantic coast and send them to him. He could not find the men on the Gulf to sail his vessels. He would dispatch brigs *Syren*, *Viper*, and *Enterprise* to cruise along the coast if they could be manned. *Syren* finally put to sea with 140 men after 52 had been drafted from the gunboats. The 11 active gunboats had to be widely scattered: 2 of them regularly convoyed military stores to Fort Stoddert, 3 were at Bay St. Louis, Cat Island, and Rigolets, and 1 was westward of New Orleans on pirate patrol. Twenty-three had recently been lost in a hurricane.[1]

The army commander, Brigadier General Wade Hampton, maintained his headquarters at Baton Rouge. He and Shaw got along well enough, but neither of them had authority over the other. In July 1811 Hampton was ordered to build a road from Muscle Shoals to Fort Stoddert, another from Stoddert to Benjamin Hawkins' Creek Agency on the Flint River, and a third from Stoddert to Baton Rouge. The purpose of this web of roads was to open up the land from the Pearl to the Perdido rivers.[2]

In the early spring of 1812 the administration for some reason determined to transfer the military command to Brigadier General James Wilkinson, Hampton's long-time enemy. Wilkinson had been a rising officer during the American Revolution and had had a minor part in both the Conway Cabal and the Newburgh Addresses. After the Revolution he served at some time or other on almost all of America's boundaries. On the southern frontier he established a lucrative connection with the government of Spain. For an annual retainer's fee he agreed to keep Spain informed on what the United States was doing in the borderlands. Even when elevated to brigadier general and made commander of the United States Army, he continued in the pay of Spain, but never in fact transmitted to her enough information to earn his fee. This connection was suspected and investigated several times, but he was always acquitted for lack of evidence. When Aaron Burr appeared in the West, Wilkinson became involved with him too, but the risk grew so great that he elected to inform against Burr, of course in such a way as to vindicate himself. In spite of all suspicions and machinations, he remained senior general of the United States Army until the outbreak of the War of 1812.[3]

Because he had economic and family interests in the Gulf region, Wilkinson was delighted to take command there. His orders reached him in Washington, and he immediately asked the secretary for clarification. Was he allowed to follow his own judgment in defending the area? Was he authorized to take Mobile and Pensacola when the moment was right? He told the President at the same time of the force he believed necessary. No less than four of the heaviest naval vessels ought to be lifted over the bar at the mouth of the Mississippi, and put into operation on the river. Needed, too, would be 40 gunboats, 6 steamers, 10,000 regulars, and 3,500 militia. The 28 companies already there, totaling 1,680 men, could not by any stretch of the imagination defend a line 600 miles long. Nine days after his appointment, his new command was enlarged to include Tennessee, Louisiana, and Mississippi Territory and was designated the Seventh Military District.[4]

When Wade Hampton sailed out of New Orleans for Baltimore on 20 May 1812, Wilkinson was still in Washington. Not until 9 July did he finally reach New Orleans and bring there the first knowledge of the declaration of war. He hastened to confer with William C. C. Claiborne, governor of the newly created state of Louisiana, and with Captain John Shaw. He and Claiborne agreed that the United States must capture Mobile and Pensacola or the Spanish would incite the Indians from those points, but Claiborne added that he could not take strong measures because Louisiana had just passed from territory to state and he was governor in expectation more than reality.[5]

The general and Captain Shaw agreed on the points where New Orleans was most vulnerable to attack, but they came to loggerheads over the chain of command. Wilkinson had the following authority from the President himself: "You will be pleased to make such disposition of the troops and such arrangements respecting the fortifications, arms, ordnance, arsenals, military and other stores, as well as the *naval force,* as your judgment may suggest." On the basis of this he issued a direct order to Shaw. Shaw replied that he would do whatever the general wanted done, but that he would resign before taking orders from an army officer. Wilkinson now wrote out ten pages in his own hand to demonstrate that the flotilla was under his orders, while Shaw expended nearly as much ink complaining to the secretary of the navy. Shaw felt, he said, "an unconquerable repugnance . . . to a deviation from the antient usages of my profession and the inevitable destruction to everything like order or discipline among naval officers. . . . Nothing of the kind has ever before been heard or thought of . . . however eminently skilled a military officer may be in the profession of arms, if he be arrayed in the amphibious garb of a naval-military commander, he will in acting under it be much less likely to acquire laurels than to bring disgrace on himself and the services. . . . In a word the military knows nothing about naval affairs." If he were forced to accept this humiliating subordination, he would request service aboard a frigate.[6]

A violent hurricane interrupted the dialogue on 18 August 1812. It blew the brig *Enterprise* out of water and buried 1 of the 10 gunboats in the mud. Driftwood was piled so high at Fort St. Philip that a man could walk on it right over the parapet. Meanwhile, the British frigate *Southampton* hovered off the mouth of the river, outside the bar, and the officers on duty at Balize and Fort St. Philip expected attack hourly.[7]

When he could pick up the controversy again, Wilkinson charged Captain Shaw with the statement that even the President had not the power to order a naval officer to serve under an army officer. Shaw had reached a "state of perfect imbecility," and the general refused to have further correspondence with him. In the end Shaw had to knuckle under. He did not resign, but never ceased to lament. When Wilkinson was away, he came under the orders of subordinate army officers. His ships, he said, "were ordered by the military chief from place to place as he thinks proper, while I have become the mere trumpet of his will and pleasure." Wilkinson, for his part, complained of the naval posture at New Orleans. Defense there depended upon fixed batteries, whereas, if Shaw had been more efficient, it could have more safely depended on ships.[8]

Wilkinson himself acted with energy and rather good strategic sense. He inspected the forts downriver, ordered them repaired, and detached some men to establish a new post at Balize. He also looked to the security of the Rigolets, which like Balize was a sensitive pass toward the city. From his own viewpoint, however, he could not do enough to offset local carelessness.[9]

The administration cautioned both Wilkinson and Shaw to be delicate in dealing with Spanish officials. Close to rupture with England, it did not want to break also with Spain. Nevertheless the provocations in the Gulf region were very great, and the pressures from the population became too heavy. "Patriots" in West Florida had revolted against Spain, and they negotiated with President Madison to be annexed. The United States occupied the terrain as far east as the Pearl River, and claimed to the Perdido but did not take possession. The occupied portion was incorporated first into Orleans Territory, and then into the state of Louisiana. This aggrandizement, including admitting Louisiana, brought threats from New England. Leaders there said that to make such an addition to the nation was a violation of the Constitution and grounds for dissolving the Union. But they did not quite secede.

William C. C. Claiborne, who, being a good Jeffersonian, had been appointed governor of Mississippi Territory in 1801, became in 1812, at the age of thirty-seven, governor of the new state of Louisiana. Where adjacent Spanish territories were concerned, he was an expansionist. "Cuba," he said, "is the real mouth of the Mississippi, and the nation possessing it can at any time command the trade of the western states. Give us Cuba and the American Union is placed beyond the reach of change."[10] To provision Fort Stoddert, he continued to pass supply vessels up the Mobile River through Spanish territory over the protest of Spanish officials. Moreover, he let it be known that interference with the passage would bring bloodshed. As far as he was concerned, the fact that the upper waters of the Mobile River ran in American territory gave to the United States the right to navigate the entire waterway, except at Mobile. Mobile remained Spanish, but the United States had to protect it from occasional private armies. Claiborne longed for express sanction from the administration for his conduct, but in its absence he persisted in his course.

Using the web of roads built by General Hampton in 1811, the United States now tried to occupy the land from the Pearl River to the Perdido. One problem lay in the fact that there were not enough persons at once loyal and literate to fill the public offices. Responsibility to fill them fell first to Governor Claiborne, who left no stone unturned. He even sent Captain Edmund P. Gaines an unsolicited commission to be the federal judge in the Pascagoula area, on the mere rumor that the captain was quitting the military service. Claiborne's responsibility ended when the area was transferred to Mississippi Territory. During the first week of September 1812 Governor David Holmes designated it as Mobile County of the Territory of Mississippi.[11]

While the rebellion took place in West Florida, the Madison administration encouraged one in East Florida. General George Mathews and Colonel John McKee of Georgia were appointed agents of the nation to receive any posts east of the Perdido tendered to them by revolutionaries. Colonel Thomas Adams Smith, USA, directed to cooperate with these two, advanced into the vicinity of St. Augustine, ostensibly to guard the patriots against attack from Spain. General Mathews, convinced that he was under orders to abet the insurgents, did his best to involve the United States Navy, under Captain Hugh Campbell, stationed at the mouth of the St. Marys River. As Mathews increased his pressure, Campbell pleaded with the secretary of the navy for instructions. Lacking these, he refused all aid at first, but in March 1812 positioned two gunboats at Fernandina on Amelia Island, he said, to avoid spilling blood. Just at this moment Mathews asserted that he had received cession from the revolutionaries of all of East Florida except St. Augustine. He therefore asked for a squadron of gunboats, not to assist actively in reducing the fort at St. Augustine, but to intercept aid to the garrison. Campbell sent *Vixen* and two gunboats, this time only to "observe."[12]

Relations with England now grew too delicate to risk offending Spain any further. Accordingly, on 4 April Secretary of State James Monroe charged Mathews with exceeding his instructions, through excess zeal, and relieved him of his command. Secretary Hamilton fired off orders to Captain Campbell to withdraw any aid he might mistakenly have afforded Mathews, and to get his ships out of Spanish waters. These orders rendered the captain, "the happiest of mortals and relieved [him] from a state of anxiety." He began at once "with pride and pleasure to carry into effect the orders of our much beloved President."[13]

Campbell's withdrawal, however, did not end American involvement. Avoiding the appearance of official participation, the administration still managed to maintain American troops on Spanish soil between the St. Marys River and St. Augustine. Spanish officials on 16 May 1812 launched a half-hearted attack on Colonel Smith's bivouac at Moosa Old Fort, just north of St. Augustine. It failed. Next, Spanish Governor Sebastian Kindelan arrived at St. Augustine on 11 June with Negro troops to reinforce the garrison. His Negro soldiers were an affront to the white people and harmed instead of helped the Spanish cause. Colonel Smith received orders to hold his ground and if attacked to advance against St. Augustine. Not long afterwards he laid siege to the place.

Meanwhile the House of Representatives conformed to the desires of the administration by passing on 25 June a bill to annex all of Florida. That same day news of the declaration of war reached Campbell. He now began to detain English vessels, and by 18 July he had impounded eight. Affairs seemed to be progressing, from President Madison's point of view, until on 3 July the United States Senate defeated the House annexation bill 16 to 14. Even this did not kill the hopes of the administration. Three days after the Senate's action Monroe wrote Governor David Mitchell of Georgia, who was General Mathews' successor, that the President thought it advisable to remove the troops from Florida, but tacitly contradicted this intent throughout the balance of the letter. Perfectly able to read between the lines, Mitchell replied, "I have carefully avoided making any proposition for withdrawing the troops under the fullest conviction that such a step was not intended."[14]

The unofficial posture arranged so cozily in Washington was uncomfortable in the extreme for Colonel Thomas Smith. Some of his men were too ill to be moved except by litters on water, and since his supply line was cut, with Campbell's withdrawal, he had to give up the siege of St. Augustine and retire toward the St. Johns River. Less restrained by public policy was Colonel Daniel Newnan of the Georgia militia, who was in northeast Florida with a militia force. His men had used up their tour of duty getting to Florida and would not be persuaded to extend it even one day. They were suffering from the climate and from hunger. Newnan made his master pitch at Picolata in September to gather a detachment to penetrate the fertile and abundant "Aulotchewan" country to the west. His promises of grants of land in the area to be invaded at length drew to him 117 men. With these, ill-equipped but hopeful of subsisting on loot, he started out on 24 September 1812. His march order was good and on Sunday 27 September he surprised a party of 75 Indians. There followed a firefight of two and one-half hours, before the Indians slipped away into the swamp behind them. Newnan had lost 3 men killed and 7 wounded, and Indian losses were thought also to be high. The red leader, King Payne, had been knocked from his white horse, and the invaders had seen him carried away. By night the Indian force seemed twice as large as Georgia's. Newnan threw up a breastwork and sent runners to Smith for help.[15]

For fourteen days Newnan's men battled against annihilation. Dissension arose among them, and supplies ran out. It was necessary to eat their horses, then gophers, alligators, and cabbage palms. Relief parties from Colonel Smith had been searching for some days, but the first group to locate them was a detachment of 14 mounted men. These supplied limited quantities of food, and helped Newnan's men fight their way back to the St. Johns. There they arrived on 11 October, 18 days out, a total of 8 men killed, 9 wounded, 8 missing, and the survivors lucky to have escaped annihilation.

Colonels Smith and Newnan fell out for a brief period, then forgot their differences and united in their mutual desire to send a second punitive expedition against the Seminoles. But, in spite of the arrival of scanty reinforcements from Georgia under General John Floyd, they were never able to get a column into motion. Meanwhile the state of Georgia seemed stirred up enough to proceed against Spain and the Florida Indians with or without the consent or aid of the United States. Mitchell, still federal commander in the Southeast, told Smith as late as 13 October that if he would capture St. Augustine, he, Mitchell, would defend him. Like many southerners he believed that victories could be won in Florida, which would offset the dismal sequence of failures in the North. Southern militiamen, he said, would not cavil at crossing the international boundary.[16]

Northward, in Tennessee, events had taken place which were to bear upon the future of Florida. From the first moment of hostilities, Andrew Jackson of Tennessee had hankered to be included in the war effort. Since 1802, when the legislature had chosen him in preference to John Sevier, he had been a major general of Tennessee militia. But, except as a boy during the Revolution, he had neither seen combat nor led troops in anything but drill. His practical experience as a soldier was negligible, and his theoretical knowledge even more so. At all times, on the other hand, he was entirely in favor of war against England and eager for personal military glory. The nature of his mood is seen in the rousing call he had issued for volunteers three months before war had been declared.

> Citizens! Your government has yielded to the impulse of the nation. . . . War is on the point of breaking out . . . and the martial hosts are summoned to the Tented Fields!
> A simple invitation is given . . . [for] 50,000 volunteers. . . . Shall we who have clamoured for war, now skulk into a corner? . . . Are we the titled Slaves of George the third? the military conscripts of Napoleon? or the frozen peasants of the Russian Czar? No—we are the free born sons . . . of the only republic now existing in the world. . . .
> Are we going to fight to satisfy the revenge or ambition of a corrupt ministry? to place another diadem on the head of an apostate republican general? . . . No . . . we are going to fight for the reestablishment of our national character . . . for the protection of our maritime citizens, to indicate our right to free trade. . . .
> The period of youth is the season for martial exploits; and how pleasing the prospect . . . to . . . *promenade* into a distant country and [witness] the grand evolutions of an army of fifty or sixty thousand men.[17]

As soon as Jackson learned of the declaration of war he wrote directly to the secretary of war offering his division to invade Canada. Within ninety days, he claimed, he could have his army before the walls of Quebec. The administration never replied to his offer. It did not choose to forget that he had given comfort to Aaron Burr during his western exploit in 1806. Neither Jackson nor Tennessee was invited to participate in defeating Britain.[18]

Finally on 21 October 1812 Tennessee received her first call. It directed that 1,500 men should go, not to Canada, but to New Orleans. The state would have to provide tents for its 1,500, but the United States at once sent forward guns for them. When the muskets arrived, they created that rare condition, a surplus of weapons for a militia army. As a result, men who were willing to burden themselves could carry two shoulder guns, their own and one of the federal muskets.[19]

The governor was empowered to appoint contractors and to draw bills on the War Department to cover expenses. The fact that the expedition was to be under a brigadier instead of a major general almost excluded Jackson, but he did not rest until he was accepted with his present grade. Thereafter he threw himself violently into details of preparation.[20]

Ostensibly the Tennessee brigade was to help General Wilkinson defend New Orleans, but Jackson and the field officers knew that its real purpose was to invade Florida. Such a purpose suited the general perfectly. "I am now at the head of 2,070 volunteers," he wrote, "the choicest of our citizens, who go at the call of their country to execute the will of the government, who have not constitutional scruples, and, if the government orders, will rejoice at the opportunity of placing the American eagle on the ramparts of Mobile, Pensacola, and St. Augustine, effectually banishing from the Southern coasts the British influence."[21]

Although Andrew Jackson could not know it, his project was even then endangered in Washington. During most of November the administration inclined to avoid irritating Spain. It relieved Governor Mitchell of the command in the southeast, and transferred it to General Thomas Pinckney, a convenient Federalist, a reliable Revolutionary veteran, who at age sixty-two was brought out of retirement to carry out the policy of Spanish appeasement. This left Colonel Smith in a weak condition, and when late in November his regular riflemen and dragoons were ordered northward, he was reduced to a nominal force, precariously camped upon the territory of a hostile power.[22]

By the last week in November, President Madison was once more willing to try the hard line in Florida. He ordered Pinckney to concentrate all forces south of Virginia at Point Peter in Georgia. At the same time the secretary of the navy told Captain Hugh Campbell to take orders from General Pinckney in order to expedite the invasion. Campbell reacted as Shaw had done at New Orleans, but he obeyed.[23]

Friends of the administration once more brought before the Senate a request that the United States occupy all of Florida. The Senate in December passed a resolution to that effect.

Meanwhile, the Tennessee brigade had finally assembled at Nashville on 10 December 1812. It consisted of two infantry regiments, with 700 men in each, one commanded by Thomas Hart Benton, the other by William Hall, and a cavalry regiment, 670 strong, under John Coffee. Jackson complained about serving under Wilkinson, and said that his men did too, but he continued with his preparations nonetheless, determined to make the best of his chance to get into the fight. Thus, on the last day of the year 1812, Governor Willie Blount sent off the final order for him to proceed toward New Orleans. "May the God of battles and the Supreme Ruler of the universe," he wrote, "aid and protect you and each of your valiant volunteers acting in the righteous cause of the best of governments." With this benediction the column at last began to move southward on 7 January 1813. The infantry boarded small flatboats on the Cumberland River and began a long, roundabout journey amidst floating ice and in bitter cold. Coffee's mounted volunteers traveled down the Natchez Trace to rendezvous with the infantry at Natchez. The infantry reached that place on 15 February, 39 days out, to find the cavalry waiting for them. At Natchez Jackson found an order from General Wilkinson dated 22 January directing him to halt there. He replied amiably that he agreed with the reasons given for the delay, and could therefore depart from the order Governor Blount had given him to go straight to New Orleans. He announced his force willing to cooperate in any way to defend the lower country. "To this end," he said, "my eyes are turned to the southeast."[24]

Wilkinson had asked for a reinforcement of 1,500 men under a brigadier general, and he was not eager to have more than that descend upon him, particularly when they were commanded by Andrew Jackson. The two had been on opposite sides of the Burr affair, and Wilkinson knew that Jackson was not easy to manage. Nor does he seem to have been informed of the true mission of the Tennessee brigade. In any event, he did not want them around New Orleans. To begin with, they would overtax his resource base, and in the second place, it was dangerous for 2,000 undisciplined militiamen to be "turned loose on this licentious community, far removed from . . . social restraints." Finally, Wilkinson wanted to remain in the Gulf area, and he thought that Jackson's presence there might dislodge him.[25]

Meanwhile, the mood had once more changed in Washington. Those opposing a policy that would antagonize Spain again gained control. Senator Samuel Smith of Maryland on 2 February 1813 proposed that only West Florida be occupied. By a sectional vote of 19 to 16 the Senate reversed its December resolution and supported Smith. Accordingly, during the first week in February orders went out to halt the Tennessee brigade.[26]

Jackson and his men remained restlessly in bivouac near Natchez for three weeks. Then he received an order from John Armstrong, dated 6 February, Armstrong's second day in office: "Sir: The causes of embodying and marching to New Orleans the corps under your command having ceased to exist, you will, on receipt of this letter, consider it as dismissed from public service, and take measures to have delivered to Major General Wilkinson all the articles of public property which may have been put into its possession." Enraged by this cold letter, Jackson wrote directly to the President. He reminded him that he had volunteered the services of Tennessee citizen soldiers at the very start of the war, and had since labored to train and discipline them properly. They soon stood ready to take the field for their nation, "To defend hur [sic] rights and repel hur Enemies without Constitutional scruples of any boundaries." When finally ordered to march in December, "It was Columbia's true sons who had walked forth." What was their reward? To be dismissed from the service 800 miles from home and told to get back the best way they could. He could not believe, Jackson continued, that the President had seen the order. He intended to disobey it, and would continue his men in United States service until they had marched back to Nashville, where he would discharge them.[27]

The return march of the frustrated Tennesseans began late in March and proceeded at eighteen miles a day. Finally, on 22 May Jackson dismissed his men in Nashville, without their having seen an enemy. Meanwhile, President Madison had approved of his conduct, and the men were promptly paid off, each of them permitted to keep a government musket. From the march back and from his unswerving determination to take care of his men, Jackson earned the nickname of "Old Hickory."[28]

With the threat of Jackson removed, General Wilkinson entered some complaints against his predecessor in command of the Seventh Military District. Hampton had left the district in bad shape and had failed to turn over any record of the disposition of the troops there. Wilkinson complained too of the Louisiana legislature, which seemed to be taking Massachusetts and Connecticut as examples. As late as August 1812 it had not bothered to enact a militia law. Nor would it permit him to enlist colored volunteers, of which he could immediately have procured 1,000. In general, he saw no energy in the legislature to undertake seriously the defense of the region.[29]

On 28 August 1812 General Wilkinson convened a council of officials to consider whether or not he had the power to seize Pensacola and Mobile. Governor Claiborne and two army officers said he possessed it, but Captain Shaw and three army officers said he did not. It happened that two days earlier the secretary of war had settled the matter, but the word took some time to reach its destination. He ordered Wilkinson to avoid creating incidents which might endanger the city and to leave the two Spanish towns alone.[30]

In 1812 the United States had added the land from the Pearl to the Perdido rivers to Mississippi Territory, but General Wilkinson received orders actually to occupy it only on 14 March 1813. He and Captain

Shaw set out joyfully to take Mobile. On 11 April, Shaw landed 400 men three miles below Fort Charlotte, which guarded that city. In the evening of 14 April Shaw anchored five of his gunboats in a close line 200 yards from the fort. The men who had been landed below now joined with 200 more, and these formed a column in front of the fort. On 15 April Wilkinson sent in a summons to surrender, and the Spanish commander, who had 50 cannon but only 80 men, complied. Thereafter General Wilkinson reconnoitered the entire area the United States had taken over and made note of places which needed his attention.[31]

He returned to New Orleans to find that the administration had imposed the strictest economy on the Gulf region. From the general's point of view, the need for money was greater rather than less. In front of him lay the Gulf of Mexico, virtually a British domain, behind him were the menacing Creeks, while to his right and left were the Choctaws and the Seminoles, both of them potential foes. He estimated that to defend the new territory he needed 2,000 more men, and 15 heavy gunboats. Captain Shaw set the number of vessels required at 41, but on 1 March 1813 he received an order to inactivate all but 13 small ships. The administration forbade both him and Wilkinson to incur major expenses without prior permission. Wilkinson had begun indispensable defensive works at New Orleans, the Perdido, Mobile Bay, the English Turn, and at the Balize, but he was obliged by direct order of the President, he said, to halt them.[32]

James Wilkinson

When General James Wilkinson had been nine months at New Orleans, Secretary Armstrong wrote him an order, dated 10 March 1813, to turn the command of the Seventh Military District over to Brigadier General Thomas J. Flournoy and to proceed at once to General Dearborn's headquarters. He accompanied the order with a friendly letter to come quickly "where the laurel grows, and where we may renew the scene of Saratoga." (The two had been associated at that great moment during the Revolution.) He soon sent along a commission (dated 2 March 1813) to be major general, thus ending Wilkinson's twenty years as brigadier general.[1]

Armstrong's motives for bringing Wilkinson into the principal theater of war are still in dispute. Henry Adams claimed that the senators from Louisiana, Tennessee, and Kentucky insisted that Wilkinson be taken out of the New Orleans command. He also asserted that Armstrong knew his man too well to intend for him any higher position than division commander under General Dearborn. These allegations may be correct, but there is another way of looking at the same facts. Armstrong could not very well relieve Dearborn until he had on hand a successor for him. He may, too, have had full confidence in his Revolutionary War crony. Finally, no less a person than Governor Isaac Shelby of Kentucky had recommended Wilkinson as the most suitable person for the vital northeastern command.

Armstrong's transfer order did not reach Wilkinson until 19 May. Meanwhile, the secretary unaccountably continued to send the general words of caution about the New Orleans area. Wilkinson finally got started toward Washington on 10 June, accompanied by his pregnant wife and her sister. Their progress by land was perforce slow and did not get them to the capital until 31 July.[2]

Somehow during the five months since Wilkinson had been ordered north, the decision had been made to place him in command of Military District Number Nine (western Pennsylvania, New York north of the Highlands, and Vermont). The very day of his arrival in Washington he was given that assignment. Before leaving Washington, he proposed an attack in the Niagara region. The secretary vetoed it. Armstrong, remembering the doleful results of the first variation from his strategy, insisted this time that the thrust be directed against the main British artery, not one of the veins. Accordingly, he gave Wilkinson a choice of two objectives: Kingston or Montreal. If the general chose Kingston, he could either attack it directly or run down the St. Lawrence far enough to choke off its support on the river. If he chose Montreal, he would work in conjunction with another army of 4,500 men stationed around Plattsburg and commanded by his arch enemy Wade Hampton. In this case, Hampton would operate under Wilkinson's orders, and the navy would protect the line of advance along the St. Lawrence. Whenever Wilkinson saw the British concentrating their strength, he was to strike at some other point.[3]

Because President Madison was deathly ill during most of the summer of 1813, his principal officers exercised a great deal of authority. Secretary Armstrong, for example, rode northward with General Wilkinson and virtually took the command post of the army with

Major General James Wilkinson

him. The secretary and the general reached Sackett's Harbor on 20 August. Armstrong said he had come north to moderate between Hampton and Wilkinson, but there is some evidence that he intended in fact to combine his function as secretary of war with that of commanding general. His detractors, too, assert that he sought the rank of lieutenant general. Ascribed to him sometimes is an anonymous note which appeared in an Albany newspaper when the campaign was concluded. "If the genius which marked the outlines of this campaign had showed in its execution, it might have pointed to the individual to be lieutenant general." There is no doubt that the broad outlines of the campaign came from him, and that for a time he himself made the critical strategic decisions in the field.[4]

Wade Hampton, aged sixty-two, was commissioned major general at the same time as Wilkinson. He had performed daring exploits with Thomas Sumter during the southern partisan campaigns of the American Revolution. After the war he left the military service and lived for twenty-five years as a civilian. He opposed the adoption of the Constitution in 1788, but later held elective offices under it. Inflamed by the *Chesapeake-Leopard* incident, he re-entered the military service in 1808 with the rank of colonel. The next year he was promoted to brigadier.[5]

Hampton protested his subordination to Wilkinson and claimed that he had been promised a separate command. His distaste for this connection was so strong that he asked to be allowed to resign from the service. A colloquy between him and the secretary followed; they seemed to get nowhere, but when Armstrong appeared in person in August, he somehow prevented Hampton from resigning. While there, the secretary argued for a descent of the Richelieu (Sorel) River and an attack on Isle aux Noix. Hampton insisted that the enemy was too strong. As the navy commander on Lake Champlain, Thomas Macdonough agreed with him. After Armstrong left, the general concentrated his 4,000 men at Cumberland Head, five miles below Plattsburg, and Macdonough based himself nearby. Together they assumed that they had put a stopper on the lake.[6]

When General Wilkinson arrived at Sackett's Harbor, he found most of his forces clustered at the extreme east and west ends of his Ninth Military District. In spite of Armstrong's directives, the general examined all of his opportunities. He believed that the line of the St. Lawrence River was especially open to attack, but that he had neither enough men nor enough river transports to assail it. This turned his attention to the other end of the district. A council of war made up of Major General Morgan Lewis, Quartermaster Robert Swartwout,

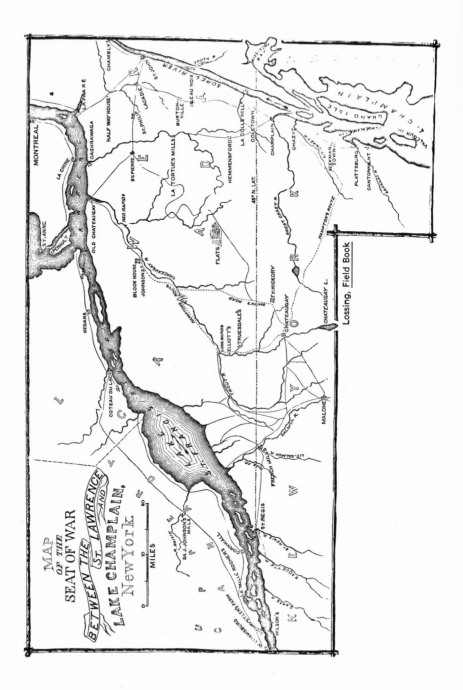

MAP
OF THE
SEAT OF WAR
BETWEEN THE
ST. LAWRENCE AND
LAKE CHAMPLAIN,
New York.

MILES

Lossing, Field Book

Brigadier General Jacob Brown, and Commodore Isaac Chauncey convened on 26 August to examine the prospects to the westward. These men estimated 3,500 American versus 2,000 British troops in the vicinity of Fort George, but they voted against an attack there.[7]

Wilkinson now went to Fort George to see the situation for himself. He did not like what he saw. "This place," he wrote Armstrong on 20 September, "neither stops a gap, extends our possession, nor covers or protects a country; it is good for naught but to command the ground it occupies, and therefore I shall dismantle and abandon it." The secretary quickly vetoed this idea. Wilkinson was doubtless right, but Fort George was at that moment the only American possession on Canadian soil. Armstrong did authorize, however, the removal of regular troops, and directed the general to turn to Peter B. Porter for the defense of the area with Indians and local militiamen. Writing twenty-seven years later, Armstrong berated Wilkinson for removing the regulars and did not then mention that he had agreed to it. On 22 September 1813 he wrote a letter which is difficult to explain other than as duplicity. He suggested to William Henry Harrison that Harrison come to Niagara, where Wilkinson would be subject to his orders. When Armstrong's conduct toward Harrison and Wilkinson at this time is considered, this particular bit of behavior is nearly impossible to interpret.[8]

Secretary Armstrong stated years later in his *Notices* that both Chauncey and Wilkinson wanted to keep the fleet at the western end of Lake Ontario in the fall of 1813. If so, it constituted an about-face for Chauncey, who had never been willing to stay away from Sackett's Harbor for any length of time. In any case, attention now turned to the source of the St. Lawrence River and the course of that river to Montreal. On 18 September, Armstrong told Wilkinson that if "Kingston or the point below [is] seized, all above perishes, because the tree is then girdled." The general appeared to concur in this and began to concentrate his troops on Grenadier Island, about half-way from Sackett's Harbor to Kingston. Here arrived the regulars from Fort George. At the same time, however, he was procuring keelboats and making other arrangements to proceed against Montreal rather than Kingston. Chauncey promised, with characteristic reservations, to protect the bivouac on Grenadier.[9]

On 5 October the secretary issued an ambiguous directive which he said had been produced in a council consisting of himself, Wilkinson, Jacob Brown, and Morgan Lewis. "If the British fleet shall not escape Commodore Chauncey and get into Kingston harbor," it read, "if the garrison of that place be not largely reinforced; and if the weather be such as will allow us to navigate the lake securely, Kingston shall be our first objective, otherwise we shall go directly to Montreal. . . ." Whether General Wilkinson could see through all the conditional clauses in the order or not, he at this time much preferred Kingston as the strategic objective. On 9 October he advised Chauncey that he would move toward Kingston the next day if the squadron would aid him. Chauncey could not help in this case, but almost testily affirmed his willingness to enter joint undertakings. "I will observe," he wrote, "that this squadron is now and always has been ready to cooperate with the army in any enterprise against the enemy, where it could be done with effect." General DeRottenburg moved his headquarters to Kingston because he believed it would soon be attacked, but the attack never came.[10]

Formation of strategy had from the first been hampered by Wilkinson's bad health. He reached the northern theater in so feeble a state that in most services he would have been adjudged unfit for duty. An especially severe attack of fever struck him on 5 October. In its grip he desired to retire from the service, but Dr. E. W. Bull, the attending surgeon, dissuaded him. John Armstrong, too, for some reason clung to him. "I would feed the old man with pap," he is supposed to have said, "sooner than leave him behind."[11]

Still sick, General Wilkinson gave the orders on 17 October 1813 which set in motion a substantial fleet and an army of 7,000 men. At the moment of its starting, no one, not even Wilkinson, seems to have known for sure whether it was going against Kingston or Montreal. The formation for its march, however, was carefully prescribed. Eight gunboats led off, followed at a distance of 360 feet by 16 boats carrying the light artillery and the elite corps. Six hundred feet behind these came 148 boats carrying 4 brigades and a reserve. The wind blew so fiercely on this flotilla for 36 hours that 15 boats went down, and it took time to re-establish order among those remaining.[12]

Two days after his order to move out, General Wilkinson was still insisting that he intended to attack lightly garrisoned and highly vulnerable Kingston. The capture of Kingston would in effect also conquer a province (Upper Canada) and at the same time eliminate 4,000 enemy troops. It would end the Indian war and destroy the British navy on Lake Ontario. If the secretary wanted the moving column to strike Montreal rather than Kingston, he must issue a direct order using the authority of the President to that effect. Armstrong made a series of strong recommendations in favor of Montreal, but never sent the peremptory order Wilkinson required.[13]

During the last two weeks of October on some account Montreal replaced Kingston. Commodore Chauncey protested the change. The

British had prepared formidable strong points to prevent the American fleet from reaching Montreal, not to mention the existence of treacherous rapids. In other ways, too, they could defend Montreal better than Kingston, and could draw help from Quebec. The army and the navy together, he said, could capture Kingston in ten days, but the navy would not be able to give equivalent help against Montreal. Having registered all these objections, he let it be known that he would do all he could to cooperate.[14]

The extant evidence does not reveal when the decision to go for Montreal was finally made. Irving Brant says Secretary Armstrong made it but never told the President. He, or whoever else was responsible, had not studied Jeffrey Amherst's similar campaign in 1760. Amherst went down the river in July with months of open weather ahead, whereas Wilkinson was going in November when any day winter weather and ice could cripple his operations. Amherst had employed 10,000 men, but Wilkinson had only 7,000. Meanwhile the population of Canada had grown. Amherst had stopped to reduce opposing strong points, but with limited numbers and the lateness of the season, Wilkinson dared not do so. Henry Adams, writing seventy years after the event, claimed that neither Armstrong nor Wilkinson really expected to reach Montreal, that they had to make a good show and intended nothing more.[15]

Wilkinson, of course, counted on the cooperation of General Hampton. At first he made suggestions through the secretary for Hampton's movements, as he considered the latter to be under Armstrong's personal direction. But after the first week in November, when Armstrong returned to Washington, Wilkinson issued orders directly to Hampton. The orders were to join his forces with Wilkinson's at St. Regis and to bring to the rendezvous three months' rations for the combined army. Armstrong had told Wilkinson that supplies around Lake Champlain were abundant.[16]

Armstrong's reasons for leaving the theater of war have been interpreted in different ways, most of them unfavorable to him. One interpretation asserts that he saw disaster ahead and was determined to dissociate himself from it. Another claims that he had never expected the attack on Montreal to succeed and saw no need to be on hand to watch it fail. A third says that he found he could not effectively mediate between Generals Wilkinson and Hampton, and a fourth puts it that he may have begun to realize the hopelessness of his aspirations to be a lieutenant general. Whatever his reasons, his departure certainly lessened any chance of success the campaign may have had.[17]

Governor Daniel D. Tompkins of New York continued to prove himself one of the best supporters of the war effort. Within two weeks he assembled between 7,000 and 8,000 militiamen. He personally saw many of the volunteer units on their way to the theater of war, and complimented them for their patriotism, their conduct while encamped, and their soldierly appearance. Even so, the New York militia did not play a decisive role in subsequent invasion attempts. Only 250 of the men Tompkins had so praised when they started actually reached General Hampton's camp, and they were in a sickly condition. No more than 60 of them were willing to enter Canada. Hampton complained that his regulars, being raw recruits, were no better than militia, and pleaded for some veterans.[18]

General Hampton never became perfectly sure what were the strategic objectives of the campaign. First he marched north from Cumberland Head on the roads leading to the bend of the St. Lawrence just south of Montreal. Severe drought had dried up drinking water on that route, and he had to return southward and follow the Chateaugay River westward. He reached Chateaugay Four Corners on 25 September with 4,000 infantry and 500 men of supporting arms. There he could threaten both the river above the city and Montreal itself. But the countryside did not, as he had hoped, rally to him. He reported it as infected with "shameful and corrupt" neutrality. After lingering about Chateaugay for one month, he decided to move into Canada, but of the 1,000 militiamen in his army only a few consented to cross the international boundary line. He left the refusers at the border with orders to raise as much "alarm" as they could, and ordered the handful who went with him to seek out and attack the enemy's citizen soldiers.[19]

He now marched down the Chateaugay River and on 22 October entered the hamlet of Spears. His motion produced some apprehension in Montreal, which had scant military manpower to draw upon. Governor Prevost, therefore, called the sedentary militia to turn out en masse. The response was not significant, but Canada had a resource in the vicinity which the governor did not know about. Charles Michel d'Irumberry de Salaberry, lieutenant colonel of the Canadian Voltigeurs, was directing the advanced troops, consisting of about 1,400 men, most of them militia. He had reconnoitered the banks of the Chateaugay and had selected the spot where he wanted to halt the American advance. His opponent, who could not avoid this spot, spent 22–24 October moving slowly through heavy forest, harassed by Indians and light troops. Then he emerged into seven miles of open farm country. Beyond that was another forest which de Salaberry had turned into one continuous abatis. Where four more-or-less parallel ravines ran at right angles down to the river, de Salaberry had erected breastworks across the road. These, on the west bank, made up his principal defensive position. His right rested upon a swamp and his left upon the river, 40 yards wide and 6 feet deep. There was just one ford, and there he built an abatis. He also destroyed all boats in the area.[20]

Hampton marched along the road on the west bank until he bumped into the principal Canadian position. He then ordered Colonel Robert Purdy to take 1,500 men, cross the river, find the ford, recross on it, and gain the Canadian rear. Purdy, who started after 9:00 P.M. on 25 October, got lost in the darkness and never reached the ford until the afternoon of 26 October 1813. There the abatis stopped him, and the parties he sent to remove it were driven back by enfilading fire. When it became apparent that Purdy would not bring off the flanking movement, Hampton ordered General George Izard to attack the central position with the main column. Izard's men went over the first earthwork with a smart bayonet charge, but from the second line came such a din of shouting and bugles that the Americans halted, certain they were facing a host. De Salaberry had duped them. Hampton called back the assaults, but he held his position until 28 October. Meanwhile a council of his officers voted to march back into the United States and Hampton concurred. Thus ended the Battle of Chateaugay.

When the invaders had returned to the United States, they went into winter quarters. On 18 October Secretary Armstrong himself had directed the quartermaster to prepare huts for 10,000 men. They must be in Canada where the men would be subject to martial law. Hampton saw a copy of this order during the night of 25 October, as he waited for Purdy's column to complete its flank march. It raised doubts in his mind about the intention of the government to push the fall campaign to any effective military conclusion.[21]

General Prevost arrived at the scene of the Battle of Chateaugay after the action was ended. But he wrote a report to Lord Bathurst which slighted de Salaberry, and did not even mention Colonel Macdonnell who had come 170 miles by water and 20 by land in 60 hours with 600 men in order to take part. He managed, however, to report that the battle had been won by French Canadians, partly because he recognized the morale value of it. No more than 300 of de Salaberry's French Canadians had repelled Hampton's offensive. The others had been ready but had not been needed. Five of them had been killed, 20 wounded or missing, at a cost of 50 United States casualties.[22]

About the time General Hampton's army returned to the United States, General Wilkinson's expedition was finally aimed beyond a doubt at Montreal. In its early stages the security on land was assigned to Brigadier General Jacob Brown. Brown knew that Commodore Chauncey had not been successful in blockading the British fleet in Kingston, and he landed his division at French Creek and took post in a thick wood. As he had expected, a naval force appeared on 1 November 1813: two brigs, two schooners, and four gunboats under the command of Captain W. H. Mulcaster. Mulcaster anchored his vessels and commenced firing, to which Brown replied with a land battery skillfully placed to protect his position from being overrun. The trees impeded the British shot, and on the second day Mulcaster withdrew, having lost one man killed and five wounded.[23]

Since Prescott was known to be studded with cannon, General Wilkinson halted his flotilla four miles upstream and landed his troops and ammunition on the American side. These passed behind Ogdensburg to a point four miles down the river. That night, under the direction of Brown who knew the river and the terrain, the flotilla ran past Prescott and picked up the hikers and the ammunition. General Prevost reported that the guns of Prescott had done heavy damage, but in fact the Americans had lost two heavy barges and one man.[24]

In trying to cooperate with Wilkinson's expedition, Commodore Chauncey first based his squadron on Long Island, then on Carlton Island, and on 9 November on Gravelly Point on the American mainland. There the weather grew bad; as he lived in dread of being frozen into the river and captured, he returned on 11 November to Sackett's Harbor and left Wilkinson's flotilla of transports to look out for itself.[25]

By 5 November the British had become certain that Wilkinson's objective was Montreal. General DeRottenburg sent a corps of observation two days later to hang on the enemy's rear whenever he landed on the Canadian shore. It consisted of 800 men detached from the Forty-ninth Foot Regiment, the second battalion of the Eighty-ninth Foot, and 3 companies of Canadian Voltigeurs, under the command of Lieutenant Colonel Joseph Morrison. Morrison started from Kingston on 7 November, and by the evening of 10 November he was pressing close upon General Wilkinson who had tied up at Crysler's Point, at the head of the rapids called the Longue Saute, to wait until General Brown had cleared some hostiles away from the other end. Wilkinson now came to the conclusion that his expedition could not run the rapids until the British corps of observation had been crippled. Being very unwell himself, he designated Brigadier General John P. Boyd of the regular army to employ about 2,000 men for this purpose.

While Boyd organized, Morrison had the opportunity to select his position. He anchored his right on the river and his left on a black ash swamp and ran his line for 700 yards along a dirt road leading from the buildings of the Crysler farm back to the swamp, at right angles to the river. A heavy log fence along the road gave his men protection. Through this position meandered some gullies which extended on out into the open field in front. On 11 November 1813 there was sleet and snow in the air and mud on the open field over which the Americans must pass in the attack. The American dragoons opened the battle on the British right, but they made no headway against mud and bullets. Some of them crouched behind trees and stayed there, whatever their officers ordered, until their ammunition was expended.[26]

Except for firing, there was only one other significant movement. The Americans had six small cannon well placed behind a ravine, and these galled the British so much that Morrison ordered an attack upon them. The Forty-ninth Foot floundered through the mud under artillery fire without the benefit of counterbattery. In ten minutes 11 of its 18 officers were hit. The attack failed. At the end of five hours twilight put an end to the action, and the Americans withdrew to their camp. Thus ended the Battle of Crysler's Farm. No more than 800 British troops had stood off 2,000 Americans, and the British corps of observation continued to exist. British losses of 22 killed, 148 wounded, and 9 missing were less than half of the American 102 killed, 237 wounded, and 100 prisoners. Quite understandably the British were exhilarated, especially since General Prevost believed that Morrison had fought against 4,000 antagonists. On the American side, considerable criticism developed against General Boyd. Secretary Armstrong also criticized General Wilkinson for failing to unite Boyd and Brown and to throw an overwhelming force against the British detachment.

On 8 November General Hampton replied to Wilkinson's order to bring his army to St. Regis, prepared to supply the combined forces. He could not come to St. Regis, he said, because he was not able to supply the combined forces. In fact, because of the shortage of supplies, his army would have to fall back to Plattsburg to the main depot there, instead of going forward. The roads in his region would not support wheeled traffic, and he could not move any more supplies than his men could carry on their backs. His forage was gone, and he had had to send his cavalry and wagon horses back to Plattsburg where they could be fed. In further extenuation, he pointed out how green and unskillful his troops were, and that he had never been able to plan for such a junction as Wilkinson now demanded because he did not

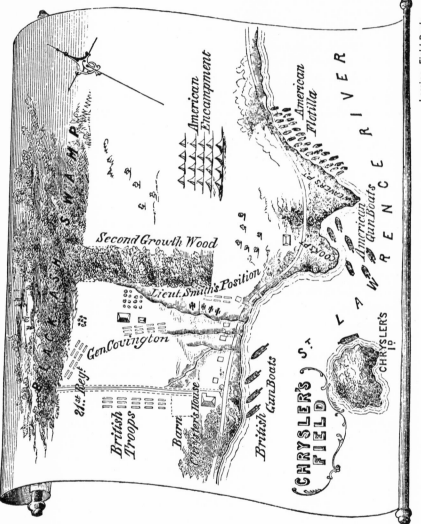

Second Growth Wood

American Encampment

American Flotilla

BEAVER'S CREEK

American GunBoats

Lieut. Smith's Position

BLACK ASH SWAMP

GenCovington

21st Regt.

British Troops

Barn

Chrisler's House

British GunBoats

COOK'S PT.

CHRYSLER'S FIELD

ST.

CHRYSLER'S ID.

LAWRENCE RIVER

know Wilkinson's plans. Having made these explanations, he went east instead of west.[27]

General Wilkinson ran his flotilla on down the river to Cornwall on the Canadian bank, just across from St. Regis, where he expected to find Hampton. There, the day after Crysler's Farm, he received Hampton's letter. "I want language to express my sorrow," he said, and added that Hampton's decision defeated the "grand objects" of his campaign. There was nothing left for him to do but settle into winter quarters at French Mills on the Salmon River, just within the borders of the United States.[28]

The move into winter quarters was made swiftly. By 15 November, Wilkinson considered himself able to protect his stores and the river flotilla, and to prepare for a strike at Montreal in the spring. In spite of the demands he had made upon Hampton, he had forty days' provisions on hand. When winter set in he intended to order 30,000 more at a price of one cent each. Provisions or not, great suffering occurred in his camp. The temperature soon dropped to 30 degrees below zero. Officers who had been appointed through political influence appropriated the pay of the dead, swindled dying soldiers, and sold government stores for personal enrichment. Sensing weakness, the British offered Americans five months' pay with a guarantee that they would not have to serve against the United States, if they would desert.[29]

At this point Wilkinson's health collapsed again. Dr. Bull certified that unless relieved for a little while he might die. But Wilkinson clung to the command. He ordered Hampton to return to Chateaugay by rapid marches to forestall an expected attack. We can guess Hampton's reply. He enumerated several reasons why he could not do it until much later. When Wilkinson received it, Dr. Bull noted that he was visibly depressed and his health visibly impaired. "For God's sake," Bull wrote to Armstrong, "harmonize, or nothing will be done with this army on this frontier." The secretary made no move at the time, but twenty-seven years later he argued that when Hampton refused to cooperate, Wilkinson ought to have relieved him. It is not known why Wilkinson did not try this; perhaps he was afraid to, for the secretary had never firmly backed up his authority over Hampton.[30]

Earlier General Hampton had asked to be allowed to resign from the army. He gave as his reasons that the campaign was nearly at an end and he could see neither honor nor profit for him in further service. Armstrong, without notifying Wilkinson, granted him permission to leave the theater, and he departed Plattsburg on 23 November 1813. He designated George Izard to act in his place, but Izard was so ill that Colonel Robert Purdy actually did the work.[31]

As soon as Wilkinson heard of Hampton's departure, he tried to stop him, but, being too late, he wrote the secretary that he wanted Hampton arrested wherever he was, as he blamed him for the failure of his campaign. This demand was shown to the President, but was never acted on, because, so Wilkinson claimed, of Hampton's wealth and influence. In March 1814 the administration accepted General Hampton's resignation.[32]

Next to go was Brigadier General Boyd. Wilkinson himself granted permission to Boyd to leave because General Brown said he would resign if he had to continue to work with Boyd. Others also found Boyd hard to get along with, especially since the Battle of Crysler's Farm. Major General Morgan Lewis referred to him as a "compound of ignorance, vanity and petulance," and said that his only military asset was a sort of battlefield bravery which "stifling reflection, blinding observation [was] better adapted to the bully of a brothel than to a soldier."[33]

General Wilkinson did not want to resign, but only to leave the front to restore his health. "I am willing to die at my post," he wrote, "but not when unable to draw my sword." He requested to go to Albany, but by late December 1813 his health was so much improved that he decided to remain with the troops.[34]

A new spurt of enthusiasm enlivened him. He pointed out to the secretary how wide the arc of his defensive posts was, from Cornwall on the St. Lawrence to Isle aux Noix in the Richelieu River. He chided Armstrong for having temporized in the Hampton matter, and complained that William Henry Harrison had passed through his district and not bothered to report. These set bad examples. Finally he implored the secretary not to send any more orders into the district except through channels. He looked forward to resuming in May the advance he had suspended in November.[35]

Captain Mulcaster of His Majesty's Navy hovered close by in Cornwall. Early in December he sent a detachment in a canoe to burn the gunboats which were frozen in at French Mills. His men got aboard, but the alarm was sounded before they could light the fires. Mulcaster asked for 1,600 men with which he asserted he could wipe out the entire American camp at French Mills. He never got them, but Secretary Armstrong must have had a similar view of the vulnerability of the winter camp, for on 20 January 1814 he directed Wilkinson to close it down, send 2,000 men and some cannon to Brown at Sackett's Harbor, and take the balance to Plattsburg. Wilkinson carried out this order between 12 and 16 February, but he had to sink or burn 328 boats, tear down his new huts, and demolish many supplies to do it.

The British sent a detachment to harass the withdrawal, and suffered the loss of 91 men, who deserted.[36]

During the ensuing winter months General Wilkinson remained at Plattsburg in a cheerful mood. Late in March, when he received word that the British were reinforcing Upper Canada, he decided to distract them by a movement along the Richelieu River, which would appear to threaten Montreal. In order to save the government $30,000 he had given up the idea of building huts for his troops at Plattsburg. Therefore it was necessary to keep them moving to keep them warm. On 30 March at the head of 4,000 men he entered Odeltown without a struggle. By 3:00 P.M. he had advanced beyond the town to where the road crossed La Cole Creek. On the south side of the creek beside the bridge was a stone mill, 50 by 30 feet, with walls 18 inches thick. A blockhouse and a sturdy barn stood on the north side, somewhat back from the stream.[37]

A British detachment of 180 men under Major Hancock occupied the mill, and Wilkinson determined that he must assail the place. At the expense of great labor, a 12-pounder and two 6-pounders were brought up through the miry roads to within 250 yards of the building. They might as well have been pea shooters for the impression they made on the thick walls and the heavy timbers which shuttered the windows. The carriage broke on an 18-pounder which was on its way forward, and it never entered the bombardment. A small Canadian garrison held the blockhouse, but Wilkinson made no attempt against it. After an hour, two companies arrived from Isle aux Noix to aid the British, and Major Hancock ordered them to charge the American cannon. After several unsuccessful assaults, they finally withdrew into the blockhouse. At the end of two and one-half hours the mill was practically undamaged and the American ammunition gone. The American officers agreed that they lacked the strength to storm the place. Meanwhile British gunfire kept coming in from a sloop and two gunboats which Captain Daniel Pring had been able to sail in close. Toward six in the evening General Wilkinson gave the order to withdraw back into the United States.

Probably less than 500 men had kept the American column of 4,000 from advancing. There were 11 British and 13 Americans killed, 46 British and 128 Americans wounded, and 4 British and 13 Americans missing. Wilkinson knew that his exploit did not help his already shaky record, and he hoped that a favorable interpretation would be put on his motives.

Although he did not know it, he had already been cashiered. Armstrong had written him on 24 March that upon receipt of the order he was to withdraw from the command of Military District Number Nine and stand ready to answer charges against him. This order reached him on 12 April 1814. Armstrong himself made the charges. The charges were neglect of duty and unofficer-like conduct. The specifications of the former: he had delayed sending troops from Fort George to Sackett's Harbor, and he had failed to accompany them when they were at last shifted; he had loitered at Sackett's Harbor and delayed going down the St. Lawrence; he had failed to protect his rear property during that descent; and he had bungled the La Cole Mill affair. Under the charge of unofficer-like conduct were these specifications: he had falsely said that he had no choice but to try to attack Montreal, he had damned the service, he had seemed to keep himself out of danger, he had been drunk on duty, and he had encouraged disobedience of orders.[38]

When he learned of these charges, Wilkinson is supposed to have said of Armstrong: "I know of his secret underworkings. . . . I am astonished at the man's audacity, when he must be sensible of the power I have over him." His trial did not take place for nearly a year. It was on 21 March 1815 that the court pronounced an honorable acquittal on all charges and specifications. Meanwhile, however, Congress had on 3 March 1815 reduced the army, and Wilkinson was not among the two major generals and four brigadiers retained. At the end of thirty-seven years of service, off and on, he had at last been let out the back door. He was not one to brook such treatment silently. In his memoirs, published two years later, he asserted with characteristic bombast, "I shall with my humble means unceasingly oppose the current corruption which menaces the constitution. . . . I despise mystery, intrigue and hypocrisy, and ardently desire to see imposture deprived of its mask, and artificial characters stripped of their borrowed plumes." Among the artificial characters in his gallery whose plumes he would have liked to pluck were John Armstrong, James Madison, and Winfield Scott.

The Nations at War

Connecticut softened her attitude toward the war effort to the extent of placing 6,000 men in federal service, but her leaders stipulated that the troops were to be used only to guard her own coastline. The state in no way abandoned her previous constitutional position, that federal officers could not be put in command of her troops, who already had their own officers, and that the governors of states were the proper judges of the times when militia ought to be placed in the service of the United States.[1]

Massachusetts put no men in federal service, but her leaders took effective steps to guard her own coast, asserting all the while that the United States was derelict in this duty. The state established a Committee for the Defense of the Sea Coast, which busied itself with purchasing stores, conferring with supply officers, and inspecting equipment. The committee had $100,000 to work with, appropriated by the legislature, and was assiduous to dispense it wisely. Above all, it had to be sure that the money was not frittered away in ineffective militia detachments. The adjutant general, who was a member of the committee, cautioned the generals that they were never to call out militia unless the selectmen and magistrates of the towns said to be threatened had given their approval.[2]

Massachusetts felt her way delicately through the legal complications of her peculiar relationship with the United States. Whenever there were squabbles between federal and militia officers over the command of the coastal forts, for example, the adjutant general hastened to point out to the state officers that all rights of war, except immediate defense, belonged to the federal government. Officers of the militia of the commonwealth occasionally joined the United States Army, and in so doing they greatly disrupted the state organization. The state was inclined to treat these officers as deserters.[3]

Generally speaking, the actions of Massachusetts in 1813 tended to make her more and more able to defend herself and less and less disposed to rely on the United States. The governor proudly contended that the militia was up to any demands made upon it. Probably the state could not have successfully defended the district of Maine, but its militia could have made a strong stand within Massachusetts itself.

Rhode Island placed no men in federal service in 1813, and New Hampshire had a mere 80 stationed at Portsmouth. Vermont presented a more complicated picture, for by a plurality of one she chose a Federalist governor, Martin Chittenden, who attempted to reverse the policy of cooperation followed by his Democratic predecessor. There was a brigade of Vermont militia garrisoning Plattsburg, while the New York militia was maneuvering to invade Canada. Chittenden ordered the Vermont unit back to its own state, but the officers, not being Federalists, flatly refused to obey. Their duty to the United States, they said, was foremost, and when state troops were in federal service the governor had no authority over them. But the rank and file did not see the matter as the officers did. Since it was harvest time, many of them left the ranks and returned home. The officers at once sent out a detachment to round these men up as deserters. In this line of duty a sergeant shot and killed a man, but was later acquitted of the charge of murder.[4]

The militia organization of Pennsylvania continued in a chaotic condition. The detachments which had been sent from it to aid Generals Smyth and Harrison had brought no honor to the state. The one at Presque Isle attached to Master Commandant Perry had been shamefully neglected by both state and nation. Its pay was several months in arrears, and its supply of arms inadequate.[5]

In contrast, several companies of 12-month volunteers reflected great honor on the state. The Pittsburgh Blues served with distinction at Mississinewa, in central Indiana, and at Fort Meigs. Having completed their year, they went home too early to take part in the Thames Battle. When Harrison gave them honorable discharges on 28 August, he stated that they, with the other volunteer companies from western Pennsylvania, were the best troops in the Northwest Army. Part of the secret of their quality was their tradition; they had been in continuous existence since well before the war, and were composed of men who enjoyed military exercises and sought the company of other men of similar tastes.[6]

Because of British marauding, thousands of citizen soldiers were called out along the shores of Chesapeake Bay. Delaware, which had not had a man in federal service in 1812, called 3,019 in 1813; Maryland jumped from 318 in 1812 to 23,539; the District of Columbia from 0 to 2,143, and Virginia from 901 to 32,121.[7]

Most of the seaboard states complained of the failure of the federal government to defend them. The Federalist legislature of Maryland charged the United States with being too preoccupied with conquest to attend to the coasts. Nearly all states appropriated money for arms and ammunition, while Virginia went so far as to authorize a state army of two regiments to serve for the duration. Within four months, however, the Virginia army was for some reason defunct. In general, though, the citizen soldiers of the southern seaboard were nearly as active as those nearer the northern theater of war. Part of their duty was to be on the alert to suppress slave insurrections, which they were sure the British were trying to stimulate. North Carolina had barred free people of color from militia service in 1812, and Georgia followed this lead in 1813.[8]

In North Carolina militia officers were accused of treasonable intercourse with the British, whose vessels were lying off the coast, but were finally proved innocent. South Carolina courts ruled that because of omissions in the state law militiamen could not be compelled to turn out to defend the coast. The legislature had to act swiftly to avoid a complete paralysis of the state militia organization.[9]

In all the states men claimed exemption from active militia duty on account of physical disability. Their claims rested on vouchers such as this one: "To their Honors the Court of enquiry: Gentlemen—I have been acquainted with . . . ever since he was a small Boy till the present time and have frequently heard him complain of a disorder in his leg also know that it is a complaint hereditary in his mothers family and I rather think he is not able to bear the fatigues of a campaign." It was frequently necessary for field commanders to weed out men who could not stand campaigning. The complaints listed on the reports of disability have a quaint sound: general debility, dropsy, consumption, inflammation of the liver, weakness of the system, general emaciation of the system, generally reduced habit, and nervous weakness.[10]

Influential groups of the English people wanted the war in America brought to a close. They believed this might be achieved if the Americans could be made to see that the two countries had the same enemy. A report from the House of Commons said, "whilst Great Britain . . . is exerting her utmost strength against the common enemy of independent nations, we have to contend against a country whose real interests in the issue of this great contest, must be the same as ours." John Wilson Croker, secretary to the Admiralty, gave his version of the error the United States was making: "There are now but two free nations . . . Great Britain and America—let the latter beware how she raises her parricidal hand against the parent country; her trade and liberty cannot long survive the downfall of British commerce and British freedom. If the citadel which now encloses and protects all that remains of European liberty be stormed, what shall defend the American union from the inroads of the despot?"[11]

Certain British officers in America did not believe that the United States had the good sense or the culture to realize what she was doing.

Henry Edward Napier, an English naval officer, contended that the core of the American character was venality: "You may always buy a Yankee in almost any rank and station," he wrote home. "[Most Americans] like the English," he observed, "as a spendthrift loves an old rich wife; the sooner we are gone the better." Lieutenant James Scott of the Royal Navy rated American women a hundred years ahead of their men in refinement of manners and ideas. He spoke of one farmer along the Potomac, who, rather than lose his herd of cattle to the invaders, offered intercourse with his daughters as an alternative. Scott was so disgusted, he claimed, that he moved out of the house into the barn, without one of the attractive daughters. *Gentleman's Magazine* charged that the United States government was offering $1,500 for Admiral Cockburn and $1,000 for Admiral Warren, dead or alive. Outraged by the American treatment of prisoners, the *Naval Chronicle* said that the United States, "Like a froward child, whose proud spirit ought to be humbled . . . should be made now to kiss the rod."[12]

Lord Jeffrey, an important Scottish legal authority, found the enemy hospitable enough to him personally. He traveled to the United States and remained there during the last three months of 1813 without molestation. Although not an official emissary, he discussed neutral rights with Monroe and dined with the President.[13]

The blockading fleet did not molest American fishermen.

Early in 1813 the Duke of Wellington asserted that General Prevost would not be able to hold any ground he might have taken or would take, and therefore that he ought to cling to a strong defensive system. Admiral Warren, on the other hand, continued to insist that the defense of Canada could best be achieved by diversionary thrusts against the United States itself. His specific recommendations seem virtually prophetic. One of them was an expedition against New Orleans. Another was to harass the Chesapeake Bay area again, this time with 6,000 to 8,000 men. He also urged the use of disaffected minorities as allies: Indians, Spaniards, and Negroes. He spoke with revulsion of "British money . . . now used in the vindictive war carried on against us." He was referring to a loan of $7 million which the United States had arranged and in which Baring Brothers of London had taken some part.[14]

The Ministry did not think enough of Admiral Warren's strategic ideas to continue him in command. During the first week in November 1813 Croker wrote him that the Lords Commissioners had decided to decentralize his command. It would split into three: the Leeward Islands, Jamaica, and Halifax. Since the only central direction of these would come from the Admiralty office itself, Warren was ordered home. "I am extremely surprised in being recalled at this moment," he wrote, "after having undertaken the command (under adverse conditions) after having zealously and faithfully served my sovereign and country under so many disadvantages." But his protest did not stop the change, although he did not actually leave his station until five months later.[15]

On the other hand the Ministers did not elect to relieve General Prevost. Lord Bathurst assured him that the Erie disaster was not debited to him. He also stated that the Ministry intended to continue to allow him wide discretion. This was the general practice when the theater of war was so far away. Below Prevost, however, the high command in Canada was almost completely revised. On 26 October 1813 Major General DeRottenburg acknowledged receipt of an order directing him to return to Europe. Lieutenant General Sir Gordon Drummond was his replacement, but did not relieve him until December. Drummond was a more energetic officer than the aging DeRottenburg, and he soon made his presence felt in Upper Canada. But Prevost sent him westward with cautious instructions: "In the present state of the war I still would have you refrain from unnecessary hostility calculated to weaken our force and widen the breach existing between the two countries and unproductive of real advantage."[16]

In the reorganization Major General George Glasgow served as deputy commander in chief in Quebec. Everything passing toward Upper Canada had to go through him, and he controlled the flow efficiently and with a sense of humor. Quebec had its own garrison, which was considered outside the combat zone. Acting informally as chief of staff to Prevost at Montreal was Major General Richard Stovin. General Procter, still in the command structure, presided over the new center wing with headquarters at Kingston. Major General Phineas Riall, who had traveled from Europe with Drummond, took over command of the right wing from General Vincent, who had asked to be relieved because of bad health. Vincent, however, stayed a while at Kingston to help until the new organization got established. Riall had headquarters at York but commanded posts as far away as the head of Lake Ontario.[17]

Commodore Yeo remained in command on the lakes, but Prevost clearly was not satisfied with him. He lectured him for consistently overestimating the American strength, and hinted other shortcomings. "I have no disposition to censure your conduct. My only complaint," he wrote, "is that you do not view as I would wish you to do the consequences of leaving in critical positions our troops exposed to the joint operations of the American fleet and army. . . ."[18]

At the bottom of the British military hierarchy, Tommy Atkins did not find 1813 different from 1812. His uniform continued to be so tight that it required three hours' preparation to put it on smoothly enough to stand inspection. The white trousers could not be kept clean except by labor which subtracted from a soldier's fighting ability. His four-inch leather stock was a miserable neckpiece, and two inches of ruffles on his breast had no purpose except show. Some units wore a heavy cap with nothing to keep it from falling off. All in all, the uniform gathered dirt, made the heat harder to bear, and did not keep out the mosquitoes. Mosquitoes were the principal foe in the Chesapeake area.[19]

Tommy's training was no better suited than his uniform to warfare in North America. He only knew how to act in elbow-to-elbow formations with his fellows, and was of little use except in conjunction with his "front rank man," or his left- or right-hand man. His weapon was clumsy both for shock and missile action. His officers did little for him. One of them wrote, "The British system of promotion, with which wealth and influence are everything, and merit nothing, was exposed . . . in all its blood-stained hideousness."[20]

The belligerents thought each other guilty of frightful atrocities. A committee of the House of Representatives made up the following list of them: mistreatment of prisoners, impressment, violation of flags of truce, and the use of Indians. The British made a countercharge regarding prisoners. Some of them agreed with the Americans about impressment, however, and laid the need of it to the brutal system of discipline in the navy. Congress, hoping to reduce impressment, passed an act on 3 March 1813 to exclude British-born sailors from American ships. The British had little to say in defense of the use of Indians, but by year's end Secretary of War John Armstrong had come to the conclusion that the United States too must use them, especially the western Indians, or lose the war. Indeed, he was willing to turn the redmen loose on the British frontier and encourage them to clear out every British person west of Kingston. But President Madison would not agree to this harsh policy.[21]

Americans could not forget the River Raisin. Their countrymen had surrendered there to British officers, yet had been slaughtered by British-Indians. Nor could they forget Hampton, Virginia. According to the American version, women were ravished there and then driven naked through the streets at bayonet point. Lieutenant Scott denied this story. One American letter referred to the British as "those half-Indian scalping assassins, those degenerate, ferocious disgraces to civilization. . . ." The same writer asserted that in Ireland the British officers stirred their toddy with Irishmen's fingers, and that in Asia the redcoats chopped up whole villages of people to test the edges of their swords.[22]

Spring and summer, 1813, were particularly critical times in American politics. After George Clinton's death, a Democratic party caucus had offered the vice presidency to John Langdon of New Hampshire. When Langdon turned it down, the caucus chose Elbridge Gerry. Although sixty-nine and not in good health, Gerry took the position and first presided over the Senate on 24 May 1813. He proved much too diligent for some of those who had selected him; he would not leave the chair in control of a president pro tempore because he feared that someone hostile to the administration, like William Giles, might be chosen.[23]

The situation of the Democratic Party was precarious. Only ten out of the eighteen states were Democratic, and the majority in both houses of Congress which could be counted on to be loyal to the party was very slim. The party's position in the Senate was weakened because its strongest supporter, William H. Crawford of Georgia, had left to become minister to France. Most damaging of all was the fact that the President, laid low by illness during much of the summer, was not expected to live. But sick as he was, Madison could not be persuaded to recommend sedition laws or other curbs on civil liberties.

In July 1813 Congress passed a bill outlawing the grain trade which in the Iberian Peninsula was feeding Wellington's army on American foodstuffs. The penalty for infraction of the law was confiscation of ship and cargo, plus a fine. But even so heavy a punishment did not stop this profitable business, primarily because a good many British ships disguised themselves as non-American neutrals and continued to take aboard grain in the United States and deliver it in Spain or Portugal. General orders were published to the United States Navy to prevent intercourse with blockaders, and to be on the lookout for violators under the "specious garb of friendly foreign flags."[24]

Late in 1812 word had reached the American government that the czar of Russia would be willing to mediate between the United States and England. President Madison at once appointed James A. Bayard and Albert Gallatin to go to Russia. Gallatin took the assignment because of his distaste for serving with John Armstrong in the cabinet, and Madison considered him to be on leave from the Treasury Department. The two emissaries set sail on 9 May 1813 with the following instructions: impressment must be eliminated; blockades must be placed upon ports only, not upon extended strips of coastline; broken voyages to carry goods from colonies to belligerents must be permitted;

trade between American ports must not be interdicted; contraband must be better defined; and the British must agree to stay out of America's inland waters.[25]

After the mission had been gone two months and ten days, the Senate rejected Gallatin as emissary because he was still secretary of the treasury. In September, however, with the Treasury matter adjusted, Gallatin's name was again proposed and this time confirmed. Meanwhile, the two envoys had reached St. Petersburg on 21 July 1813, and joined John Quincy Adams, minister there and the third special envoy. There was continuous delay before they learned on 1 November that the czar remained willing to mediate, but that Britain categorically refused his services. They could now do nothing but leave Russia and seek an opportunity for direct negotiation with England.

It was known that some American captains by collusion allowed themselves to be captured by blockaders, thereby gaining rich profits for themselves and at the same time channeling needed supplies to the British military forces. In December 1813 Madison at last got Congress to enact a sweeping embargo act. Food and contraband would not be allowed even to put to sea. This act was aimed primarily at New England, and it intensified the bitterness in that region against the administration. It did not help relations when John Armstrong began to talk in Washington about the need for conscription. There ensued a duel within the party between Armstrong and Monroe. The latter, who felt sure that conscription would ruin the party, finally won.[26]

Before his departure Gallatin had made proposals to Congress relative to certain special funds. One fund had accumulated from the sale of British ships which happened to be within reach and were confiscated at the start of the war. Gallatin wanted the fund transferred to the treasury, which was falling farther and farther behind. The House voted against his proposal 64 to 61. Some members favored the measure, but wanted the policy of nonintercourse to end, and saw no way to end it but to choke off government revenues. New England Federalists, on the other hand, favored nonimportation because it protected their growing industrial investments. Gallatin's proposal was lost between these two interests. There was another fund of about $18 million made up of fines and bonds paid by people who had imported goods when war came. Gallatin asked for it too, but Congress on 5 January 1813 voted that the fines be forgiven and the monies returned.[27]

As the need for money was increasing, and as these large funds were denied to the administration by Congress, added taxes became more and more imperative. But no financial measure got through the regular sessions early in 1813, except an act on 23 February permitting the secretary of the treasury to borrow $16 million at 6 per cent interest, and a broker's fee of ¼ per cent. The treasury could not find lenders willing to take up more than half this amount. Finally, Parish and Girard of Philadelphia took $7 million and John Jacob Astor $2 million. The net result for the treasury was that it had to issue $18,109,-377 worth of bonds to obtain $16 million, while for Parish, Girard, and Astor it resulted in a discount of $13.64 on each $100.

Due to Congress' failure to provide revenue, Madison called a special session to convene on 24 May 1813. During this session the two parties traded their traditional positions on taxes. The Federalists, who in the 1790s had enacted internal taxes, now fought them, while the Democrats pushed through taxes on carriages, auctions, sugar refineries, salt, and licenses to sell liquor. They also passed a stamp tax on legal documents, a tax on whiskey stills, and, last but not least, a direct tax of $3 million. Each state was assigned a portion of the latter. At the upper end of the quota spectrum was New York, with $431,-141.62, and at the lower end the new state of Louisiana, with $28,-295.11. A state could deduct 15 per cent if it paid before February 1814 and 10 per cent if before May. But anyway one viewed it, the Democrats had turned the dreaded tax-gatherer loose in the land, the figure who when the Federalists had been in power had represented tyranny to the Democrats.[28]

It was clearly necessary to improve the military organization. Accordingly, on 1 May 1813 regulations were promulgated which defined the duties of a general staff. This staff was not for strategic planning, but for achieving more efficient military housekeeping. It included the following departments: Quartermaster, Topographical Engineering, Adjutant and Inspector General (a dual function performed by one officer), Ordnance, Hospital, Purchasing, and Pay. Related to the staff also were the judge advocates, the chaplains, the military academy at West Point, and the commanding generals of the nine military districts with their logistical staffs. Assistants to the chief were added in four of the departments. All in all, the new arrangement at last relieved the secretary of war of some of his overload of work.[29]

Callender Irvine became commissary general of purchases. Under the old organizational chart he had issued 708 items of clothing, and had shifted away from linen for army clothes toward cotton and wool. This change of material was not only a financial saving, but also a sanitary gain. Irvine had so built up his mechanism that by late 1813 he could turn out 3,000 uniforms per week. He took the superintendent of military stores under his command, redesignated the position, and then appointed to it a civilian, Richard Cutts, who happened to be President Madison's brother-in-law. Cutts was, it appears, well qualified for his duties. Irvine sought to eliminate overlapping between his office and the quartermaster and the commissary general of ordnance.[30]

On 21 March 1813 Morgan Lewis was relieved as quartermaster general and replaced with Robert Swartwout. Swartwout was an improvement over Lewis, but was never able fully to control the department. His worst problem was that each deputy quartermaster operated independently of all others, usually under the command of some field general. In too many instances, as far as the quartermaster was concerned, the authority of the field commander overrode his own.[31]

On 18 July 1813 Eli Whitney had been awarded a contract to manufacture 15,000 muskets. He had received several thousand dollars in advance of delivery to enable him to retool, but as the months passed he remained slow about delivering the muskets. The government, for its part, often fell as much as two months behind in paying the advances due him, and he had to remind it of the obligation. The pattern of the relationship between them had been established as far back as the late 1790s, at which time Whitney had received his first contract to make muskets. His musket was a modification of the Charleville, the weapon which had been introduced into America in quantity by the French during the Revolution. The models chiefly used during the War of 1812 were from 54½ to 56½ inches long, about 10 pounds in weight, with a caliber close to .69. The bayonet for them was 14½ inches long. All were muzzleloading, single-shot, flintlock guns, with an accurate range not in excess of 75 yards. The United States employed one breechloading, single-shot musket, Hall's musket, which was put into production at Harpers Ferry in 1811. American troops never welcomed it because of its malfunctions and of injuries to the men who fired it, but ordnance believed in it and kept on hand a larger stock than its light use merited.[32]

The army and the navy cooperated during 1813 so much more than ever before that they were able to prepare together a set of regulations to govern joint operations.[33]

There were some phenomena during the year 1813 which human readjustments could not affect. A destructive hurricane struck the Gulf coast in August. It missed the Atlantic seaboard, but when winter came the bitterest cold on record gripped that region. Temperatures dropped so low that work in the navy yards as far south as Charleston had to be suspended.[34]

1813–1814

The Creek War

The loose association of Indians of the same culture pattern, called the Creek Confederation, was one of the most important Indian blocs within the United States. It was identified with an area about 300 miles square, roughly from the Tennessee River on the north to the Gulf of Mexico on the south, and from the middle of Georgia on the east to what later became the eastern boundary of the state of Mississippi on the west. Spanish, French, English, and United States agents steadily attempted to influence the Creeks, to secure their trade, and to keep them as allies. But at the time of the War of 1812 the Creeks could extract very little from any of these nations. Although there were nearly 18,000 Creeks, perhaps only 4,000 of them were warriors, and these had no more than 1,000 guns. Since they were also low on ammunition, they were not practiced marksmen, and often set the musket aside after one shot in favor of the bow and arrow.[1]

Tecumseh's visits to the Creeks had added to their restlessness. He had infected some of the younger men with his vision of an Indian confederation to expel the white man. He had promised that after the defeat of the Americans in the North, he would come south to help his kinsmen, the Creeks, complete the victory of red over white. His southern supporters were encouraged by the spectacular results of British-Indian collaboration at the River Raisin in January 1813. Little Warrior and six other Creeks had been there. Returning southward, they murdered two families on 9 February 1813 on the north bank of the Ohio River. When news of this crime reached Benjamin Hawkins, the energetic United States agent to the Creeks, he demanded that the murderers be turned over to his government. Instead, the old Creek chiefs invoked tribal justice and themselves killed Little Warrior and three of his accomplices. A younger faction, those influenced by Tecumseh, outraged by what they deemed subservience to the United States, undertook in turn to kill every leader who had taken part in the execution. They drove the Tuckabatchee chiefs finally to seek Hawkins' protection at Coweta.[2]

Benjamin Hawkins himself was as much a disruptive factor as Tecumseh. He had undertaken to turn the Creeks away from their hunting and gathering culture to a white style of agriculture. The confederation bit by bit divided over his reforms. One faction embraced them warmly while the other rejected them violently, and the two were all but irreconcilable. The immediate problem was whether to aid the United States or Britain. Agents, seeing the opportunity, began again to make overtures. Runners came from the Great Lakes area to assure the Creeks that England would supply them armament if they would help against the United States. The American Southeast was upset by unfounded rumors that Spain intended to transfer East Florida to England. The Spanish officials in Florida were not sure which way to turn, but after some prodding by British emissaries, they decided that it was to Spain's interest to help arm the Creeks. Thus, an invitation went to Peter McQueen, a half-breed Creek leader, to come to Pensacola for ammunition.[3]

When Americans in the Alabama country learned of McQueen's expedition, Colonel James Caller raised a party of 180 Mississippi militiamen from the vicinity of St. Stephen on the Tombigbee River to intercept McQueen on his return trip. An advanced detachment under Sam Dale surprised McQueen's group in camp and routed it. Caller had to round up his men, who were in pursuit, to secure the pack train which carried the precious ammunition from Pensacola. McQueen too reorganized his party and set up an ambush. At the proper moment his men rushed out from a canebrake upon Caller's detachment, but although they broke up the column, they did not recapture most of the ammunition. This action, known as the Battle of Burnt Corn Creek, 27 July 1813, is often called the opening battle of the Creek War.[4]

Just at this time Secretary Armstrong wrote to General Pinckney, commander of the Sixth Military District, that the United States was prepared to take action against the Creeks. Moreover, if it became clear that the Spanish were behind the Creeks, he said it would be justifiable to strike at Pensacola. Such words resonated in the Southeast.

Georgia set about establishing a line of forts ten miles apart along

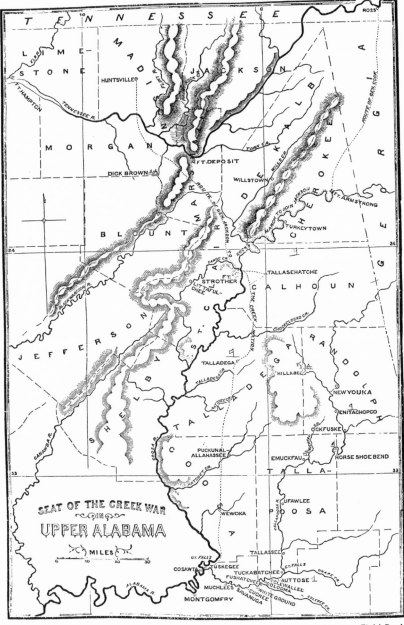

SEAT OF THE CREEK WAR
~in~
UPPER ALABAMA

MILES
0   10   20   30

Lossing, Field Book

the Creek frontier. Each fort had a garrison of eighteen or more men and a couple of horsemen, who were supposed to reconnoiter as far as the next forts in the chain. This system was expected to protect the frontier and leave Georgia free to prepare offensives into the Creek country. Tennessee had several times sent military expeditions into the Creek country as far south as East Florida. At the western borders of the Creek Confederation, American military affairs were under the direction of Brigadier General Ferdinand Claiborne of the militia of Mississippi Territory. Claiborne recognized the weakness of his sector and repeatedly urged pre-emptive strikes to gain the advantage of the initiative. Major General Thomas Flournoy, commanding general in the Seventh Military District, regularly refused to permit them, and reminded the militia general that American strategy in that zone was defensive.[5]

The people in the territory north of Fort Stoddert and between the Alabama and Tombigbee rivers sought refuge in blockhouses. A substantial number had gathered at the Mims place on Lake Tensa about ten miles north of Fort Stoddert. Claiborne sent Major Daniel Beasley and three captains of the regular army there to supervise the defense. On 7 August 1813 Claiborne himself came to inspect, and while there he ordered the construction of two more blockhouses. By late August Fort Mims consisted of seventeen buildings surrounded by a reasonably strong stockade. On the east side, where the main gate was, a second picket wall was built a few yards within the other. About 550 persons dwelt inside this defensive system. Major Beasley continued very languidly to strengthen the works, but did not seem to fear immediate attack. Thus he was skeptical when two Negro slaves dashed into the fort on 29 August to report that they had seen Indians painted for war. He ordered a mounted reconnaissance, and when it reported no signs of Indians, he had the slaves whipped for giving a false alarm.[6]

The two slaves so cruelly used had actually seen the point of a Creek war party of about 100 warriors, led by William Weatherford. Known as Red Eagle to the Creeks, Weatherford belonged, in spite of his white father, to the militant anti–United States faction of the Creeks, called the Red Sticks. He had learned of the careless security maintained at Fort Mims. When the drum call to dinner rolled in the fort at noon on 30 August 1813, the gate was not only open but was held open by drifting sand. While the whites were eating their midday meal, Weatherford's party sprinted across the cleared field in front of the east side and into the open gate. They killed Major Beasley, who too late had run to try to close the gate. White and red now shot through the portholes, and bit by bit the red drove the white back into the inner works. The defenders made their final stand in the loomhouse which was built against the northern picket wall. Using burning arrows, the Indians set this keep on fire, and by five in the afternoon they had completely overrun the entire fort and had killed 400 of the 500 persons there. They generally spared the Negroes to become their own slaves, but they showed no mercy to the whites. It is said that they seized children by the feet and brained them against the log walls. Pregnant women were disembowelled and their unborn infants tossed about. Weatherford is credited with vainly trying to stop the carnage, but his warriors believed that the British at Pensacola had offered them $5.00 for every American scalp, and they continued the harvest, often from living victims.

The price the Creeks paid for the Fort Mims massacre was in the end very high. They lost 300 to 400 of their own warriors. Moreover, they concentrated the hatred of the entire Southeast against themselves, and brought upon themselves invasion from Tennessee, Georgia, and Mississippi Territory.

The immediate reaction of the whites in the vicinity was a near panic. They blamed everybody who in any way had a connection with it. General Claiborne, in order to concentrate his forces, directed that the garrison and people at Fort Madison be shifted to Fort St. Stephen. Over local protests Colonel Joseph Carson made the shift with 500 persons, but when he had left, Captain Sam Dale marched into Fort Madison with 80 volunteers and held it.[7]

Governor Charles Cameron of New Providence Island in the Bahamas saw advantage to Britain in having the Creeks as allies, and in September 1813 he sent Captain Edward Handfield, Royal Navy, to make a contact. Handfield received on board a delegation of Creeks and Seminoles, and carried their petition for help back to Cameron. The governor forwarded this to Lord Bathurst, who, when it finally reached him, ordered all possible aid through Cameron.[8]

Many of the Creeks tried to remain friendly to the United States, but the white Americans of the Southeast, enraged by Fort Mims, drew no fine distinctions among them. The heart of the Creek Confederation was the Holy Ground, at the junction of the Coosa and Tallapoosa rivers. The best route to invade it was from Georgia by way of the United States forts on the Chattahoochee River and through the Lower Creek towns. The distance was 150 miles, 80 of it along a good road. The next best line was from Mobile up the Alabama River, also 150 miles. Most difficult of all was the route from Tennessee, mountainous and pathless, yet the principal thrust came that way.[9]

Tennessee responded militantly to the call of the secretary of war for troops to suppress the Creeks. On 25 September 1813 the legislature of the state authorized 3,500 volunteers to be added to the 1,500 Tennessee citizen soldiers already in federal service. It also appropriated $300,000 for expenses and pay. But the major general commanding the Tennessee militia, Andrew Jackson, was badly crippled and bedridden from a wound received in a street brawl. Governor Willie Blount took steps to replace him, but Jackson asserted he had a right to the command and struggled up out of bed with one arm in a sling and a bullet permanently lodged close to his heart. Meanwhile, his loyal friend John Coffee, commander of the horse troops, had reached Huntsville, south of the Tennessee border, on 4 October with 1,300 mounted men, and Major General John Cocke had assembled his division from East Tennessee at Knoxville. Jackson himself was able to join the infantry and assume overall command at Fayetteville on 7 October. Four days later he broke camp and marched his men 32 miles in 9 hours to join Coffee on the Tennessee River below Huntsville. He next sent a detachment up the river about 20 miles to establish a main base, which he called Fort Deposit. The principal column began to cut a road southward over Raccoon Mountain to the junction of the Coosa River with Canoe Creek, 40 to 50 miles distant. It completed the road in six days. At this time Jackson had with him 2,500 men and 1,300 horses. To subsist so many horses in the fall when the grass was likely to be frost-killed was a major undertaking, and the entire logistical problem was complicated by the low water level in the Tennessee River, which made it impractical as a supply route.[10]

General Jackson may not have known how he would supply his army, but he understood perfectly well what he intended to do with it. Spies informed him of the strength of the Creeks, and he considered his force able to wipe them out and take the Creek towns. Then he would proceed southward to Mobile, leaving behind him a usable road to Tennessee. Mobile would be a staging point from which to take Pensacola· to start with, and afterwards to eliminate Spain from the Floridas. He did not intend to rely on any but Tennessee troops.[11]

At the junction of the Coosa River and Canoe Creek, Jackson built his advanced supply base and called it Fort Strother. Next he detached General Coffee (a brigadier general since 24 September) to destroy Tallushatchee, a hostile town of Upper Creeks straight eastward from Strother. When within a mile of the place, Coffee prolonged his line to extend far beyond the edges of the village, and advanced it in a long loop with the ends in front. The pre-attack advance was made in the dark and at 8:00 A.M. on 3 November 1813, the center took the town by surprise. There was a brisk fight, but the ends of Coffee's loop came together and completed the encirclement. Not a single warrior escaped; 186 were known to be killed, and 84 women and children captured, at a cost to the Tennesseans of 5 killed and 41 wounded. Coffee's successful tactics of annihilation became the model for later operations.[12]

Lack of supplies continued to keep Jackson close to Fort Strother, but on 7 November a runner brought an appeal from the friendly Creek village of Talladega, which was surrounded by hostile Creeks, to come to its aid. At this time Jackson received word that part of General Cocke's column from East Tennessee, Brigadier General James White commanding, was drawing close. Accordingly, he sent word to White to hurry on to Strother and protect it, and himself set out with his force to cover the 30 miles southward toward Talladega. On the way a messenger arrived to inform him that Cocke had ordered White to ignore Jackson's order and rejoin him. This meant that there would be no garrison in Fort Strother except a few sick men, but Jackson decided to run the risk and continue on toward Talladega. Following the tried pattern of successful attack, he formed his lines in a Coffee-style loop before dawn on 9 November 1813. Mounted men were on both wingtips so that they could ride toward each other and encircle the foe. At first light an advanced detachment went forward to start the battle and draw the Indians into the center, but almost fell into an ambush. Some of the besieged friendlies ran out at the risk of their lives, seized the bridles of the horses, and turned their heads toward the as-yet-unseen danger. After four or five volleys, the advanced detachment fell back to the main line, drawing the hostile Indians with them toward annihilation, but at the critical moment one of the militia units broke and let them through the line. Except for this break, Jackson vowed that the destruction would have been as great as at Tallushatchee. In fact, only 290 Indians were killed, while around 700 escaped. The cost to the Tennessee force was 17 killed, and 83 wounded out of around 1,000 engaged.[13]

For the time being, the Tennesseans lost their momentum. Jackson had to return to Strother and bend all his energy merely to keeping an army in the Creek country. Both his militia and his 12-month volunteers believed that they had fulfilled their terms of service, and they were determined to return to Tennessee. When the militia began an unauthorized march toward home, Jackson had the volunteers drawn up across their path; but the next day he was obliged to reverse the process, that is, use the militia to keep the volunteers from departing. He himself rode up and down the lines, haranguing the sullen men, but they did not respond. Finally, he promised them that if supplies did not come in two days, he would lead the march back to Tennessee. On 17 November, true to his word, he led the column northward. Soon they encountered a train of 9 supply wagons and 150 cattle, whereupon they halted and held a barbecue. Many of the men, regardless of the agreement, had no intention of returning to Fort Strother. Having eaten, they formed column and moved off toward Tennessee. Jackson snatched a musket from someone and rode through the woods to head them off. At a bend in the trail the column came upon him with the musket leveled across the horse's neck, prepared to shoot the first man who moved forward. While general and troops glared at each other, John Coffee and several troopers ranged themselves silently beside Jackson. The men gave in, turned about, and went back to Fort Strother.

They did not remain there long. Unmoved by the general's storming, nearly all the volunteers started home on the day they reckoned their tour of duty ended. This time Jackson faced them at the turn with two small cannon, match lighted, loaded with grapeshot, and served by the regulars. No one advanced, but on the other hand when he harangued for volunteers, none came forward. Finally, on 12 December, in spite of all he could do, the men continued their march toward Tennessee. Jackson described them to his wife as "whining, complaining . . . mutineers."[14]

In the midst of this trial of wills the East Tennesseans belatedly and perversely injected themselves into the campaign. Jackson had all along been unsuccessfully trying to hurry Major General Cocke's 2,500 men to join him. There was jealousy between the militia of East and West Tennessee, and the evidence is rather strong that Cocke did not want to unite them. He well understood that union with Jackson would end his chance for any independent action. He therefore went off on his own excursion.

Eastward of Talladega about twenty miles were two towns occupied by Creeks called Hillabees. These had informed Jackson that they could not oppose the United States, whereupon he summoned their head men to confer with him. While the chiefs were away, White's brigade of Cocke's army fell upon their undefended village at dawn on 17 November, killed 60 Hillabees, and captured around 250. White reported this exploit with pride to Cocke. Jackson exploded at the news, but did nothing except say nasty things about Cocke and White.[15]

Jackson's anger made Cocke less eager than before to report to him, but a longer delay was impossible and he checked in finally at Fort Strother on 12 December. His force consisted by that time of no more than 1,450 men, who had only 10 days of service left. Jackson dismissed them without ceremony and sent General Cocke back to Tennessee to hurry along supplies and reinforcements.

As 1813 ended, Jackson's army on the fringe of the Creek heartland appeared to be disintegrating. Two of his veteran infantry brigades went home, and the mounted contingent, in spite of John Coffee's remonstrances, also returned to Tennessee. Coffee himself stood loyally by his chief. "I intend to keep my steady course," he wrote his wife, "and not be perplexed, let things go as they may." He considered Jackson's task as heavy as a man could bear, and lightened it for him where he could.[16]

Governor Blount now showed signs of softening. He saw no advantage in Jackson's remaining at his advanced post with a handful of men. Would it not be better, he wrote the general, to retire to Tennessee, closer to the source of supplies and recruits? He got back a blast: "Arouse from yr. lethargy—despise fawning smiles or snarling frowns—with energy exercise yr. functions—the campaign must rapidly progress or . . . yr. country ruined. Call out the full quota—execute the orders of the Secy. of War, arrest the officer who omits his duty . . . let popularity perish for the present. . . . Save Mobile—save the Territory—save your frontier from becoming drenched in blood. . . . What, retrograde under these circumstances? I will perish first."[17]

All the while, Georgia and Mississippi Territory withheld or applied their military strength against the Creeks without any attempt to coordinate with Tennessee and with each other. Neither General Pinckney, commanding in the Sixth Military District, General Flournoy, commanding in the Seventh, nor the secretary of war did anything to channel the efforts against the Creeks. But in October, General Flournoy had finally slipped the leash on Brigadier General Claiborne and ordered him to lay waste Creek property near the junction of the Alabama and Tombigbee rivers. Claiborne based his marches on Fort St. Stephen and achieved some devastation, but no major military actions.

At the same time Captain Sam Dale finally left Fort Madison and headed southward toward the Alabama River. His party encountered Creeks on the river. He and three others rowed out in a small boat on 12 November 1813 to intercept a war canoe, which appeared to have only two warriors in it. Boat and canoe came gunwale to gunwale and became the platform for a vicious hand-to-hand encounter. Several warriors who had been lying on the bottom of the large canoe bid fair to overpower Dale and his three supporters. The two vessels drifted apart, leaving Dale alone in the canoe with four of the foe. His ammunition was gone but he continued to fight with clubbed musket and bayonet. His associates did what they could to help him with gunfire from the other vessel. In the end Dale killed his four opponents. His canoe fight made him a legend in the Southeast.[18]

General Claiborne pushed his operations northward and established a strong point on the east bank of the Alabama River, 85 miles above Fort Stoddert. His objective was the Holy Ground. Thirty miles away, he built a stockade for his baggage, and advanced in three columns. His right column consisted of volunteers, his center of the Third United States Infantry plus some mounted volunteers, and his left of militia and four companies of Choctaws under Pushmataha. His exact strength is not known. He fell upon the Holy Ground at dawn 23 December 1813, and after some brisk shooting routed the warriors with a known loss to them of 30, against 1 of his men killed and 6 wounded. Weatherford provided the only heady drama. Hotly pursued, he galloped his horse over a high bluff into the deep water below, and safely reached the opposite shore. The invaders burned down 260 houses. They were incensed by a note they purported to have found from the Spanish governor, congratulating Red Eagle on the Mims massacre. But due to supply shortages Claiborne had to pull out of the Creek heartland and return southward to Fort St. Stephen.[19]

On 24 November 1813, Brigadier General John Floyd in command of 950 Georgia militiamen and 400 friendly Indians crossed the Chattahoochee River and marched westward toward the Holy Ground. After traversing 120 miles in 7 days, he attacked the village of Auttose on 29 November. His men killed 200 Indians and lost 11 killed and 54 wounded. They are supposed to have committed many atrocities. Henry Adams regarded this battle as proof that the Creeks had neither the fighting ability nor the fighting tools of the northern Indians. A lesser number of warriors at Tippecanoe had inflicted four times as many casualties.[20]

When Andrew Jackson learned of the success of the other columns against the Creeks, he wrote General Floyd congratulations but at the same time a lecture. The lack of coordination among the states was lamentable. He pointed out that he had got near to the heart of the Creek country, but had been left standing alone. Georgia, East Tennessee, and the supply contractors had all abandoned him, and he had had to retreat. When he was able to move forward again, he told Floyd, he expected cooperation.[21]

Central direction might have brought the campaign to a conclusion by New Year's Day 1814. As it was, more than 7,000 men had entered Creek territory from different directions and had killed 800 warriors—at least one-fifth of the Creek fighting power. They had not, however, wiped out the towns which were the center of belligerence.[22]

Jackson's admonitions and lectures seemed not to bring results. On 14 January his last seasoned Tennessee unit left, and the garrison at Fort Strother dropped to 130 men. Later the same day, however, 800 recruits arrived from Tennessee. Determined to make use of these, since they were enlisted for 60 days only, Jackson advanced toward Talladega and camped there. Besides these 800 recruits, he had 200 Creeks and Cherokees and 30 artillerymen with one 6-pounder. John Coffee, whose men had left him without a command, helped give some cohesion to this green army. Jackson, fully aware of the shortcomings of his inexperienced troops, nonetheless elected to move another 30 miles toward the Holy Ground. Heretofore the Creeks had remained on the defensive for lack of ammunition, but they now chose to attack. At daylight on 22 January 1814 near the town of Emuckfau, they struck the Tennesseans with about equal numbers. During the darkness Jackson's men held off the attack by firing at the muzzle flashes, and when daylight came Coffee led a successful charge. Next Jackson sent him with 400 men to assault Emuckfau, but seeing that it was too strong, Coffee marched back to get the cannon. At this sign of retreat, the Creeks hit Jackson's right very hard, but Coffee moved toward envelopment, and Jackson, anticipating the point of attack, put his main column in its way. Two or three volleys and a bayonet charge ended the action. Among the wounded was Coffee and among the dead was his brother-in-law. He wrote thus to his father-in-law: "Painful as it is, I must inform you that Sandy Donelson was among the slain. He fell by a ball through his head, near me. . . . In a state of war the lives of men must be lost; and the only circumstance that leaves us any satisfaction for our departed friends, is when they have acted their part well and fallen bravely defending the government we are bound to protect. . . . He is no more, but his death had been glorious. He has bequeathed his friends a valuable inheritance in the character he has acquired to his memory. . . ."[23]

With such a force as he had, with the wounded, and with the invariable supply pinch, Jackson could do nothing but turn his back on the heartland and retreat to Strother. Encouraged by this retrograde movement, the Creeks struck his rear on 24 January when his advanced units were already across Enotachopco Creek and the artillery was still in the water. Jackson had instructed the advanced units to recross in such a contingency, fan out, and strive for an envelopment. Before they could do so, the companies holding off the attack upon the rear panicked and broke. In the ensuing confusion, the officers could not for some time get the men back into formations. John Carroll, commanding 25 soldiers who remained steady, stood in the water and protected the rear, while Jackson and Coffee moved among the stragglers gradually getting them back into some sort of order. The two colonels in command of the rear guard were later court-martialed for their failure, but thanks to the coolness of others the momentary break of their units did not result in perfect rout. In the two battles of Emuckfau and Enotachopco, Jackson lost 19 killed and 76 wounded, but the Indian loss was claimed by the white men to total 190.[24]

After the Creeks had struck Jackson on 22 and 24 January 1814 and obliged him to retreat, they diverted their force eastward with better central direction than was common for Indians to attack the column from Georgia. General John Floyd, commanding this column, had advanced to Fort Mitchell on the Chattahoochee River and remained there for six weeks. Then, at the head of 1,200 volunteers, a company of mounted men, and 400 Indians, he advanced to a point 50 miles farther west. There the Creeks attacked him at dawn on 26 January 1814. As long as darkness lasted, the outcome was in doubt, but as soon as daylight came Floyd employed that tactic which rarely failed against Indians. With a charge he broke up the Creek base of fire, but at the high price of 17 killed, 132 wounded, besides 5 friendly Indians killed and 15 wounded. Moreover, he felt obliged to draw back again to Fort Mitchell. This was the last expedition which Georgia mounted to penetrate the Creek country during the War of 1812.[25]

Jackson reluctantly dismissed his army at Fort Strother because its time of service was up. When the men got back to Tennessee, their tales of the campaign stimulated volunteering. Major General Cocke raised a new army in East Tennessee for six months, and started with it toward Strother. But when his men found out that the West Tennessee detachment was enlisted for only three months, they threatened mutiny. Cocke tried to pacify them, but as the story reached Jackson, Cocke appeared as the chief inciter. Accordingly, Jackson sent orders to one of the brigadier generals to arrest all of the mutinous officers, Cocke included, and send them back to Tennessee for trial. A court-martial later cleared Cocke of Jackson's charges.[26]

While waiting at Fort Strother for reinforcements, Jackson opened roads toward the Indian country, gathered supplies, and little by little perfected the organization of his cadre. On 6 February a regiment of regulars, recruited in Tennessee, marched into the fort, 600 strong. The general counted on it, he said, "To give great strength to his arm and quell mutiny." By the end of February 1814 he had 4,000 men collected around Strother.[27]

Brigadier General Isaac Roberts of the Tennessee militia marched to join Jackson with men who were enlisted for only three months. Fearful of the general's attitude, he halted the detachment short of Strother and went on ahead. As he had anticipated, Jackson insisted that the men serve for six months. Without waiting for the decision, one company begain to return to Tennessee. Jackson proclaimed them deserters and ordered them arrested, but agreed to pardon any man who returned to duty. The company got as far as Fayetteville, Tennessee, picked up some new members, then placidly returned to Fort Strother. One of the new men was John Wood, a lad of eighteen. The day he joined was a fatal one in his short life. While on guard duty he became angry, refused to obey an order, and offered to shoot anyone who tried to coerce him. Jackson had him seized, charged with mutiny, and brought before a court-martial. Although Wood had not been with the company during its unauthorized return to Fayetteville, he was accused of having been twice mutinous. The court sentenced him to die, Jackson refused a pardon, and Wood was shot. He thus became the first militiaman since the Revolution to suffer death for a military offense. The example, though brutal, proved salutary. Men in Jackson's army jumped to do as they were told, and there was almost no insubordination during the final campaign against the Creeks.[28]

With a fairly powerful army for the first time, Andrew Jackson in the early spring of 1814 began his third advance southward out of Fort Strother toward the Holy Ground. The remainder of the Red Sticks, about 1,200 of them, had finally united and had taken up a completely defensive position. With some white help, probably Spanish, they built an earthworks across the open end of the Horseshoe Bend of the Tallapoosa River, enclosing about 300 acres. The entire peninsula made by the bend was forested and full of brush, and inside the works was a tangle of logs. At the closed end of the horseshoe the Creeks prepared a camp, amply stocked with water and food to withstand a siege.[29]

When Jackson arrived, he saw that the Indians had in fact shut themselves into a slaughter pen. Without delay, therefore, he began an attack on 27 March 1814. In the first stage the Cherokees swam the river and brought away the canoes tied at the camp. Jackson held up the next step, he said, until women and children might have a chance to escape, but it is not clear how they were to get away. At ten-thirty his 6-pounder began to fire. At the same time Coffee's men, waiting on the banks opposite the camp, either swam the river or else crossed over in the stolen canoes. At twelve-thirty the foot troops charged the earthworks, and with moderate casualties overran them. Inside the defensive position some 700 warriors were slaughtered, at a cost of 26 white men killed and 111 wounded. Now nothing stood in the way, and the Tennessee army continued on unopposed to the Holy Ground. There, Red Eagle walked into camp, found his way to Jackson's tent, and surrendered. He asked nothing for himself, but requested mercy for the starving Creek women and children. Touched by this manly approach, Jackson let him go free, and did provide some relief for his people. As William Weatherford, Red Eagle settled down in Alabama, and lived out the rest of his life as a planter.[30]

The series of battles, but especially Horseshoe Bend, had broken the fighting power of the Creek Confederation. Jackson disposed the troops to hold the advanced positions, and himself returned to Fort Deposit. His victory had made him the most famous American of the moment. His countrymen were starved for good war news, and Horseshoe Bend was the very best they had received since Perry's victory on Lake Erie. General Jackson had started up the ladder to a distinguished military career and to a more famous political one. Later, when a major general of the United States Army, he was commissioned to make the final treaty with the Creeks. On 9 August 1814 on behalf of the United States he took title in the Treaty of Fort Jackson to 20 million acres of Creek land. Almost as many Creeks had fought on the side of the United States as against them, but Jackson's treaty stripped friend and foe of lands, without discrimination.[31]

1814

Naval Actions on the Oceans

On 7 March 1814 Vice Admiral of the Red Sir Alexander Forrester Inglis Cochrane appeared at Bermuda to relieve Admiral Warren. Cochrane, the youngest son of the impecunious eighth Earl of Dundonald, had seen arduous service against the French monarchy during the American Revolution, and beginning in 1793 against the French Republic. After twenty-six years as a commissioned officer he had finally attained the rank of rear admiral in 1804. Sometime member of Parliament, Knight of the Bath, and governor of the Leeward Islands until 1814, Cochrane was well known in the navy as a competent professional. Subordinates found him easy to get along with. His fleet captain, Edward Codrington, said that his greatest weakness was too much trust in the persons around him. Cochrane's son, for example, commanded a ship in his fleet, and trafficked upon the connection. Sir John Fortescue, historian of the British army, categorized Cochrane with all Scottish admirals as greedy for loot, but Fortescue bore a continuous prejudice against the navy and possibly against the Scots.[1]

As far as is known, Warren had no personal antagonism to Cochrane, but he was slow to turn over the station to him. Moreover, Cochrane complained to his superiors that Warren did not even keep him abreast of events. Not until April Fools' Day did the command change hands.[2]

When Admiral Cochrane had been in control three weeks, he enlarged the blockade to include the entire coast of the United States. This meant that New England, which had received special consideration, was now lumped in with the rest of the nation. Cochrane was in-

Admiral Sir Alexander Cochrane

duced to do this by Congress' repeal during the spring of the embargo and nonimportation acts. Congress wanted the income which would flow from the opening of trade, and Cochrane wanted to cut it off. He also wanted to bottle up the United States naval vessels which were operating out of New England ports.[3]

Compared to American naval resources, Cochrane's command looked impressive. Two ships-of-the-line, 4 frigates, 11 sloops, and 1 schooner were stationed at Halifax or off Boston. Two frigates kept the vigil off Nantucket, and 2 ships-of-the-line, 1 frigate, and 2 sloops were off New London. There were 1 razee and 1 frigate off New York, 2 frigates off Delaware Bay, 2 ships-of-the-line, 2 frigates, 1 sloop, and 1 schooner around Chesapeake Bay, 1 razee and 3 sloops between Cape Hatteras and St. Marys River, 1 frigate, 2 sloops, and 2 schooners in the Gulf of Mexico. This totaled 6 ships-of-the-line, 13 frigates, 19 sloops, 2 razees, and 4 schooners, but the admiral insisted that he needed 17 more frigates, 21 more sloops, and 16 more small vessels. With the war in Europe ended, the Ministry could at least look at his demands without losing its composure.[4]

British naval officers had learned during the American Revolution that it was impossible during the winter to keep the northeastern coast of the United States under continuous blockade because of the strong westerly winds which drove the blockaders off station in spite of themselves. They had also learned that the vessels of the United States Navy operating out of northern ports would try to break out during foul weather, while those to the southward, where the westerly winds did not blow, would not.[5]

Gentlemen in the British navy detested blockade duty as both dull and cruel. Lieutenant Henry E. Napier recorded in his journal that his flotilla burned two vessels, but let a third go simply because it belonged to an old man with eight children who had lost $20,000 in shipping in the past two years. They burned a sloop with shingles on board, belonging to three "females" who had received the shingles as payment for teaching school, but the officers gave personal donations to recompense these three. A small shipowner was obliged to pay $200 ransom. With seven children and a heavy debt, "He with great difficulty scraped up by sixpenses and shillings the amount . . . and came on board with tears in his eyes." Napier concluded, "This is an ungenerous war against the poor, and unworthy of Englishmen."[6]

Blockade duty, although disagreeable, was effective. Combined with the operations of the mobile British fleet, it had by the summer of 1814 bottled up four vessels of the United States Navy, carrying 144 guns: *Congress, Constellation, John Adams,* and *United States. Adams,* 28 guns (not to be confused with *John Adams*, although both had 28 guns), got to sea late in the summer, only to be chased into the Penobscot River where her crew burned her on 3 September 1814, lest she fall into enemy hands.[7]

The naval odyssey which above all others captured the American imagination was that of *Essex*, a 32-gun frigate commanded by Captain David Porter. She sailed out of the Delaware River on 28 October 1812, cruised southward, rounded the Horn, and entered the Pacific Ocean. For a year she preyed on enemy shipping, and literally destroyed the British whale fishery. She took 15 prizes and converted several of them to naval use; so, whereas Porter had started with 1 ship and a crew of 319, he commanded at the maximum 7 ships, 80 guns, and 650 men. He trained his crews and enforced rules to preserve their health with uncommon efficiency. He was gone so long that it was necessary to heave his ships down in shallow water on an unknown, remote island to clean and repair them. He named the island for President Madison and became so involved in the politics and wars of the natives that only with difficulty was he able to leave the place. His cruise carried him to the Galápagos Islands where he filled the holds of his ship with the giant turtles unique to those islands. These could exist in the holds for a year without food and without care, and made excellent fresh meat for his crews.[8]

Early in 1814 Porter entered the harbor of Valparaíso, Chile. Three British men-of-war appeared, and one of them, *Phoebe*, came in and took a berth beside *Essex*. Porter was friendly with the officers, but began to fear that they meant to violate the neutrality of the port. What remained of his flotilla was no match for the British warships, and he sought to engage *Phoebe* in a single-ship duel. Even when the crew of *Essex* sang insulting songs for the benefit of the British crew, Captain James Hilyer would not agree to a fight. Finally on 28 March 1814, seventeen months to the day after his departure from Delaware Bay, Captain Porter made a run for the open sea. He was in poor luck, for a squall struck him, partially disabled his ship, and forced it on a course close to the neutral shore. Two of the British ships now openly attacked him. Porter had only one chance, to board *Phoebe*, but he could not sail close enough to do it. Because of damage to sailing gear and because of fire, he could not even run *Essex* ashore, so he allowed those of the crew who wanted to try it to jump overboard and swim the three-quarters of a mile to freedom. Finally, at 6:20 P.M., full of bitterness both at the breach of neutrality and of the gentleman's code of naval warfare, he had to strike his colors. He impugned the honor of his adversaries, but they insisted that their conduct had been ethical in all ways. Porter reported 58 killed, 66 wounded, and 31 missing. Captain Hilyer elected to parole Porter and his crew, and send them to the United States. Admiral Cochrane protested this, for he considered Porter a menace at large, and he called upon Porter to give himself up. He called in vain.

The United States brig *Frolic*, 18 guns, was captured on 20 April 1814. *Syren* too was taken. Schooner *Rattlesnake*, 14 guns, was captured on 22 June, but the schooner with which she had been teaming, *Enterprise*, escaped.[9]

The frigate *President*, rated at 44 but carrying 54 guns, remained at liberty until the end of the year. Stephen Decatur, bored with inactivity, issued a series of challenges to single-ship duels, but when these produced no action, he took advantage of a hard westerly wind and rough weather in December to make a dash for the ocean. *Macedonian*, captured from the British in 1812 and laid up during most of 1814, accompanied him. In the darkness and heavy sea, *President* ran aground and was twisted and battered for an hour and a half. Although she was badly strained, when finally free, Decatur chose to continue his dash. The British blockade commander had calculated about what would happen and where Decatur would emerge, and when *President* and *Macedonian* reached the ocean on the morning of 15 December 1814, they found four British warships waiting for them. Decatur spread full sail and wet it for speed, but *President* had lost her swiftness due to the strain. Nevertheless, there was a running fight for eighteen hours before she struck her colors. Meanwhile *Macedonian*, sailing beautifully, had outdistanced her preoccupied pursuers and escaped.[10]

Besides *Enterprise* and *Macedonian*, five other American warships of different classes remained at sea and eluded destruction or capture by the enemy until war's end. *Constitution*, 44 guns, had the satisfaction of capturing two small British naval vessels, *Cyane* and *Levant*, on 20 February 1815, but she at once had to abandon them and run for her life from a British squadron. *Hornet*, a United States 20-gun ship-sloop, captured *Penguin* after a battle in roaring westerly weather near Tristan da Cunha on 23 March 1815. Later she rounded the Cape of Good Hope, and was chased by a British 74. She outran her pursuer only by jettisoning her guns and nearly everything else. Thus shorn of power, she could do nothing but return home, where she learned that the war was over.[11]

Peacock, a war-built sloop-of-war of 24 guns, based on New York, was sometimes able to get to sea. On one foray she attacked the British brig *Epervier*, 18 guns, as the latter convoyed a small fleet of merchant vessels. The ships battered each other from 9:40 A.M. to 11:00 A.M. on 29 April 1814, but *Epervier's* fire was weak because her guns overturned with every recoil. Captain Richard H. Wales tried to board *Peacock*, but the crew would not follow him. He surrendered at 11:05 A.M. *Peacock* thus made a handsome haul, for her prize had on board $118,000 in specie. All of this money and the ship itself became legitimate booty for the captors, without the United States subtracting any share for itself, since the two vessels were of equal strength.[12]

No American ship had a better record than the sloop-of-war *Wasp*, 18 guns, Captain Johnston Blakely. On 28 June 1814 she captured and destroyed *Reindeer*, of about half her force. From 1 May to 6 July she captured a total of eight ships. On the first day of September she found herself near a flotilla of English cargo ships convoyed by war vessels. She cut out a brig, overpowered and burned it, then forced the surrender of another brig, *Avon*. At that point two large warships approached and forced her to flee. But late in September *Wasp* sank at sea, carrying down all hands.[13]

With characteristic optimism the United States continued to build naval vessels. The frigate *Guerrière*, 44 guns, was launched at Philadelphia in June 1814, and Captain Rodgers and his crew from *President* were sent to man her. Her sister ship *Java*, fine as a piece of cabinet work, was launched in August at Baltimore. But neither of these frigates was able to make its power felt during the war. Nor were the first American 74s. *Independence* was launched in June 1814 at Charlestown, Massachusetts, and *Washington* in October at Portsmouth, New Hampshire. Both of them were top-heavy and needed so many alterations that they finally served only as receiving ships. British authorities, supposing them to be as lethal in their class as the American frigates, directed their 74s to avoid tackling them on a ship-to-ship basis. Six sloops were finished during the war, and several more were on the stocks. But even when a ship was launched, the whole story had not been told. Guns and crews were nearly impossible to obtain.[14]

At the end of 1814 Congress had provided for a navy of four 74s, nine 44s, three 36s, eight sloops, and many brigs and schooners, carrying 1,300 guns, all told. There must be added to these the 125 gunboats still in service on the rivers and harbors and the lake flotilla, all of which carried a total of another 500 guns. To direct this enlarging navy, even though one of the 74s and four of the 44s had not yet been built, the secretary of the navy recommended that a flag rank be created and an admiral appointed to it. But he saw no virtue in adopting the brevet system used by the army.[15]

Henry Adams said with the benefit of hindsight that the United States Congress had been too much bemused by big ships. The war was over before the frigates and 74s, voted during the conflict, were of any use, whereas the sloops authorized in January 1813 were launched within eleven months. Moreover, it took 200 oak trees, the production of 57 acres, to build a 74, and in other ways they cost far, far more than the sloops. In addition, however industriously the United States built big ships, it still could not make much impression against Britain, which had no less than 1,000 naval vessels.[16]

Robert Fulton built the world's first steam frigate, *Fulton the First*, and launched it at New York on 31 October 1814. This unique ship was 145 feet long, 55 feet wide, with a draft of 8 feet. Each of her carronades could fire hot shot weighing 100 pounds, and she could make speeds of 3 to 4 knots against the wind. By way of defensive armor, she had timbers 5 feet thick, enlarged to 11 feet around the engine. If *Fulton the First* never attained enough readiness to be a menace in Long Island Sound, she at least frightened the British naval officers into asking for a special vessel to combat her.

Steamboats for transportation of supplies spread onto the rivers with surprising swiftness. The first one reached New Orleans on 10 January 1812 and was thereafter employed effectively on the river. The British leased a steamboat to carry troops and light freight on the St. Lawrence. But the full impact of the steamboat on war lay in the future.[17]

American merchant ships were virtually driven from the oceans. At no other time in history has the United States been so fully cut off from the sea. Imports of critical gunpowder dropped to one-sixth of the pre-war volume, a decline which did not produce military disaster only because of the rapid development of the DuPont works in Delaware to supply the deficiency. Fortunately for the United States, an effective blockade was not as decisive then as it would have been in 1776, or was to become later when nations had to have copper, rubber, and tin. Because of simpler economics and techniques, it was possible then to inconvenience a nation by blockade, but not to destroy its economy.[18]

British naval power not infrequently penetrated inland. A party of about 200 men in ship's barges started up the Connecticut River at 10:00 P.M. on 7 April 1814 to attack a quantity of shipping laid up six miles above the river's mouth. They brushed off a light militia attack, but because of adverse wind and current did not reach their quarry until 3:30 A.M. on 8 April. By 10:00 A.M. they had destroyed 27 vessels of 5,110 tons, pierced for 134 guns, and had inflicted a loss on Americans of no less than $100,000. By the time the destruction was complete, a rather amorphous defense had formed, which kept up a smart fusillade from the shores and lit the river with bonfires. Nevertheless, the ship's boats ran the narrows after dark and escaped with a loss of two killed and two wounded.[19]

In May two British war vessels drove back into New London a motley flotilla of ketches, schooners, and galleys which was attempting to move about on Long Island Sound. On rare occasions British aggression was repelled. When boats from *Endymion* were sent against a ship and a schooner becalmed off Nantucket, the becalmed vessels with uncanny accuracy shot away some of the sweeps, and, when the crippled boats clustered together, blasted them effectively. Once finally alongside, the attackers could not board the steep sides of the ships, and had to withdraw with a loss of 17 killed and 45 wounded.[20]

On 18 July Admiral Cochrane got around to issuing general orders which denounced the American conduct of war as barbarous. He cited Dover and other places in Canada, and directed commanders to lay waste towns and districts within their reach until the United States paid indemnity. He sent along, however, a secret directive which allowed local commanders to spare places that would be useful to them. He authorized them, too, to lay contributions on the inhabitants of spared places equal to the value of the unharmed property. He ordered them to bear hardest on persons known to be of the President's party.[21]

The retaliation orders were in effect one month before Admiral Cochrane informed Secretary of State Monroe of them. Three weeks later Monroe replied with a denial that Britain had either legal or moral grounds for retaliation. He cited Indian atrocities, the River Raisin massacre, and the burning of Havre de Grace as evidence. He also referred to the recent burning of the public buildings in Washington. But the United States government, he said, disavowed responsibility for the burning of Newark, Long Point, and St. Davids.[22]

Not much devastation grew out of Cochrane's retaliation order. Rear Admiral Henry Hotham, however, took it as authority to punish Stonington, Connecticut, for harboring torpedoes. Four British warships began to bombard Stonington on 9 August 1814. They ceased fire at the end of the day, but resumed it on 11 August. The fort stoutly replied, and the local militia swarmed 3,000 strong to repel the expected landing. The vessels drew off when night came and did not return. Wareham, Massachusetts, however, did not escape. Vessels there and a cloth factory worth $20,000 were burned, and 10 ships were destroyed at Scituate.[23]

American torpedoes were not very lethal, but British officers considered them engines of the devil, unfit for civilized warfare. In the same category was the "turtle boat" which Robert Fulton invented to submerge and attach torpedoes to ships' bottoms. Fulton's boat actually got beneath *Ramillies,* and its crew bored a hole in the copper sheathing, but broke the bolt which was to fasten the torpedo. After this narrow escape Captain Thomas Hardy withdrew his ships from New London, and kept them in motion at all times. He notified the Americans that prisoners of war would be aboard all his ships and would be blown up with them.[24]

Late in June the turtle boat washed ashore on Long Island. The British blockaders hastened to view the monster and to put an end to it. American militiamen were waiting for them behind the dunes, but British boats went in covered by the guns of *Maidstone* and *Sylph.* After one round the Americans fled, and the invaders proceeded to blow up the craft, which they said looked just like a stranded whale.[25]

Finally in January 1815 Admiral Cochrane withdrew his system of retaliation from towns known to disapprove of America's hostilities, most of which were in New England. He directed his subordinates at the same time to bear harder on places which harbored privateers, for it was the privateers who really hurt England. Privateers had virtually succeeded in imposing a blockade upon England itself. A privateer captain named Ordronaux sent in a mock paper declaring the east coast of the British Isles under blockade. In fact, a guardian flotilla of 3 frigates and 14 sloops did not prevent American privateers from capturing scores of vessels close to the home islands. Depredations by privateers drove insurance rates on cargo ships so high that the English shipping trade was jeopardized. The resultant melting of profits in the end helped produce in Britain a determination to bring the war to a conclusion on whatever terms.[26]

Profit-minded Americans had created a type of vessel especially well suited to commerce raiding. It was a sort of schooner with ship or brig rigging. It had speed and an uncanny ability to sail into the wind. When heavier British vessels were closing in on it, they were often astounded to see it virtually head into the wind and outrun them. It carried 16 to 18 guns and 100 to 150 sailors. It did not fight warships unless cornered, but outran them. On the other hand, it could outmaneuver and outfight armed merchantmen.

General Armstrong, one of the famous American privateers, carried 8 long 9-pounders, 1 long 42, and 90 men. She had taken $1 million in English property when cornered in September 1814 in the Portuguese port of Fayal by *Rota* and *Plantagenet.* Captain Sam C. Reid contended that the two British ships attacked him in neutral waters, but the British captains said Reid fired the first shot. Whatever the truth, they captured *General Armstrong* on 26 September 1814, but only after a fight which cost them 36 killed and 84 wounded, against 2 Americans killed and 7 wounded.[27]

American ships, the British government reported, captured 16 of their naval vessels during the war, carrying 266 guns and 2,015 seamen. The Ministry never published a figure on merchant ships captured by all sorts of American vessels, and American figures range from a low of 1,300 to a high of 2,500. On the other hand, British sources claimed the capture of 34 American naval vessels, with 400 guns and 1,956 men, not counting those on the Great Lakes. In addition they claimed the capture of 1,400 American ships and a total of 17,885 seamen. On both sides, maritime attrition, even though not known accurately, was very heavy and moved the belligerents to seek peace.[28]

Hearing that the inhabitants of Nantucket were starving, Admiral Hotham sent a naval vessel there. He was willing for the people to import goods if they would announce themselves neutral—that is, if they would pay no taxes to the United States, surrender their warlike stores to the British, and supply British ships when requested to do so. Nantucket accepted these conditions, and became neutral on 23 August 1814. Other towns in the Cape Cod area were assessed contributions ranging from $4,000 for Brewster to $1,200 for Eastham. The banks of Portland, Maine, buried their specie, while the people of Salem, expecting momentary attack, sent off 500 wagonloads of goods in a single day.[29]

One of the objects of such British strategy as had been formed was to control the land along the route which ran in a straight line from Halifax westward to Quebec. On 5 July an expedition left Halifax for this purpose. It easily took Eastport on Moose Island, the easternmost town in the United States, and the entire Bay population swore allegience to the king of England. Next, late in August, a British flotilla of boats entered the Penobscot River. The diminutive federal garrison there could do nothing but set fire to its stores and retire, while the local militia made only a pitifully weak stand. Within two weeks England controlled all of Maine east of the Penobscot. The male citizens quietly took the oath of allegiance to the king, and 100 miles of seacoast, with the land behind it, became for a second time part of the British Empire. As England did not want the area west of the river, she made no significant assaults there.[30]

The Great Lakes

At the start of the year 1814 the focal point for both belligerents remained, as before, the Great Lakes region. Neither of them, however, possessed the forces to cover all the vital points within that vast territory, nor did either have a certain knowledge of where they ought to concentrate what they had. Both of them knew, though, that they needed naval superiority on the Great Lakes. In England where no less an authority than Lord Wellington said so, the Ministry took steps to involve the Admiralty in trying to achieve it. During the third week in January 1814 J. W. Croker designated Sir James Lucas Yeo to be the naval commander on the lakes, including shore installations. Yeo had been on duty there since May 1813, but he was now for the first time freed from subordination to the admiral commanding the North Atlantic Station. At the same time he was authorized to expect all possible aid from that commander.[1]

As of early March the British were temporarily behind in the perennial shipbuilding race on Lake Ontario: 8 ships carrying 76 long guns and 108 carronades, and 2 being built, compared to 11 ships and 5 being built for the Americans. They tipped the scale in their favor, however, when on 15 April they launched *Prince Regent*, 58 guns, and *Princess Charlotte*, 42, which gave them an advantage of about 25 guns. But this margin did not make them feel able to seek out and try to destroy the American flotilla, which was, as was common with the underdog, taking refuge in its principal harbor and staying there except for occasional brief forays.[2]

The costs of the naval race were proving hard for England to bear. Guns for her ships had to be hauled by land lest they be captured, and 200 ox-teams were secretly hired in Vermont and New Hampshire to sled them. But even with the economies made possible by sledding on ice and snow, it cost £6,000 to haul 46 guns to Kingston.[3]

Manning the lake flotillas was a problem for both belligerents. It became necessary for the British to inactivate two sea-going ships in order to send the crews to the lakes. On the American side the tight blockade idled several naval vessels, so their crews were also sent to the Great Lakes. The lake service was not popular among salt-water sailors, but after the pay for it was raised by the United States, the old salts went cheerfully enough. Neither side, however, was able to find all the men it needed.

Lieutenant General Sir Gordon Drummond took charge at Kingston on 13 December 1813 as President Administering the Government of Upper Canada. In the middle of February the Parliament of Upper Canada met in a 30-day session, during which it pleased Drummond by its tractability. To begin with, it suspended the privilege of the writ of habeas corpus to make treason easier to punish. Next it acquiesced when the general resorted to martial law to procure supplies and set prices. It took the occasion, however, to point out to the Prince Regent that the war had withdrawn about 15,000 men from agriculture in Upper Canada, and that since there had been several harvest failures, the province was suffering from real hunger.[4]

Surveying Upper Canada from Kingston, General Drummond saw Detroit and the Lake Erie fleet as the best strategic objectives. He proposed to leave 1,200 men to guard the Niagara front, and pass on the ice to assail Detroit with 1,760 picked soldiers, who could easily overpower the 600 Americans reputed to be there. Not much about his picked force was orthodox. They were to be armed with bill hooks, hatchets, and axes, and were to drag their equipment over land and ice on 132 sleighs. Alternately pulling and riding, they could average 30 miles a day. General Prevost gave timid approval to this, provided it was carried out swiftly. He hastened to add that he could send no reinforcements to Drummond for the expedition. With normal cold weather, Drummond's plan would have had a good chance of success, but it was never tried because the winter remained too mild and the ice too thin.[5]

On the American side it was Secretary Armstrong who urged taking advantage of the ice and snow. As troop movements by the British along the line of the St. Lawrence were reported to him, he suggested that Montreal might be dangerously undergarrisoned and especially vulnerable to attack. Nothing came of this suggestion. Toward the end of January he presented the idea of an attack in the Niagara area to General Wilkinson. Whatever Wilkinson thought of the scheme, Armstrong on 21 February 1814 ordered Jacob Brown to invest Fort Niagara. That same day however he issued a contradictory order to Brown: if Chauncey approved, to attack Kingston as soon as the ice was out of the lake. He later asserted that he never intended for the Niagara order to be obeyed; it was to fall into British hands to deceive them, but this fact was never communicated to Brown.[6]

General Brown had to interpret his orders, and he decided that they told him to provide for the security of Sackett's Harbor, then to proceed to Niagara. As soon as Brigadier General Edmund P. Gaines arrived to assume command at Sackett's, Brown began his march. But beset by misgivings along the way, he left his column and returned. On

24 March, after conferences with Gaines and Chauncey, he once more concluded that Niagara was his objective and started out again. His force reached Batavia, 40 miles short of Niagara, on the last day of March. There he received a letter from Armstrong, dated 20 March, which told him that he had misunderstood the secretary's orders. But it also told him to continue on his present course. "Good consequences," Armstrong said, "are sometimes the results of mistakes." Brown was distressed that he had misunderstood, but glad to be at last in phase with the secretary. He prepared to concentrate near the ruins of Buffalo. There he could face both ways: toward Detroit when the time to attack it came, and toward Lake Ontario where he could harass the foe while Chauncey built up his strength. Chauncey said he would not be able to aid the army until June.[7]

With Brown near Buffalo the strategic picture was sharply altered. While at Kingston he had held the principal northern force close to the critical pressure point on the main artery of British power in Canada. Now, on the other hand, he had it placed 200 miles westward where it could not possibly achieve strategic objectives equal to the cutting of the St. Lawrence. Yet the place was not without advantages. From it he might gain control of Lakes Erie and Huron and of the trade of most of the westerly tribes of Indians.

General Brown found Major General Amos Hall of the New York militia trying to hold together a small force on the Niagara front. Since the militia of the area itself had been hopelessly demoralized, Hall had to seek his men elsewhere. The secretary of war called on Pennsylvania for 1,000 citizen soldiers, and Governor Tompkins of New York, with his usual energy, directed western New York to provide two regiments of volunteers. Ontarians and British deserters were welcomed.[8]

General Hall resigned in disgust after he failed to secure either arms or pay for his men. Brigadier General Peter B. Porter succeeded him, and Porter's first job was to recruit the two regiments from the West, as ordered by the governor. Failure to pay Hall's men made recruiting difficult, as did the scarcity of equipment; but try as he might, Tompkins could find no supplies. The going wages also hampered the attempt to raise men. The farmers in the area were paying $15.00 per month for help, whereas Porter could offer only $8.00.[9] When Secretary Armstrong attempted to procure the promised equipment, he too encountered difficulties. All the arms available to the quartermaster at Albany had been issued to militia who had wasted them. Such waste, Armstrong said, was as dangerous as the enemy himself, and he made specific proposals to stop it in the future.[10]

Now and then British foraging parties landed somewhere on the shores of Lake Ontario and confiscated supplies. In a few cases bands of militiamen materialized to oppose them, but not often. General Porter could not collect enough New York volunteers to fill even one of the two regiments he had been told to raise, but he joined Brown at the head of 500 Indians and a regiment of drafted Pennsylvania militiamen. These men had been given two weeks after notification of draft to make their arrangements. As soon as they assembled, they received some necessaries, and on the fifth day of service they were issued tents and camp kettles. On the nineteenth day they drew pay from the state. Well supplied as the regiment was, the supply wagons often could not keep up with it because of the mud, and the men still had to "Lay out without tents and had nothing to eat." At first the men underwent no drill, but spent the time in fatigue duty, hunting, fishing, reading, washing, and mending clothes. Then in May the officers began to drill one another three hours a day, and a week later started to train the enlisted men too.

Four Pennsylvanians deserted but were caught. In the words of one of the spectators, they "were drummed round the Camp with their half rations of Meet tied round their necks, with roughs march played after them." For disobedience of orders a man was drummed down the line wearing a crown of straw, a hair tail with a parcel of bones tied to it, and a head of cabbage around his neck.[11]

The Ministry in England saw clearly at the beginning of 1814 that they would soon have resources to shift from Europe to America. Private persons deluged them with advice. The least expected bit of advice came from James Stephen, an old America-hater and author of the Orders in Council. Reversing his previous recommendation to crush the United States, he announced that it was essential to make peace on any decent terms. If this was not done, France would ally with the United States, and the two in the end would force England to give up her much-cherished naval rights.[12]

Most of the gratuitous advisors disagreed with Stephen. Their line in general was that in twenty years the United States would become a deadly rival of England, equal to her in population, resources, and commerce. One of them made the case in bad metaphor: the young nation would become "a nest egg of mischief where all the violent spirits of Europe will take shelter." Sir John Sinclair insisted that all Americans, especially President Madison, hated England and sought to undermine her commerce and steal her possessions in the Western Hemisphere. This gave her the moral right to strike now for the sake of security later. There were other moral grounds for what we would now call a pre-emptive strike. The United States had shown herself indifferent through two decades to Europe's struggle to prevent Napoleon from becoming dictator of a continent; what is more, in starting a "wanton and unnecessary war" she had turned parricide and become a tool for Napoleon. The London *Times* urged between tirades against the United States that no less than 20,000 soldiers be sent across the Atlantic to insure success.[13]

As early as January 1814 Bathurst wrote to Wellington that the time had come to break up his army and send some of it to America. A month passed before the Duke replied. The larger the army operating in America, he said, the more it would be tied to the waterways. There was no prospect of easy victory in America. Since he did not argue against the shipment of his troops, the government started four regiments over during the first two months of 1814.[14]

Napoleon abdicated on 11 April 1814. Two living members of the British Ministry had helped force him to it. Castlereagh had made the decision to continue the war in Spain and to reappoint Wellington, while Liverpool had husbanded the strength of England for the long, dogged struggle.[15]

Three days after the abdication Bathurst informed Prevost that aid would be forthcoming to Canada. Just about the same time, although the Ministry did not find it out until July, Prevost was attempting to arrange an armistice. Over the opposition of Drummond and Yeo, he sent Adjutant Edward Baynes to Lake Champlain on 1 May to meet an American emissary. Nothing came of it because the United States representative had no authority to act. But as soon as word of this attempt reached Lord Bathurst, he wrote sharply to Prevost. The intention of the government, he said, was to prosecute the war more vigorously. If Prevost had signed any sort of armistice, he must inform the United States of its immediate termination.[16]

Commanders on both sides kept their attention riveted on the strategic spot where the St. Lawrence River flowed out of Lake Ontario. Generals Gaines and Brown were sure in mid-April that an attack upon Sackett's Harbor was imminent, and they rightly divined the intention of the enemy. General Prevost had indeed represented to Drummond the need to destroy the fleet at Sackett's. Drummond was as much in favor of doing this as Prevost, but he, with Yeo concurring, set the number of men needed at no less than 4,000, which was 1,000 more than could be scraped together. When Drummond asked for reinforcements to make up the difference, Prevost told him that while Lower Canada was under threat he could not expect any.[17]

On the American side, General Brown informed the secretary that although he had 3,500 troops, they were divided between Sackett's Harbor and Niagara, with the entire length of Lake Ontario between them. But even if they were concentrated, he said, he could not take the offensive. Sackett's Harbor was the best vantage point for him, and he intended to remain there unless ordered elsewhere by the secretary himself.[18]

Unable to attack Sackett's Harbor, Drummond and Yeo plotted to destroy Oswego, which was an indispensable depot on the end of the American supply line from the Hudson River to Sackett's. Lieutenant Colonel G. A. Mitchell of the Third United States Artillery reached Oswego on 30 April with a small detachment. He found the pickets of the fort rotten, the cannon few and in poor repair, and he set to work to upgrade what he could. He was never able to assemble more than 300 men, and knew full well that he could not defend the place against a determined assault, but he pitched his tents on one side of the Oswego River and hid his men in the fort on the other in order to deceive the enemy. They appeared before him on 5 May, 7 transports, 900 soldiers, and 11 gunboats, but a heavy wind drove them away. Better weather came the next day, and at 11:00 P.M. they began to come ashore again, the men wading in through waist-deep water. Mitchell posted his men in a ditch, safe from the ships' guns, and opened fire as soon as the foe's artillery cover lifted. After half an hour he ordered a planned retreat toward Sackett's. The foe moved in and captured all the cannon, as well as large stores of provisions. The British lost 19 men killed and 62 wounded, against 6 Americans killed, 38 wounded, and 25 captured.[19]

After the British had picked up or destroyed the captured goods, they evacuated Oswego. Secretary Armstrong regarded the place as important, and the Americans soon began to use it again. Late in May there arrived 21 long 32-pounders, 10 24-pounders, and 3 42-pound carronades. These guns had to be moved to Sackett's Harbor, 40 miles away, in order to be installed in the American flotilla. Chauncey gave the task to Master Commandant Melancthon Woolsey, and General Brown attached to him 150 men from the United State Rifle Regiment, under the command of Major Daniel Appling. Woolsey loaded the precious guns into 18 boats and started out of Oswego during the night of 28 May. Besides his slender crews and the riflemen, he had only 200 Indians. Conscious of their peril, his men rowed 12 hours without rest, then pulled into Sandy Creek, 16 miles from Sackett's, to hide and to recuperate. A British force commanded by Captain Stephen Popham was looking for them. Tracing his quarry to Sandy Creek, Popham sailed up the waterway as far as he could, then put his men ashore to attack. Although he did not know it, riflemen and Indians were in the woods all around him. Once his detachment was well committed, accurate fire struck them from all sides. The guns on the American boats opened upon their front. In no time Popham's force of 137 was powerless, 10 of them killed, 52 badly wounded, and the rest captured. Thus the essential guns traveled onward to Sackett's, except for two 24-pounders which disappeared with one of the boats.[20]

Since neither side could mount a decisive offensive, there were many scattered actions by local detachments. In one such, Captain A. H. Holmes led 160 American men into the countryside along the Thames River, 110 miles from Detroit. A superior British force moved out against him, and learning of its approach, he took up a strong defensive position on top of a hill. He next allowed his British opposite, Captain J. L. Barden, to lure him down by means of a ruse, but at once saw his error and regained his stronghold before he could be cut off. There 240 Canadians attacked him on three sides. Because his men were not up to complicated maneuvers, Holmes formed them in a hollow square, protected by logs and dirt. When the attackers found they could not overrun the position, they retired behind trees and kept up a galling fire until twilight, when they withdrew. Their loss was 14 killed and 52 wounded, compared to 4 Americans killed and 3 wounded. The Americans had made a fine showing, but their battle had scant strategic significance.[21]

Commodore Chauncey launched *Superior* on 1 May 1814. She was larger than the frigate *President*, carried 64 guns, and had been built in only 80 days. She virtually equalized the two Ontario flotillas, but this fact did not prevent British foraging parties from operating where they willed. A flotilla of British gunboats came to the mouth of the Genessee River and demanded the surrender of the hamlet of Charlotte. General Porter, who ranged far and wide, happened to be there. When he refused to surrender the place, the gunboats began firing from a mile away. Their fire had little effect, and they soon departed.[22]

John B. Campbell had been commissioned lieutenant colonel straight from civil life in Virginia when the war broke out in 1812. In April 1814 he was promoted to colonel, and now was stationed on Lake Erie. Determined to do something, on 14 May he loaded 800 men into prize ships, reconditioned for United States service at Put-in Bay, and sent them unopposed to Port Dover. Residents of this place had convinced him that it was a settlement of Old Tories who hated the United States and had been foremost in the looting and plundering of Buffalo and Black Rock. Accordingly, he burned three flour mills, three sawmills, three distilleries, and about twenty houses. He shot all the livestock and left the carcasses to rot (at least so the inhabitants later deposed). He was reported to have said that he burned Dover in retaliation for Buffalo, Havre de Grace, and Lewiston. When General Riall sent a courier to ask whether or not the government had sanctioned this destruction, Campbell replied that he alone had planned and executed it. Not even the victims accused his men of rape or indignities to the weak and helpless, but only of plundering and burning. Similar depredations occurred at Long Point, but these seem to have been the work of renegade Canadians who were settling old scores. Various other raiders ranged widely, spreading terror and anarchy.

Campbell reported to the secretary of war that he could have marched from Dover straight to Burlington Heights if he had had supplies. Since he did not make that march, it is hard to find profit in his foray. Captain John Sinclair, who commanded the American ships, criticized Campbell for acting on the testimony of partisan officers and citizens, "who are biast by individual motives." About one month after the destruction of Dover, an American court of inquiry found that Campbell did right in burning the public buildings and the mills, but wrong in burning the houses. Revenge, it said, was not part of warfare. Nevertheless, he was not subject to any severer discipline than a mild reprimand, but he died of wounds received at Chippewa the following July.[23]

The failure at Sandy Creek had made Commodore Yeo edgy. Early in June he reported that he was already short 280 seamen, and that when his new ship was ready he would need 640 more. His case of nerves showed in a letter to General Drummond: "I shall at all times be ready to take the Squadron into action, whenever the General Officer with whom I am acting represents to me that he thinks it necessary . . . but such Sanction or authority under existing conditions I will require, as I can never take the whole responsibility upon myself." Drummond was perfectly willing to share the responsibility, but assured the commodore that at this time he was able only to stay on the defensive.

About the middle of June the United States launched *Mohawk*. This made the total of vessels about equal, but gave the Americans 251 guns to 222 for the British, with a broadside weight of 4,188 against 2,752. The American naval service on the Great Lakes now had 3,321 men in it, which was more than double the British figure of 1,517.[24]

Secretary Armstrong, conscious of the naval advantage, urged General Brown to make the most of it. He suggested building a number of armed galleys at Sackett's Harbor to cut communications in the St. Lawrence between Kingston and Montreal. But above all he urged action in the Niagara theater, for this was the one area where the army could act on foreign soil with minimum naval assistance. The spot he picked as most vulnerable was Fort Erie, which reportedly had a garrison of no more than 300 to 400. Brown saw the strategy the same way as Armstrong: "If we can conquer or render useless to the enemy the force he has on the [Ontario] peninsula," he said, "we may hope to reach Kingston in the course of the campaign." He shaped his plans to depart Sackett's Harbor about 1 July, but did not expect much help from the navy, even though it was temporarily in the ascendant.[25]

General Brown of course could not issue orders to Commodore Chauncey. The practice of unified command did not exist. It is true General Wilkinson had been invested with it for a time at New Orleans, but the naval officers there had never ceased to oppose it. They had the force of printed regulations behind them. These stated that no army officer was to command a ship, no naval officer was to command army troops when the two services were acting together. If the navy put a detachment ashore, it must be exclusively a naval detachment commanded by a naval officer. Even though officers of the two services understood that they should share supplies for the national good, whenever the association went beyond that there was much lamentation. When Captain Hugh Campbell was ordered to consider his vessels under the command of General Pinckney, commander of the Sixth Military District, he suffered wounded pride and loss of interest in his profession. To dissuade the naval establishment in Washington from continuing this anomalous arrangement, he pointed out that it increased naval costs, while reducing those of the army. Captain J. D. Dent at Charleston reacted the same way to a similar order. "I cannot consent [to obey the orders of an officer of the army] as this arrangement is novel and the order not a general one. I will not be the first to establish the precedent. . . . My feelings as an officer compel me to disobey such an order." He preferred court-martial, he said, to service under army command. But in spite of protests, a few captains in the navy received orders from army officers during the war and obeyed them. They did not, however, consider that they were establishing a precedent. And they were right, for as late as 23 November 1814 the secretaries of war and navy issued a joint statement that the officers of one service were not to be allowed to command the forces of the other.[26]

The Niagara Theater

With the war against Napoleon finished, the Ministry in England for the first time made some elaborate plans to transfer a part of the victorious army from Europe to America, and formulated certain broad strategic objectives for the army in America. Lord Bathurst communicated the strategy to Governor Prevost in a letter written 3 June 1814. Prevost was ordered first to provide immediate protection to British possessions, then to look toward ultimate security. Under the head of immediate protection the secretary enumerated the destruction of Sackett's Harbor and of the United States naval power on the Great Lakes and on Lake Champlain. For permanent security Britain would have to control the Niagara valley and as much of the adjacent territory as Prevost should think necessary. Occupation of Detroit and Mackinac would also be essential. Britain might retain the Niagara region, but would restore the Michigan country, including Detroit, to the Indians.[1]

On Lake Ontario the actual situation was at a stalemate, but the United States dominated Lake Erie and would continue to do so as long as she maintained strength in the Niagara valley. Lake Huron, on the other hand, was securely a British preserve during all of 1814. The St. Lawrence, since the failure of Wilkinson's campaign, seemed to be a British preserve too. When everything had been weighed, the cabinet of the United States decided on 7 June to make the main drive of the campaign season against the British center at Niagara. General Prevost also viewed Niagara as the place to have a fight. There and only there could he employ British power offensively before major reinforcements came from Europe.[2]

Lieutenant General Sir Gordon Drummond had about 2,700 men and 100 officers near Niagara, and 1,700 more men and another 100 officers scattered at Long Point, Burlington, and York. This was not strength enough to contain the American attack which he expected in the Niagara theater. Drummond requested reinforcements from Prevost. The latter at once informed him that there were none to spare, and even intimated that action in that theater should be started by British forces, not the Americans.[3]

Certain Pennsylvania regiments had to be coerced to march toward Niagara. One Pennsylvanian who went willingly, however, was Private John Withrow, Jr. He reported in his journal seeing "Brigadeader Genl. Wingfield Scott." At the same time he recorded that the drill became intense, and that the regulars fought a sham battle in front of the citizen soldiers, using blank cartridges. He did not realize that what he was watching was the taking effect of the influence of Winfield Scott, a strict disciplinarian and intensive trainer. Scott was engrossed in making professionals out of the men in his brigade of regulars. For three months, while he was idle at Buffalo, he drilled and inspected them. Also, since suitable blue cloth was not available, he uniformed them in short gray jackets, white trousers, and tall leather hats, never knowing that he was thereby designing the uniform of future cadets at West Point.[4]

Major General Jacob Brown, following Armstrong's suggestion, directed the opening American offensive against Fort Erie. On 3 July his force easily overpowered the garrison of 10 officers and 155 men without loss of life on either side. This gave his army a foothold in Canada, from which it began cautiously to advance northward. One hundred and twenty Pennsylvanians refused to cross over into Canada (they were within their legal rights), but 480 did accompany the invading column.[5]

Major General Phineas Riall knew that his enemy had come into Canada, but not that he had captured Fort Erie. Assuming that most of the invasion force would be besieging Erie, he marched southward, only to run into American engineers, with some infantry, building a bridge across the Chippewa River. He used two 24-pounders and a line of skirmishers to break up the work, then he took position north of the river. On the night of 4 July 1814, when Brown's army camped behind Street's Creek, the opposing forces lay about a mile and a half apart. General Brown himself reached camp around 11:00 P.M.[6]

There was a plain three-quarters of a mile wide between Street's Creek and the Chippewa River. It was bounded on the west by thick woods and on the east by the Niagara River, about a mile above the great falls. Brown and others were up with daylight, reconnoitering and skirmishing. British Indians galled the American force from the woods. Late in the afternoon Brown ordered Porter to drive them out. Porter led out 400 Indians and 300 Pennsylvania volunteers, crossed Street's Creek, and plunged into the forest. After his men had handily cleared the woods, they bumped into a column of British regulars. Perhaps John Withrow's account of what happened is the most remarkable of all. "We marched down to near Chapaway, and General Porter called on our Regiment for some vollinteers to go out on a Scout and about 200 of our Regiment with 450 indians advanced within a mile of Chipawa when we met some of the enemy we drove them till their main body the let loose their artilery on us when we

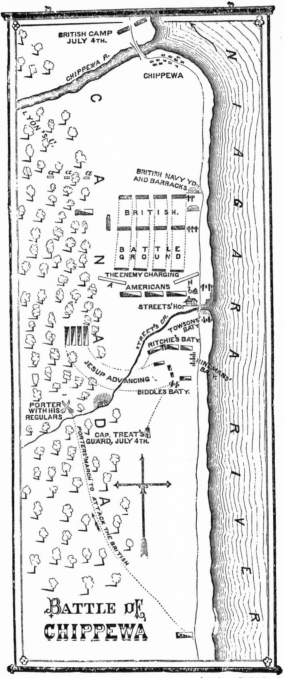

were obliged to retreat a short Distance till general Scott Came to our assistance with the regulars which soon Compelled the enemy to retreat to their fort. . . ."

General Brown described the same action, and at first reported that the militia fled in all directions. General Porter took exception to this. Even when Brown modified his version to say that he did not expect the militia to stand against British regulars, Porter still protested. His men deserved not faint praise but commendation, for they had done double the work of any other troops. Although tired and half a mile ahead of all support, they had attacked the British regulars twice. For a force which had been designated only a scouting party, they had performed beyond the call of duty.

Brown reached the conclusion that the British were actually advancing in force. Late in the afternoon he ordered Winfield Scott to bring his brigade onto the plain. Scott was just in the act of doing this for another reason: to drill his men on the open ground, for he did not believe that the enemy was there in force. In a very short time his brigade was crossing the bridge over Street's Creek where to his surprise it came under fire from three heavy cannon. Now training told. His column of 1,500 men passed over the bridge under fire and formed flawlessly into line of battle. Their skill came as a shock to General Riall, who had been carelessly watching their movement. "Those are regulars, by God," he said and began to reassess his position. With his back to the Chippewa, 150 yards wide where the bridge crossed it, he was in a precarious situation against disciplined troops.

Of four batteries of artillery on the American side, Nathan Towson's was closest to the enemy. From its position just south of the mouth of Street's Creek it now heavily attacked the enemy line. This preparation was followed by a battle in classical eighteenth-century style, the only one during the war in which numbers were about equal.

Scott begain to notice that the British regiments were handled unevenly, and that they often exposed their flanks. His line worked its way forward, alternately halting to fire, then advancing again, until at 80 paces he bellowed above the din that Americans must now prove their ability to handle bayonets. Then he personally led the Eleventh Infantry against one of the temporary flanks. His charge broke the British cohesion and pushed their units backward toward the bridge over the Chippewa. A strong pursuit might have trapped them, but the Americans, stunned by what they had already done, did not make it. Riall was able to march back across the bridge and tear up the planking.

British losses in this, the Battle of Chippewa, were not far from one-third of the force engaged: 148 killed and 321 wounded. Such casualties showed the accuracy of American fire, both from shoulder arms and from artillery. American losses were 60 killed, 235 wounded. General Brown was elated with the performance and repeatedly requested brevet promotions for General Scott, Major Henry Leavenworth, commanding the Ninth Infantry, Major John McNeil, Twenty-second, and Major Thomas S. Jesup of the Twenty-fifth.

On 7 or 8 July Riall had to retire to Fort George because the Americans had cut a road from Street's Creek to Lyon's Creek, where they could cross and turn his flank. Brown moved his men into the erstwhile British works behind the Chippewa, then onward to Queenston, which to his surprise was also evacuated. Leaving garrisons at both places, he advanced to the shores of Lake Ontario in the hope of meeting Commodore Chauncey there on 10 July. Army and navy would then assail Burlington together. General Drummond feared just this strategy. Riall believed that none of the three forts, Niagara, George, or Mississaga, could withstand heavy attack. He proposed to place minimum garrisons in them, take 900 men, meet a detachment of troops from Burlington, and travel with this force over the short hills and Lundy's Lane to the enemy's rear.[7]

The American plan was foiled when Chauncey did not appear. Both sides had expected him because Yeo had lifted his blockade of Sackett's Harbor, and because the American flotilla held a slight advantage at the moment. Disappointed and annoyed, General Brown wrote to Chauncey on 13 July: "For God's sake let me see you; Sir James will not fight . . . at all events have the politeness to let me know what aid I am to expect from the fleet on Lake Ontario . . . this army can march and fight all over the area if the fleet will carry the supplies." He assured the commodore that working together they could take Burlington, York, and finally Kingston. Chauncey did not reply, probably because of illness, nor did his flotilla do anything except keep on building vessels. Paralysis seemed to Secretary Jones to have struck the lake service, and on 28 July he ordered Captain Stephen Decatur to proceed to the lakes and take over from Chauncey. Very soon Jones learned of Chauncey's illness and suspended the order; Decatur, who anticipated the new assignment, never did get it.[8]

Finally on 10 August Chauncey was able to reply to his critics. He told the secretary that he was sorry to have disappointed the public, but that even if he had been well he could not have accomplished what was expected of him. His ships were not ready. Even so, he had brought two frigates and two sloops to completion much faster than had been done by the ocean-going fleet. Brown had had no grounds to expect aid from him, he continued, for Chauncey had informed him that he could not take his flotilla to the head of the lake unless the enemy did so. Nor could the two services have collaborated in any case because of the shallowness of the water. Finally, he explained that he had not passed the command to his second because he had daily expected to be up and active.[9]

He replied to General Brown much more harshly. The fleet could not have got within two miles of Fort George or nine miles of Burlington Heights. To Brown's tactless statement that "this army can march and fight all over this area if the fleet will carry the supplies," he responded with hauteur, "The Secretary of the Navy has honored us with a higher destiny—we are intended to seek and to fight the enemy's fleet . . . I shall not be diverted . . . by any sinister attempt to render us subordinate to, or an appendage of, the Army."[10]

When Brown finally received this letter on 4 September, he was not much impressed. There was no basis for Chauncey to be offended by what he, Brown, had said, unless he considered the flotilla his own property, not the government's. It was the government which had led Brown to expect cooperation from the navy. As for the barrier to cooperation which Chauncey contended the shallow water created, this shallowness simply did not exist. With supplies which only the navy could have transported, the army might have gained control of the head of Lake Ontario.[11]

While vainly waiting for the navy, Brown had taken a brigade and made a reconnaissance in force at Fort George. He found that there was no chance to overpower the place without the help of heavy naval guns. General Riall was of the same mind. Under existing conditions he could defend Fort George with the 600 men in it, and Fort Mississaga with its 400 men. Thus, when Brown learned later that the naval guns he had expected were blockaded in at Sackett's Harbor, he pulled back southward to the Chippewa River. On 19 July the Americans evacuated and burned Queenston and St. Davids. Fire did not consume much of Queenston, but it wiped out the forty houses which had made up St. Davids. Lieutenant Colonel Isaac Stone denied that he had ordered this destruction, but he was relieved by Brown and immediately retired from the military service.[12]

For some reason General Brown decided to take another look at Fort George. He ordered General Scott to try to draw the foe out of his works there, but Scott had no success. While Brown's reconnaissance force was forward, General Riall had an army of maneuver at a short distance outside the fort, but Brown did not seek to attack and destroy this. Instead, he dropped back swiftly to protect his communications. Riall's column of maneuver followed closely. Meanwhile Lieutenant General Drummond was coming westward to involve himself personally in the Niagara theater. He ordered Riall to retire toward Burlington if he were attacked. He even spelled out the tactics for his subordinate to use: first repulse the American light troops; find an open place and plant his cannon in the center of it; then concentrate his force there and protect the flanks with light troops, militia, and Indians. All of this was to create a diversion so that the garrison at Mississaga could destroy the cannon which Americans were supposed to be emplacing to bombard Fort George.[13]

At the very time when Brown's second reconnaissance of Fort George brought his force closest to the head of the lake, the British were executing eight men there for treason. Seven more were sentenced to death, pending a directive from England, but three of these men died and the other four were promised their lives if they would get out of Canada forever and leave all their property there.[14]

On the night of 24 July the American force camped upon the Chippewa battlefield. Early the next morning General Riall sent out a column of 950 men to take up a defensive position north of it. The British line strung out along Lundy's Lane, which here ran over a low hill and in front of a church. At mid-morning, 25 July, it was three miles away from the body of 2,600 Americans. Although General Brown did not know it, this was the only time he might have taken advantage of superior numbers. The moment soon passed, for General Drummond now interjected himself with reinforcements into the conflict. He took 500 men, landed on the American side, and marched upon Lewiston to break up the American camp there and to threaten the magazine at Fort Schlosser. When he discovered that the foe had already abandoned Lewiston, he recrossed the river about 4:00 P.M. to join Riall. He could have accomplished more had he stayed on the American side and threatened Black Rock and Buffalo, for these movements with a large enough force would have obliged the United States commanders to abandon the Canadian side of the river altogether. As it was, General Brown determined to protect his communications on the American side by attacking on the Canadian bank. Somewhere between 4:00 and 5:00 P.M. he ordered Winfield Scott to advance along the Queenston road.[15]

Although it was five o'clock when Scott got into motion, the heat was intense. After marching two and one-half miles he learned that the foe occupied the little hill along Lundy's Lane. He believed his 1,070 men about equal to the British detachment, and with his usual

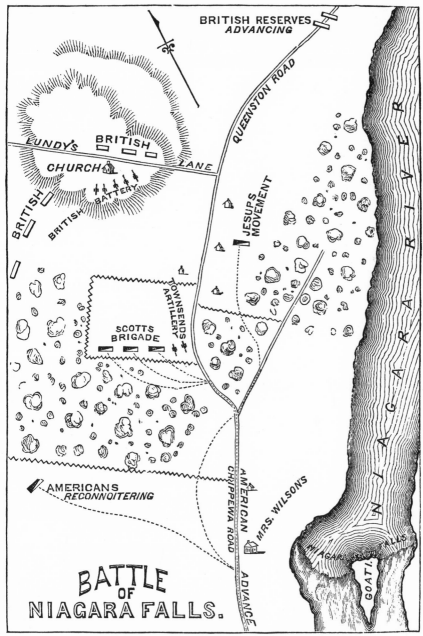

BATTLE OF NIAGARA FALLS.

aggressiveness he prepared to attack. Another half-mile brought him to the foot of the slope, where his men with the skill of professionals deployed from column into line under the fire of four or five cannon. As Scott launched the first attack about 6:00 P.M. General Riall, convinced that he was outnumbered, gave the order to withdraw. General Drummond arrived on the field just then with reinforcements and overruled him. Scott's attack with 1,000 men now struck a foe who numbered between 1,600 and 1,800.

The British position followed Lundy's Lane and a road at right angles to it, but was more a crescent than a square angle. Irregulars held the flanks; cannon were on the hill in the center. The American order of battle from left to right was: Ninth, Eleventh, Twenty-second, and Twenty-fifth infantry regiments. Scott's thrust was directed against the center and left of the enemy, and was in danger of being overlapped by the British right. Major T. S. Jesup, leading the Twenty-fifth, got upon the British left flank and rear, but was pushed back by the reserves. Scott personally led several charges which broke up the British left but did not dislodge the rest of the line. The battle went on in twilight and then darkness. General Brown arrived and at once sent to the rear for reinforcements. By 8:00 P.M. Scott's units were reduced to about 600 effectives. They hung onto the left of the British line like a boxer in a clinch. It would not have been difficult to envelop and wipe them out, but the British did not know it, for it was hard to distinguish friend from foe. Fighting swirled around the cannon, and in more than one instance cannoneers limbered up and brought off an enemy piece, mistaking it for their own.

The battle took a new turn about nine o'clock. The Second Brigade commanded by Brigadier General E. W. Ripley, and Porter's militia and Indian brigade arrived, 1,300 strong. At the same time Colonel Hercules Scott brought 1,230 reinforcements and some cannon to the British. Now there were about 2,100 Americans and 3,000 British on the field, but the American performance was such that General Drummond estimated their strength at 5,000.

Scott's brigade was badly cut up and in need of relief. General Brown therefore decided to form a new front using Ripley and Porter. This maneuver could not be made, however, until the cannon on the hill were silenced. About 10:00 P.M. Brown told Ripley to silence them. Ripley himself took the Twenty-third Infantry to strike once more at the British left, and gave to Colonel James Miller with 300 men from the Twenty-first the attack against the battery proper. The two columns advanced in bright moonlight that was streaked with the comet-like tails of the British Congreve rockets. Miller worked his men up through brush to a rail fence, fifteen yards from the hostile cannon. He ordered them to rest their guns on the fence, take careful aim, fire once, and rush the battery. They were inside the British position before the defenders knew they were threatened. Meanwhile Ripley, in an equally brilliant action, had broken the British left, composed of fresh, veteran reinforcements, and pushed it back half a mile.

The remainder of the battle centered on the seven cannon Miller captured. The British made repeated charges to retake them, and the opposing lines stood a few yards apart blazing at each other's muzzle flashes. Toward midnight both Generals Brown and Scott were badly wounded. As Brown was carried off, he ordered Ripley to withdraw, rest until dawn, then if need be resume the battle. Ripley's withdrawal, as the British reported it, was virtually a rout. Equipment was thrown into the rapids, but no one thought to spike the cannon which fell to the British in operating condition. Whatever the nature of their retreat, the Americans straggled into their camp on the Chippewa between one and two on the morning of 26 July.

About dawn Ripley began to gather a force to return to the battlefield as ordered. But it was nine o'clock before he had 1,500 weary men on the march. He encountered a British force of twice this size drawn up for battle a mile south of the field. He countermarched, and Drummond did not trouble to follow him. Brown always criticized Ripley's countermarch, but Ripley could expect no reinforcements and was already outnumbered two to one.

Losses were fearful in this, the Battle of Lundy's Lane: 171 Americans, 84 British killed; 572 Americans, 559 British wounded. Counting captured or missing men the figures came to 880 British and 855 American casualties. Lord Bathurst expressed concern over such numbers, but complimented Prevost on the conduct of the troops because he had been led to believe that they were greatly outnumbered.

Several Americans, then or later, chose to criticize their generals. Wilkinson said that Brown incurred needless slaughter, and that Scott "like a maniac ranged the field in quest of blood, regardless from what side it flowed." Secretary Armstrong thought that Brown ought to have moved past Riall's flank and struck at his communications toward Burlington. He ought also to have kept the battle from becoming a series of fights among detachments. Both these men, of course, had personal reasons for finding fault.

General Peter B. Porter also had personal reasons, but of a different sort: those of a citizen soldier serving with regulars. He said that the field ought never to have been abandoned, and that the citizen soldiers could have held it if the regulars could not. When Brown and Scott had been eliminated, he had for a moment seen a chance for himself to take command, but General Ripley had got in the way. "It is certain," he said, "that no militia general is to gain any military fame while united to a regular force and commanded by their officers. I have been brigadiered till I am quite satisfied." He also objected that the militia were used as virtual servants of the regulars. Because five of his companies had been detached to do guard duty, he could only bring 300 men from his brigade into the battle. If Porter was piqued at Brown, his pique was not reciprocated. General Brown said that Porter had immortalized his name amidst the hottest fire at both Chippewa and Lundy's Lane. He recommended his promotion to major general.

Brown's Niagara campaign did not in the end secure for the United States a foothold in Canada. On the other hand, it precluded any sort of British offensive in an area designated by the Ministry, no less, as essential to the ultimate security of Canada. It was not in Brown's nature to sit in the presence of the enemy and not fight him. He knew nothing of the eighteenth-century doctrine of warfare against enemy lines of communication. Even if he had, only the navy could have struck at those lines, and he was never able to bring Commodore Chauncey into the campaign.[16]

Porter and Brown were both indignant over the response of their native state to the British threat. Instead of rallying to the defense, the frontier dwellers, from the soldiers' point of view, had skulked. "Is it possible," Porter asked the governor, "that the state of New York will sit with her arms folded and see this army . . . sacrificed? Do not think I despond. I feel prouder and richer and better than the miserable speculators who are hoarding up their gold." Brown took up the theme when only 300 men out of 1,000 called made an appearance. "I doubt," he said, "if a parallel can be found for the state of things existing upon this frontier. A gallant little army struggling with the enemies of their country . . . left by that country to struggle alone, within sight and within hearing." Persons who avoided militia duty, he recommended, should lose the right to vote.[17]

The American commanders had good reason to worry about the reluctance of the populace to turn out, for General Drummond had received reinforcements. Moreover, the garrison at Fort Erie, the last point on Canadian soil held by Americans, was only 2,125 men, without much hope of reinforcements except through local militia. The fort was not completed and seemed very difficult to defend.

Drummond now had superior numbers, beginning his operations with 3,150 men. He detached 600 of them to destroy the American depots at Buffalo and Black Rock. This detachment commanded by Lieutenant Colonel J. G. P. Tucker landed downstream from Black Rock on 4 August and marched southward. At Conjocheta Creek 250 to 300 American riflemen were waiting for them beyond the stream and behind a long breastwork under the command of Major Lodowick Morgan. The defenders had taken down the bridge, and their rifles kept the invaders from crossing by any other means. After three hours the British gave up the attempt and retreated with losses of 11 killed, 17 wounded, and 4 missing. Their officers said it was the devastating accuracy of the American riflemen which had foiled them.[18]

To assail Fort Erie itself, General Drummond sent to Fort George for heavy cannon. While waiting for them, he dispatched a picked detachment of 75 men to capture three American schooners which lay in the lake opposite Fort Erie. These men cut eight miles of trail through the woods, then on their shoulders carried a captain's gig and five bateaux over it to launch in Lake Erie. They now rowed toward the vessels in silence, and when challenged claimed they were provisioners. But once close, they had to fight. They captured *Somers* and *Ohio*, but *Porcupine* cut her cable and drifted out of danger. They lost 2 killed and 4 wounded against 1 killed and 7 wounded.[19]

Fort Erie was less a fortress than an entrenched camp about 750 yards long by 250 yards at the widest point. Since Brown had lost confidence in Ripley, Brigadier General Edmund P. Gaines commanded there. The British opened fire on 13 August with six guns, which they expected to be able to breach the curtains. Their preparation continued into the next day, when General Drummond issued his attack orders. His strongest column, 1,300 men, was to strike the southern tip of the camp, anchored on Snake Hill. Another column, 550 men, was to storm the curtain between Fort Erie and the shoreline at the northernmost extremity. Old Fort Erie formed the elbow there, where the works turned from north to east and ran to the water's edge. About 200 men were told off to attack the long defensive mound running from the old fort on the north to Snake Hill on the south. All British columns, totaling 2,100 men, were to strike simultaneously, while a reserve of about 1,000 men waited for an opening.[20]

The columns began to march to their points of departure at 4:00 P.M., 14 August. There were no flints in the shoulder arms; the men were to rely on the bayonet. Shortly after 2:00 A.M. a brief artillery preparation illuminated the night. General Gaines, who had been expecting the attack, peered anxiously into the dark and saw the col-

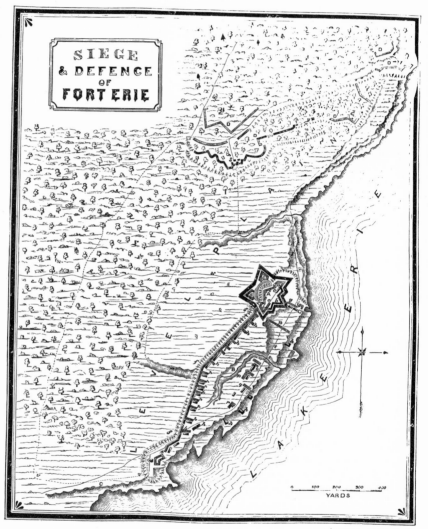

SIEGE & DEFENCE of FORT ERIE

Lossing, *Field Book*

umns moving into position by the light of the violent cannon fire. Suddenly the artillery ceased, and the attack columns began to move. Six cannon and 250 men on Snake Hill fought back the attackers there. A few men attempted to wade along the unfortified shore and come in, but they were all captured. The center column of attack got nowhere, but at the north Colonel Hercules Scott led his men into one of the rear bastions of the old fort in the face of 6 cannon and 800 men. Here the antagonists fought hand to hand for more than two hours with bayonets, pikes, and spears. Gaines drew men from his left to try to win back this bastion, but to no avail. What finally dislodged the dogged attackers was the accidental explosion of a powder magazine, which killed Colonel Scott and many of his men. By 6:00 A.M. on 15 August the assault was repulsed everywhere with fearful losses: for the British 57 killed, 307 wounded, and 538 captured or missing; for the Americans 17 killed, 56 wounded, and 11 missing, plus 9 killed and 36 wounded during the preliminary bombardment.

Since the Battle of Chippewa 40 days earlier, the British army had lost 2,300 men in the Niagara theater without achieving a single clear-cut military advantage. Even with the diversion of resources from Europe, such losses could not be replaced in Upper Canada. Some of the subordinate officers blamed General Drummond for the failure. Drummond fixed upon Major General Louis Charles deWatteville's regiment, made up entirely of foreigners, as his scapegoat. Except for their bad conduct, he said, the attack on Snake Hill would have succeeded. This line of reasoning did not convince General Prevost, who delicately censured Drummond for relying too heavily on a foreign regiment and for failing to prepare sufficiently for a night attack, which is always precarious. He hinted too that Drummond had allowed himself to be pushed by the opinion of others into making the attack. In England, two months to the day after the Erie disaster, Lord Bathurst deplored the severe losses, but ascribed them and the failure to accident rather than to poor leadership.

General Drummond continued to be fascinated by Fort Erie. He perfected 3 batteries 500 yards from the northern faces of the old fort. These, he believed, would breach the walls whenever he ordered it. Meanwhile ominous numbers of militia were forming on the American side of the Niagara River, while his own troops were being depleted through sickness. The longer he sat before Erie the more his position deteriorated. When the heavy rains came in September, he had no alternative, for he lacked the power to withdraw his batteries through the deep mud.[21]

General Gaines had been wounded on 15 August, and Jacob Brown, although still handicapped by his Lundy's Lane wound, took command at Fort Erie on 2 September. General Ripley, backed by a council of officers, favored evacuation of the fort. Brown would neither accept evacuation nor sit in the fort and look out passively at the enemy. He was encouraged by the improved response of the militia when 1,500 of them volunteered to cross into Canada with General Porter. Abetted by Porter, he determined to launch a sortie against the nagging British batteries. General Porter was to lead one column of 1,200 men, mostly volunteers, out of Snake Hill on a long flank march through the woods to Battery Number 3. Porter was supposed to interpose himself between that battery and the British camp, two miles distant, then wipe out the battery. At the same time, James Miller, recently promoted brigadier and placed in command of Winfield Scott's First Brigade, was to move through a ravine which ran at right angles from the long earthworks of the fort to the front of Battery Number 3. At an appointed time, he was to assault the abatis and earthworks and join Porter within the British position.

Porter's men worked all day on 16 September cutting a track through the heavy forest. The British had no sentries out, and were not aware of what was in train. Porter started his column along the new trail at noon on 17 September, still undetected by the foe. Miller and Porter attacked in concert at 3:00 P.M. Porter had occasion to pass from one of his columns to the other with only an aide and a handful of men. Suddenly 80 or 90 enemy soldiers were upon him. He rushed them, seized their weapons, threw them to the ground, and demanded a surrender. A fight commenced but before the superior British numbers could tell, a body of Americans appeared and drove the enemy away. Meanwhile Porter's men overran Battery Number 3, blew up the magazine, and spiked the cannon. Miller now joined Porter, and the united force stormed and took Battery Number 2. Even though torrential rain poured down, this part of the sortie was completed within half an hour. But Battery Number 1 held out against the attack.

The whole affair was a great credit to the Americans. Their casualties as attackers were less than the defenders: 609 British, 511 Americans. Moreover, as soon as the rains permitted it, Drummond pulled back. General Brown was elated: "The militia of New York," he wrote, "have redeemed their character." Porter chimed in for them that they had proved themselves the equals in steadiness and bravery of the heroes of Chippewa and Lundy's Lane. It was no small accomplishment for citizen soldiers to successfully assault entrenched regulars. Perhaps to save his face, Drummond reported that there were 5,000 attackers.

Shifting his eyes away from Niagara for a time, Secretary Armstrong urged the President to order the navy to give up the idea of blockading Kingston and to betake itself to the head of the lake, where the action was. In conjunction with the army it could cut British communications westward, and force the British fleet to come out of Kingston and fight. On his own, Commodore Chauncey ventured on 1 August to sail westward, but once in the Niagara area he became too uneasy about his base to remain. He therefore left *Jefferson*, *Sylph*, and *Oneida* to watch some British vessels in the Niagara River, and hastened back to Sackett's. Once there he seemed more eager to bring on a fight than ever before. He even left four ships' guns ashore, thereby nearly equalizing the gun power, in the hope that the British flotilla would accept the equal terms. They did not do so. Meanwhile, due to naval ascendency, American troops could go from one end of the lake to the other by ship transport in two days, whereas the British, forced to march, could not make the trip in less than sixteen days.[22]

Partly due to American control of Lake Ontario, the resources of Upper Canada were exhausted. Such supplies as got through had to come by bateaux. There was no alternate route by land, for the road from Kingston to Niagara simply could not support heavy wagon traffic. In some counties, Lincoln for example, militia commanders were told to demand up to 12 bushels of wheat from every grower, and pay $2.50 a bushel for it. Two-thirds of the British army, General Prevost said, was eating beef supplied by contractors from Vermont and New York. Specie as well as beef flowed in a steady stream from New England into Canada. Such economic interdependence made General Prevost cautious. He wrote the Ministry on 12 July that he intended to remain on the defensive until Yeo had once again secured control of Lake Ontario. His letter shocked the government when it came to them 40 days later. With Napoleon out of the way, the Ministry expected offensive activity and thought that it had provided the means to carry it on. Thus on 22 August Lord Bathurst categorically told Prevost that there ought to be aggressive moves made at least against the United States Navy around Lakes Ontario and Champlain.[23]

Major General George Izard, in command of American forces around Lake Champlain, verified the movement of beef from New England to the British army: "Like herds of buffaloes they press through the forest making paths for themselves." He had not the manpower to stretch a solid cordon of troops to stop this traffic. Izard suggested that the best use of his men might be to cut the St. Lawrence River line somewhere. Secretary Armstrong had always liked this idea, but he now decided against it. He chose for some reason, perhaps the American control of Lake Ontario, to push the war in the Ontario vicinity. To that end he ordered George Izard to march his force overland to Sackett's Harbor. Izard, aware that the reinforcements from Europe were concentrating for a blow in the Champlain theater, protested the order, but when Armstrong repeated it, Izard marched. On 29 August he left Plattsburg with 4,000 men. Armstrong's decision, which prompted this move, is surely one of the most misguided of the entire war, for 10,000 British veterans of the Napoleonic conflict were concentrating close to the area which Izard was abandoning.[24]

General Izard's column covered 280 miles in 20 days and reached Sackett's Harbor on 17 September. Armstrong claimed that the proper route would only have taken 10 days, but his judgment about this movement is not to be trusted. Izard found no work to do at the harbor, so he decided to comply with General Brown's request that he come to Fort Erie and help there. Heavy weather prevented embarkation until 21 September, but by 27 September he was at Batavia conferring with Brown. Being senior, he assumed the command. Brown never objected to this, but with characteristic bluntness told the secretary of war that he had no confidence in Izard.

No one on either side knew what General Izard was going to do. Drummond thought he might go west from Fort Erie and strike at the British rear by way of the Grand River. General Prevost believed that he would only act defensively to give some relief to the overstrained militia of the Niagara region. Izard himself wanted to attack Fort Niagara, but Brown and Porter persuaded him to cross into Canada and advance to the Chippewa River. On 15 October he fired across the river with cannon and then drew back. Drummond reported him gone from his front, but did not understand why. He could concentrate 2,800 troops, but estimated the Americans at 8,000 (they actually had about 6,300 fit for duty). Drummond lamented that he was badly outnumbered, Izard that he had an efficient army but no worthy strategic objective for it.[25]

On 10 September 1814, Yeo launched *Lawrence* at Kingston, a warship of oceanic magnitude. By early October she had her full complement of 110 guns, which gave the British 294 guns afloat to 230 for the Americans. Commodore Chauncey at once drew back into Sackett's Harbor. Izard said that this move "defeated all the objects of the operations by land in this quarter," and began to talk about winter quarters. General Drummond was not as enthusiastic about the new ship as might have been expected, for he too had learned not to anticipate much cooperation from the navy. He and Prevost agreed that the navies on the lakes had concentrated so much on beating each other as to grow oblivious to the needs of the army. Instead of prompt, cheerful cooperation, every demand brought from the naval commanders complaints that it would endanger the fleet.

The most aggressive thing that Izard did was to detach 900 men under Brigadier General Daniel Bissell to burn mills and otherwise attack the enemy's food supply. Bissell's march accomplished little and cost 67 casualties. On 21 October Izard had begun constructing winter quarters at Black Rock. General Drummond, convinced that there would be no further offensive, departed for Kingston, leaving Major General Richard Stovin in charge on the Niagara.[26]

The American high command began to worry again about Sackett's Harbor. Secretary Armstrong called upon Governor Tompkins for substantial detachments from the exhausted militia there. Because the situation was delicate, Tompkins sent Washington Irving to Sackett's Harbor as his personal representative. Irving reported on 3 October that there were 800 regulars and 2,000 militiamen close by, but that the entire concentration "seems to be affected with those insufficiencies and those numerous wants that so generally prevail in our military establishment." General Izard dispatched General Brown to Sackett's with 2,000 men and meant to go there soon himself.[27]

On 5 November Izard ordered that Fort Erie be abandoned and blown up. With this the Americans gave up their only holding in Canada. To be commander under such conditions depressed General Izard. He was perhaps the best trained of all the American generals, but at all points he seemed to be foiled in his use of what he admitted was a fine military force. It was difficult for him to adjust to the dynamics of a citizen-soldier army, and he recommended that the command be reinvested in General Brown: "Where a portion of the forces is composed of irregular troops," he said, "I have no hesitation in acknowledging my conviction of his being better qualified than I to make them useful in the public service." He offered to resign, but was refused.[28]

In anticipation of the campaign of 1815 the British began to construct two gunboats at Chippewa and two massive ships-of-the-line, 120 guns each, at Kingston. General Prevost advised Bathurst that the future safety of Canada depended on maintaining naval ascendency on Lakes Huron, Erie, and Ontario. He therefore requested that an admiral be assigned to the lake service. The Ministry did not accept this recommendation, but did decide to replace Commodore Yeo. On 12 December Captain E. W. C. R. Owen was ordered to proceed to the lakes and take command. He was told that he must do better than Yeo had done in communicating with the Admiralty. Yeo, therefore, departed his command on 23 March 1815, and on 16 May reported his arrival at Liverpool.[29]

All the while the naval building race on the lakes continued apace. On Christmas day the British launched *Psyche*, 55 guns, at Kingston. Her frame had been built in England and freighted across the ocean. It had cost £2,588 to ship the frame from Montreal to Kingston, and £2,000 to haul 6 of her guns by land from Quebec to Kingston. The frame for a sister ship had also been made in England, but because of the costs had never been assembled. The expense of the naval race soared for both belligerents. President Madison over protests by Secretary Jones diverted funds for two ocean-going 74s into building on the lakes.[30]

Detroit was the center of United States power west of Niagara, but the garrison there was pared in September to 68 regulars (20 of them at Malden). Lewis Cass, governor of Michigan Territory, informed the government that this put Detroit in serious danger, but the troops sent from Detroit to Niagara were not ordered back. Instead the secretary called upon the governor of Ohio to send a regiment of militia at once.

Cass recommended laying waste the rich grain lands along the Grand River, but he was not heeded. Nevertheless depredations were the usual style of operation. Early in September an American detachment all but destroyed Port Talbot. Late in October Brigadier General Duncan McArthur sent 600 volunteers, 500 United States Rangers, and 70 Indians to burn mills in the area north of Lake Erie. The expedition moved 150 miles before it met any opposition. It ransacked Oxford, less than 50 miles from the head of the lake, on 4 November. McArthur announced that resisters would suffer destruction of their property. He now discovered that high water prevented him from crossing the Grand River, and he began slowly to retreat toward Detroit in the face of increasing opposition. He had succeeded in destroying every mill west of the Grand River, and his force had lived off the land. As a result, the British could maintain neither troops nor Indians there, and they could not consider establishing a shipyard for use in rebuilding the navy on Lake Erie.[31]

The Northwest

Relations with the western Indians depended to a degree on who controlled Lakes Ontario and Erie, but victories and defeats on those two were only slowly reflected on Lakes Huron and Michigan. Military actions at these westernmost lakes and the other peripheries were all but independent of the chief movements of the war.

England worked harder than the United States at the Indian connection and overtaxed her long line of communications to feed her red allies. The Indians in the Niagara region consumed 40 barrels of flour every day, and General Riall said that he could not continue to provide so much and maintain his army. General Drummond, with no more than 3,000 troops, had to issue up to 8,000 daily rations. Indians who in the past had depended upon Detroit now went to Mackinac, and Lieutenant Colonel Robert McDouall, who took command there in May 1814, required 300 rations per day for the Indians and the same amount for his troops. In addition, the red allies had to be paid, and the British worked out a sort of piece-work rate for them. A prisoner delivered alive was valued at $5.00. A chief who lost an eye or a limb in the British service might receive an annuity of $100 per year for life.[1]

The Americans followed no such intricate system. Beginning in the spring of 1814 they paid every warrior who professed loyalty to the United States 75 cents per day. As far as they were concerned there were no neutral Indians; all were either friends or enemies. In the Old Northwest all Indians except Wyandots, Delawares, and Shawnees were enemies. Plans were made to put these three tribes into some sort of enclave to shelter them from the British influence.

Although there was strong American sentiment for punishing the allies of Britain, a treaty was signed with many of them on 22 July 1814. The red signatories agreed thereafter to aid the United States and to supply warriors in numbers stipulated by the United States. The redmen also agreed not to make peace without American concurrence. In return, the United States promised to confirm the boundaries which had existed between them and the Indians when the war commenced. William Henry Harrison and Lewis Cass signed for the United States. Harrison had resigned from the army as major general on 31 May 1814, and Cass had resigned as brigadier general at about the same time. The latter resumed his duties as governor of Michigan Territory.[2]

Two weeks after this treaty was completed, the government singled out for punishment the Potawatamis, who had not signed it. Brigadier General Duncan McArthur received orders to raise 1,000 men in the Detroit region and with them destroy crops and villages. McArthur made some forays, but no major campaign. As he saw it, every isolated house in Michigan could not possibly be defended. Moreover, Indian spies easily came and went from Detroit, carrying back news of any American preparations there. McArthur saw no solution to the problem except to move the friendly Indians into the interior of the United States, then lay waste the adjacent areas of Canada. Since the British had by this time committed extensive depredations along the east coast, a policy of devastation would not be considered immoral. John Armstrong had in the past favored a similar system, but on 3 September 1814 he had been succeeded by James Monroe as secretary of war. Monroe would not sanction this kind of warfare.[3]

Red-headed Robert Dickson, British agent for the northern Indians, surveyed the western scene with complacence. Even the July treaty did not seem to him to harm his country's cause appreciably. There was only one American strongpoint left close to the Great Lakes in the Illinois and Iowa country, namely, Fort Clark at Peoria with a garrison of 100 men. Since the fighting men of the Mississippi Valley were drained away to the Creek War in the South, it would be possible, Dickson believed, to capture even St. Louis with no more than 600 men. "The crisis is not far off," he wrote, "when I trust in God that the Tyrant will be humbled and the Scoundrel American Democrats be obliged to go on their knees to Britain." The tyrant Napoleon did fall, and the British agents to the Indians addressed their charges with confidence. Robert McDouall told a meeting of chiefs at Mackinac that Britain securely held the Niagara valley and also Kingston. The king, he said, had defeated his enemies in Europe and could now bring all of his great power to bear upon the United States. If the chiefs supported Britain loyally, English traders would soon be among them, and Britain would look out for them in the peace settlement.[4]

McDouall had had 30 large bateaux built in Nottawasaga Bay the previous winter and had brought them with him when he came in May 1814 to assume command at Mackinac. His cruise through waters still filled with ice had been heroic and his arrival at Mackinac decisive, for, as General Prevost reported to the Ministry, the situation at Mackinac influenced the Indians as far south as New Orleans and as far west as the Pacific Ocean.[5]

Governor William Clark of Missouri Territory appeared early in June at Prairie du Chien. There he built a fort and garrisoned it with 60 regulars from the Seventh Regiment. His prime purpose was to influence the Indians. Little trouble was to be expected from the Sacs, Foxes, and Sioux, but the Winnebagos, Wild Oats, and part of the Kickapoos would be enemies as long as the British could continue to supply them.

McDouall constituted a force of 400 Indians and 150 white men to try to drive Clark's garrison away. Lieutenant Colonel William McKay commanded this expedition, and he arrived before the fort at Prairie du Chien on 17 July with his men, three gunboats, a brass 3-pounder, and one artilleryman. When Lieutenant Joseph Perkins, commanding the skimpy garrison, refused to surrender, McKay directed his cannon at an armored gunboat which lay beside the fort. It dropped safely downstream out of range. He tried to dig a tunnel, but had no success. The fourth day he was about to fire hot shot with his scant remaining ammunition when the garrison raised a white flag. Their ammunition was gone and their well dry. They surrendered and received parole. A British officer accompanied them on their march to prevent the Indians from harming them.

McKay himself could not advance farther into Illinois because he could not rely on his Indians, but a large band of the latter carried out a significant foray on their own. McKay provided them with kegs of powder to use against the gunboats which had brought the American detachment to Prairie du Chien. They found six boats moored at one of the rapids, the crews carelessly camped ashore. These they completely surprised on 22 July, killed 100 crewmen, and captured 5 cannon. McKay had thought the redmen useless at Prairie du Chien and a severe trial to him in general, but now he freely reported that this had been a brilliant coup.[6]

Early in June George Croghan, of Fort Stephenson fame, received orders to team with Captain John Sinclair of the navy to destroy British strength on Lake Huron. The ultimate locus of power on Huron was Mackinac, but Croghan took time to loot St. Josephs and did not appear at Mackinac before 4 August. He had 700 men with him, and Captain Sinclair's flotilla of 5 ships. This force looked formidable to McDouall because McKay was absent at Prairie du Chien, and the agent resolved that he must strike rather than wait to be struck and be cooped up in the fort. Accordingly, with 200 white men and some Indians he attacked Croghan soon after his landing. He killed 16, wounded 60 Americans, and captured 2 armed schooners. One of the dead was Major A. H. Holmes, who had fought so skillful a defense action on the Thames in March. So heavy a list of casualties required explanation from the American officers to their superiors. General McArthur laid it on the treachery of the residents of Detroit, who, he said, informed the British of Croghan's every move.

Croghan could of course do nothing but leave Mackinac in British hands. On his way south however he paused to attack the blockhouse at the mouth of the Nottawasaga River. The garrison of the place, being hopelessly outnumbered, themselves blew up their stronghold and with it the schooner *Nancy*. What hurt was that *Nancy* had six months' supplies aboard for Mackinac; these could in no way be replaced. Despite the victory at Mackinac, British control of Lake Huron was now endangered, for Croghan left *Tigress* and *Scorpion* to cut communications between Mackinac and the rest of Canada. On the other hand, these two vessels and nothing more constituted the military power of the United States on the lake.[7]

Less than two weeks after the destruction of the blockhouse and of *Nancy*, Lieutenant Andrew H. Bulger led a detachment out of Mackinac in two boats. On the night of 3 September, he worked his way undetected within 100 yards of *Tigress*, then his men rushed and overpowered her 30-man crew. Now he used *Tigress* to approach *Scorpion* which was anchored 15 miles away. Once more the crew rushed and overpowered the unsuspecting men. In this manner American power was altogether eliminated from Lake Huron.[8]

General Benjamin Howard, in command of the Eighth Military District since Harrison's resignation, wanted an effort made to establish American control at the headwaters of the Mississippi River. He prepared eight large gunboats protected against musketry by heavy planking with rifle slits along the sides. About 350 men were put on the boats under the command of Major Zachary Taylor. This flotilla proceeded upstream until forced by a heavy wind to tie up on an island just north of the mouth of the Rock River. A force of 1,200 Indians and 20 English soldiers gathered to strike at them there. Lieutenant Duncan Graham, the British commander, was able to emplace three small cannon within 300 yards of Taylor's island anchorage, and he opened fire with them on 5 September. While the enemy cannon barked, Taylor held a council of his officers. It voted not to continue up the river. Accordingly, they weighed anchor and dropped down to the mouth of the Des Moines River, harassed all the way by the enemy Indians. At this point the crews of five of the boats erected what they called Fort Johnson, to replace Fort Madison which had been abandoned the year before. The British expected the new fort to be used as a staging area against Prairie du Chien, but in fact it was abandoned within a few weeks.[9]

In September 1814 General Benjamin Howard died. The administration moved swiftly to fill the vacancy, and a month later Colonel William Russell turned up at St. Louis to take command of the Eighth

Military District. He found no United States military force at all north
of the mouth of the Illinois River, and a lack of resources throughout
his entire command. Governor William Clark of Missouri Territory
asserted that there was not a field officer of the regular service left in
either Missouri or Illinois Territory. Russell, as commander of the
United States Mounted Rangers, designed his defense around them. By
moving constantly along critical lines of communication, the Rangers
were to try to awe the Indians into keeping quiet. If more was necessary, he planned to cut down the Indian corn in the fields. His eye was
upon the Mississippi River, down which British influence radiated from
Mackinac. He was in favor of pulling his outposts in quite close and
relying on mobility.[10]

The legislative council for Missouri saw no hope for their territory,
or so they represented matters to the Congress, unless a substantial body
of regulars was sent at once to their aid. Missouri, they insisted, was
ringed about with 6,000 warriors, whereas the whole number of their
enrolled militia came only to 3,400.[11]

Washington

Chesapeake Bay was continuously attractive to the British because it
enabled them to project their sea power deep into the United States.
Admiral Sir George Cockburn had in 1813 gradually learned the Chesapeake waters better than most American pilots, and had become inci-
dentally a devil figure in the area. When he was promoted from rear
admiral of the blue to rear admiral of the white, *Niles' Register* grumbled, "The ruffian will be anxious to deserve this distinction by some
act of great atrocity and meanness. . . ." To guard against him and the
likes of him, Congress authorized the construction of a special flotilla
of gunboats, called barges, for use in the upper bay. In August 1813
Captain Joshua Barney had been made a commodore to supervise the
building of them, to raise their crews, and to command the flotilla.
Using the new tool, he was expected to keep the foe below the Potomac River well away from Washington.[1]

Barney was a naval veteran of the Revolution. He had gone to France with Monroe in 1796, and had stayed there to become a commodore in the French naval service. He had directed depredations of French privateers upon English commerce and possibly upon some American ships as well. He was a symbol of the American-French connection and a seasoned hater of England. Inasmuch as he had been the commander of a trading vessel at the age of sixteen, he was at fifty-five a highly qualified sailor.

By April 1814 Barney was in command of 26 barge-gunboats and 900 men, based on Baltimore. While cruising in the bay on the lookout for vessels engaged in illegal commerce, he encountered a 74, 3 schooners, and 7 barges sailing together. Hopelessly outclassed, he made for the Patuxent River where the heavy ships could not follow him. The British flotilla took station off the mouth of the Patuxent and burned a schooner to try to lure Barney out. He would not come out. Next, on 6 June, Captain Sir Robert Barrie brought his light ships into the river, whereupon Barney worked his way out of reach six miles up Leonard's Creek. Since gunfire could occasionally reach him, he decided to attack his molesters. So vigorous was his strike that the British flotilla retreated, and *St. Lawrence* grounded on her way downstream. Only by stationing officers in the tops to direct fire from the other ships was Barrie able to keep the stranded ship from falling into American hands. On 10 June he counterattacked up Leonard's Creek with 21 barges, a rocket ship, and 2 schooners, but Barney assailed them so fiercely with 13 barges that they withdrew. Barrie now decided to send out a detachment of marines and Negro troops to harry the countryside. Even though this detachment destroyed 2,500 hogsheads of tobacco and penetrated to Marlboro, 18 miles from Washington, it still did not force the Americans out to fight.[2]

Secretary Jones considered the American flotilla to be hopelessly bottled up in Leonard's Creek, and he gave the order to destroy it. But just at that moment Commissary General of Ordnance Decius Wadsworth volunteered to try to liberate it. With 600 men he advanced to the mouth of the creek and emplaced two 18-pound long cannon on the reverse side of a hill where they were free from counterbattery fire. Under the protection of their fire, he attacked with a small fleet of barges. Notwithstanding that his cannon recoiled halfway down the hill with each discharge, his attack was so effective that on 26 June a part of Barney's flotilla was able to sail out of Leonard's Creek into the Patuxent. This backed the British out into the Potomac. There they captured Leonardtown on 18 July without firing a shot, but they did not destroy it. Two days later they met sharper resistance on the Nominy River, but in the end they captured two schooners, quantities of tobacco, and four prisoners. In addition, 135 slaves followed them. At the Yeocomico River they also had to fight. By this time Cockburn with only 500 men had penetrated 10 miles inland in heavily wooded country. He was forming the conclusion that his detachments could go anywhere they chose in the bay area, that all the American forces must be clustered around Washington, Annapolis, and Baltimore.[3]

"Jonathan is so confounded," Captain Joseph Nourse reported to Cockburn, "that he does not know when or where to look for us, and I do believe that he is at this moment so undecided and unprepared that it would require little force to burn Washington, and I hope soon to put the first torch to it myself." He was about right. The American government could not decide whether there was need to make provision to defend its capital. Certain observers expected an attack there. If the British struck Washington, they could disrupt government, disgrace the administration, destroy the Navy Yard and two important iron works, and adversely affect the peace negotiations already in progress. To counter such an attack, the Americans needed to maintain an advanced defensive posture. The British fleet could be blocked in if it passed too far up the crooked, shoal-water rivers. Fire rafts, amphibious infantry, and active cavalry detachments ought to be employed, and a telegraphic system should start at once. In contrast to this point of view, John Armstrong acknowledged no grounds on which the foe would find it worthwhile to attack the capital. He assured the President that he would take any action necessary to defend the place. In fact, however, he kept his attention turned so consistently elsewhere that it was difficult to provide even for such irregular troops as did turn out in the vicinity. He never considered the British prisoners brought before him as anything but foragers.[4]

President Madison announced at a cabinet meeting on 1 July that he expected an attack upon Washington. The next day the Tenth Military District was created. Secretary Armstrong wanted Moses Porter to command it, but Madison himself chose Brigadier General William H. Winder. Winder had been captured in 1813 at Beaver Dam, and was released early in 1814 to go to Washington to negotiate the exchange of prisoners. While he was there, he received from the President appointment as the United States representative in all negotiations for the exchange of prisoners. Through his efforts a convention was agreed upon 16 April 1814, and the machinery for a general exchange of prisoners was set in motion. A personal connection made Winder especially available: He was the nephew of Levin Winder, Federalist governor of Maryland, who was hypercritical of the conduct of the war. If kinsman William commanded in the bay area, the governor might become more cooperative. Nevertheless, Secretary Armstrong was offended by the selection.[5]

No more than 500 regulars were in the new Tenth Military District, and half of them were shut up in forts. The government therefore decided on a massive alert of 93,500 militia, and it was on Independence Day that the nearby states were notified of their quotas. Winder, however, was not permitted to call any of this horde of citizen soldiers into active service until there was imminent danger. On 12 July he received permission to call out 6,000 from Maryland, but his uncle's administration responded so sluggishly that he had no more than 250 under his control six weeks later. He had no authority over any detachment until it was organized, equipped, and formally turned over to him by the War Department. It was never known how many of the 6,000 from Maryland actually entered the service, for no reports were made.[6]

On 17 July the government gave Winder permission to call for the following additional increments: Pennsylvania 5,000, Virginia 2,000, and the District of Columbia 2,000. The troops he could legally call into federal service now totaled 15,000, but the number he actually had in the ranks never did exceed a few hundred. Naturally, Winder called for regulars, marines, and sailors. His request prompted Secretary Jones on 8 August to direct three of the navy's finest captains to repair to Washington and aid the defense there. They were John Rodgers, Oliver H. Perry, and David Porter.

As of 23 July the men who were to make up the Maryland quota had not yet even been detached. Nevertheless, General Winder summoned all of them into federal service and tried to find supplies for them. Some Maryland militia were already in state service, guarding the coast, and most of these were put on the federal payroll in lieu of the new quota which had been called for but could not seem to be raised. They continued to do as federal employees what they had done for the state.[7]

The situation in Pennsylvania was worse yet. The legislature at its last session had completely revamped the militia law, and the new law had invalidated all commissions issued under previous statutes. As a result none of the standing militia could be compelled to serve and nothing could be done to change matters until October. The governor tried to fill the state's quota with volunteers, but he could not. In effect, Pennsylvania had in the very midst of war accidentally legislated herself out of the fight for three critical months. Virginia was in better shape legally, but she too was not able to meet her quota.[8]

The facts justified President Madison and others who worried about the security of Washington. As early as 1812 Generals Prevost and

Brock had suggested to Admiral Warren the need for a diversion southward to take pressure off Canada. In November 1812 Warren had
asked for a "flying army" of 3,000 men to be used at his discretion.
Admiral Cockburn's harassment of the Chesapeake region grew out of
this request. Cockburn's success led Admiral Warren once more to
call the attention of the Lords Commissioners to Chesapeake Bay as
a strategic objective for 1814. When Vice Admiral Sir Alexander
Cochrane replaced Warren, he adopted as his own Warren's project
for the bay area. All the while Admiral Cockburn continued the harassment with limited means. Americans of various sorts aided him. Men
whose property he threatened warned him of impending attacks in
return for protection, and disaffected blacks guided his detachments in
the night.[9]

Back in England the means were at hand to mount a diversion in
force somewhere on the Atlantic coast. For some Englishmen there
was an opportunity "to retaliate upon the Americans," as the chancellor of the exchequer put it, "for the outrages they had committed."
The Ministry dispatched a fleet of 12 troopships from the Garonne
on 2 July 1814. On board were about 3,000 men from Wellington's
army; they were commanded by Major General Robert Ross. During
25 years of commissioned service Ross, forty-eight years old in 1814,
had fought the French in Egypt, Italy, Portugal, Spain, and in France
proper. He had consistently displayed the dash characteristic of those
generals who had risen to high command under Wellington. Earl
Bathurst himself instructed him to be guided by Admiral Cochrane's
plans (the point to be attacked was left to Cochrane's discretion), and
by his own judgment and experience. He specified that the expedition
was no more than a diversion, and that Ross must not operate very
far from the coast. While afloat and during embarkation Ross was
under naval command, but the admiral had been directed to consult
him on all strategic decisions. It was the general's privilege to refuse
to commit his troops to any operation which seemed to him "unsuit-
able."[10]

The fleet of troopships anchored off Bermuda on 24 July, where
about 900 additional men came aboard. Ross now reorganized his army
into three brigades commanded by Colonels William Thornton, Arthur
Brooke, and Charles Malcolm. Cochrane met Ross at Bermuda and
the two conferred.

Cochrane had been doing some hard thinking about strategic objectives, and had taken Fleet Captain Edward Codrington into his
confidence. The two sat on deck in shirt sleeves and examined the
possibilities. Cochrane had made up his mind that Chesapeake Bay

would not do until October because of the fever season. Codrington
tried to hold him to this line of reasoning, but after the interview
with Ross, Cochrane for some reason switched back to the bay. The
most credible explanation for his about-face is Cockburn's success in
marauding in spite of chills and fever. In any case the expedition cleared
Bermuda on 3 August, and sighted Cape Charles on the fourteenth.
It then sailed into Chesapeake Bay with 20 warships and several transports. The troops expected Ross to lead them Wellington-style, and
there was temporary consternation when a senior, Major General
Gerard Gosselin, appeared, but his orders were for Canada and he soon
departed.[11]

Admiral Cockburn sought and received permission to accompany
the land force, and as he knew the territory well, Cochrane asked him
what was the best point of debarkation. Since Washington was always
Cockburn's objective, he unhesitatingly recommended Benedict on the
Patuxent, 45 miles from the capital on a good road. At that village
there would be scant danger from Fort Washington on the Potomac,
there would be quiet water for anchorage, quarters for troops, plenty
of horses, and forage for the army. Within 48 hours after occupying
Benedict, Cockburn claimed, Washington could be taken almost without opposition. In addition, there were roads leading to both Annapolis and Baltimore, and guides were available to conduct them
anywhere in the area. Admiral Cochrane followed Cockburn's advice.[12]

Three days' rations—three pounds of pork and seven and one-half
pounds of bread—were cooked on board and issued to each man.
By 3:00 P.M. Saturday 20 August around 4,500 men were established
in a strong position two miles above the village of Benedict. The inhabitants had deserted the place. Horses were not as abundant as Cockburn had claimed, and when the column moved out at dawn on 21
August none but general officers and their staffs rode. Only one
6-pounder and two 3-pounders were with the force. The column was
well screened by flankers, and a flotilla of boats kept abreast of its
right flank. At the head were Ross and Cockburn. (Admiral Cochrane
had remained with the fleet.) The column halted at Nottingham when
evening came, having covered 20 miles without hostile incident. Many
of the men had fallen out, though, weakened by the sea voyage and
debilitated by the high humidity and a temperature close to 90 degrees.[13]

Next morning, Monday, 22 August, the march was under way at
seven o'clock, but Ross halted it at Upper Marlboro to thrash out with
Cockburn which route to take. In the distance they heard the explo-

sions as Commodore Barney blew up his barges. Cockburn continued to argue for Washington, and Ross at length agreed. One route toward that city led to the banks of the eastern branch of the Potomac where two bridges spanned the river. The commanders ruled this out as being too heavily defended and too dependent upon the two bridges. At Old Fields they could continue northwest, instead of turning west, and reach Bladensburg. This route was eight miles the longer, but at Bladensburg they could ford the eastern branch of the Potomac. Ross and Cockburn selected this course in the hope of achieving surprise. Their debate, and subsequent preparations, had delayed the march from mid-day 22 August to 4:00 P.M. 23 August. The advance started so late in the day was to continue into the night in order to put the troops into position in the morning. The marines stayed at Upper Marlboro to make it a stronghold to retire upon, if there should be a failure.[14]

The troops were resting at two o'clock on the morning of 24 August when a courier on a lathered horse found General Ross and Admiral Cockburn at "Melwood," the Digges estate. The messenger carried an order from Admiral Cochrane to return to Benedict and re-embark. Ross said it left no room for discretion, but Cockburn insisted that they were past the point of return. The two walked and talked, and the staff at a distance could hear Cockburn arguing for continuing the advance. At dawn they saw Ross strike his forehead and announce, "Well, we will proceed." The march now resumed on the direct route to Washington, and its direction convinced the United States officers guarding the eastern approaches to the city that they must resort to extremes. Accordingly, between eight and eight-thirty on the morning of 24 August Captain John O. Creighton of the navy destroyed the bridges east of Washington. At about the same time, the British column reached the crossroads at Old Fields and swung onto the road which ran northwest into Bladensburg.

At the time the British landed, General Winder had controlled about 1,700 troops. He at once issued an alarm call to Pennsylvania for a regiment and summoned en masse the militia of Baltimore and two counties of Maryland. He published notices in newspapers urging companies and individuals to hurry to Bladensburg without delay, not waiting for the usual militia processes to work themselves out. When the *National Intelligencer* printed the general's order, it added, "We feel assured that the number and bravery of our men will afford complete protection to the city." Similar confidence in numbers without cohesion and in bravery became the military policy of the United States in future years, and was to be the cause of many disasters.[15]

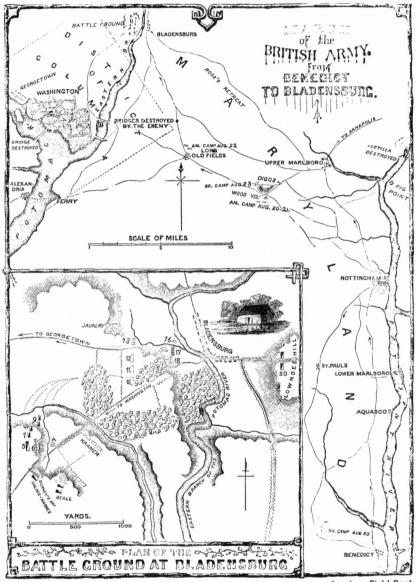

MAP of the BRITISH ARMY, from BENEDICT TO BLADENSBURG.

PLAN OF THE BATTLE GROUND AT BLADENSBURG

Lossing, Field Book

Citizens outside the militia organization bestirred themselves. In one small Virginia town a prominent lawyer mounted a wagon and called on his neighbors to follow him against the enemy. A company formed behind him, scraped up some equipment, and began the march. In Washington militia exempts hastily organized and joined the movement. At Bladensburg the people volunteered to dig earthworks, and Winder, who had neglected to have it done before, sent a trained engineer to supervise them. The newspapers urged all free people of color to go to Bladensburg to help dig, and about 500 of them answered this call.[16]

Everyone neglected the simplest and most obvious tactics of all: to fell trees across the roads, tear up bridges, and harass the enemy column as it passed through the heavy forest. (Armstrong later claimed that he advised Winder to do the harassment.) For 40 miles the invaders traversed the thick woods and scarcely caught sight of an American.[17]

By 23 August citizen soldiers began swarming into District Number Ten. Winder had about 2,000 of them with him at the Woodyard, 10 miles southeast of Washington. The enemy were vulnerable while in column, with their flank to him, but he made no attempt to strike them. His camp, only a few miles from the British position, was very noisy, and a spy could have picked up the countersign 50 yards from any outpost.[18]

On 23 August the militia called en masse by General Winder began to reach the Washington area. For a while on Tuesday two regiments of drafted militia from the vicinity of Baltimore, commanded by Brigadier General Tobias Stansbury, occupied a strong position east of Bladensburg. Winder sent orders to Stansbury to stay where he was and fight the enemy if he came that way. Disgruntled because he thought Winder was recklessly hazarding the Maryland troops, Stansbury called a council of his officers. He and they decided to disobey the order and to cross the eastern branch and take position on the slope beyond it. At that point the eastern branch was 40 yards wide, but only 3 feet deep, with a firm bottom and gently sloping banks. The road crossed the branch on a wooden bridge. General Stansbury claimed that he ordered it destroyed, but the bridge remained intact.[19]

In its new position Stansbury's brigade was joined about five in the afternoon of 23 August by 1,000 men commanded by Colonel Joseph Sterrett. The core of this reinforcement was the Fifth Maryland Volunteer Infantry, recruited from the best society in Baltimore. It had left the city in full dress: blue jackets faced with red, white pantaloons, black gaiters, white cross-belts, and heavy leather helmets topped with two sweeping plumes, one red and one black. The streets of Baltimore were lined with spectators, shouting, waving handkerchiefs, and crying. The spirits of Private John Pendleton Kennedy soared. The eighteen-year-old volunteer and his friends had their stores in a wagon, and they hired a Negro camp follower to cook for them. Even if the second day out was too hot for their winter uniforms and leather helmets, even if most of the boys were heavily encumbered with over-coat, blanket, three shirts, stockings, underwear, and in Kennedy's case a pair of dancing pumps, still the march was a lark to them. That night, when they joined Stansbury, they had a sumptuous meal of ham and chicken, and then lighted cigars and lay chatting around the fire. Hardly had they gotten to sleep when they were up again, forming for an attack. Since they had to throw on their vivid uniforms in the darkness, Kennedy put on his dancing pumps and had no chance to change. Near dawn they were permitted to lie down in the field be-side the road, but in a short while were marching back the way they had come. All their marching and countermarching during the night resulted from false alarms, but it tired the men out just the same.[20]

When the Annapolis militia pitched camp Tuesday night, they soon found that they were within half a mile of the British pickets. This discovery caused a disorderly removal in which tents were rolled up so loosely that they would not fit into the wagons and a few of them had to be left behind. The men were ordered to keep their guns loaded, whereupon one of them shot a companion in the thigh and another killed a horse. Seeing their lives imperiled by their own com-panions, two men deserted.[21]

Even as the British made their final march upon Bladensburg, Winder's troops were not concentrated, yet 6,000 American men, more or less, were within 30 miles of Washington, supposedly ready to fight. They were opposed by 4,500 British soldiers, unquestionably ready to fight and tightly concentrated, whose way into the hostile land had thus far been shockingly free of opposition.

.About 10:00 A.M. 24 August word came to Winder that the enemy was indeed marching toward Bladensburg. Winder was just then in the vicinity of the Navy Yard at Washington, conferring with the President and other officials. He started the troops off and himself galloped toward Bladensburg. The President and the cabinet also took the Bladensburg road, with Monroe loping along far ahead of the others, including General Winder.[22]

At Bladensburg, General Stansbury was arranging his tired men quite effectively. The two companies of Baltimore artillery were placed in an imperfect barbette close to the river. Unfortunately their cannon, which ought to have been able to sweep the bridge from end to end, could only shoot obliquely across it. Five companies of riflemen were stationed along the bank to the left of the cannon, and in an orchard some distance back of them stood the main force. The river protected the center and left, thick woods and a deep ravine the right. The road to Washington ran through their position up a gentle slope a mile and a quarter to its summit.[23]

About this time the militia from Annapolis under Colonel William Beall came in on the double, just barely ahead of the British. They passed through Stansbury's lines and took position at the top of the slope.

Monroe outdistanced the other officers of the government and reached Stansbury's position about eleven-thirty. Without consulting the general, he began to rearrange the troops. When he had finished, the Baltimore artillery and their cover of riflemen were left to face the first assault by themselves. The nearest troops were 500 yards behind, so situated that the orchard no longer protected them, nor could they observe the action on the bank of the river.[24]

The Baltimore artillery and the riflemen had already begun to fire when the first reinforcements reached the field from Washington. General Walter Smith of the District militia disposed his men on the same ridge with Beall's Marylanders, and laid six cannon to fire across the pike. Presently Commodore Joshua Barney arrived on the double with 500 sailors and marines and took a position between Smith and Beall, blocking the Washington Pike with his five big naval guns. The American force was now all on the field, arranged in three lines. Down by the river was the Baltimore artillery and its support of riflemen. The second line consisted of General Stansbury's three regiments and the third line of Colonel Beall's and Joshua Barney's units. None of the lines was in a position to support any other line; indeed, the first two did not know that the third was behind them. Even to a lieutenant of Maryland cavalry, looking over the field from the top of the hill, the American army seemed dangerously scattered. George Gleig, a subaltern with the British army who was nearing the scene from the bottom of the slope, later wrote, "They seemed country people, who would have been much more appropriately employed in attending to their agricultural occupations than in standing with muskets in their hands on the brow of a bare green hill."

The British brigades held tightly together internally in their approach to Bladensburg, but a distance of about a mile opened up between them. Not choosing to rest the tired men, Ross threw them against the American position. The light brigade in the lead crossed the bridge and advanced straight down the road, but the militia artillery drove them back to the shelter of the willows on the west bank where they huddled to wait for support. In a few minutes the second brigade arrived, crossed, and turned to its right, where very shortly it got upon the end of the militia line and forced a retreat. This exposed the left flank of the American second line. General Winder now ordered the Fifth Maryland Regiment, which occupied the center of the second line, to hold at all cost while he tried to rally the collapsing left. A council of Maryland officers decided that his order, as they were outnumbered five to one, doomed them to certain destruction. They ordered a retreat.

In spite of the fact that the first line did not re-form on it, the second held for a time. But when the Fifth Maryland began to draw back, disorder quickly set in. The British Congreve rockets abetted it. They shrieked in flight, and the citizen soldiers had no way of knowing that they really did very little harm. When it is recalled that these rockets unnerved French veterans, the reaction of the American irregulars is not surprising. The officers yelled and exerted themselves to stop the rout, and Stansbury's swearing could be heard above the din of battle. To no avail.

When the attackers struck the third line they found themselves for the first time in serious trouble. Commodore Barney's guns tore them up, and at the same time the militia on the flanks poured in on them an effective fire. It was Winder himself who caused the dislocation of the third line, for on some account he ordered the militia there to retire while they were still fighting firmly. Not well enough trained to retreat in good order, before long they broke ranks and fled. Only the sailors and marines kept the field until overrun.

Before rout had set in, General Winder ordered the Maryland cavalry on top of the slope to charge. This was an unusual order to give green horsemen, and the cavalry commander protested that his men and horses had not had the training to gallop headlong into enemy fire. In the end there was no mounted charge; indeed when the wave of the advancing foe reached the top of the crest, some cavalrymen began to slip away into the woods, and in spite of the bawling of their officers, the rest could not seem to form into any sort of defensive line. They, too, were soon a part of the disorganized retreat.

Thus, by 4:00 P.M. the notorious Battle of Bladensburg came to an end. While it lasted American fire had been very effective, killing 64 and wounding 185 of the enemy, against an American loss of only 71.

The British detachment rested two hours and then began the seven-mile march to Washington. The third brigade, which had not been in the fight, passed through the other two, and took the van with General Ross, Admiral Cockburn, and their aides. Although it was dark when they reached the town, Ross and Cockburn were conspicuous because of their white horses and lace hats. When they were close to Albert Gallatin's house, a body of 300 Americans opened fire on them and killed Ross' horse. This detachment was soon dispersed and two of the buildings set on fire.

Flames now sprang up in every quarter. All of the public buildings were fired, and a few private ones. Commodore Thomas Tingey, commandant of the Washington Navy Yard, followed standing orders from the secretary of the navy and blew up the yard on the eastern branch of the Potomac. The flames from it flared high into the darkness. George Gleig said of the sight, "Except for the burning of St. Sebastian's I do not recollect to have witnessed a scene more striking or more sublime." Admiral Cockburn seemed also to enjoy the spectacle. Still conspicuous on his white horse, followed by a black colt, he made ironic inquiries for the President and joked heavily with the people standing about. He personally supervised the wrecking of the office of the *National Intelligencer*, and told his workers to "destroy all C's so they can't abuse my name." Certain officers entered the White House before it was ignited and ate a meal set on the table for the President. Commander James Scott traded his dirty shirt for a clean one found there.[25]

Americans lost no time in denouncing the burning of their capital. *Niles' Register* pointed out that Napoleon himself had never stooped so low, although he had entered many an enemy capital. The paper claimed that in protest against the burning none of the foreign ministers would come to a grand banquet given in Vienna by the Duke of Wellington. Even British periodicals became critical of the incident. The *Annual Register* excoriated the British commanders as "More suitable to the times of barbarism. If there is such a thing as humanized war, its principle must consist in inflicting no other evils upon the enemy than are necessary to promote the success of warlike operations." But General Ross, reporting directly to Earl Bathurst, made no apology. On the contrary, he listed with pride the stores captured: 206 cannon, 500 barrels of powder, 40 barrels of fine-grain powder, and 100,000 musket cartridges.[26]

Depredations continued throughout 25 August, but during the afternoon a violent storm put out the fires. If there was any discussion between Ross and Cockburn as to what they should do next, it is not of record. They decided to use the cover of darkness to go back to their transports. To this end the inhabitants were put under a curfew at 8:00 P.M. to keep them from spying. The injured had to be left behind, and Commodore Barney, who had received kind treatment since his wounding and capture at Bladensburg, pledged himself to speak for them. Campfires were left burning brightly, and at nine o'clock the column moved out. On 26 August it was delayed from three until noon by trees blown down in the storm. That night it bivouacked at Upper Marlboro, and on 27 August reached Nottingham over repaired bridges. (Some Americans had finally gotten around to tearing them up.) It re-embarked at Benedict on 30 August. During the entire withdrawal no one caught even a glimpse of the foe.[27]

As for the Americans, their rout continued through Washington and beyond. Neither officers nor men could be roused to set up a proper camp or guard, and those who were halted just dropped where they stood. About 3,000 men were listed as missing, but no one knew for sure, since there were no returns. General Winder himself was not accessible. He retreated northwest with such men as he could rally, and about midnight he halted at Montgomery Court House, now Rockville, 16 miles from Washington. Then when he learned of the British withdrawal on the night of 25 August, he assumed that the next point of attack would be Baltimore, and he started eastward to travel the 30-odd miles to that city.

When the rockets had begun to fly at Bladensburg, President Madison had informed his cabinet that they ought to retire and leave the field to military men. Hardly had the official party returned to the capital when they had to move on unceremoniously. Madison had arranged that in such an event the others were to rejoin him at Frederick, Maryland, 50 miles away. He set out for Virginia instead, accompanied by Secretary Jones and Attorney General Rush. On 25 August his and his wife's routes intersected at an inn, and they continued their flight together. They were sometimes insulted by people who blamed Madison for what had happened. The same day Monroe caught up with the Commander in Chief, then returned across the Potomac to rejoin Winder's army. Secretaries Armstrong and Campbell followed the original plan and rode to Frederick. They waited there for the others, who never came. Madison returned to Washington during the evening of 27 August, and on Sunday, 28 August, with the few officials who had arrived he attempted to put the government back into operation.[28]

The British navy lay perilously close by. Based upon Tangier Island opposite the mouth of the Potomac, it dominated the rivers flowing into Chesapeake Bay. Admiral Cochrane had sent a few small vessels with Cockburn, but had ordered two frigates, two rocket ships, two bomb ships, and one schooner up the Potomac. This flotilla, commanded by Captain James Gordon, was to support the Patuxent expedition and give it something to fall back on if hard pressed. American warships rarely tried to negotiate the shoal waters into which Gordon was ordered without unloading their guns on shore. But Gordon started upstream on 19 August and in 5 days covered 50 miles, every foot of it by warping.* One or another of his ships was aground twenty times. But the Americans offered no resistance. The flotilla reached Maryland Point and had just anchored there, 40 miles below Washington, when Ross' army ignited that city. The violent storm which put out the fires in the capital the next day also damaged the rigging of the ships and slowed down their advance. Not until Saturday, 27 August, did Gordon warp up to Fort Warburton or Washington and prepare to shell it. The commandant there, Captain Samuel T. Dyson, evacuated the place, whereupon the British blew it up. Next the flotilla appeared before defenseless Alexandria on 28 August and sent in demands. Gordon's ultimatum allowed almost no time, and the town council agreed to turn over all naval stores, ordnance, and ships, including those recently sunk to avoid capture. In return, Gordon spared Alexandria. During the next three days the fleet loaded 21 prize ships with goods and burned what they could not carry. In addition to the ships, the British confiscated at least 16,000 barrels of flour, 1,000 hogsheads of tobacco, 150 bales of cotton, and $5,000 worth of wine. *Niles' Register* called the British action base and barbarous, and branded the Alexandria reaction cowardly.[29]

Secretary Jones had sent Commodores Rodgers, Porter, and Perry to attack the hostile fleet on its way down the river. Gordon began the descent on the last day of August and encountered cannon fire for the first time on 4 and again on 5 September, Commodore Porter had set up a battery of 13 cannon at White House, a few miles below Mount Vernon, and had gathered some Virginia militia to protect it. He opened fire as soon as the flotilla was in range. One of the bomb ships grounded, and Gordon had to shift the ballast in all his ships to list them so that they could fire high enough to reach the shore cannon. Porter moved his pieces behind the hill and began to use grape shot. Although Gordon had 173 guns on his ships, he found it necessary to land a party to assail Porter's battery. The Virginia militia defended the guns gallantly for a while, losing 11 killed and 18 wounded, before they permitted them to be captured. Commodore Rodgers, while he did

* To warp a ship is to move it along by hauling on ropes or warps attached to a fixed object.

not achieve as much as Porter, did send three fire ships into the flotilla, but without effect. In the end, the American effort to stop the descent concluded on 6 September and the British reached the bay with all ships intact, but with 7 men killed and 35 wounded.

While Gordon's flotilla was in the Potomac, Sir Peter Parker led a naval detachment to harass the head of the bay. He reconnoitered both Annapolis and Baltimore, but then he was ordered back to the main fleet before he had a chance to fight. He sailed southward looking for excitement. When he heard from a Negro of the activity of the militia near Chestertown, Maryland, he prepared to go ashore for "one more frolic with the Yankees." He landed 124 men at 11:00 P.M. on 30 August. Twenty of them were armed with pikes. He then eagerly led them inland five miles, decoyed by the Americans, to a clearing in the woods where the militia made a stand. His men could see the foe because of the bright moonlight, and they fired and charged. There was a succession of fierce thrusts and counterthrusts. Parker himself was killed at the age of twenty-eight, together with 17 of his men and another 27 wounded. The American force consisted of 170 men and 2 cannon, but Parker's successor reported them at 500 and 5. This, the Battle of Caulk's Field, only hurt the British, for in addition to the casualties they suffered the loss of 40 sailors, who it is presumed took advantage of the confusion to desert.[30]

The Chesapeake campaign produced many accusations in America. John Armstrong, who was the target of most of them, chose to blame the citizen soldiers. "If all the troops assembled at Bladensburg had been faithful to themselves, and to their country," he wrote, "the enemy would have been beaten . . . the determining cause of the failure is to be found in that love of life which in many corps predominated over love of country and of honor." Commodore Barney took more or less the same line. With 2,000 militiamen from Kentucky instead of Maryland and the District, he said, the outcome would have been different. The Englishman George Gleig agreed with Armstrong and Barney: "Had [the American troops] conducted themselves with coolness and resolution, it is not conceivable how the battle could have been won."[31]

Many citizens, in contrast, became openly hostile to John Armstrong. Before Armstrong returned from Frederick, Monroe took over the duties of the War Department on an interim basis and did what he could to bring about Armstrong's removal. Some of the District militia passed resolutions refusing ever again to serve under Armstrong as secretary. They and others saw a conspiracy among officers and leaders to escape blame by alleging bad conduct on the part of the citizen soldiers. Some persons denounced Armstrong to his face. He arrived in Washington on 29 August and conferred that evening with the President. Madison told him of negative public sentiment toward the administration and especially toward him. The secretary offered to resign, but the President countered with the suggestion that he retire temporarily. Armstrong left Washington, and when he got to Baltimore wrote out his resignation. Madison accepted it at once, and James Monroe stepped in officially as acting secretary of war. Three weeks later he was confirmed as permanent in the post, and thus became the secretary of two major departments, state and war. In the state post he had little to do, but in the other he could not hope to keep up with his duties.

Baltimore

While the Washington diversion was in progress, the British commanders found it necessary to consider their next moves. Since their instructions not to hold captured ground were explicit, none of the three recommended the occupation of Washington. For a time Admiral Cochrane insisted that the expedition must clear out of Chesapeake Bay to escape the deadliest enemies of all, malaria and yellow fever. As late as 28 August he held to his intention to transfer to Rhode Island until November.[1]

Thirty days before the start of the Washington campaign, Admiral Cockburn had spoken in favor of attacking Baltimore on the roads leading from the District of Columbia. From the land side Baltimore was vulnerable, but on the water side ships drawing 16 feet could not approach within 5 miles of the city. Cockburn and Ross considered the approach by land, but agreed that it was not viable unless several heavy vessels were standing by in the upper part of the bay to retreat to in case of calamity. Under the circumstances they did not think it was worthwhile to press Cochrane for this naval aid, and with no more backward looks they foreclosed that approach.

The day after the army was re-embarked at Benedict, General Ross voiced his desire to advance without delay against Baltimore by water. At first Cochrane refused. He spoke about the fever and his determination to transfer to Rhode Island. It is possible, too, that he was peeved

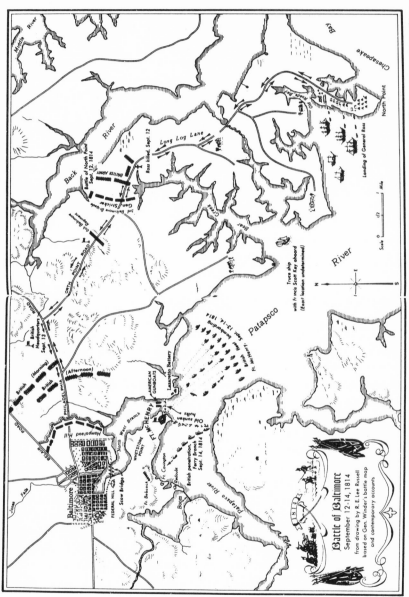

Battle of Baltimore
September 12-14, 1814
from drawing by R. E. Lee Russell
based on Gen. Winder's battle map
and contemporary accounts

because the excursion he had tried to halt had been so romantically successful. Fleet Captain Codrington sided with his chief and tried to persuade Ross to give up the venture, but Admiral Cockburn and Quartermaster Sir George de Lacy Evans abetted the general. Cockburn must have decided to overlook the problems in the water approach, which had in no way grown smaller. In any case the debate continued on board the flagship through the first week in September.

Finally, on 7 September Admiral Cochrane reversed himself and authorized a move on Baltimore. Captain Codrington claimed that Ross and Cockburn nagged him into the shift. Quartermaster Evans, on the other hand, contended that newspaper information convinced Cochrane that the city was vulnerable. But Cochrane himself, when reporting to the government, did not mention any of these influences. He ascribed the change to the equinoctial storms which made it impossible for the fleet to leave Chesapeake Bay. Forced to remain, it was natural for him and Ross to decide on a demonstration against Baltimore, which, if all went well, could turn into a full-scale attack. Whatever the reasons for it, Cochrane's vacillation helped occasion a delay of eight precious days. Some of the delay was inevitable, since the fleet had to be reunited before the new excursion could begin. The last of Gordon's flotilla did not rejoin from the Potomac until 10 September.

The reunited fleet now began to transport the army, which was to make the main effort. The fleet also supplied 1,000 sailors for use ashore. The ships anchored toward evening on Sunday 11 September at the mouth of the Patapsco River, and three American cannon by prearrangement announced their arrival to the citizenry of Baltimore.[2]

Baltimore had 40,000 inhabitants, which made it the third largest city in the United States. It had ample resources to repel the attack if they could be marshaled. The day of Bladensburg there had been created a Committee of Vigilance and Safety which met daily thereafter, with Mayor Edward Johnson as chairman. This committee resolved to draft every white male between sixteen and fifty years of age, and to provide him with a firearm and accessories. Next it offered the command of the defenses to Samuel Smith, major general of Maryland militia, United States senator, Revolutionary veteran, Federalist, and outspoken opponent of the Madison administration. Because General Winder was the commander of the military district which included Baltimore and his uncle was the governor of the state, Smith would not undertake the command unless the governor approved. But when Levin Winder agreed, Smith refused to yield to William Winder or to the three celebrated commodores of the United States Navy sent to Baltimore by the secretary. Smith took over the command completely.[3]

The city papers let it be known that elderly men "who are able to carry a firelock and willing to render a last service to their country and posterity" were invited to form a company. Exempt citizens were asked, on hearing a fire alarm, to go to the station and give aid. "This request becomes the more necessary as the members [of the fire squads] generally are engaged in military duty." The doctors of the city who were not already militia surgeons were asked to join some corps which had no surgeon.

As the days went by, nearly 9,000 men collected close to Baltimore. Supplies had to be impressed for their use, and all wagons were requisitioned to haul ammunition. Many men had neither blankets, tents, nor many other necessities. Only liquor was in oversupply, so the committee required grog shops to close at nine in the evening, and doubled the town watch during the daytime. It was necessary to give public aid to the families of some militiamen who were on duty. Public funds were exhausted and General Smith was said to have mortgaged his own property to help replenish them. The federal government could send neither supplies nor money to Baltimore; indeed, at the height of the defense effort the War Department requested that the city return nineteen field guns on loan. The state of Maryland did no better. It agreed to forward muskets to the city, but when the boxes were opened, they were found to contain not muskets, but old government records.

Baltimore dug. The whole town was divided into sectors, and each sector was assigned a portion of earthwork to construct. Beginning on 27 August, people of all stations blistered their hands with shovels and picks. Since it would not have been possible to ring the whole town with earthworks, General Smith gambled that the British would approach by water, and did not fortify the inland routes.[4]

When General Winder reached Baltimore from Washington with part of his column, Smith made it crystal clear that he, Smith, was in command. Winder then requested that he be created a major general in the regular service to outrank the general from Baltimore, but in the end he had to serve under Smith and to accept unimportant field commands. Samuel Smith was old and seasoned enough in politics never to lose control of the situation.[5]

The British had decided while on their way to Baltimore that North Point was the place to go ashore because the fleet could there protect the army's flanks. Even though it turned out that the water was too shallow for the navy to afford flank protection, Ross began his disembarkation at North Point, roughly fourteen miles from Baltimore, at 3:00 A.M. on 12 September 1814. At eight o'clock the column moved off along a good road to the northwest. It marched in three brigades with a short distance separating them; the six cannon and two howitzers were put between the second and first brigades. About halfway to Baltimore they encountered the Americans strongly posted behind high pilings. The United States force there consisted of 3,185 men under the command of Brigadier General John Stricker of the Baltimore militia. Stricker had been sent out early enough to take up his position between the upper waters of Bear Creek and Back River where the peninsula was about one mile wide. He had had time to erect the pilings for his front and to secure his flanks on open water and swamp. He had also sent 150 riflemen forward of his line, but most of these had retired behind the pilings by the time the British arrived.[6]

When his column struck Stricker's position, General Ross rode forward to reconnoiter. He returned to the column to order the light infantry forward on the double, and had started back to the American position when he was knocked off his white horse by a bullet through his right arm and into his chest. It had been fired by one of two boys, Daniel Wells or Henry G. McComas, who had not retreated with the other riflemen. Both the boys were later killed, and quarter was denied other American sharpshooters. Ross lay unseen until the light infantry found his body.

Colonel Arthur Brooke now took over the British command. About 10:00 A.M. he ordered artillery fire. British salvos did considerable execution upon the most exposed part of the American line, while the light infantry had to lie down to wait out the heavy fire returned by the Americans. As at Bladensburg, screaming Congreve rockets unnerved the Americans. Brooke started a regiment to try to reach the enemy's left flank, and after an appropriate interval ordered an attack across the entire position. At first this seemed successful, for in fifteen minutes the Americans fell back to a prepared line 300 yards behind the advanced one, and soon withdrew about half a mile more to the reserve position. Finally, between three and three-forty-five in the afternoon Stricker ordered a retreat to his final prepared position nearer to the city. The British camped on the battlefield, but American resistance had been such that Brooke reported it as the work of 6,000 men instead of half of that, which it really was.

Even though Admiral Cochrane knew that his large ships could not get close to the city, he hoped to place some of them where they could destroy Fort McHenry and then move up the northwest branch of the Patapsco to flank the American defenses. Accordingly, his five bomb and rocket vessels took position about five miles from the city and three from McHenry (which was as close as they could get), and at dawn on 13 September they began a bombardment. The frigates formed a line farther down the river, too far away to add to the cannonade.

Major George Armistead commanded not only Fort McHenry, but also the Lazaretto Battery and the gunboats which were anchored in the entrance to the northwest branch. He had a garrison of about 1,000 men. His cannon could not reach the attacking ships, which managed to drop an occasional round into his works. But the luck of his crews improved when at 2:00 P.M. several British vessels drew within two miles to exploit what they thought was a breach. The American cannoneers drove these back out of range in half an hour. Next, Cochrane sent 1,200 British sailors in barges at one on the morning of 14 September to try to pass over the sunken hulks in the main channel of the Patapsco to land and approach the city from the southwest. But the fire from the forts and batteries very soon drove the sailors back to their ships. After this failure the flotilla began to drop downstream. Americans estimated that it had fired 1,500 or more rounds. Of these, 400 had hit within the defenses, but the rest had burst more or less harmlessly overhead. These latter were the "bombs bursting in air" immortalized by Francis Scott Key. He was a resident of Georgetown, but was at Baltimore serving with a volunteer artillery battery. In fact, while the bombardment raged he was aboard *Minden*, a cartel ship on which he had gone to interview Admiral Cochrane about the release of a prisoner. His total poetic product was "The Star Spangled Banner," later to become the national anthem. The last rounds struck Fort McHenry about 7:00 A.M., but the entire bombardment had killed only four and wounded twenty-four Americans.

Not long after the naval bombardment had commenced, Colonel Brooke started his column up the road toward the last of the American prepared positions. After a five-mile march he found himself confronted by a very strong earthwork. The American left flank was dangling, but Brooke did not see this. Cochrane had warned Brooke not to storm any strongholds unless he was sure of carrying them. On the other hand, the admiral had assured Brooke that the navy would soon be in position to give his men immediate aid. Brooke called a council of war which estimated the force in front of them at 100 cannon and 15,000 men. Notwithstanding this and Cochrane's warning, the council voted to assault the works at night. While rain poured down, Brooke tried to lure the Americans out of their defenses, but in vain. Then, toward evening came word from Admiral Cochrane that the navy could not help after all. Brooke called another council of war and announced that he would not carry out the assault without the unanimous consent of the officers. When this was not given, the plans were voided. About 3:00 A.M. campfires were left burning, and the column marched silently out, aided by bright moonlight, to return to its shipping.

The next morning, when the retreat was discovered, General Smith allowed a small pursuit, but his heart was not in it. His objective had been limited to the saving of Baltimore. "When you fight our citizens against the British regulars," he said, "you're staking dollars against cents." Bladensburg was at least partly redeemed. The *National Intelligencer* said that the militia and volunteers stood on higher grounds in self-confidence, in the affection of the country, and the respect of the foe than ever before.

Just two days after the Battle of North Point the British flotilla departed down the river. As soon as the wind permitted, it dropped toward the lower bay. On 19 September Admiral Cochrane sailed for Halifax, and Cockburn for Bermuda. This left Rear Admiral Pultney Malcolm in charge. On 27 September he returned the fleet to the vicinity of the Potomac River, then on 14 October took most of it off to join a grand rendezvous at Jamaica. Thus, once and for all, ended the British campaigns in Chesapeake waters. The 1814 campaign had cost Britain and the United States about the same number of casualties, from 300 to 325 each. It had cost an enormous amount in ill-will. Hezekiah Niles, who lived in Baltimore and who had to suspend publication of his *Register* at the height of the threat, proposed that a monument be erected on the spot where General Ross fell, with the following inscription: "By the Just Dispensation of the Almighty near this Spot was Slain, September 12, 1814, the Leader of a Host of Barbarians who destroyed the Capitol of the United States . . . and devoted the Populous City of Baltimore to rape, robbery, and conflagration." He dedicated volume 6 of the *Register* "To Remembrance of the Baltimore Militia who Withstood the choicest Troops of the Foe, September 13, 1814, and Died in Defense of their altars and firesides, their wives and their little ones. Whose gallant hearts shielded the virgin from pollution, and the matron from insult; who preserved this city from plunder and conflagration and all the murdering business of war waged by a new race of Goths, outraging the ordinances of God and the laws of humanity. . . ." Conspicuous by its absence here is any reference to the part played by the United States in saving Baltimore, which part, in truth, did not amount to very much.[7]

Niles claimed that a shore party had smashed organ pipes in churches, opened coffins in search of loot, and wantonly broken up property they could not carry away. He was probably guilty of exaggeration, but there was some vandalism. Admiral Cochrane attempted to stop it by ordering that no party was to go ashore without an officer, and that soldiers caught stealing would receive 48 lashes in the presence of the persons they had robbed. Where goods were confiscated for the fleet's use, Cochrane set a uniform price scale to be paid in coin.[8]

Ill-will did not grow within Americans only. Fleet Captain Codrington wanted not just to defeat but to squelch the Baltimoreans. He saw retaliation as the best way to shorten a war with such people. "I do not believe," he wrote to his wife, "there is anywhere a more detestable race of people." During the oppressive August heat on "this oven of a river," he concluded that America was not a fit habitation for social man. Americans were to him meanly acquisitive, and capable of betraying their country, a brother, or any other cause for personal gain. Chronicler Gleig did not write off the Americans and their environment as Codrington did, but agreed with him that you had to fight a democracy with savage weapons: fire, looting, and ruthless preying upon commerce.

Three times during the Chesapeake campaign, British personnel reported poisoned wine placed in their way by Americans, but they never preserved the evidence long enough to prove it. They charged their foes also with other uncivilized practices. There was the case of a Captain James Scott who was lured into an ambush by a flag of truce. Luckily Scott escaped from this treachery, and learning who his opponents were, he led a detachment in the night to drag the leader, a colonel of militia, out of bed. The colonel was brought to the fleet and badly scared, but in the end he was freed without injury or loss. There was the case also of a British sergeant who refused to surrender and fought fiercely until badly wounded. An American lieutenant put a pistol to his head and killed him. To the British this was "cruel cowardice," but an American newspaper summarized the demise of the sergeant thus: "This hardy Briton died a victim of rash valor."

The English met face to face the institution of slavery in the Chesapeake Bay area. The officers were opposed to it, influenced by the crusade, begun in England in the 1790s, to outlaw the slave trade and to abolish slavery in English possessions. Nevertheless, when Lord Bathurst issued instructions to General Ross, he cautioned him not to encourage Negro insurrection, but to accept black refugees and enlist them in the British colonial corps if possible. Admiral Cockburn relied heavily on ex-slaves to guide his detachments. This may have prompted Cochrane to write him on 1 July, "The great point to be attained is the cordial support of the Black population." Cockburn was directed to arm the blacks. One gratis adviser of the government recommended that a harsh ultimatum be delivered to the United States. If the Americans rejected it, Britain should at once conquer Maryland and

Virginia, free the slaves, and make them citizens of Great Britain.[9]

Most of the English commanders took pleasure in using the West Indian black troops in the Chesapeake Bay area, and spoke well of their performance. They assumed that the use of Negroes as soldiers would at once give Britain needed manpower and at the same time engender despair in the United States. In any case, substantial numbers of blacks followed Cockburn's detachments back to the fleet. Most of them did not want to enter British military service, but they came in such numbers that captains of ships appealed for instructions and for help. After the fall of Washington swarms of slaves implored Ross to take them with him, but he refused, thus violating at least the spirit of his instructions, simply because he could not make provision for such hordes.

More and more it became necessary for the British commanders and their government to adopt some sort of policy toward American Negro slavery. Their attitude was influenced by the conviction that while Britain struggled to keep a tyrant from dominating the world, America had knifed her in the back. A good way to get revenge in part was through the institution of Negro slavery.

At first English officials looked upon the escaped slaves as potential replacements to enter their West Indian regiments or as recruits for certain Canadian units which could not seem to attain full strength. Inciting slave insurrection was discouraged, except in one instance. When Americans announced that they would retaliate upon British subjects for atrocities committed by British Indians, Lord Bathurst announced, but only in government circles, that if the American policy was carried out, British commanders would be instructed to encourage the Negroes to revolt. Neither the American nor the British threat was ever put into effect.[10]

Admiral Warren had always viewed the use of black troops as a way to humiliate southern Americans. Admiral Cochrane saw their use more arithmetically, as an addition to one force and a subtraction from the other. He ordered that runaways were either to be recruited into appropriate military units or to be sent off as free persons to certain British possessions. But he never spelled out what possessions would receive free Negroes and treat them as citizens. The proclamations he issued were intended to align not only Indians but also Negroes with his country. Admiral Cockburn induced desertion of slaves by sending ex-slaves among them with the British message. Cockburn did not expect much out of them as soldiers, but someone, perhaps Captain Hugh Pigot, convinced Cochrane that they had special military advantages. They were all skilled horsemen who might bring horses with them when they defected. They could be trained as cavalry and counted on to scare Americans above all other types of troops. Their hatred of slavery would render them as fierce and ruthless as Cossacks. Because Americans loathed the idea of the black man armed, these troops would shock and unsettle them.[11]

By late September Cochrane could report no more than 300 ex-slaves in military service. Most of these blacks were combined with some detached companies into a new battalion of the Royal Colonial Marines. About 1,000 runaways, who had not been willing to become soldiers, were shipped off to Halifax in October 1814. They arrived there nearly naked and desperately in need of warm clothing. About as many were sent to Bermuda, where they became the responsibility of the local naval officers. The latter put the men to work in the naval yards at two shillings per day, plus rations, but the senior commander, Commodore Andrew Evans, reported that they were "very riotous." Evans added, "Their general character is so useless, their capacity for improvement so doubtful, and their sloth so invincible" that he did not know what to do with them. Race prejudice might have colored his estimate, but there is no way of being sure. In any event, he asked for a ship on which to sequester them until some better disposition could be found, because the local residents did not want them on the island as free persons.[12]

It was charged that Admiral Cochrane carried some runaway blacks to his plantation in Trinidad and reinslaved them for his own use. He denied this categorically, and stated that as of the end of 1814 no United States Negroes had been shipped anywhere except to Halifax and Bermuda.[13]

When he later gave the command of the North American Station to Rear Admiral Malcolm, Cochrane ordered him to try to get future runaways to enlist in the West Indian regiments. Those who would not were to be urged, but not forced, to return to their masters. This was the exact opposite of Cochrane's previous policy. Under it slaves had been encouraged to escape and seek British protection. The shift was due to expediency alone. Since Britain had not conquered America, the British officers had the problem of what to do with a helpless crowd of Negro refugees, but it would disappear if the refugees once more became slaves. Cochrane's solution was perfectly human, but the very opposite of humane.[14]

About 3,600 slaves detached themselves from their owners during the War of 1812. Since slavery was an active institution in Bermuda and the Bahamas, there was no permanent place for them in these islands as free persons. Most of them, therefore, were shipped to New Brunswick and Nova Scotia. The few who remained in the islands, presumably as free people, begat issue whose descendents still live there. Those dumped in Canada became for a time a heavy burden upon the communities. Some of them were eventually colonized in Sierra Leone, but most of them remained and their successors live there yet.[15]

During and after the Baltimore campaign, the entire east coast was thrown into alarm. No American knew the British plans, but it was assumed that they would include the destruction of seacoast towns and attacks on seacoast cities. Chesapeake Bay always appeared a sound objective, and Governor James Barbour of Virginia despaired of being able to defend it. He asked that the United States return to fundless Virginia money which it had borrowed in the past, but the treasury of course could not comply. His consternation was multiplied when he received a demand from Monroe dated 2 October that Virginia organize 4,000 militiamen and march them toward Washington, armed if possible with rifles. All Barbour could do was send the militia gathered for the defense of Richmond, but they had to go without firearms.[16]

While the flotilla was watering at Tangier Island, Colonel Brooke sent about 1,000 men ashore in the vicinity of the Nominy River. Half of this detachment struck at Black Point, the other at Monday Point. They secured provisions and captured some arms at a cost of one officer killed and two enlisted men wounded. Another landing party, 200 strong, went ashore at Parker's Point. It had to cope with 1,000 Virginia militiamen, and was lucky to extricate itself and get back aboard ship. When Norfolk appeared to be threatened, Governor Barbour asked that North Carolina take over its defense, since Virginia could do no more.[17]

Secretary Monroe expected another attack in the Chesapeake area when the British had picked up their reinforcements in the West Indies. He called for militia from Virginia and Pennsylvania, and ordered General Winfield Scott to take command of the Tenth Military District, if his wounds would permit it. Scott came and Winder was sent off to the northern frontier. After one month of Scott, Generals Samuel Smith and John Stricker of the Maryland militia resigned, and Robert Goodloe Harper took over at Baltimore.[18]

On 1 December a British landing party captured the village of Tappahannock, forty miles from the mouth of the Rappahannock River, and, so Americans claimed, wantonly plundered it. Militia contested their return trip down the river and inflicted several casualties. Meanwhile, the number of British troops in the Chesapeake area was slowly declining, until by mid-January 1815 the secretary of war felt safe in authorizing the discharge of an entire brigade of Virginia militia from the federal service. Reduction of the numbers of militia on active duty was something he and the President had long been striving toward.[19]

There was a bustle of volunteer activity at Philadelphia, and the Pennsylvania Bank loaned the government $200,000 to be used to defend the city. Monroe requested the governor to make all avenues to the city difficult to the enemy by felling trees, moving supplies, and so forth. Next, on 23 September he notified Brigadier General Joseph Bloomfield that higher rank was needed in his space, and that therefore Major General Edmund P. Gaines would relieve him in the Fourth Military District (eastern Pennsylvania, New Jersey, and Delaware). Gaines assumed the command on 9 October 1814.[20]

Efforts were made, of course, to strengthen New York City and the area around it. Secretary Jones sent Commodore Decatur there to take charge of naval affairs. But because most of the troops there were citizen soldiers from New York state, Governor Tompkins seemed the man most likely to inspire them. Accordingly, the President relieved Morgan Lewis as commander of the Third District and installed Tompkins. DeWitt Clinton, representing the governor's political rivals, protested the change. He was personally aggrieved, for although a major general of New York militia, he was one of those Tompkins had kept out of active command throughout the war.[21]

The governor of New Jersey protested that Tompkins became commander of New Jersey militia on New Jersey soil, and that this arrangement was illegal. Monroe took time to frame his reply. The federal government, he said, took militia officers under its control when it summoned their units into federal service. The governor of a state, being an officer in the militia, entered federal service with the troops of the state, if the United States desired him. Tompkins then lost all the attributes of governorship when in federal service and appointed to command the military district, except that of commander in chief of his own militia. Therefore his authority did not encroach on the powers vested by election in the governor of New Jersey. Monroe then cited the command arrangement during the Whiskey Rebellion, when Governor Richard Howell of New Jersey and Governor Thomas Mifflin of Pennsylvania had served under the military command of Governor Henry Lee of Virginia. It is not known how far this explanation satisfied the governor of New Jersey, but Tompkins continued to command the Third Military District until April 1815. All the while he was a state commander in chief and the commander of a United States military district without holding military rank or commission.

Lake Champlain

The British Ministry expected Lieutenant General Sir George Prevost to strike the main blow against the United States from Canada. Certain people in Canada for political or personal reasons did not like Sir George, and other people wished to see him removed because they doubted his competence as a military commander. The groups never combined sufficiently to displace him. Prevost himself continued to ask for reinforcements, not with a view to offensive action, but merely to enable him to maintain the defensive in Canada. Early in the year he complained that the promised increments would arrive too late to be of use during the campaign season of 1814. While he was most discouraged, he suggested to Bathurst that the Canadians might desert the British cause if help from England did not come soon. Earl Bathurst rebutted the suggestion by saying that Canadians could not be indifferent to the exertions which England was making for the liberties of Europe.[1]

The last battle of the Peninsular War was fought at Toulouse on 11 April 1814. Early in June two powerful naval convoys left Bordeaux and the Gironde River to conduct to America 60 transports loaded with troops. The vessels from these convoys which were consigned to Canada reached Quebec during the third week in August, after a voyage of two and one-half months. By the end of August at least 13,000 veteran troops had passed from Europe into Canada. They raised the total of nonmilitia troops in Canada to about 30,000. British sea power had made it possible to transfer so many men from one continent to another, and British sea power would have to insure the safe arrival every day of 45 tons of supplies for them.[2]

General Prevost organized about 10,500 infantrymen into a division for offensive use. His selection of Major General Francis DeRottenburg to command the division was a questionable decision, both because DeRottenburg was too old and because he was not held in high regard by the three young Wellington protégés who commanded the brigades: Frederick Philipse Robinson, Thomas Brisbane, and Manley Power, all major generals. These young veterans were skeptical not only of DeRottenburg, but of Prevost himself, because of his foreign birth and his lack of experience in combat. After all, they had been considered and nominated as his best by Wellington himself and had fought against, and had been commanded by, the masters of the craft. On still other grounds they doubted the competence of

Lieutenant Thomas Macdonough

Prevost. He had on 4 June 1814 promoted his adjutant general, Edward Baynes, from colonel to major general. This promotion placed in the top echelon of command another officer with scant combat experience, who appeared to owe his rise to influence and good luck. And finally, the Duke of Wellington had never been fussy about such surface matters as uniform, whereas Prevost issued orders that dress regulations be enforced to the letter.[3]

Prevost attached 536 royal artillerymen and 300 light dragoons to the offensive division. He also organized under the command of Major General James Kempt a fourth brigade of 3,500 to 4,000 men to serve as a reserve. The reserve brigade was stationed at Montreal, and Prevost moved his own headquarters from Chambly to Montreal, the better to control his impressive forces. The troops in Lower Canada totaled about 18,000. Neither Prevost nor his detractors doubted the success of the offensive which he was now to begin.

It was up to General Prevost to determine how his army of veterans would be used. He made a personal reconnaissance of Sackett's Harbor and concluded that the place could not be captured. The American fleet on Lake Ontario was too strong, and Prevost could not supply his forces in a region now picked clean of provisions. Soon he settled upon the Richelieu (Sorel) River and Lake Champlain line for his operations. Here was a natural invasion route, a fertile valley where an army of up to 12,000 could be subsisted. Moreover, it lay altogether in the United States, and control of it would provide a valuable counter in the negotiations for peace. Finally, if that valley was in British hands it would assure the continuation of the meat supply from New York and Vermont, on which the army had come to depend.[4]

While Prevost made up his mind, the American commanders tried to guess what he would do with his growing army. Toward the end of April, Secretary Armstrong had placed Major General George Izard in command of the land forces around Lake Champlain, and bombarded him with advice. In reply, Izard complained that his force consisted of inexperienced officers and green troops with too little time left in their enlistment to teach them the essential skills. Some Negro troops from New England appeared, but since many white officers and men refused to serve with them, they were organized into a segregated pioneer corps. Besides the ill-will this engendered, Izard had to contend with a high rate of desertion and a severe shortage of supplies.[5]

Lieutenant Thomas Macdonough had been the naval commander on Lake Champlain since the fall of 1813. He was trying to build an American flotilla at Vergennes on Otter Creek in Vermont, off the southern part of Lake Champlain. British Captain Daniel Pring left his base at Isle aux Noix with a brig, three sloops, and twelve galleys and appeared off the mouth of Otter Creek on 14 May 1814. Macdonough called upon the governor of Vermont for a brigade of militia, and determined to try to make his force appear more formidable than it was. The seven cannon he had planted at the mouth kept the enemy flotilla out of Otter Creek, and he used his own ships to try to bluff Pring into withdrawing. Pring did withdraw, primarily because he had no landing party, and returned to Isle aux Noix.[6]

Secretary Armstrong learned of the Otter Creek incident ten days later, and at once directed Izard to advance to the head of Lake Champlain and erect there such fortifications as would close the lake to the British. Izard found that the enemy already occupied the points indicated by Armstrong, and decided to concentrate at Plattsburg instead. He began to erect rather formidable strongpoints south of the town. On 3 September Macdonough brought his three warships and some gunboats into Plattsburg Bay. His flagship *Saratoga*, 8 long guns and 18 carronades, had been launched on 11 April, only 40 days after the trees in her had been cut from the forest. Next was *Ticonderoga*, with 12 long guns and 5 short, and third was *Preble*, 7 long guns. Macdonough received word from Washington that no added naval force could be sent to him. He called the Brown brothers back from New York City and commissioned them late in June to build a sloop as fast as possible. They built *Eagle*, 8 long guns and 12 carronades, and the sloop was ready for use on 15 August. Ten days later the British launched *Confiance*, 31 long and 6 short guns, at Isle aux Noix, but she was far from being combat ready.[7]

Izard set out on his march westward on 29 August in reluctant obedience to Armstrong's orders. General Alexander Macomb, as already told, took command at Plattsburg. Izard took with him 4,000 men, leaving Macomb with only 1,500, of which all but a few hundred were green militiamen. Less than a week after Izard's departure from Plattsburg, Prevost began moving southward with 12,000 men. General Benjamin Mooers of the New York militia now issued a call for the organization in his district to fall out en masse. Only 700 men responded, but they hung like gnats about the advancing British column. Prevost did not even bother to deploy his men from column to line to cope with them. Macomb was forced to put invalids into his three forts and two blockhouses, and ordered them to defend to the death. On 6 September he sent forward two regular detachments, each about 200 strong, to stall the enemy's advance on the two main roads from the north. These men gamely contested the ground. Some militiamen rallied to them, but then dissolved when a squadron of New York dragoons, with red coats like the British, approached from the south and convinced them that they were surrounded. [8]

When the British column was within a mile of the main American position, Macomb's advanced parties fell back, fighting in good order. Prevost found the American line on an elevated ridge south of the Saranac River, protected by two blockhouses and three forts, all well supplied with cannon. The Americans had removed the planking from the only two bridges, making it necessary for the invaders to go three miles upstream to ford the river. Prevost ordered an immediate assault, but canceled it when he discovered that no guide could lead his force to the fords. Now his men occupied houses on the north bank and kept up a nasty fire from the upper stories, until their nests were destroyed by hot shot from cannon. The American galleys harassed the British army with their guns. All through the day of 6 September British parties tried without success to cross over the plankless bridges. Sometime during that day Prevost reached the portentous decision not to attack on land until the fleet came up. For the next four days he brought forward and emplaced his cannon.

Governor Martin Chittenden of Vermont had receded from his intransigent posture of 1813, but he still did not feel that he had the power to call out Vermont militia for service in New York. The best he could bring himself to do was to issue a proclamation urging volunteers to go to the aid of the United States Army. The response was enthusiastic, and by 10 September 2,500 Vermont volunteers, commanded by a major general, were at Plattsburg behind Macomb's well-constructed works.

On 2 September Captain George Downie replaced Captain Peter Fisher as the British naval commander on Lake Champlain. This change was ordered by Sir James Yeo, who believed that Fisher had too violent a temper to be entrusted with separate command. General Prevost at once wrote Downie that the army needed naval support and was waiting for it. There came a flurry of correspondence. Downie sent word to the general on 8 September that *Confiance* was not ready. He could not hazard the squadron against a superior force until this, his flagship, was fully prepared. He intended to remain anchored at Chazy until all her guns were in place.

Though Prevost could not command Downie, he could certainly influence him through rank and prestige. This influence finally prevailed. On 9 September Downie agreed to take his ships onto Plattsburg Bay before dawn the next day and attack the American flotilla. Most of the crew on *Confiance* at this time were landlubbers who had

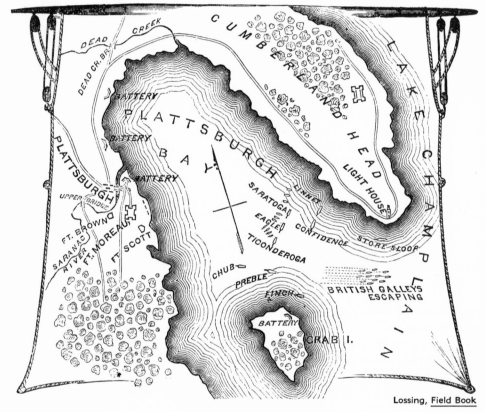

Battle of Plattsburg Bay

been aboard only four days. Men and officers were still unacquainted with one another, and they had had only two chances to practice with their guns. Even so, they had found that the rate of fire was dangerously slow because the decks were so rough that it was hard to push the guns over them. They had found too that to make the guns work they had to employ several makeshift firing devices.

Downie's squadron consisted of the frigate *Confiance* with 37 guns, the brig *Linnet* 16, the sloop *Chubb* 11, the sloop *Finch* 10, and 12 gunboats carrying among them 16 guns. Of the total armament, 60 were long guns which could throw 1,128 pounds of metal, 30 were carronades capable of throwing 736 pounds. The Americans had the frigate *Saratoga* with 26 guns, the brig *Eagle* 20, the schooner *Ticonderoga* 17, the sloop *Preble* 7, and 10 gunboats mounting 16 guns. Their 45 long guns could throw only 759 pounds of metal, but the carronades, 41 in all, could throw 1,274 pounds.

Macdonough's intelligence service had given him quite accurate information about the enemy, and he was determined to fight at anchor. C. S. Forester said that the American profited from his study of the ways by which Nelson had beaten anchored fleets on the Nile and at Copenhagen. Macdonough chose a position about 2 miles from the mainland, out of reach of the shore batteries if these latter should fall into British hands. He placed *Preble* just beyond shoal water off the north end of Crab Island, stern to the island; then *Ticonderoga* 200 yards northward, stern to *Preble*'s bow; then at another 100 yards *Saratoga*; and at the point *Eagle*. Forming a second line 40 yards westward, the gunboats filled the intervals between the front-line ships. When his flotilla was in position, Macdonough put out kedge anchors* off the sides of the bows of each of the first-line ships, with the hawsers underwater. Now he could, if he needed to, wind his ships around to retire the starboard broadsides and present the larboard. Finally he picked his anchorage so that the English ships would have to round Cumberland Head and then beat upwind to reach the Americans. Since there was no room for them to anchor broadside out of American carronade range, the British could not utilize their advantage in long guns.

Downie was unable to make his approach on 10 September because the winds were adverse, but he sailed from Chazy at 3:30 A.M. on

---

* A kedge anchor was a small anchor which could be carried forward, let go, and be used as a firm grip toward which the ship could be hauled by heaving round on the capstan (a winch) which wound in the hawser attached to the anchor.

11 September to keep his rendezvous. He thought Prevost had agreed that when the naval signal guns were fired, the army would start the land battle. Between 7:30 and 8:30 A.M. the flotilla rounded Cumberland Head, with the wind in the northwest, shifted from line ahead to line abreast, and steered for the American line. Downie now fired his signal guns. At this time a large part of the army was cooking breakfast and continued to do so. General Robinson's brigade, it is true, was in motion under orders from Prevost to march three miles upstream, cross the fords, and assail the American flank. But Robinson had been told not to attack before ten o'clock.

Downie's plan was for *Chubb, Linnet,* and *Confiance* to concentrate their force on *Eagle,* eliminate her, and then turn their full power upon *Saratoga.* The gunboats would help *Finch* fight *Preble* and *Ticonderoga.* His principal reliance was placed on the new, but not well prepared, flagship *Confiance,* far more powerful than any other vessel present. But while the British ships tacked in bows on, they took severe punishment from the American long guns. Macdonough himself sighted the first guns, and the shot carried from bow to stern through *Confiance,* wreaking destruction. When finally they got into position opposite the American line, however, the British anchored their ships and with perfect discipline under heavy fire swung them around until their broadsides bore. Captain Downie ordered his gunners to take careful aim, and the full larboard broadside of *Confiance* smashed into *Saratoga,* killing or wounding 40 members of the crew. The blast broke open chicken coops on *Saratoga*'s deck. One rooster flew up to light on a gun, there flapped his wings, and crowed. The American crew took this to be a most favorable omen; its members regained their composure and fell to work. No later rounds by the British were as effective as the first one. Mostly they were too high and did no more than cut up the rigging.

During the first fifteen minutes of the battle an American round shot knocked a British gun from its carriage into Captain Downie, at the groin, and without even breaking the skin the blow killed him instantly. For the first half-hour *Chubb* and *Linnet* closely engaged *Eagle* as planned. Then *Chubb* went out of control, drifted through the center of the American line, approached the western shore, and there had to surrender. Her commander was later charged with bad conduct, but he was cleared when the testimony revealed that his vessel had become unmanageable, that he himself was wounded, and that only 6 of his men were left on deck. Soon after *Chubb*'s surrender, *Eagle* cut her cables and took position between *Saratoga* and *Ticonderoga.* The brig took a southerly heading, brought her larboard broadside into the battle, and wrought damage upon *Confiance*. At about the same time *Preble* was disabled and drifted off westward before the wind. While *Finch* engaged *Ticonderoga*, 4 of the British gunboats moved in upon the latter's stern. But Captain Stephen Cassin and his crew gallantly put out a fire and kept *Ticonderoga* in action.

At mid-point of the battle it seemed as if the end had come for the American flotilla. Macdonough himself was once knocked down by the head of Midshipman Bellamy, torn off by a round shot, and was again knocked down by flying debris. Then all of *Saratoga*'s starboard battery was silenced by enemy shot. Now Macdonough diverted all his attention to winding his ship around until her larboard battery was able to bear. Lieutenant James Robertson, commanding *Confiance* after Downie's fall, ordered the same maneuver, but without the sort of advanced preparation Macdonough had seen to. *Confiance*'s lines fouled when the ship was stern to *Saratoga*, and she took such severe punishment—at least so Robertson reported—that the crews refused to stand to their battle stations. Thus, about ten-thirty in the morning *Confiance* struck her colors. Now the fresh broadsides of *Saratoga* and *Eagle* converged on *Linnet* and soon forced her surrender too. *Finch* went out of control and drifted into the shoals on the north side of Crab Island. Several of the British gunboats now fled; they seemed to hang back from the battle all along.

By 10:30 A.M. this lake battle—tiny but one of the most decisive in American history—was finished. No more than 1,800 men were involved in it, around one-tenth of the number in the Battle of Trafalgar in 1805. The American dead totaled 47, the British 57; the American wounded were 58, the British at least 100. It was an overall casualty rate of about 14 per cent. The numbers were insignificant, but the consequences were tremendous.

When the British squadron came into view around Cumberland Head, General Prevost ordered a cannonade all along the American line. The firing continued until the middle of the afternoon. The general also arranged for assaults across the Saranac River, but he counted on a much longer naval battle than he got. General Robinson began his attack as ordered at 10:00 A.M., but his guide got lost and Robinson could not cross the river until later. Once started, however, his men quickly scattered the American militia. Robinson believed he had broken the American left flank. Then he received a shocking message from Adjutant Baynes: "I am directed to inform you that the 'Confiance' and the Brig having struck their colours in consequence of the Frigate having grounded, it will no longer be prudent to persevere in the Service committed to your charge, and it is therefore the Orders of the Commander of the Forces that you immediately return with the troops under your command." The general and his staff were dumbfounded by this order, and the enlisted men obeyed it sullenly. Instantly upon learning of the defeat of the naval squadron, General Prevost apparently had decided to halt the land battle. Not long afterwards he also pulled his army back into Canada. He ordered vast quantities of stores destroyed, and he had reached Chazy, 8 miles away, before General Macomb even knew he had departed. Macomb reported that he did not pursue the British because of torrential rains. He was lucky to have escaped destruction.

Casualties in the land campaign were roughly equal: 37 Americans, 35 British killed; 63 Americans, 47 British wounded. But at least 300 British soldiers deserted.[9]

Prevost's retreat ended the major British offensive planned for North America, and it eventually affected the peace negotiations. Henry Goulburn said, "If we had either burnt Baltimore or held Plattsburg, I believe we could have had peace on our own terms." General Prevost of course had much explaining to do. He withdrew hastily, he said, because the roads were becoming impassable, because food was scarce, and because his own force was dwindling through desertions, while the Americans were waxing. Most of all, once the flank of his army lay open on the lake side, he considered its position untenable. He explained it to Bathurst: "Your Lordship must have been aware from my previous despatches that no Offensive Operations could be carried out within the Enemy's Territory for the destruction of his Naval Establishments without Naval Support. . . . The disastrous and unlooked for result of the Naval Contest by depriving me of the only means by which I could avail myself of any advantage I might gain, rendered a perseverance in the attack of the Enemy's position highly imprudent as well as hazardous. Under the circumstances I had to determine whether I should consider my own fame by gratifying the ardor of the troops in persevering in the attack, or consult the more substantial interest of my country by withdrawing the Army which was yet uncrippled for the security of these provinces."[10]

Commodore Yeo did not agree that the result of the naval battle was "unlooked for." He became convinced that Prevost had hurried Downie into a foredoomed attack. Much later he made formal charges: Prevost had led Downie to expect full cooperation from the army, but had not given it; Prevost had disregarded the pre-arranged signal for joint attack, and had failed to storm the United

States' position during the naval engagement as he had agreed to do; if he had stormed the American works as early as 6 September, he could have taken them with small loss; he could have achieved gains by attacking the Americans even after the defeat of the British flotilla, for this would have forced the American vessels out into the open lake; and finally, Prevost had goaded Downie into attacking before his flotilla was adequately prepared.[11]

The Duke of Wellington agreed with Prevost's thesis that control of the lake was essential to victory. But he considered that the campaign had been managed as "ill as possible." He advised the Ministry to remove Prevost because "He had gone to war about trifles with the general officers I sent him, which are certainly the best of their rank in the army." Lord Liverpool, for his part, became convinced that Prevost had lost the confidence of his army. General Robinson reported that the destruction of supplies was "precipitate and wasteful." Certain critics blamed Prevost for Britain's having lost naval control of the lakes. A coterie of civilians sent nothing but bad reports about him from Canada. They asserted that the army was near mutiny over the bumbling of Plattsburg and the campaign. To prevent this from being known in England, they said, Prevost had sent personal emissaries to the Ministry schooled to distort the truth. In Canada he was the unwitting instrument of the "insidious designs of the set of villains who hover around the throne. . . . Had any man with common abilities been at the head of this government, unbiased by the invidious counsels of fools and sycophants," the failure of the campaign would not have occurred.[12]

It suited Lord Liverpool to listen to Prevost's detractors, for his own conscience pricked him sometimes. He admitted that it was a mistake to have sent most of the veteran reinforcements to Prevost, who had proved incompetent. He never acknowledged that he and the Ministry might be blameable for having maintained an incompetent man in a position of power. Moreover, he did not charge the failure entirely to Prevost. He had become convinced that England could not hope to dominate Lake Champlain under any circumstances.

Was Prevost right in withdrawing his splendid army after the naval defeat? It seems unlikely that the small American naval force, even with land help, could have trapped his powerful column very soon. Therefore, he ought to have stayed to take the American position at Plattsburg, which would have forced Macdonough to find a new base. Coordinated action by the British army and navy might have beaten the American forces, which were perfectly uncoordinated.

Lord Bathurst sent a messenger to Canada to revoke Prevost's commission as governor of Canada and to recall him to England to face Yeo's charges. Prevost let the secretary know that the use of a junior officer humiliated him. Nevertheless, he arrived in England early in the fall of 1815 to find himself already condemned by a naval hearing. He demanded an army court-martial and was granted one. After some delay, the date for it was set on 15 January 1816. Prevost never attended it, and it was never held, because, worn out by worry and humiliation, he died on 5 January at the age of forty-nine. In the century and one-half since that day he has had more detractors than defenders.

The States and the United States

By early 1814 it had become apparent that Old and New England were not going to become active allies, so, for the first time during the war the former became an immediate threat to the latter. Massachusetts saw this danger and tried to prepare herself to repel it. Throughout the state, including the District of Maine, there were only around 600 regulars. These were scattered in tiny detachments in various forts, and many officials in the state would have preferred to see them replaced by militiamen. Now and again vessels of the United States Navy entered New England harbors, but instead of giving protection, they required it. Generally, however, they received adequate cooperation from the state militias.[1]

The War Department, hoping to improve relations between the state and the United States, placed Henry Dearborn in command of Military District Number One, which included Massachusetts. Early in July, when Dearborn called for 1,200 men to serve for three months, the first federal call upon Massachusetts in two years, the state met his request promptly and fully. But when he called again two months later, he received only a polite refusal. The governor said that the July detachment had caused so many "objections and inconveniences" that it could not be repeated. Nevertheless he called the men out, but designated a Massachusetts major general to command them.[2]

Massachusetts' militia, with 70,000 men, was in far better condition than the troops of any other state. Her Federalist administration kept the system efficient, according to Henry Adams, in order to use it sometime to affect the balance of power within the nation. New England Federalists in general were sure that the United States would soon sink into military exhaustion, and Massachusetts would then be able to enforce a peace settlement satisfactory to her.[3]

After the British burned Washington, Massachusetts lost what scant confidence she had had in the central government and turned very seriously to the business of defending herself. At the same time she attempted to draw closer to the other New England states. Conditions daily grew more favorable for a rebirth of the New England Confederation of the seventeenth century. More and more Massachusetts regarded her militia as a state army only. Orders read, "Continue your exertions to obtain military knowledge and perfect yourselves in discipline, and you will thereby answer the just expectations of the government of Massachusetts."[4]

Militia commanders noted with indignation the presence of federal recruiting officers in their camps, and they ruled that any soldier who left to enlist in the regular service would be treated as a deserter. Federal law and practice contradicted this. Two men who left their militia units to join the United States forces were caught and confined by state authorities. The regular officer who had recruited them threatened to seize and hold two militia men as hostages until they were freed. Massachusetts refused, as formally as if it were negotiating with a foreign power, to give General Dearborn a strength report, but, careful to stay within the law, punctually sent the annual report of her militia to the secretary of war. When Dearborn requested that the state return some cannon loaned her, Massachusetts, as if to show that she need not rely on the federal government for anything, sent back the borrowed pieces at once.[5]

In Maine lead was so scarce that spoons had to be melted down to make bullets. Serviceable weapons were also scarce among field troops. Men with good firearms often hired substitutes who carried "miserable weapons of self-destruction." The hired substitutes were too frequently old men or boys, who gave out after the first long march and had to be released. It was recommended that the officers who accepted them in the first place should be subject to heavy fines. W. H. Sumner, later to become one of the ablest of all state adjutant generals, found the trials of the Massachusetts system (the best) too much for his patience. A system of defense by militia, he said, "is the most troublesome and expensive, as well as the least efficient that could have been devised by a wise people." He, like Washington,

was goaded by immediate aggravations into strong denunciation of
the system, but, also like Washington, later became a champion of
well-disciplined militia.[6]

Thirty-two Massachusetts towns sent remonstrances against the war
to the General Court, and the court heartily responded with its own
complaint of what was happening to America. The state, the complaint ran, had cheerfully surrendered part of her sovereignty to the
central government. Since it did so, forces had developed in the South
and West not contemplated when the Constitution was put into operation. As a result, the once powerful voice of New England had been
reduced to "the feeble expression of colonial complaints, unattended
to and disregarded." Weak and profligate rulers meanwhile had har-
rassed commerce with a view to annihilating it. Finally, the war
faction had put together a veteran army of 60,000 men, which they
might someday use to subvert liberty. The *Boston Centinal* stated in
September that it considered the Union already practically dissolved.[7]

Governor Strong called the General Court into special session on
5 October, and informed it that the United States was failing in
its task of defending the nation. "Let us, relying on the support and
direction of Providence," he said, "unite in such measures for our
safety as the times demand. . . ." He meant that the state would
have to take over where the United States had failed. The General
Court joined him in castigating the central government for carrying
on a ruinous war and for draining New England's population and
treasure for the "protection of their favorite enterprises."[8]

On 20 October it authorized the creation of a state army of 10,000
men, and granted the power to borrow as much as $100,000 to
support it. State officials soon found out however that to afford this
luxury they would have to get back from the United States government certain of the main sources of revenue, such as the duty on
imports. Therefore Governor Strong suspended the operation of the
act until funds became available. The General Court concurred in
this. There was no need for this army, the legislators said for the
record, as long as militiamen continued to answer calls to duty rapidly
and with a will.[9]

Specie flowed toward New England from the rest of the country,
and most of it ended up in the Massachusetts banks. Banks everywhere but in New England suspended specie payment, and their
currency fluctuated wildly in value. The United States government
had rather large deposits of paper money from local banks of the
South and West, but the New England banks would not give it
specie for them. Large quantities of British goods were smuggled

downward from Quebec into New England in return for specie; thus hard money flowed northward to Canada rather than southward into the United States.[10]

Secretary Monroe urged Governor Strong to help raise money in Massachusetts for the federal government. Monroe declared that Congress was placing its finances on a sound basis, but he did not for a minute convince Strong of this. Privately Monroe lamented the deterioration of Massachusetts. During the Revolution that state would have expelled the invader single-handed, but now would not even lend money to enable someone else to do the fighting.[11]

Not all of New England followed Massachusetts' lead. On 19 September 1814 the governor of Vermont issued a proclamation that the war had now changed from a party activity to a matter of common national concern. He urged the people of Vermont to unite behind the war effort. Such insults to our sovereignty as the tribute exacted from the town of Alexandria, Virginia, he said, were of a kind that the whole people must undertake to revenge.[12] Nevertheless, the change of heart came so late in the year that in 1814 Vermont supplied only 777 men to the federal service, compared with 2,232 men the previous year.

Connecticut furnished militia for federal service but endlessly fussed about it. Governor John Cotton Smith made it clear that the United States had no right to make requisitions upon his state for troops, and that he supplied militiamen as a free gift and nothing more. He bickered with the War Department over the organization of the Connecticut militia in federal service. There were four regiments divided into two brigades. Federal officers kept trying to reorganize them into three regiments combined into one brigade in order to conform to regular army tables of organization. But Governor Smith would never permit this because he insisted that the regular tables did not apply. He stood foursquare on the provisions of the Militia Act of 1792.[13]

Because there were two brigades, Governor Smith supplied a major general. Back from the secretary of war came the protest that the Connecticut detachment required no more than one brigadier general. If the Connecticut major general were accepted, he would outrank the federal district commander, and would have to take command of the district. In indignant response to all this, Smith removed the Connecticut militia for a time from the jurisdicion of the federal district commander, and used them to defend the state's own coast. In the latter activity he paid little attention to such plans as the government had for overall coastal defense.[14]

All in all, Connecticut supplied about as many men in 1814 as she had in each of the previous two years. New Hampshire supplied 5,000 more men than she had in the two previous years combined, Massachusetts, 2,400, and Rhode Island, 873.[15]

From the time of the adoption of the Constitution to the outbreak of the War of 1812, Massachusetts had paid $30 million in taxes into the United States treasury. Her share of the direct tax of 1814 was $316,000, which she paid. In addition, federal agents collected $1,600,000 in customs and $198,000 in internal taxes in Massachusetts. The total of $2,114,000 of taxes collected in the state in 1814 was four times more than those paid in Virginia that year. Moreover, six regular regiments were raised in Massachusetts in 1814, compared to three in Virginia. New England raised thirteen regiments, New Jersey, New York, and Pennsylvania raised fifteen, while all the states from Delaware southward raised ten. Only New York supplied more men than Massachusetts to the regular army.[16]

Secretary Monroe, always an optimist, concocted a plan to re-conquer eastern Maine, but when he tried to interest the New England states in it he met no enthusiasm. Therefore, he told Dearborn to appeal directly to corps of citizen soldiers. When this failed to produce an army, sadly on 2 January 1815 he had to notify interested persons that no attack would take place. Massachusetts refused to raise either men or money to redeem eastern Maine. It may be that she intended ultimately to take the province back by state means only, when the federal government had shown its virtual powerlessness, but in fact eastern Maine remained a British province until the Treaty of Ghent restored it to the United States.[17]

Before the capture of Washington, Madison had issued a call for a special session of Congress; but when it convened on 19 September it had difficulty finding a meeting place in the capital. Once settled into makeshift quarters, it spent its time considering the bankruptcy of the government, then turned to the military problem. On 10 October the first English conditions for peace reached Washington. One of the conditions was the cession to Great Britain of that portion of Maine occupied by the British army. Another contemplated the establishment of a permanent Indian country in the Northwest. Since these conditions could not possibly be honored, the end of war seemed nowhere in view.[18]

On 17 October James Monroe submitted the administration's military projection to the Senate Military Committee. It was founded on the proposition that militia was too expensive and too inefficient. He proposed instead an increase of the standing army to a total of

100,000. Forty thousand of these would be a highly mobile force to shuttle up and down the coast. Since it had never been possible to recruit the regular army above 35,000, the 100,000 figure obviously carried with it some sort of conscription. Monroe offered several ways to raise this big army, but championed only one: divide the men from eighteen to forty-five years of age into classes of 100 and require each class to provide four men to serve for the duration. Should any of the four become a casualty or desert, the class would be responsible for replacing him. He insisted that his project was constitutional and less compulsive than the militia system.[19]

The committee did not even offer Monroe's proposal to the Senate. Instead it presented two inconsequential bills, one to make the regular service slightly more attractive and the other to raise 80,000 militiamen. These latter would not be obligated to operate outside their own or adjoining states, but their term would be an unprecedented two years. Supporters of the war opposed a two-year militia, and contended that nine months was the outside limit allowed in common law. One of them called the act "the first step on the odious ground of conscription." Senator David Daggett of Connecticut said that such militia turned citizen soldiers into regulars and stole from the states their only constitutional military protection. Other New England senators joined Daggett to make it clear that militias were necessary state armies which would be undermined if men were drawn away for two years. In spite of them, however, the bill passed the Senate 19 to 12. It now went to the House, where much the same arguments were heard, but in the end it became law. At the same time Congress enacted the measure to improve the conditions of the regular military service. In reality it had sidestepped the critical issues and left the administration to wage an increasingly desperate war with 30,000 regulars and a fluctuating horde of six-month militia. The two-year militia was in fact never raised.[20]

At the seat of government President Madison had a constant battle to keep a competent team of administrators. When Albert Gallatin went to Europe in May 1813, Madison designated William Jones to be acting secretary of the treasury. Thus, from May 1813 to March 1814 Jones held two portfolios. When Gallatin resigned in March, the Senate confirmed him as peace emissary, and the President persuaded George Washington Campbell to become secretary of the treasury. By October of 1814 Campbell was tired of trying to conduct the war without funds, and he resigned. Now Madison, with some difficulty, persuaded Alexander James Dallas to take the post, and Dallas finished out the war in that important position.[21]

No one in the Madison administration worked so hard to build a personal political machine as Gideon Granger, the postmaster general. He went so far as to ignore some of the appointments suggested to him by the President. In time Madison asked him to resign, whereupon he threatened to stir up some old scandals he claimed to know about. It is not known what these were, for in March 1814 he went out without airing them, and Return Jonathan Meigs, erstwhile governor of Ohio, took his place.[22]

Congress did not help the problem of the President in maintaining executive competence when it cut the salaries of clerks. At the time when the duties of clerks multiplied, their salaries shrank. At the same time Congress refused to make the pay of the secretaries of the two military departments equal to that of the secretary of the treasury. This seems a strange decision in time of war.[23]

On 23 November 1814 Vice President Elbridge Gerry died. His death did not much alter the conduct of the war, but it did place Rufus King, a Federalist, next in line to be President if something should happen to Madison. The Senate countered this threat by electing John Gaillard of South Carolina president pro tempore, but for two years thereafter the United States had no vice president. This lack did not create a real void in the active administration, but the resignation of William Jones did. On 1 December he left the Navy Office to devote his attention to personal affairs, for he was verging on bankruptcy. After he left, the chief clerk of the department carried on for a time, then Benjamin W. Crowninshield, like Jones a merchant engaged in shipping, accepted the post.[24]

No weight of vicissitudes stopped the administration's dreams of ultimate victory. In a proclamation on 8 September 1814 the President called upon all Americans to "unite their hearts and hands" to defeat the "barbarous" enemy. He had read Albert Gallatin's enumeration of what the peace delegation needed to strengthen its bargaining power: to defend New Orleans, retake eastern Maine, subjugate the Indians, and gain a patch of territory somewhere from Canada. This was a big order, but the administration gave the impression that it expected to be able to deliver it.[25]

Major General Jacob Brown now appeared in Washington to plan a major offensive in Canada for the campaigning season of 1815. He had Monroe's assurance that there would be an army of 40,000 men "to carry the war into Canada." Fifteen thousand of them would be regulars, the balance citizen soldiers drawn primarily from New York and Vermont, with some help from Pennsylvania, Ohio, and western Virginia.[26]

The authorized strength of the regular army when 1814 began had been 58,250, but only 30,000 were actually enrolled. To try to fill the ranks Congress had in January tripled the bounty for enlistment, and in addition had given each soldier 320 acres of public land. Subsequent legislation raised the authorized size to 62,773, organized into 46 infantry regiments, 4 rifle regiments, the corps of artillery, 1 regiment of light artillery, 1 regiment of dragoons, the engineer corps, and some rangers. But the number actually enlisted stayed around 30,000.[27]

1814–1815

Pensacola and Mobile

It was comforting to officials of the United States government when Governor W. C. C. Claiborne gave assurance that if the area were attacked the Louisiana Creoles would loyally serve the nation. He was not so sure, on the other hand, that the free blacks would. While he was in military command there, General James Wilkinson rarely gave his superiors any such comfort. He designated as especially vulnerable 240 miles of coastline from Bayou Teche on the west to Lake Pontchartrain on the east. Within this sensitive coastal zone he named six likely lines of military approach to the city. Any commander trying to guard this danger zone would need no less than 4 heavy warships, 40 gunboats, 6 steamboats, and some smaller vessels. From the army he would need 10,000 regular soldiers and from Louisiana and Mississippi 3,500 militiamen.[1]

No nation previously holding New Orleans had ever made adequate provisions to defend her, and neither did the United States. Meanwhile the city grew more and more desirable as a military prize. A fortune in cotton, estimated at £3,500,000 sterling lay blockaded in the city. Sir John Fortescue, historian of the British army and no lover of the navy, claimed that the Scottish admirals, Cochrane, Cockburn, and Malcolm, who ran the naval establishment in North America, could not possibly take their eyes off such a treasure. Throughout British history, he argued, the admirals, especially the Scots, had always chosen objectives with a view to booty.*[2]

* The contention that Admiral Cochrane rested his strategy primarily on the prospect of loot is affirmed by Carson I. A. Ritchie, "Louisiana Campaign," pp.

It cannot accurately be determined when British strategists took their first squint at New Orleans. As far back as the fall of 1812 Generals Brock and Prevost had suggested to Admiral Warren that there should be a diversion to the south somewhere to relieve the pressure on Canada. After Warren had surveyed the broad region in which he commanded, he adopted this suggestion, but as his own contribution to it he specified New Orleans and the Gulf coast as the best targets. He requested that 3,100 men be sent to him at Halifax to use to the southward. They might seize New Orleans, then turn it over to a regiment of blacks. Warren favored the military use of Negroes in the American South in order to add manpower to Britain, subtract it from the United States, and affront American race prejudice. Apparently he did not guess that the employment of blacks might make southern Americans fight like tigers, but more probably he didn't care what it stimulated them to do. If Warren had an eye for the wealth of New Orleans, he did not say so, then or later, but he did mention that its capture would cut off the resources of several states, especially Kentucky, Tennessee and Ohio, which were centers of activism against Canada.[3]

During the summer of 1813 John Armstrong ordered the Third Infantry to leave New Orleans and move northward. When Governor Claiborne and Brigadier General Thomas J. Flournoy protested this drain, the secretary assured them that England knew better than to apply her small disposable force at so remote and precarious a place. Nor would the capture of New Orleans help the British protect Canada, which he rightly recognized as the center of their strategy. So the Third Regiment left New Orleans in July. Armstrong, it happens, was right at the time. Napoleon had not yet been halted, except in Russia; the Battle of Leipzig lay three and one-half months in the future. Thus, still entirely preoccupied with Napoleon, the British high command left unnoticed Admiral Warren's suggestion for an attack on the Crescent City.[4]

Late in 1813, however, a new ingredient commenced to percolate into British strategic thinking. The commanders in America began to believe that certain privilegeless groups in the Gulf region might be susceptible to enticements to join England against the United States. At least one Louisianian saw this danger. "If the Creeks should

---

33, 42, 43. Ritchie founded his opinion on Fortescue's statements and more particularly on private accusations made by the Duke of Wellington to the family of Pakenham. There is no proof that Wellington knew what he was talking about, and of course his statements to the bereaved family were more likely than not to indicate a scapegoat.

invade us," he wrote, "we have no force to resist them." Panton, Leslie and Company, an English firm trading in Spanish territory, had seen this possibility for some time, and had communicated it to Governor Charles Cameron of New Providence Island. This started a communication between Cameron and the Creek Indians. Certain of their chiefs wrote him in November 1813 that their people were in fact at war with the "Mericans, fiting in defense of our Rights and in behalf of our old friends the British Government." But they could not continue the fight unless they received powder, lead, arms, and gunflints from England. They indicated that from the mouth of the Apalachicola River the British could maintain contact not only with them, but also with the Choctaws, Chickasaws, and Cherokees. These, the "Red people of the fore nations," with the aid of a small British army, could conquer the western country.[5]

When Admiral Cochrane succeeded Warren in command of the North American station, he received two ideas which fused into a strategy. One, to attack the Gulf coast, came from Warren; and the other, to use Indians, Negroes, and possibly pirates as allies, came in part from Warren and in part from Governor Cameron. To check out the possibilities, Cochrane on 14 March 1814 instructed Captain Hugh Pigot to load his ship *Orpheus* with 2,000 stands of arms and 300,000 ball cartridges and take it to New Providence to consult with Governor Cameron as to the best place to make contact with the Creeks. He was of the opinion that the cheapest and best way "to draw off the attention of the Americans from His Majesty's possessions in Canada" was to supply the Indians in the Gulf region.[6]

Pigot anchored *Orpheus* near the mouth of the Apalachicola River on 10 May. On 20 May he assembled ten chiefs on board and talked with them. He commissioned George Woodbine to be brevet captain of marines and agent to the Creek nation. He gave Woodbine the means to feed many Red Stick Creeks who had migrated south after their defeat by Jackson in March and were starving in the swamps around Pensacola. Woodbine took ashore with him a sergeant and a corporal to instruct the Indians in the use of the bayonet. He estimated that there were 2,800 warriors close by whom it would be possible to make into soldiers in eight to ten weeks. He began to issue arms to the Creeks for them to keep, in order to show contrast with the United States, which sometimes issued arms but took them back after each fight.

Pigot adopted Woodbine's estimates of numbers and his enthusiasm for the Indians. He informed Cochrane with confidence that Britain could count on both Creeks and Choctaws, and that these two nations,

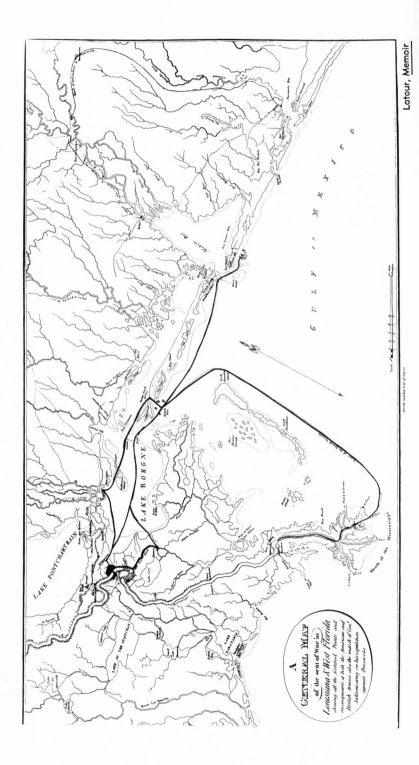

A
GENERAL MAP
of the seat of War in
Louisiana & West Florida
showing all the fortified Points and
encampments of both the American and
British Armies also the march of Gen.l
Jackson's army in his expedition
against Pensacola

GULF OF MEXICO

LAKE PONTCHARTRAIN

LAKE BORGNE

aided by a handful of British troops and a few gunboats, could capture Baton Rouge, then New Orleans. He also mentioned as possible allies the Baratarians, 800 men inured to fighting. Finally, he sent along with his report letters from several Creek chiefs. The chiefs thanked the admiral for the weapons, asserted that they had always been "Englishmen," and agreed with Pigot that the Americans could be driven out of the Gulf region.[7]

Pigot's letter turned Admiral Cochrane toward a line of strategy which was to end six months later in the fateful fight at New Orleans. Cochrane informed the Admiralty that given 3,000 troops he could land at Mobile, rally Indians, disaffected Frenchmen, and Spaniards, and drive the United States out of Louisiana and the Floridas. The best time to do this would be in October and November. Meanwhile he would continue to issue muskets and ammunition and even two cannon to the Creeks.[8]

The more Cochrane thought about the Indians as the key to the penetration of the Gulf coast, the better he liked the idea. These redmen, after all, had been subjected to relentless aggression by Americans ever since the Revolutionary War. They were ripe for England's cause and would be fully loyal if they were restored to the condition they had enjoyed under Britain. When the war was over, the British must give them back their lands. He voiced the hope that Negroes from Georgia and the Carolinas would also join with Britain in the fight. By proclamation he pointed out to the Indians that the United States "forges chains" for them, whereas the British strove to make them free and to restore their land.[9]

The date probably meant nothing to the admiral, but it was 4 July when he penned his instructions to the officer he had designated to take the enlarged Indian-aid party ashore. His choice was Edward Nicolls.* Nicolls was then a brevet major in the Royal Marines with the local rank of lieutenant colonel. If he succeeded in raising a battalion of 500 warriors, he would become a colonel. Cochrane warned Nicolls not to assume too much authority among the Indians. He was to hold their good will, try to prevent them from committing barbarous acts, find out as much as possible about the vulnerability of New Orleans, determine whether or not the Indians would aid in the capture of that city, avoid hostile acts toward England's ally Spain, and actively aid this ally if she entered with England into the war. Woodbine was put under Nicolls' command, and the entire detachment placed upon the supplementary list of the Third Battalion of Royal

* This man's name according to his own signature was Nicolls. It appears constantly in print as Nicholls. I prefer to spell it as the man himself spelled it.

Marines. Finally, *Hermes* and *Caron*, under the command of Captain Henry Percy, were assigned to supply the shore party.[10]

Before Nicolls was ready to land, Admiral Cochrane for an unknown reason recalculated his estimate of the force needed to secure control of the Gulf coast. In mid-July he wrote to Bathurst that he could do the job with only 2,000 British soldiers, 1,000 less than he had requested three weeks earlier. The same number popped into the head of George Woodbine, who was out among the Indians. He said that with 2,000 men his country could take over the entire area from the St. Marys River to the Mississippi.[11]

After the Battle of Leipzig in October 1813 the Ministry in England could soon begin to shift some troops to America. Their basic strategy, however, remained rather hazy until unforeseen events opened up unexpected opportunities. By the beginning of 1814 Bathurst had begun a search among Wellington's lieutenants for the proper general to command south of Canada. He offered the assignment first to Sir John Hope. Hope replied that his wounds made it impossible for him to accept, but added cryptically that there were many reasons why he declined this particular service. Now Sir Thomas Picton and Sir Rowland Hill came under consideration, and Hill was in the end invested with the command. But the exact nature of the campaign he was to conduct never became clear. Indeed, he was factored out when the Ministry finally decided late in July to adopt Admiral Cochrane's plan to attack New Orleans.[12]

The Admiralty stated that December was the best time and Negril Point on the western tip of Jamaica the best staging area for this campaign. During the second week in August, Bathurst told Ross that what had been Hill's expedition was now going to the Gulf of Mexico, but Hill was no longer part of it because the force Cochrane recommended did not need a general of such high rank. Instead Ross himself was to be provided with 5,000 men for it. Bathurst informed him that his authority was limited only by Cochrane's plans. He must carefully study intelligence of the enemy, strive for the goodwill of the Indians, woo Spain, and if possible enlist liberated blacks into the West Indian regiments.[13]

The same day, 10 August 1814, Bathurst also informed Admiral Cochrane, through the Lords Commissioners, that the government had approved his New Orleans plan. The Ministry, he said, had harbored the intention to strike this city for a long time, but had first vacillated, then had abandoned it. Cochrane's offer to do the job with fewer men was what had caused them to revive the intention and put it into effect. The admiral was to expect the force assigned to the campaign to meet him at Negril Bay on or after 20 November. He would also find there 20 shallow-draft vessels and armament for the Indians. The rest was up to him in consultation with Ross. The two of them could even give up the Louisiana project if they preferred some other plan to it.[14]

September 1814 was the happiest month the harried administration of Lord Liverpool had ever known. Napoleon had been banished, and a glittering Congress was in session in Vienna to design the post-war world. General Prevost had 20,000 troops, with which it was assumed he could win the war at the north. An effective diversion was in progress in Chesapeake Bay. To cap everything, news of the success at Washington reached London on the twenty-seventh. Full of elation, Liverpool sent off praises to Ross, doubled his forces from 5,000 to 10,000, and gave him two major generals as subordinates. Ross and Cochrane were allowed virtually a free hand, but the Ministry expected them to win.[15]

There were certain reasons to doubt success, but Cochrane does not seem to have known them, so of course the Ministers did not. Captain Woodbine continued to send optimistic reports about Indian cooperation, which were founded on faulty intelligence.* He did not know that the Creek Confederation was too deeply divided within itself to make a united stand. Nor did he comprehend how badly Andrew Jackson's campaign had wrecked the Red Stick Creeks, or that the hatred between Lower Creeks and Red Sticks was too great to allow them to reunite. He apparently did not know that the Choctaws, Chickasaws, and Cherokees were already actually siding with the United States. Contrary to his assumptions, whatever aid the British received from the Indians would have to come from the small Florida bands, Mikasukis, Alachuas, and the recently migrated Red Sticks, all loosely known as Seminoles.[16]

Captain Henry Percy's squadron, arrived early in August 1814 off Pensacola with Edward Nicolls and his command aboard. Nicolls wanted to make Pensacola his base for inland operations, but Percy would not agree to it unless the Spaniards requested a British landing there. Since the Spaniards had virtually turned the defense of Pensacola over to George Woodbine, it was he who actually invited his country-

---

* On 9 August 1814, the very day when Woodbine was talking about massive Indian aid to the British, Andrew Jackson met with certain Indian leaders at the confluence of the Coosa and Tallapoosa rivers and exacted from them two-thirds of all Creek lands. This forced some Creeks toward England, since the Lower Creeks also lost land, though they had supported the United States against the Red Sticks. Woodbine's expectation of a Creek alliance was therefore at least reasonable.

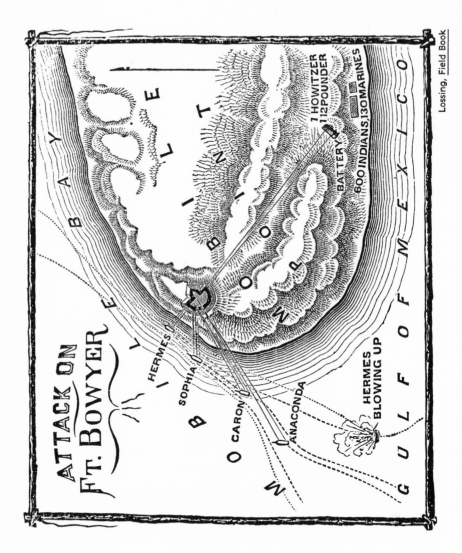

ATTACK ON FT. BOWYER

BAY

POINT

B O O M B

HERMES

SOPHIA

O CARON

ANACONDA

HERMES
BLOWING UP

7 HOWITZER
112 POUNDER

BATTERY

600 INDIANS, 130 MARINES

GULF OF MEXICO

Lossing, Field Book

men to come ashore. Nicolls, 3 other officers, a surgeon, 11 noncommissioned officers, and 97 enlisted men landed and occupied Fort San Miguel. Besides their own arms, they carried 3 field pieces, 1,000 stands of arms, and 300 British uniforms for the Indians. Every member of the detachment had received a month's pay in advance, and Nicolls carried with him $1,000 in specie to meet extraordinary expenses.[17]

Nicolls now proclaimed Britain's power to punish insolent America. Persons who wished to escape chastisement, he said, must display a French, Spanish, or English flag. He especially addressed the Kentuckians, who had borne the brunt of the war in the West for the United States, yet had received nothing for it but casualties. England was fighting for the freedom of the world, so by supporting her they could embrace the cause of liberty. Even if they elected to remain neutral, they could grow rich trading with England for silver and gold. He also especially exhorted Louisianians to liberate from a "faithless, imbecile government your paternal soil," and ended by promising aid to everyone oppressed by the Americans.[18]

Although Admiral Cochrane did not realize it, the foundations upon which he had based his strategy for the Gulf campaign were breaking down. The case of the Indians has just been told. Next was Mobile, a place the British must hold if they were to conquer the Gulf coast. The key to it was Fort Bowyer which commanded the entrance to Mobile Bay. Aware of its importance, Andrew Jackson had taken pains to strengthen Bowyer, but Captain Percy deemed it vulnerable anyway. He put ashore an assault party under Nicolls on 12 September 1814, but because of adverse wind and tide he could not support the detachment from the sea. On 15 September he sailed into the bay with 4 war vessels and opened a bombardment upon the fort. After three hours, Bowyer still showed no sign of surrender, but one of Percy's ships had been sunk. Nicolls, back aboard because he was sick, dragged himself on deck during the gun duel. It was his misfortune to be wounded in the head and leg and blinded in his right eye. Percy withdrew the next day the remaining 3 vessels of his flotilla. Nicolls, ever an optimist, asserted that although the fort still was American, the attack had drawn American forces out of the Creek country. Even so, without Bowyer the British could not take and use essential Mobile.[19]

In spite of his wounds, Nicolls kept on trying to raise an effective body of Indian warriors. His subordinate Woodbine received permission to pay for Indian services on a graduated scale which ran from two dollars a day for a chief to fifty cents for each Negro slave furnished by an Indian. Nicolls expected to be able to penetrate into Georgia, using Seminole and Lower Creek support. When the month passed without an advance in any direction, he explained to Admiral Cochrane that his health was wretched and that the pro-British Indians had to be rescued first from virtual starvation before they could be efficiently used. He even wrote to Andrew Jackson to accuse him of inciting the Indians to barbarous acts and paying a bounty for scalps. Nevertheless, though he did his best to suppress barbarism among his own allies, a party of Red Sticks cooked and ate selected portions of certain Americans. Such cannibalism was by this time very rare among the Creeks.[20]

The pirates of Barataria were led by Jean Laffite and were a disaffected group, about 800 strong, to whom some British officers looked for cooperation. On 29 August 1814, the British brig *Sophia* anchored off Laffite's stronghold, and Captain Nicholas Lockyer urged Laffite to establish a British connection. Laffite stalled his visitors, indeed almost held them prisoners, while he revealed their overture to the authorities of Louisiana. When he offered his services to the United States, he was sharply rebuffed; but he still declined the British alliance. If Lockyer became overbearing and threatened Laffite, the Americans became out and out violent. On 14 August a naval detachment commanded by Commodore Daniel Patterson destroyed their establishment. Thus, in spite of American policy, another possible ally fell away from the British cause, and another prop caved in which had seemed to support Admiral Cochrane's strategy.[21]

Unaware that his Gulf strategy had been accepted in England, Admiral Cochrane wrote in September from Chesapeake Bay of other plans. The climate of the bay area was forcing him to go north, probably to capture Rhode Island. He could take that state and lead the Americans to believe that Lord Hill was on his way to attack New York. Once the fever and hurricane season was past in the South, he could return there to attack those vulnerable coasts. A small force, made up half of blacks, could harry the southern shores until America was obliged to make a peace to Britain's liking.[22]

Meanwhile the first of the reinforcements for Ross were shipped from Plymouth under the command of Major General John Keane. Keane was a tall, youthful, black-whiskered Irishman, with a good record in the Napoleonic wars. He carried dispatches to Ross and orders that if something should have happened to Ross, he was to take command himself. In that case, he must maintain good relations with Admiral Cochrane. He must aid the people of Louisiana, if they so desired, to reattach themselves to Spain, but must "discountenance any proposition of the inhabitants to place themselves under the dominion of Great Britain." The prime objects of the expedition were to close American commerce on the Mississippi and to occupy space which might be useful in bargaining for peace terms. It was up to him and Cochrane to decide how they intended to approach New Orleans and what their objectives were to be once the city was captured.[23]

When Admiral Cochrane received news of the approval of his New Orleans strategy, he turned away from Rhode Island. Even though the hurricane season was in mid-career, he made for the West Indies. No shadow of doubt of success crossed his mind, and he detached Admiral Cockburn with 1,500 men to land on Cumberland Island to create a diversion. After the subjection of the Crescent City, the forces could reunite and conquer Georgia and the Carolinas. He continued to expect aid from thousands of Indians and Negroes. He got off a note to Governor Prevost to notify him of the diversion in his favor and to request that the First Battalion of the Royal Marines be sent him from Canada.[24]

In England Lord Bathurst appointed John Lambert the second major general to work under Ross. Then on 17 October word reached London of the death of Robert Ross. Lambert was senior to Keane and was ordered to supersede him until a general of higher grade should reach America. The search for this senior officer now began. There was already on file a request from the Prince Regent that Sir Edward Pakenham be used in America if there was an appropriate space for him. Pakenham was the Duke of Wellington's brother-in-law and had been battle tested under the duke. Without much hesitation he was chosen, and on 24 October given a copy of Ross' instructions to guide him. Bathurst added nothing to these orders, except the admonition that strict discipline must be maintained, looting suppressed, and booty taken be handled through the Admiralty courts.[25]

Even while Pakenham was still in England, the Ministers were weighing the value of sending the Duke of Wellington himself to America in the dual role of military commander and chief peace negotiator. Wellington was very blunt about the United States: he neither held any grudges against it nor saw military grounds to claim concessions from it unless the New Orleans campaign succeeded. Control of the Great Lakes was the key to success in America, and until that was achieved even he himself probably could make slight headway. "I suspect," he said, the public "will never be quiet till I shall go there." With customary candor he told Bathurst that the government could not spare him out of Europe before 15 April 1815. After that date he said, "It will be for you to consider whether I can be more useful to you there, here, or elsewhere." Later he specified that he would not accept the command in America unless a serious effort had first been made to secure peace without annexing any territory.[26]

Brigadier General Thomas Flournoy had asked the administration very early in the year that he be relieved of the command of the Seventh Military District. The government responded by appointing Andrew Jackson on 28 May. There was no question about Jackson's energy or devotion to the cause, but from the administration's point of view he was a little too much determined to liberate Florida from Spain. Still, since Secretary Monroe knew that the British had turned south, but did not know what their target was, the new general's orders in September remained discretionary. Monroe sent out alerts to the governors of Georgia, Tennessee, and Kentucky to have militia detachments in readiness. The militias of Mississippi and Louisiana were too much occupied with Indians and the fear of black insurrection to be counted on. Monroe's perennially optimistic spirit shone at this time. With reference to England's projected southern campaign he wrote, "In this as in all their other disorganizing and visionary projects, they will be defeated by the virtue and gallantry of our people." Such rhetoric found sympathy in General Jackson, who proclaimed his own version of it. "I well know," he said, "that every man whose soul beats high at the proud title of freeman . . . will rally round the eagle of Columbia. . . ."[27]

Secretary Monroe told Jackson to expect 7,500 militiamen from his own state of Tennessee, 2,500 from Kentucky, and 2,500 from Georgia. Meanwhile Governor Claiborne of Louisiana raised as many men as he could. He placed detachments at vulnerable points of access to give warning of the approach of the enemy, but he concentrated most of the Louisiana force near New Orleans. He and his people had confidence in Andrew Jackson and looked forward to his arrival.[28]

While suspense built up at New Orleans and Washington, Andrew Jackson went about his private business of conquering West Florida. Monroe warned him in a letter dated 28 October to avoid bringing on a contest with Spain. Jackson had already appeared before Pensacola on 7 November with 4,000 men, a mixture of regulars and Tennessee and Mississippi volunteers. (Monroe's letter did not reach him until the war was over.) Within the town Nicolls and Captain James Gordon had been trying to goad the Spanish governor into making some preparations for defense. Since he refused, they began to shift their Indians away from Pensacola, and it was too late when the governor finally made a frantic call on them on 6 November. Jackson ordered a charge into the main street and the town capitulated. The commander of San Miguel held out for a few hours, but when the Americans prepared to storm the works, he too surrendered. The British officers now blew up Fort Barrancas and the fort on Santa Rosa Island, and then decamped.[29]

Monroe, still unaware of what had occurred, wrote, one month to the day after the conquest of Pensacola, that he hoped his earlier letters had prevented acts which would aggravate Spain. Diplomatically, of course, Jackson's capture of Pensacola was dangerous, but from a purely military standpoint it made good sense. Pensacola was the finest harbor along the coast, and whoever controlled it had good lines of access into the interior of the United States. As long as England dominated the place, even if it was nominally Spanish, it was also a nest of anti-American spies.*

The British now concentrated their detachment at Prospect Bluff on the Apalachicola River, a position Nicolls had selected six months before. In spite of its being on Spanish ground, he built an installation there with no cost to the government except tools and labor. The Spaniards protested this violation of their sovereignty, but, since they had no power behind their protests, the Liverpool Ministry let the building continue. Nicolls soon began to incite the Indians to make small forays into the United States. While their attacks accomplished little, they did add to the sum of false intelligence upon which the British high command was working, for the marauders brought back word that thousands of Negroes in Georgia and Louisiana would rally to a British force the moment it invaded.[30]

Meanwhile the main British invasion force was taking shape in the West Indies. The army from Chesapeake Bay under Colonel Arthur Brooke reached Negril Bay on 19 November. On 24 November it was joined by the detachment General Keane had brought from England. There were now 6,000 soldiers on hand, not counting sailors and marines. Keane and Admiral Cochrane left for the Gulf coast on 25 November with four vessels. The next day the balance of the force headed for the United States in a naval convoy commanded by Rear Admiral Pultney Malcolm. As they approached the hostile shore, Cochrane and Keane composed a thumping proclamation "To the Great and Illustrious Chiefs of the Creek and Other Indian Nations."

* Brown, *Amphibious*, p. 26, contends that Monroe only saved face with his restraints upon the capture of Pensacola; he did not intend for the order forbidding Jackson to attack to reach Jackson on time. Monroe remonstrated later so as to implicate Jackson but leave the government uninvolved. SW to Jackson, 7 Dec. 1814, M6R7.

They asked for help from the Indians and explained to them the ethics of taking the British side. "The same principle of justice which led our Father to wage a war of twenty years in favor of the oppressed Nations of Europe, animates him now in support of his Indian children. And by the efforts of his Warriors, he hopes to obtain for them the restoration of those lands of which the People of Bad Spirit have basely robbed them."[31]

When some of the pro-British chiefs came aboard, Edward Codrington, who had received notice of his promotion to be rear admiral on 9 October, thought them poor creatures to have as allies. Cappachamico, Hopsi or Perryman, and the Prophet Francis (Hillis Hadjo) were wearing one layer of clothes over another, and had tied the several trousers around their waists without bothering to get into the legs. Codrington liked their native headdress: the skin and plumage of a handsome bird, with the beak pointing down the forehead and the wings spread out over the ears, but the chiefs discarded these in favor of gold-laced cocked hats. With this millinery, and the sergeant's jackets supplied by the admiral, they looked to him like "dressed up apes."[32]

Not until 21 November did Andrew Jackson pry himself loose from Florida and head for New Orleans. Whatever the administration thought of his lingering, it was probably justified in a military way. He knew that the United States had to hold both Pensacola and Mobile in order to defend New Orleans from attack by way of the Mississippi River north of the city. Meanwhile, he had acquired the best maps available for the New Orleans area, and made plans for his shift there. As soon as General James Winchester arrived on 20 November to take command at Mobile, Jackson set out. He reached New Orleans on 2 December, dirty, unpolished, and emaciated from long illness. But neither dirt nor lack of polish nor sickness nullified his energy. The very day of his arrival he reviewed the volunteer companies of the city, most of them part Negro, and complimented them on their appearance. He quickly saw that these 900 men and about 1,200 more who were around the city were not enough, and he sent out hurry-up calls for others already on their way.[33]

Governor Blount of Tennessee had been able on 20 November to start 2,500 men, by no means well supplied or well armed, down the river from Nashville. At the same time, 3,000 more gathered at Knoxville but never shipped out. Monroe now requisitioned rather meekly on Kentucky. Kentucky raised the quota he set, but relied on the United States to supply and transport it. Her detachment sat and waited on the river bank for quartermaster officers and transports to appear, but when they did not come, one Kentucky officer borrowed enough money on his own credit to hire flatboats. Since the flatboats were old and leaky, they had to be repaired almost every day, and the progress of the Kentucky troops was perforce very slow.[34]

Although it was known in Washington that the need for firearms was very great in New Orleans, the War Department did not issue orders until 2 November to ship 4,000 muskets down the river from Pittsburgh. The barges loaded with these muskets moved languidly with the current just a little ahead of the Tennessee troops.

Jackson, like Winder, occupied himself at first in detailed reconnaissance. He found that the local people knew little about the terrain, and he did not rely on the professional engineers. What he saw was, in Marquis James' expressive terms, a country that was "neither land nor water, but a geological laboratory where land [was] being made." Where the forming soil was too unstable to support trees, marsh reeds reared "their bright green blades six feet high, tough as hemp and sharp as knives."[35]

When Jackson had seen the lay of the land, he gave orders that all bayous which led from the Gulf toward New Orleans be obstructed, and that batteries be erected at certain points. His announcement that the city could be defended if his orders were carried out gave heart to the residents. They had confidence in him. Governor Claiborne let it be known that he would not serve under any other officer, but in spite of his lack of military experience he did want to be appointed second in command. Jackson avoided the political pitfalls of this situation by leaving the post of vice commander unfilled. As time passed, Claiborne began to feel that the general was purposely keeping the governor out of the firing line.[36]

The British advanced party anchored off Ship Island on 8 December 1814. Admiral Cochrane found then that the destination of his expedition was well known. He found too that he did not have the shallow-draft vessels promised him, nor any source from which to acquire them. On 11 and 12 December the main fleet joined him at Ship Island, and on the next day all hands moved to Cat Island, 80 miles from New Orleans.[37]

New Orleans

As far as Captain John Shaw of the United States Navy was concerned, the entire Gulf coast between the Pearl and Pascagoula rivers lay open to the invaders. The land before them was high and dry, open pinewoods laced with good roads, and there were supplies and guides to be obtained. If an invader made an amphibious landing in this strip of shoreline, his natural objectives would be first Natchez, then Baton Rouge, and last New Orleans. This was the route to use if heavy reliance was to be placed on Indian allies. Cochrane and Keane eliminated it in part because it required control of Pensacola and Mobile, which they did not have, and in part because their force was so large that they no longer thought it necessary to rely on Indians or any other minority group. They believed themselves able to strike directly at New Orleans.[1]

Their problem then became that of choosing among several possible lines of access to the city. Farthest west was the Bayou Teche. Once up it a short distance, they could follow an open land route eastward for 90 miles, then cross the Mississippi. Since the crossing would have to be made in the presence of the enemy, and the march made through his territory, they turned away from this route. They also rejected the next most westerly, the Bayou LaFourche.[2]

The most obvious path seemed to be one or the other of the mouths of the Mississippi River; but closer inspection revealed a number of problems. First, warships could not get over the bar, where there was no more than 15 feet of water. Second, if the wind was light, such ships as could cross the bar might have to wait days to do it. Once inside, the wind had to be just right to give a ship headway against the current, which ran between 2 and 5 miles an hour. With the best wind, the trip of 100 miles would take 6 days. At the halfway mark was Fort St. Philip, which, it was proved later, could stop hostile ships. These problems and others caused the planners to rule out the river approach.

Between Bayou LaFourche and the mouths of the Mississippi was a route from Lake Barataria. It wound through lakes and bayous, having a depth of at least 7 feet everywhere, then opened into a canal. After 6 miles the canal ended a few hundred yards short of the bank of the Mississippi, and a mile upstream from the city. The whole passage was about 50 miles long, and certain qualified persons considered it the best way of all. Had the British secured Laffite's cooperation, they almost certainly would have taken it. Governor Claiborne saw the eligibility of this route and stationed a volunteer company at the old pirate base. After some consideration, the British decided against this line of approach.

Certain advisers considered Lake Pontchartrain the only route, and Cochrane intended to go that way. The problem was the two shallow inlets, called Rigolets and Chef Menteur, having no more than 8 feet of water, through which it was necessary to go to get into the lake with boats. A fort, Petites Coquilles, and some batteries guarded the way to both of these. Even so, this way was so attractive that the British left their options to it open to the very last. Finally they may have given it up because they lacked knowledge of the true strength of Petites Coquilles.

Lake Borgne appeared eligible because there were several routes from it toward the city. The strategists soon ruled out the one which ran through waterways to the English Turn, 14 miles below New Orleans, because the waterways were not navigable for anything but small boats, and once at the turn the invader would confront 2,000 American citizen soldiers stationed there with some cannon. Even so, by mid-December Cochrane and Keane had apparently decided that their approach would be either through Lake Borgne or Lake Pontchartrain, and they determined to establish an intermediate base closer to them than Cat Island.

They chose Isle aux Pois (Peas Island) in the mouth of the Pearl River because ships could ride at anchor there and troops could camp ashore. Before they could occupy it, however, they had to reckon with a small flotilla of 5 nameless Jeffersonian gunboats, Numbers 5, 23, 156, 162, and 163, under the command of pugnacious Lieutenant Thomas Ap Catesby Jones.

Jones first discovered the British fleet at dawn on 10 December anchored between Cat and Ship islands. During the next two days he reconnoitered them, and on 13 December sailed for Bay St. Louis. When he learned that the foe was moving in that direction too, he made haste toward Rigolets to plug up the narrows, but was foiled by contrary winds. In the end he had to anchor his 5 gunboats by the stern, facing northward in the mile-wide strip of shallow water between Malheureux Island and Point Claire on the mainland. He put springs on his cables in order to be able to wind his larboard broadsides into action, and with 23 guns and 185 men awaited the moves of the enemy. They came at 10:30 A.M. on 14 December 1814. Three columns of ship's boats, 42 to 45 in all, armed with 43 guns and loaded with 1,200 men, swept toward him under the command of Captain Lockyer. The American guns punished them severely while they rowed bows-on into his broadsides, but they closed in anyway, boarded, and by noon had captured all of his ships. Both Jones and Lockyer had been severely wounded early in the encounter, and Jones was not able to make his official report for three months.[3]

Losses were 17 British and 6 Americans killed, 77 British and 35 Americans wounded. The fight was a tactical disaster, but it had delayed the British about 6 days and earned Jackson more time to improve the defenses of New Orleans. On the other hand, since Jones never had any chance against such odds, he perhaps ought to have blown up his ships. As it was, they fell in usable condition into British hands. Some good came from the lies told by the captured crews, which convinced the invaders that a very large force awaited them at New Orleans. Some harm, however, stemmed from the limited naval help Andrew Jackson could count on after this loss. He had left only *Carolina*, *Louisiana*, and one gunboat, and he could not strike the British amphibious operation afloat, when it was most vulnerable. He could only surrender the initiative and wait for his opponent to make the moves.

The British began to disembark on Isle aux Pois on 16 December, and by 19 December had settled into primitive quarters. Even Admiral Cochrane had for shelter no more than a shed thatched with reeds, through which the sharp wind blew unhampered. Ice stood an inch thick on the water tubs, and Admiral Codrington marveled how his commander endured the continuous cold and the absence of comforts. But stand it Cochrane did. He and Keane sent out Lieutenant John Peddie of the army and Captain P. Spencer of the navy to reconnoiter a likely route out of Lake Borgne called Bayou Bienvenu. This bayou, 100 yards wide and navigable for good-sized boats 12 miles from its mouth, was the main waterway draining the area south of Lake Pontchartrain. Several other streams meandered southward and westward from Bayou Bienvenu, and were intersected by canals which in turn led almost to the Mississippi River itself. Peddie and Spencer found the mouth of the bayou closer to the anchorage of the battle fleet than any other, and the only one not blocked. They made their way into it, thence into Bayou Mazant, thence into one of the canals, and on 21 December, disguised in blue smocks, found themselves standing on the river road, eight miles from New Orleans.[4]

Upon their return they gave this route their enthusiastic endorsement, and Cochrane, Malcolm, and Keane, or an unknown combination of them, decided to use it. Since the beachhead was 57 miles from the fleet and 24 from Isle aux Pois, the sailors were obliged to undergo terrible physical exertion. All the ships' boats could not carry more than 2,200 men in one trip, which meant that the sailors had to row day and night to transport soldiers and supplies. The soldiers, too, had to sit long hours in cramped positions in the cold.

Andrew Jackson was reconnoitering the Plain of Gentilly, where he expected an attack, when word reached him on 15 December of the defeat of Jones' gunboat flotilla. He returned to town at a gallop, and issued crisis orders to his scattered and approaching forces. General John Coffee's orders read, "You must not sleep until you reach me or arrive within striking distance." The next day he placed New Orleans under martial law.[5]

General Coffee received his order on 17 December, and the following morning he began the march with 1,250 men, all who were fit out of 2,000. Before the end of the first day's march he had to slough off another 400 men who could not keep up, but the remaining 850 covered 135 miles in three days to reach the city. They did not impress the city folk very much, dirty as they were, unshaven, their hunting shirts and pants of a home-dyed dingy color, their skin caps with the tails on, and belts of untanned deer skin. But each man carried a tomahawk, a hunting knife, and a long rifle. A squadron of Mississippi dragoons came in with them.[6]

The Tennessee brigade commanded by Major General William Carroll arrived on 21 December. They may have looked more respectable than Coffee's volunteers, but only one in ten of them had started from home with a firearm. By good luck, however, they had caught up with the loitering flatboats carrying muskets from Pittsburgh, and had received arms and begun to drill aboard their boats.[7]

At 10:00 A.M., 22 December, Lieutenant Colonel William Thornton, a seasoned officer in the British service, led the advanced column from Isle aux Pois to the mainland. This column of about 1,850 men, organized as a light brigade, consisted of the Fourth, Eighty-fifth, and Ninety-fifth Foot Regiments, with some rocketeers and two 3-pounder cannon. By sunset it was northeast of the entrance to Bienvenu, waiting for darkness to conceal its landing. Finally at midnight its point went ashore, guided by fishermen who lived in a village of 200 to 300 persons, a mile and one-half from the mouth. Because of their warning, Thornton was able to surprise and capture the tiny detachment of Americans posted in the village.[8]

It was broad daylight when the British point reached the head of Bayou Mazant. General Keane had accompanied the advance, and now he decided to get to the river road by way of the Villeré Canal. Its length was 8 miles, the first quarter of which required a bridge of boats in some places. By ten o'clock the entire advanced party had landed and was toiling toward the river road through the swampy terrain. Thirty American militiamen were loitering around the Villeré house when a detachment of British soldiers surprised and captured them. Major Gabriel Villeré, their commander, jumped out of a window, and made his way through the swamp to carry the alarm to General Jackson.

After leaving the canal, Thornton advanced about half a mile toward New Orleans and halted. He had only 1,600 men. Certain officers recommended to General Keane that the column stay in the tall reeds until ready to advance. Thornton, in contrast, wanted to push on without delay as far as possible. Informants told him that the city had only 5,000 defenders, and that a swift thrust would capture it. General Keane, however, believed Joseph Ducros, a prisoner, who inflated the number to 10,000. He ordered Thornton to put his brigade into bivouac and wait for reinforcements. The men began happily to hunt up firewood, forage for edibles, and otherwise to prepare for a quiet, comfortable night.

A rumor of the British presence reached Jackson at noon, and Villeré soon confirmed it. The desperate situation was exactly the sort which triggered Jackson into his finest leadership. By the eternal, he said, the invaders must be fought this very evening. He ordered the town ransacked for firearms, and every able-bodied man, enrolled in some military unit, called out. Major Jean Baptiste Plauché's uniformed battalion of French and Spanish Creoles double-timed all the way from Bayou St. Johns, others made extra exertions, and by sunset Jackson had accumulated a force of about 2,100 men. These advanced to the LaRonde plantation, undetected by the British, and took a position concealed by an avenue of trees. Separating them from the foe was a cultivated area about 1,200 yards wide, bounded on the north by a swamp and on the south by the Mississippi, here 1,000 yards across. John Coffee, commanding 730 volunteers of various sorts, was on the left of the line near the swamp. Next to him was the Seventh United States Infantry, 465 men, then the Forty-fourth Infantry, then Plauché's battalion, and finally a battalion of volunteer Negro refugees from Santo Domingo, commanded by Major Louis Daquin. Beyond them were 18 Choctaws.[9]

The American schooner *Carolina*, carrying 14 guns and 95 men, slipped unnoticed in the gloaming into position to enfilade the British camp, now brightly illuminated by campfires. Jackson had agreed with Commodore Daniel Patterson that her first fire would commence the battle. At 7:30 P.M. of a short December day her guns spoke. They threw the British camp into confusion. Half an hour later Jackson moved forward to the attack. In the total darkness friends were indistinguishable from foes. Men blundered into enemy formations and were captured; compatriots fired at each other. *Carolina*'s fire became less deadly in the black night, and the British were able to form themselves into a line of sorts. Still, confusion reigned. The firing could be heard at the English Turn, and the Louisiana militiamen there demanded that Brigadier General David B. Morgan lead them toward it. As a result, 350 of them reached the British rear during the hottest part of the fight. They stayed where they were until morning because they knew not whether friend or foe was before them. Then, since the action seemed to have ended and they could not open communication with Jackson, they marched back the way they had come. In contrast, the British Ninety-third Foot Regiment arrived during the battle and helped throw back a determined American assault.

One participant said the battle was over by nine-thirty; another contended it continued until three in the morning. Whatever its duration, the casualties were severe: 46 British and 24 Americans killed, 167 British and 115 Americans wounded, 64 British and 74 Americans missing. This totaled 277 casualties out of 1,600 British engaged, and 213 out of 2,100 Americans. In spite of losses, Colonel Thornton wanted to move on toward the city the next day, but Keane decided to wait for the rest of his army. His force rose to 4,700 on 24 December, and he caused them all to stand in formation throughout the daylight hours without fires to be ready should Jackson strike. He apparently did not know that Jackson had no more than 1,950 men in his line and that Thornton himself was missing the best opportunity he would ever have to use superior numbers. Gleig had no duties to keep him in place. He wandered over the battlefield and noted that the dead and wounded appeared more grisly than usual, due to the high incidence of cut and thrust wounds.

Jackson drew his thin force back 2 miles, sent word into the city that anyone found on the streets without a pass would be arrested, and consulted his engineers. The engineers began to erect on the Macarté plantation an earthwork 30 yards behind the Rodriguez Canal, which was 4 feet deep and 20 feet wide. Because of Keane's decision to halt, Jackson had time to make his works strong. Slaves, citizen soldiers, and regulars labored side by side with pick and shovel. Meanwhile, the British could get no rest because of American snipers. Guards at outposts were safe in European warfare, but knowing no such convention, American sharpshooters picked off every one they could see.[10]

In New Orleans officials lifted the proscription upon Jean Laffite

and released Dominique You from prison. Jackson refused all appeals
to take the Baratarians into military service, but when Laffite himself
came, asked to help, and gave an inventory of his resources, the general changed his mind. He was influenced primarily by the precious
supply of artillery ammunition the Baratarians could produce, for his
own ammunition was critically low.[11]

Jackson had not heard from his government in two months, but he
was not one to brood over what he could not control. Thus, when the
preparations for his defensive line were in train—he had scarcely slept
during the three days since news of the British presence—he lay down
on the night of 26 December for an extended rest.[12]

The Americans had heard loud cheering from the British camp on
Christmas Day. Those cheers celebrated the arrival of reinforcements
and of Lieutenant General Sir Edward Pakenham, accompanied by
Major General Sir Samuel Gibbs. Pakenham, Gibbs, Cochrane, Malcolm, and Keane conferred for the first time in the Villeré parlor.
Subordinates outside the parlor strained their ears to hear what went
on. Pakenham, the listeners reported, was angry when he saw the precarious position in which his army was placed. They also said that
Admiral Cochrane scornfully volunteered to lead his sailors and marines against New Orleans if Pakenham would not commit his army
to the business as it stood. The soldiers, he is supposed to have said,
"could then bring up the baggage." This conversation seems more
imaginary than real, for there is no reason to believe that Admiral
Cochrane did not fully respect the conventions which governed joint
action between army and navy. These strictly forbade the naval commander involved in an amphibious operation to interfere with the arrangements of the commander of the ground forces, once the landing
had taken place.[13]

In theory, at least, Pakenham could have successfully backed out of
the position if it had seemed hopeless to him. If he did so, it would be
necessary to advance along another route, but no route was known to
be any easier. As one of the British officers said, you could approach
the city only if "assisted by the aerial flight of the bird of prey or
astride the alligator's scaly back." Whatever his reasons, Pakenham
elected to remain where Cochrane and Keane had placed his army.[14]

His artillery was under the capable command of Lieutenant Colonel
Sir Alexander Dickson, a Wellington veteran. Dickson now concentrated on getting rid of *Carolina*. By 26 December a furnace for hot
shot was built, and gunfire could be opened. The schooner had been
crippled in the night battle of 23 December and had been immobilized
by contrary winds since that night. The hot shot from Dickson's can-

non fell heavily on the ship, and blew it up at 9:00 A.M. on 27 December. This action cost one-third of the British supply of ammunition, but it was well worth the price because *Carolina* carried four times the artillery force the British had to oppose to it. *Louisiana*, which had been harassing the British flank with her 22 guns, also became a target, but her crew of 170 men succeeded in warping her out of range.[15]

About this time Jackson attempted to flood the British position by cutting the levee on the Jumonville plantation, but the water level was so low that this probably hindered rather than helped his defense. By his orders the buildings on the Chalmette plantation were knocked down to open up the area in front of his earthworks. Since he continued to expect a British advance on the Plain of Gentilly, he kept the First Regiment of Louisiana militia there and a detachment of it at the Piernas Canal, a possible route to his rear. On 27 December, however, he drew in this regiment and added it to his force on the river bank. He was now convinced that Pakenham meant to make his main thrust that way.

He was right. Pakenham organized his army into two wings, one under Keane and the other under Gibbs, and on 28 December he moved it, 8,000 strong, 2 miles forward. There to his surprise it ran into a line of formidable works. American volunteer dragoons had scoured the area between the armies and had prevented British reconnaissance. The American engineer, Major A. Lacarrière Latour, considered this particular British movement a mere show of force, staged in the vain hope that the green Americans would break at the sight of heavy columns of Napoleon's conquerors maneuvering flawlessly.[16]

Louisiana enjoyed a gunner's field day. During seven hours she fired 800 rounds at those magnificent columns. Some 4,000 infantrymen also banged away from behind the earthworks. All American units were in the line who had been there on 23 December, and in addition Major Pierre LaCoste's battalion of free men of color, the Second Louisiana militia, and several batteries of artillery. In a short time the artillery had dismantled the light field pieces which the foe had brought forward with great labor. The heavy fire, too, had forced the British footsoldiers to lie on the ground. It took much prodding to get them up, withdraw them to LaRonde's plantation, and put them into bivouac.[17]

During the excitement someone reported to Andrew Jackson that the Louisiana legislature was about to surrender to the invaders. With his attention on the army before him, Jackson rejoined that if this should prove true, the assembly ought to be shut down. To his astonishment, men-at-arms closed it, and he found himself confronted by angry legislators who suspected him of aspiring to become a military dictator. In three days the legislature was back in session, but Jackson's image was tarnished, especially for the Louisiana Creoles.[18]

At the recommendation of some residents, Jackson extended his line one-quarter of a mile into the swamp, making the line a mile long, and bent it toward his rear to prevent envelopment. To give employment to excess citizen soldiers and to hedge against disaster, he ordered the construction of two more defensive lines closer to New Orleans. Most important of all, he added 8 batteries of cannon to the main line. Battery number 1 was 70 feet from the river bank, had 3 cannon, and was commanded by Captain Enoch Humphreys, United States Artillery. Battery number 2 was 90 yards to the left of number 1 and consisted of 1 24-pounder handled by crewmen from *Carolina*. Battery number 3 was 50 yards beyond number 2, contained 2 24-pounders, and was directed by the Baratarian leaders Dominique You and Renato Beluche. Battery number 4 was 20 yards beyond number 3 and consisted of 1 32-pounder also served by crewmen from *Carolina*. Battery number 5 had 2 light guns manned by regular army artillerymen and was 190 yards from number 4. Battery number 6 was a single 12-pounder directed by Garrigues Flaujeac, a member of the Louisiana legislature, and was 36 yards from number 5. There was another interval of 190 yards to an 18-pounder and a 6-pounder operated by regular artillerymen and denominated battery number 7. Finally, at the end of the line there was 1 small carronade manned by Tennesseans. In addition, Commodore Patterson had emplaced 2 12-pounders on the right bank to fire across the Mississippi.[19]

Otherwise the right bank was ignored until very late. Then, apparently realizing the danger, Jackson summoned David Morgan's detachment from the English Turn and sent it across the river. At Jackson's order, Major Latour started building a line of earthworks. But after some indecision Morgan gave up Latour's line and chose another, 300 yards longer, about a mile downstream from Jackson's position on the left bank. Morgan never completed more than 200 yards of earthworks so that his right flank, besides dangling, had no protection except a shallow ditch in front of it. Commodore Patterson helped Morgan mount 3 cannon, and since Morgan had no more than 350 militiamen, Patterson also joined him in frequent requests for reinforcements. Jackson ordered Latour to construct a backup defense line along the Boisgervais Canal. This was done efficiently.[20]

On 4 January 1815 a brigade from Kentucky, 2,250 men commanded by General John Thomas, arrived in New Orleans. They were, Jackson said, "The worst provided body of men, perhaps, that ever went 1,500 miles from home to help a sister state." The only camp equipment they had was one kettle per 80 men, few had arms, and many wore clothes so ragged they had to hold them together by hand! Unlike the Tennesseans they had not been paid when they left home because no federal officer had been on hand. Lacking tents and blankets, they slept out in the weather. The legislature of Louisiana voted $6,000 to relieve their distress, and private sources added $12,000. Louisiana women took some of the blankets bought by these funds and made clothes for them. But New Orleans could find firearms for only 500 of them. Jackson ordered all the armed members to join Morgan on the right bank of the river on 7 January, but only 250 of them actually got there.

Meanwhile, the area of one and one-half miles between the hostile lines on the left bank was the scene of constant activity. On 29 December the Mississippi Dragoons performed evolutions for an hour or more within 200 yards of the enemy, with no more loss than three men and two horses wounded slightly. The American army gave them three cheers, and the general complimented them. Parties of marksmen left the breastworks and advanced close enough to British outposts to cause great annoyance and no small loss of life. In the fringes of the swamp Tennessee riflemen stalked the enemy like wild beasts. One sharpshooter, lying concealed, killed three guards in succession and took their gear before the sergeant of the guard abandoned the outpost.[21]

Admiral Cochrane now recommended that heavy guns be brought up from the battle fleet to knock down the American earthworks. When Pakenham agreed, the admiral once more set his sailors at killing labor. During the next three days they rowed 24 18- and 24-pounders from the ships, then dragged them through the canal. These guns were established in batteries on the night of 31 December. One battery was laid to fire on *Louisiana* and at American artillery on the right bank, but the other three bore upon the earthworks. The platforms were so light that the guns, it turned out, recoiled off them with every shot. The mounds built up before them were too low also. On the other hand, the emplaced guns could throw 35 pounds more metal than the American cannon (260 to 225); but this put a heavy strain on the British supply of ammunition. Even though that supply was insufficient, Pakenham ordered the attack to proceed.[22]

He formed two columns of infantry to exploit the breaches which the artillery was expected to open. They were to attack at dawn on New Year's Day, 1815, in dense formations with no flints in their muskets. That dawn was dimmed by fog. At first the British could not see that the American army was in parade formation some distance behind the earthworks, preparing for a grand review. About eight o'clock the fog lifted suddenly, and the gunners had a view of their unexpected target. Had they opened fire with scatter-shot rather than demolition rounds, they would have wreaked fearful havoc. At it was, with their opening salvo they drove Jackson and his staff out of the Macarté mansion. Not much injured, the American forces hurried to their own earthworks, and the artillerymen began counterbattery fire. Within 40 minutes American cannon fire had wrecked 5 English pieces, and disabled 8 more. By afternoon the British artillery was all but silenced, and Pakenham had to issue the humiliating order to withdraw without guns. The infantry could do little, for it was earthbound. During the night, once more with heavy labor, the British brought off most of their cannon. They had lost 26 killed to 11 Americans, and 41 wounded to 23 Americans. British morale had been injured; indeed, Admiral Codrington referred to the action as a discredit to the Royal Artillery. Of course the failure did not rest with the artillery alone.

General Pakenham now insisted that nothing more be done until General Lambert arrived with the Seventh Fusiliers and the Forty-third Foot, totaling 1,600 men, from Wellington's army. They arrived at the anchorage on New Year's Day and were hustled forward, but each man was required to weight himself down with a cannon ball in his knapsack to make up for the recent serious depletion. At this stage Pakenham apparently saw no course open to him except to hurl his enlarged army against the American left-bank position, and to try a flanking movement on the right bank. Admiral Cochrane gave assurance that his sailors could open up the Villeré Canal to drag boats from Bayou Mazant to the river, and set his men to one more herculean task. This required building a dam to raise the water level in the canal. Pakenham doubted if a strong enough dam could be built, but he agreed to the attempt.[23]

Cochrane also sent 6 vessels to the mouth of the Mississippi River to try to force their way in, sail upstream, and attack Fort St. Philip. Aware of this threat, Andrew Jackson approached Henry Shreve, an enterprising civilian steamboat captain, with a request that he run by the British batteries below New Orleans and carry essential supplies to the fort. Shreve agreed and succeeded. Pakenham, anticipating a delay of at least two weeks in the subjugation of St. Philip, decided to proceed with the assault on Chalmette Plain, and set 8 January as the date.

During the night of 7 and 8 January the sailors had to try to drag 50 boats through the Villeré Canal. The dam Admiral Cochrane had built to raise the water level broke, leaving only 18 inches in the ditch. As a result only a few of the boats could be brought to the river. Twelve hundred men were assigned to cross under the command of

Lieutenant Colonel William Thornton, but only 350 could go at a time. Since the entire battle was to begin with the action on the right bank, all of the timing was dislocated by the shortage of boats.[24]

Under the battle plan for the left bank, Major General Gibbs was to command the column assigned to make the main thrust about 200 yards from the swamp. His column contained the Fourth, Twenty-first, and Forty-fourth Foot regiments, and the First West Indian Regiment, about 2,100 men. The Forty-fourth was to lead, and its van was to carry fascines and throw them in the ditch, which was 4 feet deep. The next wave was to plant ladders against the earthwork and lead the climb into the enemy position. No one was to shoot until he had reached the ditch. Lieutenant Colonel Thomas Mullins, commander of the Forty-fourth, could not conceal his belief that his regiment was being sacrificed to earn glory for others. He did not oversee the gathering of fascines and ladders, and grew gloomier about the outcome of the assault. The regiment picked up his dark mood.

Major General Keane commanded a second column, 1,200 strong, made up of the Ninety-third Highland and the Ninety-fifth Rifle regiments. If Thornton captured the cannon on the right bank, Keane was to assault the river side of the American line, but if Gibbs should make a breakthrough, Keane was to pour his men into it. A small third column, made up of one company from each of the Seventh, Forty-third, Ninety-third, and First West Indian regiments was placed under Lieutenant Colonel Robert Rennie for the purpose of advancing along the road close to the river bank. Finally, Pakenham left General Lambert in command of a reserve, which had in it 1,400 men from the Seventh and Forty-third Foot regiments.

According to American legend, vehemently denied by British participants, the British password on this fateful night was "beauty and booty." General Pakenham rose at 5:00 A.M. and waited impatiently for the shots from the right bank which were to signal the opening of the battle. When daylight came, shrouded by heavy fog, with no sign from the other shore, he decided to put the main advance on the left bank in motion anyhow. A rocket was fired, skirmishers moved out, and the three columns began their movement. Gibbs' column came to a halt because no one had brought forward the fascines and ladders. Now quite suddenly the fog lifted, and the Americans began to fire. Commodore Patterson's artillery from the right bank struck Keane in the flank. Battery number 1 shotgunned Lieutenant Colonel Rennie's formation on the road. Batteries 2, 3, and 4 blasted away at the British artillery, which had been established during the night in the old New Year's Day emplacements. The other batteries took the bright-colored columns, 60 men wide, as targets. Behind number 7, the point at which Gibb's column was more or less aimed, two ranks of General Carroll's Tennesseans aimed and fired carefully. Back of them stood a rank or two of Kentuckians, who pushed forward to fire when the Tennessee boys were loading.[25]

As soon as General Keane realized that the American cannon on the right bank had not been silenced according to schedule, he obliqued his column toward Gibbs'. This left Rennie in charge on the river side of the field, and his detachment forced its way into a parapet which stood on the river bank detached from the main earthwork. But once in this parapet, there was no place for his men to hide from the concentrated American fire. Rennie and many of his men fell. Keane too encountered a sheet of bullets which within twenty-five minutes broke up his column and forced his men to hug the ground.

Gibbs' column, after waiting for fascines and ladders, had resumed its forward motion, but contrary to orders had halted once more to fire. The Seventh and Forty-third, seasoned veterans that they were, had they been in the front instead of the reserve, would probably not have made this mistake. Gibbs' men when motionless became prime targets, and once more had to hug the dirt; all but 2 companies of the point, which reached the ditch, made steps up the mound with their bayonets and attained the parapet. The rest of the column could not come to their support, and they were all killed or captured.

Now Sir Samuel Gibbs rode forward to get his men off the ground and into motion. He authorized them for the first time to lay aside their 30-pound packs. Some rose and tried to follow the general, but could not do it. They were facing men who were now loading and firing individually as fast as they could. There was much talking and joking among these executioners, but not on the field in front of them. Gibbs fell mortally wounded; Keane dropped too and was carried unconscious to the rear. General Lambert ordered the reserve forward, but in no time it too was pinned down. Sir Edward Pakenham, once reproved by Wellington for needlessly exposing himself, galloped to where the men were cowering against the earth. As he shouted at them, his horse fell dead, and threw him so violently as to wrench his shoulder. Though seriously crippled, he commandeered another mount from a junior officer, and resumed his effort to rally the army. He was hit again and killed, 300 yards from the American works. This shifted the command to General Lambert, who had never been briefed to take it. Appalled by the scene, Lambert halted the attack on the left bank, and sent Lieutenant Colonel Dickson to make an estimate of the situation on the right bank.

The battle on that bank had not developed according to plan. By 3:00 A.M. Lieutenant Colonel Thornton had known that he would not have the boats to ferry all of his men across the river. Accordingly, he had returned two-thirds of them to Gibbs and Keane, and prepared to do what he could with 450 men. His landing took place a mile downstream from the American earthworks, much later than planned. Thus Thornton was not yet in contact with the enemy when firing began on the other side of the river, but he hastened forward to join in the battle he was supposed to have started. His men first encountered the 250 exhausted Kentuckians, who had arrived in the area about four that morning and had marched without rest ever since. They pushed them back easily to the extreme right of General Morgan's line, where, protected only by a ditch, they manned 300 yards. Beyond them was a gap of 200 yards, then a forlorn hope of 16 men with no protection at all for their right flank. For a short time the Kentuckians held in their new position, then they decamped and ran full speed for the rear. Commodore Patterson had opened with one battery (the only one not laid to fire across the river) against the attackers, but soon he could no longer enfilade the British line without killing his own countrymen. He spiked his cannon, boarded *Louisiana,* and floated safely into the river. About this time the entire American force fell back in confusion. It did not take on any cohesion again until it reached the Line Boisgervais. At that point General Jean Humbert, a refugee from the French revolutionary armies, arrived and informed Brigadier General Morgan that Jackson had sent him to take command. Morgan would not yield to him without a written order, so Humbert returned to the left bank via the city. Governor Claiborne too turned up on the Boisgervais, hoping to get into the active fighting somewhere, but Morgan also refused to surrender the command to him. Claiborne left, more than ever convinced that General Jackson was purposely denying him the chance to earn military glory.[26]

Colonel Thornton, lacking the forces to take the Boisgervais, halted to await reinforcements and orders. This was the posture in which Lieutenant Colonel Dickson found him. Dickson was a seasoned and talented artilleryman, but also primarily defense-minded. He saw slight opportunity on the right bank, and recommended to General Lambert that Thornton's force be withdrawn. Admiral Codrington and Colonel John Fox Burgoyne opposed this policy, arguing that with reinforcements Thornton could break through the Boisgervais line and continue straight onward to the bank of the river opposite New Orleans. From that point it would be a simple matter to fire rockets into the highly inflammable city. But Lambert adopted Dickson's advice and sent

Thornton orders to return to the left bank. At the same time he requested General Jackson to agree to an armistice to run until the following day. Jackson was willing on condition that neither side reinforce the right bank. Inasmuch as Lambert had already ordered withdrawal there, he readily concurred.

General Lambert's decision to withdraw from the right bank extricated the American army from a very serious threat. Someone was obviously to blame for the existence of such a serious menace to the American cause. The most convenient scapegoat was the Kentucky militia, and General Jackson charged them with the whole blame. His thesis was that they had cravenly abandoned their line. He did not choose to recognize that they were ill-disciplined, ill-provided, had been up all night, and had marched five miles through the mud just before the British struck them. Commodore Patterson and the Kentucky officers themselves also blamed the enlisted militiamen. No one at the time charged General Jackson with negligence, but it is now plain that he had made insufficient provision to defend a flank which was obviously vulnerable.

There have been few battles in which the casualties were as one-sided as on 8 January 1815. There were 192 British and 13 American men killed; 1,265 British and 13 Americans wounded; 484 British and 19 Americans missing. This totals 1,941 to 45, a ratio of almost 29 to 1. Counting roughly 5,800 British and 4,300 Americans in the battle, the loss ratio was 34 per cent to 1.6 per cent of the forces engaged. From the night battle of 23 December to the conclusion of the battle of 8 January, the totals read: 378 British, 57 Americans killed; 1,518 British, 186 Americans wounded; 548 British, 93 Americans missing. Thus there were 2,444 British casualties against 336 American, a ratio of about 7 to 1.

Elements of the British army blamed Colonel Mullins and the Forty-fourth Foot for the disaster because of their failure to bring up the fascines and ladders. Mullins was later court-martialed and cashiered. He was of course in command only because Colonel Arthur Brooke, though present, did not take part in the fight. Brooke answered persons who accused him of malingering with the statement that he had already transferred the command to Mullins and was waiting to go on leave. He had requested leave in part because he felt disgraced. He had taken over command of an army when Ross had been killed at Baltimore, but he later had been reduced once more to regimental command with no mark of royal favor. The deceased Lieutenant General Pakenham was charged with the following errors: keeping his headquarters too far back, leaving the troops confused as to their assignments, heedlessly exposing himself, failing to assail the American lines while they were most vulnerable, and proceeding with the battle on the left bank without having secured the right bank. General Keane, of course, was found at fault too. Most critics agree that an attack with his entire force early in the campaign might have succeeded, but the navy shares the blame here for failing to provide enough boats to get the entire force where it was needed when needed. Sir John Fortescue labeled the entire action as buccaneering rather than military campaigning, and faulted Keane for failing to push ahead with Thornton's light brigade plus the reinforcements which arrived on 24 December.[27]

In the last analysis Admiral Cochrane was more responsible than any other person. He picked New Orleans as the objective, and also for the most part he picked the route to attack it. His decisions in these matters were based on faulty intelligence. Indians, Negroes, and pirates did not rally to help as he had been led to expect. Neither did the mass of the inhabitants come to Britain's side as he had expected. Fortescue chose to call the admiral's expectations "a piece of folly so childish that it ought to have warned the British ministers against listening to any of his projects." But when the success of the operations which Cochrane had witnessed in the Chesapeake Bay area is weighed into the judgment, Fortescue's charge seems ill-considered. His accusation that Cochrane put the army into a cul-de-sac for the sake of loot has already been evaluated.

Meanwhile in England nearly all public figures took the fall of New Orleans for granted. In mid-December Castlereagh informed the Congress of Vienna that most of the large American seaports could be assumed to be burned already, and the Great Lakes, the Mississippi Valley, and New Orleans under the control of Britain's armed forces. At the time of the night battle of 23 December, Liverpool wrote to Castlereagh that he expected Pakenham to complete the conquest of New Orleans and to be in Chesapeake and Delaware bays by mid-February.[28]

General Lambert heard none of this optimism, but he lived in the midst of a deteriorating situation. He considered his forces in grave danger of destruction, and dared not move them forward or backward. The only encouraging development was that his wounded men were recovering more rapidly than usual. Many of the wounds were made by buckshot, and were therefore light. Accordingly, he set the able-bodied to work building a road back to Bayou Mazant, and preparing a strong position one mile from Lake Borgne. At the end of ten days he felt able to draw his army back to this strong point, except for 6 crippled 18-pounders and 2 carronades which could not be moved. On

27 January he re-embarked the army, but it could not sail away from the anchorage until 4 February because of adverse winds.[29]

It would have heartened General Lambert to know that Andrew Jackson was as much alarmed as he was. Far from contemplating an offensive, Jackson was concerned about the next British attack. To repel it he asked for a total of 5,000 regulars. The citizen soldiers who had saved New Orleans were the finest in the world, he said, but they could not be relied on for extended duty. Until reinforcements came, Jackson confined his activity to harassment of British working parties and enticement of their soldiers to desert.[30]

At the time when the inhabitants of New Orleans expected to relax a little from the rigors of war, General Jackson tightened up his internal security. It is true he lifted martial law on 21 January, but he reimposed it again in a few days. When in March a citizen criticized the continuation of martial law, Jackson had him jailed. In response Judge Dominick Hall issued a writ of habeas corpus, but the general, instead of honoring it, jailed him too. After peace was officially proclaimed, Hall charged Jackson with contempt of court and imposed a fine upon him, but wealthy citizens of New Orleans, far gone in hero worship, raised the money to pay the fine.

Foiled at New Orleans, the British commanders aimed once more at Mobile, from which they could also penetrate the interior. The first step of course was to take Fort Bowyer. To this end they established their main staging zone on Dauphine Island, about four miles from Bowyer, then fanned out their vessels to encircle the fort on the north, west, and south. This left the east open, but on 8 February 1815 they landed 5,000 men two and one-half miles to the east of the fort to close the ring. There was an inlet on the north side of the peninsula, which ran two-thirds of the way across, and the British extended this the rest of the way across the peninsula with a strong trench. Behind the inlet, they emplaced several cannon. Bowyer was now cut off completely. Inside the fort, Major William Lawrence, in command of 320 men, did what he could to foil the encirclement, but availed little. On 9 February the besiegers opened approach trenches, which by the eleventh they had dug to within forty yards of the curtain. General Lambert now called upon Lawrence to surrender. Argument over terms occupied the balance of the day, but toward evening a capitulation with honor was arranged. At noon on 12 February 1815, Fort Bowyer changed hands. The victors did not, however, proceed against Mobile.[31]

At a part of the strategy to gain control of southeastern United States, Admiral Cochrane sent Cockburn to operate in the Atlantic against the Georgia and Florida coasts. Cockburn on 10 January successfully invaded Cumberland Island, then took the American battery at Point Petre, then the town of St. Marys, Georgia. He also occupied St. Simons Island, but abandoned it after removing Negroes and merchandise. Next he sent boats 50 miles up the St. Marys River to try to make contact with Colonel Nicolls, who had orders to advance northeastward from Prospect Bluff on the Apalachicola River. American officials in Savannah declared martial law as British efforts continued successful on the South Atlantic coast.[32]

Admiral Cochrane now once more returned to heavy reliance upon Indians as allies. He directed Lambert to organize two bodies of Indians and Negroes, combined with some British soldiers. One was to harass the interior of Georgia and try to reach the Atlantic coast to make contact with Admiral Cockburn. The other was to take Fort Stoddert on the Tombigbee River, then work downstream toward Mobile. The Prospect Bluff fortification could protect the families of those redmen who were aiding England, and also serve as a base for either body to fall back on in case of unforeseen disaster. This activity would oblige sizable American forces to guard Mobile and New Orleans, and would occupy the militias of Tennessee and Kentucky. It would therefore keep some American power out of Canada. Lying behind this strategy too was the English policy to recover for the Indians the lands which greedy Americans had seized.[33]

In February 1815 Admiral Cochrane sailed to Chesapeake Bay where he could keep in better touch with all parts of the North American command. He left Rear Admiral Pultney Malcolm in charge in the Gulf region with special instructions relative to the Indians. The installation at Prospect Bluff was the key to British intercourse with them. Through it the redmen could grow rich trading with England. Until their old lands were returned to them, Malcolm was to leave three war vessels to protect Prospect Bluff.[34]

While the British continued to menace Mobile from Fort Bowyer, Andrew Jackson carried out in that city the notorious execution of six citizen soldiers. They had been members of the detachment of Tennesseans left in the heart of the Creek Country after the Battle of Horseshoe Bend. In the fall of 1814 they had been eager to go home to take care of their farms, but could not persuade Jackson to permit it. They argued with the general over their term of service. They contended that it was three months, and some of their officers let it be known that they would march their units home at the end of that time. Certain noncommissioned officers and privates, not bothering to wait for the officers, left before the argument was settled, at the time when they considered their tour was up. They did not get Jackson's permission either to leave or to carry off the rations they took to feed themselves on the way home.[35]

General Jackson was not likely to overlook such conduct. He made charges against these "deserters," and had them seized to be held for court-martial. They were tried at Mobile in December 1814. The court ruled that two captains be dismissed from the service, and that one of them have his sword broken over his back and be denied the right ever again to hold any sort of commission from the United States. It ruled that 197 enlisted men, charged with mutiny and desertion, be required to make up their lost time, forfeit half their pay, suffer one side of their heads to be shaved, and be drummed out of camp. But the ringleaders, one sergeant, and five privates, charged with robbery, mutiny, and desertion, were sentenced to be shot. They were executed on 21 February in Mobile. The newspapers of the time hardly noticed the event, but it would rise in the future to plague Jackson when he became a candidate for president.[36]

Peace

The Negotiations

A growing number of influential men in the United States considered the federal government exhausted and incapable of providing for the national defense. Senator Jeremiah Mason of New Hampshire stated the solution which many of them had come to accept. "Should the national defense be abandoned by the general government," he said, "I trust the people, if still retaining a good portion of their resources, may rally under their State governments against foreign invasion." Artemus Ward gave his version of this point of view in the House: "the resources of the States will be applied with more economy and with greater effect in the defense of the country under the state governments than under the government of the United States."[1]

Massachusetts, Rhode Island, New York, Maryland, Virginia, South Carolina, and Kentucky took steps to constitute their own armies. But all of them soon found that they could not afford an independent military force. Indeed they stipulated that if their armies actually materialized it would be up to the United States to support them. Since the federal government never agreed to this condition, the state armies were in fact not raised.[2]

The antiwar faction in New England reached the end of its patience late in 1814. The General Court of Massachusetts called for a meeting of the states to amend the Constitution, and on 19 October elected 12 men to be delegates to it. But only 215 out of 500 legislators elected them, and 75 of the dissenters signed a paper protesting that the proposed convention was in fact both unconstitutional and dangerous to the Union.[3]

Governor John Cotton Smith of Connecticut convened the legislature of his state in special session to consider Massachusett's call. He told it that Madison's administration had entered a coalition with the "fearful tyrant of Europe." Moreover, it had levied heavy taxes upon Connecticut and had not spent the money to the state's advantage. It had left Connecticut's coastline utterly undefended. On account of these abuses he recommended that his state send delegates, and the legislature complied.[4]

In the end, representatives from Massachusetts, Connecticut, Rhode Island, two New Hampshire counties, and one county in Vermont met in Hartford during December. They concurred that the Madison government had been guilty of the following abuses: placing regular army officers illegally in command of local militia forces; proposing to reclassify the militia in an unconstitutional way; representing only the agrarian interest of the nation and discriminating against commerce; trying so hard to acquire Canada as to neglect the coastline and therefore obliging the states to try to defend their own coasts with insufficient resources; purposely pitting state against state in order to keep one section in control of the federal government; excluding able men from its councils because they had refused to follow the party line; depriving judges of office in violation of the Constitution; using tax policy to curry political favor; using the federal patronage to keep one section in power; and weakening the commercial regions of the nation by encouraging the admission of western states.[5]

Having made their indictment, the Hartford delegates passed a series of resolutions designed to prevent "weak and profligate" policy from undermining the Union. The Constitution must be amended so that in the future: (1) representative and direct taxes would be apportioned according to the number of free persons in each state, thus eliminating the slave as three-fifths of a person; (2) new states would come into the Union only by a two-thirds vote of both houses of Congress; (3) Congress could not interdict commerce except by a two-thirds vote; (4) no agency of the government could enforce an embargo for more than sixty days; (5) a two-thirds vote in Congress would be necessary to declare war; (6) naturalized citizens could never hold office in the federal government; (7) a President would be allowed only one term and might not be chosen from the same geographical area as his predecessor. It is plain that the thrust of these proposed amendments was to curb the power of the political center and to terminate the Virginia dynasty.[6]

Twenty-six delegates signed these resolutions and hurried them off to Washington in the care of Harrison Grey Otis. Although Otis and his two companions did not know it, they were competing in a three-way race. H.M.S. *Favorite* was under full sail toward Washington with the news of peace, while a courier was riding hard from the southwest to bring word of the Battle of New Orleans. All three messages were in Washington by 5 February, but the Hartford delegates decided to withhold their resolutions under the circumstances.[7]

Much earlier the United States peace commissioners, Albert Gallatin, James A. Bayard, Jonathan Russell, Henry Clay, and John Quincy Adams, were converging upon Gothenburg in Sweden. All five of them knew how essential peace was for their country, but they also knew that they dared not alienate territory to get it and that they must secure a clear definition of, and a sharp limitation on, naval blockade.[8]

The British Ministry, for its part, was in no hurry to negotiate except on its own terms because military affairs were going well in Europe. Many influential persons advised it to take a hard line with the United States. Canadians said there must be no peace until Canada was made perfectly secure from its predatory neighbor to the south. Certain advisers assured the Ministry that through financial exhaustion, monetary collapse, threatened insurrection, and imminent Negro revolt, the United States was about to cave in. *Gentleman's Magazine* represented one slant of the hard anti-America line. "Our forbearance has been despised as weakness," it said, "if we cannot gain their gratitude for our patience, at least [it is time] to awake in them something like respect for our power." Another slant of hard-line reasoning was that in the future the United States would become England's most dangerous rival for world trade and would be ready to fight to gain trade advantages. The natural thing to do was to strike to cripple American growth before it was too late.[9]

British shipping interests wanted the war to end because the depredations of American privateers had pushed marine insurance rates so high that they were operating at a disadvantage in international competition. Large landowners wanted peace because they considered the war taxes unbearable. Both of these interests urged the government not to set out to humiliate the United States, for this would make her continue the fight, even though exhausted. They did not want British policy to unite Americans behind the war, and they deplored the destruction of Washington because of the hatred of Britain it kindled in the United States. There was too much loose talk in England, they said—for example, discussion of capturing and executing President Madison. Finally, they urged moderation because it would force the Madison administration either to make peace or to suffer political defeat. In either case Madison would be out, a step necessary before there could be peace.[10]

Gallatin and Bayard, through the courtesy of Lord Castlereagh, were allowed to stay in London for a time. There they saw the rising ill-will directed toward their country. They read the 24 May issue of the London *Times* which said, "Strike! Chastise the savages, for such they are." When the czar of Russia came to the city following Napoleon's abdication, Gallatin sought and obtained an interview with him because he was believed to be friendly to the United States. Gallatin hoped to use the czar's outstanding popularity in England to aid his own country, but he could gain no statement from that powerful ruler except a private expression of sympathy.[11]

Gallatin sought to get his associates to move from Gothenburg to Ghent, Belgium, in the hope that the British government might thus be led actually to begin negotiations. In time he arranged this shift, and when he himself reached Ghent on 6 July, the other commissioners were there waiting for him. Although John Quincy Adams was titular head of the American commission, it was Gallatin who had to try to keep the strong personalities from refusing to work with one another.[12]

One month to the day after Gallatin's arrival, British commissioners appeared at Ghent. Castlereagh, following a policy of purposeful delay, had taken his time about appointing them. The chairman was Lord James Gambier, a secondary naval person, and the other members were Henry Goulburn, undersecretary to Lord Bathurst in the Colonial Office, and William Adams, Doctor of Civil Laws. In selecting so weak a trio, Castlereagh had repeated the error made in 1783 by Lord Shelburne when he had also chosen second-rate commissioners to negotiate with Americans. The English team was further handicapped by the determination of the Ministry to control even the details of the proceedings. The members had no notion of what their government intended to do, and they had no power to do other than transmit messages between the Ministry and the American commissioners. They were no match for the Americans.[13]

At the first joint meeting on 8 August the British commissioners presented the demands of conquerors. They refused to discuss impressment, insisted that the Canadian border must be adjusted in Canada's favor, and stated categorically that the Indians must receive back most of the Old Northwest. The Americans had no authority to negotiate on such terms, and they declined to make a reply until after reflection.

This first session might have been the last if instructions dated 27 June had not come from Monroe that very evening, authorizing the Americans to yield, if necessary, on impressment.[14]

Spurred by fur traders and perhaps by humanitarian motives, the British Ministry instructed its delegates to stand firm for the Indians. At the second meeting, 19 August, Gambier announced that his government wanted the line set by the Treaty of Greenville of 1795 as the border of the Indian territory.* This meant giving back to the Indians what had since become Ohio and what later became Indiana, Illinois, Wisconsin, and Michigan. In the same vein, he said that England must control all military installations on the Great Lakes. The reasoning here was that with those posts in English possession, there was no threat to the security of the United States, but if the opposite was true, the United States could commence any future war in the very heart of Canada. He insisted next that England must have the right to navigate the Mississippi River. Finally, his country had to acquire enough of Maine to provide a land route from Halifax to Quebec.[15]

Since the Americans could find nothing to negotiate in these demands, the second session, like the first, ended as if it might be the last. Indeed, there was no meeting for the next three months. Instead the two commissions carried on a correspondence. At the start of it John Quincy Adams framed a reply to the British demands of 19 August which he and his colleagues believed would end negotiations once and for all. They made preparations to go home. At this point, however, the Ministry realized that if the talks ended now, England would appear to have wrecked them because of imperialistic ambitions. The war might even become popular in the United States. Liverpool, Castlereagh, and Bathurst therefore took pains to prepare new instructions. The post-Napoleonic offensive in America might give them greater bargaining power than before.

Early in September the Ministry began to soften its demands. They told the commissioners to give up the buffer state for the Indians. Under these instructions, Gambier forwarded a fourth note on 8 October to the American delegation. It proposed the same status and territory for the Indians as they had enjoyed in 1811. John Quincy Adams objected to this, but his colleagues brought him around. Thus, the Indian item became the first one agreed upon by the two commissions. It constituted a turning point.[16]

Each delegation now began to prepare its version of a treaty. In the

---

* Negotiated by Anthony Wayne after the Battle of Fallen Timbers, this treaty brought to the United States 50 million acres of land in the Northwest Territory, including Detroit and the future site of Chicago.

beginning the Americans labored under the disadvantage imposed by the burning of Washington, but this was more than offset when on 17 October news reached London of Baltimore, Plattsburg, and Fort Erie. By common consent, no delegate any longer raised the issue of impressment. The need had passed. Also, the Ministry told its commissioners to cease demanding exclusive military control on the Great Lakes. But to keep the Americans busy the British delegates raised issue after issue. Late in October they questioned the right of the Americans to cure fish on certain British-owned shores, and to fish in certain waters. John Quincy Adams was incensed. Next, they reaffirmed their right, confirmed by the Treaty of 1783, to navigate the Mississippi River. Now Henry Clay became incensed, but neither he nor Adams would support the special interest of the other. It took all of Gallatin's tact and patience to push these issues out of the foreground.[17]

As 1814 drew to a close, negotiations went badly for the British at Vienna, affairs in France did not promise to remain stable, and pressure in England to gain relief from taxes mounted higher and higher. The Prime Minister warned Castlereagh that it might be impossible to continue taxes at their high level just for the American war. Englishmen, having been at war for twenty-one years, were all but in rebellion over the tax rates. Since 1795 England had wrung out £57 million to pay foreign armies to fight on the continent of Europe, and the bill for this had been passed to the taxpayers.[18]

Liverpool now solicited an opinion from the Duke of Wellington. The Duke replied, "In regard to your present negotiations, I confess that I think you have no right from the state of the war to demand any concession of territory from America." With this and Plattsburg, Baltimore, and Erie, Liverpool knew that England could not impose demands upon the United States unless she was willing to carry on another full year of war. Moreover, he had concluded that even if the war went on for a very long time, it could not in the end guarantee a perfectly secure frontier for Canada. The United States had access to Canada during all seasons, whereas Great Britain could get to the principal cities and to the interior via the St. Lawrence River only six months out of each year. For these reasons he sent word to the commissioners at Ghent to get as good a settlement as possible. "Although our peace will not be very creditable compared with our overture," Bathurst wrote them, "yet it will be the best thing which can happen, particularly if it is soon concluded."[19]

These developments brought about on 1 December the first meeting of the two commissions since 19 August. In this and in subsequent meetings, the Americans became more, the British less, confident.

After several more meetings, the eight commissioners completed a document and signed it on Christmas Eve. It was more truly a cessation of hostilities than a treaty because it left most of the major issues open for future discussion and, everyone hoped, for settlement. Arrangements to pay for property taken or destroyed by illegal means were so ambiguous as to be virtually meaningless. Nothing at all was said about impressment, neutral rights, fishing rights, or navigation of the Mississippi River. Boundary problems were to be turned over to a joint commission. Only the clause relating to the Indians could be called specific.[20]

The British commissioners got the document to the foreign office on 26 December. The Ministry then set out to have it processed swiftly. They hoped to slip it through before there could be any public meetings or parliamentary resolutions about it. Lord Liverpool was aware how much ill-will there was in England against the United States, and that the treaty would hurt British pride. On the other hand, he counted on the unpopularity of the war to help move the matter to completion without an uproar. His wishes were gratified, and the treaty agreed to in short order. But it did not reach the United States until 11 February, and did not come before the Senate until the fifteenth. On 16 February the Senate voted for it, 35 to 0. By the time that word of this reached England, Napoleon was once more at large. Since the Ministry had also had news of the disaster at New Orleans, they were relieved and gratified at the prompt American ratification.[21]

The Treaty of Ghent

Article I of the Treaty of Ghent gives the impression that slaves and other private property were to be restored to their owners, but the wording is so ambiguous that one can suspect the signers of really trying to avoid the issue. In subsequent years the American government insisted that Britain was obligated either to return the slaves or to pay for them. British officials categorically refused to return the Negroes themselves on two grounds: unwillingness to remand them to slavery and disagreement as to what the treaty required. Finally in 1818 the two parties agreed that the czar of Russia could resolve the dispute. Four years later he found for the United States. By this time, of course, no one expected that the slaves themselves would be returned. The Canadians declared that to repatriate those Negroes would be to incur for them torture and death in "the land of the free and the home of the brave." The negotiators therefore had to find a price which both parties would accept. In 1824 they fixed upon $580 for every slave from Louisiana, $390 from Alabama, Georgia, and South Carolina, and $280 for all others. These prices were not acceptable to the two governments, and the matter remained unresolved for another three years. Finally in 1827 England agreed through diplomatic channels to pay £250,000 (about $1,204,960) in full settlement for all sorts of private property carried away during the war. This action legally freed about 3,600 former slaves.[1]

Article IX related to the Indians. It stipulated that the United States would guarantee to the redmen the same status and territory which they had had in 1811. This substantial concession does not seem to have troubled the American commissioners because they believed that it would be interpreted in specific cases to the advantage of the United States. In the light of subsequent history it is hard to see how they could have agreed to it in good faith. Surely they did not really intend to give back to the Indians the land ceded after the Battle of Tippecanoe in the north and Horseshoe Bend in the south.

Article IX caused Britons in contact with the redmen much distress. When Robert McDouall in far off Mackinac finally learned of it on 1 May, he protested to his government. His prediction was that the United States would stop the issue of powder to the natives, increase the sale of whiskey, and within fifty years wipe out all Indians east of the Rockies. The Indians themselves saw about the same future as McDouall. They watched with dismay the withdrawal of troops and dismantling of forts. "Father," said one of the chiefs, "you promised us repeatedly that this place would not be given up; and if you actually intend to abandon us to our inveterate enemy, who always sought our destruction, it would be better that you had us killed at once, rather than to expose us to a lingering death." In spite of such appeals, the British government went ahead with its planned withdrawal. Meanwhile the United States gave every impression of trying to live up to Article IX. From July to October 1815 it signed fifteen treaties with divers Indian tribes guaranteeing them their status as of 1811. But in none of these did it return an acre of land.[2]

The reaction of the British Indian agents in the southeast was similar to McDouall's. Lieutenant Colonel Edward Nicolls had stayed on at the fort at Prospect Bluff during the first half of 1815. He continued while there to complain to his American counterpart, Benjamin Hawkins. Upon the testimony of a Seminole chief, Bowlegs, he protested American attacks on villages of the Florida Indians in April. He warned Hawkins that Britain stood behind the redmen in what amounted to an offensive-defensive alliance and would see that her allies had enough arms to defend themselves. He stressed the significance of the fort the British had built at Prospect Bluff, which they intended to turn over to the Indians. Finally, he protested the running of the boundary lines set by the Treaty of Fort Jackson. Not only was that document a false treaty, but also it was in violation of Article IX.[3]

Nicolls and other British commanders in the Gulf region probably recognized by the middle of 1815 that the Americans would never live up to the provisions of Article IX. They recognized that no group in the United States would be willing to annul Jackson's treaty and give 20 million acres back to the Indians. On the other hand they saw that an attempt to enforce the article might renew the war.[4]

The Indians and British agents were not the only persons disillusioned with the United States. John Strachan, Bishop at York in Canada, when he heard that Thomas Jefferson had referred to the British activity in Washington as "vandalism," addressed a long indictment to him. It was the United States, he said, which had set the tone of brutality with the destruction of York and the plundering of private property which went with it, the burning of Newark, the systematic plundering which he claimed Wilkinson's army had done, General Brown's needless leveling of the country between Fort Erie and Chippewa, and Colonel Campbell's destruction of Dover. Americans, he claimed, had mistreated prisoners, violated flags of truce, and detained officers who were on official missions. Kentuckians had shown particular brutality to the Indians.[5]

There was room for endless argument about prisoners. In 1812 the British had sent to England 23 captives to be tried for treason. By late 1813 the United States had put 128 prisoners in close confinement as hostages for them. These and other prisoners were finally released when an exchange agreement was negotiated. Some Americans, however, mostly captured privateersmen, remained imprisoned at Dartmoor. Their circumstances were bad, and when no shipping was forthcoming to take them home, they rioted on 6 April 1815. Their guards killed 5 and wounded 34 of them. Had this incident been known in America, it might have caused some sort of retaliation.[6]

One fixed British objective was to secure Canada against the United

States. Commodore Yeo did not consider that the naval forces on the Great Lakes were able to achieve this. All they could do was make Kingston secure and sally from it in response to specific threats. Britain only remained in Canada, in his opinion, due to the "impolicy of [American] plans, the disunion of the commanders and lastly between them and their Minister of War." The Duke of Wellington expressed much the same view. He professed astonishment that "the officers of the army and navy were able to defend those provinces. . . . I can attribute their having been able to defend them as they did only to the inexperience of the officers of the United States in the operations of war. . . ."[7]

At war's end there were 25,975 British troops in Canada, but all defense plans were made on the supposition that so large a number could not be maintained in peacetime. At the start, after all, there had been only 8,125 soldiers. To help strengthen security, it was planned to grant land on which the soldiers in foreign regiments, such as duMeuron's and deWatteville's could settle down. This "barrier population" would receive rations for the first six months and could get farm tools at reduced prices. Later their families would be sent to join them at the government's expense.[8]

Roughly 398,000 American militiamen served during the war for less than six months, and another 60,000 enrolled for slightly longer terms. This was a more wasteful use of manpower than during the American Revolution, when only 164,000 men had served such short hitches. Long-termers during the Revolution totaled 231,000, but in the War of 1812 only 50,000. Some militiamen are known to have engaged for as many as ten short tours of duty. This kind of coming and going was prodigal of supplies, for short-termers as often as not carried home articles of issue which it was nearly impossible to replace. Blankets were in such short supply that recruits were asked to bring their own. The commissary general issued a greatcoat every two years in lieu of a scarce blanket. Not only did the short-term system increase the cost of supplies, it also vastly enlarged the pension lists for generations in the future.[9]

Albert Gallatin said, "The war has been productive of evil and good, but I think that the good preponderates. . . . The war renewed and reinstated the National Feelings and character which the Revolution had given, and which were daily lessened. The people now have more general objects of attachment with which their pride and political opinions are connected. They are more American; they feel and act more as a nation, and I hope that the permanency of the Union is thereby secured."[10]

Even though American defeats were numerous, the stature of the United States was enlarged among the nations. The early single-ship victories helped cause the growth of respect, and so did the ability of the federal government to reform the army in the midst of military operations while diplomatically isolated. The change which other countries respected amounted to an increase in the power of the federal government. The feeble conduct of the war at its outset seemed to demonstrate that the central authority had grown flabby since the Revolution. It appeared to some people that the Continental Congress, impotent as it had been, had still shown more coordinating power than the Madison administration could muster in 1812. The necessities of war forced upon a reluctant United States some centralization, and the process proved to be irreversible. Army management was enlarged and solidified, the general staff was put together, and institutional aid was given to the military secretaries to carry out their logistical, technical, and training duties. These changes became the bases for the permanent reforms completed between 1816 and 1818 under the direction of John C. Calhoun as secretary of war.[11]

Manufacturing had been given a smart fillip by embargo, nonintercourse, and the war itself. Some scholars have claimed that the resulting expansion was equal to that of two decades in peacetime. In any event, President Madison was aware of the enlarged manufacturing interests, and to protect them he recommended that the wartime duties on imports be retained for two years after the peace. New England, still primarily devoted to shipping, opposed this extension, but Madison commanded enough support in Congress to get it enacted into law in April 1814.[12]

The cost of the War of 1812 to the United States was $105 million. In a way, it was a sound investment in national rights and the reaffirmation of national independence. Financing the war was very difficult at the time. Baring Brothers, a banking firm of the enemy country, handled routine accounts for the United States overseas, but the firm would take on no loans. The loans were in the end absorbed by wealthy Americans at great hazard—also, as it turned out, at great profit to them. The interest rate they received was high even for that day, and the principal of the loans was discounted 12 per cent to them. Once the war was over, the United States easily handled the war costs. Two decades after peace the nation had paid off its entire bonded indebtedness, the only time it has ever been able to do so. All in all, the War of 1812 required of the American people only one-tenth of the financial exertion, in proportion to population and resources, which the Civil War was later to exact from them.[13]

The economic cost to Britain was much greater. The British public debt was £451,700,000 in 1800, but it was £840,850,000 in 1815. Much of this increase has of course to be charged to the war in Europe. Probably the only advantage which England purchased through the War of 1812 was a closer tie with Canada. War tended to link the older eastern part of Canada more closely than before with the new western section and to create a Canadian national identity. It also gave Great Britain and Canada at least one common bond, a deep dislike and distrust of the United States.[14]

The Napoleonic wars demonstrated that the British military system was as much in need of reform as that of the United States. Even Wellington complained that his army was often out of control, a condition that the French historian Élie Halévy ascribed to the social gap that existed between officers and enlisted men. Major General Jacob Brown considered the British enlisted man less effective than the American, perhaps because of the social gulf between the grades. Frederick II and Napoleon, two great captains, had seen the need for a different relationship. Napoleon's officers were able to work their way up from the ranks, to become military professionals. British officers, in contrast, were gentlemen first and soldiers second; if they became professionals, it was to some degree by accident. They were drawn from the English governing class, and with that class they were more interested in reducing government expenses than in developing an efficient military system. Members of the English ruling class were champions of the counterrevolution in Europe. It was because of them that in England "the net effect of the revolutionary decade was to demonstrate or to consolidate the strength of the established order." In the United States the reverse was true.[15]

Notes

Explanation

The short citations in the notes are tied alphabetically to the entries in Sources Cited, where full bibliographical information is given, and the short citations are repeated at the end of each entry. The following abbreviations are used in the notes:

AC	*Annals of Congress.*
Adm	Admiralty Records, London. Adm/1/502/143: Admiralty Records, class 1, folio or volume 502, page 143.
AG	Adjutant General.
AGLR	Adjutant General (U.S.), Letters Received.
AGLS	Adjutant General (U.S.), Letters Sent.
ASPMA	American State Papers, Military Affairs.
CO	Colonial Office Records, London. CO/42/318/25: Colonial Office Records, class 42, folio or volume 318, page 25.
DAB	*Dictionary of American Biography.*
DNB	*Dictionary of National Bibliography.*
HC	House of Commons.
HL	House of Lords.
HR	House of Representatives.
MPHC	Michigan Pioneer and Historical Collection.
MR	Microfilm reels in the National Archives. M125R23/42: Microfilm group 125, reel 23, page 42. M149R10/H282: Microfilm 149, reel 10, document 282 received and filed under the first letter of the sender's last name for the pertinent year.
MS(S)	Manuscript(s).
NA	National Archives
PAC	Public Archives of Canada, Ottawa. PAC/C1218/131: Public Archives, folio C1218, page 131.
SN	Secretary of the Navy.
SW	Secretary of War.
Sen. Doc.	Senate Document in the U.S. Congress Serial Set.
TP	*Territorial Papers of the United States.*
USSL	*United States Statutes at Large.*
WO	War Office Records, London. WO/1/141/27: War Office Records, class 1, folio or volume 141, page 27.
WOLR	War Office (U.S.), Letters Received.
WOLS	War Office (U.S.), Letters Sent.
WRHS	Western Reserve Historical Society.

The United States

1. Act of 12 April 1808, *USSL*, 2:481; Mahon, "Organization," p. 58.
2. *AC*, 12 Cong., 1 sess., 23:35 ff.
3. Ibid., p. 731.
4. Act of 11 Jan. 1812, *USSL*, 2:671; Adams, *History*, bk. 6, pp. 149–53.
5. SW to HR, 27 Jan. 1810, MS, NA; *AC*, 12 Cong., 1 sess., 23:58; Acts of 14 Jan., 6 Feb., 10 April 1812, *USSL*, 2:674, 676, 705.
6. Risch, *Quartermaster*, pp. 117–24, 136–42; White, *Jeffersonians*, pp. 233–36.
7. White, *Jeffersonians*, pp. 217–18; Adams, *History*, bk. 6, pp. 168, 206, 392, 395–96; *DAB.*
8. *DAB*; Brant, *Madison*, pp. 125–26.
9. Hitsman, *Incredible*, p. 21; Lossing, *Field Book*, p. 184.

10. SN to Rodgers, 9 April 1812, M149R10/38; vice versa, 29 April 1812, M125R23/53.

11. SN to Rodgers, 21 May 1812, M149R10/41–42; vice versa, 3 June 1812, M125R23/56.

12. SN to Decatur, 21 May 1812, M149R10/41–42; vice versa, 8 June 1812, M125R24/42.

13. Rodgers to SN, 19 June 1812, M125R24; Mahan, *Sea Power, 1812,* 2:317, 319, 321.

14. Brant, *Madison,* pp. 13–18.

15. Adams, *History,* bk. 6, p. 163.

16. Ibid.; Albion, *Sea Lanes,* p. 97; Byron, *War of 1812,* pp. 8–10; White, *Nation,* p. 5.

17. These sources apply to this and the next 2 paragraphs: Rodgers to SN, 11 June 1812, M125R24/10; Roosevelt, *Naval War,* pp. 39, 48, 51, 62; Chapelle, *Sailing Navy,* pp. 127–28, 130–32, 165.

18. Chapelle, *Sailing Navy,* pp. 182, 186, 188, 212, 234; Forester, *Fighting Sail,* p. 125; Roosevelt, *Naval War,* p. 176.

19. Chapelle, *Sailing Navy,* pp. 179–241.

20. Mahan, *Sea Power, 1812,* 2:87; Roosevelt, *Naval War,* p. 57; James, *Naval History,* 6:149, 475.

21. Roosevelt, *Naval War,* pp. 37, 39.

22. Albion, *Sea Lanes,* p. 112.

23. "Returns," 22 March 1804, 20 Feb. 1811, ASPMA, 1:168–72, 293–301; see also *Statistical History of the United States* for population and debt figures.

24. Adams, *History,* bk. 6, pp. 137–38.

England and Canada

1. Heckscher, *Continental,* pp. 61, 64; *Niles' Register,* 2:284.

2. Adams, *History,* bk. 6, p. 2.

3. Mahan, *Sea Power, 1812,* 1:379; Bryant, *Age of Elegance,* pp. 33–38.

4. Bryant, *Age of Elegance,* p. 67; *DNB;* Yonge, *Liverpool,* passim.

5. *DNB;* Perkins, *Prologue,* p. 12; *Annual Register,* 1814, p. 342.

6. Baugh, *Naval,* pp. 6, 64.

7. Fortescue, *History,* 10:202.

8. Hitsman, *Incredible,* pp. 30–33.

9. "Return of the Effective Strength of the British Army," HC, *Journal,* vol. 69, 1813–14.

10. Baugh, *Naval,* pp. 64–65, 73.

11. *DNB.*

12. Hitsman, *Incredible,* p. 41.

13. Foster to Sawyer, 15 June 1812, Adm/1/502/143.

14. Prevost to Torrens, 12 Jan. 1812, PAC/C1218/131; Fortescue, *History,* 9:326–27.

15. Pirtle, *Tippecanoe,* pp. 8 ff.; Lucas, *Canadian War,* p. 5; Craig, *Upper Canada,* p. 36; Cruikshank, "Indians," p. 326.

16. Simcoe to Dundas, 23 Feb. 1784, CO/42/318; Mahan, *Sea Power, 1812,* 1:304; Stacey, "Another Look," p. 42.

17. Hitsman, *Incredible,* p. 24; *DNB;* Mahon, "Command," pp. 219–20, 230–33.

18. Craig, *Upper Canada,* pp. 17–19; Christie, *Military,* pp. 47–48; Brock to Liverpool, 23 March 1813, CO/42/352/8.

19. Hitsman, *Incredible,* pp. 14, 20, 34; Lucas, *Canadian War,* p. 9; Christie, *Military,* p. 44; Mahan, *Sea Power, 1812,* 1:291n; "Return of the Effective Strength of the British Land Forces in North America," 25 May 1812, HL,

Sess. Papers, 1813, 8:27; Liverpool to Prevost, 2 April, 20 April 1812, CO/43/23/52.

20. Hitsman, "Prevost's Conduct," pp. 34, 37; Brock to Prevost, 25 Feb. 1812, PAC/C676/92–95.

21. Brock to Prevost, just cited; to Liverpool, 23 March 1812, CO/42/352/8.

22. Craig, *Upper Canada*, pp. 68, 71–72; Stanley, *Soldiers*, pp. 154–55; Brock to Prevost, 6 Feb. 1812, PAC/C676.

Tippecanoe

1. Tucker, *Tecumseh*, passim.

2. Ibid., pp. 123, 164; Pirtle, *Tippecanoe*, p. 6; Harrison to SW, 10 July, 7 Aug. 1811, Harrison, *Messages*, 1:534, 549.

3. Harrison to SW, 6 Aug. 1811, Harrison, *Messages*, 1:545–48; Cotterill, *Southern Indians*, pp. 166 ff.

4. Tucker, *Tecumseh*, pp. 89–110.

5. Harrison to SW, 13 Aug. 1811, Harrison, *Messages*, 1:554–55; Cleaves, *Old Tippecanoe*, pp. 85, 86.

6. SW to President, 21 Aug. 1811, Harrison to SW, 17 Sept. 1811, Harrison, *Messages*, 1:563, 571–75; vice versa, 18 Sept. 1811, *TP: Indiana*, 8:133–34.

7. Walker, *Journal*, "Return of Harrison's Forces," 18 Sept. 1811, in Harrison, *Messages*, 1:695 ff., 597–98; Cleaves, *Old Tippecanoe*, p. 88.

8. "General Order," 22 Sept., 25 Sept., 27 Sept. 1811, Harrison to SW, 7 Aug., 13 Oct. 1811, Harrison, *Messages*, 1:587–88, 593, 551, 600; same, 2 Nov., 13 Nov. 1811, M221R44/H2, H17.

9. Cleaves, *Old Tippecanoe*, pp. 90, 93; Walker, *Journal*, pp. 12, 16.

10. Harrison to SW, 13 Nov. 1811, M221R44/H2; Adams, *History*, bk. 6, pp. 97, 99; Cleaves, *Old Tippecanoe*, pp. 91, 92, 96.

11. Walker, *Journal*, pp. 17 ff.; Pirtle, *Tippecanoe*, pp. 8, 39, 40, 41, 45, 46; Harrison to SW, 18 Nov. 1811, Harrison, *Messages*, 1:618–31.

12. "Snelling's Estimate," "Funk's Narrative," in Harrison, *Messages*, 1:680, 720; "Shabonee's Account," pp. 353–57; Pirtle, *Tippecanoe*, p. 62; Cleaves, *Old Tippecanoe*, p. 98.

13. Harrison to SW, 18 Nov. 1811, to Charles Scott, 13 Dec. 1811, "Funk's Narrative," in Harrison, *Messages*, 1:618–31, 668–69, 723; Walker, *Journal*, pp. 20, 34.

14. Pirtle, *Tippecanoe*, pp. 80, 81; "Funk's Narrative," in Harrison, *Messages*, 1:722.

15. Pirtle, *Tippecanoe*, p. 69; Cleaves, *Old Tippecanoe*, pp. 99, 101.

16. Cleaves, *Old Tippecanoe*, pp. 103–5; Pirtle, *Tippecanoe*, p. 70; Adams, *History*, bk. 6, p. 100; Harrison to SW, 26 Nov. 1811, "Return of Casualties," Harrison, *Messages*, 1:651, 637.

17. Snelling to Harrison, 20 Nov. 1811, Harrison, *Messages*, 1:644; Tucker, *Tecumseh*, pp. 229–31.

18. Jackson to Harrison, 28 Nov. 1811, AGLR/H2.

19. Cleaves, *Old Tippecanoe*, pp. 105–6; "Statement of Officers," 19 Nov. 1811, in Harrison, *Messages*, 1:634.

Reaction to the War

1. Borden, *Bayard*, pp. 187–90; Coggeshall, *Privateers*, p. xxxvii.

2. Adams, *History*, bk. 6, pp. 230, 233, 235; Acts of 26 June, 6 July 1812, *USSL*, 2:764, 784–85; Upton, *Military*, p. 92.

3. Smith to SW, 2 July 1812, Griswold to SW, 18 Aug. 1812, ASPMA, 1:325–26.

4. Strong to SW, 5 Aug. 1812, ASPMA, 1:323; *Niles' Register*, 2:355; "General Orders," 3 July 1812, Mass. Orderly.

5. "Volunteers from Each State During the War of 1812," *Sen. Doc. 100*, 15 Feb. 1812, 16 Cong., 2 sess.; SW to Commanding Officer, Newport, 18 Aug. 1812, WOLS.

6. *Niles' Register*, 2:372-80, 3:322, 353, 388-89; Adams, *History*, bk. 6, p. 406.

7. *Montreal Herald*, 27 June 1812.

8. Hitsman, *Incredible*, pp. 37, 45; Prevost to Liverpool, 6 July 1812, CO/42/147/115.

9. Prevost to Brock, 7 July, 10 July 1812, PAC/C1218/301, 306; vice versa, 12 July 1812, Brock to . . . 29 July 1812, PAC/C676/150-52, 239-41; Prevost to Liverpool, 15 July 1812, PAC/C1218/308-12; "Regulations," 10 July 1812, in *Niles' Register*, 2:368, 3:87.

10. Prevost to Liverpool, 18 July 1812, CO/42/147/24; Hitsman, *Incredible*, p. 46; Freer to Glasgow, 23 July 1812, to Robinson, 6 Aug. 1812, PAC/C1218/334, 356.

11. Mahan, *Sea Power, 1812*, 1:388; Horsman, *Causes*, chs. 9, 10.

12. "Observations upon the Present War with the United States," 18 June 1812 (author unknown, probably James Stephen), Liverpool Papers, 38386/195-96.

13. "Observations upon American Affairs," 16 Sept. 1812 (author unknown), ibid., 38363/12-16.

14. Brock to Prevost, 28 Sept. 1812, Warren Papers; Prevost to Bathurst, 8 Oct. 1812, CO/42/147/207 ff.; vice versa, 10 Aug. 1812, CO/42/23/70; "Memo on Indian Expenses," CO/42/148/129-30.

15. Macpherson to Freer, 5 July 1812, PAC/C676; Hitsman, *Incredible*, pp. 52, 94.

16. *DAB*.

17. Eckert, "Jones," pp. 150-51; SW to Dearborn, 28 May 1812, M6R5/409; Brant, *Madison*, pp. 39, 45.

18. SW to Dearborn, 26 June 1812, M6R5/458.

19. Dearborn to SW, 10 July, 13 July, 28 July 1812, M221R43/D109(6), D112(6); vice versa, 1 Aug. 1812, M6R6/199.

20. SW to Dearborn, 26 July 1812, M6R5/458; vice versa, 30 July 1812, M221R43/D120(6).

21. Brant, *Madison*, p. 53; Burt, *US & GB*, p. 46.

22. Hitsman, *Incredible*, p. 49; SN to Gordon, 23 June 1812, "Circular," SN, 14 July 1812, M149R10/72, 99; Chauncey to SN, 23 July 1812, Bainbridge to SN, n.d., M125R24/61, 64.

23. Rodgers to SN, 21 June 1812, M125R24/46; James, *Naval History*, 6:122; "Account of H.M.S. Belvidera," 23 June 1812, Adm/1; Roosevelt, *Naval History*, p. 64; Forester, *Fighting Sail*, p. 30.

24. SN to Decatur, 22 June 1812, M149R10/66.

25. Forester, *Fighting Sail*, pp. 27, 30, 33.

26. Hull to SN, 20 June 1812, Chauncey to SN, 17 July 1812, M125R24/43; Broke to Croker, 30 July 1812, Adm/2/4358.

27. Hull to SN, 27 July 1812, M125R24/127; Forester, *Fighting Sail*, p. 50; Roosevelt, *Naval War*, p. 74.

28. Hull to SN, 2 Aug. 1812, M125R24.

29. Bainbridge to SN, 11 July 1812, M125R24/102.

30. Porter to SN, 12 July, 2 Aug., 8 Aug. 1812, M125R24/104, 154, M125R25/15a; James, *Naval History*, 5:363-64.

31. James, *Naval History*, 6:127-29; Porter to SN, 15 Aug., 3 Sept. 1812, M125R24/178, M125R25/12; Roosevelt, *Naval History*, p. 69; *Niles' Register*, 4:62.

William Hull

1. Hull to SW, 17 Dec. 1811, WOLR/H67(6); *DAB*; Gilpin, *War in Northwest*, p. 24.

2. Gilpin, *War in Northwest*, p. 28.

3. Ibid., p. 31; SW to Meigs, 26 March 1812, M6R5; McArthur to Worthington, 19 May 1812, Cass to Worthington, 16 May 1812, in *Worthington*, pp. 89, 90; Wadsworth to SW, 26 Aug. 1812, WRHS, tract 3.

4. Hull to SW, 6 March 1812, WOLR/H168(6); Brant, *Madison*, pp. 43, 46; Burt, *US & GB*, p. 46.

5. Hull to SW, 13 May, 9 June, 11 June 1812, WOLR; Gilpin, *War in Northwest*, p. 60.

6. Hull to SW, 18 June, 24 June 1812, WOLR/H275, H281.

7. Hitsman, *Incredible*, p. 55; Gilpin, *War in Northwest*, p. 55.

8. These sources apply to this and the next paragraph: SW to Hull, 24 June 1812, M6R5/457; vice versa, 7 July 1812, WOLR/H334(6); Gilpin, *War in Northwest*, p. 57.

9. St. George to Brock, 8 July, 15 July 1812, PAC/C676; "Hull Proclamation," 13 July 1812, Brock to Prevost, 20 July 1812, MPHC, 15:106–7, 115.

10. Gilpin, *War in Northwest*, pp. 75–76.

11. Hitsman, *Incredible*, p. 65.

12. Gilpin, *War in Northwest*, pp. 79, 82–83; Walker, *Journal*, p. 56; Lucas, *Journal*, p. 35.

13. Hull to Meigs, 11 July 1812, in Williams, *Brush*, pp. 12, 13, 16.

14. Williams, *Brush*, pp. 25, 27; Gilpin, *War in Northwest*, pp. 95–98; Armstrong, *Notices*, 1:25; Dalliba, *Narrative*, p. 8.

15. Dalliba, *Narrative*, p. 10.

16. Ibid., pp. 12, 15, 26, 35, 36; Procter to Brock, 26 July, 11 Aug. 1812, PAC/C676; Armstrong, *Notices*, 1:26–30; Gilpin, *War in Northwest*, pp. 102–3; Hull to SW, 13 Aug. 1812, Brannan, *Letters*, p. 38.

17. Hull to SW, 26 Aug. 1812, Brannan, *Letters*, pp. 45–46; same, 22 July 1812, WOLR/H332.

18. Roberts to AG, 17 July 1812, MPHC, 15:109; Hitsman, *Incredible*, p. 38; Hanks to Hull, 4 Aug. 1812, M222R8; Harrison to SW, 12 Aug. 1812, *TP: Indiana*, 8:189–93.

19. Hull to SW, 4 Aug. 1812, WOLR/H336; "Cass Testimony," in Hull, *Trial*; Gilpin, *War in Northwest*, pp. 107, 111; Hull, *Memoirs*, p. 64; Cass to SW, 10 Sept. 1812, in Brannan, *Letters*, p. 56.

20. Hull to SW, 26 Aug. 1812, in Brannan, *Letters*, p. 47; Brock to Prevost, 17 Aug. 1812, in *Niles' Register*, 3:266–67.

21. Brock to Prevost, just cited; Hitsman, *Incredible*, p. 74; Gilpin, *War in Northwest*, pp. 114–15.

22. Brock to Prevost, 17 Aug. 1812, in *Niles' Register*, 3:266–67; same, 1 Sept. 1812, CO/42/147/177.

23. Brock to Prevost, last cited; same, 17 Aug. 1812, in *Niles' Register*, 3:266–67; Cass to SW, 10 Sept. 1812, M221R43/C462(6)E; Gilpin, *War in Northwest*, pp. 117–18, 121.

24. "Proclamation," 21 Aug. 1812, in *Niles' Register*, 3:92.

25. Hitsman, *Incredible*, p. 79; *Anderson*, p. 18; Lucas, *Journal*, p. 35; Hatch, *A Chapter*, pp. 44–47, 75.

26. Hull, *Trial*.

27. Hull, *Memoirs*, pp. 12 ff., 54, 66, 80, 91, 95; Cass to SW, 10 Sept. 1812, M221R43/C462(6)E; Whistler to SW, 6 Oct. 1812, M222R6; Gilpin, *War in Northwest*, p. 121.

28. Prevost to Bathurst, 17 Aug. 1812, PAC/C1219/13–17; to Dearborn, 2 Aug. 1812, M222R6; Dearborn to SW, 8 Aug. 1812, M221R43/D158(6).

29. Dearborn to Baynes, 8 Aug. 1812, MPHC, 15:127; Prevost to Bathurst, 17 Aug., 24 Aug. 1812, PAC/C1219/13–17; Hitsman, *Incredible*, p. 78; Mahan, *Sea Power, 1812*, 1:352; Armstrong, *Notices*, 1:97; Adams, *History*, bk. 6, pp. 324–25.

30. Dearborn to SW, 15 Aug. 1812, M221R43/D130(6).

31. These sources apply to this and the next paragraph: Cass to SW, 10 Sept. 1812, M221R43/C462(6)E; McArthur to Worthington, 7 July 1812, in *Worthington*, p. 106; Armstrong, *Notices*, 1:36, 43, 46; Jesup to Cushing, 6 Jan. 1813, M222R8; Mahan, *Sea Power, 1812*, 1:348, 366.

32. Brant, *Madison*, pp. 73, 74.

33. The account of Fort Dearborn is based on Lossing, *Field Book*, pp. 303–10.

British Strategy

1. Croker to Warren, 3 Aug. 1812, Adm/2/1375/33.

2. Mahan, *Sea Power, 1812*, 1:390.

3. Warren to Croker, 5 Oct. 1812, Adm/1/502/303; Mahan, *Sea Power, 1812*, 3:391.

4. Warren to Melville, 7 Oct., 11 Nov., 18 Nov. 1812, Warren Papers.

5. "Minutes of the Privy Council Meeting," 21 Aug. 1812, WO/744/95; Sawyer to Croker, 7 Sept. 1812, Warren to Croker, 18 Oct. 1812, Adm/1/502/280, 327.

6. Bathurst to Prevost, 10 Aug. 1812, in Hitsman, *Incredible*, p. 56; Warren to Croker, 5 Oct. 1812, Adm/1/502/303.

7. Prevost to Frederick, 17 Oct. 1812, to Brock, 14 Sept. 1812, PAC/C1218/447, 441–43.

8. Brock to Prevost, 28 Sept. 1812, Warren Papers; Prevost to Bathurst, 8 Oct. 1812, CO/42/147/207.

9. Bathurst to Prevost, 11 Feb., 13 Aug. 1813, CO/43/23/91, PAC/C679/421–22.

10. Prevost to Bathurst, 6 June, 12 Aug., 15 Sept. 1813, PAC/C1219/53, 101, CO/42/151/146; Hitsman, *Incredible*, p. 112.

Naval Actions on the Oceans

1. Hull to SN, 28 Aug., 30 Aug. 1812, Dacres to Sawyer, 12 Sept. 1812, in *Niles' Register*, 3:28, 254; James, *Naval History*, 6:142–57; Roosevelt, *Naval War*, pp. 75–82; Coggeshall, *Privateers*, pp. 27–31; Forester, *Fighting Sail*, pp. 64–68.

2. Perkins, *Castlereagh*, p. 19; Mahan, *Sea Power, 1812*, 1:402–3.

3. SN to Officers, 28 July 1812, to Hull, 9 Sept. 1812, M149R10/115, 119, 123, 138; Hull to SN, 1 Sept. 1812, Bainbridge to SN, 2 Sept. 1812, M125R25; same, 10 Feb. 1812, M125R23.

4. Rodgers to SN, 31 Aug., 1 Sept. 1812, M125R24/2, 222; Sawyer to Croker, 17 Sept. 1812, Adm/1/502/265.

5. SN to Decatur and Rodgers, 9 Sept. 1812, M149R10.

6. Whinyates to Warren, 23 Oct. 1812, Adm/1/502/341; Jones to SN, 24 Nov. 1812, in *Niles' Register*, 2:217; Roosevelt, *Naval History*, pp. 84–89; James, *Naval History*, 6:159–63.

7. James, *Naval History*, 6:164–76; Roosevelt, *Naval War*, pp. 91–98; Carden to Croker, 25 Oct. 1812, Decatur to SN, 30 Oct. 1812, in *Niles' Register*, 4:52, 3:253; vice versa, 29 Dec. 1812, 3 Feb. 1813, M149R10; "Bainbridge Journal," M125R26; SN to Jones, 1 Feb. 1813, M149R10/241; Forester, *Fighting Sail*, pp. 107–10.

8. Bainbridge to SN, 3 Jan. 1813, Chads to Croker, 31 Dec. 1812, in *Niles' Register*, 4:273–74, 3:410–13; James, *Naval History*, 6:187–96; Roosevelt, *Naval War*, pp. 100–109.

9. Warren to Croker, 29 Dec. 1812, 25 Jan. 1813, Adm/1/503/49, 119.

10. "Naval Force on the American Station," *HL Sess. Papers*, 1813, 8:1; "Ships Captured by the United States," *Niles' Register*, 3:122; Mahan, *Sea Power, 1812*, 1:382.

William Henry Harrison

1. McAfee, *History*, p. 120.

2. Wadsworth to SW, 26 Aug. 1812, in Whittlesey, *Papers, 1812*, p. 3; SW to Ohio officers, 5 Sept. 1812, WOLS; Beall to Wadsworth, 13 Sept. 1812, WRHS, tract 12, p. 2; Perkins to Wadsworth, 11 Sept. 1812, WRHS, tract 18, p. 2.

3. Harrison to SW, 14 Jan. 1812, in *Harrison and the War*, p. 3; same, 28 July 1812, to Scott, 14 July 1812, Harrison, *Messages*, 2:73–74, 80.

4. SW to Harrison, 22 Aug. 1812, in Harrison, *Messages*, 2:92.

5. Harrison to SW, 14 April, 22 April 1812, M6R45/H203, H215; Cleaves, *Old Tippecanoe*, p. 46; Adams, *History*, bk. 6, p. 77.

6. Harrison to SW, 28 Aug. 1812, Harrison, *Messages*, 2:99–101; Gibson to SW, 2 Sept. 1812, *TP: Indiana*, 8:197–98; Gilpin, *War in Northwest*, pp. 131–32, 140–41; SW to Harrison, 17 Sept. 1812, M6R6/150; Brant, *Madison*, pp. 82–85; Johnson to President, 18 Sept. 1812, in Cleaves, *Old Tippecanoe*, p. 120.

7. Harrison to SW, 21 Sept. 1812, Harrison, *Messages*, 2:145–47; same, 24 Sept. 1812, in *Harrison and the War*, p. 33.

8. Shelby to SW, 5 Sept. 1812, in Harrison, *Messages*, 2:114.

9. "General Orders," Governor of Pennsylvania, Pa. Historical Comm.

10. Woodward to Secretary of Treasury, 7 Sept. 1812, *TP: Michigan*, 10:400–401.

11. Bathurst to Wellington, 6 Oct. 1812, Wellington, *Supp. Des.*, 7:442.

12. Gilpin, *War in Northwest*, pp. 137–38; Taylor to Harrison, 10 Sept. 1812, in *Niles' Register*, 3:90; Lossing, *Field Book*, pp. 317–18, 334.

13. Lossing, *Field Book*, pp. 313–14; Procter to Brock, 9 Sept. 1812, Brock to Prevost, 18 Sept. 1812, in MPHC, 15:145–47; Slocum, "Origin," pp. 253–77.

14. Muir to Procter, 30 Sept. 1812, PAC/C677/102; Prevost to Brock, n.d., PAC/C1218/444; Procter to Brock, 3 Oct. 1812, in MPHC, 15:155; Lossing, *Field Book*, pp. 325–27; McAfee, *History*, pp. 137–38, 145.

15. Harrison to SW, 21 Sept., 24 Sept. 1812, in *Harrison and the War*, pp. 31–34.

16. Shelby to Harrison, 1 Nov. 1812, in Harrison, *Messages*, 2:192; Gilpin, *War in Northwest*, pp. 147–49.

17. Johnson to Howard, 7 Jan. 1812, Clark to SW, 13 Feb. 1812, Howard to SW, 19 March 1812, *TP: Louisiana-Missouri*, 14:506, 518, 533; Gilpin, *War in Northwest*, pp. 34, 35, 38, 39, 65, 129; *TP: Illinois*, 15:347; Hamilton to Russell, 18 July 1813, M221R53/H232; Russell to Posey, 25 July 1813, in Harrison, *Messages*, 2:497.

18. Edwards, *Illinois*, pp. 68–69; Alvord, *Illinois*, p. 447; Russell to SW, 31 Oct. 1812, *TP: Illinois*, 16:268–69; "Petition, Territorial Legislature of Illinois," 30 Nov. 1812, ibid., p. 271; Edwards to SW, 25 Dec. 1812, M222R5; to President, 16 Jan. 1813, to SW, 13 March, 14 March 1813, *TP: Illinois*, 16:285–88, 303–6; Bond to Edwards, 7 Feb., 13 Feb., 25 Feb. 1813, *Edwards Papers*, pp. 94, 95, 97.

19. Hopkins to Shelby, 27 Nov. 1812, in *Niles' Register*, 3:264–65; Gilpin, *War in Northwest*, pp. 149–50.

20. Harrison to SW, 27 Sept. 1812, in *Harrison and the War*, pp. 35–36.

21. Harrison to SW, 13 Oct., 22 Oct. 1812, Harrison, *Messages,* 2:173, 185; Morrison to Clay, 24 Dec. 1812, M222R6; Armstrong, *Notices,* 1:87.

22. Harrison to SW, 27 Sept., 22 Oct., 12 Dec. 1812, Harrison, *Messages,* 2:185, 242; SW to Harrison, 26 Dec. 1812, M6R6.

23. These sources apply to this and the next paragraph: Harrison to SW, 13 Oct., 22 Oct., 15 Nov. 1812, Harrison, *Messages,* 2:156, 177, 185 ff., 211-15; same, 24 Sept., 27 Sept. 1812, in *Harrison and the War,* pp. 33-35; Morrison to Clay, 24 Dec. 1812, M222R6.

24. Harrison to SW, 27 Sept., 13 Oct. 1812, in *Harrison and the War,* pp. 36, 42; Worthington to Harrison, 28 Nov. 1812, *TP: Indiana,* 8:216-19.

25. Cruikshank, "H & P," pp. 138-39; Gilpin, *War in Northwest,* pp. 150-52; Tupper to Harrison, 12 Oct. 1812, in *Niles' Register,* 3:167.

26. Tupper to Harrison, just cited; Slocum, "Origin," p. 263; Cruikshank, "H & P," p. 140; Harrison to SW, 14 Dec. 1812, Harrison, *Messages,* 2:246; Tupper to Harrison, 16 Nov. 1812, M6R45/H432(6).

27. These sources apply to this and the next paragraph: Harrison to SW, 15 Nov. 1812, Campbell to Harrison, 25 Dec. 1812, in Harrison, *Messages,* 2:211, 253-65; Lossing, *Field Book,* pp. 346-48; Cruikshank, "H & P," pp. 145-46; *Pittsburgh Gazette,* 22 Jan. 1813, Morrison to Clay, 24 Dec. 1812, M222R6; Niebaum, "Pittsburgh Blues."

28. Wadsworth to SW, 20 Nov. 1812, in WRHS, tract 12, p. 3.

29. Benton, "Northern Ohio," pp. 29-107; Adams, *History,* bk. 6, pp. 96-97; Darnell, *Journal,* p. 34.

30. McAfee, *History,* pp. 138-45; Brown, *Views,* pp. 43, 109, 111; *Harrison and the War,* pp. 141-42; Lindley, "Captain Cushing."

31. Brown, *Views,* p. 111.

The Niagara Theater

1. SW to Tompkins, 24 March 1812, M6R5; Brant, *Madison,* p. 44; "General Orders," 23 June 1812, Tompkins, *Public Papers,* 1:13, 14.

2. SW to Tompkins, 3 Feb. 1812, WOLS; Hitsman, *Incredible,* p. 51.

3. "General Orders," 13 July 1812, Tompkins, *Public Papers,* 1:270; Van Rensselaer, *Narrative,* p. 10.

4. Dearborn to SW, 29 Aug. 1812, WOLR/D141(6); to Prevost, 26 Aug. 1812, MPHC, 15:136; Prevost to Bathurst, 24 Aug. 1812, in Hitsman, *Incredible,* p. 38.

5. Brock to Prevost, 7 Sept. 1812, PAC/C677/66-67; to brother, 18 Sept. 1812, in Coffin, *1812,* p. 54.

6. Dearborn to SW, 14 Sept. 1812, M221R43; Brant, *Madison,* p. 89; Adams, *History,* bk. 6, p. 30; Van Rensselaer to Smyth, 30 Sept. 1812, in Van Rensselaer, *Narrative,* appendix p. 67.

7. Adams, *History,* bk. 6, pp. 29-30; Lossing, *Field Book,* p. 390; Wadsworth to . . . 26 Aug. 1812, M221R43.

8. Brant, *Madison,* p. 89; Van Rensselaer, *Narrative,* p. 20.

9. Lossing, *Field Book,* pp. 392-94.

10. Van Rensselaer to Dearborn, 14 Oct. 1812, Chrystie to AG, 22 Dec. 1812, in Armstrong, *Notices,* 1:254-58, 207-12.

11. Lossing, *Field Book,* pp. 394-96.

12. Ibid., pp. 397-99; Van Rensselaer, *Narrative,* pp. 24-30.

13. Lossing, *Field Book,* pp. 399-501; Scott to SW, 29 Dec. 1812, M221R57/S64.

14. Scott to SW, just cited; Meade to Tompkins, 9 Nov. 1812, Tompkins, "Letters," p. 70; Armstrong, *Notices,* 1:106, 253.

15. Scott to SW, 29 Dec. 1812, M221R57/S64; Lucas, *Canadian War*, p. 52; Lossing, *Field Book*, pp. 400–403; CO/42/148/17–19.

16. Dearborn to SW, 21 Oct. 1812, M221R43/D209(6); "Apology of Smyth," M221R57/S228.

17. IG Report, 5 Oct. 1812, Livingston to Smyth, 4 Nov. 1812, Parker to Smyth, 30 Oct. 1812, Smyth to SW, 20 Oct. 1812, ASPMA, 1:492, 496, 495, 493.

18. Smyth to SW, just cited.

19. Dearborn to Smyth, 31 Oct., 28 Oct. 1812, to Van Rensselaer, 13 Oct. 1812, M221R52/D109(6), D29(7); Smyth to SW, 9 Nov. 1812, ASPMA, 1:497; Clarke, *Militia of Pa.*, 1:187; Read to Governor of Pa., 12 June 1812, "General Order," 5 Sept. 1812, Snyder Papers; Tannehill.

20. Smyth, "Proclamation," 10 Nov. 1812, CO/42/148/112.

21. "Reply to Smyth's Proclamation," ibid.; SW to Smyth, 25 Nov. 1812, M6R6/236.

22. Lucas, *Canadian War*, p. 57; Myers to Sheaffe, 22 Oct. 1812, PAC/C277/200–201; *Niles' Register*, 3:250.

23. Smyth to Tannehill, 21 Nov. 1812, vice versa, 22 Nov. 1812, in *Niles' Register*, 4:249.

24. Smyth to Dearborn, 4 Dec. 1812, in *Niles' Register*, 3:283–85; Sheaffe to Prevost, 23 Nov. 1812, CO/42/354/5; Winder to Smyth, 7 Dec. 1812, M222R6; Bisshop to Sheaffe, 1 Dec. 1812, CO/42/148/105.

25. These sources apply to this and the next paragraph: Smyth to New York Committee, 4 Dec. 1812, Brannan, *Letters*, p. 97; Lossing, *Field Book*, pp. 430–31; "General Orders," 24 Nov. 1812, Tannehill; Smyth to Dearborn, 4 Dec. 1812, in *Niles' Register*, 3:283.

26. "Roster," n.d., ADC to Smyth, 8 Dec. 1812, ASPMA, 1:499, 507; Tannehill, 2 Dec. 1812.

27. Smyth to New York Committee, 4 Dec. 1812, Porter to Public, 14 Dec. 1812, Brannan, *Letters*, pp. 97, 105–9; Lossing, *Field Book*, p. 432; "Apology of Smyth," M221R57/S228; McMaster, *History*, 4:16; SW to Dearborn, 19 Dec. 1812, M6R6/254; Prevost to Sheaffe, 1 Jan. 1813, PAC/C1220/84.

The Great Lakes and the St. Lawrence River

1. Prevost to Liverpool, 14 April 1812, PAC/C1218/207; Grey to . . . 29 Jan. 1812, MPHC, 15:73.

2. Mahan, *Sea Power, 1812*, 1:362; *DAB*; Chauncey to SN, 24 Sept., 21 Oct., 5 Nov. 1812, M125R25/75, 106, 137, 162; to Dearborn, 1 Nov. 1812, WOLR/D227(6); to SN, 11 June 1812, Woolsey to Chauncey, 7 Sept. 1812, M222R5; Chauncey to SN, 8 Dec. 1812, M125R33/31.

3. *Niles' Register*, 4:159; Mahan, *Sea Power, 1812*, 1:362; Prevost to Liverpool, 14 April 1812, PAC/C1218/207.

4. Lossing, *Field Book*, pp. 367–69.

5. Stacey, "Chauncey's Attack," p. 127; Lossing, *Field Book*, pp. 369–70; Prevost to Bathurst, 26 Oct. 1812, CO/42/148/3, 12, 13.

6. Stacey, "Ships," pp. 317–18; Chauncey to SN, 8 Dec. 1812, M125R33/31.

7. Chauncey to SN, 4 Nov., 6 Nov. 1812, M125R25/164, 167.

8. Lossing, *Field Book*, pp. 371–72; Chauncey to SN, 13 Nov. 1812, in *Niles' Register*, 3:206; Vincent to Sheaffe, 11 Nov. 1812, PAC/C228/80; Hitsman, "Alarm," pp. 129–30.

9. Hitsman, "Alarm," p. 132; Chauncey to SN, 17 Nov., 9 Dec. 1812, Specifications for *Madison*, M125R25/183, 210, 192; Mahan, *Sea Power, 1812*, 1:362, 366, 2:59.

10. Same sources as note 9; Grey to Prevost, 3 Dec. 1812, vice versa, 19 Dec. 1812, in MPHC, 15:191–92, 201.

11. Prevost to Grey, just cited; to Sheaffe, 3 Dec. 1812, PAC/C1220/47; to Bathurst, 21 Nov. 1812, CO/42/148/51.

12. Woolsey to Chauncey, 7 Sept. 1812, M222R5; Coffin, *1812*, p. 55; . . . to Prevost, 11 Oct. 1812, in MPHC, 15:164–65; Mahan, *Sea Power, 1812*, 1:354.

13. Mahan, *Sea Power, 1812*, 1:375, 377; Chauncey to SN, 8 Oct. 1812, Elliott to Chauncey, 14 Sept. 1812, M125R25.

14. Prevost to Warren, 31 Dec. 1812, Warren Papers.

15. These sources apply to this and the next paragraph: Christie, *Military*, pp. 79–81; Hitsman, *Incredible*, pp. 96, 99; Lossing, *Field Book*, pp. 372, 374.

16. These sources apply to this and the next paragraph: Hitsman, *Incredible*, p. 98; Brown to Tompkins, 1 Sept., 10 Sept., 1 Oct., 11 Oct. 1812, Tompkins, "Letters," pp. 17, 131, 63.

17. Dearborn to Tompkins, 21 Aug. 1812, Tompkins, "Letters," to SW, 29 Aug. 1812, M221R43; *Niles' Register*, 2:383; Chauncey to SN, 12 Sept. 1812, M125R25/40; Tompkins to SW, 20 June 1812, WOLR/T109(6).

18. SN to Macdonough, 28 Sept. 1812, M149R10/165; SW to Dearborn, 28 Sept. 1812, M6R6/172; vice versa, 16 Oct. 1812, M221R43.

19. Lossing, *Field Book*, pp. 375–76; "General Orders," 27 Nov. 1812, CO/42/148/67.

20. Dearborn to SW, 8 Nov. 1812, M221R43/D227(6).

21. Same, 24 Nov. 1812, M221R43/D254(6); Hitsman, *Incredible*, p. 102.

22. Hitsman, *Incredible*, p. 102; Lossing, *Field Book*, p. 369.

23. Dearborn to SW, 11 Dec. 1812, M221R43/D262(6).

The Nations at War

1. Prevost to Bathurst, 24 Sept. 1812, PAC/C1219/38; CO/42/147/79; McMaster, *History*, 4:1–3; *Niles' Register*, 2:395, 3:356.

2. Allen to Warren, 7 Dec. 1812, Warren Papers; Mahan, *Sea Power, 1812*, 1:290.

3. Prevost to Bathurst, 5 Nov. 1812, CO/42/148/7; same, 28 Nov. 1812, CO/42/148/61; vice versa, 9 Dec. 1812, CO/42/147/239.

4. Beckwith to Warren, 22 Nov. 1812, Adm/1/503/51; Croker to War Dept., 18 Dec. 1812, Adm/2/1375/320–24.

5. James, *Naval History*, 6:29; Wellington, *Supp. Des.*, 13:10; *Naval Chronicle*, 29:32; *Naval Chronology*, 3:217–18.

6. McMaster, *History*, 4:193–201; Barlow, "Congress," pp. 8, 9, 21.

7. Barlow, "Congress," p. 203; Brant, *Madison*, pp. 96–113.

8. Brant, *Madison*, p. 107.

9. Adams, *History*, bk. 6, pp. 418 ff.; McMaster, *History*, 4:201; Barlow, "Congress," p. 39.

10. Barlow, "Congress," p. 147; Monroe to House and Senate Military Committees, 23 Dec. 1812, *War Office Reports to Congress*, 1:245; USSL, 2:788.

11. AC, 12 Cong., 2 sess., 25:459, 474, 538, 628, 637.

12. Acts of 6 July, 12 Dec. 1812, USSL, 2:785, 788.

13. AC, 12 Cong., 2 sess., 25:498.

14. Brant, *Madison*, p. 133; *Niles' Register*, 3:306–9; AC, 12 Cong., 2 sess., 25:922.

15. Examples: Georgia, Act of 7 Dec. 1812, Lamar, *Compilation*, p. 439; New Hampshire, Act of 17 Dec. 1812, N.H., *Public Acts*, 1812; Pennsylvania, Act of 10 Dec. 1812, Pa., *SL*, vol. 18; North Carolina, N.C., *Laws*, ch. 1.

16. Adams, *History*, bk. 6, pp. 38, 166.

17. Tucker, *Poltroons*, p. 274; Brant, *Madison*, pp. 127, 128, 315.

18. Brant, *Madison*, p. 166; "Register, United States Army," 27 Dec. 1813, ASPMA, 1:384–425; Davie to SW, 4 April 1813, M221R521/D101(7).

19. "Register, U.S. Army," just cited.
20. "General Orders," 19 March 1813, in *Niles' Register*, 4:65.
21. Armstrong to SW, 2 Jan. 1812, in Armstrong, *Notices*, 1:234–41.
22. *DAB*; White, *Jeffersonians*, pp. 271–72; Eckert, "Jones," passim.
23. SN to Smith, 21 March 1813, to Dent, 9 April 1813, to Lewis, 23 April 1813, to Perry, 18 Aug. 1813, to Barney, 15 Sept. 1813, M149R10/314, 316, 342, 368, M149R11/54, 55, 86; Eckert, "Jones," p. 47.
24. *Times* (London), 9 Feb. 1813, quoted in Tucker, *Poltroons*, p. 275.

Riverine Warfare and Blockade

1. "Declaration of His Majesty's Government," 9 Jan. 1813, *Naval Chronicle*, 29:141–49.
2. *Buffalo Gazette*, in Cruikshank, *Doc. Hist.*, *Niagara*, 5:122; Tucker, *Poltroons*, p. 287.
3. James, *Naval History*, 6:29; *Naval Chronology*, 3:217–18; Croker to Warren, 9 Jan. 1813, Adm/2/1375/365; *Naval Chronicle*, 29:32.
4. *Naval Chronicle*, 30:204; Croker to Warren, 26 March, 28 April 1813, Adm/2/1376/179, 231; vice versa, 13 Nov. 1813, Warren, "Proclamation," 16 Nov. 1813, Capel to Warren, 11 May 1813, Adm/1/504/278, 351, 87; *Annual Register*, 1813, p. 38.
5. Croker to Warren, 25 May, 19 June 1813, Adm/2/1377/21–22, 88 (see also pp. 159, 163–64, 167); Warren to Melville, 22 July 1813, Warren Papers.
6. Cockburn to Warren, 6 June 1813, Adm/1/504/16; *Niles' Register*, 4:144, 325, 5:6, 27, 28; *Naval Chronicle*, 30:348; James, *Naval History*, 6:348; Scott, *Recollections*, 3:173–74; Lossing, *Field Book*, pp. 692–93.
7. Cockburn Papers, no. 43; "Naval Recollections," in *United Services Journal*, 1841, pt. 1, p. 456; Marine, *Invasion*, p. 23.
8. Burdett to Warren, 9 Feb. 1813, Cockburn Papers, no. 38.
9. Gordon to SN, 13 March, 15 April, 2 May 1813, M125R27, M149R10, M125R28.
10. Gordon to SN, 13 March 1813, M125R27; Winder to President, 26 April 1813, in Marine, *Invasion*, p. 30; Smith to SW, 6 May 1813, M221R57/S172; Wadsworth to SW, 26 April 1813, M221R58/W153; Warren to Croker, 28 May 1813, Adm 1/503/278–79.
11. Cockburn to Burnett, 5 March 1813, Cockburn Papers, no. 43; Scott, *Recollections*, 3:78, 80, 82, 84, 85, 87, 88, 92; Warren to Croker, 28 May 1813, Adm/1/503/278–79.
12. Cockburn to Beresford, 7 March 1813, Cockburn Papers, no. 43; Haslet to SW, 24 March 1813, M221R53/H70; Tucker, *Poltroons*, p. 288; *Niles' Register*, 4:118; McMaster, *History*, 4:123.
13. SN to Murray, 22 March 1813, to Kennedy, 29 March 1813, M149R10/318, 325.
14. Warren to Melville, 19 March 1813, Warren Papers; to Croker, 20 April 1813, Adm/1/503/239; Scott, *Recollections*, 3:97; Cockburn to Warren, 29 April 1813, Adm/1/503/328–30; Warren to Croker, 28 May 1813, Adm/1/503/278–79.
15. Scott, *Recollections*, 3:100–102, 135–36; *Niles' Register*, 4:182–83; Tucker, *Poltroons*, pp. 292–93; Marine, *Invasion*, p. 30; James, *Naval History*, 6:330; Cockburn to Warren, 29 April 1813, Adm/1/503/331–34.
16. Bathurst to Beckwith, 18 March 1813, CO/43/23/97–111.
17. Stewart to SN, 13 May 1813, M125R28/S26; Warren to Prevost, 7 June 1813, PAC/C679/43.
18. "Cockburn Memo," 11 June 1813, Lumley to Cockburn, 12 June 1813, Hickey to Cockburn, 15 June 1813, Cockburn Papers, no. 43.
19. Same sources as note 18; Taylor to SW, 20 June 1813, M221R57/T95;

Scott, *Recollections*, 3:137–39; Cassin to SN, 21 June 1813, in *Niles' Register*, 4:291.

20. Cockburn to Warren, 29 April 1813, Adm/1/503/335–39; Scott, *Recollections*, 3:112–13, 115, 149n.

21. Taylor to SW, 17 March 1813, M221R57/T48.

22. These sources apply to this and the next 2 paragraphs: Taylor to SW, 18 June, 19 June, 23 June 1813, Sawyer to SW, 27 June 1813, M221R57/T93, T91, T101, S255; Warren to Cockburn, 21 June 1813, Cockburn Papers, no. 38; Warren to Croker, 24 June 1813, Adm/1/503/371; to Melville, 23 June 1813, Warren Papers; Cassin to SN, 23 June 1813, Beatty to Taylor, 25 June 1813, in *Niles' Register*, 4:292, 324; Scott, *Recollections*, 3:141–42.

23. Crutchfield to SW, 25 June 1813, M221R57/T107; Lossing, *Field Book*, pp. 681–84; *Niles' Register*, 4:309; James, *Naval History*, 6:339.

24. James, *Naval History*, 6:342; Warren to Cockburn, 30 June 1813, Cockburn to Napier, 12 July 1813, Cockburn Papers, no. 38; Cockburn to Warren, 12 July 1813, Adm/1/504/11–12; Blount to SW, 19 July 1813, M221R50/B271.

25. Lloyd to Warren, 14 July 1813, Rattray to Warren, 14 July 1813, Warren to Croker, 29 July 1813, Adm/1/504/31, 36.

26. Morrison to SN, 18 July 1813, M125R30; vice versa, 12 Aug. 1813, M149R11/47; Marine, *Invasion*, pp. 55–57.

27. Warren to Croker, 14 Aug., 23 Aug. 1813, Adm/1/504/70–71; to Melville, 24 Aug., 16 Sept. 1813, Warren Papers; Byron, *War of 1812*, p. 31.

28. Warren to Prevost, 21 Sept. 1813, PAC/C680/97; to Melville, 24 Aug. 1813, Warren Papers; Parker to Barbour, 21 Aug. 1813, M221R50/B303; Evans to Cockburn, 1 Oct. 1813, Cockburn Papers, no. 38.

29. Warren to Cockburn, 30 Aug. 1813, Cockburn Papers, no. 38, pp. 194–95.

30. Mahan, *Sea Power, 1812*, 2:21; Hitsman, *Incredible*, p. 141; Adams, *War of 1812*, p. 129.

Naval Actions on the Oceans

1. These sources apply to this and the next paragraph: Wright to . . . 26 March 1813, Adm/1/503/245; Lawrence to SN, 19 March 1813, M125R27; Roosevelt, *Naval History*, pp. 141–43; Mahan, *Sea Power, 1812*, 2:9; James, *Naval History*, 6:279.

2. These sources apply to this and the next 2 paragraphs: Broke to Lawrence, n.d. 1813, Bainbridge to SN, 3 June 1813, Budd to SN, 15 June 1813, M125R29; Broke to Capel, 6 June 1813, Adm/1/503/322; *Niles' Register*, 5:5, 29, 57; James, *Naval History*, 6:285–99; James, *Occurrences*, pp. lix, lxi, 215–32; *Naval Chronicle*, 33:1–20.

3. Purcell, "Ship," pp. 83–94.

4. Gordon to Pickell, 25 May 1813, Pigot to Hardy, 29 April 1813, Adm/1/503/304, 314; Coggeshall, *Privateers*, pp. 106–8.

5. Coote to Oliver, 22 Oct. 1813, Adm/1/504/342; *Niles' Register*, 4:308.

6. *Niles' Register*, 5:14; Coggeshall, *Privateers*, pp. 172–77.

7. Shead to Angus, 6 Aug. 1813, in *Niles' Register*, 4:423; James, *Naval History*, 6:343–45.

8. James, *Naval History*, 6:320; Watson to SN, 2 March 1815, in James, *Occurrences*, pp. lxvi, lxix; Roosevelt, *Naval War*, pp. 169–71.

9. These sources apply to this and the next paragraph: James, *Naval History*, 6:317–18; McCreery to Gordon, 6 Sept. 1813, Adm/1/504/152; McCall to SN, 7 Sept. 1813, Tillinghast to Hull, 9 Sept. 1813, M125R31; Albion, *Sea Lanes*, p. 117.

10. Warren to Croker, 22 Feb. 1813, Adm/1/503/134.

11. Same, 20 Nov., 30 Dec. 1813, Adm/1/504/279, Adm/1/505/44–45, 49.

12. Bainbridge to SN, 22 June, 15 Dec. 1813, M125R29, M125R33; Morris

to SN, 23 May 1813, M125R28; SN to Stewart, 3 June 1813, M145R10/454; Hitsman, *Incredible,* p. 217; Lossing, *Field Book,* p. 616.

13. SN to Lewis, 16 May 1813, to Bainbridge, 1 Aug. 1813, to Ridgely, 31 Aug. 1813, M149R10/420, M149R11/32, 50, 70; Tingey to SN, 20 Feb. 1813, M125R26/97; Wadsworth to SW, 13 Nov. 1812, 2 Jan., 7 Jan. 1813, M221R8/W337(6), M221R58/W39.

The River Raisin

1. These sources apply to this and the next paragraph: Harrison to SW, 4 Jan., 6 Jan. 1813, M221R53/H13, Harrison, *Messages,* 2:300–305.

2. Monroe to Harrison, 17 Jan. 1813, M6R6/269.

3. Tucker, *Poltroons,* pp. 228–31; Harrison to SW, 20 Jan. 1813, Lewis to Winchester, 20 Jan. 1813, in Harrison, *Messages,* 2:316, 319–24; Darnell, *Journal,* p. 45.

4. Darnell, *Journal,* pp. 50–56, 64–66; Armstrong, *Notices,* 1:197–99; Cruikshank, "H & P," pp. 152–64; Kingsford, *History,* 8:300; McClanahan to Harrison, 26 Jan. 1813, in Harrison, *Messages,* 2:338–41: Procter to Sheaffe, 25 Jan. 1813, CO/42/354/20–22, 51–53; Winchester to SW, 23 Jan., 11 Feb. 1813, M221R58/W58, W67; Hitsman, *Incredible,* p. 114; "Squire Reynolds' Narrative," in Coffin, *1812,* pp. 203–6; Cleaves, *Old Tippecanoe,* pp. 142–44; Dudley, "Battle," pp. 1–4; Woodward to Monroe, 31 Jan. 1813, in MPHC, 15:234.

5. Procter to Sheaffe, 1 Feb. 1813, PAC/C678/61–63.

6. Richard to John Gano, n.d., "Gano Papers," p. 34.

7. These sources apply to this and the next paragraph: Harrison to Meigs, 24 Jan., 26 Jan. 1813, Harrison, *Messages,* 2:329–31, 335–38; Cleaves, *Old Tippecanoe,* pp. 151–52.

8. Prevost to Bathurst, 16 Jan. 1813, PAC/C1270/111; Hitsman, *Incredible,* p. 108; Kingsford, *History,* 8:286.

9. Harrison to SW, 11 Feb. 1813, Harrison, *Messages,* 2:356–60; McAfee, *History,* p. 266.

10. McAfee, *History,* p. 277.

11. Items on life at Fort Meigs are drawn mostly from Lindley, "Captain Cushing."

12. SW to Harrison, 5 March, 17 March 1813, vice versa, 17 March 1813, in Harrison, *Messages,* 2:378–80, 386, 387–92.

13. Harrison to SW, 16 Feb. 1813, *TP: Indiana,* 8:237; SW to Howard, 10 April 1813, M6R6/359.

14. SW to Dearborn, 6 Feb. 1813, WOLS; SW to Harrison, 5 March 1813, vice versa, 17 March 1813, in Harrison, *Messages,* 2:378–80, 387–92.

15. SW to Harrison, 3 April, 4 April 1813, M6R6/360–61; Armstrong, *Notices,* 1:245–48.

16. Act of 20 Jan. 1813, USSL, 2:791; Upton, *Military Policy,* p. 105; SW to Harrison, 3 April 1813, M6R6/360–61; AG to Baldwin, 9 March 1813, AGLS.

17. Freer to Johnson, 14 Jan. 1813, PAC/C257/17; Prevost to Bathurst, 26 Jan. 1813, CO/42/150/9; "Register, U.S. Army," 27 Dec. 1813, ASPMA, 1:384–425.

18. Howard to SW, 3 Sept., 28 Oct. 1813, M221R53/H234, H267; Clark to SW, 12 Sept. 1813, M221R51/C232.

Lake Champlain

1. Prevost to Bathurst, 1 Aug. 1813, CO/42/151/95.

2. Taylor to Stovin, 3 June 1813, DeRottenburg to Glasgow, 5 June 1813, PAC/C679/50, 64; Prevost to Bathurst, 4 July 1813, CO/42/150/61; Mahan,

Sea Power, 1812, 2:358; Kingsford, *History,* 8:358; Horsman, *War of 1812,* p. 49.

3. DeRottenburg to Brinton, 9 June 1813, PAC/C679/71; Prevost to Bathurst, 18 July 1813, *HL Sess. Papers,* 4:291; Everard to Warren, 21 July 1813, Adm/1/504/160 ff.

4. SN to Macdonough, 17 June 1813, M149R10/469; Hampton to SW, 13 July 1813, M221R53/H186.

5. "Instructions to Col. Murray," 27 July 1813, PAC/C679/291; Hitsman, *Incredible,* pp. 144-45; *Niles' Register,* 4:388; Kingsford, *History,* 8:360; Coffin, *1812,* p. 190; Mooers to Tompkins, 8 Aug. 1813, Tompkins, "Letters," p. 107.

6. Everard to Prevost, 3 Aug. 1813, PAC/C679/340; Bankhead to SW, 2 Aug. 1813, M221R50/B281.

Lake Ontario

1. Armstrong to SW, 2 Jan. 1812, to Dearborn, 10 Feb., 24 Feb. 1813, in Armstrong, *Notices,* 1:234-41, 221-23; to Cabinet, 8 Feb. 1813, M6R6/461.

2. Chauncey to SN, 21 Feb., 18 March 1813, vice versa, 5 Feb. 1813, M125R26/99, M125R27/58, M149R10/245; Dearborn to SW, 3 March, 14 March 1813, M221R52/D68(7), D82(7).

3. Same sources as note 2.

4. SW to Dearborn, 29 March, 19 April 1813, M6R6/338, 439.

5. Same sources as note 4.

6. Croker to captains, 8 March 1813, to Goulborn, 9 March 1813, to Yeo, 19 March 1813, Adm/2/1376/182-83, 250-54, 259, 261, 283, CO/42/152/228; Hitsman, *Incredible,* p. 106.

7. *DNB;* Forester, *Fighting Sail,* p. 98; Cruikshank, "Contest, 1812-13," p. 182.

8. Forsyth to Dearborn, 8 Feb. 1813, M221R52/D45(7); Presser to DeRottenburg, 7 Feb. 1813, in Lossing, *Field Book,* p. 576.

9. Lossing, *Field Book,* p. 578; Macdonnell to Harvey, 22 Feb., 25 Feb. 1813, PAC/C678/95-96, 100-102; to Prevost, 23 Feb. 1813, in James, *Naval History,* 6:393-94; *Niles' Register,* 4:50; Hitsman, "Alarm," p. 135; Cruikshank, *Doc. Hist., Niagara,* 5:77; Hitsman, *Incredible,* pp. 119-20.

10. Hitsman, *Incredible,* pp. 119-20; Prevost to Bathurst, 27 Feb. 1813, PAC/C1220/197-202.

11. Dearborn to SW, 25 Feb. 1813, M221R52/D62(7); Brown to Tompkins, 1 March 1813, Tompkins, "Letters," p. 83.

12. SW to Dearborn, 10 March 1813, M6R6/314; Sheaffe to Bathurst, 5 April 1813, CO/42/354/95.

13. Vandeventer to SW, 15 March, 1 April, 5 April 1813, M221R58, M222R9; "Force on the Lakes," 24 July 1813, *HL Sess. Papers,* 4:295-97; Cruikshank, "Contest, 1812-13," p. 180.

14. Chauncey to SN, 24 April 1813, M125R28; *Niles' Register,* 4:304; Lossing, *Field Book,* p. 587; Tucker, *Poltroons,* pp. 243-44.

15. These sources apply to this and the next 4 paragraphs: Tucker, *Poltroons,* pp. 246-52; *Niles' Register,* 4:178-79, 225-26; Lossing, *Field Book,* pp. 586-90; Sheaffe to Prevost, 5 May 1813, PAC/C1219/39-41.

16. Dearborn to SW, 3 May 1813, M221R52/D144(7); Tucker, *Poltroons,* p. 252.

17. Lucas, *Canadian War,* p. 89; Stacey, "Another Look," p. 44; Hitsman, *Incredible,* p. 127.

18. Hitsman, *Incredible,* p. 124; Dearborn to SW, 11 Feb., 5 March 1814, M221R52/D200(7); Armstrong, *Notices,* 1:132; Cruikshank, *Doc. Hist., Niagara,* 5:192-206; Prevost to Sheaffe, 22 July 1813, PAC/C1221/106.

19. These sources apply to this and the next 2 paragraphs: Prevost to Torrens, 10 Feb. 1813, to Bathurst, 21 April, 26 May 1813, to Procter, 20 June 1813, to

York, 23 June 1813, PAC/C1220/169, 315–21, PAC/C1219/44–45, MPHC, 15: 319, PAC/C1220/408–10; "General Orders," 22 April 1813, Wood, *Documents,* 2:88; Hitsman, *Incredible,* pp. 137–38; Kingsford, *History,* 8:346–47.

20. These sources apply to this and the next paragraph: Chauncey to SN, 7 May, 11 May, 17 May, 28 May 1813, M125R28/101, 136, 148, 190; SW to Lewis, 10 March 1813, M6R6/319; Vincent to Sheaffe, 20 May 1813, to Prevost, 28 May 1813, Harvey to Baynes, 25 May 1813, "Casualty Report," Fowler to Baynes, 29 May 1813, PAC/C678/305, 318–21, 311–12, 339–41, 327–35; Cruikshank, "Fort George," pp. 19–28; *Niles' Register,* 4:239; Mills, *Perry,* pp. 64–67; Tucker, *Poltroons,* pp. 307–8; Coffin, *1812,* pp. 126 ff.

21. Bisshop to Vincent, 18 March 1813, PAC/C678/136–40.

22. Barclay to Freer, 9 May 1813, Wood, *Documents,* 2:115; Prevost to Bathurst, 18 May 1813, CO/42/150/157; Yeo to Croker, 26 May 1813, Cruikshank, *Doc. Hist., Niagara,* 5:244; Cruikshank, "Contest, 1812–13," p. 192.

23. These sources apply to this and the next 5 paragraphs: Baynes to Prevost, 30 May 1813, PAC/C678/347–53; Prevost to Bathurst, 1 June 1813, PAC/C1219/45–47; Brown to SW, 1 June 1813, M221R50/B204; Herkimer to SW, 1 July 1813, M222R8; Armstrong, *Notices,* 1:143–46; *Niles' Register,* 4:241–42; *Mil. and Naval Mag.,* 1:21; Coffin, *1812,* pp. 132–39; Fortescue, *History,* 9:316; Hitsman, "Prevost's Conduct," p. 40; Hitsman, *Incredible,* p. 132; Kingsford, *History,* 8:272–74.

24. These sources apply to this and the next 2 paragraphs: Kingsford, *History,* 8:276–86; Vincent to Baynes, 31 May 1813, to Prevost, 2 June, 6 June 1813, Prevost to Bathurst, 14 June 1813, PAC/C679/1, 38, 354, 27–34; Burn to Dearborn, n.d., WOLR/D135(7); Lossing, *Field Book,* pp. 603–5; Armstrong, *Notices,* 1:135–42; Coffin, *1812,* p. 142; Cruikshank, "Stoney Creek," pp. 4–19.

25. Evans to Harvey, 10 June 1813, PAC/C679/74–75.

26. Dearborn to SW, 8 June 1813, M221R52/D139(7); vice versa, 19 June 1813, M6R6/459–60.

27. Cruikshank, "Stoney Creek," pp. 20, 25; Boerstler to . . . 1 Jan. 1813, M221R50.

28. Vincent to Prevost, 6 June 1813, CO/42/151/21; Harvey to Baynes, 6 June 1813, PAC/C679/38–39.

29. Prevost to Vincent, 18 June 1813, PAC/C1221/153.

30. These sources apply to this and the next 4 paragraphs: Bisshop to Vincent, 24 June 1813, Boerstler to Dearborn, 25 June 1813, PAC/C679/130–34; Dearborn to SW, 25 June 1813, "Narrative of Major Chapin," in *Niles' Register,* 4:305–6, 373; Roach, "Journal," pp. 148–51; Cruikshank, "Stoney Creek," pp. 26–32; Cruikshank, "Beechwoods," pp. 6–30.

31. Chauncey to SN, 18 June, 24 June 1813, M125R29/77, 104; SN to Crane, 26 June 1813, M149R10/481.

32. Woolsey to Chauncey, 19 June 1813, Chauncey to SN, 24 June 1813, M125R29.

33. Bathurst to Prevost, 1 July 1813, PAC/C679/164–67; vice versa, 3 July 1813, CO/42/151/47; Cruikshank, "Contest, 1812–13," pp. 191–92; Hitsman, *Incredible,* p. 135.

34. SW to Lewis, 9 July 1813, M6R7/11; officers to Dearborn, 15 July 1813, in *Niles' Register,* 4:371; Brant, *Madison,* p. 203; Tucker, *Poltroons,* p. 413.

35. SW to Lewis, 9 July 1813, M6R7/11.

36. Porter to SW, 27 July 1813, M222R9.

37. Clark to Harvey, 5 July 1813, PAC/C679/187; Lossing, *Field Book,* p. 626; Cruikshank, "Stoney Creek," pp. 33–38.

38. DeRottenburg to Prevost, 9 July 1813, PAC/C679/210.

39. Ibid.; Clark to Harvey, 12 July 1813, PAC/C679/230–33; Cruikshank, "Stoney Creek," pp. 40–42; Lossing, *Field Book,* p. 627; Armstrong, *Notices,* 1:147.

40. Armstrong, *Notices*, 1:147; Prevost to Bathurst, 18 July 1813, PAC/
C1219/78–80; DeRottenburg to Prevost, 20 July 1813, PAC/C679/264.

41. Chauncey to SN, 12 June 1813, M125R29; *Niles' Register*, 4:374; Mahan,
Sea Power, 1812, 2:51–53.

42. Chauncey to SN, 4 Aug. 1813, in *Niles' Register*, 4:405; . . . to Prevost,
1 Aug. 1813, PAC/C679/309.

43. Boyd to SW, 27 July, 8 Aug. 1813, M221R50/B270, B287; Chauncey to
SN, 13 Aug., 19 Aug. 1813, M125R30; Yeo to Warren, 10 Aug. 1813, to
Prevost, 11 Aug. 1813, Adm/1/504/168; Cruikshank, *Doc. Hist., Niagara*, 7:7,
29; Cruikshank, "Contest, 1812–13," p. 200; Cruikshank, "Stoney Creek," pp.
49–61; Hitsman, *Incredible*, p. 146.

44. Yeo to Prevost, 11 Aug. 1813, Cruikshank, *Doc. Hist., Niagara*, 7:7;
Cruikshank, "Contest, 1812–13," p. 202.

45. Same sources as note 44.

46. Chauncey to SN, 13 Sept. 1813, M125R31/43; Hitsman, *Incredible*, pp.
148–49; Roosevelt, *Naval War*, p. 202.

47. Prevost to Bathurst, 25 Aug., 15 Sept., 22 Sept. 1813, to Yeo, 22 Sept.
1813, PAC/C1219/103–9, PAC/C1221/159, 162–63; DeRottenburg to Prevost,
5 Sept., 17 Sept. 1813, PAC/C680/22–24, 68; Cruikshank, "Stoney Creek," pp.
62–72; Kingsford, *History*, 8:345.

48. These sources apply to this and the next paragraph: Chauncey to SN,
25 Sept., 1 Oct. 1813, M125R31; Yeo to Warren, 29 Sept. 1813, Adm/1/504/
325; Prevost to Bathurst, 8 Oct. 1813, PAC/C1221/302; Cruikshank, "Contest,
1812–13," pp. 209–10; Cruikshank, "Stoney Creek," pp. 73–76; Roosevelt, *Naval
War*, p. 203; Mahan, *Sea Power, 1812*, 2:106–9.

49. These sources apply to this and the next paragraph: Chauncey to SN,
6 Oct., 8 Oct. 1813, M125R31/125, 147.

50. Prevost to Yeo, 12 Oct. 1813, PAC/C1221/182.

51. Chapelle, *Sailing Navy*, pp. 273, 302, 339, 274, 296.

Fort Meigs

1. Harrison to SW, 21 April 1813, vice versa, 27 April 1813, in Harrison,
Messages, 1:425, 428; Risch, *Quartermaster*, pp. 159–64, 172.

2. "Wood's Journal," pp. 371–72; Melish, *Atlas*, p. 10.

3. Shelby to SW, 21 Feb. 1813, to Harrison, 20 March, 27 March, 4 April
1813, M221R57/S78, H78, M221R53; Harrison, *Messages*, 2:398–99, 414.

4. These sources apply to this and the next 6 paragraphs: Harrison to SW,
5 May, 9 May, 13 May, 8 June 1813, in Harrison, *Messages*, 2:431, 442–47,
465–67; Clay to Harrison, 9 May 1813, in *Niles' Register*, 4:192–93; "Embarkation Return," Procter to Prevost, 14 May 1813, "Casualty Report," PAC/C678/
251–54, 262; Cleaves, *Old Tippecanoe*, pp. 171–72; Armstrong, *Notices*, 1:164;
Adams, *War of 1812*, pp. 59, 60, 69; Lossing, *Field Book*, pp. 482n, 484; McAfee,
History, p. 278.

5. Procter to McDouall, 19 June 1813, DeRottenburg to Procter, 1 July 1813,
PAC/C679/110, 218; Prevost to DeRottenburg, 23 July 1813, PAC/C1221/143.

6. McAfee, *History*, pp. 302, 313; Brown, *Views*, p. 56.

7. Gano to Van Horne, 17 Jan. 1813, "Gano Papers," 16:25.

8. Wingate to Gano, 30 Jan. 1813, Kisling to Gano, 2 Feb. 1813, Meigs to
Gano, 2 March 1813, Meek to Gano, 18 Jan., 21 Jan. 1813, "Gano Papers,"
16:38, 40, 55, 28, 29; McAfee, *History*, p. 275.

9. Procter to Prevost, 13 July 1813, PAC/C679/224–29.

10. Harrison to SW, 23 July 1813, M221R53/H196; Lossing, *Field Book*, p.
498.

11. Clay to Harrison, 28 July 1813, M221R53/H200; Jesup to SW, 15 July

1813, M222R81; Harrison to SW, 24 July 1813, to Croghan, 29 July, 30 July 1813, vice versa, 30 July 1813, in Harrison, *Messages*, 2:496, 502–3.

12. "Disembarkation Return," 1 Aug. 1813, PAC/C679(2)/370; Croghan to Harrison, 5 Aug. 1813, to Editor, *Liberty Hall*, 27 Aug. 1813, in Harrison, *Messages*, 2:514–16, 527–29; *Niles' Register*, 5:7–9; Cleaves, *Old Tippecanoe*, pp. 181–82; Lossing, *Field Book*, p. 502; Armstrong, *Notices*, 1:179–81.

13. Procter to Prevost, 9 Aug. 1813, DeRottenburg to Procter, 22 Aug. 1813, in MPHC, 15:347–49, 357; Prevost to Procter, 22 Aug. 1813, in Hitsman, *Incredible*, p. 151; Prevost to Bathurst, 25 Aug. 1813, CO/42/151/138.

14. Croghan to Editor, *Liberty Hall*, 27 Aug. 1813, in Harrison, *Messages*, 2:527–29.

Lake Erie

1. Chauncey to SN, 1 Jan. 1813, M125R26/1.
2. Same, 8 Jan. 1813, M125R26/13.
3. Same, 20 Jan., 4 Feb., 5 Feb. 1813, M125R26/25, 47, 50.
4. SN to Perry, 6 Oct. 1812, 8 Feb. 1813, M149R10/168, 248.
5. Burt, *US & GB*, p. 329; Dutton, *Perry*, pp. 1–72 passim.
6. Same sources as note 5; SN to Chauncey, 27 Jan. 1813, M149R10/231–32.
7. Freer to Myers, 22 April 1813, PAC/C1220/329–30; Barclay, "Court-Martial," in Paullin, *Erie*, pp. 155–58; Chauncey to SN, 29 May 1813, M125R28/196; Barclay to Yeo, 1 June, 16 June 1813, in *Anecdotes of Erie*, pp. 17, 22; to Vincent, 17 June 1813, Wood, *Documents*, 2:246.
8. These sources apply to this and the next paragraph: Barclay to Vincent, just cited; Vincent to Prevost, 18 July 1813, Procter to MacDonald, 4 July 1813, to Prevost, 11 July, 13 July 1813, DeRottenburg to Baynes, 22 July 1813, PAC/C679/107, 177–78, 220–23, 272–74; Prevost to Bathurst, 18 July 1813, *HL Sess. Papers*, 4:290–91; Barclay to Yeo, 10 July, 16 July 1813, in *Anecdotes of Erie*, pp. 23–26.
9. Chauncey to Perry, 14 July 1813, M125R29/194; Mahan, *Sea Power, 1812*, 2:64–66.
10. Barclay to Prevost, 16 July 1813, in *Anecdotes of Erie*, pp. 26–27; DeRottenburg to Baynes, 22 July 1813, PAC/C679(2)/272–74; Mahan, *Sea Power, 1812*, 2:63; Barclay, "Court-Martial," in Paullin, *Erie*, pp. 59–61.
11. Procter to Prevost, 18 Aug. 1813, PAC/C679(2)/447; Tucker, *Poltroons*, pp. 316–17; Forester, *Fighting Sail*, pp. 178–79; Mills, *Perry*, pp. 86–91; Dutton, *Perry*, pp. 86, 98, 103, 105.
12. These sources apply to this and the next 14 paragraphs: Procter to Prevost, 26 Aug. 1813, in MPHC, 15:360; Barclay to Yeo, 6 Oct., 12 Oct. 1813, Yeo to Warren, 10 Oct. 1813, "Usher Parsons' Accounts," in *Anecdotes of Erie*, pp. 37, 41–47, 53–54; Prevost to Yeo, 14 Sept., 16 Sept. 1813, to Bathurst, 8 Oct. 1813, PAC/C1221/159–61, 119–22; to Procter, 23 Sept. 1813, DeRottenburg to Prevost, 10 Sept. 1813, PAC/C680/112, 58; Inglis to Barclay, 10 Sept. 1813, CO/42/152/51–57; Yeo to Warren, 14 Nov. 1813, Adm/1/2737/n.p.; Perry to SN, 10 Sept. 1813, M125R31; to Harrison, 10 Sept. 1813, in Harrison, *Messages*, 2:539; "British Squadron on Erie," PAC/C679/200; Hitsman, *Incredible*, pp. 152–53; Dutton, *Perry*, pp. 105–72 passim; Mills, *Perry*, pp. 107–90 passim; Elliott, *Biographical*, pp. 28–190 passim; James, *Occurrences*, pp. 284–85, 292, 294 ff.; Forester, *Fighting Sail*, pp. 182–85; Mahan, *Sea Power, 1812*, 2:76–77; Elliott, "Court of Inquiry," Barclay, "Court-Martial," in Paullin, *Erie*, pp. 135–202; Adams, *War of 1812*, pp. 67–69; Ward, *Manual*, pp. 77–79.
13. Yeo to Warren, 10 Oct. 1813, in *Anecdotes of Erie*, pp. 46–47; Prevost to Procter, 23 Sept. 1813, PAC/C680/112.
14. Bathurst to Prevost, 5 Nov. 1813, *HL Sess. Papers*, 4:332; *Gentleman's Magazine*. Nov. 1813, p. 491.

15. Barclay, "Court-Martial," in Paullin, *Erie*, pp. 136–68.

16. SN to Perry, 18 April 1814, M149R11/287, 337–38; Dutton, *Perry*, p. 209.

17. Perry to Elliott, 18 June 1818, in *Documents in Relation*, pp. 22–23; vice versa, 7 July 1818, in *Elliott, Biographical*, pp. 207, 211, 213, 222.

The Northwest

1. Harrison to Shelby, 20 July, 12 Sept. 1813, vice versa, 8 Aug., 11 Aug. 1813, Harrison to SW, 11 Aug. 1813, in Harrison, *Messages*, 2:493, 539, 518–19, 521–23.

2. Handbill, in McAfee, *History*, pp. 363–64; Young, *Thames*, p. 31.

3. Shelby to Harrison, 8 Aug. 1813, in Harrison, *Messages*, 2:518–19; vice versa, 18 Aug. 1813, in McAfee, *History*, pp. 366–67.

4. "Gano Papers," 2 July 1813, 16:64; Harrison to Meigs, 8 Aug. 1813, in McAfee, *History*, pp. 356–57.

5. Harrison to Shelby, 12 Sept. 1813, in Harrison, *Messages*, 2:539.

6. McAfee, *History*, p. 414.

7. Procter to Sheaffe, 4 Feb. 1813, PAC/C678/70–73; to Prevost, 3 Sept. 1813, to DeRottenburg, 12 Sept. 1813, Harvey to Procter, 17 Sept. 1813, Glasgow to Freer, 10 Sept. 1813, PAC/C680/7, 71, 48, 75–77; "Proclamation," 13 Sept. 1813, Cruikshank, *Doc. Hist., Niagara*, 7:124; Prevost to Bathurst, 22 Sept. 1813, CO/42/151/154–55.

8. Perry to SN, 24 Sept. 1813, M125R31/81; "General Orders," 27 Sept. 1813, in Harrison, *Messages*, 2:546–48.

9. These sources apply to this and the next paragraph: DeRottenburg to Prevost, 28 Sept. 1813, PAC/C680/121; Harrison to SW, 9 Oct. 1813, M222R8; Coffin, *1812*, pp. 220–25; Fortescue, *History*, 9:335–36; Zaslow, *Border*, p. 116.

10. These sources apply to this and the next paragraph: McAfee, *History*, pp. 308, 313, 316–17; Coffin, *1812*, p. 236; Harrison to SW, 23 May, 9 July 1813, M221R53/H149, H179; to Johnson, 11 June 1813, vice versa, 9 July 1813, in Harrison, *Messages*, 2:468, 487.

11. These sources apply to this and the next 4 paragraphs: Harrison to SW, 9 Oct. 1813, Harrison, *Messages*, 2:558–65; Hall to Harvey, 5 Oct. 1813, PAC/C680/205; Coffin, *1812*, pp. 225–35; Cleaves, *Old Tippecanoe*, p. 199; Hitsman, *Incredible*, p. 155; Tucker, *Poltroons*, pp. 338, 343; Johnson to Armstrong, 22 Dec. 1834, in Armstrong, *Notices*, 1:232; McAfee, *History*, p. 429.

12. "General Orders," 24 Nov. 1813, CO/42/152/59.

13. Procter to DeRottenburg, 23 Oct., 16 Nov. 1813, PAC/C680/273–82, 259–60.

14. Procter to Drummond, 14 Jan. 1814, PAC/C680/302, "Court-Martial Record," 21 Dec. 1814, WO/91/513–17.

15. Fortescue, *History*, 9:335–36.

16. Young, *Thames*, p. 108.

17. McAfee, *History*, p. 433; Quaife, "Shelby's Army," p. 154.

18. Perry to SN, 18 Oct. 1813, M125R32/16.

19. Chauncey to Perry, 9 Oct., 13 Oct. 1813, M125R31/153, 168; Perry to SN, 18 Oct., 25 Oct. 1813, M125R32/16, 48; Dutton, *Perry*, pp. 209, 212.

20. Harrison to SW, 10 Oct. 1813, M221R53/H247–48.

21. Gano to Meigs, 10 Nov., 10 Dec. 1813, "Gano Papers," 16:98, 18:11.

22. Vincent to DeRottenburg, 11 Aug. 1813, DeRottenburg to Prevost, 14 Oct. 1813, PAC/C680/212, 235; Kingsford, *History*, 8:376.

23. Porter to Wilkinson, 17 Sept. 1813, Brannan, *Letters*, p. 194; Scott to Wilkinson, 11 Oct. 1813, ASPMA, 1:482.

24. Scott to Wilkinson, just cited; Lossing, *Field Book*, p. 632*n*.

25. Harrison to SW, 11 Nov. 1813, M221R53/H271; Chauncey to SN, 12 Nov., 21 Nov. 1813, M125R32/99, 114; Cleaves, *Old Tippecanoe*, pp. 209–10.

26. Cleaves, *Old Tippecanoe*, pp. 210–11; Harrison to SW, 21 Dec. 1813, M221R53/H274; vice versa, 8 Jan. 1814, M6R7.

27. Cleaves, *Old Tippecanoe*, pp. 216–23; Barlow, "Congress," pp. 84, 85; SW to McArthur, 28 May 1814, M6R7/210.

28. Zaslow, *Border*, pp. 230–32; Kingsford, *History*, 8:376–78, 445; Medcalf to Bostwick, 25 Dec. 1813, in MPHC, 15:458–59; Bostwick to . . . 14 Nov. 1813, PAC/C681/142.

29. SW to McClure, 27 Nov. 1813, vice versa, 13 Dec., 25 Dec. 1813, ASPMA, 1:486–87; McClure to Tompkins, 10 Dec. 1813, Tompkins, "Letters," p. 142; Murray to Vincent, 12 Dec. 1813, PAC/C681/217, 237.

30. Murray to Vincent, just cited; SW to CO, Fort George, 4 Oct. 1813, Cruikshank, *Doc. Hist., Niagara*, 7:193; McClure, *Causes*, p. 18; Tucker, *Poltroons*, p. 419.

31. Drummond to Prevost, 18 Dec. 1813, Frazer to Harvey, 22 Dec. 1813, PAC/C681/240–43, 303; SW to Wilkinson, 1 Jan., 6 Jan. 1814, M6R7.

32. Murray to Drummond, 19 Dec. 1813, PAC/C681/249–51; Cruikshank, "Drummond," pp. 18–22; McClure, *Causes*, p. 25.

33. McClure to Tompkins, 21 Dec. 1813, Tompkins, "Letters," p. 144; to SW, 25 Dec. 1813, ASPMA, 1:487.

34. Hall to Tompkins, 6 Jan. 1814, Tompkins, "Letters," p. 148; Lossing, *Field Book*, p. 635.

35. Drummond to Riall, 29 Dec. 1813, PAC/C681/312–14; vice versa, 1 Jan. 1814, *Annual Register*, 1814, appendix pp. 146–47; Drummond to Prevost, 2 Jan. 1814, PAC/C1221/183–85; Hall to Tompkins, 6 Jan. 1814, Wadsworth to Tompkins, 6 Jan. 1814, Tompkins, "Letters," pp. 148, 151; Tompkins to SW, 2 Jan. 1814, M221R57/T194; Cass to SW, 12 Jan. 1814, M221R51/C303; Cruikshank, "Drummond," pp. 25–28; Lossing, *Field Book*, p. 632.

36. Same sources as note 35.

The Southeast

1. Shaw to SN, 3 Feb., 27 Oct. 1812, M125R23/88, 147; Hampton to Pike, 6 Feb. 1812, WOLR/H123.

2. Wilkinson to SW, 11 April, 18 May 1812, Madison to Wilkinson, 15 April 1812, SW to Hampton, 20 July 1811, M6R5/177, W98(6), W139; vice versa, 19 May 1812, WOLR.

3. Jacobs, *Wilkinson*, passim; *DAB*.

4. Wilkinson to SW, 11 April 1812, M221R49/W139.

5. Same, 13 July 1812, M222R6/W259; Claiborne to Monroe, 20 July 1812, Claiborne, *Letterbook*, 6:132.

6. Shaw to SN, 11 July, 4 Aug., 17 Aug. 1812, 18 Jan. 1813, M125R24; to Wilkinson, 11 Aug. 1812, M125R26/23; Wilkinson to Shaw, 7 Aug., 10 Aug., 18 Aug. 1812, M222R49.

7. Wilkinson to SW, 22 Aug. 1812, M222R49; Shaw to SN, 23 Aug. 1812, M125R24.

8. Wilkinson to SW, 1 Oct. 1812, M221R49.

9. Wilkinson to SW, 28 Aug. 1812, 17 Jan. 1813, M222R6, M221R58/W51.

10. Claiborne to Secretary of State, 24 Dec. 1810, Claiborne, *Letterbook*, 5:63.

11. Claiborne to Folch, 29 June 1811, to Maxent, 7 July 1811, ibid., 1:281, 284, 292; Claiborne to Gaines, 15 Aug. 1811, M6R5/335; Holmes to Wilkinson, 7 Sept. 1812, in *TP: Mississippi*, 6:321.

12. SW to Smith, 26 Jan. 1811, M6R5; Campbell to SN, 27 Feb., 21 March 1812, Mathews to Campbell, 14 March, 2 April 1812, M125R23/60, 83, 76; for the detailed story of the Patriot War see Patrick, *Fiasco*.

13. Monroe to Mathews, 4 April 1812, M222R6; SN to Campbell, 8 April

1812, M149R10/12; vice versa, 11 April, 25 April 1812, M125R23/147, 115.

14. Mitchell to Monroe, 17 July 1812, *State Papers*, 9:164–65; Campbell to SN, 27 June, 18 July 1812, M125R24/67, 121; Patrick, *Fiasco*, pp. 136 ff.

15. Patrick, *Fiasco*, pp. 195–210; Newnan to Mitchell, 19 Oct. 1812, Brannan, *Letters*, p. 78.

16. Mitchell to Smith, 13 Oct. 1812, M222R6; Patrick, *Fiasco*, pp. 211, 220.

17. 7 March 1812, in Jackson, *Correspondence*, 1:220.

18. James, *Border Captain*, p. 152.

19. SW to Governor of Tennessee, 21 Oct. 1812, WOLS/6/205.

20. "Regimental Order," 19 Jan. 1813, Jackson Papers, p. 83.

21. Lossing, *Field Book*, p. 743.

22. Patrick, *Fiasco*, pp. 213, 218; Smith to . . . 14 Nov. 1812, M222R6.

23. SW to Pinckney, 27 Nov. 1812, M6R6/237; Campbell to SN, 26 Dec. 1812, 13 Feb. 1813, M125R25/221, M125R26.

24. Lossing, *Field Book*, pp. 742–43; Jackson to SW, 29 Nov. 1812, Blount to Jackson, 31 Dec. 1812, M222R5; Jackson to Wilkinson, 20 Feb. 1813, M222R8.

25. Wilkinson to SW, 19 Feb. 1813, M222R8/W63.

26. Cox, *West Florida*, p. 615; Adams, *War of 1812*, pp. 106–7.

27. Jackson to President, 15 March 1813, SW to Jackson, 22 March 1813, Jackson, *Correspondence*, 1:292, 300; Brant, *Madison*, p. 141; Armstrong to Jackson, 6 Feb. 1813, in Lossing, *Field Book*, p. 743.

28. Lossing, *Field Book*, p. 744.

29. Wilkinson to SW, 22 July, 1 Oct. 1812, M221R49.

30. "Minutes, Council of War," 28 Aug. 1812, M221R49; SW to Wilkinson, 26 Aug. 1812, M6R6/99.

31. Wilkinson to SW, 3 April, 16 April 1813, M221R58/W148; Shaw to SN, 19 April 1813, M125R28; *Niles' Register*, 4:224; Wilkinson, *Memoirs*, 1:507, 518, 521–22, 524.

32. Wilkinson, *Memoirs*, 1:524; Wilkinson to SW, 23 May 1813, M221R58/W176.

James Wilkinson

1. These sources apply to this and the next paragraph: SW to Wilkinson, 10 March 1813, M6R6/313; Shelby to Harrison, 4 April 1813, in Harrison, *Messages*, 2:413; Adams, *War of 1812*, p. 91; Brant, *Madison*, p. 168.

2. SW to Wilkinson, 27 May 1813, M6R6/443; vice versa, 6 July 1813, M221R58/W203.

3. SW to Tompkins, 13 July 1813, WOLS/7/14; SW to Wilkinson, 8 Aug., 9 Aug., 10 Aug. 1813, M6R7/59, 33; Hitsman, *Incredible*, p. 161.

4. Brant, *Madison*, pp. 219, 221–22, 226, 253; Tucker, *Poltroons*, p. 414.

5. *DAB*.

6. Hampton to SW, 22 Aug., 31 Aug., 7 Sept., 15 Sept. 1813, M222R8.

7. "Minutes, Council," 26 Aug. 1813, in Armstrong, *Notices*, 2:198–200; Wilkinson to SW, 30 Aug. 1813, Cruikshank, *Doc. Hist., Niagara*, 7:88–89.

8. SW to Wilkinson, 18 Sept., 22 Sept. 1813, vice versa, 20 Sept. 1813, Cruikshank, *Doc. Hist., Niagara*, 7:146, 151, 157; SW to Harrison, 22 Sept. 1813, M6R7/96; Armstrong, *Notices*, 2:31–39.

9. Armstrong, *Notices*, 2:203–5; SW to Wilkinson, 18 Sept. 1813, Cruikshank, *Doc. Hist., Niagara*, 7:146; vice versa, 20 Sept. 1813, M222R9.

10. "Armstrong Directive," 5 Oct. 1813, in Wilkinson, *Memoirs*, 3:193, 197, 355–56; Wilkinson to Chauncey, 9 Oct. 1813, vice versa, 9 Oct. 1813, Cruikshank, *Doc. Hist., Niagara*, 7:216; DeRottenburg to Prevost, 3 Oct. 1813, PAC/C680/137.

11. Wilkinson, *Memoirs*, 3:353–54, 366, 369.

12. "Order of Sailing," ibid., p. 138; Prevost to Yeo, 12 Oct. 1813, PAC/C1221/183.

13. Wilkinson to SW, 19 Oct. 1813, M222R9.

14. Chauncey to SN, 30 Oct. 1813, M125R32/63.

15. SW to Harrison, 3 Nov. 1813, M6R7/101, 98; Adams, *War of 1812*, pp. 91, 93, 96, 98.

16. Wilkinson to SW, 1 Nov. 1813, to Hampton, 6 Nov. 1813, M222R9.

17. Adams, *War of 1812*, pp. 96, 98; Brant, *Madison*, p. 253.

18. "General Orders," 18 Sept. 1813, in Tompkins, "Letters," p. 487; Hampton to SW, 25 Sept., 4 Oct. 1813, ASPMA, 1:459–60.

19. Hampton letters, just cited; Hampton to SW, 22 Sept. 1813, M221R53/H289; "Thayer Report," M221R57/T233.

20. These sources apply to this and the next paragraph: "Thayer Report," just cited; Prevost to Bathurst, 30 Oct. 1813, PAC/C1219/124–26; Hampton to SW, 1 Nov. 1813, M221R53/H292; Kingsford, *History*, 8:366–68; Wood, *Documents*, 2:401–10; Coffin, *1812*, pp. 247–64; Hitsman, *Incredible*, pp. 164–67; Zaslow, *Border*, p. 65.

21. SW to Swartwout, 16 Oct. 1813, in Wilkinson, *Memoirs*, 3:70–71 (the correct date appears to be 18 Oct., see M6R7/94).

22. Kingsford, *History*, 8:368.

23. Mulcaster to Yeo, 2 Nov. 1813, Adm/11/505/185; Wilkinson, *Memoirs*, 3:200–204; Lossing, *Field Book*, p. 648.

24. Lossing, *Field Book*, pp. 649–51; Wilkinson, *Memoirs*, 3:200–204, 233; Prevost to Bathurst, 15 Nov. 1813, PAC/C1219/135–40.

25. Chauncey to SN, 11 Nov. 1813, M125R32/93.

26. These sources apply to this and the next paragraph: Morrison to De-Rottenburg, 12 Nov. 1813, PAC/C681/62–64; "General Orders," 14 Nov. 1813, M222R8; Prevost to Bathurst, 15 Nov. 1813, PAC/C1219/135–40; Zaslow, *Border*, pp. 65–82; Hitsman, *Incredible*, pp. 168–70; Lossing, *Field Book*, pp. 651–53; Armstrong, *Notices*, 2:42.

27. Hampton to Wilkinson, 8 Nov. 1813, M222R8/H282; to SW, 12 Nov. 1813, M221R53.

28. Wilkinson to SW, 12 Nov. 1813, M222R9.

29. Wilkinson to SW, 15 Nov. 1813, M222R9; Lossing, *Field Book*, p. 657.

30. Bull to SW, 17 Nov., 7 Dec. 1813, M221R50/B353, M221R51/B430; Wilkinson to Hampton, 17 Nov. 1813, M222R9/W251; vice versa, 20 Nov. 1813, M221R58; Armstrong, *Notices*, 2:44.

31. Hampton to SW, 1 Nov., 31 Dec. 1813, M222R8; Izard to Wilkinson, 3 Dec. 1813, M222R9.

32. Wilkinson to SW, 24 Nov., 26 Nov. 1813, M221R58, M222R9; SW to Hampton, 5 Jan., 19 Jan. 1814, M6R7/112, 141; Wilkinson, *Memoirs*, 3:196.

33. Lewis to SW, 5 July 1813, M222R8.

34. Wilkinson to SW, 7 Dec. 1813, M221R58/W259.

35. Same, 24 Dec., 26 Dec. 1813, M222R9.

36. Mulcaster to Prevost, 2 Dec. 1813, PAC/C681/188–91; Prevost to Bathurst, 12 March 1814, PAC/C1219/194–96; SW to Wilkinson, 20 Jan. 1814, M6R7/111; vice versa, 12 Feb. 1814, M221R58/W302.

37. These sources apply to this and the next 2 paragraphs: Wilkinson to SW, 25 March, 31 March 1814, M221R58/W329; *Niles' Register*, 6:131; Wilkinson, *Memoirs*, 3:172–84; Prevost to Bathurst, 31 March 1814, PAC/C1219/201–2; Kingsford, *History*, 8:439–42.

38. These sources apply to this and the next paragraph: SW to Wilkinson, 24 March 1814, M6R7/147; vice versa, 5 March, 12 March 1814, M221R58/W337, W344; Wood to SW, 6 April 1814, M221R58; Wilkinson, *Memoirs*, 3:2, 16–19, 40, 55 ff., 612, 605, 618, 644, 646; Tucker, *Poltroons*, p. 417.

The Nations at War

1. SW to Burbeck, 18 July 1813, WOLS.
2. Act of 16 June 1813, "Message," 27 Jan. 1813, AG to Governor, 20 April, 21 April 1813, to Major General, Maine District, 25 April 1813, to Irish, 3 May 1813, Mass., "AG Letterbook A."
3. AG to Atherton, 1 Dec. 1813, Mass., "AG Letterbook B."
4. Hemenway, *Vermont*, s.v. "Chittenden, Martin"; "Proclamation," 10 Nov. 1813, . . . to Chittenden, n.d., Brannan, *Letters*, pp. 261–62; Van de Water, *Champlain*, pp. 255–56.
5. Letters of Colonel Rees Hill, in Snyder Papers, vol. 53.
6. Niebaum, "Pittsburgh Blues," pp. 263–64.
7. *Sen. Doc. 100*, 16 Cong., 2 sess.
8. "Resolution," 29 May 1813, in Marine, *Invasion*, p. 30; Act of 18 Feb. 1813, Va., *Acts*, 1813; Dancy to AG, 16 July 1813, N.C., AG "Letterbook," 1811–13.
9. AG to Bell, 5 Oct. 1813, vice versa, n.d., AG to Pugh, 5 Oct. 1813, N.C., AG "Letterbook," 1811–13; N.C., "Militia Returns," 1813–17; Wallace, *South Carolina*, 2:390–91.
10. N.C. "Militia Papers"; "Orderly Book," Graham Papers.
11. "Commons' Reply to Regent," 5 Nov. 1813, HC, *Journal*, 1813–14, p. 8; Croker, *Key*, p. 18.
12. Scott, *Recollections*, 3:166, 185; *Gentleman's Magazine*, vol. 83, pt. 2, p. 491; *Naval Chronicle*, 30:225; Napier, *Journal*, p. 18.
13. Napier, *Journal*, pp. xv, 20.
14. Wellington to Bathurst, 10 Feb. 1813, Wellington, *Dispatches*, 10:108; Warren to Melville, 26 Oct. 1813, Warren Papers; to Liverpool, 16 Nov. 1813, Liverpool Papers, 38255; Mahon, "British Strategy."
15. Croker to Warren, 4 Nov. 1813, Adm/2/1378/146–49; Warren to Melville, 3 Feb. 1814, Warren Papers.
16. Baynes to DeRottenburg, 16 Sept. 1813, PAC/C1219/115–17; Prevost to Drummond, 19 Oct. 1813, vice versa, 18 Dec. 1813, Bathurst to Prevost, 5 Dec. 1813, PAC/C681/326, 240–43, 196–206; DeRottenburg to Freer, 26 Oct. 1813, PAC/C680/247; Hitsman, *Incredible*, p. 172.
17. Glasgow to . . . 26 Oct. 1813, PAC/C680/375; "Organization of the Army," PAC/C1221; Prevost to Bathurst, 30 Oct. 1813, CO/42/151/230.
18. Prevost to Yeo, 6 Oct. 1813, PAC/C1221/173–74.
19. Cooper, *Rough Notes*, pp. 145–49; Mitchell, "British Troops," pp. 85, 92; Scott, *Recollections*, 3:160.
20. Mitchell, "British Troops," pp. 85, 92.
21. "Albion" to Liverpool, 25 May 1813, Liverpool Papers, 38253; "Report of the Committee of the House of Representatives," in *Niles' Register*, 4:379; SW to Harrison, 29 Nov. 1813, in Harrison, *Messages*, 2:613–16; Mahan, *Sea Power, 1812*, 1:392.
22. These sources apply to this and the next paragraph: Lewis to Crutchfield, 23 May 1813, Warren to Melville, 6 July 1813, Warren Papers; McKeehan to Niles, 24 May 1813, in Harrison, *Messages*, 2:461; *Niles' Register*, 7:269; Scott, *Recollections*, 3:150–51, 155.
23. These sources apply to this and the next paragraph: Learned, "Gerry," pp. 94–97; Adams, *History*, bk. 7, p. 51; Brant, *Madison*, pp. 193, 197.
24. "General Orders," 29 July 1813, M149R11; Galpin, "Grain Trade," p. 40.
25. These sources apply to this and the next paragraph: Burt, *US & GB*, p. 346; Engelman, *Peace*, pp. 29, 42, 46, 55, 67, 81–82, 86; Brant, *Madison*, pp. 159–82.
26. Brant, *Madison*, p. 230; Mahan, *Sea Power, 1812*, 2:176; Adams, *History*, bk. 7, pp. 369–73; McMaster, *History*, 4:223–27.
27. These sources apply to this and the next paragraph: McMaster, *History*,

4:209; Gallatin to SW, 17 April 1813, M222R9; Adams, *History*, bk. 6, pp. 438, 443–44, 448; Nielson, *Financial History*, pp. 8 43–49.

28. Nielson, *Financial History*, pp. 28, 42, 45; Act of 2 Aug. 1813, in *Niles' Register*, 5:17–21; Adams, *History*, bk. 7, p. 53; McMaster, *History*, 4:216.

29. White, *Jeffersonians*, p. 237; Risch, *Quartermaster*, pp. 142–43, 146.

30. "Report of Clothes Issued," n.d. 1812, Irvine to SW, n.d. July 1813, M222R8.

31. Risch, *Quartermaster*, pp. 149–53.

32. Whitney to SW, 3 March 1813, M221R58/W68; Russell, *Guns*, pp. 151–57.

33. SN to Macdonough, 28 June 1813, M149R10.

34. Dent to SN, 16 Feb., 28 Aug. 1813, M124R26, M125R20.

The Creek War

1. Adams, *War of 1812*, pp. 110, 117; Swanton, *Early History*, p. 443.

2. Adams, *War of 1812*, pp. 114–15; *Niles' Register*, 4:135.

3. Simpson to SW, 14 May 1813, M221R57/S213; Halbert, *Creek War*, pp. 92, 127; Cotterill, *Southern Indians*, p. 177; Pound, *Hawkins*, p. 223.

4. Holmes to SW, 30 Aug. 1813, in *TP: Mississippi*, 6:396; Rowland, *Jackson*, p. 67; Lossing, *Field Book*, pp. 748–49.

5. Blackshear to Mitchell, 13 Aug. 1813, Blackshear, "Memoir," pp. 412–13; Claiborne to SW, 28 Aug. 1813, M221R51/C231; Halbert, *Creek War*, p. 267; Thomason, "Governor Early," p. 226.

6. These sources apply to this and the next 2 paragraphs: Claiborne to Flournoy, 3 Sept. 1813, M221R53/C238; Sewall to SW, 4 Sept. 1813, M221R57/S315; Lossing, *Field Book*, pp. 752–57.

7. Lossing, *Field Book*, pp. 761–72.

8. Owsley, "British Activities," pp. 114–15.

9. Adams, *War of 1812*, pp. 117–18.

10. Lossing, *Field Book*, p. 758; James, *Border Captain*, pp. 166–67.

11. James, *Border Captain*, pp. 166–67.

12. Ibid., p. 168; Armstrong, *Notices*, 2:51.

13. Jackson to Blount, 11 Nov. 1813, M221R50; James, *Border Captain*, p. 170.

14. Jackson to Mrs. Jackson, 9 Dec., 29 Dec. 1813, Jackson, "Letters," p. 113.

15. White to Cocke, 24 Nov. 1813, M221R51/C257; Halbert, *Creek War*, p. 271.

16. Coffee to Mrs. Coffee, 22 Dec. 1813, Coffee, "Letters," p. 178.

17. James, *Border Captain*, p. 176; Blount to Jackson, 22 Dec. 1813, M221R50.

18. Lossing, *Field Book*, pp. 769–70.

19. Ibid., p. 772; Claiborne to Blount, 1 Jan. 1814, M221R51/B407(7).

20. Lossing, *Field Book*, pp. 768–69; Adams, *War of 1812*, p. 121.

21. Jackson to Floyd, 27 Dec. 1813, M221R8.

22. Adams, *War of 1812*, p. 122.

23. James, *Border Captain*, pp. 176–78; Lossing, *Field Book*, p. 774; Coffee to Donelson, 28 Jan. 1814, Coffee, "Letters," p. 179.

24. Jackson to Pinckney, 29 Jan. 1814, Brannan, *Letters*, p. 299; James, *Border Captain*, p. 178.

25. Lossing, *Field Book*, pp. 776–77.

26. Adams, *History*, bk. 7, p. 252.

27. Jackson to Lewis, 21 Feb. 1814, in Parton, *Jackson*, 1:502.

28. Parton, *Jackson*, 1:505–7.

29. Lossing, *Field Book*, p. 777.

30. James, *Border Captain*, pp. 183–84; *Niles' Register*, 6:130–31.

31. Jackson to Blount, 28 April 1814, M221R51/B505; SW to Jackson, 24 May 1814, M6R7.

Naval Actions on the Oceans

1. *DNB*; Codrington to Mrs. Codrington, 12 Nov., 10 Dec. 1814, Codrington Papers.

2. Cochrane to Croker, 7 March, 31 March 1814, Adm/1/505/317, 419–20.

3. Same, 25 April, 28 April, 30 May 1814, Adm/1/506/26, 38, 246, 244; *Annual Register*, 1814, p. 179.

4. Cochrane to Croker, 26 May 1814, Cockburn Papers, no. 38.

5. Vice versa, 31 May 1814, Adm/2/1380/178; Mahan, *Sea Power, 1812*, 2:311–12.

6. Quoted in Albion, *Sea Lanes*, pp. 123–24.

7. Morris, *Autobiography*, pp. 60, 64; Morris to SN, 20 Sept. 1814, in *Niles' Register*, 6:267, 132, 150, 7:62–63; Griffith to Croker, 9 Sept. 1814, Adm/1/507/130, 133; SN to Decatur, 4 April 1814, to Stewart, 19 April 1814, to Bainbridge, 20 May 1814, M149R11/265, 392, 318.

8. These sources apply to this and the next paragraph: Porter to SN, 7 Sept. 1812, 2 July 1813, M125R25; same, 3 July 1814, in *Niles' Register*, 6:338–42; Porter, *Journal*, passim; Cochrane to Croker, 2 Sept. 1814, Adm/1/507/61; James, *Naval History*, 6:308–17; Forester, *Fighting Sail*, p. 212; Roosevelt, *Naval War*, p. 68.

9. Creighton to SN 9 March 1814, in *Niles' Register*, 6:69–70, 12; SN to Bainbridge, 7 Feb. 1814, M149R11/213; James, *Naval History*, 6:422.

10. James, *Naval History*, 6:527–30; SN to Rodgers, 26 Feb., 12 March 1814, M149R11/226, 238; Hayes to Hotham, 17 Jan. 1815, Adm/1/508/387–88; Forester, *Fighting Sail*, pp. 259–61.

11. Forester, *Fighting Sail*, pp. 257–58, 275–76; Collier to Griffith, 12 March 1815, Adm/1/509/252, 255; James, *Naval History*, 6:cxcvi.

12. James, *Naval History*, 6:424–26; Wales to Croker, 8 May 1814, Adm/1/506/564; *Niles' Register*, 2:411, 6:195–96.

13. Blakely to SN, 8 July, 11 Sept. 1814, in *Niles' Register*, 7:114, 174, 192; James, *Naval History*, 6:431–33.

14. SN to Rodgers, 16 April 1814, M149R11/279; *Niles' Register*, 6:267, 391; Chapelle, *Sailing Navy*; Croker to admirals, 25 Nov. 1814, Adm/2/1381/46.

15. SN to Senate, 22 Feb. 1814, "Report of the Senate Naval Committee," 28 Nov. 1814, in *Niles' Register*, 6:73–74, 7:221.

16. "Naval Report," 15 Nov. 1814, ibid., 7:211; Adams, *War of 1812*, pp. 150–52.

17. Adm/1/507/439, 449; Claiborne, *Letterbook*, 6:41n; Freer to Molson, 15 Dec. 1812, PAC/C1220/56.

18. Albion, *Sea Lanes*, pp. 32, 110, 115.

19. Smith to SW, 9 April 1814, M221R57/S465; Coote to Capel, 9 April 1814, Adm/1/506/274–76, 280; James, *Naval History*, 6:473.

20. Burdett to Capel, 30 May 1814, Adm/1/506/44–45; Hope to Hotham, 11 Oct. 1814, Adm/1/507/474.

21. "Cochrane Order," 18 July 1814, Cruikshank, *Doc. Hist., Niagara*, 2:414; Cochrane to captains, 18 July 1814, to Hardy, 4 Sept. 1814, Cochrane Papers, 2346.

22. Cochrane to Monroe, 18 Aug. 1814, vice versa, 6 Sept. 1814, in Latour, *Memoir*, appendix pp. i–iv.

23. "Report," Cochrane Papers, 2332; Hotham to Cochrane, 13 Aug. 1814, Adm/1/506/24–28; *Niles' Register*, 6:280, 428–29.

24. Scott, *Recollections*, 3:68–70; *Gentleman's Magazine*, vol. 83, pt. 2, pp. 285, 388.

25. Burdett to Paget, 29 June 1814, Adm/1/506/451.

26. Cochrane to Griffith & Hotham, 5 Jan. 1815, Adm/1/508/274.

27. Lloyd to Brown, 28 Sept. 1814, Adm/1/508/453–54; *Niles' Register*,

7:253, Supp. 167–72; McMaster, *History*, 4:112, 115–16; Roosevelt, *Naval War*, pp. 68–71; Forester, *Fighting Sail*, p. 86.

28. "Accounts Relating to American Seamen . . ." *HL Sess. Papers*, 4:21–24; "An Account of All Ships Taken . . ." CO/42/160/94–95; Mahan, *Sea Power, 1812*, 2:220; Byron, *War of 1812*, pp. 14, 53.

29. Hotham to Newton, 21 Aug. 1814, Cochrane Papers, 2332; Cochrane to Croker, 5 Oct. 1814, Adm/1/507/249; WO/1/142/411–64; McMaster, *History*, 4:133.

30. Griffith to Croker, 25 Aug., 27 Sept. 1814, Adm/1/506/539, Adm/1/507/304; *Annual Register*, 1814, pp. 181, 189–90; *Niles' Register*, 6:388–89.

Naval Actions on the Great Lakes

1. Bathurst to Admiralty, 1 Jan., 11 Jan. 1814, CO/43/50/214, 219; to Prevost, 20 Jan. 1814, CO/43/23/270; Croker to Yeo, 24 Jan. 1814, to Cochrane, 24 Jan. 1814, Adm/2/1379/100, 30.

2. "Statement of the Navy on Ontario," 26 Jan. 1814, PAC/C219/191–92; Zaslow, *Border*, pp. 169–71.

3. Croker to Griffith, 9 Feb. 1814, Adm/2/1379/171; SN to Macdonough, 17 March, 18 April 1814, M149R11/242, 286; *Niles' Register*, 6:150; Cruikshank, "Contest, 1814," p. 101.

4. Drummond to Bathurst, 18 Jan., 5 April, 28 May 1814, CO/42/355/4, 49, 82–83; "Address to Prince Regent," March 1814, CO/42/156/225b; "Address to Prince Regent by House of Commons, Upper Canada," 14 March 1814, CO/42/161/40; Hitsman, *Incredible*, p. 180.

5. Drummond to Prevost, 21 Jan., 19 Feb. 1814, vice versa, 29 Jan. 1814, CO/42/156/77–78, 83; same, 9 Dec. 1813, in Hitsman, *Incredible*, p. 177; Wood, *Documents*, 3:38–39.

6. SW to Wilkinson, 1 Jan., 30 Jan. 1814, M6R7.

7. SW to Brown, 21 Feb., 28 Feb. 1814, in Wilkinson, *Memoirs*, 1:642, 648; same, 20 March 1814, in Armstrong, *Notices*, 2:213; vice versa, 24 March, 31 March, 8 April 1814, M221R51/B471(7), B472(7), B479(7); SW to Scott, 20 March 1814, M6R7; Hitsman, *Incredible*, p. 183.

8. SW to Governor of Pa., 15 Jan. 1814, WOLS; "General Orders," 13 March 1814, in Tompkins, *Public Papers*, 1:478.

9. Porter to Tompkins, 8 April, 26 May 1814, Tompkins, "Letters," p. 170; vice versa, 17 May 1814, Cruikshank, *Doc. Hist., Niagara*, 2:396, 399.

10. SW to Brown, 8 June 1814, WOLS.

11. Withrow, "Journal."

12. Stephen to Liverpool, 22 March 1814, Liverpool Papers, 38257.

13. Sinclair to Liverpool, unsigned memos to Liverpool, Liverpool Papers, 38257/179, 38365/176, 38572/n.p.; *Times* (London), quoted in *Niles' Register*, 6:307, 370.

14. Wellington to Bathurst, 22 Feb. 1814, Wellington, *Dispatches*, 9:525–26; Bathurst to Prevost, 5 March 1814, CO/43/23/287–89.

15. Fortescue, *Statesmen*, p. 259.

16. Bathurst to Prevost, 14 April, 11 July 1814, CO/43/23/291, 306; Kingsford, *History*, 8:529.

17. Gaines to SW, 13 April, 14 April 1814, M221R53/G123–24; vice versa, 26 April 1814, M6R7/223; Brown to SW, 25 April 1814, M221R51/B487; "Statement of Forces . . ." 28 April 1814, Drummond to Prevost, 27 April, 3 May 1814, MPHC, 15:539, 549; vice versa, 30 April 1814, Wood, *Documents*, 3:49.

18. Brown to SW, 29 April 1814, M221R51/B488.

19. Ibid.; Mitchell to Brown, 8 May 1814, M221R51/B510; Drummond to

Prevost, 27 April, 7 May 1814, MPHC, 15:540; Prevost to Bathurst, 18 May 1814, PAC/C1219/220–27; *Annual Register*, 1814, p. 197; Yeo to Croker, 9 May 1814, Wood, *Documents*, 3:49, 61–63; Baynes to Bathurst, 12 May 1814, in *Niles' Register*, 6:49, 212; "General Orders," 12 May 1814, Adm/1/506/106; Cruikshank, "Contest, 1814," pp. 118–20.

20. SW to Brown, 25 May 1814, to Izard, 25 May 1814, to Scott, 25 May 1814, M6R7/204–5, 211, 215; Garden to SW, 6 June 1814, M221R59; Chauncey to SN, 2 June 1814, in *Niles' Register*, 6:243, 266; Popham to Yeo, 1 June 1814, PAC/C1219/230–31; Drummond to Prevost, 2 June 1814, Wood, *Documents*, 3:73–74; Bathurst to Prevost, 21 Aug. 1814, CO/43/23/161b; *Annual Register*, 1814, p. 180.

21. Holmes to Butler, 10 March 1814, M221R51/B465(7); *Niles' Register*, 6:116–17; Borden to Stewart, 13 March 1814, MPHC, 15:516.

22. *Niles' Register*, 6:179, 214.

23. Campbell to SW, 18 May 1814, M221R51/C365; Sinclair to SN, 19 May 1814, "Court of Inquiry," in Zaslow, *Border*, p. 235; Drummond to Prevost, 27 May 1814, MPHC, 15:565; "Deposition," 31 May 1814, Cruikshank, *Documents, Niagara*, pp. 16, 17; "Opinion of the Court," 19 June 1814, in *Niles' Register*, 6:359; Hitsman, *Incredible*, p. 193.

24. "Yeo Report," 2 June 1814, CO/42/156/333; Yeo to Drummond, 3 June 1814, vice versa, 6 June 1814, Wood, *Documents*, 3:76–79; James, *Naval History*, 6:486; "Strength on Ontario," 18 June 1814, in *Niles' Register*, 6:267.

25. SW to Brown, 10 June 1814, to Izard, 10 June 1814, M6R7/261, 279; Brown to SW, 17 June 1814, M221R59.

'26. Samples of the controversy over unified command are: SN to COs, Naval Yards, 20 June 1812, M149R10/64, 65, 179; SN to Shaw, 12 Oct. 1812, M222R5; to Patterson, 18 Oct. 1813, M149R11/123; Dent to SN, 26 Oct. 1812, M125R25; Campbell to SN, 13 Feb. 1813, M125R26/66; "Regulations . . . when acting in concert," n.d., M6R6/355; "Joint Statement," 23 Nov. 1814, in Eckert, "Jones."

The Niagara Theater

1. Bathurst to Prevost, 3 June 1814, CO/43/23/296–301.

2. SW to Gaines, 16 June 1814, M6R7/238; Mahan, *Sea Power, 1812*, 2:290.

3. Drummond to Prevost, 21 June 1814, in Hitsman, *Incredible*, p. 194.

4. Withrow, "Journal."

5. Porter to Tompkins, 3 July 1814, Cruikshank, *Doc. Hist., Niagara*, 1:26; Brown to SW, 6 July 1814, M221R59.

6. These sources apply to this and the next 7 paragraphs: Brown to SW, 6 July, 7 July 1814, "Merritt's Journal," Drummond to Prevost, 7 July 1814, Wood, *Documents*, 3:111, 82; "Scott Report," 15 July 1814, in *Niles' Register*, 6:399–400 (see also p. 354); Hindman to AG, n.d., Porter to Tompkins, 29 July 1814, Mackonochie to Glasgow, 9 Aug. 1814, Letter to *Boston Centinal*, 7 July 1814, "Brown's Diary," Porter to Stone, 26 May 1840, Cruikshank, *Doc. Hist., Niagara*, 1:44, 101, 49, 2:463–64, 360–66; Brown to SW, 18 July 1814, M221R59; Riall to Drummond, 6 July 1814, in *Annual Register*, 1814, pp. 199–201; Hitsman, *Incredible*, p. 195; Adams, *War of 1812*, pp. 173–79.

7. Riall to Drummond, 8 July 1814, "Brown's Diary," Cruikshank, *Doc. Hist., Niagara*, 1:54, 2:465–67; Riall to Drummond, 12 July 1814, Drummond to Prevost, 11 July 1814, Wood, *Documents*, 3:133–34, 123–25; Brown to SW, 11 July 1814, M221R59.

8. "Naval Strength, Ontario," 23 July 1814, Brown to Chauncey, 13 July 1814, in *Niles' Register*, 6:356, 7:38; Prevost to Bathurst, 12 July 1814, PAC/C1219/243–44; SN to Decatur, 28 July 1814, to Chauncey, 3 Aug. 1814, in Armstrong, *Notices*, 2:240, 239.

9. Chauncey to SN, 10 Aug. 1814, Cruikshank, *Doc. Hist., Niagara,* 1:126.

10. Chauncey to Brown, 10 Aug. 1814, in *Niles' Register,* 7:38–39.

11. Vice versa, 4 Sept. 1814, ibid., 7:121; Armstrong, *Notices,* 2:237–38.

12. Drummond to Prevost, 13 July 1814, "Merritt's Journal," Wood, *Documents,* 3:126–29, 618; Tucker to Riall, 15 July 1814, Porter to Brown, 16 July 1814, Riall to Drummond, 17 July, 19 July 1814, McFarland to Mrs. McFarland, n.d., Stone to Tompkins, 25 July 1814, Brown to SW, 25 July 1814, Cruikshank, *Doc. Hist., Niagara,* 1:66, 68, 71, 73, 74, 87; Prevost to Cochrane, 3 Aug. 1814, CO/42/157/124; Cruikshank, "Lundy's Lane"; Cruikshank, "Disaffection," p. 47.

13. Harvey to Riall, 23 July 1814, "Jesup Narrative," Cruikshank, *Doc. Hist., Niagara,* 1:82–83, 2:476; Riall to Drummond, 21 July 1814, Wood, *Documents,* 3:140; Brown to SW, 22 July 1814, M221R59; Cruikshank, "Lundy's Lane," p. 23.

14. Zaslow, *Border,* p. 247.

15. These sources apply to this and the next 9 paragraphs: Brown to SW, n.d., Wood, *Documents,* 3:157–64; Miller to . . . 28 July 1814, Officers, 11th Regiment, to . . . 2 Aug. 1814, Porter to Tompkins, 29 July 1814, Cruikshank, *Documents, Niagara,* pp. 105–6, 110–11; "Brown's Diary," Leavenworth to . . . 15 Jan. 1815, Pentland to Wilkinson, 16 Dec. 1816, "Jesup Narrative," Cruikshank, *Doc. Hist., Niagara,* 2:335–42, 355, 375, 468–71, 478; Drummond to Prevost, 27 July 1814, in *Annual Register,* 1814, pp. 203–8; Bathurst to Prevost, 7 Oct. 1814, CO/43/23/168b; Cruikshank, "Lundy's Lane"; "Report of Capt. Ketchum," in *Niles' Register,* 6:438; Hitsman, *Incredible,* p. 196.

16. Porter to Tompkins, 29 July 1814, H. Scott to brother, 12 Aug. 1814, Cruikshank, *Doc. Hist., Niagara,* 1:101, 130; Brown to Backus, 7 Aug. 1814, Cruikshank, *Documents, Niagara,* p. 56; Wilkinson, *Memoirs,* 1:708; Armstrong, *Notices,* 2:113–18; Cruikshank, "Lundy's Lane."

17. Brown to Tompkins, 1 Aug., 19 Aug., 21 Aug. 1814, Cruikshank, *Documents, Niagara,* pp. 54, 67, 68; Porter to Tompkins, 9 Aug. 1814, Cruikshank, *Doc. Hist., Niagara,* 2:431.

18. "General Orders," 1 Aug. 1814, Wood, *Documents,* 3:171–74, 177; Morgan to Brown, 5 Aug. 1814, in *Niles' Register,* 6:437, 428; Drummond to Prevost, 4 Aug. 1814, Tucker to Drummond, 4 Aug. 1814, CO/42/157/134, 136.

19. Drummond to Prevost, 4 Aug. 1814, CO/42/157/134; James, *Naval History,* 6:492; Kingsford, *History,* 8:495.

20. These sources apply to this and the next 2 paragraphs: Drummond to Prevost, 12 Aug. 1814, vice versa, 26 Aug. 1814, Ripley to Gaines, 17 Aug. 1814, McMahon to Jarvis, 22 Aug. 1814, Trimble v. Gaines, 2 Sept. 1816, Cruikshank, *Doc. Hist., Niagara,* 1:132, 174, 156, 167, 160 (see also 2:220); Gaines to SW, n.d. Aug. 1814, in *Niles' Register,* 6:19–20; Drummond to Fischer, 14 Aug. 1814, vice versa, 15 Aug. 1814, Drummond to Prevost, 15 Aug., 16 Aug. 1814, Fischer to ADC, 15 Aug. 1814, Wood, *Documents,* 3:185–88, 190–91, 209–12; Bathurst to Prevost, 15 Oct. 1814, CO/43/23/269.

21. These sources apply to this and the next 3 paragraphs: Drummond to Prevost, 30 Aug., 2 Sept., 9 Sept., 11 Sept., 14 Sept. 1814, Brown to Tompkins, 20 Sept. 1814, deWatteville to Drummond, 19 Sept. 1814, Cruikshank, *Doc. Hist., Niagara,* 1:189–90, 196, 198, 100, 257, 207, 259–60; Porter to Brown, 22 Sept. 1814, Brown to SW, 29 Sept. 1814, in *Niles' Register,* 7:101–2, 221; Brown to Tompkins, 20 Sept. 1814, Tompkins, "Letters," p. 19; to SW, 18 Sept. 1814, M221R59.

22. Prevost to Bathurst, 5 Aug. 1814, Wood, *Documents,* 3:345–46; same, 14 Aug. 1814, Cruikshank, *Doc. Hist., Niagara,* 1:177; SW to President, 28 July 1814, in Armstrong, *Notices,* 2:243; Cruikshank, "Contest, 1814," pp. 132–35.

23. Drummond to Yeo, 18 Aug. 1814, "General Orders," 25 Aug. 1814, Prevost to Bathurst, 27 Aug. 1814, Cruikshank, *Doc. Hist., Niagara,* 1:182, 179–80;

Robinson to Prevost, 27 Aug. 1814, PAC/C1219/276; Prevost to Bathurst, 12 July 1814, CO/42/157/19; vice versa, 22 Aug. 1814, CO/43/23/163.

24. SW to Izard, 27 Sept. 1814, M6R7/375; Brown to Izard, 31 Aug. 1814, in Armstrong, *Notices*, 2:100*n*, 102–4; same, 10 Sept. 1814, Izard to SW, 28 Sept. 1814, Drummond to Prevost, 2 Oct. 1814, Cruikshank, *Doc. Hist., Niagara*, 1:197, 233, 238.

25. Drummond to Prevost, 21 Sept., 24 Sept. 1814, Prevost to Bathurst, 11 Oct., 18 Oct. 1814, Izard to SW, 16 Oct. 1814, Cruikshank, *Doc. Hist., Niagara*, 1:225, 228, 245–46, 254–56; Prevost to Drummond, 11 Oct. 1814, Cruikshank, *Documents, Niagara*, p. 244; Cruikshank, "Contest, 1814," pp. 148–49; Drummond to Prevost, 10 Oct., 15 Oct. 1814, Wood, *Documents*, 3:208–10, 217–18; same, 12 Oct., 18 Oct. 1814, CO/42/355/164, 169; Prevost to Bathurst, 18 Oct. 1814, CO/42/157/200; Hitsman, *Incredible*, pp. 229–30.

26. Bissell to Izard, 22 Oct. 1814, in *Niles' Register*, 7:171–72; Drummond to Prevost, 23 Oct. 1814, Cruikshank, *Documents, Niagara*, pp. 266, 270; Cruikshank, *Doc. Hist., Niagara*, 2:272–73.

27. Irving to Tompkins, 3 Oct. 1814, Widrig to Tompkins, 5 Oct. 1814, Tompkins, "Letters," pp. 19, 20; SW to Tompkins, 22 Oct. 1814, M6R7/402.

28. SW to Izard, 24 Oct. 1814, M6R7/409; Yeo to Croker, 24 Oct. 1814, Adm/1/2737/214; Prevost to Bathurst, 1 Nov., 5 Nov. 1814, CO/42/157/274–76; Drummond to Prevost, 5 Nov. 1814, Wood, *Documents*, 3:239–44; Izard to SW, 8 Nov. 1814, Cruikshank, *Doc. Hist., Niagara*, 2:298.

29. Prevost to Bathurst, 7 Oct., 16 Nov., 19 Nov. 1814, CO/42/157/242–43, 341, 360; Croker to Owen, 12 Dec. 1814, Adm/2/1381/68; Yeo to Croker, 23 March, 16 May 1815, Adm 1/2738/81–82; Drummond to Prevost, 9 Nov. 1814, Yeo to Drummond, 14 Nov. 1814, Wood, *Documents*, 3:245–48, 291–92.

30. "Agent's Report," 2 Feb. 1815, Prevost to Bathurst, 14 Feb. 1815, CO/42/161/37–38, 35; Cruikshank, "Contest, 1814," pp. 155–58.

31. SW to Scott, 19 Oct., 24 Oct. 1814, to Governor of Ohio, 25 Oct. 1814, M6R7/382, 409, 392; Cass to SW, 4 Sept., 30 Sept. 1814, *TP: Michigan*, 10:482, 487; Prevost to Bathurst, 21 Nov. 1814, PAC/C1219/325–26; McArthur to SW, 18 Nov. 1814, in *Niles' Register*, 7:282; Drummond to Yeo, 13 Nov. 1814, Wood, *Documents*, 3:290–91; Zaslow, *Border*, pp. 236–38.

The Northwest

1. Drummond to Prevost, 25 April 1814, Cruikshank, *Doc. Hist., Niagara*, 1:11; McDouall to Prevost, 20 July 1814, PAC/C1219/219–20; Cruikshank, "Stoney Creek," p. 48.

2. Worthington et al. to SW, 18 March 1814, M221R58/W335; SW to Governor of Mich. Territory, 4 March 1814, M6R7/258; "Treaty . . ." 22 July 1814, Kappler, *Indian Treaties*, 2:105–7.

3. SW to McArthur, 2 Aug., 6 Aug., 8 Aug. 1814, vice versa, 6 Feb. 1815, *TP: Michigan*, 10:471–74, 503–4.

4. Dickson to Low, 4 Feb. 1814, "Dickson Papers," pp. 289–91; McDouall to Drummond, 26 May 1814, Wood, *Documents*, 3:272; McDouall to chiefs, n.d., CO/42/157/15–16.

5. Prevost to Bathurst, 18 May 1814, CO/42/156/294.

6. Prevost to Bathurst, 2 Aug. 1814, CO/42/157/97–98; Clark to SW, 24 June, 31 July 1814, Perkins to Howard, n.d. Aug. 1814, *TP: Louisiana and Missouri*, 14:775–76, 781, 785; "Anderson Narrative," Grignon, "Recollections," WRHS, 9:193–99, 3:274–75; McDouall to Drummond, 16 July 1814, McKay to McDouall, 27 July 1814, Wood, *Documents*, 3:253–56, 257–65; Howard to SW, 15 July 1814, *TP: Illinois*, 16:445; Pratt, "Fur Trade," p. 263.

7. SW to Croghan, 2 June 1814, to Brown, 10 June 1814, M6R7/215, 261;

Prevost to Bathurst, 10 July 1814, McDouall to Prevost, 14 Aug. 1814, PAC/
C1219/234–36, 281–85; Croghan to SW, 9 Aug. 1814, to McArthur, 23 Aug.
1814, in *Niles' Register*, 7:4–6, 18; Crookshank to Turgnand, 21 Aug. 1814,
MPHC, 15:636; Armstrong, *Notices*, 2:74 ff.; Stanley, "Operations," pp. 98–100.
    8. Bulger to McDouall, 7 Sept. 1814, Wood, *Documents*, 3:279–81; Sinclair
to SN, 28 Oct. 1814, in *Niles' Register*, 7:156.
    9. Taylor to Howard, 6 Sept. 1814, in *Niles' Register*, 7:137; McDouall to
Drummond, 2 Oct. 1814, CO/42/157/339; Graham to Anderson, 7 Sept. 1814,
Anderson to McDouall, 11 Oct. 1814, "Anderson Journal," WRHS, 9:226–30,
243–44.
    10. Clark to SW, 18 Sept. 1814, Russell to SW, 20 Oct., 4 Dec. 1814, *TP:
Louisiana and Missouri*, 14:787–88, 796, 800–801.
    11. "Memorial to Congress," 26 Dec. 1814, ibid., 14:808–10.

Washington

    1. SN to Barney, 20 Aug., 2 Sept. 1813, 18 Feb. 1814, M149R11/56–57, 72,
219; *Niles' Register*, 7:133.
    2. Barrie to Cockburn, 1 June, 11 June, 19 June 1814, Adm/1/507/74, 79,
81; Barrie to SN, 3 June, 9 June, 11 June, 13 June 1814, in *Niles' Register*, 6:
245, 268–69; DeConde, *Entangling*, pp. 496–97; Marine, *Invasion*, pp. 60–70.
    3. Marine, *Invasion*, pp. 60–70; Wadsworth to SW, 26 June 1814, in *Niles'
Register*, 6:300–301 (see also p. 279); "Operations in Chesapeake," Adm/1/507/
101, 108, 110, 117, 119, 121; Cockburn to Cochrane, 4 Aug. 1814, Adm/1/507/
112.
    4. Nourse to Cockburn, 23 July 1814, Cockburn Papers, no. 38, pp. 370–71;
Tatham to SW, 3 June 1813, M111R9; McKenney, *Memoirs*, 1:5.
    5. Prevost to Bathurst, 27 March 1814, PAC/C1219/198–99; SW to Harri-
son, 23 April 1814, M6R7/171; *Niles' Register*, 7:249; Brant, *Madison*, pp. 271,
279, 299; Barlow, "Congress," p. 226; Ingraham, *Capture*, pp. 13, 17; Armstrong, *Examination*, pp. 5n, 6, 9–11.
    6. SW to Governors, 4 July 1814, M6R7: "Inquiry into the Causes of the
Capture of Washington," ASPMA, 1:524–99, "Résumé," in *Niles' Register*,
7:249–50.
    7. Winder to SW, 20 July, 23 July, 13 Aug. 1814, ASPMA, 1:544, 539, 546.
    8. Secretary of Commonwealth to SW, 25 July 1814, ASPMA, 1:551; SW to
Governor of Va., 18 July 1814, WOLS.
    9. Warren to Melville, 18 Nov. 1812, 26 Oct. 1814, Warren Papers; Scott,
Recollections, 3:187, 189, 191, 240, 261.
    10. Bathurst to Ross, n.d., WO/6/2/1–3; Smith, *Autobiography*, 1:196–97;
Evans, "Memo"; *DNB*.
    11. Gleig, *Narrative*, pp. 41, 84–87, 94; Codrington to Mrs. Codrington, 13
July, 18 July 1814, in Bouchier, *Memoir*, 1:310; same, 30 July 1814, Codring-
ton Papers; Smith, *Autobiography*, 1:194–95; Cochrane to Croker, 23 July 1814,
Adm/1/506/443; to Bathurst, 14 July 1814, WO/1/141/12–13; Evans,
"Memo," pp. 1–4.
    12. Scott, *Recollections*, 3:239–40; Cockburn to Cochrane, 17 July 1814,
Cockburn Papers, no. 45.
    13. Gleig, *Narrative*, pp. 91–95; Evans, "Memo," pp. 2–3.
    14. These sources apply to this and the next paragraph: Evans, "Memo," p.
4; Scott, *Recollections*, 3:280–84; Robinson, "New Light," pp. 285–90; Gleig,
Narrative, pp. 97–108.
    15. "Winder's Narrative," Winder to SW, 19 Aug. 1814, ASPMA, 1:552–60,
549; "District Order," in *National Intelligencer*, 18 Aug. 1814.
    16. *National Intelligencer*, just cited.

17. Ibid., 21 Aug. 1814; Williams, *Invasion*, pp. 367–71; Adams, *War of 1812*, p. 220; Gleig, *Narrative*, p. 105; "Armstrong Narrative," 17 Oct. 1814, ASPMA, 1:539.

18. Williams, *Invasion*, p. 175.

19. Ibid., pp. 153 ff.; "Stansbury's Report," 15 Nov. 1814, "Winder's Narrative," ASPMA, 1:552–60.

20. Tuckerman, *Kennedy*, pp. 64–80.

21. Sprigg to Hughes, 25 Aug. 1814, Manuscripts Division, Library of Congress.

22. Swanson, *Perilous Fight*, pp. 22–24.

23. Williams, *Invasion*, p. 179.

24. These sources apply to this and the following 7 paragraphs: Monroe to Committee, 13 Nov. 1814, Rush to Committee, 15 Oct. 1814, "Winder's Narrative," "Sterrett's Statement," "Stansbury's Report," "Callett's Statement," ASPMA, 1:536, 541, 548, 552–60, 583; Gleig, *Narrative*, pp. 109–25; Evans, "Memo," pp. 5–14; Barney to SN, 29 Aug. 1814, in *Niles' Register*, 7:7–8 (see also appendix p. 159); Swanson, *Perilous Fight*, passim; Williams, *Invasion*, pp. 179–225; McKenney, *Memoirs*, 1:5–6; Ingraham, *Capture*, passim; Hadel, "Bladensburg," pp. 155–67, 197–210; Brant, *Madison*, pp. 284–304; Cockburn to Cochrane, 22 Aug. 1814, in *Annual Register*, 1814, p. 225.

25. Gleig, *Narrative*, pp. 129–38, 152–55; Cockburn to Cochrane, 27 Aug. 1814, in *Annual Register*, 1814, pp. 226–29; SN to Creighton, 24 Aug. 1814, M149R11/448; Tingey to SN, 27 Aug. 1814, in *Niles' Register*, 7:49–50; Brant, *Madison*, p. 316; Scott, *Recollections*, 3:295–300; McMaster, *History*, 4:144.

26. *Naval Chronicle*, 32:249–50, 330; *Niles' Register*, 7:1, 203; Ross to Bathurst, 30 Aug. 1814, in *Annual Register*, 1814, pp. 218–21 (see also p. 185); Fortescue, *History*, 10:146.

27. Gleig, *Narrative*, pp. 141–45; Evans, "Memo."

28. "Winder's Narrative," ASPMA, 1:552–60; Brant, *Madison*, pp. 306–12.

29. These sources apply to this and the next paragraph: Cochrane to Croker, 2 Sept. 1814, Gordon to Cochrane, 9 Sept. 1814, in *Annual Register*, 1814, pp. 222–23, 241–43 (see also pp. 185–86); Hungerford to SW, 6 Sept. 1814, Brannan, *Letters*, p. 409; Porter to SN, 7 Sept. 1814, Rodgers to SN, 9 Sept. 1814, in *Niles' Register*, 7:33–37 (see also pp. 10, 250–52); "Report, Vigilance Committee," 7 Sept. 1814, ibid., supplement p. 140; Gleig, *Narrative*, pp. 160–61; Napier, *Life*, 1:76–86; "Congratulations to Gordon," 19 Sept. 1814, Codrington Papers (Tonnant Memo Book).

30. Parker to Cochrane, 29 Aug. 1814, Cochrane Papers, 2329/15; Creaso to Cochrane, 1 Sept. 1814, Adm/1/506/9–13; *Niles' Register*, 7:11; Byron, *War of 1812*, p. 60.

31. These sources apply to this and the next paragraph: "Statement," ASPMA, 1:539–40; Armstrong to Editor, 3 Sept. 1814, in *Niles' Register*, 7:6–7; Gleig, *Narrative*, p. 125; Marine, *Invasion*, p. 70; McKenney, *Memoirs*, 1:6, 7, 17; Williams, *Invasion*, p. 79; Armstrong, *Examination*, pp. 13–14.

Baltimore

1. These sources apply to this and the next 3 paragraphs: Cockburn to Cochrane, 17 July 1814, Cockburn Papers, no. 45; Cochrane to Bathurst, 28 Aug. 1814, Ross to Bathurst, 2 Sept. 1814, WO/1/141/27–28, 59; Cochrane to Croker, 17 Sept. 1814, Adm/1/507/171–75; Scott, *Recollections*, 3:331, 344; "Goldsborough Statement," p. 231; Evans, "Memo," p. 18; Codrington to Mrs. Codrington, 10 Sept. 1814, in Bourchier, *Memoir*, 1:319; Codrington to Bunbury, 15 Sept. 1814, Bunbury Papers; Fortescue, *History*, 10:140; Smith, *Autobiography*, 1:200–206.

2. Evans, "Memo"; Byron, *War of 1812*, pp. 63 ff.

3. These sources apply to this and the next 2 paragraphs: Swanson, *Perilous Fight*, pp. 154, 199–211; Robinson, "Controversy," pp. 179, 183, 190–91.

4. Swanson, *Perilous Fight*, pp. 182, 193, 195, 222, 275–78, 280.

5. Robinson, "Controversy," pp. 177–98.

6. These sources apply to this and the next 6 paragraphs: Evans, "Memo," pp. 19–26; Cochrane to Croker, 17 Sept. 1814, Brooke to Bathurst, 17 Sept. 1814, in *Annual Register*, 1814, pp. 234–36, 229–32; Cockburn to Cochrane, 15 Sept. 1814, Adm/1/507/95, 96; Gleig, *Narrative*, pp. 174–200; Stricker to Smith, 15 Sept. 1814, Smith to SW, 19 Sept. 1814, "General Orders," 19 Sept. 1814, Armistead to SW, 24 Sept. 1814, in *Niles' Register*, 7:23–30, 40; editorial remarks on Brooke letter, ibid., 7:200–201; James, *Naval History*, 6:464–69.

7. *Niles' Register*, 6:flyleaf, 7:158.

8. These sources apply to this and the next 2 paragraphs: Cockburn to Cochrane, 21 July 1814, Claxton to Hardy, 16 Sept. 1814, Cochrane Papers, 2333, 2329; "General Memo," 22 Aug., 25 Aug., 18 Sept. 1814, Codrington Papers (Tonnant Memo Book); Scott, *Recollections*, 3:189, 191, 193, 210, 215, 221–22, 225–27; letter to editor, 14 Aug. 1814, *Niles' Register*, 7:51.

9. Harriott to Treasury, 5 May 1814, Liverpool Papers, 38157/111; Ross to Cockburn, 29 May 1814, Cockburn to Cochrane, 23 June 1814, Adm/1/507/57, 68; Bathurst to Ross, n.d., WO/6/2/1–3; Cochrane to Cockburn, 1 July 1814, vice versa, 21 July 1814, Cochrane Papers, 2346, 2333; Nourse to Cockburn, 4 Aug. 1814, Cockburn Papers, no. 38; Gleig, *Narrative*, p. 149.

10. Bathurst to Torrens, 4 Jan. 1814, to Croker, 19 Jan. 1814, Goulburn to Torrens, 20 Jan. 1814, CO/43/40/216, 224, 229; Bathurst to Admiralty, n.d. 1814, WO/6/2/49–51; "Proclamation," 2 April 1814, in *Niles' Register*, 6:242.

11. Cochrane to Cockburn, 8 April 1814, Cockburn Papers, no. 38/247; to Bathurst, 14 July 1814, WO/1/141/9–13; Cockburn to Cochrane, 13 April 1814, Cochrane Papers, 2333.

12. Cochrane to Cockburn, 26 May 1814, Evans to Cockburn, 28 Nov. 1814, Cockburn Papers, no. 38/296, 468–70; Cochrane to Croker, 27 Sept. 1814, Adm/1/507/248; Gordon to Harrison, 20 Oct. 1814, CO/43/51/64; Carr, "Naval History," p. 22; Riddell, "Slavery," p. 374.

13. Cochrane to Bathurst, 31 Dec. 1814, WO/1/141/191.

14. Cochrane to Malcolm, 17 Feb. 1815, WO/1/143/38.

15. Perkins, *Castlereagh*, p. 166; Carr, "Naval History," p. 22; Riddell, "Slavery," pp. 374–75.

16. SW to major generals, 7 Sept. 1814, M6R7/428; Barbour to SW, 13 Sept., 30 Sept., 13 Oct. 1814, M221R59; vice versa, 2 Oct. 1814, WOLS/7/330.

17. Brooke to Bathurst, 7 Oct. 1814, WO/1/141/99; Barrie to Cockburn, 31 Oct. 1814, Adm/1/509/194; SW to Pinckney, 5 Oct. 1814, to Scott, 28 Oct. 1814, M6R7/379, 405; Barbour to SW, 31 Oct. 1814, M221R59; Byron, *War of 1812*, p. 81.

18. SW to Scott, 19 Oct. 1814, WOLS/7/380–81; *Niles Register*, 7:170; Robinson, "Controversy," pp. 196–98.

19. Barrie to Cockburn, 7 Dec. 1814, Adm/1/509/188; SW to Barbour, 14 Jan. 1815, M6R8; *Niles' Register*, 7:283.

20. Secretary of Pa. to SW, 27 Aug. 1814, ASPMA, 1:551; SW to Bloomfield, 4 Sept., 5 Sept. 1814, to Smith, 19 Sept. 1814, to Scott, 19 Sept. 1814, to Snider, 21 Sept. 1814, M6R7; SW to Pa. Committee of Defense, 5 Oct. 1814, Bloomfield to SW, 10 Oct. 1814, M221R59; SW to Bloomfield, 23 Sept. 1814, to President, Bank of Pa., 2 Oct. 1814, to Governor of Pa., 2 Oct. 1814, WOLS/7/313, 336, 338; McMaster, *History*, 4:151–54.

21. These sources apply to this and the next paragraph: SN to Decatur, 8 Aug. 1814, M149R11/395; SW to Lewis, 15 Oct. 1814, to Clinton, 21 Oct. 1814, to Governor of N.J., 22 Nov. 1814, WOLS/7/374, 428.

Lake Champlain

1. Prevost to Bathurst, 14 Jan. 1814, vice versa, 20 Jan. 1814, PAC/C1219/188, 277.

2. Keith to Croker, 17 May, 31 May, 2 June 1814, Schonberg to Croker, 22 Aug. 1814, WO/1/735/77, 167, 219, 471; Forester, *Fighting Sail*, pp. 5, 8.

3. Bathurst to Prevost, 3 June 1814, in Hitsman, *Incredible*, pp. 219–20, 249–51 (see also p. 190); vice versa, 12 July, 29 July 1814, PAC/C1219/242, 180; same, 26 June 1814, CO/42/156/347; "General Orders," 19 June 1814, Wood, *Documents*, 3:338.

4. Adams, *War of 1812*, pp. 201–2; Coffin, *1812*, p. 179; Prevost, *Public Life*, p. 142.

5. SW to Izard, 28 April, 18 May 1814, M6R7/186, 197; vice versa, 7 May, 3 July 1814, Izard, *Correspondence*, pp. 2, 46.

6. Muller, *Proudest Day*, pp. 237–42; Forester, *Fighting Sail*, p. 10; Richards, *Memoir*, pp. 74, 90, 94.

7. SW to Izard, 25 May, 21 June, 30 June, 2 July, 10 Aug. 1814, M6R7; Prevost to Bathurst, 27 Aug. 1814, CO/42/157/156.

8. These sources apply to this and the next 12 paragraphs: Fisher to Croker, 15 Sept. 1814, Yeo to Croker, 17 Sept., 29 Sept. 1814, Adm/1/2737/181, 179, 206; "Court-martial of McGhie (Chub)," 11 Sept. 1815, Adm/1/5451; "Stores Lost at Plattsburg," CO/42/161/152–54; Robinson to Merry, 22 Sept. 1814, Bathurst MSS, 76:290–93; Robinson, "Plattsburg," pp. 507–18; Izard to Tompkins, 25 Aug. 1814, Macomb to Tompkins, 1 Sept., 9 Sept. 1814, Mooers to Tompkins, 4 Sept., 9 Sept. 1814, Tompkins, "Letters," pp. 17–19; Macdonough to SN, 13 Sept. 1814, Macomb to SW, 15 Sept. 1814, Henly to SN, 12 Sept. 1814, in *Niles' Register*, 7:41–42, 60–61, Supplement, p. 135; Prevost to Bathurst, 11 Sept. 1814, Pring to Yeo, 12 Sept. 1814, Yeo to Croker, 24 Sept. 1814, in *Annual Register*, 1814, pp. 213–15; Cochrane to Gordon, 20 Sept. 1814, Prevost to Bathurst, 22 Sept. 1814, Robertson to Pring, 12 Sept., 15 Sept. 1814, Yeo to Croker, 29 Sept. 1814, Downie to Prevost, 8 Sept. 1814, Sinclair to Baynes, 20 March 1815, "Plattsburg Court-Martial," Aug. 1815, Pring to Yeo, 17 Sept. 1814, Wood, *Documents*, 3:361–64, 373–76, 383–86, 377–78, 380, 397–480; Mahan, *Sea Power, 1812*, 2:367–72; Kingsford, *History*, 8:539–40; Fortescue, *History*, 10:126–33; Shortt, *Canada*, 3:262; Hitsman, *Incredible*, pp. 224–28; Muller, *Proudest Day*, pp. 306, 312, 324; Cooper, *Navy*, 2:212–16; Forester, *Fighting Sail*, p. 88.

9. Macomb to SW, 15 Sept. 1814, in *Niles' Register*, 7:61.

10. Prevost to Bathurst, 22 Sept. 1814, Wood, *Documents*, 3:364–66; Goulburn quoted in Ross, "Naval Officer," pp. 71–95.

11. Yeo to Croker, 5 Sept. 1815, Adm/1/2738/140–44.

12. These sources apply to this and the next 2 paragraphs: Wellington to Bathurst, 22 Feb., 30 Oct. 1814, to Liverpool, 9 Nov. 1814, Wellington, *Dispatches*, 9:525, Wellington, *Supp. Des.*, 9:425–26; Robinson to Merry, 22 Sept. 1814, Bathurst MSS, 76:290–93 (see also p. 302); Robinson, "Plattsburg," pp. 507–18; Croker to Yeo, 12 Dec. 1814, Adm/1/1381/74; Prevost to Bathurst, 11 May, 24 May 1815, "Prevost v. Kay," *Quebec Gazette*, 30 March 1815, CO/42/161/71, 170–79, 180, 182, 184; Codrington to Mrs. Codrington, 28 Sept., 2 Oct. 1814, Codrington Papers; Prevost, *Public Life*, pp. 146–75; *Veritas*, pp. 89, 108, 110, 118–19, 121–22; "Heriot on Canada War," Oct. 1814, PAC/C680/362; Pring to Yeo, 17 Sept. 1814, Alicia Cockburn to Sandys, 20 Oct. 1814, Prevost to Bathurst, 20 Dec. 1814, Wood, *Documents*, 3:385–91, 393. Analyses by historians: Mahan, *Sea Power, 1812*, 2:367–73; Forester, *Fighting Sail*, pp. 6, 10 ff., 236–39; Kingsford, *History*, 8:194, 539–40; Fortescue, *History*, 10:126–33; Shortt, *Canada*, 3:262–64; Hitsman, *Incredible*, pp. 224–25, 231.

The States and the United States

1. The state's efforts to prepare herself may be traced in "General Orders IV," Mass. Coast Defense, and in Mass., "AG Letterbook B."

2. Dearborn to Strong, 8 July 1814, *HR Doc. 81,* 15 Cong., 1 sess.; vice versa, 7 Sept. 1814, ASPMA, 1:613.

3. Adams, *War of 1812,* p. 257.

4. "Orderly Book," 6 Oct. 1814, Mass., Cambridge Lt. Inf.

5. "Brigade Orders," 24 Sept. 1814, ibid.; Sumner to Adjutant General, Mass., 6 Oct. 1814, Mass. Coast Defense, 1:108; Adjutant General, Mass., to Governor of Mass., 21 Dec. 1814, to Board of War, 30 Dec. 1814, vice versa, 2 Jan. 1815, Mass., "AG Letterbook B."

6. Sumner to Adjutant General, 28 Sept., 6 Oct. 1814, Mass. Coast Defense.

7. "Report of the Joint Committee of the Massachusetts General Court," 4 Feb. 1814, ibid., 6:5–6; *Boston Centinal,* 10 Sept. 1814.

8. Governor of Mass. to General Court, 5 Oct. 1814, "Report of the Committee of the Massachusetts House of Representatives," 8 Oct. 1814, "Minority Report," 15 Oct. 1814, in *Niles' Register,* 7:114, 149–50, 153–55.

9. Act of 20 Oct. 1814, "Report," 8 Feb. 1815, Mass., *Resolves,* 1815, p. 607.

10. Mahan, *Sea Power, 1812,* 2:297.

11. Monroe to Strong, 1 Dec. 1814, WOLS.

12. *Niles' Register,* 7:65.

13. Governor of Conn. to SW, 25 Aug. 1814, ASPMA, 1:618.

14. Ibid., 1:617–21; McMaster, *History,* 4:244.

15. *Sen. Doc. 100,* 16 Cong., 2 sess.; Adams, *War of 1812,* p. 256.

16. Adams, *War of 1812,* pp. 262–63.

17. SW to Dearborn, 14 Nov. 1814, M6R7; to King, 2 Jan. 1815, M6R8; Mass., *Resolves,* 8 Feb. 1815.

18. Brant, *Madison,* p. 353.

19. SW to Senate Military Committee, 17 Oct. 1814, ASPMA, 1:514.

20. Sen. debate, *AC,* 28:58–109; HR debate, *AC,* 28:482–91, 530–41, 770–976.

21. Brant, *Madison,* p. 330.

22. Ibid., pp. 243–45.

23. Barlow, "Congress," p. 86.

24. Brant, *Madison,* pp. 329, 349; Eckert, "Jones," pp. 55–63.

25. "Proclamation," 8 Sept. 1814, in *Annual Register,* 1814, pp. 449–50; Brant, *Madison,* p. 353.

26. Brant, *Madison,* p. 366; SW to Brown, 10 Feb. 1815, WOLS Confidential, p. 53.

27. Acts of 28 Jan., 10 Feb. 1814, *USSL,* 3:96; Adams, *History,* bk. 7, pp. 381, 384.

Pensacola and Mobile

1. Claiborne to SW, 31 Aug. 1811, Claiborne, *Letterbook,* 1:349–50; Wilkinson to SW, 28 March 1812, in Wilkinson, *Memoirs,* 1:472–73, 478.

2. Adams, *History,* bk. 7, p. 226; Fortescue, *History,* 10:150–51.

3. Warren to Melville, 11 Oct., 18 Nov. 1812, Warren Papers.

4. Claiborne to Flournoy, 21 June 1813, Claiborne, *Letterbook,* 6:227; SW to Flournoy, 4 July 1813, M6R7/5–6.

5. Windship to Plumer, 1 Nov. 1813, 18 Feb. 1814, Chiefs to Governor, 11 Nov. 1813, CO/23/60.

6. Cochrane to Cameron and Pigot, 25 March 1814, Cochrane Papers, 2346; Cameron to Bathurst, 20 Oct. 1813, CO/23/60.

7. Pigot to Cochrane, 8 June 1814, Adm/1/506/394–96.

8. Cochrane to Croker, 20 June 1814, Adm/1/506/391.

9. Same, 22 June 1814, Adm/1/506/343; "Proclamation," 1 July 1814, WO/1/143/156–57.

10. Cochrane to Nicolls, 4 July 1814, to Percy, 5 July 1814, Adm/1/506/480–82, 486.

11. Cochrane to Bathurst, 14 July 1814, WO/1/141/9–11; Woodbine to Cochrane, 25 July 1814, Cochrane Papers, 2328/35.

12. Hope to Bathurst, 2 May 1814, WO/1/142/1; Bathurst to Wellington, 28 Jan. 1814, vice versa, 30 Oct. 1814, Wellington, *Supp. Des.*, 8:547, Bathurst MSS, p. 302.

13. Melville to Domett, 23 July 1814, vice versa, 26 July 1814, WO/1/142/519, 525–27; Bathurst to Ross, 30 July, 10 Aug. 1814, WO/6/2/5–8.

14. Croker to Cochrane, 10 Aug. 1814, WO/1/141/15–24.

15. Same, 28 Sept. 1814, WO/6/2/19–24.

16. Woodbine to Cochrane, 9 Aug. 1814, Cochrane Papers, 2328/56; Percy to Cochrane, 9 Sept. 1814, Adm/1/505/152–53; Lawrence to Jackson, 15 Sept. 1814, in *Niles' Register*, 7:93; Cotterill, *Southern Indians*, p. 188.

17. Cochrane to Croker, 25 Aug. 1814, Adm/1/506/478.

18. "Proclamation," 29 Aug. 1814, in *Niles' Register*, 7:134–35.

19. Percy to Cochrane, 29 Aug. 1814, Adm/1/505; same, 16 Sept. 1814, Nicolls to Cochrane, 12 Aug. 1814, Cochrane Papers, 2328/83, 59; Brown, *Amphibious*, p. 46.

20. Nicolls to Cochrane, a continuing report beginning 12 Aug. 1814, Woodbine to Nicolls, 27 Oct. 1814, Cochrane Papers, 2328/83, 60, 99, 171a.

21. Nicolls to Laffite, 31 Aug. 1814, Percy to Laffite, 1 Sept. 1814, in Latour, *Memoir*, appendix pp. ix–x; Percy to Cochrane, 9 Sept. 1814, Adm/1/505; Walker, *Jackson*, p. 59.

22. Cochrane to Bathurst, 2 Sept. 1814, WO/1/141/62–66.

23. Bathurst to Ross, 6 Sept. 1814, Bunbury to Keane, 12 Sept. 1814, WO/6/2/11, 15; Keith to Croker, 13 Sept. 1814, WO/1/735/415; "Recollections, Expedition," p. 495.

24. Liverpool to Wellington, 27 Sept. 1814, Wellington, *Supp. Des.*, 9:290; Cochrane to Croker, 3 Oct. 1814, Adm/1/4360; to Prevost, 5 Oct. 1814, Adm/1/508/131.

25. Bathurst to Lambert, 5 Oct., 18 Oct. 1814, to Pakenham, 24 Oct. 1814, WO/6/2/24–25, 26–29; Torrens to Wellington, 14 April 1814, Liverpool to Castlereagh, 21 Oct. 1814, Wellington, *Supp. Des.*, 9:85, 367; "Recollections, Expedition," pp. 507, 514; Walker, *Jackson*, pp. 199, 201–2, 210.

26. Liverpool to Wellington, 4 Nov., 13 Nov. 1814, vice versa, 18 Nov. 1814, Bathurst to Wellington, 4 Nov. 1814, Wellington, *Supp. Des.*, 9:406, 430, 436, 416.

27. SW to Flournoy, 8 Feb., 26 May 1814, to Jackson, 28 May, 5 Sept., 27 Sept. 1814, M6R7; "Proclamation," in Latour, *Memoir*, appendix pp. xxix–xxx.

28. SW to Blount, 14 Oct. 1814, to Jackson, 21 Oct. 1814, M6R7.

29. Nicolls to Cochrane, 9 Nov. 1814, Gordon to Cochrane, 18 Nov. 1814, Cochrane Papers, 2328/103 ff., 109–10; Latour, *Memoir*, pp. 45–48; Jackson to Early, 16 Nov. 1814, in *Niles' Register*, 7:271; Monroe to Jackson, 28 Oct. 1814, in Brown, *Amphibious*, p. 26.

30. Hamilton to Bathurst, 14 Dec. 1814, WO/1/143/197; "Nicolls' Report," Cochrane Papers, 2328/61.

31. "Proclamation," 5 Dec. 1814, WO/1/141/249.

32. Codrington to Mrs. Codrington, 14 Dec. 1814, in Bourchier, *Memoir*, 1:329.

33. Parton, *Jackson*, 2:25–27, 30; Brown, *Amphibious*, pp. 46, 55, 58, 64, 186.

34. SW to Governor of Ky., 3 Oct. 1814, WOLS.

35. James, *Border Captain*, p. 221.

36. Claiborne to Monroe, 9 Dec. 1814, Claiborne, *Letterbook*, 6:321; Latour, *Memoir*, pp. 54–55.

37. Cochrane to Croker, 7 Dec. 1814, Adm/1/508/395–96.

New Orleans

1. Shaw to Patterson, 21 Dec. 1813, M125R33/94; Keane, "Journal," p. 395.

2. These sources apply to this and the next 5 paragraphs: Darby to Wilkinson, 28 April 1816, in Wilkinson, *Memoirs*, 1:505–6; Graham to Brooks, 18 Nov. 1814, WO/1/143/79–81; Gleig, *Narrative*, pp. 257–59; Walker, *Jackson*, pp. 31, 36, 37, 40, 58, 59; James to Stirling, 15 Nov. 1812, Hotham Papers.

3. These sources apply to this and the next paragraph: Jones to Patterson, 12 March 1815, in Latour, *Memoir*, appendix pp. xxxiii–xxxv (see also pp. 58–62); Cochrane to Croker, 16 Dec. 1814, in *Annual Register*, 1815, pp. 153–54; Gleig, *Narrative*, p. 263; Forester, *Fighting Sail*, p. 271; Brown, *Amphibious*, pp. 79–82.

4. These sources apply to this and the next paragraph: Shaw to Patterson, 8 Dec. 1813, M125R33; Jones to Wilkinson, 16 Aug. 1815, Flood to Wilkinson, 8 Dec. 1815, in Wilkinson, *Memoirs*, 1:555–56; "Considerations," Cochrane Papers, 2330/163–70; Claiborne to Fromentin, 24 Oct. 1814, to Jackson, 28 Oct., 4 Nov. 1814, to McRae, 4 Nov. 1814, Claiborne, *Letterbook*, 6:285, 297–98, 306–9; Walker, *Jackson*, pp. 113–14; Brooks, *Siege*, pp. 50, 52, 73, 81–83, 124; Gleig, *Narrative*, pp. 143, 261; Keane, "Journal," p. 395; Bourchier, *Memoir*, 1:329–34.

5. Parton, *Jackson*, 2:56.

6. Ibid., 2:65–66; James, *Border Captain*, pp. 214–15.

7. Parton, *Jackson*, 2:35.

8. These sources apply to this and the next 2 paragraphs: Keane, "Journal," pp. 395–96; Keane to Pakenham, 26 Dec. 1814, in *Annual Register*, 1815, pp. 144–45; Latour, *Memoir*, pp. 78, 82–87; Cooke, *Narrative*, pp. 187–88; Walker, *Jackson*, p. 130; Forrest, *Journal*, pp. 23–28.

9. These sources apply to this and the next 2 paragraphs: SN to Henley, 8 July 1814, to Patterson, 8 July 1814, M149R11/366, 369; Keane to Pakenham, 26 Dec. 1814, in *Annual Register*, 1815, pp. 144–46; Cooke, *Narrative*, pp. 189–99; Latour, *Memoir*, pp. 58, 88–101, 237–44; Gleig, *Narrative*, pp. 289–98; Walker, *Jackson*, pp. 130 ff.; Smith, *New Orleans*, pp. 40 ff.; Brooks, *Siege*, pp. 138–52; Dickson, "Artillery," pp. 29–32.

10. Cochrane to Croker, 18 Jan. 1815, in *Annual Register*, 1815, pp. 155–57; Dickson, "Artillery," pp. 89–98; Brooks, *Siege*, pp. 162–78; Forrest, *Journal*, pp. 32–37.

11. deGrummond, *Baratarians;* Brown, *Amphibious*, p. 87.

12. James, *Border Captain*, p. 247.

13. Pakenham to Cochrane, 18 Dec. 1814, Cochrane Papers, 2330/43; Walker, *Jackson*, p. 212; Brooks, *Siege*, pp. 172, 292 (Brooks' notes do not support his analysis of the command decisions); Fortescue, *History*, 10:162–63; Brown, *Amphibious*, pp. 111–12.

14. Cooke, *Narrative*, p. 178.

15. These sources apply to this and the next paragraph: Keane, "Journal," p. 397; Shaw to SN, 12 March 1813, M125R27; Henley to Patterson, 28 Dec. 1814, in Latour, *Memoir*, appendix pp. xlvii–xlviii (see also pp. 117–19, 129); Brooks, *Siege*, pp. 178–79; Ritchie, "Louisiana," p. 46; Dickson, "Artillery," p. 99.

16. Dickson, "Artillery," p. 179; Latour, *Memoir*, p. 124.

17. Patterson to SN, 29 Dec. 1814, in Latour, *Memoir*, appendix pp. xlix–l (see also pp. 120–25); Keane, "Journal," p. 397; Dickson, "Artillery," pp. 101–4; Brooks, *Siege*, pp. 180–82, 187–89, 191–95.

18. Brooks, *Siege*, pp. 185–86, 190–91; James, *Border Captain*, pp. 147–49, 251–52.

19. Latour, *Memoir*, pp. 147–48; Smith, *New Orleans*, p. 31.

20. These sources apply to this and the next paragraph: Smith, *New Orleans*, p. 66; Latour, *Memoir*, pp. 165–69; Adams, "New Orleans," p. 357; Parton, *Jackson*, 2:36.

21. Parton, *Jackson*, 2:147, 152–54; Brooks, *Siege*, pp. 191–201; Walker, *Jackson*, pp. 224, 299.

22. These sources apply to this and the next paragraph: Walker, *Jackson*, pp. 239, 375; Keane, "Journal," pp. 398–99; Patterson to SN, 2 Jan., 13 Jan. 1815, in Latour, *Memoir*, appendix pp. l–li, lx (see also pp. 132–35); Bourchier, *Memoir*, 1:334; Dickson, "Artillery," pp. 109–12, 148–50; Brown, *Amphibious*, pp. 126–27; Brooks, *Siege*, pp. 201–7.

23. These sources apply to this and the next paragraph: Brooks, *Siege*, pp. 208–26; Cooper, *Rough Notes*, pp. 126–29; Latour, *Memoir*, pp. 138–40; Cooke, *Narrative*, pp. 157–65, 202, 216, 225; Dickson, "Artillery," pp. 151–59; Forrest, *Journal*, pp. 37–44.

24. These sources apply to this and the next 2 paragraphs: "Attack Order," 7 Jan. 1815, Codrington Papers; Gleig, *Narrative*, pp. 330–31.

25. These sources apply to this and the next 3 paragraphs: Lambert to Bathurst, 10 Jan. 1815, Jackson to SW, 9 Jan. 1815, in Latour, *Memoir*, appendix pp. cxlix–cliii, lii–liv (see also pp. 153–64); Smith, *Autobiography*, pp. 235–39; Cooke, *Narrative*, pp. 225–50; Cooper, *Rough Notes*, pp. 130–32; "Contemporary Account," pp. 11–15; Walker, *Jackson*, p. 92; Gleig, *Narrative*, pp. 329 ff.; Fortescue, *History*, 10:155–77; Brooks, *Siege*, pp. 227–52; James, *Border Captain*, pp. 253–70; Adams, *War of 1812*, pp. 315–21; Dickson, "Artillery," pp. 159–70; Ritchie, "Louisiana," pp. 75 ff.

26. These sources apply to this and the next 3 paragraphs: Ritchie, "Louisiana," pp. 68–74; Gleig, *Narrative*, pp. 34–43; Walker, *Jackson*, p. 294; Patterson to SN, 13 Jan. 1815, Jackson to SW, 9 Jan. 1815, in Latour, *Memoir*, appendix pp. lx–lxiv, lii–liv (see also appendix pp. clxx–clxxv); Thornton to Pakenham, 8 Jan. 1815, in *Annual Register*, 1815, pp. 147–49.

27. These sources apply to this and the next paragraph: British government documents in WO/6/2/479–508; Brooke to Bunbury, 28 March 1815, WO/1/141/202; Bourchier, *Memoir*, 1:336–39; Cooke, *Narrative*, pp. 150–56; Forrest to Prevost, 28 Jan. 1815, Murray Papers, pp. 76–79; Gleig, *Narrative*, pp. 380–83; Latour, *Memoir*, pp. 246–48; Fortescue, *History*, 10:150–59, 164–77.

28. Liverpool to Castlereagh, 23 Dec. 1814, Wellington, *Supp. Des.*, 9:495; Walker, *Jackson*, p. 58.

29. Lambert to Bathurst, 28 Jan. 1815, in *Annual Register*, 1815, pp. 149–50; same, 19 Jan. 1815, WO/1/141/239–41; Gleig, *Narrative*, pp. 346–59; Dickson, "Artillery," pp. 170–78; Brooks, *Siege*, pp. 253–74.

30. These sources apply to this and the next paragraph: Jackson to SW, 25 Jan. 1815, Jackson, *Correspondence*, 2:151; Latour, *Memoir*, pp. 187–97; James, *Border Captain*, pp. 275–76, 284–86.

31. Latour, *Memoir*, pp. 207–15, appendix pp. lxxxvii–xc; Dickson, "Artillery," pp. 213–27.

32. Williams to Barrie, 14 Jan. 1815, Ramsey to Cockburn, 28 Jan. 1815, Phillot to Cockburn, 26 Feb. 1815, Adm/1/509/163, 178; Barrie to Cockburn, 14 Jan. 1815, Cockburn Papers, no. 38/483–84; Cochrane to Croker, 14 Feb. 1815, in *Niles' Register*, 7:361 ff.

33. Cochrane to Lambert, 3 Feb. 1815, WO/1/143/53–63.

34. Cochrane to Malcolm, 17 Feb. 1815, WO/1/143/37–43.

35. Parton, *Jackson*, 2:277–300.

36. Ibid.

The Negotiations

1. Adams, *War of 1812*, pp. 268–69.

2. Ibid., pp. 272–74.

3. Governor of Mass. to General Court, 5 Oct. 1814, "Report of the Committee of the Massachusetts House of Representatives," 8 Oct. 1814, "Minority Report," 15 Oct. 1814, in *Niles' Register*, 7:114, 149–50, 153–55.

4. Governor of Conn. to SW, 25 Aug. 1814, ASPMA, 1:617–21; McMaster, *History*, 4:244.

5. "Report of the Hartford Convention," 4 Jan. 1815, in *Niles' Register,* 7:305–13.

6. Ibid.

7. Perkins, *Castlereagh,* p. 140.

8. Burt, *US & GB,* pp. 347–48; Engelman, *Peace,* p. 87; Brant, *Madison,* p. 34.

9. "Heads of a Reply to American Commissioners," n.d., "Memo on the United States," Liverpool Papers, 38365/153 ff.; *Gentleman's Magazine,* vol. 84, pt. 1, p. 85, pt. 2, p. 596; *Quebec Mercury,* 15 Nov. 1814, quoted in *Niles' Register,* 7:270; Adm/1/508/92–97; Arbuthnot to . . . 2 Sept. 1814, Liverpool Papers, 38259/91–102.

10. Editorial, *Naval Chronicle,* 31:419 (see also 32:137–44); Milne, "Letters," p. 293.

11. Engelman, *Peace,* pp. 88, 92, 112.

12. Ibid., pp. 89, 95, 106, 114.

13. Ibid., pp. 121, 131.

14. Ibid., pp. 132–37; Burt, *US & GB,* p. 352.

15. Engelman, *Peace,* pp. 146, 186; "Draft of Note to American Emissaries," 24 Aug. 1814, Liverpool Papers, 38259/51–53; "Memo on the United States," ibid., 38365/153 ff.; Liverpool to Bathurst, 11 Sept. 1814, Wellington, *Supp. Des.,* 9:247.

16. Liverpool to Castlereagh, 18 Nov. 1814, in Yonge, *Liverpool,* 2:12; Engelman, *Peace,* pp. 175, 186, 203.

17. Engelman, *Peace,* pp. 200–203, 232, 275–76; Adams, *War of 1812,* pp. 342–44.

18. Engelman, *Peace,* p. 253; Liverpool to Castlereagh, 18 Nov. 1814, in Yonge, *Liverpool,* 2:12; Perkins, *Castlereagh,* p. 99.

19. Wellington to Liverpool, 9 Nov. 1814, Liverpool to Canning, 28 Dec. 1814, Wellington, *Supp. Des.,* 9:425–26, 513; Liverpool to Castlereagh, 18 Nov. 1814, in Yonge, *Liverpool,* 2:12; Engelman, *Peace,* pp. 253–55.

20. Engelman, *Peace,* pp. 276, 283; Miller, *Treaties,* 2:581; Burt, *US & GB,* pp. 357, 375.

21. Engelman, *Peace,* pp. 283, 288; Liverpool to Canning, 28 Dec. 1814, Wellington, *Supp. Des.,* 9:513; Kingsford, *History,* 8:574.

The Treaty of Ghent

1. Riddell, "Slavery," pp. 374–75; Miller, *Treaties,* 2:574–75.

2. "Memorial of Fur Traders," 7 May 1814, Liverpool Papers, 38257/279; Cochrane to Croker, 22 June 1814, Adm/1/506/343; Liverpool to Bathurst, 11 Sept. 1814, Wellington, *Supp. Des.,* 9:240; McDouall to Foster, 15 May 1815, Wood, *Documents,* 3:533–35; "Report of Council," 3 June 1815, in Anderson, "Personal Narrative," p. 143.

3. Nicolls to Hawkins, 28 April, 12 May, 12 June 1815, WO/1/143/161, 151, 165–66.

4. WO/1/144/144–45, 174–75.

5. Strachan to Jefferson, 30 Jan. 1815, in Kingsford, *History,* 8:585–96.

6. Drummond to Prevost, 12 Nov. 1814, CO/42/157/374–91; *United Services Journal,* 1836, pt. 2, p. 505; Robinson, "Retaliation," pp. 65 ff.; Perkins, *Castlereagh,* p. 165.

7. Yeo to Melville, 30 May 1815, Adm/1/2738/83–85; Wellington to Select Committee, House of Commons, 15 April 1828, in Hitsman, *Incredible,* p. 240.

8. Bathurst to Prevost, 12 July, 15 Sept. 1814, CO/43/23/310 ff., 165; "Distribution of Troops," 8 Nov. 1814, Cruikshank, *Documents, Niagara,* 2:459 (also in CO/42/157/336).

9. Irvine to SW, 14 Jan. 1813, M222R8; "Militia Enrolled," *Sen. Doc. 100,* 16 Cong., 2 sess., p. 58; Upton, *Military,* pp. 137–42.

10. Gallatin to Lyon, 7 May 1816, Gallatin, *Writings,* 1:700.

11. Adams, *History,* bk. 6, p. 418; White, *Jeffersonians,* pp. 239, 263–64; Brant, *Madison,* pp. 376–78, 399.

12. President to Congress, 1 April 1814, in *Niles' Register,* 7:79; McMaster, *History,* 4:229; White, *Jeffersonians,* pp. 253–55.

13. Adams, *History,* bk. 7, p. 385; Perkins, *Castlereagh,* pp. 28, 29, 151.

14. Perkins, *Castlereagh,* pp. 161, 175; Clode, *Military,* vol. 1; Shortt, *Canada,* 3:215.

15. Halévy, *England in 1815,* pp. 87, 94; Brown to Izard, 11 Sept. 1814, Izard, *Correspondence,* p. 87; Palmer, *Revolution,* 2:459, 461.

Bibliography

Sources Cited

(*The short citations used in the notes are given in brackets.*)

Adams, Henry. *History of the United States of America during the Administration of James Madison.* 2 vols. Bks. 5–9 of *History of the United States of America during the Administrations of Thomas Jefferson and James Madison* (New York: Charles Scribner's Sons, 1889–91). New York: Albert and Charles Boni, 1930. [Adams, *History.*]
———. *The War of 1812.* Edited by H. A. DeWeerd. Harrisburg, Pa.: Infantry Journal Press, 1944. [Adams, *War of 1812.*]
Adams, Reed M. B. "New Orleans and the War of 1812." *Louisiana Historical Quarterly* 16 (1933): 221–34, 479–503, 681–703; 17 (1934): 169–82, 349–63, 502–23. [Adams, "New Orleans."]
Admiralty Office Papers, Secretary's Department. In Letters [Adm/1/502–9]; Out Letters [Adm/2/1375–82]; Captains' Letters [Adm/1/2737–38]; In Letters, Departmental [Adm/1/4020–22, 4224–31]; Secret In Letters [Adm/1/4358–60]. London, Public Records Office.
Albion, Robert G., and Pope, Jennie. *Sea Lanes in Wartime.* New York, 1942. [Albion, *Sea Lanes.*]
Alvord, Clarence W. *The Illinois Country, 1673 to 1818.* Vol. 1. Springfield: Illinois Centennial Commission, 1920. [Alvord, *Illinois.*]
American State Papers, Military Affairs. 7 vols. Washington, 1832–60. [ASPMA.]
[Anderson, John.] "A Short History of the Life of John Anderson." Transcribed by Richard C. Knopf from Michigan State Archives. Stenciled at Columbus, Ohio, 1956. ["Anderson."]
Anderson, Thomas G. "Personal Narrative of Captain Thomas G. Anderson." *Reports and Collections of the State Historical Society of Wisconsin,* 1880, 1881, 1882. [Anderson, "Personal Narrative."]
"Anecdotes of the Lake Erie Area, War of 1812." Transcribed by Richard C. Knopf. Stenciled at Columbus, Ohio, 1957. ["Anecdotes of Erie."]
Annals of Congress. 42 vols. Washington, 1832–56. [*AC.*]
Annual Register (London), 1813, 1814, 1815. Vols. 55–57. [*Annual Register.*]
Armstrong, John. *Notices of the War of 1812.* 2 vols. New York: Wiley and Putnam, 1840. [Armstrong, *Notices.*]

Armstrong, Kosciuszko. *Examination of Thomas L. McKenney's Reply to the Review of His Narrative.* . . . New York, 1847. [Armstrong, *Examination.*]

Barlow, William R. "Congress during the War of 1812." Ph.D. dissertation, Ohio State University, 1961. [Barlow, "Congress."]

[Bathurst, Lord.] *Report on the Manuscripts of Earl Bathurst Preserved at Cirencester Park.* Prepared by Francis Bickley. Historical Manuscript Commission. Vol. 76. London: His Majesty's Stationery Office, 1923. [Bathurst MSS.]

Baugh, Daniel A. *British Naval Administration in the Age of Walpole.* Princeton: Princeton University Press, 1965. [Baugh, *Naval.*]

Benton, Elbert J. "Northern Ohio during the War of 1812." Western Reserve Historical Society. Tract no. 92, pt. 2. Cleveland, 1913. [Benton, "Northern Ohio."]

[Blackshear, David.] "Memoir of Brigadier General David Blackshear." In *Bench and Bar of Georgia,* edited by Stephen F. Miller, 1:354–483. 2 vols. Philadelphia, 1858. [Blackshear, "Memoir."]

Borden, Morton. *The Federalism of James A. Bayard.* New York: Columbia University Press, 1955. [Borden, *Bayard.*]

Boston *Centinal,* 10 September 1814. [Boston *Centinal.*]

Bourchier, Lady. *A Memoir of the Life of Admiral Sir Edward Codrington.* 2 vols. London, 1873. [Bourchier, *Memoir.*]

Brannan, John, comp. *Official Letters of the Military and Naval Officers of the United States during the War with Great Britain in the Years 1812, 13, 14, and 15.* Washington, 1823. [Brannan, *Letters.*]

Brant, Irving. *James Madison.* Vol. 6, *Commander-in-Chief.* Indianapolis: Bobbs-Merrill Co., 1961. [Brant, *Madison.*]

Brooks, Charles B. *The Siege of New Orleans.* Seattle: University of Washington Press, 1961. [Brooks, *Siege.*]

Brown, Roger H. *The Republic in Peril: 1812.* New York: Columbia University Press, 1964. [Brown, *The Republic.*]

Brown, Samuel R. *Views of the Campaigns of the Northwest Army.* Burlington, Vt., 1814. [Brown, *Views.*]

Brown, Wilburt S. *The Amphibious Campaign for West Florida and Louisiana, 1814–15: A Critical Review of Strategy and Tactics at New Orleans.* University: University of Alabama Press, 1969. [Brown, *Amphibious.*]

Bryant, Arthur. *The Age of Elegance: England, 1812–1822.* Baltimore: Penguin Books, 1958. [Bryant, *Age of Elegance.*]

Bunbury Family Records. Records Office, Bury St. Edmunds, England. [Bunbury Papers.]

Burt, A. L. *The United States, Great Britain, and British North America from the Revolution to the Establishment of Peace After the War of 1812.* New Haven: Yale University Press, 1940. [Burt, *US & GB.*]

Byron, Gilbert. *The War of 1812 on the Chesapeake Bay.* Baltimore, 1964. [Byron, *War of 1812.*]

Carr, H. J. "Naval History of Bermuda." *Bermuda Historical Quarterly,* vol. 8, 1951. [Carr, "Naval History."]

Chapelle, Howard I. *History of the American Sailing Navy: The Ships and Their Development.* New York: W. W. Norton & Co., 1949. [Chapelle, *Sailing Navy.*]

Christie, Robert. *The Military and Naval Operations in the Canadas during the Late War with the United States.* Quebec, 1818. [Christie, *Military.*]

Claiborne, W. C. C. *Official Letter Books of W. C. C. Claiborne, 1801–1816.* Edited by Dunbar Rowland. 6 vols. Jackson, Miss.: State Department of Archives and History, 1917. [Claiborne, *Letterbook.*]

Clark, Emmons. *History of the Second Company of the Seventh Regiment (National Guard) N. Y. S. Militia.* New York: J. G. Gregory, 1864. [Clark, *Second Company.*]

Clarke, William P. *Official History of the Militia and National Guard of the State of Pennsylvania.* 3 vols. Philadelphia, 1909. [Clarke, *Militia of Pa.*]

Cleaves, Freeman. *Old Tippecanoe: William Henry Harrison and His Time.* New York: Charles Scribner's Sons, 1939. [Cleaves, *Old Tippecanoe.*]

Clode, Charles M. *The Military Forces of the Crown: Their Administration and Government.* 2 vols. London, 1869. [Clode, *Military.*]

Cochrane, Vice Admiral Alexander F. I. Papers. Edinburgh, National Library of Scotland. [Cochrane Papers.]

Cockburn, Rear Admiral George. Papers. Washington, Library of Congress. [Cockburn Papers.]

Codrington, Admiral Edward. Papers. Greenwich, England, National Maritime Museum. Contains, among other things, the Tonnant Memo Book, to which special reference is made in the notes. [Codrington Papers.]

Coffee, John. "Letters, John Coffee to John Donelson." *American Historical Review,* vol. 6, 1901. [Coffee, "Letters."]

Coffin, William F. *1812: The War and Its Moral, A Canadian Chronicle.* Montreal, 1864. [Coffin, *1812.*]

Coggeshall, George. *History of American Privateers and Letters of Marque during Our War with England in the Years 1812, '13, and '14.* 3d ed. New York, 1861. [Coggeshall, *Privateers.*]

Colonial Office Papers, British. In Letters [CO/42/147–61, 352–55]; Intergovernmental Letters [CO/43/23, 40–51]; Sessional and Council Papers [CO/45/45, 53, 54, 140, 141]. London, Public Records Office.

"Contemporary Account of the Battle of New Orleans by a Soldier in the Ranks, A." *Louisiana Historical Quarterly,* vol. 9, 1926. ["Contemporary Account."]

Cooke, John Henry. *A Narrative of Events in the South of France and of the Attack on New Orleans in 1814 and 1815.* London 1835. [Cooke, *Narrative.*]

Cooper, James Fenimore. *History of the Navy of the United States of America.* 2 vols. Philadelphia, 1839. [Cooper, *Navy.*]

Cooper, John Spencer. *Rough Notes of Seven Campaigns.* London, 1869. [Cooper, *Rough Notes.*]

Cotterill, Robert S. *The Southern Indians: The Story of the Civilized Tribes Before Removal.* Norman: University of Oklahoma Press, 1954. [Cotterill, *Southern Indians.*]

Cox, Isaac J. *The West Florida Controversy, 1798–1813: A Study in American Diplomacy.* Baltimore: Johns Hopkins Press, 1918. [Cox, *West Florida.*]

Craig, Gerald M. *Upper Canada: The Formative Years, 1784–1841.* Toronto: McClelland & Stewart; New York: Oxford University Press, 1963. [Craig, *Upper Canada.*]

Croker, John Wilson. *A Key to the Orders in Council.* London, 1812. [Croker, *Key.*]

Cruikshank, Ernest A. "The Battle of Fort George." In *Niagara Historical Society Transactions.* No. 1. Niagara-on-the-Lake, Ontario, 1896. [Cruikshank, "Fort George."]

———. "The Battle of Lundy's Lane." In *Lundy's Lane Historical Society Publications, 1893.* Welland, Ontario, 1893. [Cruikshank, "Lundy's Lane."]

———. "The Battle of Stoney Creek and the Blockade of Fort George." In *Niagara Historical Society Transactions, 1898.* Niagara-on-the-Lake, Ontario, 1898. [Cruikshank, "Stoney Creek."]

———. "The Contest for the Command of Lake Ontario in 1812 and 1813." In *Transactions of the Royal Society of Canada.* 3d ser., vol. 10, sec. 2. Ottawa, 1916. Reprinted in Zaslow, *Border.* [Cruikshank, "Contest, 1812–13."]

————. "Contest for the Command of Lake Ontario in 1814." In *Ontario Historical Society Papers and Records*. Vol. 21. Toronto, 1924. [Cruikshank, "Contest, 1814."]

————. *Documentary History of the Campaigns upon the Niagara Frontier in 1813 and 1814*. 9 vols. Welland, Ontario: Lundy's Lane Historical Society, n.d. [Cruikshank, *Doc. Hist., Niagara*.]

————. *Documents Relating to the Invasion of the Niagara Peninsula by the United States Force Commanded by General Jacob Brown in July and August, 1814*. Document no. 33. Niagara-on-the-Lake, Ontario: Niagara Historical Society, 1920. [Cruikshank, *Documents, Niagara*.]

————. "Drummond's Winter Campaign, 1813." In *Lundy's Lane Historical Society Publications, 1897*. Welland, Ontario, 1897. Reprinted in Zaslow, *Border*. [Cruikshank, "Drummond."]

————. "The Employment of Indians in the War of 1812." In *American Historical Association, Annual Report, 1895*. Washington, 1895. [Cruikshank, "Indians."]

————. "The Fight in the Beechwoods." In *Lundy's Lane Historical Society Publications, 1895*. Welland, Ontario, 1895. [Cruikshank, "Beechwoods."]

————. "Harrison and Procter." In *Royal Society of Canada Proceedings*. 3d ser., vol. 4, sec. 2. Ottawa, 1910. [Cruikshank, "H & P."]

————. "A Study of Disaffection in Upper Canada." In *Transactions of the Royal Society of Canada*. 3d ser., vol. 6, sec. 2. Ottawa, 1913. Reprinted in Zaslow, *Border*. [Cruikshank, "Disaffection."]

Dalliba, James. *A Narrative of the Battle of Brownstown*. New York, 1816. [Dalliba, *Narrative*.]

Darnell, Elias. *A Journal . . . of Those Heroic Kentucky Volunteers and Regulars Commanded by General Winchester in the Years 1812–1813*. Philadelphia, 1843. [Darnell, *Journal*.]

De Conde, Alexander. *Entangling Alliance: Politics and Diplomacy under George Washington*. Durham, N.C.: Duke University Press, 1958. [DeConde, *Entangling*.]

de Grummond, Jane L. *The Baratarians and the Battle of New Orleans*. Baton Rouge: Louisiana State University Press, 1961. [deGrummond, *Baratarians*.]

Dickson, Sir Alexander. "Artillery Services in North America in 1814 and 1815: Being Extracts from the Journal of Sir Alexander Dickson." Introduction and notes by J. H. Leslie. *Journal of the Society for Army Historical Research*, vol. 8, 1929. Dickson's journal is also reprinted in Ritchie, "Louisiana." [Dickson, "Artillery."]

Dickson, Robert. "Dickson and Grignon Papers." In *Collections*. Wisconsin State Historical Society Publications, vol. 11. Madison, 1888. ["Dickson Papers."]

Dictionary of American Biography. 22 vols. New York: Charles Scribner's Sons, 1928–58. [*DAB*.]

Dictionary of National Biography. 22 vols. Oxford: Oxford University Press, 1917–. [*DNB*.]

Documents in Relation to the Differences Which Subsisted Between the Late Commodore O. H. Perry and Captain Jesse D. Elliott. Boston, 1834. [*Documents in Relation*.]

Dudley, Thomas P. "Battle and Massacre at Frenchtown, Michigan, January, 1813." Western Reserve and Northern Historical Society Tract No. 1. Cleveland, 1870. [Dudley, "Battle."]

Dutton, Charles J. *Oliver Hazard Perry*. New York, 1935. [Dutton, *Perry*.]

Eckert, Edward K. "William Jones and the Role of the Secretary of the Navy in the War of 1812." Ph.D. dissertation, University of Florida, 1969. [Eckert, "Jones."]

Edwards, Ninian. *The Edwards Papers.* Edited by E. B. Washburne. Collections of the Chicago Historical Society, vol. 3. Chicago, 1884. [*Edwards Papers.*]

Edwards, Ninian W. *History of Illinois, 1778–1833, and the Life and Times of Ninian Edwards.* Springfield, Ill., 1870. [Edwards, *Illinois.*]

Elliott, Commodore Jesse D., *A Biographical Notice of, Containing a Review of the Controversy Between Him and the Late Commodore Perry.* Philadelphia, 1835. [*Elliott, Biographical.*]

Engelman, Fred L. *The Peace of Christmas Eve.* New York: Harcourt, Brace, 1962. [Engelman, *Peace.*]

Evans, Sir George de Lacey. "Memo of Operations on the Shores of the Chesapeake." Sir George Murray Papers. Vol. 120. Edinburgh, National Library of Scotland. [Evans, "Memo."]

Forester, C. S. *The Age of Fighting Sail: The Story of the Naval War of 1812.* Garden City, N.Y.: Doubleday & Co., 1956. [Forester, *Fighting Sail.*]

Forrest, C. R. *The Battle of New Orleans—A British View: The Journal of Major C. R. Forrest, Asst. QM General, 34th Regiment of Foot.* Introduction and annotations by Hugh F. Rankin. New Orleans: Hauser Press, 1961. Reprinted in Dickson, "Artillery." [Forrest, *Journal.*]

Fortescue, Sir John W. *British Statesmen of the Great War, 1793–1814.* Oxford: Oxford University Press, 1961. [Fortescue, *Statesmen.*]

———. *A History of the British Army.* 13 vols. London: Macmillan Co., 1899–1930. [Fortescue, *History.*]

Gallatin, Albert. *Writings of Albert Gallatin.* Edited by Henry Adams. 3 vols. Philadelphia, 1879. [Gallatin, *Writings.*]

Galpin, W. F. "The American Grain Trade to the Spanish Peninsula, 1810–14." *American Historical Review,* vol. 28, 1922. [Galpin, "Grain Trade."]

Gano, John S. and Richard. "Selections from the Gano Papers." *Quarterly Publication of the Historical and Philosophical Society of Ohio,* vols. 15–18, 1920. ["Gano Papers."]

Gentleman's Magazine (London). Vols. 83–85, 1813–15. [*Gentleman's Magazine.*]

Gilpin, Alec R. *The War of 1812 in the Old Northwest.* East Lansing: Michigan State University Press, 1958. [Gilpin, *War in Northwest.*]

[Gleig, George R.] *A Narrative of the Campaigns of the British Army at Washington, Baltimore, and New Orleans. . . .* Philadelphia, 1821. [Gleig, *Narrative.*]

"Goldsborough Statement." *Maryland Historical Magazine,* vol. 40, 1945. ["Goldsborough Statement."]

Graham, Joseph. Joseph Graham Papers. File no. 1, 1813–19. Raleigh, North Carolina Department of History and Archives. [Graham Papers.]

Hadel, Albert K. "The Battle of Bladensburg." *Maryland Historical Magazine,* vol. 1, 1906. [Hadel, "Bladensburg."]

Halbert, H. S., and Ball, T. H. *The Creek War of 1813 and 1814.* Chicago, 1895. [Halbert, *Creek War.*]

Halévy, Elie. *A History of the English People in the Nineteenth Century.* 2d ed. Translated by E. I. Watkin and R. B. McCallum. Vol. 1, *England in 1815.* London: Ernest Benn, 1949. [Halévy, *England in 1815.*]

Harrison, William Henry. *Messages and Letters of William Henry Harrison.* Edited by Logan Esary. 2 vols. Indiana Historical Collections, vols. 8–9. Indianapolis, 1922. [Harrison, *Messages.*]

———. *William Henry Harrison and the War of 1812.* Documents . . . transcribed by Richard C. Knopf. Columbus, Ohio, 1957. [*Harrison and the War.*]

Hatch, William S. *A Chapter in the War of 1812 in the Northwest.* . . . Cincinnati, 1872. [Hatch, *A Chapter.*]

Heckscher, Eli F. *The Continental System: An Economic Interpretation.* Edited by Harald Westergaard. New York: H. Milford, 1922. [Heckscher, *Continental.*]

Hemenway, Abby M., ed. *Vermont Historical Gazeteer.* 5 vols. Burlington, Vt., 1867–91. [Hemenway, *Vermont.*]

Hitsman, J. Mackay. "Alarm on Lake Ontario, Winter, 1812–13." *Military Affairs,* vol. 23, 1959. Reprinted in Zaslow, *Border.* [Hitsman, "Alarm."]

———. *The Incredible War of 1812: A Military History.* Toronto: University of Toronto Press, 1965. [Hitsman, *Incredible.*]

———. "Sir George Prevost's Conduct of the Canadian War of 1812." In *Canadian Historical Association Report,* 1962. [Hitsman, "Prevost's Conduct."]

Horsman, Reginald. *The Causes of the War of 1812.* Philadelphia: University of Pennsylvania Press, 1962. [Horsman, *Causes.*]

———. *The War of 1812.* New York: Alfred A. Knopf, 1969. [Horsman, *War of 1812.*]

Hotham, Sir Henry. Papers of Vice Admiral Sir Henry Hotham. East Riding County Records Office, Beverly, Yorkshire, England. [Hotham Papers.]

House of Commons, British. *House of Commons Journal.* Vol. 69, 1813–14. [HC, *Journal.*]

House of Lords, British. *House of Lords Sessional Papers.* Vols. 4, 8, 1815. [HL, *Sess. Papers.*]

House of Representatives, U.S. *House Document 81.* 15 Cong., 1 sess., 1817–18. [*HR Doc. 81.*]

Hull, William. *Memoirs of the Campaign of the Northwest Army.* Boston, 1824. [Hull, *Memoirs.*]

[———.] *Report of the Trial of Brigadier General William Hull.* . . . New York, 1814. [Hull, *Trial.*]

Ingraham, Edward D. *Sketch of the Events Which Preceded the Capture of Washington.* Philadelphia, 1849. [Ingraham, *Capture.*]

Izard, George. *Official Correspondence.* . . . Philadelphia, 1816. [Izard, *Correspondence.*]

Jackson, Andrew. Andrew Jackson Papers. Vol. 1. Washington, Library of Congress. [Jackson Papers.]

———. *Correspondence of Andrew Jackson.* Edited by John Spencer Bassett. 7 vols. Washington: Carnegie Institution, 1926–35. [Jackson, *Correspondence.*]

———. "Letters of Andrew Jackson. . . ." Edited by Avery O. Craven. In *Henry E. Huntington Library Bulletin.* No. 3. San Marino, Calif., 1933. [Jackson, "Letters."]

Jacobs, James Ripley. *Tarnished Warrior: Major-General James Wilkinson.* New York: Macmillan Co., 1938. [Jacobs, *Wilkinson.*]

James, Marquis. *Andrew Jackson.* Vol. 1, *The Border Captain.* Indianapolis: Bobbs-Merrill Co., 1933. [James, *Border Captain.*]

James, William. *Full and Correct Account of the Chief Naval Occurrences of the Late War Between Great Britain and the United States.* . . . London, 1817. [James, *Occurrences.*]

———. *The Naval History of Great Britain from the Declaration of War by France in 1793, to the Accession of George IV.* 6 vols. London, 1826. [James, *Naval History.*]

Kappler, Charles J., ed. *Indian Affairs: Laws and Treaties.* 2 vols. Washington,

1904. Printed as *Senate Document 319*, 58 Cong., 2 sess., 1903–4. [Kappler, *Indian Treaties*.]

Keane, John. "A Journal of Operations Against New Orleans Submitted by . . . Major General John Keane." In Wellington, *Supp. Des.*, vol. 10. [Keane, "Journal."]

Kingsford, William. *The History of Canada, 1608–1841*. 10 vols. London, 1887–98. [Kingsford, *History*.]

Lamar, Lucius. Q. C. *Compilation of the Laws of . . . Georgia*. Augusta, Ga., 1821. [Lamar, *Compilation*.]

Latour, Major A. Lacarrière. *Historical Memoir of the War in West Florida and Louisiana in 1814–15*. Translated by H. P. Nugent. Reprinted in facsimile with an introduction and index by Jane Lucas de Grummond. Floridiana Facsimile Series, edited by Rembert W. Patrick. Gainesville: University of Florida Press, 1964. [Latour, *Memoir*.]

Learned, Henry B. "Gerry and the Presidential Succession in 1813." *American Historical Review*, vol. 22, 1916. [Learned, "Gerry."]

Lindley, Harlow, ed. "Captain Cushing in the War of 1812." In *Ohio Historical Society Collections*. Vol. 11, 1944. [Lindley, "Captain Cushing."]

Liverpool, Lord. Liverpool Papers. Additional MSS, folios 38190–489, 38564–81. London, British Museum. The Napoleonic Wars are covered in 38194, 38196, 38248–60, 38327, 38362–65, 38379, 38474, 38564, 38572, 38577. [Liverpool Papers.]

Lossing, Benson J. *The Pictorial Field-Book of the War of 1812; or, Illustrations, by Pen and Pencil, of the History, Biography, Scenery, Relics, and Traditions of the Last War for American Independence*. New York: Harper & Bros., 1867. [Lossing, *Field Book*.]

Lucas, C. P. *The Canadian War of 1812*. Oxford: Oxford University Press, 1906. [Lucas, *Canadian War*.]

Lucas, Robert. *The Robert Lucas Journal of the War of 1812 during the Campaign under General Hull*. Edited by John C. Parrish. Iowa City, 1906. [Lucas, *Journal*.]

McAfee, Robert B. *History of the Late War in the Western Country*. Bowling Green, Ohio, 1816. [McAfee, *History*.]

McClure, George. *Causes of the Destruction of Towns on the Niagara Frontier.* . . . Bath, N.Y., 1817. [McClure, *Causes*.]

McKenney, Thomas L. *Memoirs, Official and Personal, with Sketches of Travels among Northern and Southern Indians, Embracing a War Excursion, and Descriptions of Scenes along the Western Borders*. 2 vols. in 1. New York, 1847. Vol. 1 contains McKenney's "Reply to Kosciuszko Armstrong's Assault upon Colonel McKenney's Narrative." [McKenney, *Memoirs*.]

McMaster, John Bach. *A History of the People of the United States, from the Revolution to the Civil War*. 8 vols. New York: D. Appleton & Co., 1883–1913. [McMaster, *History*.]

Mahan, Alfred T. *Sea Power in Its Relation to the War of 1812*. 2 vols. Boston: Little, Brown & Co., 1919. [Mahan, *Sea Power, 1812*.]

Mahon, John K. "British Command Decisions Relative to the Battle of New Orleans." *Louisiana History*, vol. 6, 1965. [Mahon, "Command."]

———. "British Strategy and Southern Indians, War of 1812." *Florida Historical Quarterly*, vol. 44, 1966. [Mahon, "British Strategy."]

———. "History of the Organization of United States Infantry." In *The Army Lineage Book*. Vol. 2, *Infantry*. Washington, 1953. [Mahon, "Organization."]

Mann, James. *Medical Sketches of the Campaigns of 1812, 13, 14*. Dedham, Mass., 1817. [Mann, *Medical*.]

Marine, William M. *The British Invasion of Maryland, 1812–1815*. Baltimore, 1913. [Marine, *Invasion*.]

Massachusetts. AG "Letterbook A, B." 2 vols. Boston, Mass. Adjutant General, Military Archives. [Mass., AG "Letterbook."]

———. Cambridge Light Infantry Orderly Book, Camp South Boston. Washington, U.S. National Archives. [Mass., Cambridge Lt. Inf.]

———. Coast Defense Letters and Papers. Boston, Mass. Adjutant General, Military Archives. [Mass., Coast Defense.]

———. Massachusetts Orderly Books. Item 19, box 9, as listed in *Preliminary Inventory of the Records of the Adjutant General's Office*, compiled by Lucille H. Pendell and Elizabeth Bethel. Washington, U.S. National Archives. [Mass., Orderly Book.]

———. *Resolves of the General Court of Massachusetts*, 1810–15. Separately bound for each session. [Mass., *Resolves*.]

Melish, John. *Military and Topographical Atlas*. . . . Philadelphia, 1813. [Melish, *Atlas*.]

Michigan Pioneer and Historical Society Collections. 40 vols. Lansing, Mich.: Michigan Pioneer and Historical Society, 1876–1929. [MPHC.]

Microfilm Records in the United States National Archives. Washington, U.S. National Archives. [Citations are to microfilm group number, reel number, and page or document number. Sample: M125R23/42.]

Military and Naval Magazine of the United States (Washington), 1833–36. 6 vols. [*Mil. and Naval Mag.*]

Miller, David Hunter, ed. *Treaties and Other International Acts of the United States of America*. Washington, 1931–. [Miller, *Treaties*.]

Mills, James C. *Oliver Hazard Perry and the Battle of Lake Erie*. Detroit, 1913. [Mills, *Perry*.]

[Milne, Sir David.] "Letters Written During the War of 1812 by a British Naval Commander in American Waters." *William and Mary Quarterly*, 2d ser., vol. 10, 1930. [Milne, "Letters."]

Mitchell, Major J. "British Troops in America." *United Services Journal* (London), 1836. [Mitchell, "British Troops."]

Montreal Herald, The, 27 June 1812. [*Montreal Herald*.]

Morris, Charles. *The Autobiography of Commodore Charles Morris*. Annapolis, Md., 1880. [Morris, *Autobiography*.]

Muller, Charles G. *The Proudest Day: Macdonough on Lake Champlain*. New York: John Day Co., 1960. [Muller, *Proudest Day*.]

Murray, Sir George. Sir George Murray Papers. Edinburgh, National Library of Scotland. [Murray Papers.]

Napier, Edward H. D. E. *The Life and Correspondence of Admiral Sir Charles Napier*. 2 vols. London, 1862. [Napier, *Life*.]

Napier, Henry Edward. *New England Blockade in 1814: The Journal of Henry Edward Napier*. . . . Edited by W. M. Whitehill. Salem, Mass., 1939. [Napier, *Journal*.]

National Archives, U.S. See Microfilm Records in the United States National Archives.

National Intelligencer (Washington), 18 August, 21 August 1814. [*National Intelligencer*.]

Naval Chronicle (London), 1749–1818. [*Naval Chronicle*.]

Naval Chronology of Great Britain . . . 1803–1815, The. Edited by James J. Ralph. 3 vols. London, 1820. [*Naval Chronology*.]

New Hampshire. *Public Acts and Laws of New Hampshire*. Exeter, N.H., 1810–15. Bound separately for each session. [N.H., *Public Acts*.]

Niebaum, John H. "The Pittsburgh Blues." *Western Pennsylvania Historical Magazine*, vols. 4–5, 1921. [Niebaum, "Pittsburgh Blues."]

Nielson, Peter R. *Financial History of the United States, 1811–1816*. Washington: Catholic University of America, 1926. [Nielson, *Financial History*.]

Niles' Weekly Register (Baltimore), 1811–49. [*Niles' Register*.]

North Carolina. Adjutant General, "Letterbook," 1807–17. 3 vols. Raleigh, North Carolina Department of History and Archives. [N.C., AG "Letterbook."]

———. *Laws of North Carolina*, 1810–15. Separately bound for each session. [N.C., *Laws*.]

———. "Militia Papers." Durham, N.C., Duke University Library. [N.C., "Militia Papers."]

———. "Militia Returns, Orders of Officers," 1811–13. Raleigh, North Carolina Department of History and Archives. [N.C., "Militia Returns."]

Owsley, Frank L., Jr. "British and Indian Activities in Spanish West Florida during the War of 1812." *Florida Historical Quarterly*, vol. 46, 1967. [Owsley, "British Activities."]

Palmer, Robert R. *The Age of the Democratic Revolution: A Political History of Europe and America, 1760–1800*. 2 vols. Princeton: Princeton University Press, 1959, 1964. [Palmer, *Revolution*.]

Parton, James. *Life of Andrew Jackson*. 3 vols. New York: Mason Bros., 1861. [Parton, *Jackson*.]

Patrick, Rembert W. *Florida Fiasco: Rampant Rebels on the Georgia-Florida Border, 1810–1815*. Athens: University of Georgia Press, 1954. [Patrick, *Fiasco*.]

Paullin, Charles O., ed. *The Battle of Lake Erie: A Collection of Documents*. Cleveland, 1918. [Paullin, *Erie*.]

Pennsylvania. Archives of Pennsylvania. Harrisburg, Pennsylvania Historical Commission, Division of Public Records. [Pa., Archives.]

———. *Pennsylvania Archives*. 9 series, 138 vols. Philadelphia, 1852–1949. [*Pa. Archives*.]

———. *Statutes at Large*. Compiled by James T. Mitchell et al. Harrisburg, 1915. [Pa., *SL*.]

Perkins, Bradford. *Castlereagh and Adams: England and the United States, 1812–1823*. Berkeley: University of California Press, 1964. [Perkins, *Castlereagh*.]

———. *Prologue to War: England and the United States, 1805–1812*. Berkeley: University of California Press, 1961. [Perkins, *Prologue*.]

Pirtle, Alfred. *The Battle of Tippecanoe*. Louisville, Ky.: J. P. Morton & Co., 1900. [Pirtle, *Tippecanoe*.]

Pittsburgh Gazette, 22 Jan. 1813. [*Pittsburgh Gazette*.]

Porter, David. *Journal of a Cruise Made to the Pacific Ocean in the United States Frigate* Essex, *1812, 1813, 1814*. 2 vols. New York, 1822. [Porter, *Journal*.]

Pound, Merritt B. *Benjamin Hawkins, Indian Agent*. Athens: University of Georgia Press, 1951. [Pound, *Hawkins*.]

Pratt, Julius W. "Fur Trade Strategy and the American Left Flank in the War of 1812." *American Historical Review*, vol. 40, 1935. [Pratt, "Fur Trade."]

Prevost, Sir George, *Some Account of the Public Life of the Late Lieutenant General. . . .* London, 1823. [Prevost, *Public Life*.]

Public Archives of Canada. Ottawa. [PAC.]

Purcell, Hugh D. "Don't Give Up the Ship." *United States Naval Institute Proceedings*, vol. 91, May 1965. [Purcell, "Ship."]

Quaife, Milo M. "General Shelby's Army in the Thames Campaign." *Filson Club Historical Quarterly*, vol. 10, 1936. [Quaife, "Shelby's Army."]
———. "General William Hull and His Critics." *Ohio Archeological and Historical Quarterly*, vol. 47, 1938. [Quaife, "Hull."]

"Recollections of the Expedition to the Chesapeake and against New Orleans in the Years 1814–15." By an old subaltern. *United Services Journal* (London), 1840. ["Recollections, Expedition."]
Richards, George H. *Memoir of Alexander Macomb*. . . . New York, 1833. [Richards, *Memoir*.]
Riddell, William R. "Slavery in Canada." *Journal of Negro History*, vol. 5, 1920. [Riddell, "Slavery."]
Risch, Erna. *Quartermaster Support of the Army: A History of the Corps, 1775–1939*. Washington, 1962. [Risch, *Quartermaster*.]
Ritchie, Carson I. A. "British Documents on the Louisiana Campaign." *Louisiana Historical Quarterly*, vol. 44, 1961. [Ritchie, "Louisiana."]
Roach, Issac. "Journal, 1812–24." *Pennsylvania Magazine of History and Biography*, vol. 17, 1893. [Roach, "Journal."]
Robinson, C. W. "The Expedition to Plattsburg . . . 1814." *Journal of the Royal United Services Institute*, vol. 61, 1916. [Robinson, "Plattsburg."]
Robinson, Ralph. "Controversy over the Command at Baltimore in the War of 1812." *Maryland Historical Magazine*, vol. 39, 1944. [Robinson, "Controversy."]
———. "New Light on Three Episodes of the British Invasion of Maryland in 1814." *Maryland Historical Magazine*, vol. 37, 1942. [Robinson, "New Light."]
———. "Retaliation for the Treatment of Prisoners in the War of 1812." *American Historical Review*, vol. 49, 1943. [Robinson, "Retaliation."]
———. "The Use of Rockets by the British in the War of 1812." *Maryland Historical Magazine*, vol. 40, 1945. [Robinson, "Rockets."]
Roosevelt, Theodore. *The Naval War of 1812*. New York, 1927. [Roosevelt, *Naval War*.]
Ross, R. D. "The Naval Officer, 1793–1815." *Army Quarterly*, vol. 78, April 1959. [Ross, "Naval Officer."]
Rowland, Eron (Mrs. Dunbar Rowland). *Andrew Jackson's Campaign against the British, or the Mississippi Territory in the War of 1812, Concerning the Military Operations of the Americans, Creek Indians, British, and Spanish, 1813–1815*. New York, 1926. [Rowland, *Jackson*.]
Russell, Carl P. *Guns on the Early Frontiers: A History of Firearms from Colonial Times through the Years of the Western Fur Trade*. Berkeley: University of California Press, 1957. [Russell, *Guns*.]

Scott, James. *Recollections of a Naval Life*. 3 vols. London, 1834. [Scott, *Recollections*.]
Senate Document 100. 16 Cong., 2 sess., 1820–21. Contains "A Statement of the Number of Militia from Each State . . . During the War of 1812." [*Sen. Doc. 100*.]
"Shabonee's Account of Tippecanoe." Edited by J. Wesley Whickar. *Indiana Magazine of History*, vol. 17, 1922. ["Shabonee's Account."]
Shortt, Adam, and Doughty, A. J. *Canada and Its Provinces*. 23 vols. Toronto, 1913–17. [Shortt, *Canada*.]
Slocum, Charles E. "The Origin, Description, and Service of Fort Winchester." *Ohio Archeological and Historical Society Publications*, vol. 9, 1901. [Slocum, "Origin."]
Smith, Harry George W. *Autobiography*. . . . 2 vols. London, 1902. [Smith, *Autobiography*.]

Smith, Zachariah F. *The Battle of New Orleans, Including the Previous Engagements between the Americans and the British, the Indians, and the Spanish Which Led to the Final Conflict on the 8th of January, 1815.* Louisville, Ky.: J. P. Morton & Co., 1904. [Smith, *New Orleans.*]

Snyder, Simon. Simon Snyder Papers. Harrisburg, Pennsylvania Historical Commission, Division of Public Records. [Snyder Papers.]

Stacey, C. P. "Another Look at the Battle of Lake Erie." *Canadian Historical Review,* vol. 39, 1958. Reprinted in Mason, *After Tippecanoe* (see Additional Readings). [Stacey, "Another Look."]

——. "Commodore Chauncey's Attack on Kingston Harbor, November 10, 1812." *Canadian Historical Review,* vol. 32, 1951. [Stacey, "Chauncey's Attack."]

——. "The Ships of the British Squadron on Lake Ontario, 1812–1814." *Canadian Historical Review,* vol. 34, 1953. [Stacey, "Ships."]

Stanley, George F. G. "British Operations in the American Northwest, 1812–1815." *Journal of the Society for Army Historical Research,* vol. 22, 1943. [Stanley, "Operations."]

——. *Canada's Soldiers, 1604–1954: The Military History of an Unmilitary People.* Toronto: Macmillan, 1954. [Stanley, *Soldiers.*]

State Papers and Public Documents of the United States. Boston: T. B. Wait & Sons, 1817. [*State Papers.*]

Swanson, Neil H. *The Perilous Fight.* New York, 1945. [Swanson, *Perilous Fight.*]

Swanton, John R. *Early History of the Creek Indians and Their Neighbors.* Bulletin no. 73. Washington: Smithsonian Institution, Bureau of American Ethnology, 1922. [Swanton, *Early History.*]

[Tannehill, Adamson.] Orderly Book, General Adamson Tannehill's Brigade, War of 1812. Ann Arbor, University of Michigan, Clements Library. [Tannehill.]

Territorial Papers of the United States. Edited by Clarence E. Carter. Washington, 1934–. [*TP: Illinois, TP: Indiana, TP: Michigan, TP: Mississippi.*]

Thomason, Hugh M. "Governor Peter Early and the Creek Indian Frontier, 1813–1815." *Georgia Historical Quarterly,* vol. 45, 1961. [Thomason, "Governor Early."]

Tompkins, Daniel D. "Letters to Daniel D. Tompkins, Governor of New York, 1812–14." Item no. 19 in *Preliminary Inventory of the Records of the Adjutant General's Office.* Washington, U.S. National Archives. [Tompkins, "Letters."]

——. *Public Papers of Daniel D. Tompkins, Military.* Introduction by Hugh Hastings. 3 vols. New York, 1898–1902. [Tompkins, *Public Papers.*]

Tucker, Glenn. *Poltroons and Patriots: A Popular Account of the War of 1812.* Indianapolis: Bobbs-Merrill Co., 1954. [Tucker, *Poltroons.*]

——. *Tecumseh: Vision of Glory.* Indianapolis: Bobbs-Merrill Co., 1956. [Tucker, *Tecumseh.*]

Tuckerman, Henry T. *The Life of John Pendleton Kennedy.* New York, 1871. [Tuckerman, *Kennedy.*]

United Services Journal (London), 1829–43. [*United Services Journal.*]

United States Statutes at Large, 1810–15. [*USSL.*]

Upton, Emory. *The Military Policy of the United States.* Washington: Government Printing Office, 1917. [Upton, *Military Policy.*]

Van de Water, Frederic F. *Lake Champlain and Lake George.* Indianapolis: Bobbs-Merrill Co., 1946. [Van de Water, *Champlain.*]

Van Rensselaer, Solomon. *A Narrative of the Affair at Queenstown in the War of 1812.* New York, 1836. [Van Rensselaer, *Narrative.*]

Veritas [pseud.]. *The Letters of Veritas . . . Containing a Succinct Narrative of the Military Administration of Sir George Prevost during His Command in the Canadas.* Montreal, 1815. Originally published in the *Montreal Herald.* [Veritas.]

Virginia. *Acts Passed at a General Assembly of the Commonwealth of Virginia, 1808–42.* The laws for each session are separately bound. [Va., *Acts.*]

Walker, Adam. *Journal of Two Campaigns . . . in Michigan and Indiana Territories. . . .* Keane, N.H., 1816. Also in Harrison, *Messages,* vol. 1; both sources cited. [Walker, *Journal.*]

Walker, Alexander. *Jackson and New Orleans.* New York, 1856. [Walker, *Jackson.*]

Wallace, David D. *The History of South Carolina.* 4 vols. New York: American Historical Society, 1934. [Wallace, *South Carolina.*]

Ward, James A. *Manual of Naval Tactics.* New York, 1859. [Ward, *Manual.*]

War Office, Letters Received, U.S. Washington, U.S. National Archives. [WOLR.]

War Office, Letters Sent, U.S. Washington, U.S. National Archives. [WOLS.]

War Office Records, British. London, Public Records Office. [WO.]

War Office Reports to Congress, U.S. Vol. 1, 1812. Washington, U.S. National Archives. [War Office Reports to Congress.]

Warren, Sir John Borlase. Warren Papers. Greenwich, England, National Maritime Museum. [Warren Papers.]

Wellington, Duke of. *The Dispatches of Field Marshal the Duke of Wellington . . . from 1799 to 1818.* Compiled by Lieutenant Colonel Gurwood. London, 1837–39. [Wellington, *Dispatches.*]

————. *Supplementary Despatches: Correspondence and Memoranda of Field Marshal Arthur Duke of Wellington.* 15 vols. London, 1858–72. [Wellington, *Supp. Des.*]

Western Reserve Historical Society. Tracts and Other Publications. Cleveland. [WRHS.]

White, Leonard D. *The Jeffersonians: A Study in Administrative History, 1801–1829.* New York: Macmillan Co., 1951. [White, *Jeffersonians.*]

White, Patrick C. T. *A Nation on Trial: America and the War of 1812.* New York: John Wiley & Sons, 1965. [White, *Nation.*]

Whittlesey, Elisha, ed. "Papers Relating to the War of 1812." Western Reserve Historical Society. Tract no. 3. Cleveland. [Whittlesey, "Papers, 1812."]

Wilkinson, James. *Memoirs of My Own Times.* 3 vols. Philadelphia, 1816. [Wilkinson, *Memoirs.*]

Williams, John S. *History of the Invasion and Capture of Washington and of the Events Which Preceded and Followed.* New York, 1857. [Williams, *Invasion.*]

Williams, Samuel. *The Expedition of Captain Henry Brush.* Cincinnati, 1870. [Williams, *Brush.*]

Winder, William H. "The Narrative of General Winder." *American State Papers, Military Affairs,* 1:552–60. Washington, D.C. ["Winder's Narrative."]

Withrow, John, Jr. "The Journal of John Withrow, Jr., While Serving a Tour of Duty." Harrisburg, Pennsylvania Historical Commission, Division of Public Records. [Withrow, "Journal."]

Wood, Eleazer D. "Eleazer D. Wood's Journal of the Northwestern Campaign." In *Campaigns of the War of 1812 . . .* edited by George W. Cullum. New York, 1879. ["Wood's Journal."]

Wood, William C. H. *Select British Documents of the Canadian War of 1812.* 3 vols. Publications of the Champlain Historical Society, vols. 13, 15, 17. Toronto, 1920–28. [Wood, *Documents.*]

Worthington, Thomas. *Thomas Worthington and the War of 1812.* Edited by Richard C. Knopf. Columbus, Ohio, 1957.

Yonge, Charles D. *Life and Administration of Robert Banks, Second Earl of Liverpool.* London, 1868. [Yonge, *Liverpool.*]

Young, Bennett H. *The Battle of the Thames.* Filson Club Publications, no. 18. Louisville, Ky., 1903. [Young, *Thames.*]

Zaslow, Morris, ed. *The Defended Border: Upper Canada and the War of 1812.* Toronto: University of Toronto Press, 1964. [Zaslow, *Border.*]

Additional Readings

Adams, Charles F. "Wednesday, August 19, 1812, 6:30 P.M.: The Birth of a World Power." *American Historical Review*, vol. 18, 1913.

Anderson, David D. "The Battle of Fort Stephenson. . . ." *Northwest Ohio Quarterly*, vol. 33, 1961.

Andreas, A. T. *History of Cook County, Illinois.* Chicago, 1884.

Armstrong, John. *Hints to Young Generals. By an Old Soldier.* Kingston, N.Y., 1812.

Army Quarterly and Defence Journal (London), 1958–1965. Vols. 76–89.

Arthur, Stanley C. *The Story of the Battle of New Orleans.* New Orleans: Louisiana Historical Society, 1915.

Atherton, William. *Narrative. . . .* Frankfort, Ky., 1842.

Babcock, James T. "The Campaign of 1814 on the Niagara Frontier." *Niagara Frontier*, vol. 10, 1963.

Babcock, Louis L. *The War of 1812 on the Niagara Frontier. Buffalo Historical Society Publications*, vol. 29. Buffalo, N.Y., 1927.

Bacon, Mrs. Lydia B. "Mrs. Lydia B. Bacon's Journal, 1811–1812." Edited by Mary M. Crawford. *Indiana Magazine of History*, vol. 41, 1945.

Bancroft, George. *History of the Battle of Lake Erie, and Miscellaneous Papers.* New York, 1891.

Barlow, William R. "Ohio's Congressmen and the War of 1812." *Ohio History*, vol. 72, 1963.

Barnes, James. *Naval Actions of the War of 1812.* New York, 1896.

Bassett, John Spencer, ed. *Major Howell Tatum's Journal while Topographical Engineer (1814) to General Jackson.* Smith College Studies in History, vol. 7. Northampton, Mass., 1921–22.

"Battle of Sackett's Harbor, The." *Military and Naval Magazine of the United States*, vol. 1, 1833.

Baylies, Nicholas. *Eleazer Wheelock Ripley of the War of 1812.* Des Moines, Iowa, 1890.

Blakeslee, Samuel. "Narrative of Colonel Samuel Blakeslee, a Defender of Buffalo." In *Buffalo Historical Society Publications*, vol. 8. Buffalo, N.Y., 1905.

Bond, Beverly W., Jr. "William Henry Harrison in the War of 1812." *Mississippi Valley Historical Review*, vol. 13, 1927.

Boom, Aaron M. "John Coffee, Citizen Soldier." *Tennessee Historical Quarterly*, vol. 22, 1963.

Booth, Mordecai. "The Capture of Washington in 1814 as Described by Mordecai Booth." Edited by Ray W. Irwin. *Americana*, vol. 28, 1934. Booth's is said to be one of two eyewitness accounts of the event.

Bourne, Alexander. "The Siege of Fort Meigs, Year 1813: An Eyewitness Account by Colonel Alexander Bourne." *Northwest Ohio Quarterly*, vols. 17, 18, 1945, 1946.

Boyd, John P. *Documents and Facts Relating to Military Events during the Late War*. Boston, 1816.

Boyd, Mark F. "Events at Prospect Bluff on the Apalachicola River, 1808–1818." *Florida Historical Quarterly*, vol. 16, 1937.

Brackenridge, Hugh M. *History of the Late War.* . . . N.p., 1817–18.

Brady, William Y. "The 22d Regiment in the War of 1812." *Western Pennsylvania Historical Magazine*, vol. 32, 1949.

Brightfield, Myron F. *John Wilson Croker*. Berkeley: University of California Press, 1940. The work is focused on Croker's literary life.

Brown, Everett S., ed. "Letters from Louisiana, 1813–1814." *Mississippi Valley Historical Review*, vol. 11, 1925.

Brown, Kenneth L. "Mr. Madison's Secretary of the Navy." *United States Naval Institute Proceedings*, vol. 73, 1947.

Brown, Samuel R. *An Authentic History of the Second War for Independence*. 2 vols. Auburn, N.Y., 1815.

Burt, A. Blanche. "A Sketch of Captain Robert Heriott Barclay, RN." In *Ontario Historical Society Papers and Records*, vol. 14. Toronto, 1916.

Cady, John F. "Western Opinion and the War of 1812." In *Ohio Archeological and Historical Society Publications*. Vol. 33. Columbus, 1925.

Carmichael-Smyth, Sir James. *Précis of the Wars in Canada from 1755 to . . . 1814*. London, 1826.

Carr, Albert H. Z. *The Coming of War: An Account of the Remarkable Events Leading to the War of 1812*. Garden City, N.Y.: Doubleday & Co., 1960.

Carter, Samuel, III. *Blaze of Glory*. New York: St. Martin's Press, 1971. See for the Battle of New Orleans.

Casey, Powell A. *Louisiana in the War of 1812*. Baton Rouge: Louisiana State University Press, 1963.

Cassell, Frank A. "Baltimore in 1813: A Study of Urban Defense." *Military Affairs*, vol. 33, 1969.

Christian, Thomas. "Sortie at Fort Meigs, May 1813." In *Western Reserve Historical and Archeological Tracts*, no. 23, 1870.

Claiborne, Nathaniel H. *Notes on the War in the South*. Richmond, Va., 1819.

Coffee, John. "Letters of John Coffee to His Wife, 1813–1815." Edited by John H. DeWitt. *Tennessee Historical Quarterly*, vol. 2, 1916.

Coleman, Christopher B. "The Ohio Valley in the Preliminaries of the War of 1812." *Mississippi Valley Historical Review*, vol. 7, 1920.

Coles, Harry L. *The War of 1812*. Chicago: University of Chicago Press, 1965.

Cooper, James Fenimore. *Lives of Distinguished American Naval Officers*. 2 vols. Philadelphia, 1846.

Cramer, C. H. "Duncan McArthur, the Military Phase." *Ohio Archeological and Historical Quarterly*, vol. 46, 1937.

Croker, John Wilson. *The Correspondence and Diaries of the Late . . .*

John Wilson Croker. Edited by Louis J. Jennings. 3 vols. London, 1884. The period of the War of 1812 is covered in the first 100 pages of vol. 1.

Cruikshank, E. A., ed. *Documents Relating to the Invasion of Canada and the Surrender of Detroit*. Canadian Archives Publications, no. 7. Ottawa, 1912.

Curzon, S. A. "The Story of Laura Secord. . . ." In *Lundy's Lane Historical Society Publications, 1898*. Welland, Ontario, 1898. Reprinted in Zaslow, *Border*.

Cushing, Captain Samuel. "The Siege of Fort Meigs." Edited by P. L. Rainwater. *Mississippi Valley Historical Review*, vol. 19, 1932. A letter from the captain.

Dalton, Samuel. "Letters of Samuel Dalton of Salem, an Impressed Seaman, 1803–1814." In *Essex Institute Historical Collections*. Vol. 68. Salem, Mass., 1932.

Davies, George E. "Robert Smith and the Navy." *Maryland Historical Magazine*, vol. 14, 1919.

Davis, T. Frederick. "U.S.S. Peacock in the War of 1812: A Fight off the Florida Coast." *Florida Historical Quarterly*, vol. 16, 1938.

Deane, John. *Deane's Manual of the History and Science of Firearms*. London, 1858.

Dearborn, Henry A. S. *Defense of General Henry Dearborn against the Attack of General William Hull*. New York, 1814. Bound with [Hull], *Report of the Trial of Brigadier General William Hull*.

DeWitt, John H. "General James Winchester, 1752–1826." *Tennessee Historical Quarterly*, vol. 1, 1915.

Dobbins, William W., ed. "The Dobbins Papers." In *Buffalo Historical Society Publications*. Vol. 8. Buffalo, N.Y., 1905. Dobbins was a sailing master under Perry at Presque Isle.

Doster, James F., ed. "Letters Relating to the Tragedy of Fort Mims. . . ." *Alabama Review*, vol. 14, 1961.

Douglas, R. Alan. "Weapons of the War of 1812." *Michigan History*, vol. 47, 1963.

Douglass, David B. "An Original Narrative of the Niagara Campaign of 1814." Edited by John T. Horton. *Niagara Frontier*, vol. 11, 1964. The narrative was written later by Captain Douglass, but it contains useful detail.

Duane, William. *A Handbook for Infantry*. Philadelphia, 1813.

———. *A Handbook for Riflemen*. Philadelphia, 1813.

Edgar, Lady Matilda. *General Brock*. Toronto: Morang & Co., 1904.

———. *Ten Years of Peace and War, Upper Canada, 1805–1815: Being the Ridout Letters*. London, 1891.

Elliott, Charles W. "The Indispensable Conquest." *Infantry Journal*, vol. 45, 1938. The article deals with Wilkinson's St. Lawrence campaign.

Evans, A. A. "Journal of . . . Constitution, 1812, by A. A. Evans, Surgeon, U.S. Navy." *Pennsylvania Magazine of History and Biography*, vol. 19, 1895–96. This is a detailed and valuable account.

Everest, Allan S. "Alexander Macomb at Plattsburg." *New York History*, vol. 44, 1963.

———. *British Objectives at the Battle of Plattsburg*. Champlain, N.Y., 1960. The work is based on secondary sources.

Everett, Donald E. "Emigrés and Militiamen: Free Persons of Color in New Orleans, 1803–1815." *Journal of Negro History*, vol. 38, 1953.

Fairchild, G. M., Jr. *The Journal of an American Prisoner at Fort Walden and Quebec in the War of 1812*. Quebec, 1909.

Fisher, Ruth Anna, ed. "The Surrender of Pensacola as Told by the British." *American Historical Review*, vol. 54, 1949. The text is a letter of Captain Gordon to Admiral Cochrane.

Footner, Hulbert. *Sailor of Fortune: The Life and Adventures of Commodore Barney, U.S.N.* New York: Harper & Bros., 1940.

Forester, C. S. "Victory on Lake Champlain." *American Heritage*, vol. 15, 1963.

Fortescue, J. W. *The County Lieutenancies and the Army, 1803–14.* London, 1909.

Fortier, Alcée. *A History of Louisiana.* 4 vols. New York, 1904. Vol. 3 contains the material on the War of 1812.

Gayarre, Charles. "Historical Sketch of Pierre and Jean Laffite." *Magazine of American History*, vol. 10, 1883.

"General Court-Martial for the Trial of Brevet Lieutenant Colonel Mullins." *Louisiana Historical Quarterly*, vol. 9, 1926.

Gilleland, J. C. *History of the Late War.* Baltimore, 1817. It is very brief.

Goodman, Warren. "Origins of the War of 1812: A Survey of Changing Interpretations." *Mississippi Valley Historical Review*, vol. 28, 1941. Reprinted in William A. Williams, *The Shaping of American Diplomacy.* 2 vols. Chicago: Rand McNally, 1956.

Green, James A. *William Henry Harrison: His Life and Times.* Richmond, Va.: Garrett & Massie, 1941.

Grignon, Augustin. "Augustin Grignon's Recollections." In *Reports and Collections of the State Historical Society of Wisconsin.* Vol. 3 (1856). Madison, 1857.

Guernsey, R. S. *New York City and Vicinity during the War of 1812.* . . . 2 vols. New York, 1889, 1895.

Hacker, Louis M. "Western Land Hunger and the War of 1812: A Conjecture." *Mississippi Valley Historical Review*, vol. 10, 1924.

Hamilton, Edward P. "The Battle of Plattsburg." *Vermont History*, vol. 31, 1963.

Hamilton, Captain Robert. "The Expeditions of Major General Samuel Hopkins up the Wabash, 1812: The Letters of Captain Robert Hamilton." *Indiana Magazine of History*, vol. 43, 1947.

Hare, John S. "Military Punishments in the War of 1812." *Journal of the American Military Institute*, vol. 4, 1940.

Hay, George. "Recollections of the War of 1812 by George Hay, Eighth Marquis of Tweedale." Edited by Lewis Einstein. *American Historical Review*, vol. 32, 1926. Hay describes the Chippewa action.

Haynes, Robert. "The Secretary of War and the War of 1812." *Louisiana History*, vol. 5, 1964.

Headley, Joel T. *The Second War with England.* 2 vols. New York, 1853. This is one of the best of the early histories.

Heaton, Herbert. "Non-importation, 1806–1812." *Journal of Economic History*, vol. 1, 1941.

Hitsman, J. Mackay. "David Parrish and the War of 1812." *Military Affairs*, vol. 26, 1962–63.

Horsman, Reginald. "British Indian Policy in the Northwest, 1807–1812." *Mississippi Valley Historical Review*, vol. 45, 1958.

———. *Matthew Elliott: British Indian Agent.* Detroit: Wayne State University Press, 1964.

———. "Wisconsin and the War of 1812." *Wisconsin Magazine of History*, vol. 46, 1962.

Hoskinson, Mrs. James. "Exploits of John Dickson." In *Buffalo Historical*

Society Publications. Vol. 8. Buffalo, N.Y., 1905. Dickson was on *Adams* in battle with *Caledonia.*

House of Representatives, U.S. *House Document 10* ("Irregulars in the War of 1812"). 24 Cong., 2 sess., Dec. 13, 1836. This is a complete listing insofar as one exists.

———. *House Document 146* ("Correspondence between Andrew Jackson and the War Department during the Creek War"). 20 Cong., 1 sess., Feb. 18, 1828.

———. *House Report 140* ("The Trial of Certain Tennessee Militiamen"). 20 Cong., 1 sess., Feb. 11, 1828. Among those tried were the men Jackson caused to be executed.

Hoyt, William D., Jr., ed. "Civilian Defense in Baltimore, 1814–15: Minutes of the Committee of Vigilance and Safety." *Maryland Historical Magazine,* vols. 39–40, 1944–45.

Hunt, Gilbert J. *The Late War.* . . . New York, 1816.

"Incidents of the War of 1812. From the *Baltimore Patriot.*" *Maryland Historical Magazine,* vol. 32, 1937.

Ingersoll, Charles J. *Historical Sketch of the Second War between Great Britain and America.* 2d ed. Philadelphia, 1852. The book reflects the violent prejudices of the period.

Irving, L. H., comp. *Officers of the British Forces in Canada during the War of 1812.* . . . Welland, Ontario: Canadian Military Institute, 1908. This is an enumeration with some biography of militia and regulars.

Jones, Wilbur D., ed. "A British View of the War of 1812 and the Peace Negotiations." *Mississippi Valley Historical Review,* vol. 45, 1958.

Jordan, Walter K. "A New Letter about the Massacre at Fort Dearborn." Edited by John D. Barnhart. *Indiana Magazine of History,* vol. 41, 1945. Corporal Jordan was a participant.

Kaplan, Lawrence S. "France and Madison's Decision for War, 1812." *Mississippi Valley Historical Review,* vol. 50, 1964.

———, ed. "A New Englander Defends the War of 1812: Senator Varnum to Judge Thacher." *Mid-America,* vol. 46, 1964.

Kaufman, Martin. "War Sentiment in Western Pennsylvania, 1812." *Pennsylvania History,* vol. 31, 1964.

Kennedy, John P. *Memoirs of the Life of William Wirt, Attorney General of the United States.* 2 vols. Philadelphia, 1849. The book contains some data on Bladensburg.

Kentucky. *Military History of Kentucky.* American Guide Series. Frankfort, Ky., 1939.

Kerr, W. B. "The Occupation of York." *Canadian Historical Review,* vol. 5, 1924.

Kinzie, Mrs. John H. *Wau-bun, the "Early Day" in the North-west.* Chicago, 1855. Mrs. Kinzie was at the massacre in Chicago.

Kissinger, Henry A. *A World Restored: Metternich, Castlereagh, and the Problems of Peace, 1812–1822.* Boston: Houghton Mifflin Co., 1957.

Knapp, Horace S. *History of the Maumee Valley.* Toledo, Ohio, 1872. Chap. 2 is on the War of 1812.

Lambert, Robert S., ed. "The Conduct of the Militia at Tippecanoe: Elihu Stout's Controversy with Colonel John P. Boyd." *Indiana Magazine of History,* vol. 51, 1955.

Larrabee, Charles. "Lieutenant Charles Larrabee's Account of the Battle of

Tippecanoe. . . ." Edited by Florence G. Watts. *Indiana Magazine of History*, vol. 57, 1961.

Latimer, Margaret K. "South Carolina: A Protagonist of the War of 1812." *American Historical Review*, vol. 61, 1956.

"Law and Grignon Papers, 1794–1821." In *Reports and Collections of the State Historical Society of Wisconsin*. Vol. 10 (1883). Madison, 1888.

Lloyd, Christopher. *The Navy and the Slave Trade: The Suppression of the African Slave Trade in the Nineteenth Century*. Toronto: Longmans Green & Co., 1949.

Lord, Walter. *The Dawn's Early Light*. New York: W. W. Norton & Co., Inc., 1972.

Lyman, Olin L. *Commodore Oliver Hazard Perry and the War on the Lakes*. New York: New Amsterdam Book Co., 1905.

McCown, Mary H., ed. "The J. Hartsell Memoir: The Journal of a Tennessee Captain in the War of 1812." In *East Tennessee Historical Society Publications*. No. 11. Knoxville, 1939.

McKee, Margaret M. "Services of Supply in the War of 1812." *Quartermaster Review*, vols. 6–7, 1927.

"Major General Henry Lee and Lieutenant General Sir George Beckwith on Peace in 1813." *American Historical Review*, vol. 32, 1927.

Marigny, Bernard. "Reflections on the Campaign of General Andrew Jackson in Louisiana. . . ." *Louisiana Historical Quarterly*, vol. 6, 1923. The article was first printed in 1848.

Marshall, John. *Royal Naval Biography*. . . . 4 vols. London, 1823–33.

Martell, J. S. "A Sidelight on Federalist Strategy." *American Historical Review*, vol. 43, 1938.

Mason, Philip P. *After Tippecanoe: Some Aspects of the War of 1812*. East Lansing: Michigan State University Press, 1963.

"Massachusetts Volunteer at the Battle of New Orleans, A." *Louisiana Historical Quarterly*, vol. 9, 1926.

Military Monitor (New York), 1812–14.

Miller, Howard S., and Clarke, Jack A. "Ships in the Wilderness. . . ." *Ohio History*, vol. 71, 1962. Jesup was sent to build invasion craft at Cleveland.

Mills, George H., comp. "Documents Relating to the Battle of Stoney Creek." In *Wentworth Historical Society Papers*, vol. 2, 1899. Correspondence among the British leaders.

Montreal Gazette, 1811–14. Microfilms were read.

Morgan, David B. "General David B. Morgan's Defense of the Conduct of the Louisiana Militia in the Battle on the Left Side of the River." *Louisiana Historical Quarterly*, vol. 9, 1926.

———. "David B. Morgan to Andrew Jackson, January 11, 1815." *Louisiana Historical Quarterly*, vol. 2, 1919.

Morse, Edward C. "Captain Ogden's Troop of Horse in the Battle of New Orleans." *Louisiana Historical Quarterly*, vol. 10, 1927.

Mullaly, Franklin E. "The Battle of Baltimore." *Maryland Historical Magazine*, vol. 54, 1959.

Muller, Charles G. "Commodore and Mrs. Thomas Macdonough." *Delaware History*, vol. 9, 1960.

Murdock, Richard K. "The Battle of Orleans, Masachusetts, 1814. . . ." *American Neptune*, vol. 24.

———. "A British Report on West Florida and Louisiana, November, 1812." *Florida Historical Quarterly*, vol. 43, 1964.

Naylor, Isaac. "The Battle of Tippecanoe as Described by Judge Isaac Naylor, a Participant." *Indiana Magazine of History*, vol. 2, 1906.

Nereus (pseud.). *The Letters on the Subject of the Naval War with America Which Appeared in the Courier under the Signature of Nereus.* London, 1813. These letters are ascribed by some historians to John Wilson Croker.

Newmyer, R. Kent. "Joseph Story and the War of 1812. . . ." *Historian*, vol. 26, 1964.

Niles, John M. *The Life of Oliver Hazard Perry. . . .* Hartford, Conn., 1821.

Nolte, Vincent. *The Memoirs of Vincent Nolte.* New York: G. H. Watt, 1934.

"Ohio and the War of 1812." In *Ohio Archeological and Historical Society Publications.* Vol. 28, 1919. Extracts from *The Trump of Fame*, first newspaper in the Western Reserve.

Ord, Robert W. "Memoranda Respecting Mobile. . . ." *Louisiana Historical Quarterly*, vol. 44, 1961. Contains a fine description of Fort Bowyer.

"Orderly Book of Harrisburg Volunteer Company of Artillery, Captain Richard M. Craig, 1814." *Pennsylvania Magazine of History and Biography*, vol. 37, 1913.

Palmer, Peter S. *History of Lake Champlain. . . .* Albany, N.Y., 1866.

Palmer, T. H., ed. *Historical Register of the United States.* 4 vols. Philadelphia, 1814–16. Consists mostly of reprints of official reports of both belligerents.

Palmerston Papers. "Army Estimates," 1812, 1813, 1814, 1815. Additional MSS 48423–26. London, British Museum. Although Palmerston was Secretary at War, 1809–28, these are the only items in his papers relative to that position.

Patrick, Rembert W. "Letters of the Invaders of East Florida, 1812." *Florida Historical Quarterly*, vol. 28, 1949–50.

Patterson, John. "The Letters of John Patterson." *Western Pennsylvania Historical Magazine*, vol. 23, 1940.

[Paulding, James Kirk.] *The Lay of the Scottish Fiddle: A Tale of Havre de Grace.* New York, 1813.

Paullin, Charles O. *Commodore John Rodgers, Captain, Commodore, and Senior Officer of the American Navy, 1773–1838.* Cleveland: Arthur H. Clark Co., 1910.

Peckham, Howard H. "Commodore Perry's Captive." *Ohio History*, vol. 72, 1963. The article relates Robert Barclay's career after his capture at Put-In-Bay.

Pellew, George. *Life and Correspondence of . . . Henry Addington, First Viscount Sidmouth.* London, 1847.

[Perkins, J. H.] *Annals of the West.* St. Louis: James R. Albach, 1852. It gives a fine account of the Indian wars in the Northwest.

Petrie, Sir Charles. *Lord Liverpool and His Times.* London: James Barrie, 1954. The War of 1812 is little more than mentioned.

Phillips, W. A., and Reede, A. H. *Neutrality: Its History, Economics, and Law.* 4 vols. Vol. 2, *The Napoleonic Period.* New York: Columbia University Press, 1936.

Pomeroy, Earl S. "The Lebanon Blues in the Baltimore Campaign." *Military Affairs*, vol. 12, 1948. This is an orderly book of the time.

Pratt, Julius. *Expansionists of 1812.* New York: Macmillan Co., 1925.

——. "Western Aims in the War of 1812." *Mississippi Valley Historical Review*, vol. 12, 1925.

Quaife, Milo M. "A Diary of the War of 1812." *Mississippi Valley Historical Review*, vol. 1, 1914. The diarist was a scout in the Detroit campaign, 1812.

——, ed. *War on the Detroit: The Chronicles of Thomas . . . de Boucherville and the Capitulation, by an Ohio Volunteer.* Chicago: Lakeside Press, 1940.

448   BIBLIOGRAPHY

Read, David B. *The Life and Times of Major General Sir Isaac Brock.* Toronto, 1894.

Review of a Pamphlet Purporting to Be Documents in Relation to the Differences Which Subsisted between the Late Commodore Oliver Hazard Perry and Captain Jesse D. Elliott, A. By a Citizen of Massachusetts. Boston, 1834.

Richardson's War of 1812. Edited by Alexander C. Casselman, Toronto, 1902. Richardson was captured by the U.S. forces at the Thames. The book was first published in 1842.

Richmond, Sir Herbert W. *Statesmen and Sea Power.* Oxford: Oxford University Press, 1946.

Risjord, Norman K. "1812: Conservatives, War Hawks, and the Nation's Honor." *William and Mary Quarterly*, 3d ser., vol. 18, 1961.

Roske, Ralph J., and Donley, Richard W. "The Perry-Elliott Controversy: A Bitter Footnote to the Battle of Lake Erie." *Northwest Ohio Quarterly*, vol. 34, 1962.

Schillinger, William. "Journal of Ensign William Schillinger, a Soldier in the War of 1812." Edited by James A. Green. *Ohio Archeological and Historical Quarterly*, vol. 41, 1932.

Scott, Winfield. *The Autobiography of Lieutenant General Winfield Scott.* 2 vols. New York, 1864.

Severance, Frank H., ed. "The Case of Brigadier General Alexander Smyth." In *Buffalo Historical Society Publications.* Vol. 18. Buffalo, N.Y., 1914. The article consists of contemporary letters, and it is essential to an understanding of Smyth's situation.

————. "Papers Relating to the War of 1812 on the Niagara Front." In *Buffalo Historical Society Publications.* Vol. 5. Buffalo, N.Y., 1902.

Shaw, John. "Narrative of John Shaw. Dictated to Lyman C. Draper." In *Wisconsin State Historical Society Publications.* Vol. 2. Madison, 1903. Shaw was a contractor and soldier; his narrative was first published in 1856.

Sheaffe, Sir Roger Hale. "The Letterbook of General Sir Roger Hale Sheaffe." In *Buffalo Historical Society Publications.* Vol. 17. Buffalo, N.Y., 1913. The letters are useful but not significant.

Sholes, Stanton. "Stanton Sholes' Narrative of the Northwest Campaign of 1813." Edited by Milo M. Quaife. *Mississippi Valley Historical Review*, vol. 15, 1929.

Sidway, Mrs. Jonathan. "Recollections of the Burning of Buffalo. . . ." In *Buffalo Historical Society Publications.* Vol. 9. Buffalo, N.Y., 1906.

Smith, Thomas Adam. "United States Troops in Spanish East Florida, 1812–1813." Edited by T. Frederick Davis. *Florida Historical Quarterly*, vols. 9–10, 1930–31, 1931–32. It consists of letters of Colonel Smith.

Smith, W. L. G. *The Life and Times of Lewis Cass*, New York, 1856.

Snider, C. H., Jr. *In the Wake of the 1812ers: War on the Great Lakes.* Toronto, 1913. The work is fairly sound, but it is in the extreme Romantic mood. With very slight changes it was reprinted in 1926 as *The Story of the Nancy and Other 1812ers.*

Stacey, C. P. "An American Plan for a Canadian Campaign: Secretary James Monroe to Major General Jacob Brown, February, 1815." *American Historical Review*, vol. 46, 1941. Reprinted in Zaslow, *Border.*

————. "The War of 1812 in Canadian History." *Ontario History*, vol. 50, 1958. This was an after-dinner speech.

————, ed. "Upper Canada at War, 1814: Captain Armstrong Reports." *Ontario History*, vol. 48, 1956. It consists of two contemporary letters.

Stanley, G. F. "The Indians in the War of 1812." *Canadian Historical Review*, vol. 31, 1950.

Stubbs, Samuel. *A Compendious Account of the Most Important Battles of the*

Late War. . . . Boston, 1817. Reprinted in the *Magazine of History*, extra issue 152, 1929.

Tait, James. "The Journal of James Tait for the Year 1813." Edited by Peter A. Brannan. *Alabama Historical Quarterly*, vol. 2, 1940. Tait was a volunteer in the Creek War.

[Tipton, John.] "Account of the Battle of Tippecanoe." In *Indiana Historical Collections*. Vol. 25. Indianapolis, 1942.

Tod, Major. *Correspondence of Major Tod, War of 1812*. Western Reserve and Northern Ohio Historical Tracts. Nos. 15, 17. Cleveland, 1873.

Todd, Frederick P. "The Militia and Volunteers of the District of Columbia, 1783–1820." In *District of Columbia Historical Society Records*. Vol. 50. Washington, 1952.

Twiggs, John. "Letters from General John Twiggs' Order Book." *Georgia Historical Quarterly*, vol. 11, 1927. The letters relate to trouble on the southeastern border.

Vansittart Papers. 9 vols. Additional MSS nos. 31229–37. London, British Museum. Nicholas Vansittart became chancellor of the exchequer in May 1812, but there is nothing in his papers relative to the American war.

Walker, Norman McF. "The Geographical Nomenclature of Louisiana." *Magazine of American History*, vol. 10, 1883.

War, The (New York), 1812–14. Edited by Samuel Woodworth. Weekly.

"War Hawks of 1812, The." *Indiana Magazine of History*, vol. 60, 1964. The June issue is devoted to the topic; four major articles.

Weekes, William M. "The War of 1812: Civil Authority and Martial Law in Upper Canada." *Ontario History*, vol. 68, 1956.

West, Elizabeth H. "A Prelude to the Creek War of 1813–1814." *Florida Historical Quarterly*, vol. 18, 1940. A letter from John to James Innerarity shows the deteriorating relationships.

Wheeler, Owen. *The War Office: Past and Present*. London, 1914.

Whittlesey, Charles. *General Wadsworth's Division, War of 1812*. Western Reserve Historical Society Tracts, no. 51. Cleveland, 1879.

Williams, Mentor S. "John Kinzie's Narrative of the Fort Dearborn Massacre." *Journal of the Illinois State Historical Society*, vol. 46, 1953.

Wilson, John. "Captain John Wilson and Some Military Matters in Maine in the War of 1812." Edited by Henry S. Burrage. *Maine Historical Society Collections and Proceedings*, 2d series, vol. 10, 1899.

Winchester, James. *Papers and Orderly Book of Brigadier General James Winchester*. Compiled by C. M. Burton. Michigan Pioneer and Historical Collections, vol. 31. Lansing, Mich., 1902.

Winsor, Justin. *Narrative and Critical History of America*. 8 vols. Boston, 1888–89. Vol. 2 contains the material on the War of 1812 and a good bibliography of it.

Wood, William C. H. *The War with the United States*. Chronicles of Canada Series. Toronto: Glasgow, Brook & Co., 1915.

Wright, J. Leitch. "A Note on the First Seminole War. . . ." *Journal of Southern History*, vol. 34, 1960.

Zimmerman, James F. *Impressment of American Seamen*. New York: Columbia University, 1925. This is a diplomatic history of the subject.

Index

Mahon, John K
   The War of 1812 [by] John K. Mahon. Gainesville, University of Florida Press, 1972.

   xii, 476 p. illus. 25 cm. $12.50

   Bibliography: p. [429]–449.

   1. United States—History—War of 1812—Campaigns and battles.
I. Title.

265342 E355.M33   973.5'23   79-137856
       ISBN 0-8130-0318-0   MARC
       Library of Congress   73 [4]

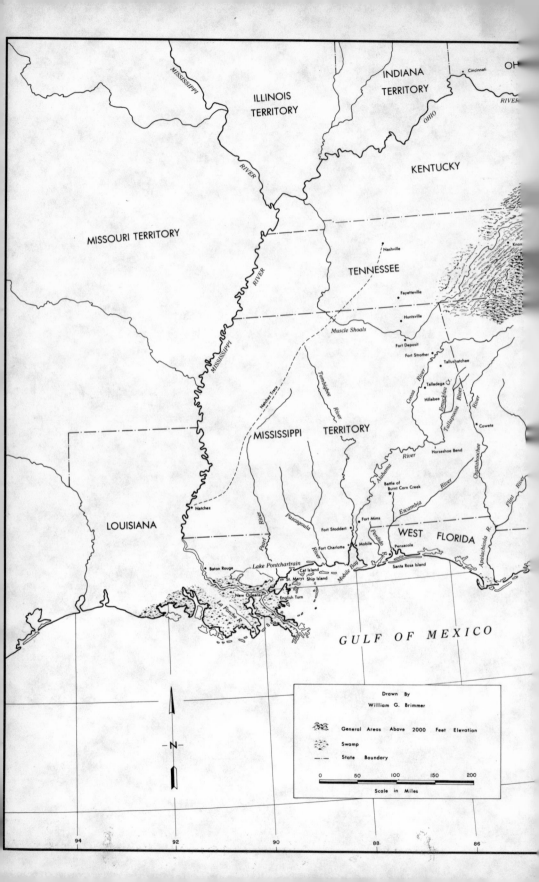